WORKS ISSUED BY
THE HAKLUYT SOCIETY

Series Editors
W. F. Ryan
Michael Brennan

THE GUIANA TRAVELS OF ROBERT SCHOMBURGK
1835–1844

Volume I: Explorations on Behalf of
the Royal Geographical Society 1835–1839

THIRD SERIES
NO. 16
(Issued for 2005)

Figure 1: Robert Schomburgk (c. 1840). Reproduced from editor's copy.

THE GUIANA TRAVELS
OF
ROBERT SCHOMBURGK
1835–1844

VOLUME I: EXPLORATIONS ON BEHALF
OF THE ROYAL GEOGRAPHICAL SOCIETY
1835–1839

Edited by

Peter Rivière

Published by
Ashgate
for
THE HAKLUYT SOCIETY
LONDON
2006

Published for The Hakluyt Society by

Ashgate Publishing Limited
Gower House
Croft Road
Aldershot
Hants GU11 3HR
England

Ashgate Publishing Company
Suite 420
101 Cherry Street
Burlington
VT 05401-4405
USA

Ashgate website: http://www.ashgate.com

British Library Cataloguing in Publication Data
The Guiana travels of Robert Schomburgk 1835–1844
Volume I: Explorations on behalf of the Royal Geographical Society 1835–1839. –
(Hakluyt Society. Third series)
1. Schomburgk, Robert H. (Robert Hermann), Sir, 1804–1865 – Travel – Guiana 2. Guiana –
Discovery and exploration – German
I. Rivière, Peter II. Hakluyt Society
918.8'042

Library of Congress Cataloging-in-Publication Data
The Guiana travels of Robert Schomburgk 1835–1844 / edited by Peter Rivière.
p. cm. – (Works issued by the Hakluyt Society, ISSN 0072–9396 ; third ser., no. 16)
Includes bibliographical references.
ISBN 0–904180–86–7 (alk. paper)
1. Guyana – Discovery and exploration – British. 2. Guyana – Description and travel. 3. Royal
Geographical Society (Great Britain). 4. Schomburgk, Robert H. (Robert Hermann), Sir, 1804–1865
– Travel – Guyana. I. Rivière, Peter. II. Series.
F2384.G85 2006
918.81042–dc22
2005024025

ISBN–13: 978–0–904180–86–2
ISBN–10: 0–904180–86–7
ISSN 0072 9396

Typeset by Waveney Typesetters, Wymondham, Norfolk.
Printed and bound in Great Britain by
the University Press, Cambridge.

CONTENTS

ILLUSTRATIONS

MAPS

PREFACE

In the entrance hall of Lowther House, the home of the Royal Geographical Society in Kensington Gore, there hang boards on which are recorded the names of the Society's medal winners. There, as recipient of the Gold Medal in 1840, is that of Robert H. Schomburgk.[1] Nor was this the only honour to be bestowed upon him; among many others which he received was a knighthood from Queen Victoria in 1844. He was on familiar terms with Darwin, Hooker, Bentham and most of the luminaries of mid-nineteenth-century science. He never, however, achieved the popular recognition that many scientific travellers of the period, such as Livingstone, Burton, and others whose names appear on those boards, did. Today his name is little known outside a handful of specialists in natural history and historians of Guiana.[2] There may be more than one reason for this.

First, although Schomburgk published extensively, his publications are mainly to be found in learned journals. He never wrote a popular book, although in 1841 he told Sir William Jardine of a two-volume work he had planned, entitled *Fragments of Natural History and Incidents of Travels, the Result of a Four Years' Ramble through the Wilds of Guiana*.[3] He later expressed to William Hooker, Director of the Kew Botanic Gardens, rather mixed feelings about his failure to have done so. He wrote:

> It is a most remarkable fact that I never could bring myself to sit down, and write a detailed account of my travels in these regions. The hope, when I returned in 1844 of being able to continue them, and the many proofs, how cautious a traveller ought to be, not to trust to first impressions, and to be very guarded in his conclusions, these circumstances combined, have been the reason that I hesitated to arrange my notes.[4]

It is almost certainly for this reason that he is often confused with his younger and better known brother, Richard, whose two-volume *Travels in British Guiana*,[5] while full of scientific observations, is more readable, being closer to the genre of travel writing.

---

[1] It was in fact the Patron's Medal for 1839. See *Journal of the Royal Geographical Society* (hereafter *JRGS*), 10, 1841, pp. xli, xlvi–xlvii.

[2] The term 'Guiana' is used throughout the editorial text of this volume to refer to the geographical area contained by the coast from the mouth of the Orinoco to that of the Amazon, and then by the Amazon, Rio Negro, Cassiquiare Canal, and Orinoco River. British Guiana is used to refer to the former British colony; Guyana to the modern state.

[3] Royal Scottish Museum, Jardine Papers (hereafter RSM, JP), Letter of Schomburgk to Jardine, 18 August 1841.

[4] Royal Botanic Gardens, Kew, Director's Correspondence, Miscellaneous Letters (hereafter RBGK, DC), Volume LXXI, 353. Letter of Schomburgk to Hooker, 21 April 1854.

[5] *Travels in British Guiana 1840–1844*, transl. and ed. by W. E. Roth, 2 vols, Georgetown, *Daily Chronicle*, 1922. This is a translation of *Reisen in Britisch-Guiana in den Jahren 1840–1844*, 3 vols, Leipzig, Verlagsbuchhandlung von J. J. Webber, 1847–8. The third volume, entitled *Versuch einer Fauna und Flora von Britisch-Guiana*, and containing contributions by various specialists, was not translated into English.

Indeed, so much better known is Richard that Robert's exploits are often attributed to him, and botanists often claim that the epidendroid genus of orchid, *Schomburgkia*, was named by George Bentham after Richard rather than Robert.[1]

Second, Robert Schomburgk spent very few years of his life in Britain; the total is barely five and the rest of the time he was in fairly remote parts of the world. Finally, and this is something by which he often used to explain any slight or reversal, he was not British but German.

The journey for which Schomburgk was awarded the Patron's Medal by the Royal Geographical Society was overland from Georgetown in British Guiana to Esmeralda on the Orinoco in Venezuela. He there joined his survey to that of Baron Alexander von Humboldt made in 1800, and returned to Georgetown by the way of the Cassiquiare Canal, Rio Negro and Rio Branco. His knighthood was conferred in recognition of his services as boundary commissioner for British Guiana. His reports of the journeys he made in Guiana between 1835 and 1844 constitute the contents of these two volumes. Admittedly versions of his accounts were published in the *Journal of the Royal Geographical Society*, but they are only versions. In each case the original manuscripts were heavily amended; nor did the editorial hand limit itself to abridgement, but undertook radical alterations of the text (and meaning) and even, on occasions, it was not above making additions. A more detailed discussion of these changes will be found in the Introduction,[2] and the only point to be made here is that this is the first time that Schomburgk's full and original manuscripts have been published.

These manuscripts are held by the Royal Geographical Society, London, and The National Archives, Kew. I am extremely grateful to both organizations for permitting their publication. At the Royal Geographical Society I would like especially to acknowledge the help of the successive Directors, John Hemming and Rita Gardner, the Archivist, Andrew Tatham and the Map Curator, Francis Herbert. At the (then) Public Record Office (now The National Archives), the Director, Sarah Tyacke, who fortuitously and conveniently also happened at the time to be President of the Hakluyt Society, smoothed certain paths. I would also like to thank Professor William Ryan of the Warburg Institute who started out as the series editor of these volumes, Professor Robin Law of the University of Stirling who then took up the baton, and Dr Michael Brennan of Leeds University who finished the task, for all their assistance and advice. I am also grateful for the support received from the British Academy, and for funds provided by the Board of the Faculty of Anthropology and Geography, the Institute of Social and Cultural Anthropology and the Interfaculty Committee for Latin American Studies of the University of Oxford, which went towards covering some of my expenses in the preparation of this work.

I have received help in editing this volume from a very large number of people from many different backgrounds. I would like to thank (in alphabetical order): Katy Archer, Melinda Babcock, Jim Bennett, Isabella Birkin, Martin Brendell, Alison Brown, Nick Brown, Eithne Carlin, Bonnie and Jean-Pierre Chaumeil, Barry Clarke, Colin Clarke, Simon Chaplin, Audrey and Robin Colson, Juul van Dam, Gina Douglas, John Dransfield, Joseph Eytle, Kate Flint, Geoffrey Forster, Robert Fox, Germán Freire, David

---

[1] See Peter Rivière, 'Confused Identities – the Schomburgk Brothers', *The Orchid Review*, 112, 2004, pp. 51–5.
[2] See below, p. 28.

Hammond, Stephen Harris, Deiter Heinen, Francis Herbert, Jim Holt, Elizabeth Hsu, Simon Humphries, Bryn Hyacinth, Cees and Ineke Koelewijn, Rob Kruszynski, Colin McCarthy, Emilio Cordero Michel, Heather Montgomery, Mike Morris, Heather O'Donoghue, Pauline Payne, Laura Peers, Cheryl Piggott, Laura Rival, Timothy Rood, Peter Savill, Gwendoline Schomburgk, Ian Schomburgk, Sarah Strong, Hugh Torrens, Bernardo Vega, Aparecida Vilaça, Adrian Webb, and Neil Whitehead. Some of these people I know well, others I have never met but even so they responded to my questions, which came out of the blue, with great kindness and thoroughness; indeed, the preparation of this work has left me convinced that both the ideal and the practice of scholarly cooperation are alive and well. To these named individuals, and I must apologize to anyone whom I have inadvertently failed to mention, must be added very many anonymous librarians and archivists who have fielded my queries and provided help. Without the assistance of all of them, be it great or small, this volume would not be as good as it is (to whatever degree that might be judged).

Another good reason why this work should appear as a publication of the Hakluyt Society is that Schomburgk himself was, from a very early date in its existence, a member of the Council of the Society and was also responsible for editing one of its most successful early volumes, Ralegh's *Discovery of the Large, Rich, and Beautiful Empire of Guiana* (1848).[1] (A new edition of Ralegh's work, edited by Joyce Lorimer, is also being published in 2006 by the Hakluyt Society.) That Schomburgk's own writings on Guiana should now be published by the Hakluyt Society seems an entirely fitting tribute.

These volumes, as well as presenting Schomburgk's South American travels, are arranged so that they provide a brief biography of the traveller. No such work exists. The longest biographical sketch, revised by myself, is to be found in the *Oxford Dictionary of National Biography*. I have for some years tried to interest publishers in a full biography of Schomburgk, but without success, the common response being 'No-one knows who he is'. Publishers seem willing to produce biographies of people of whom there are already numerous such works, but shy away from forgotten, but equally worthy subjects. That Schomburgk is such a worthy subject, and deserves resurrecting, I have no doubts about, and I hope readers, by the time they reach the end of these two volumes, will agree with me.

---

[1] *The Discovery of the Large, Rich, and Beautiful Empire of Guiana, with a Relation of the Great and Golden City of Manoa (which the Spaniards call El Dorado), etc. Performed in the Year 1595, by Sir Walter Ralegh, Knt.*, The Hakluyt Society, 1st ser. 3, London, 1848.

INTRODUCTION

Robert Hermann Schomburgk – The Man

We do not know a great deal about Schomburgk's early life and for what we do, we have to rely mainly on his own account.[1] He was born in Freiburg on the Unstrut River, then in Thuringia but later in the Prussian Province of Saxony, on 5 June 1804. His father was Johann Friedrich Ludwig Schomburgk, assistant pastor in Freiburg between 1801 and 1820 and then in Voigstedt until 1847, soon after which year he died of cholera. His mother was Christine Juliane who died in 1827. He was the eldest of their five children: Linna Theresia born in 1806, Alfred Otto in 1809, Moritz Richard in 1811, and Ludwig Julius in 1819.[2]

Schomburgk received much of his primary education from his father, and, according to him, he developed a love of botany from a very early age. He left home to start his career as an apprentice to a merchant Krieger in Naumberg at the age of fourteen. In 1823 he entered the employment of his uncle, Henry Schomburgk, who had a business in Leipzig. This city allowed greater opportunities to study botany and, as well as attending lectures at the local university, he took private lessons. He also made various botanical excursions to Hesse, the Rhine region, Hartz and Thuringia.

Schomburgk recalled in 1840 that he had from an early age wished to travel outside Europe, but he had refrained from doing so as a result of some promise to his mother. He was later to tell George Bentham[3] that he had left Germany 'chiefly in consequence of political causes'.[4] Whatever the reason it was the year after his mother's death in 1827

---

[1] The introduction to the first part of Schomburgk's *Fishes of Guiana* (in *The Naturalist's Library*, conducted by Sir William Jardine, Vol. 32 (Ichthyology, Vol. III), Edinburgh, W. H. Lizars, 1841) contains the most detailed information on his early life. The details were provided by Schomburgk himself, but he asked the editor, Sir William Jardine, to disguise the fact and to make it appear that he had 'received the information partly through conversation with me, partly through the public papers in Germany as an autobiography would no doubt appear <u>arrogant</u> and absurd' (RSM, JP, Letter of Schomburgk to Jardine, 5 December 1840. Emphasis in the original). An updated version, now entitled 'Autobiographie', is to be found in *Leopoldina*, 1, 1859, pp. 34–9.

[2] Except for Richard who joined Robert in Guiana in 1840–43, the other three siblings play little or no part in this volume. Otto became embroiled in politics while a student at the University of Halle in the 1830s and left Germany, together with Richard, for Australia after the political upheaval of 1848. They were joined in 1850 by Linna and Julius, following the death of their father. Richard was to become Director of the Adelaide Botanic Museum from 1865–91, in which latter year he died. For further information, see Pauline Payne, 'Dr Richard Schomburgk and Adelaide Botanic Gardens, 1865–1891', unpublished PhD thesis, University of Adelaide, 1992.

[3] George Bentham (1800–84), botanist, Secretary of the (now Royal) Horticultural Society (1829–40), and President of the Linnean Society (1863–74). He was responsible for describing many of the plants which Schomburgk collected.

[4] Royal Botanic Gardens, Kew, Bentham Correspondence (hereafter RBGK, BC), IX/355, Letter of Schomburgk to Bentham, 17 November 1838. This was the period of the Liberal Movement, the political upheaval in Germany that reached its climax in the 1848 Revolution.

that he took an opportunity to act as supercargo for a flock of Merino sheep that were being sent to the USA as a speculation. On arrival there he obtained employment with a counting-house in Richmond, Virginia.

He did not remain long in North America because in October 1829 he embarked at New York for St Thomas, the Danish possession in the Virgin Islands. The business enterprises he had entered into in the States, and which he continued on St Thomas, turned out badly and he suffered severe losses. These were made worse when in 1830, a fire destroyed his account and invoice books together with his library and other possessions. It is this event which made him decide to abandon a life in commerce and devote himself instead to natural history.

The period 1830 to 1835, Schomburgk's time in the Caribbean, is covered more fully in this Introduction; that from 1835 to 1844 in South America forms the focus of this volume; and the last two decades of his life are the subject of the Epilogue (which will be found in Volume II). However, it might be helpful to the reader if a summary of his career is also provided here.

Schomburgk persuaded the Royal Geographical Society to patronize and support explorations in the interior of British Guiana. He arrived in that country in 1835 and his first expedition, September 1835 to March 1836, was a tentative exploration up the Essequibo and Rupununi Rivers. The first part of the second expedition was an unsuccessful attempt to ascend the Corentyne River in October 1836 and the second part an ascent of the Berbice River between November 1836 and March 1837. His third expedition lasted from September 1837 until June 1839. During the first part he ascended to the source of the Essequibo, and after spending the wet season at the Brazilian Fort São Joaquim, at the junction of the Takutu River and Rio Branco, he journeyed via Mount Roraima to Esmeralda on the Orinoco where he connected his survey with that of Alexander von Humboldt. He then returned via the Cassiquiare Canal, the Rio Negro and Rio Branco. In the summer of 1839 Schomburgk sailed for London to receive in the following year the Royal Geographical Society's Patron's Medal for his exploits.

As a result of what were seen as Brazilian incursions against Amerindians on the Rupununi savannahs, it was decided that the boundaries of the colony, until then undefined, should be settled. In 1840 he was appointed boundary commissioner to survey the frontiers. He returned to British Guiana in January 1841 and conducted his first boundary expedition to the delta of the Orinoco and the north-west between April and July that year. The next boundary to be surveyed was that with Brazil along the Takutu and Surumu Rivers, and with Venezuela from Roraima to the Cuyuni River which was completed between December 1841 and January 1843. The final part of the survey covered the frontier with Dutch Guiana (modern Surinam) along the Corentyne River and was conducted between February and October 1843.

Schomburgk returned to London in mid-1844, to be rewarded with a knighthood. After some three years spent in literary and other activities, as well as angling for preferment, he was appointed in September 1847 the first ever British consul to Santo Domingo, in the newly independent Dominican Republic, where he took up his post in January 1848. He stayed there until May 1857 when he was transferred to the British consulship in Bangkok. While there his health steadily deteriorated, and he retired sick to England in the summer of 1864 and, after a stay of a few months, went to Berlin where he died in March 1865.

Although there are numerous letters and reports by Schomburgk, these are virtually all of a formal and official nature. Very few personal letters exist, and the nearest we get to such material are some of his letters to Sir William Hooker and Sir William Jardine[1] in which he did on occasion express some personal feelings. For example, from Santo Domingo in 1850, he wrote to Hooker:

> Here I stand alone, growing old, and have no person with whom to exchange my ideas, whom to cherish. It is very ridiculous, but I have frequently thought that I threw one chance away, and this was when you put the two Misses W. under my protection; the elder of whom I thought pretty and most amiable. Though Lady Hooker wished me to visit there again I felt ashamed of having neglected the family for two years and could never muster courage enough to return.[2]

As well as remaining unmarried, we know Schomburgk drank, but did not smoke, and was a devout Christian. He was fairly short in stature, and from his first expedition onwards experienced recurring ill health. As well as malaria and yellow fever, he suffered from severe rheumatic fever and later in life from poor eyesight.[3] There is also evidence that he suffered from epilepsy. The young artist, Edward Goodall,[4] who accompanied the second and third boundary surveys, recorded in his diary for 1 October 1841: 'I came home, went to bed but was soon roused by Mr. Schomburgk having one of the most dreadful epileptic fits I ever saw'.[5] Earlier the same year, Schomburgk mentioned in a letter to Jardine that he had suffered two attacks of 'nervous debility' which may well refer to the same thing.[6] However, except for a reference to a 'nervous

---

[1] Sir William Hooker (1785–1865) was Professor of Botany at Glasgow University and then Director of Kew Gardens. Sir William Jardine (1800–74), the 7th baronet, commenced and edited the *Naturalist's Library* series, in which numerous volumes were published between 1833 and 1845, including Schomburgk's *Fishes of Guiana*. It is not clear how Schomburgk became acquainted with Hooker, but the first letter which we know of between them, which is some years before they met, is from Hooker to Schomburgk, dated 21 November 1834. It is possible, even likely, that Hooker would have become aware of Schomburgk if approached, and this is equally likely, through John Lindley asking if he wanted to subscribe for one of Schomburgk's botanical collections. They continued to correspond until the year before both their deaths and Schomburgk's letters are be found in the archives of the Royal Botanic Gardens at Kew. Hooker, while still at Glasgow, was responsible for introducing Schomburgk to Jardine in 1839. In 1876, Jardine's widow (his second wife) married Sir Joseph Hooker, Sir William's son , who succeeded him as Director of Kew Gardens.

[2] RBGK, DC, LXX/290. Letter of Schomburgk to Hooker, 1 December 1850. The incident referred to took place in November 1839 when Schomburgk escorted the two young women, the Misses Wood, on a train from Glasgow, where they had all been staying with the Hookers (William Hooker was then Professor of Botany at Glasgow University), to Liverpool. In fact Schomburgk never married, although an informal union in Georgetown did produce a son whose descendants live today in England.

[3] This complaint may well have been glaucoma of which the Schomburgk family has a history (personal communication, Ian Schomburgk, 29 May 1994).

[4] Edward Angelo Goodall (1819–1908). For a brief biographical sketch of Goodall and the reproduction of a number of the paintings he made in British Guiana, see M. N. Menezes, 'Introduction' to Edward Goodall, *Sketches of Amerindian Tribes 1841–1843*, London, British Museum Publications, pp. 11–30. There is a collection of Goodall's work in the British Library (Add. MSS 16936–16939). Goodall kept a diary from his arrival in Georgetown on 28 July 1841 until it abruptly ends on 13 June 1842. See Edward Goodall, 'The Diary of Edward Goodall Esq. During his Sojourn in Georgetown from 28th July to 11th December 1841', *Journal of the British Guiana Museum and Zoo*, 35, 1962, pp. 39–53; and 'Edward Goodall's Diary 23rd December 1841–13th June, 1842 (on the Essequibo & Rupununi Rivers)', *Journal of the British Guiana Museum and Zoo*, 36, 1962, pp. 47–64 (hereafter Goodall, 'Diary' and 'Goodall's Diary').

[5] Goodall, 'Diary', p. 46.

[6] RSM, JP, Letter of Schomburgk to Jardine, 18 August 1841.

attack' in 1855,[1] which once again may be the same complaint, no other mention of this problem has been noted.

Almost as trying to him as his physical well-being, was his nationality. He never achieved the British nationality he so eagerly sought. He wrote to the Secretary of the Royal Geographical Society in 1835, just before leaving the Virgin Islands for British Guiana, in these words:

> The neglect I have met with from the ministers at Berlin and the circumstance that political opinions are the reason for my being expatriated, however still more: that a younger brother of mine, associated with the late political Society in Prussia has been treated in a manner which one would have expected only to meet with in the Annals of the Spanish Inquisition, have separated the last link which connected me with that power, who has usurped the Dominion over my own native country, Thuringia. Do not consider me an enthusiast if I say with a pride that can not be equalled: England is now my adopted country!!²

It was not, however, until Schomburgk was in Santo Domingo that we have evidence of his making serious attempts at naturalization. There were then a series of letters in which the topic was brought up. For example, in a letter to Lord Palmerston in 1850, he stated that until then, because his father had been alive and other members of his family had been living in Prussia, he had not applied for British citizenship. Now that his father was dead, two brothers were in Australia and his remaining brother and sister were about to follow, all to become subjects of 'a Sovereign whom I have served since She ascended the Throne', he also wished to have British citizenship. He noted that the lack of such citizenship had not barred him from either knighthood or consulship.[3] The insurmountable problem was that of residence on British soil and Schomburgk never achieved his wish.

We can also garner certain things about Schomburgk's character from his official writings. He often felt seriously misunderstood, on many occasions with good reason. To a large extent this was and remains a common feeling of those in the field that those sitting at home completely fail to appreciate the difficulties encountered. He was certainly punctilious in his behaviour and worked and tried very hard.[4] He clearly felt uncomfortable about any drop in personal standards and etiquette. It is understandable that, when at Esmeralda, he worried about returning to British Guiana via the Rio Negro because he had no suitable clothes in which to meet Brazilian citizens. But to hide in a hut because he did not want Amerindians to see the state of his clothes is more difficult to appreciate.[5] Indeed clothes seemed of great importance to Schomburgk.

---

[1] RBGK, DC, LXXI, Letter of Schomburgk to Hooker, 7 March 1855.

[2] Royal Geographical Society, Schomburgk Correspondence 1834–40 (hereafter RGS, RHS 1834–40), Letter of Schomburgk to Maconochie, 2 July 1835. The brother in question was Otto, who, Schomburgk later mentioned to Bentham, had been sentenced to thirty years in prison. Schomburgk appealed to Humboldt for help which seems to have been effective (RBGK, BC, IX, Letter of Schomburgk to Bentham, 17 November 1838).

[3] Kew, The National Archives, Foreign Office (hereafter TNA, FO) 23/7, Letter of Schomburgk to Palmerston, 25 June 1850.

[4] Perhaps too hard for some! There is a letter from Sir John Barrow at the Admiralty to the Royal Geographical Society, just dated 13 October although the year is probably 1837, a postscript to which reads 'He [Schomburgk] is too fond of work to accomplish much' (RGS Corres 1834–40).

[5] See below p. 253 and p. 363.

William Crichton, Inspector-General of Police in British Guiana, described Schomburgk attending a church service in the interior, as dressed 'in Full Regimentals with a sword as long as himself nearly – a chapeau Bras with a Plume above it a yard in length at least'.[1] It was possibly this same dress uniform that Schomburgk hung on to, despite having to abandon his scientific collections, on the Corentyne in 1843.[2] It was clothes, among other things, that gave rise to a diplomatic incident involving the French consul in Santo Domingo in April 1852.[3]

Edward Goodall has left us with some of the best personal, if irreverent, descriptions of Schomburgk. On first meeting Schomburgk on 30 July 1841, he wrote, 'he seems a very nice little man but rather petulant, however. It is too soon for me to think of giving an opinion at present, as he is very agreeable and kind. That may perhaps wear off when we get into the bush.'[4] Goodall's caution proved well founded and his diary has various entries which read along similar lines to these: 'the little man in a damned bad mood'; or 'worked himself into a towering passion and tried to drown what I said'.[5]

Even if short-tempered, Schomburgk certainly possessed other qualities without which he could not possibly have led expeditions that covered thousands of miles in the interior of Guiana with an increasing degree of success. He was much concerned about the welfare of the members of his expeditions, both Amerindian and non-Amerindian, and was proud of the fact that, with the exception of one fatal accident on the Berbice, his journeys had been remarkably free of calamities. On a personal note, having been closely involved with him for the past decade, I am not certain that I would have liked Schomburgk, but I certainly admire him and am sure that he was someone to be trusted.[6]

The Road to British Guiana

On 27 August 1830 Schomburgk wrote from St John in the Virgin Islands to the Linnean Society in London, sending a collection of 100 plants collected on that island as a token of esteem. He informed the Society that his plans were to travel to the other Virgin Islands and offered to collect for members of the Society, as well as plants, fishes 'preserved after a new method' and seeds of plants 'distinguished for their beauty and singularity'. He went on to explain that he was 'without any protection [patronage] from his own country' and with a wish to explore foreign countries he had to depend on what he got for his collections. His greatest wish was to travel through Kentucky, Indiana, Ohio, Georgia and Florida but he could see no possibility of realizing such a project unless some Society looked favourably upon his plans. He stated that he had a

[1] Kew, The National Archives, Colonial Office (hereafter TNA, CO) 111/195, Journal submitted by Crichton to Light, 20 February 1842.

[2] See Volume II, chap. 3.

[3] TNA, FO 23/13, Letters of Schomburgk to Foreign Office, 12 April, 25 June, 3 July 1852.

[4] Goodall, 'Diary', p. 39.

[5] Ibid., pp. 54–55. Goodall does come across as a slightly bumptious and ill-disciplined young man. Even so he accompanied Schomburgk on the difficult expedition down the Corentyne in 1843 and received much praise from Schomburgk.

[6] Or to put it rather differently, I would have been happy to go on a tiger hunt with him, but might have chosen different company to have a drink with afterwards.

strong constitution, and that from his youth botany had been his favourite subject. A list of referees, comprising scholars in Germany, Alsace, New York and Martinique, was provided together with the names of those who were able to pronounce on his moral conduct. He concluded: 'I really should feel happy, if you Gentlemen could do something for me and if America not agreeable to you, I would go to any place you pointed out to me; besides english, I am acquainted with french & spanish.'[1]

On 16 October, Schomburgk wrote again to the Linnean Society, this time from Tortola in the British Virgin Islands. He sent a duplicate of his earlier letter and expressed the hope that it would not be found odd that he should return to the same subject without awaiting a reply. However, he was so anxious that the Society should accept his services, he was providing the names of two further referees. He then gave in greater detail, under eight headings, the objects of natural history of which he proposed to make collections. They were 1) dried plants, 2) skins of animals and birds, 3) fishes, 4) shells, 5) insects, 6) remarkable plants and fruits preserved in glasses, 7) seeds, and 8) drawings of objects which change their form or colour when preserved. Under the last heading he prided himself as an expert drawer of natural objects.[2]

Whereas the western part of America was where he would have liked to go because the plain had been so little visited, if this was not agreeable to the Society, he proposed that he should take up a suggestion by Professor Reichenbach[3] of Dresden that he should proceed to French Guiana to continue the work begun by Aublet.[4] But in the end he was willing to go anywhere the Society suggested. As for recompense, he did not wish to do it for personal gain but just to be provided with the means to undertake his scientific explorations. He thought that the Society would wish to help him enrich science and he would leave it entirely to the Society's generosity to make the conditions. There is no evidence that Schomburgk ever received a reply from the Linnean Society (and he was later to complain that he had rarely received any acknowledgement from that Society for communications that he had sent them), but his life took a dramatic and unexpected turn at this point.

Schomburgk happened to be on the island of Anegada, the most north-easterly of the British Virgin Islands, in March and April 1831 when three shipwrecks occurred; those of the British brig *Frances*, the American brig *Lewis* and the Spanish schooner *Restaudora*. Shipwrecks were not unusual occurrences on Anegada because of its low contours (it only reaches to some 30 feet above sea level), extensive coral reefs combined with a strong current flowing to the north-west, that had been the grave of numerous ships over the centuries. He later claimed that it was the wreck of the *Restaudora* that had sunk with its load of slaves, who were still visible beneath the water chained to their benches, that motivated him to re-survey and correct the charts of the area, although he believed that the strong currents were also to blame for the frequency of wrecks.

He had already had some surveying experience but received further instruction from

---

[1] Linnean Society MSS, Loose Letters, Letter of Schomburgk to Secretary, 27 August 1830.

[2] Evidence for this exists in his drawings, now held in the Natural History Museum, London (581.9 (881) SCH.F).

[3] Heinrich Gottlieb Ludwig Reichenbach (1793–1879), German botanist.

[4] Jean Baptiste Christophe Fusée Aublet (1720–1778), French botanist and author of *Historie des plantes de Guiane Françoise*, 4 vols, London and Paris, Pierre-Francois Didot jeune, 1775.

the Danish military commander and the harbour master at St Thomas. He returned to Anegada in August 1831 and spent three months surveying the island at his own expense. His efforts were not entirely appreciated by the islanders, who had made a comfortable living from salvaging cargo from the wrecks, and his efforts were obstructed even to the extent of physical assault on one occasion.

On completion, Schomburgk sent his chart to the Admiralty and submitted two articles to the recently founded Royal Geographical Society. One of which, being a geographical description of Anegada, was published, whereas the other, which remains unpublished, consisted of extracts from his survey journal and is mainly concerned with his techniques.[1]

It may be presumed that the submission of these articles was Schomburgk's first contact with the Royal Geographical Society, and he was extremely fortunate to have done so through its first secretary, Captain Alexander Maconochie RN,[2] who proved a staunch supporter of Schomburgk. While the first extant letter between Schomburgk and the Royal Geographical Society is dated 2 July 1832, there is reference in it to two earlier communications. On 2 July Schomburgk wrote to Maconochie from Tortola in response to a letter from the latter dated 6 June.[3] In his letter Schomburgk thanks Maconochie for the favourable opinion of his article, 'Remarks on the Island of Anegada', and asks that he be permitted to correspond with the society. He has also been in touch with John Barrow concerning his chart, but had been unaware that Barrow held such an important position at the Admiralty and, when he became aware, he was mortified that he had failed to treat him with the respect his rank deserved.[4]

At this point Schomburgk tried to interest the Royal Geographical Society in his future research, following his failure with the Linnean Society. As before, he laid out his plans for going to the United States. He stressed that he was not a professional or mechanical collector but a contributor to the learned societies of which he was a member or with which he corresponded. In future, however, as result of certain events that have deprived him of his financial security, he explains, he will have to try to derive

---

[1] See Schomburgk, 'Remarks on Anegada', *JRGS*, 2, 1832, pp. 152–70. The manuscript of the unpublished piece is to be found in the archives of the Royal Geographical Society, shelfmark JMS 5/2.

[2] Captain Alexander Maconochie (1787–1860) went on to become famous as the reforming governor of the penal settlement on Norfolk Island. There are two biographies of him: John V. Barry, *Alexander Maconochie of Norfolk Island: A Study of a Pioneer in Penal Reform*, Melbourne, Oxford University Press, 1958; and John Clay, *Maconochie's Experiment*, London, John Murray, 2001.

[3] Royal Geographical Society, Schomburgk Correspondence 1830–33 (hereafter RGS, RHS 1830–33), Letter of Schomburgk to Maconochie, 2 July 1832. The Royal Geographical Society did not start keeping copies of out letters until 1836., but fortunately Schomburgk had the practice of summarizing the letters to which he was replying, so that it is possible to get a fairly good idea of the contents of the letters written to him.

[4] John Barrow (1764–1848) was Second Secretary to the Admiralty, the most senior civil service position there, from 1804 to 1845 with a short break in 1806–7. He was elected a Fellow of the Royal Society in 1806, and became one of the first Vice-Presidents and Chairman of the Royal Geographical Society when it was founded in 1830. With a naval officer, Maconochie, as the latter Society's secretary, he exercised an enormous degree of influence within it, as he did on all government-sponsored exploration during the first half of the 19th century. Regardless of what *faux pas* Schomburgk might have made in addressing him, it seems unlikely that Schomburgk would have met with Barrow's favour; not only was he not a naval officer he was a foreigner as well. Barrow appears to have been as much prejudiced in favour of the former as he was against the latter. See Fergus Fleming, *Barrow's Boys*, London, Granta Books, 1998, for an account of Barrow's influence on exploration during the first part of the 19th century.

some income from his pursuit of natural history. Botany will not occupy his whole time and he is very willing to send communications to the Royal Geographical Society and, in turn, will obey and execute to the best of his powers, any instructions with which the Society might favour him. He also hopes that he will be able to defray the cost of travel and research by selling botanical collections. What sort of price, Schomburgk asked Maconochie, would such collections command and would there be enough subscribers to cover the cost of travelling expenses? He did not want remuneration above his costs because his research was gratification enough. Those were his intentions, he wrote, but if the Society thought he might be better employed elsewhere as a naturalist and geographer, his plans were not so fixed that they could not be changed. Most of all he would like to be employed as an assistant surveyor or naturalist on one of the Society's expeditions.[1]

Maconochie wrote to John Lindley,[2] Professor of Botany at the University of London (later University College London), about Schomburgk's questions and plans. Lindley's response was of crucial significance. He replied that there was already a botanist (Drummond)[3] sending back good collections from the area that Schomburgk proposed to visit and suggested that he should instead turn his attention to the sources of the Orinoco River and the country within 200 miles of Santa Fé de Bogotá, in Colombia. As for botanical specimens, the going rate was £2.10s.0d per 100 species, but the problem was that Schomburgk was unknown to British naturalists and they would not give him any commission. He suggested that Schomburgk might send him some parcels of dried specimens from Tortola and he would show them around among botanists. He would not pay for the Tortola specimens, except for well-preserved orchids at 9d a species. Schomburgk acted on this suggestion and on 12 May 1833 despatched a parcel to Lindley. He knew by August that the boat carrying the specimens had arrived safely and looked forward to Lindley's comments. By October, he found it strange that he had still not heard anything and it was not until February 1834 that it emerged that the package had not been taken off the boat and had crossed the Atlantic three times before being delivered.[4]

On 5 November 1833, Schomburgk wrote to Maconochie, commenting on Lindley's recommendation that he should turn his interest to South America. He was disappointed that someone else had anticipated his proposal for the Mississippi region, and considered Lindley's suggestion too risky a venture to be undertaken 'individually'. In North America he would be able to underwrite his summer's botanizing by teaching botany, mathematics and languages during the winter. If part of the expenses of the South American journey can be assured him, there was no one happier to undertake it and he flattered himself that he possessed the perseverance and physical powers to

---

[1] RGS, RHS 1830–33, Letter of Schomburgk to Maconochie, 2 July 1832.

[2] John Lindley (1799–1865), appointed first Professor of Botany of the University of London in 1829. He was much involved, with George Bentham, in the running of the Horticultural Society. For a recent set of critical essays on Lindley, see William T. Stearn, ed., *John Lindley 1799–1856. Gardener, Botanist and Pioneer Orchidologist*, Woodbridge, Antique Collectors' Club and Royal Horticultural Society, 1998.

[3] Thomas Drummond (1780–1835) collected in Canada, the United States and Texas from 1831 and died in Havana in March 1835.

[4] RGS, RHS 1830–33, Letters of Schomburgk to Maconochie, 2 July 1832, 5 November 1832, 12 April 1833, 30 May 1833, 5 August 1833, 7 October 1833; RGS, RHS 1834–40, Letter of Schomburgk to Maconochie, 7 February 1834.

contend with it. The patronage of the Royal Geographical Society would be very valuable, if the South American project were to be undertaken.[1]

In February 1833, Schomburgk wrote two letters to Maconochie, one of them confidential, in which he reported that he had received further financial setbacks. When he had written to Maconochie and Lindley in the previous November he had had sufficient funds to cover the cost of the proposed expedition's equipment (instruments, charts, books, etc.) and the expenses of the first year, the success of which, he hoped, would have encouraged the 'scientific public' to invest in its prolongation. This money had all been lost so that now the only way forward was for Schomburgk to rely on Maconochie's and his friends' influence and encouragement, and substantial protection from the Royal Geographical Society. Schomburgk himself was willing to dedicate all the money he could to the venture and had written to other institutions soliciting support.[2]

In his official letter of the same date, Schomburgk acknowledged enthusiastically news of his impending election as a Corresponding Member of the Royal Geographical Society. It was an honour, he wrote, that would encourage him to dedicate a greater part of his future researches to geography. When, however, in April 1834, he received official notification of his election he turned this round, and wrote that he expected that the Society would now feel that much more anxious that his South American expedition be crowned with success, clearly hinting at patronage and financial support.[3]

Maconochie's letter also contained some questions about the proposed expedition and, in response, Schomburgk considered both the obstacles to its successful completion and the qualities he possessed that would achieve that end. He went on to list his qualifications among which were a command of German, French, Italian and English, and he was learning Spanish (despite the fact he had earlier told the Linnean Society he was acquainted with that language). Although he had obtained some of Alexander von Humboldt's volumes,[4] without access to a library he has been unable to make a detailed plan, but he craved the Society's substantial assistance 'in exploring the Rivers Orinoco and Amazon in Geographical and botanical respects'. The survey instruments he owned were too large and cumbersome, but he had been offered, for $150, a box containing a pocket sextant by Troughton,[5] a Schmalcalder[6] azimuth compass, an artificial horizon, microscope, camera lucida, and a pocket telescope. In addition he would also need thermometers, barometers, hygrometers, pluviometer, pendulum, dipping needle, and a good chronometer, without which the undertaking would be useless. Equally indispensable would be powerful recommendations to the British authorities in Guiana as well as to influential persons in Colombia.[7]

By January 1833 Schomburgk had become concerned about his chart of Anegada which he had sent to the Admiralty the previous September. Barrow had seemed to

[1] RGS, RHS 1830–33, Letter of Schomburgk to Maconochie, 5 November 1832.

[2] RGS, RHS 1830–33, Confidential letter of Schomburgk to Maconochie, 9 February 33.

[3] RGS, RHS 1830–33, Letters of Schomburgk to Maconochie, 9 February 1833, 12 April 1833.

[4] Alexander von Humboldt (1769–1859), who explored the Orinoco and regions of Columbia in 1799–1804, ranks among the greatest geographers of the 19th century. Schomburgk saw him as a hero and someone to emulate. The two men were unacquainted in 1833 but later became good friends.

[5] Edward Troughton (1753–1835), of the scientific instrument makers Troughton and Simms of London.

[6] Charles Augustus Schmalcalder (c. 1786–1843), instrument maker of Strand, London.

[7] RGS, RHS 1830–33, Letter of Schomburgk to Maconochie, 9 February 1833.

acknowledge receipt on 14 December when he wrote to say that he had been instructed by his Lordships to inform Schomburgk that it was not usual for a chart to be dedicated to His Majesty, as Schomburgk had requested. Schomburgk was upset by his unintentional breach of etiquette, but even more by the fact that Barrow's letter gave no indication of what the Admiralty's intentions were with regard to the chart. Finally, in April 1833, Schomburgk heard that the Admiralty had approved his chart and that it was to be engraved and published. Although Schomburgk was pleased with this news, he bemoaned the fact that he was to get so little reward for his time, cost and health. However, the saga of the chart was not yet over as later in the year the Admiralty reversed its decision about publishing it. Schomburgk was mortified by this, but the Admiralty then changed its mind yet again and went ahead and published it.[1] In 1834 it was described in *The Nautical Magazine* as 'very valuable' and that it 'should be in the possession of every West India trader'.[2]

During 1832–3, Schomburgk had been carrying out other surveys in the Virgin Islands, but so disillusioned had he become over his treatment with regard to the Anegada chart that he more than once threatened, in his letters to Maconochie, to give the whole thing up. In fact he continued with it and in due course submitted his findings on tides and sea conditions around the Virgin Islands to the Royal Geographical Society which published them in the *Journal* in 1835.[3] He also submitted in 1833 an article entitled 'On the Originating Cause and the Further Development of Hurricanes in the West-Indies' which was not published.[4]

At the same time Schomburgk was beginning to draw up plans for his South American project. He was concerned about lack of proper support from home now that he had been deprived of his own funds. He cannot expect, he wrote, to find:

> encouragement and proper means in the country I am to explore – and furthermore will my tale receive credit amongst a suspicious race (I do not allude to the uncivilized Indians on whom I confide with more security than to the lords of the soil, the Portuguese, the Colombian,[5] etc), if I am not provided with credentials or letters of recommendation.

He wanted to take his time and not 'run through the country like a mechanical collector of plants'. He intended to make observations on:

1) geographical features, rivers, productions of the soil, climate, etc.;
2) the character of the inhabitants, whether trade with them may be possible and in what goods, and whether 'civilization' has been attempted among them; and

---

[1] RGS, RHS 1830–33, Letters of Schomburgk to Maconochie, 6 January 1833, 9 February 1833, 12 April 1833, 5 August 1833. Although there is no evidence for it this change of heart may have been occasioned by Captain Barnett of HMS *Jackdaw* who had been off Anegada in June 1833 and had expressed complete satisfaction in the chart. At a later date the survey schooner *Lark* checked the accuracy of Schomburgk's work and found that it did him 'infinite credit' (RGS, RHS, 1834–40, Letter of Schomburgk to Maconochie, 20 April 1836).

[2] See *The Nautical Magazine*, 3, 1834, p. 368.

[3] See Schomburgk, 'Remarks on the Heavy Swell Along Some of the West-India Islands, Commonly Called "Ground" or "North Sea": and on the Set and Velocity of the Tides, and the Effects Produced by Their Transporting Power, Among the Virgin Islands', *JRGS*, 5, 1835, pp. 23–38.

[4] The manuscript is held in the archives of the Royal Geographical Society, shelfmark JMS 20/1. William Faraday reviewed it for publication and wrote 'Much of the Philosophy ... is not at all fit for the present time & and the rest requires far more *rigorous proof* than is given in the paper'.

[5] Schomburgk almost invariably wrote 'Portuguese' rather than 'Brazilian'; except in direct quotations, this practice has not been followed. Colombian also covers modern Venezuelan.

3) to make collections of minerals, plants and animals.

What he needed was proper support from the authorities, the necessary surveying instruments, and funds to cover the first two years of the expedition. After that he would be able to fund himself from the income received from his plant collections.[1]

His initial plan had been to go to Maracaibo or Santa Marta on the Venezuelan coast and from there travel overland to Bogotá, but he was very willing to change this in order to explore first 'the central ridge between the basin of the Orinoco along the whole of the Guyana coast and the Amazon'. He would ascend the latter river to examine the natural products and the scope for trade with the tribes before heading north to the Orinoco. He planned to leave the Virgin Islands after the autumnal equinox and go to British Guiana where he would stay while collecting information. To cover the cost of his passage to British Guiana and the initial equipment, he would like the necessary money provided in Tortola. Furthermore, when he arrived in British Guiana he would expect to find the means for starting the expedition, instructions for disposing of collections, observations and manuscripts. He did not mind whether the books, instruments and charts which he needed were delivered to him in Tortola or British Guiana. As for the source of funding he felt that if his plan was laid before the government 'in an influential and imposing manner', it would help. The unexplored Amazon region doubtless offered 'new resources to the mercantile interest' that might help in the present state of depression. He himself had written to the Berlin Horticultural Society which might be willing to collaborate with the Royal Geographical Society in this venture.[2]

Nothing moved fast and in August 1833, Schomburgk, in reply to a non-extant letter from Maconochie, wrote that he was unhappy about progress and that after ten months planning things seemed to have retreated rather than advanced. He was worried that the obstacles that have arisen were the result of his nationality but trusted that this was not a consideration within the scientific community. The problem was that the Royal Geographical Society was considering another candidate to undertake the exploration. Schomburgk either was told this or deduced it because he pointed out that he had been four years in the West Indies and that his constitution was now well adapted, and certainly better so than someone sent out from England, for the proposed venture. Furthermore, he added, he required only his expenses; he was not undertaking the journey for 'lucre' and his reward would be success.[3]

One can also see why he felt no advance had been made because the same unseen letter posed various questions to him, most of which he had already answered. The first question was 'what outfit would you absolutely require?'. To which he replied that he would be as economical as possible but he did not see why he should pay expenses out of his own pocket as no benefit accrued to him. Immediately he needed £50 for the passage to British Guiana. The second question was 'what instruments does he require?'. The instruments he listed are similar to those that he mentioned in his letter of 9 February, but additions included a theodolite and chain, a reflecting telescope, and

[1] RGS, RHS 1830–33, Letter of Schomburgk to Maconochie, 12 April 1833.
[2] RGS, RHS 1830–33, Letter of Schomburgk to Maconochie, 12 April 1833.
[3] RGS, RHS 1830–33, Letter of Schomburgk to Maconochie, 5 August 1833. RGS, Council Minute Book, 1830–41, Minute of 25 January 1834.

Wollaston's[1] apparatus for measuring height by boiling point. The third question was 'what books does he need?'. He listed three works of Humboldt, his journeys, astronomical observations and his equinoctial plants. He proposed an encyclopaedia of plants, one or two works on geodesical surveying, the nautical almanac for 1834 and a formular for recording barometric and thermometric measurements. To the question what other equipment he needed Schomburgk answered several dozen assorted drawing pencils, some notebooks, a small chest of indispensable medicines, and several muskets with powder and shot. As for the size of the expedition he suggested one literate and numerate person and four to six Indians or mixed Indian/Negroes, and four horses or mules to carry the instruments and plant collections. His answers to these last two questions indicated that he had very little idea of the conditions which he was going to encounter.[2]

The annual cost of the expedition Schomburgk was unable to estimate but he had certain proposals to make. He would operate under the strictest economies and suggested that the Royal Geographical Society determine the sum that it thought adequate and deposit it with the Governor of British Guiana. The latter, if he considered Schomburgk qualified to undertake the expedition but that it should cost less than the sum provided, would pass judgement and Schomburgk would accept his ruling. Should the Governor not approve of him, the £50 travelling money from Tortola to British Guiana was not to be refunded. From the time that Schomburgk and the Royal Geographical Society come to an agreement, the former's services would belong to the latter for four years. During the first two of these, the Royal Geographical Society would pay all expenses, and all the observations, notes, charts, drawings made by Schomburgk during the four years would be its property. The money from plant collections made during the first two years would cover the expenses of years three and four, and the income from such collections made during those years would go to cover the cost of Schomburgk's return journey and convalescence. As well as the twelve sets of plants for the subscribers found by Lindley, Schomburgk would seek to make further sets, two of which would go to the Royal Geographical Society and one he would keep for himself. After the second year he had the right to decide whether to continue the expedition but this decision must be reached by the end of the third year.[3]

As for what he proposed to do, the first two years would be spent on the examination of Guiana from the basin of the Orinoco to the mouth of the Amazon; years three and four on the journey to Bogotá, the route of which would be determined by the Royal Geographical Society. If after the fourth year, his health and funds permitting, he decided to extend his researches for a further two years, then during that time all his notes, drawings and other productions would belong to him.[4]

He was to be provided with letters from influential people, preferably the Colonial Office, to the Dutch, French, Brazilian and Colombian authorities, so that there would be no difficulties about crossing their territories. While he would take the greatest care of all equipment, he was not to be held responsible for any damage or loss. The instruments were to be returned to the Governor of British Guiana or other designated person on

[1] William Hyde Wollaston (1766–1828), English physicist.
[2] RGS, RHS 1830–33, Letter of Schomburgk to Maconochie, 5 August 1833.
[3] RGS, RHS 1830–33, Letter of Schomburgk to Maconochie, 5 August 1833.
[4] RGS, RHS 1830–33, Letter of Schomburgk to Maconochie, 5 August 1833.

completion of the expedition. He hoped that this letter, together with earlier ones, would be enough to enable the Council of the Royal Geographical Society to reach a decision.[1]

In mid-September he was in a position to elaborate further on his plans mainly, it would appear, because he had obtained more volumes of Humboldt's *Personal Narrative*. He claimed that no scientific traveller had visited Guiana since Humboldt, who had visited only a small part of the region and had not investigated the Pacaraima Mountains. His plans now embraced an examination of the Imataca Mountains, an ascent of the Cuyuni River to its source, followed by a crossing to the Mazaruni River by which he would make his way back to the Essequibo. He also proposed to ascend the Rupununi River to its source, then cross to that of the Takutu and follow the latter to its junction with the Rio Branco where the Brazilian Fort São Joaquim was located. If he has been provided with suitable letters to the Brazilian authorities, he will make his base at the fort and from there explore the Pacaraima Mountains and the rivers flowing south from them. It was in this area that geographers, for the past two centuries, had placed Ralegh's El Dorado. At São Joaquim he would be able to learn whether it would be feasible to reach from there the source of the Orinoco or whether it would be more advisable to travel via the Rio Negro and the Cassiquiare Canal to Esmeralda and make the attempt from there.[2]

Despite the 'Mosquitos and the resignation of all comforts' Schomburgk would stay some time in the vicinity of Esmeralda as Humboldt had left much to be investigated in the area. After he had done this and completed the main aim of the expedition, the discovery of the source of the Orinoco, for which he would have to win over the Guiacas and Guaharibos[3] Indians with presents of hatchets, knives and fishing utensils, he proposed to make his base at the Mission of Maypures and explore the plains between the Rivers Vichada, Meta and Guaviare. Alternatively he could base himself at San Fernando de Atabapo and travel by the Temi and Tuamini rivers[4] to the Rio Negro and thence to the Amazon. It would be up to Council to decide how far he should ascend the Amazon, but he could then follow one of its tributaries to reach Bogotá.[5]

Schomburgk reckoned that he would need four years to undertake this expedition as he wanted to travel slowly, choosing central points from which to carry out investigations. He noted that Humboldt had observed that a traveller was welcome at the missions and thus able to spend a year on the banks of the Rivers Atabapo, Tuamini and Negro. This, together with another year among the mountains near Esmeralda would

---

[1] RGS, RHS 1830–33, Letter of Schomburgk to Maconochie, 5 August 1833.

[2] RGS, RHS 1830–33, Letter of Schomburgk to Maconochie, 15 September 1833.

[3] Among the names used for local groups of the present day Yanomami. Guiaca is usually spelt Waica.

[4] The Tuamini is not marked on the 1:500,000 map of the Servicio Autónomo de Geografía Nacional of Venezuela. Schomburgk, however, has taken his information from Humboldt. See his *Personal Narrative of Travels to the Equinoctial Regions of the New Continent During the Years 1799–1804*, transl. by Thomasina Ross, 3 vols, London, George Bell & Sons, 1907, II, p. 351, who stated that the Tuamini is a tributary of the Temi and on its banks was to be found the mission of Javita, spelt Yavita on the modern map. Yavita lies on a left bank tributary of the Temi (itself a tributary of the Atabapo) which is perhaps the Tuamini, and is at the northern end of the short portage between the Amazon and Orinoco river systems. It was crossed by Humboldt in 1800 and by Richard Spruce in 1854. See Spruce, *Notes of a Botanist on the Amazon and Andes*, 2 vols, London, Macmillan, 1908, I, p. 451. Alfred Wallace made Yavita his base for several weeks in 1851: *A Narrative of Travels on the Amazon and Rio Negro*, London, New York & Melbourne, Ward, Lock & Co., 1890. See Chapter IX entitled 'Javíta'.

[5] RGS, RHS 1830–33, Letter of Schomburgk to Maconochie, 15 September 1833.

prove botanically very fruitful. Thus Humboldt had suggested that a traveller should be provided with letters from the Generals of the different religious orders (Capuchins, Franciscans and Dominicans). Schomburgk suggested that the Royal Geographical Society, through its extensive connections, might be able to secure such letters, despite the fact that he was a Lutheran.[1]

Schomburgk also made other detailed changes to his August plan. Because of the climate, he would have to despatch plant collections at every opportunity. The journey between Fort São Joaquim and Esmeralda would have to be done in canoes so that the mules would have to be dispensed with at that point. As far as the number of expedition members was concerned this would have to be determined by him according to circumstances. He would like to add a quicksilver horizon to the list of instruments he required because Humboldt repeatedly regretted the lack of one since the mosquitos made it impossible to level instruments. Additional books he wanted were La Condamine[2] and, if he were to explore the Caroní River, a copy of the account of a journey on this river in 1820.[3] Pins and boxes would be required if a collection of insects were to be made, and the advice of an experienced entomologist. A map of his proposed route was being prepared and would be forwarded in due course.[4]

On 7 October Schomburgk sent part of the map (the rest was sent a month later) and more details.[5] He had also received the good news from Baron Schlechtendal,[6] editor of *Linnaea*, who occupied the Chair of Botany at Halle and had advised him to go ahead with the journey and had found him 10 subscribers for plants at £2 per 100 species.[7]

Progress was very slow and, on 5 November, Schomburgk complained to Maconochie that he had not heard from him since 10 June, but then he reacted with dismay when he did. Maconochie wrote on 12 December with the news that the Council had still not reached a decision. Schomburgk responded by pointing out that if the Royal Geographical Society refused to help he would suffer a great and undeserved hardship. He had only remained in the West Indies because of the proposed expedition and had refused employment at one of the Western Colleges in America in order to be free to undertake it. Maconochie had also noted that Schomburgk's estimate for outfitting the expedition was thought to be 'on too complete a scale' and may have to be cut back, to which the latter replied that that was up to the Royal Geographical Society, but if he did not have the instruments he could not take observations and his workload would be reduced accordingly.[8]

---

[1] RGS, RHS 1830–33, Letter of Schomburgk to Maconochie, 15 September 1833.

[2] La Condamine, Charles Marie de, *Relation abrégée d'un voyage fait dans l'intérieur de l'Amérique Méridionale*, Paris, chez la Veuve Pissot, 1745.

[3] Anon., 'Journal of a Trip from St. Thome de Angostura, in Spanish Guayana, to the Capuchin Missions of the Caroni', *The Quarterly Journal of Science, Literature, and the Arts*, 8, 1820, pp. 260–87; and 'Journal of an Excursion from St. Thome de Angostura, in Spanish Guayana, to the Capuchin Missions of the Caroni', ibid., 9, 1820, pp. 1–32.

[4] RGS, RHS 1830–33, Letter of Schomburgk to Maconochie, 15 September 1833.

[5] This map is to be found in the Map Room of the Royal Geographical Society (Shelfmark: Venezuela S/S2). There is also an associated manuscript (JMS 6/9) entitled 'Remarks to Accompany a Map of the rivers Orinoco, Essequebo, Branco, &c &c'.

[6] Diederich Franz Leonhard von Schlechtendal (1794–1866).

[7] RGS, RHS 1830–33, Letter of Schomburgk to Maconochie, 7 October 1833.

[8] RGS, RHS 1830–33, Letter of Schomburgk to Maconochie, 5 November 1833; RGS, RHS 1834–40, Letter of Schomburgk to Maconochie, 7 February 1834.

By mid-March 1834, Schomburgk had still heard nothing, and he 'prepared for the worst' but at the same time was ready to leave for British Guiana if the news were favourable. In fact, it more or less was, because on 18 March Schomburgk received Maconochie's letter of 6 February that informed him that the Royal Geographical Society had voted him £50 towards outfitting the expedition and £50 a year for three years to cover expenses. Furthermore, Maconochie was convinced that the government would provide an additional £100–200 a year together with a small advance towards outfitting. Schomburgk, while expressing heartfelt gratitude to Maconochie for his exertions on his behalf, was not exactly overjoyed by this news. He pointed out that the project could not go ahead without government support and what the Royal Geographical Society had offered was too small even for arrangements to be made. He repeated his condition that he was to receive £50 for his passage from Tortola to Demerara and stated that he could not be expected to provide instruments and other equipment out of that sum. On the question of instruments, he appreciated that the Royal Geographical Society should decide what he would take with him. He noted that in an earlier letter it had been claimed that he 'would not be able to lay down the ground with the exactness and particularity at which [he] seemed to aim, particularly if otherwise engaged in collecting and procuring plants and insects'. Even so, he argued a theodolite and chain would be indispensable and it would be a pity if, for the want of a little effort on the part of the Royal Geographical Society to procure a few instruments (which would be returned to it), he would have to neglect points of interest to science. He would now await anxiously to hear whether he was to proceed to British Guiana in June.[1]

Maconochie was able to inform Schomburgk in May that Lord Stanley, Secretary of State for the Colonies, had approved the expedition and only the decision of the Treasury was outstanding. The Royal Geographical Society's proposal to the government had been for joint funding of two expeditions, one in Southern Africa and the other in Guiana, both of great scientific and commercial importance and interest. The Society had proposed to put up £500 if the government would contribute £1,000. By July, however, Lord Stanley had resigned from office and the decision was stalled. Schomburgk once again voiced the feeling that he had been badly done by as he had turned down other offers and he was surprised that the discouragements had not worn out his patience. Even so he has made no other plans and would await the final decision, which if it arrived soon would still allow time for some exploration before the next wet season.[2]

In November 1834 the government had decided to patronize the expedition and the Council of the Royal Geographical Society agreed formally to engage Schomburgk's services and issued detailed instructions to him.[3] Schomburgk was to undertake two distinct objectives: the first of these was to investigate the physical and astronomical geography of the interior of British Guiana, and the second to connect his survey with that of Humboldt on the Orinoco. The second was not to be begun until the first was completed and the whole expedition was to last three years from

---

[1] RGS, RHS 1834–40, Letters of Schomburgk to Maconochie, 14 March 1834, 26 March 1834.

[2] RGS, RHS 1834–40, Letter of Schomburgk to Maconochie, 25 August 1834.

[3] The instructions were contained in two letters, of 13 and 19 November 1834. There are no extant copies of the originals but they were reproduced in 'Report of the Royal Geographical Society for 1835' in the *JRGS*, 6, 1836, pp. 7–11.

the date of his initial departure from Georgetown, capital of British Guiana. The sum available, to be administered by the Royal Geographical Society, was £900 in total; £600 during the first year and £300 spread over the next two. He was to proceed to British Guiana where he would receive instructions, in the name of the Royal Geographical Society, from the governor. All geographical information obtained during the three years would belong to the Royal Geographical Society, but the collections of natural history would remain Schomburgk's property, save that the Society was to have one set of any collections of dried plants, birds, fishes or insects which it would present, in his name, to the British Museum, and one set of geological specimens to be presented to the Geological Society of London. A draft for £50 was enclosed with the letter as a first payment out of the £600 for the first year to cover the costs of travelling to British Guiana, and his negotiation of it would be taken as an agreement to the terms laid down.

Alongside these formal instructions some more general views of the Society were conveyed to Schomburgk and it is worth examining these in a little more detail as they reflect on the fairness of the criticism that was later levelled at Schomburgk. It was pointed out that the objectives were more limited than those originally proposed by Schomburgk. The reason for this was to ensure that full justice be done to the physical geography of the colony in return for the British government's patronage.

> Accordingly, the Council wishes you to understand most distinctly that, for the first year, or eighteen months, every thing is to be subordinate to the object of thoroughly investigating the physical character and resources of that portion of the central ridge traversing this part of South America, which furnishes tributaries to the Demerara, Essequibo, and other rivers flowing into the Atlantic, within, or immediately contiguous to the British colony of Guiana.

Investigations were to cover mineral composition, soil and climate, origin, course and navigability of the rivers, human, plant and animal life, and the actual state and future capabilities of the colony. Only when these researches had been completed was Schomburgk 'to pass the mountains' and connect his survey with that of Humboldt. The Royal Geographical Society directed that Esmeralda should not be reached via the Rio Branco and Rio Negro, as these regions were already well known, but overland by the upper reaches of the Orinoco. His explorations could not now begin before August 1835 so it proposed that he delay his arrival in Georgetown until June. On the other hand if he wanted to arrive earlier and explore up the Cuyuni River to the Imataca Mountains, as he had originally proposed, then he may do so but only with the agreement of the governor and he would get no additional funding for this journey. The instructions closed with a rather grudging admission that some things had to be left to his own judgement and discretion.[1]

There appears to have been a letter from the Royal Geographical Society dated 18 December 1834 which authorized Schomburgk's departure for Demerara. However, that letter, as well as the two earlier letters reproduced in the 'Annual Report of the Royal Geographical Society' and two letters from Schomburgk to the Society (in January and February 1835), are missing. Accordingly it is difficult to put together what happened during early 1835. There was certainly one further complication. There had

---

[1] Report of the Royal Geographical Society for 1835, pp. 9–11.

been another change of government[1] shortly after the decision to help fund the expedition had been made, but initially it was not thought that this would affect things. That, however, was not the case and on 1 April 1835 Maconochie informed Schomburgk that the matter was to be reconsidered and urged him to remain in Tortola until further orders. A month later the matter was settled and on 13 June Schomburgk wrote to say that he would depart for British Guiana at the earliest opportunity but, in the absence of any direct route, he would have to travel via Barbados.[2]

Schomburgk left Tortola for St Thomas on 4 July to catch the steamboat to Barbados but it failed to arrive and it was only on the 16th of the month that he finally got away. There was a further delay in Barbados and it was not until Monday, 3 August 1835 that he arrived in Georgetown, capital of British Guiana.[3]

British Guiana in the 1830s

The British Guiana in which Schomburgk found himself in August 1835 had had a complex colonial history. The Dutch had been the first to colonize the three rivers, Essequibo, Demerara and Berbice. During the seventeenth and eighteenth centuries they had successfully hung on to their colonies but during the Napoleonic wars the colonies changed hands several times between the Dutch, French and British. The British took final *de facto* possession of the three colonies in 1803 under the Terms of Capitulation which were formally confirmed by the Convention of London in 1814. Under the Convention all Dutch colonies were restored to the Netherlands except for the Cape of Good Hope, Demerara, Essequibo and Berbice, for which Britain paid three million pounds sterling. The three colonies were amalgamated as British Guiana with its capital at Georgetown in 1831.

The colony's economy was heavily dependent on sugar and during the 1830s the planters were worried about a threat to their operation. In 1834 slavery had been abolished and the planters were wondering who exactly was going to work their plantations once the five-year period of apprenticeship, during which ex-slaves had to continue working for their former masters, had expired. The answer was to be indentured labour, mainly from the South Asian subcontinent, but that is not part of this story. More important was the fact that the planters saw the government in London, and more immediately its representative in the form of the governor, as responsible for their woes. They were disinclined to be cooperative and the peculiar constitution of British Guiana, partly based as it was on a Dutch constitution of 1795, and accepted in 1803 under the Terms of Capitulation, allowed them to exercise that disinclination.

The constitutional bodies consisted of the Court of Policy presided over by the governor appointed in London. This body consisted of five ex-officio members, including the governor, and five colonial members appointed by an electoral college, the College of Kiezers.[4] Then there was the College of Financial Representatives which

---

[1] Melbourne was dismissed as Prime Minister by William IV in November 1834, and Robert Peel took over in December. He resigned in April 1835 and Melbourne returned to the post.

[2] RGS, RHS 1834–40, Letters of Schomburgk to Maconochie, 21 April 1835, 19 May 1835, 13 June 1835.

[3] RGS, RHS 1834–40, Letters of Schomburgk to Maconochie, 2 July 1835, 15 July 1835, 8 August 1835.

[4] This name was merely a retention of the Dutch form. Kiezer in Dutch means elector.

had six members elected by the College of Kiezers. The Court of Policy and College of Financial Representatives came together in the Combined Court which body had the final say on financial matters. The plantocracy, because of the strict qualification of the franchise, had a built-in majority. This made them, if not *de facto* rulers of the colony, a group to be reckoned with and it often made things very difficult for the governor and exasperated the government back in London when it refused to accept any responsibility, financial or otherwise, for certain matters relating to the colony. In due course this was to impinge directly on Schomburgk's activities when the Combined Court declined to contribute to the cost of surveying the colony's boundaries.

The plantations, like most of the population, were within a few miles of the coast, and as a visitor in 1831 wrote: 'The merchants and planters on the coast ridicule the idea of expeditions into the interior, attended as they are with risk, discomfort and no profit.'[1] Indeed, unlike their Dutch predecessors, the British tended to ignore the interior and its Amerindian inhabitants.[2] Admittedly the Dutch had been operating in a different political environment and, as well as trading with the Amerindians, they had recruited them to keep the African slave population in order and the Spanish in Venezuela at bay. As part of this policy the Dutch had set up, on the courses of the main rivers, posts which could control the flow of people and goods, although the Amerindians had no difficulty in circumventing them whenever they wanted. Nor could it be said that the far interior was unknown. The Dutch were almost certainly aware in the seventeenth century of the route, via the Pirara portage, from the Essequibo to the Rio Branco and thus to Portuguese territory, and they may even have travelled it. In 1639, a Spanish priest, Christoval de Acuña, reported the possession by the Amerindians on the Rio Negro of Dutch goods. This, however, does not prove that the trade was carried on directly by the Dutch; indeed Amerindian intermediaries are much more likely to have been responsible for the conveyance of the merchandise. A hundred years later, an official expedition into the interior, headed by the German surgeon Nicolas Horstman, was mounted. Horstman descended the Rio Branco and it is unlikely that he would have been heard of again if he had not met the French scientist La Condamine, to whom he gave an account of his journey and a sketch map of it. These papers were taken back to France and the information contained in them incorporated into Jean d'Anville's 1748 map of South America, the first to give even a vaguely accurate picture of the region where the fabled Lake Parima and El Dorado were supposed to be located.[3]

---

[1] J. E. Alexander, *Transatlantic Sketches, Comprising Visits to the Most Interesting Scenes in North and South America and the West Indies with Notes on Negro Slavery and Canadian Emigration*, London, Richard Bentley, 1833, p. 77.

[2] See M. N. Menezes, *British Policy Towards the Amerindians in British Guiana 1803–1873*, Oxford, Clarendon Press, 1977, for an account of British involvement with the native population during the 19th century.

[3] It would be too much of a diversion to explain how the site of Lake Parima came to be located here. The story is well told by John Hemming, *The Search for El Dorado*, London, Joseph, 1978. The idea proved obstinately persistent and on D'Anville's 1760 map it is back again, and is marked as the source of tributaries of the Rio Branco, Cuyuni and Orinoco. As late as 1844, an American writer, Jacob Van Heuvel, *El Dorado; Being a Narrative of the Circumstances Which Gave Rise to Reports in the Sixteenth Century, of the Existence of a Rich and Splendid City in South America, to Which that Name was Given, and Which Led to Many Enterprises in Search of it; Including a Defence of Sir Walter Raleigh, in Regard to the Relations Made by him Respecting it, etc.*, New York, J. Winchester, New World Press, 1844, resurrected it. Schomburgk responded fiercely to this claim. See 1845, 'On the Lake Parima (The "El Dorado" of Sir Walter Raleigh) and the Geography of Guiana', *Simmonds's Colonial Magazine*, 5, pp. 381–91.

Under British rule, there were, of course, those who ventured into the interior; the most famous being the naturalist Charles Waterton who made four such journeys between 1812 and 1824.[1] Before that, however, in 1810 a medical doctor, John Hancock,[2] and two companions had been sent by the government on a mission to discover the number and strength of the Amerindian population in the interior and whether they represented any threat to the colony. Both Waterton and Hancock travelled as far as the Portuguese Fort São Joaquim at the junction of the Takutu and Rio Branco, and a later pair of travellers, Smith and Gullifer,[3] continued down the latter river to the Amazon. It is also clear that there must have been unrecorded but frequent comings and goings of free coloured and Amerindians between the coast and the interior.

Thus while the interior was regarded as economically unimportant, routes into and through it were known. At the same time detailed geographical knowledge of it was extraordinarily limited. Humboldt had commented early in the century that in the interior of Guiana, where Lake Parima was reputed to be, there were '48,000 square leagues upon which there is not a single astronomical observation'.[4] Nothing had changed by the mid-1830s and even the limits of the colony were unknown. The Corentyne River marked the eastern boundary with Dutch Guiana, but otherwise the frontiers, those with Brazil and Venezuela, were undefined and nobody had given much thought to them. Some idea of this can be derived from the 1833 map, mentioned above, that Schomburgk constructed, with information derived from Humboldt, to go with his proposal to the Royal Geographical Society for a 'scientific journey' in South America. This shows, for example, the frontier between British Guiana and Venezuela running along the Essequibo, south of the Potaro River, until it meets French Guiana which stretches across the south of British Guiana; nor are Brazil and British Guiana shown as sharing a common boundary.[5] It is not intended

[1] Charles Waterton (1782–1865). His *Wanderings in South America, the North-West of the United States, and the Antilles, in the Years 1812, 1816, 1820 and 1824 with Original Instructions for the Perfect Preservation of Birds and for Cabinets of Natural History*, London, J. Mawman, 1825, has been republished on numerous occasions since its first edition. Beyond his brilliant and amusing account of his travels, Waterton is best known for his eccentricities. See Julia Blackburn, *Charles Waterton: 1782–1865*, London, Bodley Head, 1989, for a recent biography.

[2] John Hancock resided for twenty-four years (1804–28) in British Guiana, as a practising physician. He made a number of trips into the interior and published on various matters relating to the colony, in particular his *Observations on the Climate, Soil, and Productions of British Guiana, and on the Advantages of Emigration to, and Colonizing the Interior of that Country*, London, James Fraser; John Hatchard and Son; and George Mann, 1835.

[3] Gullifer was a Royal Navy lieutenant, and Smith a British merchant from Caracas. They journeyed into the interior of British Guiana in 1820. They travelled down the Rio Branco to Manaus where Smith died. Gullifer then made his way to Trinidad where he committed suicide. There is reference to an account of the journey written by Gullifer which at one point was in Schomburgk's possession (see below p. 282). No trace of it has been found.

[4] Humboldt, *Voyage aux régions équinoxiales du Nouveau Continent, fait en 1799, 1800, 1801, 1803 et 1804*, 13 vols, Paris, Librairée Grecque-Latine-Allemande, 1816–31, II, p. 682.

[5] Schomburgk modified his ideas soon after reaching British Guiana in August 1835. He produced a sketch map based on the work of William Hilhouse and J. E. Alexander which gives a better representation of the colony, although still leaving the Venezuelan boundary along the Essequibo. A reproduction of this map is to be found in Graham Burnett, *Masters of All They Surveyed. Exploration, Geography, and a British El Dorado*, Chicago and London, University of Chicago Press, 2000, p. 73. He states that it was 'recently discovered in the Archives of the University of Guyana' but by the time his book was published, it had disappeared again (p. 74 and fn. 16).

to enter here into a discussion of the boundary question since a summary of it can be found in Volume II, Appendix 1, 'The Boundary Dispute'; rather, mention is made of it merely to draw attention to just how empty was the map on which Schomburgk set to work.

The Native Peoples of British Guiana

In 1840, Schomburgk estimated the native population of British Guiana as 7,000; a figure far below that of William Hilhouse, Quartermaster-General of the Indians, who in 1825 had put the figure 'between 15,000 and 20,000' in the part of the country north of the Rupununi River.[1] Whereas this demonstrates the difficulty of estimating the size of a native population in the interior of a country such as British Guiana, Hilhouse's figure is more likely. One reason for Schomburgk's low estimate is that by 1840, although he had travelled widely in the south of the country, he had not been in the north-west, the region with the highest density of Amerindians. Today the Amerindian population of Guyana is over 30,000.

The Native Peoples were divided, more perhaps by the colonists than the Amerindians themselves, into a number of distinct tribal groups. The Amerindian names for groups of people tended to be localized and changing. This meant that the same group of people, perhaps no more than a collection of a few settlements, was called different names by their different neighbours. Furthermore some of these names are merely nicknames, and a name such as Serekong (an Akawaio sub-group), means little more than 'the people here'. The constant shifting of settlements also contributed to the problem. Thus the population of a named community might move as a whole to a different site, or it could split up and become absorbed into other communities, thus losing its identity rather than disappearing. That said, since the arrival of the Europeans there had been a huge decline in the native population and with it great changes in the political and social organization in the region. Evidence points to the previous existence of far more complex arrangements than existed in the mid-nineteenth century. While the process of depopulation was still underway in the 1830–40s, mainly as a result of smallpox and other imported diseases, the extinction of whole tribes which Schomburgk reported,[2] needs to be treated with caution. To add to this general confusion the main tribal groups recognized at the period were not territorially discrete, but villages belonging to different groups were intermingled with one another.

Although there is a fair amount of ethnographic information in Schomburgk's reports, he published little of a purely ethnographic nature. A paper by Schomburgk on Indo-American traditions was read to what Schomburgk called the Antiquarian Society

---

[1] See Schomburgk, *A Description of British Guiana, Geographical and Statistical: Exhibiting its Resources and Capabilities, Together with the Present and Future Condition and Prospects of the Colony*, London, Simpkin, Marshall & Co., 1840, p. 51; William Hilhouse, *Indian Notices: or Sketches of the Habits, Characters, Languages, Superstitions, Soil, and Climate of the Several Nations; with Remarks on their Capacity for Colonization, Present Government and Suggestions for Future Improvements and Civilization. Also, the Icthyology of the Fresh Waters of the Interior*, Georgetown, National Commission for Research Materials, 1978 [1825], p. 7.

[2] See, for example, Volume II, chap. 3, on the fate of the Amaripa.

of London in 1836,[1] but it is not until 1844, after he had completed his South American journeys, that he presented a paper to the Ethnological Society of London 'On the Natives of Guiana'.[2] He lists thirteen different tribes, and since there is very frequent reference to them in his reports, it is worth considering them altogether here, although where each first appears in his reports, there is a brief comment to help the reader.

The Arawaaks lived along the full length of the coast and not far inland; a distribution not much different from today. The name is spelt Arawak today which is also the name of the language group to which they belong. Their self-designation was Lokono, meaning 'The People', but today, even among themselves, this name has been superseded by Arawak.

The Warraus, spelt today Warao, mainly lived, as they do today, in the Orinoco Delta, but communities then also existed on the Corentyne River which are no longer found there. The Warao language is independent.

The Caribs or Caribisi, the former name being the standard spelling today, inhabited the lower reaches of the Essequibo, Mazaruni, Cuyuni and Corentyne rivers. It would appear that in Schomburgk's time they had recently abandoned the middle reaches of some of these rivers and moved downstream. The name Carib also denotes one of the major language groups of the region.

Accawais or Waccawaios, usually spelt Akawaio today, are a Carib-speaking group who were and are mainly concentrated in the Upper Cuyuni and Mazaruni, although in Schomburgk's day their settlements were also found on the Demerara and Berbice. These people are also found, together with the Patamona, on the Venezuelan savannahs. The Akawaio and the Patamona consider themselves to constitute a group called Kapon.

The Macusi, usually Macushi today, are another Carib-speaking group who lived and live mainly on the Rupununi savannahs north of the Kanuku Mountains and south of the Pacaraima range and across the frontier into Brazil.

The Arècūnãs, spelt Arecuna today, are a Carib-speaking group who live to the north-west of the Macushi to whom they are very closely related. The Macushi and Arecuna, together with the Kamarakoto and Taurepan, two groups not mentioned by Schomburgk, identify themselves as a single people called Pemon.

Wapisianas, usually Wapishiana today, are an Arawak-speaking group who inhabited, as they still do now, an arc stretching from the Southern Rupununi savannahs northwestward on to the Rio Branco savannahs.

Atorãis or Atórias, an Arawak-speaking group, lived south of the Wapishiana and

---

[1] A copy of this paper, entitled 'Fragments of Indo-American Traditions, and a description of the painted Rocks at the Cataract of Waraputa' is to be found among the Pigott papers in the Bodleian Library, Oxford (Bod MS Pigott c.3). According to Humboldt, a paper on Macushi religious traditions was read to the Société des Antiquaires on 17 November 1836 ('Sur quelques points importans de la géographie de la Guyane', *Nouvelles annales des voyages et des sciences géographiques*, 74 (14, 3rd Series), pp. 137–80, 1837, p. 176), and the Secretary of the Royal Geographical Society forwarded to the 'Antiquarian Society' on 15 November 1836 a paper by Schomburgk entitled 'Fragments of Indo-American Traditions' (Royal Geographical Society, Letter Book (hereafter RGS, LB), 1836–40). Presumably the society being referred to is the Society of Antiquaries, but its records for that period are rather sparse, and it has no record of such a paper. Schomburgk in this paper refers to another paper by him on the original descent of the Caribs that had been read to the Society at an earlier date; no trace of this paper has been discovered.

[2] It was not published until 1848. See Schomburgk, 'On the Natives of Guiana', *Journal of the Ethnological Society of London*, 1, pp. 253–76.

were very similar to them. Very few of them survived in Schomburgk's time and they finally disappeared or had become absorbed by the Wapishiana by the middle of the twentieth century.

The Taruma lived in the upper tributaries of the Essequibo River. There is evidence to suggest that they had fled from the Rio Negro and settled in the region. Schomburgk reported that there were 400 of them, but by the first quarter of the twentieth century they had heavily intermarried with the Waiwai and all but disappeared. Linguistically they were not related to other groups in the region.

Woyawais, known today as Waiwai, a Carib-speaking people, have inhabited, since first reported, the Upper Essequibo and Upper Trombetas Rivers. Over the decades the Waiwai have absorbed a number of small neighbouring groups, or, which may be more accurate, the name Waiwai has prevailed for an amalgamation of a number of small neighbouring groups.

Maopityans, the modern day Mawayena, lived among the tributaries of the Upper Trombetas. Although Schomburgk stated that they were rapidly approaching extinction, a few Mawayena have survived till today and are to be found living in Waiwai or Trio settlements. They are Arawak-speaking.

The Pianaghotto, whom Schomburgk found living in the upper tributaries of the Corentyne River, were a Carib-speaking group and almost certainly a sub-group of the Trio. Although they no longer exist this is probably because the name died out rather than the people.

Drios, known today as the Trio, were found by Schomburgk in the Upper Corentyne. They are a Carib-speaking people who live today either side of the Brazil–Surinam frontier.

Whereas these are the Native People with whom Schomburgk had most contact, and of whom, accordingly, there are the most numerous references in his reports, on his journey to Esmeralda, which took him well beyond the boundaries of British Guiana, he met members of many other tribal groupings. Rather than introduce them here, comments on these people will be found at the appropriate places in the text.

All the native peoples whom Schomburgk met in the interior were broadly similar in their social and cultural characteristics, although, as mentioned above, in many aspects they had undergone far-reaching changes over the previous three hundred years. They were shifting cultivators and their main staple was the root, bitter cassava, supplemented by a range of other cultivated, semi-cultivated and wild crops. They hunted and fished, and although communities were basically self-sufficient, considerable trade was undertaken and European goods, above all metal cutting tools such as knives and axes, had been incorporated into their economies. Their settlements were small, averaging around thirty people, and often no more than a single house. Settlements were relocated frequently and there was considerable movement of people between them. The composition of settlements was kin-based and the village leader was closer to the head of a family than a chief and had little authority beyond his personal influence. Settlements were autonomous and there was no overarching political structure, although a number of settlements through the density of their interactions would form a vague group. The shaman, who filled the roles of medical practitioner, priest, prophet and counsellor, was an important figure throughout the region. This is because the Amerindian's explanation of mundane events involved an invisible world, the realm of spirits, and it was the shaman's ability to communicate with it that gave him the insight to deal with the unknown and unexpected.[1]

Schomburgk's views of the Amerindian might be summed up as those of evangelical humanitarianism. He saw them as benighted children for whom salvation lay in their christianization, which he regarded as synonymous with civilization, and used the words almost interchangeably. He originally thought that this could be attained by persuading them to abandon their jungle haunts and to settle near the coast. This would have the added advantage of protecting them from abduction or exploitation by Portuguese or Spanish neighbours. He soon came to realize that there was little hope of getting them to move, and that civilization would have to be brought to them. He greatly applauded the founding of the first mission in the interior in 1838, but, as a result of observing the abduction of a group of Wapishiana in August that year,[2] he became only too aware that if the Amerindians were to receive protection that they must live under British sovereignty; this, in turn, meant defining boundaries. Indeed it was this incident that politicized Schomburgk.[3]

Schomburgk saw the Amerindian as innocent because, unaware of civilized behaviour, his actions fell short of it. There is a good example of this in the 'Report of the Boundary Commission's First Expedition'[4] where Schomburgk argued that an Amerindian, who had revenged the death of his kinsfolk by killing the sorcerer responsible, should not be tried by English law, the principles of which were unknown to the accused who, in terms of Amerindian tenets, had behaved perfectly properly. He was also critical, intolerant and mocking of what he regarded as their superstitions, but, unlike many of his contemporaries, he was convinced that the Amerindian was not condemned permanently to a brutal and savage existence, and inevitable extinction, but had the potential for development to a higher plane if properly treated and educated.[5]

Schomburgk as Scientist

In keeping with most scientific travellers of his day, Schomburgk contributed to every branch of natural history. He published works on botany, geography, geology, zoology, ornithology, ichthyology, entomology and ethnology. It is, however, as a botanist that he is best known. As already noted, he had limited formal education and no qualifications in the subject; he was for the most part self-taught. Although, as we have seen, he claimed not to be a mere collector, it is as a collector that he is best remembered in the botanical world. His collections are large and valuable, and distributed in herbaria

---

[1] For an introduction to the Amerindian societies of the region, see Peter Rivière, *Individual and Society in Guiana. A Comparative Study of Amerindian Social Organization*, Cambridge, Cambridge University Press, 1984.

[2] See below, pp. 291–4.

[3] See Peter Rivière, 'From Science to Imperialism: Robert Schomburgk's Humanitarianism', *Archives of Natural History*, 25, 1998, pp. 1–8.

[4] See Volume II, chap. 1.

[5] His views are succinctly stated in *Twelve Views in the Interior of Guiana: from Drawings Executed by Mr. Charles Bentley, after Sketches Taken During the Expedition Carried on in the Years 1835 to 1839, under the Direction of the Royal Geographical Society of London, and Aided by Her Majesty's Government*, London, Ackermann & Co., 1841, pp. 37–8. In certain particulars, such as the equation between civilization and christianization, Schomburgk's views coincide closely with the influential evangelical Clapham Sect. In others, such as the potential for development, they tend to differ.

across Europe and the United States of America.[1] For example, he presented to the Natural History Department of the British Museum, 248 original water-colours of plants, and 2,190 plant specimens together with a further 125 specimens of woods and fruits.[2] His collections contain some new genera and many new species, although his critics might say that it would have been almost impossible not to have made such discoveries given how little botanical investigation had taken place in the region and just how rich and diverse the flora of tropical South America is. Although he undertook the description of some his finds, this task fell mainly to George Bentham who between 1839 and 1848 published, mainly in the *Journal of Botany*, seventeen pieces, amounting to some 330 pages, entitled 'Enumeration of plants collected by Mr. Schomburgk in British Guiana', as well as various other articles on specific plants. However, one must be careful not to underplay Schomburgk's ability to provide scientific descriptions of his finds; for example, his two descriptions of the same plant, the Snake Nut tree, exhibit his technical skill.[3]

Like most, if not all, scientific travellers of his day, Schomburgk made collections of virtually everything. For example, the Natural History Departments of the British Museum received numerous fossils and 126 birds.[4] The geological collections originally went to the Geological Society of London, and then to the Natural History Museum when the former's collections were dispersed in 1911.[5] The Museum of Mankind holds a large collection of what were then known as native curiosities, and a number of other British museums, such as the Cuming Museum in Southwark, contain ethnographic objects collected by him. The Royal College of Surgeons was the beneficiary of Amerindian and other skeletal remains which he had either surreptitiously exhumed or bought; those that were not destroyed during the Second World War are now in the Natural History Museum.[6] In many cases his collections of objects were just that. For example, the Amerindian artefacts which he collected, and which are now in the Museum of Mankind in London, appear to have come with only minimal description. An exception to this is his work on fish which resulted in a lavishly illustrated, two-volume *Fishes of Guiana* in Jardine's *Naturalist's Library* series. Nor were British institutions the only recipients of his collections; his botanical specimens, for example, are to be found today in over twenty herbaria across Europe and the United States of America.

Perhaps next to his botanical work, Schomburgk is best remembered as a geographical surveyor. We have already noted that he more or less taught himself surveying with

---

[1] See Juul van Dam, 'The Guyanan Plant Collections of Robert and Richard Schomburgk', in *Flora of the Guianas*, ed. M. J. Jansen-Jacobs, Royal Botanic Gardens, Kew, 2002. for a detailed description of both Robert and Richard Schomburgk's collections.

[2] *The History of the Collections Contained in the Natural History Departments of the British Museum*, 2 vols, London, Trustees of the British Museum, 1904–6, I, pp. 47 & 85.

[3] See, Schomburgk, 'Description of the Snake-nut Tree of Guiana', *Annals of Natural History or, Magazine of Zoology, Botany and Geology*, 5, 1840, pp. 202–4, and 'A Description of *Ophiocaryon paradoxum*, on the Snake Nut Tree of Guiana', *London Journal of Botany*, 4, 1845 pp. 375–8.

[4] *History of the Collections*, I, p. 323; Vol. II, p. 247.

[5] D. T. Moore, J. C. Thackray, & D. L. Morgan, 'A Short History of the Geological Society of London, 1807–1911, with a Catalogue of the British and Irish Accessions, and Notes on Surviving Collections', *The Bulletin of the British Museum of Natural History (Historical Series)*, 19, 1991, pp. 51–160, see pp. 60–61.

[6] He had earlier collected sea shells, but sold his collection to help fund his South American travels (RGS, RHS 1834–40, Letter of Schomburgk to Maconochie, 19 September 1835).

the help of the Danish harbour master and others at St Thomas. His first attempt at this new skill, the chart of Anegada, was found to be of high quality when checked by a Royal Navy survey ship. Similar praise was given to him for his survey of the mouth of the Corentyne River,[1] and for the accuracy of his surveying which he demonstrated when he connected his 1835 and 1837 surveys at Primo's Inlet on the Essequibo.[2] It cannot be said that he did not make mistakes, as, for example, his serious miscalculation of distance travelled when he claimed to be south of the Equator in his journey to the sources of the Essequibo in 1837.[3] However, given the conditions under which he had to work, the setbacks he encountered and the instruments available to him, his surveys of the interior of Guiana are a remarkable achievement.[4] He achieved them mainly through conscientious hard work and attention to detail. All this is very apparent from his reports and was recognized by one who followed in his footsteps. The Senior Boundary Commissioner, following the survey conducted as a result of the boundary arbitration at the end of the nineteenth century, wrote:

> In concluding this report we cannot omit to draw attention to the very excellent work done by Sir Robert Schomburgk who travelled in this colony on behalf of the Royal Geographical Society and the British Government. We found on the whole that our results agreed fairly with those obtained by him, and when we contrast the conditions of travelling at the present day with those that obtained when he was an explorer, we can only wonder at his endurance, patience and skill, and metaphorically speaking, take off our hats in respect to his memory.[5]

However, one might note here one oddity of Schomburgk that somehow fails to fit with his success as a geographer: he, on frequent occasions, managed to reverse directions. For example, and there are lots of actual examples in the texts that follow, he often described the course of a river, not in the conventional way of the direction in which it flows, but from that in which he was facing. Thus, if he is travelling north and meets a river flowing SW, he is likely to describe its course as NE.

Finally there is Schomburgk as a writer. We have already noted that he never produced a popular account of his South American travels, although his *Twelve Views in the Interior of Guiana* (1841), a sort of coffee-table book, comes close. He did, however, publish extensively. A list of most of his publications is to be found before the list of the works cited at the end of Volume II of this edition. As is apparent, most of these are on geographical and natural history matters and they naturally follow the pattern of his career. Thus the earliest publications relate to the West Indies, and these are followed in turn by those on South America, Barbados, Santo Domingo and the Dominican Republic, and finally Thailand. One also finds that he concentrated on a particular topic for a while; for example, at the end of the 1840s, he turned his attention to Amerindian ethnography and languages and published a series of articles on these topics. Some

---

[1] See below, p. 231.

[2] See Schomburgk, 'Diary of an Ascent of the River Berbice in British Guayana, 1837', *JRGS*, 7, 1837, pp. 302–50, editor's footnote, pp. 333–4.

[3] See below, p. 249.

[4] Burnett, *Masters of All They Surveyed*, provides a deconstructionist critique of Schomburgk's survey work, but he is less concerned with an assessment of his achievements, than with map-making as a handmaiden to empire building.

[5] TNA CO 111/544, Letter of Perkins to Government Secretary, British Guiana, 9 January 1905.

pieces seem less easy to categorize, including his 'On the Manufacture of Beet-root Sugar in the German Custom-House League or Zollverein' (1848),[1] although this probably reflects a general interest in the sugar industry and competition faced by the West Indies. There are also a few articles of a more popular nature, such as his 'Steam-boat Voyage to Barbados' (1847).[2] Most of Schomburgk's publications are difficult to find today unless one has access to a scholarly library with a good collection of nine-teenth-century periodicals.

The Manuscripts and Editorial Conventions Adopted

The main text of these volumes consists of the manuscript reports of Schomburgk's travels in South America between 1835 and 1843. They readily divide into two parts. The first three expeditions (1835–9) were conducted under the auspices of the Royal Geographical Society, although with some subvention from the British Government. The second three (1841–3) were undertaken as Boundary Commissioner, and thus directly under government direction. Except for the last part of the second survey, the journey from Roraima via the Cuyuni River to Georgetown on which no report was probably prepared, reports of all these journeys were published in the *Journal of the Royal Geographical Society*. These reports are based on the manuscripts and, although they are often very long, they are, in many cases, highly abbreviated and edited versions of the original. The manuscripts from the first three journeys have suffered most in this way whereas those from the boundary expedition were published with rather less editorial interference. There are two possible reasons for this. The first is that, as Schomburgk's reputation and authority increased, there was less inclination to mess about with his version. The second is that there was a change of editor of the *Journal*, to someone with less inclination to tamper. During the earlier period, Captain John Washington RN,[3] who succeeded Maconochie as Secretary to the Royal Geographical Society, appears to have had editorial responsibility for the *Journal*, and he certainly rewrote Schomburgk's report on the first expedition.

The manuscripts of the reports on the first three expeditions, those to the interior of British Guiana in 1835–6, up the Corentyne and Berbice Rivers in 1836–7, and to the sources of the Essequibo and to Esmeralda in 1837–9, are in the archives of the Royal Geographical Society in London. The manuscript of the first boundary survey, that of the north-west in 1841, is among the Colonial Office papers in The National Archives at Kew; the Colonial Office transmitting to the Royal Geographical Society a version with matters relating to the boundary and Venezuelans' treatment of Amerindians excised. There is no copy of the manuscript report of the second boundary survey, that of the Takutu River in 1842, among the Colonial Office papers, but it does exist in the archives of the Royal Geographical Society. The report on the second part of that survey, that of the Surumu and Cotingo Rivers to Roraima and from there by the

---

[1] 'On the Manufacture of Beet-root Sugar in the German Custom-house League or Zollverein', *Simmonds's Colonial Magazine*, 14, 1848, pp. 134–40.

[2] 'Steam-boat Voyage to Barbados', *Bentley's Miscellany*, 22, 1847, pp. 30–41.

[3] John Washington (1800–63), later Rear Admiral and Admiralty Hydrographer (1855–62). He was Secretary of the Royal Geographical Society (1836–41) and elected Fellow of the Royal Society in 1845.

Cuyuni River to Georgetown, was almost certainly never written. The reason for this was that Schomburgk left Georgetown again within a bare three weeks of his arrival in order to avoid imminent instructions from London to cancel the Corentyne survey. For this part of the survey it is necessary to rely on a relatively sketchy account contained in a letter of 23 January 1843 from Schomburgk to the Governor of British Guiana. Finally, the manuscript of the third boundary survey, that of the Corentyne in 1843, is in the Royal Geographical Society archives, and once again the Colonial Office does not appear to have retained a copy.

Rather more detail about these various manuscripts is provided individually before their transcription. Some general remarks, however, may be made here. We know Schomburgk kept a journal because he made numerous references to it. What happened to these journals and what language they were written in we do not know. At a guess Schomburgk took them back with him to Germany in 1864, a few months before he died. There has been no reference to them since his death and if they remained in Germany, they were possibly, even probably, destroyed during the Second World War.[1] The reports were constructed from the journal entries. Some of the reports are in Schomburgk's own handwriting, others are not. It is likely that some of these were dictated and we know that Schomburgk employed a 'copyist'. The condition of the manuscripts is variable, but overall there is remarkably little which is illegible. The main problem, and this applies particularly to the earlier rather than the later manuscripts, is the amount of alteration which has taken place. This includes crossing-out and writing over the top. Some of this has been done by Schomburgk himself, but a large proportion has been done by an editorial hand.

The editorial convention adopted to deal with this has been to incorporate the changes that are clearly in Schomburgk's hand, to ignore those in another hand and to reproduce the original as far as possible. This leaves a small number of cases where authorship remains uncertain and which is the correct reading if more than one is possible. These have been dealt with case by case and duly noted.

Schomburgk, it must be remembered, was a native German speaker and to the best of our knowledge learnt no English until he went to North America in 1827. By the time his first extant letters to the Linnean Society were written in 1830, he had a competent demand of the language which improved steadily and rapidly. His spelling, however, and often that of his copyists is erratic, and whereas there are some consistent mistakes, the same word is frequently spelt differently within a few lines of each other. Mistakes are sufficiently common that were they to be marked by 'sic' it would become an irritant to the reader. Accordingly they have been transcribed as in the manuscripts without comment. Schomburgk also uses on occasion the wrong word, and where he does this the probable word is suggested in a footnote. Schomburgk is also inconsistent in his use of capitalization; some words such as Canoe is almost invariably written so, whereas others, like savannah, may or may not be. Once again the usage in the manuscripts has been followed in the transcription.

---

[1] Another possible fate is that they were inherited by his family in Australia, perhaps by Richard, and destroyed during the First World War. There is a Schomburgk family tradition that, one night during a period of intense anti-German feeling when it was inadvisable to have any association with that country, a bonfire was made of all family papers that were in German (Personal communication, Pauline Payne).

Very similar difficulties were encountered with the punctuation, and in places the punctuation or the lack of it makes it difficult to follow the meaning of a passage. Where this is the case suitable punctuation has been provided within square brackets, and in those cases where a full stop has been added, the first letter of the following word has been capitalized and included within the square bracket. All diacritics and other symbols, such as double or single inverted commas, have been retained as in the original.

Where words are illegible and it has been impossible even to guess at it, the missing word or words are replaced by [illegible]. If it is possible to make an informed guess at the word, the word is placed in square brackets; on occasions where part of the word is missing as a result of a torn sheet, part of a word may appear in square brackets.

In a number of the manuscripts the pages are not in their original order. In every case it has been possible to identify the original order and they have been returned to it in the transcription. Where this has been done it has been duly noted. Related to this is the matter of the manuscripts' pagination. There is often more than one set, and the sheets have clearly been numbered for different purposes on different occasions. It has sometimes been difficult to sort these out, but a comment on the pagination will be found in the introduction to each individual manuscript and at the appropriate places in the manuscript.

The question of how much explanatory annotation should be included is a tricky one, and in editing Schomburgk's work, I have very much in mind Froude's strictures on the inadequacy of the editorial work in the first two volumes that the Hakluyt Society published, those that preceded Schomburgk's.[1] On the other hand I hate being patronized by footnotes. I hope that I have managed to steer a course between providing too much information and not enough. The guidelines I have set myself fall under different headings and these can be briefly outlined.

Where an individual is first referred to in the text, I have provided the briefest biographical details, simply to identify the person. For example, the footnote for the Governor of British Guiana in 1835 reads: 'Sir James Carmichael Smyth (1779–1838), a military engineer who served on Wellington's staff at Waterloo. He was Governor-in-Chief of the Bahamas 1829–33, and Governor of British Guiana, 1833–8.' As might be imagined, absolutely no information has been obtainable on some of the colonists in British Guiana and other minor characters whom Schomburgk mentioned; in such cases, rather than a note saying that nothing has been found, no comment has been made.

For reports such as these, maps are an essential accompaniment; the Royal Geographical Society has kindly permitted the use of the maps that accompanied the original *Journal* articles and the Leeds Library has kindly supplied copies of their illustrations. Because of the poor condition of all published copies of the 1836 and 1837 maps, flat and unfolded proof copies of these, held by the Royal Geographical Society, have been used. The only difference between the proofs and the final versions is that on the 1836 proof some coastal shading is absent and Schomburgk has been misspelt Schombergk. The 1840 map is taken from a bound volume in which the map has been cut into sections and remounted on cloth. On these maps will be found many, but not

[1] James Froude, 'England's Forgotten Worthies', *The Westminster Review*, 2 (new series), July–October 1852, pp. 32–67, p. 35.

all, of the geographical features referred to in the manuscripts. In many cases rather different names or spellings are in use today; where this is the case and it has been possible to identify the feature in question, the modern name is provided in a footnote. These names, which are those used in the editorial matter and the index, have been taken from the following sources which are referred to, where necessary, as the 'reference maps':

For Guyana, a 1:500,000 map in four sheets has been used. The south-east, south-west and north-west sheets were published by the Ministry of Defence of the United Kingdom in 1966, and the north-east sheet by the Guyana Government in 1972. As these maps are relatively expensive, it might be noted that the International Travel Map of Guyana (sheet 748) on a scale of 1:850,000 appears to be based on the 1:500,000 maps and is cheap and easily available.

For Brazil, the reference maps are the 1961 1:1,000,000 map of the Território do Rio Branco (modern day Roraima) of the Instituto Brasileiro de Geografia e Estatística and the 1983 1:2,500,000 map of Amazônia Legal published by the Ministério das Minas e Energia.

For Venezuela, the reference maps are the relevant sheets (NA 19–I, NA 19–II, NA 20–III, NA 20–IV, NB 20–I, NB 20–II, NB 20–III, NC 20–II) of the 1:500,000 series of the Servicio Autónomo de Geografía y Cartografía Nacional, first edition of 1974–77 or second edition of 2000.

Those geographical features identified and named by Schomburgk but which do not appear on any of the reference maps are not noted as unidentified; in other words their non-identification is to be read as such rather than this fact being spelt out on each occasion. They are mainly small creeks and low hills, although there are also rather more major features, usually hills or mountains, which it has not been possible to identify.

A word of warning needs to be made with reference to population settlements. The Amerindian practice of moving their settlements relatively frequently, means that the location of a settlement recorded by Schomburgk may not be the same as that today, although if it is a name taken from a geographical feature it is likely to be in the same neighbourhood. Another problem with naming is that the different Amerindian groups know, or used to know, the same feature by different names; a fact of which Schomburgk became fully aware.

A number of footnotes concern the elucidation of local matters; as, for example, the difference between a canoe and a corial. This information has been provided as economically as possible; in the case of the more complex matters, a reference to an appropriate literary source is given, in case the reader wishes to pursue the topic further. Without doubt the most difficult thing has been to identify the various faunal and floral species that Schomburgk referred to. The main reason for this is that the scientific classifications have for the most part changed since his time. A high rate of success can be claimed with regard to birds, animals, reptiles and fish,[1] but by far the largest number of

---

[1] For mammals, I have relied heavily on Robert Murphey, 'Mammalia Americae Australe. A Table of Taxonomic and Vernacular Names', *Ciencia Interamericana*, 17, 1–4, 1976, pp. 16–32, 18–30, 26–35, and Jaime Tello, *Mamiferos de Venezuela*, Caracas, Fundación La Salle de Ciencias Naturales, 1979; for birds, Dorothy Snyder, *The Birds of Guyana*, Salem, Mass., Peabody Museum, 1966, and James Peters, *Check-list of Birds of the World*, 16 vols, Cambridge, Mass., Harvard University Press, 1931–87; for fish, Joseph Nelson, *Fishes of the World*, New York, John Wiley, 1984; and for amphibians, Darrel Frost, ed., *Amphibian Species of the World*, Lawrence, Kansas, Allen Press and Association of Systematics Collections, 1985.

references are to botanical species and it has proved impossible to identify all of these. This is partly because Schomburgk himself identified them wrongly and also because either of the frequent changes in the scientific nomenclature of plants or of the numerous synonyms that exist. Great help in unravelling this is Juul van Dam's 'The Guyanan Plant Collections of Robert and Richard Schomburgk', but frequently, although van Dam lists both the original and current scientific names of all the plants in the collections, the former names do not appear in the manuscripts. Where it does occur, the current name given by van Dam may not agree with that provided by another authority. For example, van Dam gives as the original name for a member of the Vandoid family of orchid, *Zygopetalum rostratum*, and its current name as *Zygosepalum labiosum*. On the other hand, Dunsterville and Garay continue to use *Zygopetalum rostratum*.[1] Such an example can be multiplied many times, often with several synonyms involved.

Thanks mainly to the volume *Check-list of Woody Plants of Guyana* (Mennega et al.)[2] most of those trees and bushes that Schomburgk referred to by their vernacular names have been identified, and a list of them will be found in Volume II, Appendix 2, 'Glossary of Vernacular Plant Names'.

A great deal of assistance was also derived from an on-line database of the National Museum of Natural History of the Smithsonian Institute, Washington.[3] This is a checklist of plants of the Guianas, covering French Guyana, Surinam, Guyana, and for some plant families the Venezuelan states of Amazonas, Bolivar and Amacuro; but excluding Brazil.[4] In other words it covers most of the area where Schomburgk made his collections. This checklist has been taken as authoritative when deciding whether a particular plant family, genus or species is present in the flora area.

Where the taxonomic name in the manuscript coincides with its present name it passes unnoted; where the current taxonomic name is different or it has been impossible to identify it, this is noted.

Whether it is a matter of identifying geographical features or flora or fauna, the identification is made only on the first occurrence. After that, the index may be used for cross-referencing. For example, at the first mention of the Conuco Mountains there is a footnote reading Kanuku Mountains; in the index under 'Conuco' or any other variant of that spelling, the reader is directed to 'Kanuku'.

Finally, before the 'Works Cited' at the end of Volume II is a list of Schomburgk's publications. These are ordered chronologically although the titles are listed alphabetically within any single year in accordance with Hakluyt Society house style. The point of this is to give the reader a biographical overview of his literary production. Schomburgk's titles are not repeated in 'Works Cited' and references to his work include dates to help readers identify the source.

---

[1] Dam, *Guyanan Plant Collections*, p. 199; G. Dunsterville and L. Garay, *Venezuela Orchids Illustrated*, 6 vols, London, Andre Deutsche, 1959–76, see I, p. 246. I am extremely grateful for the great deal of assistance that Juul van Dam has given in helping to sort out the identification of many of the plants mentioned by Schomburgk in his manuscripts.

[2] E. A. Mennega, W. C. M. Tammens-de Rooij, M. J. Jansen-Jacobs, eds, *Check-list of Woody Plants of Guyana: based on D. B. Fanshawe's "Check-list of the Indigenous Woody Plants of British Guiana"*, Ede, The Tropenbos Foundation, 1988.

[3] See http://www.mnh.si.edu/biodiversity/bdg/planthtml/. It is referred to as NMNH Check-list.

[4] Much help in the identification of Brazilian plants has been derived from M. P. Corrêa, *Dicionário das plantas úteis do Brasil e das exóticas cultivadas*, 6 vols, Rio de Janeiro, Imprensa Nacional, 1926–78.

CHAPTER 1

The First Expedition into the Interior: 1835–1836

On his arrival in Georgetown, on 3 August 1835, Schomburgk wasted no time in calling on the governor, Sir James Carmichael Smyth,[1] with whom he was to get along well and who made up for the failure of the funds from the Royal Geographical Society to arrive by advancing him £150 from the 'Military Chest'. Smyth wrote to Maconochie about Schomburgk, stating that: 'from what I have had the pleasure of seeing of him I apprehend he is exactly the sort of man to carry the views of the Society into effect. He seems a great enthusiast; active and intelligent – of his scientific qualifications I do not pretend to be able to judge.' He also expressed his concern about the funds available to Schomburgk, referring to them as a 'ridiculously small sum'.[2]

Without delay Schomburgk began to make detailed plans for his first expedition into the interior. He reported to Maconochie that he would be unable to ascend the Demerara River and then cross over to the Essequibo as he had planned, because the Arawak chief on the former river was not on friendly terms with the mainly Carib-speaking tribes of the latter. Instead he would have to proceed the whole way up the Essequibo to its confluence with the Rupununi which he hoped to reach by beginning of October, and make a camp from which to carry out investigations. If the season was not too far advanced he would try to proceed to the source of the Essequibo. He imagined that if this lay in the mountains, he would find 'luxuriant valleys and fertile plains' and if food was available he would camp there for the short rainy season (December–January). He had started to recruit expedition members. He hoped these would include Lieutenant James Haining of the 65th Regiment if leave could be arranged for him. Otherwise he would need fourteen men to handle two canoes (clearly having discovered that mules are not a means of transport in that part of the world).[3]

Schomburgk appeared to have been welcomed and well treated by both the governor and the residents of Georgetown. The one exception to this was William Hilhouse,[4] who was widely regarded as the colonist with the greatest experience of the interior and its native inhabitants, on whose behalf he endlessly campaigned. He had a reputation for being a difficult character and a thorn in the side of authority. Schomburgk met him only once before his first expedition and complained that he 'alone has kept back with that information I thought I should receive from him'. The

---

[1] Sir James Carmichael Smyth (1779–1838), a military engineer who served on Wellington's staff at Waterloo. He was Governor-in-Chief of the Bahamas, 1829–33, and Governor of British Guiana, 1833–8.

[2] RGS Corres 1834–40, Letter of Schomburgk to Maconochie, 8 August 1835; RGS Corres 1834–40, Letter of Smyth to Maconochie, 5 August 1835.

[3] RGS Corres 1834–40, Letter of Schomburgk to Maconochie, 8 August 1835.

[4] For a brief biographical sketch of Hilhouse, see Menezes's 'Introduction' to the 1978 edition of Hilhouse's *Indian Notices* of 1825.

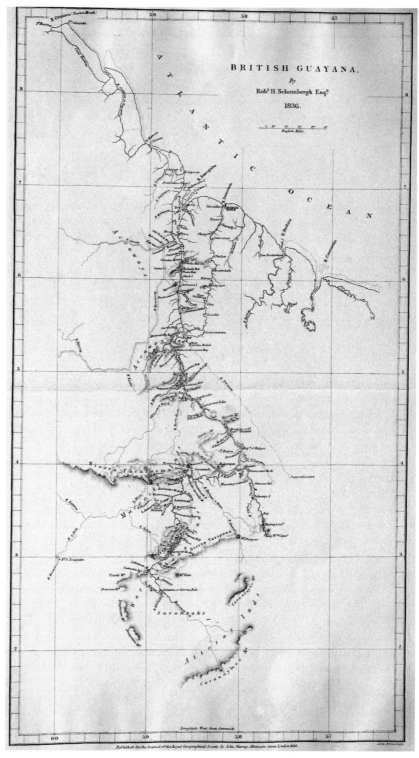

Map 1: 'British Guayana. By Robt. H. Schombergk Esqr. 1836.' Proof copy, illustrating route of the first expedition. Included by permission of the Royal Geographical Society, London.

governor warned Schomburgk not to trust Hilhouse's information and generally to keep clear of him.[1] Schomburgk passed this information back to the Royal Geographical Society in case it appeared odd that he had not availed himself of Hilhouse's expertise. Presumably unknown to Schomburgk, Hilhouse was simultaneously writing to the Society about Schomburgk. Hilhouse described him as appearing 'not unqualified for his task – he is of a light weight, active, & temperate, three great points in the exploring of our rivers'. He continued that he had advised Schomburgk to tackle the Essequibo although whether he also told him that it was 'the best object for a training expedition' and that if he gets through it 'safe & sound he will require no further instruction' is not clear.[2]

Soon after his arrival in British Guiana Schomburgk made his first foray into the interior;[3] this was to the mouth of the Cuyuni River in order to get the assistance of the postholder[4] in recruiting paddlers for his canoes. It is his account of this journey that constitutes Schomburgk's first report to the Royal Geographical Society on his South American travels.

This report, entitled 'An Excursion to the Post at the Mouth of the Cayuni', forms part of Schomburgk's manuscript at the Royal Geographical Society, and is catalogued as 'JMS.6/13(e)'. The total manuscript JMS 6/13 is composed of five distinct parts, of which (a) comprises the first, second and third reports of the first expedition, dated respectively Annay, 29 October 1835; Curassawaak, 15 January 1836; and Georgetown, 1 April 1836; and 'Geographical Memoir to Accompany the Map of the Essequebo and its tributary the Rupununy, &c &c'. Part (b) is entitled 'An Abstract of Mr. Schomburgk's First Report to the Royal Geographical Society of London', and it is not clear who prepared it or for what purpose. Part (c) is 'Abstract of Reports by J Washington (Editor)' and is Washington's redrafted version of the first report as it appeared in the *Journal of the Royal Geographical Society*.[5] Part (d) is 'Account of Expenses Incurred During the First and Second Expedition in the Interior of British Guiana'. Finally, as mentioned above, part (e) is 'An excursion to the Post at the mouth of the Cayuni'. A water-colour of the expedition's departure from the post at Cayuni on 1 October which formed part of the original manuscript has been archived separately as LMS/RHS/1 (see Fig 2).

Reproduced here are parts (a) and (e), and in order to provide the correct chronology the latter has been placed before the former. Part (e) was not published, although some

---

[1] Hilhouse had no high regard for Smyth of whom he wrote 'I hear our L[t]. Gov[r.] has given Schomberg great assistance – which as far as words go, I know may be true – but further – except as clap trap – he would not give a farthing for all the discoveries in the world. He is a perfect miser as regards Scientific research' (RGS Corres 1834–40, Postscript to letter of Hilhouse to Maconochie, 10 October 1835).

[2] RGS Corres 1834–40, Letter of Schomburgk to Maconochie, 19 September 1835; Letter of Hilhouse to Maconochie, 17 August 1835.

[3] It has not been possible to identify the exact dates of this excursion, but in 'Account of Expenses' the cost of it is dated 'August' (JMS 6/13(d), p. 12). The manuscript (e) is dated 21 September 1835.

[4] The scheme of postholders was a continuation of the Dutch policy of maintaining outposts on the major rivers. The postholder's job was to regulate trade and maintain harmonious relationships with the Amerindians. Between 1803 and 1838 postholders were subordinate to an unsalaried Protector of Indians. In 1838, Protectors were replaced by salaried Superintendents of Rivers and Creeks, and in 1843 the job of postholder was merged with that of superintendent. For a full account of this, see Menezes, *British Policy Towards the Amerindians*, chapters 3 & 4.

[5] See Schomburgk, 'Report of an Expedition into the Interior of British Guayana, in 1835–36', *JRGS*, 6, 1836, pp. 224–84.

information was taken from it and incorporated in the published version of the first report. Nor was the 'Memoir' contained in part (a) published, although lengthy passages of it are to be found in the published versions of all three reports. Schomburgk's original reports underwent a fairly severe redrafting at the hand of Washington before they were published, and this is particularly true of the first report which has undergone a massive rewriting. Whereas all his reports were edited to some degree, the fact that this earliest one suffered most is not too surprising. He had had little experience of preparing such a thing; he was writing in a foreign language, and it is likely that as he became increasingly well known there was a corresponding reluctance to tamper with his words.

As far as possible everything published has been returned to the form in which Schomburgk submitted the documents to the Royal Geographical Society. There have been some difficulties in doing this. Pages from one document are to be found displaced in another document, and even within one document the order of the pages has been changed. It is believed that the order as presented here is as it was originally, and where it differs from the order to be found in the documents today, this has been indicated.

A comment has already been made in the Introduction concerning the inconsistency of Schomburgk's spelling, capitalization and punctuation; the situation with regard to the report on the first expedition not being helped by the fact that he forgot to take his dictionary with him, and on occasions used the wrong word.[1] These failings are particularly bad in these early manuscripts. The same name will be spelt differently in the same sentence, a word will or will not be capitalized in an almost random fashion, and punctuation is a rather hit-and-miss affair. No attempt has been made to change or correct any of these features, nor has the text been littered with the word 'sic', especially where readers will have no difficulty in working out for themselves what is intended.

Part (e) consists of fourteen numbered pages of writing, and a cover sheet with title, all in Schomburgk's handwriting. To the original cover sheet has been added in different handwriting, 'Sept 21 – 1835 with remarks on a map of the Orinoco, Essequibo & Rio Branco'. It is not clear whether this is a reference to the 1833 document entitled 'Remarks to accompany a Map of the rivers Orinoco, Essequebo, Branco, &c &c' and is shelf marked JMS 6/9 and the map Venezuela S/S2. There are also two additional newer cover sheets, one of which states that the document is composed of fifteen pages, which is correct if these two later sheets are discounted.

AN EXCURSION TO THE POST AT THE MOUTH OF THE CAYUNI[2] BY R. H. SCHOMBURGK

Having been honoured by the Royal Geographical Society of London with an expedition into the interior of British Guiana, I found on my arrival in Demerara that it would be of importance and advantage to the object of the Expedition if I engaged the necessary crew for manning the Corials[3] at the Post up the Essequibo, the more so since I

---

[1] RGS Corres 1834–40, Letter of Schomburgk to Maconochie, 29 October 1835.

[2] Cuyuni River.

[3] The canoe and the corial of the region are similarly constructed craft, both being made from a hollowed-out tree trunk, and thus usually referred to as dugouts. Both words are of Amerindian origin, but there is not agreement about the differences between them. For Schomburgk the corial is pointed at both ends, whereas the canoe has its ends squared off and filled with triangular pieces of wood. *Fishes of Guiana*, I, 1841, p. 92.

had been given to understand that several free coloured people who lived there, had been already up the Essequibo and crossed by the Reponony[1] to the Fort Saint Joaquim.[2] I was likewise anxious to ascertain the state of the river, whether it had returned to it banks, or, whether higher up it was still overflowing. Provided with letters by his Excellency the Governor to the Postholder to afford me every assistance in selecting the crew, I congratulated myself of being able to avail myself of an opportunity to perform my trip in the company of M[r.] Teshmaker[3] and his amiable family. M[r.] Teshmaker is perhaps known to the Geographical world as having been M[r.] Hillhouse's compagnion de Voyage, during his trip up the Massaroony[4] and to judge from his amiable disposition and his knowledge of Indian manners, he must have been a great acquisition to M[r.] Hillhouse.[5]

Arrived at Wakenham, we made every preparation for our departure, and as it was resolved that we were to make our trip to the "Post" in a Schooner, we took a Corial in tow, in order to resort to it when wind and tide should fail us.

We left Warkenham in the afternoon, favoured in the commencement by a strong sea breeze and tide, which combined, acted upon the Schooner and made her walk through the waters; but, scarcely had we passed the Channel between Leguan and the northern point of Hog Island, when the wind began to fail, and the tide to ebb.

We reached Fort Island[6] in the evening and came to anchor. What a change! what vicissitudes have befallen this Island! before the Seat of Government, the great Store of the Dutch West India Company; hundreds of vessels loaded and unloaded on its shores; and what remains of its grandeur? the vestiges of a Wharf, on which the vessels of the Company delivered and received their Cargoes, a brick building that jointly was used as Church and Court House, and a Fort in decay.

The tide was not favourable until 11 o'Clock next morning – our hammocks were therefore slung in the hall of one of the inhabitants who welcomed us to the bare walls of her house. This was my first essay of passing a night in a hammock, and only the fear of being ridiculed could reconcile me to the uncomfortable couch, which it must prove to every novice until he has accustomed himself to it. The wind was still so light in the morning that our vessel could not have stemmed the opposing tide. I sauntered therefore out to take a view of Fort Island; my steps were directed first to the Fort, but few yards distant from our lodgings. The outer works are as much in decay as the main-hold; the first partly undermined by the water, fall over in large masses, and give an evidence of the good cement and the faithful work of the builder who, though he could not hinder the element from encroaching, when unguarded prevented the Walls from falling in pell mell. That part of the fort which was used as quarters for the Officers and the deposit of stores, has been covered with a pointed roof – the rafters are still extant,

---

[1] Rupununi River.

[2] Fort São Joaquim, situated at the confluence of the River Takutu and Rio Branco.

[3] Thomas Teschmaker, a proprietor of Wakenaam Island at the mouth of the Essequibo.

[4] Mazaruni River.

[5] Hilhouse's account of this journey is to be found in 'Journal of a Voyage up the Massaroony in 1831', *JRGS*, 4, 1834, pp. 25–40.

[6] Fort Island, earlier known as Flag Island, was the Dutch capital of the Colony of Essequibo from 1739 until the end of the 18th century when, as a result of the merger of the administrations of Demerara and Essequibo, the capital of the former, Stabroek (later Georgetown), became the main centre and that of the latter gradually fell into disuse.

but the shingles have been of less durability, and have made sundry openings for the admittance of the Sun's rays, and the discharge of watery clouds – and while the still covered parts are used as a temporary Stable, the adjoining stronghold served as a conventicle to a large number of Bats, all hushed in silence, and contemplation of perhaps some mighty point of last nights discourse, until we took it upon ourselves to wake them out of their lethargy.

I went next to the Church, a simple brick building, thatched with Palm-leaves; on my way thither I passed almost all the houses which comprise the present settlement, and I seldom saw, comparatively speaking, such a number of miserable hovels, destitute of the slightest indication of industry. The discovery of a Gold Mine could not have produced a greater astonishment to me when at last I observed a small spot fenced in and planted with a few vegetables. The inhabitants consist of coloured people and liberated Slaves of the Dutch West India Company and their descendants.

I found the Church open, a few pews, the pulpit, & wooden tables containing the Commandments, were its whole adornment. I observed in the nave of the Church, the Tombstone of Johannes Baker, Commandant of Fort Island, who died in February 1772.

The Congregation confess themselves to the rites of the Dutch Reformed Church; but, there is likewise a Methodist Chapel here.

The Sea breeze sets in almost regularly with the tide, as soon as the water commenced therefore to wash (the common expression for the flood tide) we set sail.

The Scenery becomes now most interesting, as far as the eye can range, an impenetrable forest is visible, the noble trees of which present a variety of tints from the darkest green to the lightest shade of yellow. The prospect opened between two Islands; in the distance presented themselves the blue Mountains, most properly so called from the bluish tint which appears to surround them. The wind became contrary and blew from the land, and instead of advancing, the reflux of the tide drifted our Schooner to the northward; we were therefore obliged to come to anchor. Our anchorage was South of Hog Island, and both banks of the River became for the first time visible – before us was "Lowe" Island.[1] The Sun had but a short distance to travel, when we resolved to enter the Corial in order to reach Itaka before nightfall. Our paddles were soon in motion and their force overcame tide & wind, and brought us after the elapse of two hours to our nights lodging. I observed here the first rocks in place, after my landing at Demerara. It was something new, and as it was already dark when we arrived in Itaka, I received the first notion of their presence by hurting my foot against a ledge which traversed the path. They are granitic and as the right bank of the river projects here somewhat, they extend into river. I presume these are the first traces of rocks which show themselves above ground south of the mouth of the Essequibo – the circumstance must have struck the aborigines; Itaka signifies in the Indian language "Rock". They are covered during high water and have proved several times fatal to vessels.

The same causes which prevented us the previous day to make much progress, prevailed the succeeding day. In consequence of the fullness of the river, the influence of the flood tide became weaker and weaker the more we ascended – we did not make more than about 10 miles when we were obliged to come to anchor again, not far from Ampa, a Settlement on the river's right bank. There are but few Islands in that vicinity,

[1] Probably Lau Lau Island.

those we saw consisted apparently only of rocks on which some trees had taken root. Three of similar origin on the eastern shore are called the brothers, and three on the Western the Sisters. A singular shaped rock which with a little stress of imagination might be taken for a gigantic head, is of great importance to the superstitious Skipper. It is fruitful of mischief to point at him with the finger, and frequently he is said to have punished such frivolous behaviour, with a blast of his full cheeks which drove the unfortunate vessel ashore or unmasted her; but still severer he punishes the audacious mortal who should laugh at his grave visage – such boldness is only to be atoned for by death, and the unfortunate dies in the course of twelve months.

We were so much in want of a little wind, that we took a particular pleasure in pointing at him, but, as we observed that he was apparently in too good a humour as to take notice of our temerity, we even laughed at him most heartily – however, he was determined not to gratify us even with a breath of wind.[1] The Monkey by his mournful cry – the "Ho-a'you," a bird which has received its name from the similarity which its note bears with that word,[2] and the confused cries of parrots, Macaws &c had informed us of the approach of day – "up Anchor" was therefore our first occupation. It was a lovely view which lay before us – two narrow Islands, running almost parellel with each other, hid partly the confluence of the Cayuni with the Essequibo, while the latter river still continued to show by the break of the hills, its southern course; Sloping hills at intervals invelloped in whitish fog closed the horizon and by their hoary appearance, brought a European Landscape at harvest time in our recollection. We were delighted, and the only regret felt at that moment was the absence of wind to favour our progress – the Corial was therefore manned and we entered soon the Cayuni river, after it has received the waters of the Massarony.

The Southern point at the confluence of the Cayuni with the Essequibo is called Barteka,[3] and is at present inhabited by a Missionary of the Methodist persuasion, a Mr Armstrong, whose name I shall have opportunity to mention again;[4] a few miles further west, on the right bank of the Cayuni is the habitation of the Postholder*

> *The Postholder's duty is to try to attach the Indians to his Post, to prevent as far as in his power, fighting between the Tribes and to give a quarterly report to the Protector of Indians, what is going on amongst them, and likewise to prevent people from passing up the river without a passport from the Lieutenant Governor or the Protector.

---

[1] Schomburgk never completely cured himself of mocking what he regarded as native superstitions. However, he was not above turning to magical practices to further his own purpose. On the Upper Essequibo in 1837, he made the image of a young woman and sacrificed it to the spirits in order to overcome Amerindian objections to passing a particular spot. Schomburgk himself never recorded this, but the American ethnographer, William Farabee, was told about it by the local Amerindians when he travelled the route nearly eighty years later. It would appear that Schomburgk's magic was so powerful that it was still then efficacious. See W. C. Farabee, 'A Pioneer in Amazonia: The Narrative of a Journey from Manaos to Georgetown', *Bulletin of the Geographical Society of Philadelphia*, 15, 1917, pp. 57–103, p. 72.

[2] The 'Who-you' bird, the White-necked Nighthawk or Pauraque (*Nyctidromous albicollis*).

[3] Bartica.

[4] John Armstrong was a catechist of the Church Missionary Society who had been responsible for founding the Bartica mission in 1831. Although Schomburgk does not mention it Armstrong had made a journey into the interior in 1833 and stayed some weeks at Pirara, a location central to Schomburgk's future travels. Armstrong seems to have been a difficult person and was often in dispute with the local committee of the Church Missionary Society. He resigned from the Society in 1836 and after his ordination the same year was sent by the Bishop of Barbados to look after the parish of Anguilla. See Peter Rivière, *Absent-minded Imperialism. Britain and the Expansion of Empire in Nineteenth-century Brazil*, London, Tauris Academic Studies, pp. 10–20.

for the Essequibo,[1] it is a beautiful situation, affording a view of the three rivers Cayuni, Massaroony, and Essequibo. The House is built of wood, thatched with the leaves of the Eta, the roof projects several feet beyond the walls, and rests at its termination on several posts, forming a commodious gallery or verandah. I consider the house about 50 to 60 feet above the level of the river, the elevation consists of immense blocks of granite, not so much approaching stratification as in Itaka.[2]

The morning after our arrival at the Post, we made an excursion a little way up the River Massaroony. We kept for some time the bank of the Cayuni in order to pay a visit to an Arowaack[3] settlement, the Captain of which is known to the Colonists by the name of "Frederick".

On our landing, Captain Frederick came forward to welcome us, and setting himself complacently upon a bench before one of the huts, he began to converse with Mr Teschmaker in the Dutch creole language.

There was nothing peculiar which struck me in his appearance, his dress consisted of a common check shirt without any further sign of the exalted situation he bore among his family. The huts consisted of Posts fixed firmly in the ground, with a thatched roof; under the roof their Hammocks were slung and their utensils of War, Chase, and domestic purpose kept from the immediate contact with the weather. Their Women were occupied with baking cassava bread, and so assiduous at their work as scarcely to venture a look at the new commers. We attempted to elicit some words, but after we succeeded they were given with bent down eyes, and the old Matrons present, looked as angry as if we had committed a crime against State and Church; and so it really was, since a smile or a complacent mien to any male but the husband, is severely punished by the latter. The Women, like the Men are "Tattoed". One of Captain Frederick's daughters was formerly attached to a white person in the Colony, but she was reputed[4] by her soi disant husband, and lives now with her father. Ka-yeeni shows still remnants of having been once handsome among her race, and her brother Arre-owa (i.e. Tiger)[5] is one of the finest and most intelligent young men I have seen of his Nation.

We passed Cartabo[6] point at the confluence of the Massaroony with the Cayuni; once the seat of Government, at the first settlement towards the close of the 16th. Century; for the protection of which the fortifications at the small island Kykoverall, under the command of Joost van Den Hoog,[7] were well calculated. At the latter period and very

---

[1] The Postholder for the Essequibo at the time was T. Richardson, but he was away and Schomburgk failed to contact him on this occasion but met various coloured people who lived in the vicinity and who had travelled as far as the nearest Brazilian settlement, Fort São Joaquim, on the Rio Branco (RGS, Corres 1834–40, Letter of Schomburgk to Maconochie, 19 September 1835).

[2] This house is represented in Figure 2 (p. 45).

[3] Arawak.

[4] Presumably Schomburgk intended 'repudiated'.

[5] There are no tigers in South America but the word was and is used colloquially in Guyana to refer to various members of the wildcat family, especially jaguars.

[6] Kartabu.

[7] James Rodway, *History of British Guiana From the Year 1668 to the Present Time*, 3 vols, Georgetown, J. Thomson, 1891–94, I, p. 4, calls him ter Hoogen, an influential Dutch gentleman, after whom the fort was initially called. Kyk-over-al, meaning 'See over all', was the main Dutch centre in the Essequibo from 1622 to 1718 when, finding the island site rather cramped, it was moved to Cartabo or Kartabu on the river bank nearby. As already noted, the centre was then moved to Flag or Fort Island in 1739.

likely in the commencement of the 17th Century the Colonists removed, to Fort Island. A few posts in the river which were left from a former wharf, some Cocoa trees and occasionally a heap of bricks partly sunk in the alluvial soil, is all what remains from the former settlement.

Along the banks of the rivers, but chiefly about the junction, live a great many free coloured people, who having intermixed with the Indians, have adopted their manners. Their names are mostly of dutch origin, and there is no doubt that European blood flowed in the veins of their ancestors. At present they resemble much more to Indians in appearance than to Africans.

We paid a visit to one of their settlements, the Patriach of which Saunder Cornelius, might have finished his four score years. Their houses do not differ much from Indian huts, distinguishing themselves only by being Wattled, and their floors somewhat raised and planked, however, there was a large Shed or Logis, which appeared to belong to the community in general. The indolence of these people approaches to the proverbial laziness of the Indians, without being able to be raised to activity by a stimulus, which certainly is not to be denied to the Indian.

We found Saunder's settlement partly in consternation, one of the young men of the little Colony, married to a grand daughter of the Patriarch, was suspected to have been poisoned by an Indian; the suspicion had been reported to the authorities, but as no post mortem examination had taken place, and as there were no proofs, nothing decisively had been done as yet.[1]

We did not proceed further, there was still however a Carabice[2] Settlement to be visited and the fortifications at Kyk-over-all to be seen, which lay on our way home.

We saw about six huts, which did not differ materially from those of the Arawaacks; but in their figure and customs the Carabisce are different; they do not tattoo like the Arawaacks, and use the Roucou[3] with which they anoint themselves; the legs receive a larger quantity of that dye than the other parts of the body. The females tie a piece of cotton stuff firm round their ankle and another a little below the joint of the knee, by which the calf is pressed out forcibly, and receives a most unatural shape. Their under lip is perforated by pins with the head inward and their points protruding beyond the chin.*

*If not otherwise occupied their tongue plays constantly with the head of the pins; the volubility of that organ is therefore more innocently employed than with us; This peculiar method of embellishment makes another observation obvious – the Carabisce is not fond of kissing, a better preventative could not have been adopted than these pointed palisades. Our gallantry towards the fair Sex is considered a most contemptible custom.

One of the Women had her ears perforated and two pieces of Bamboo, three quarters of an Inch in diameter which served her in lieu of Earings; it is quite natural to expect that the lower part of the ear was enlarged and was almost transparent. We observed a small hut of conical shape, just of sufficient width to afford room to one person; in that hut I

---

[1] References to death from poisoning occur at several points in Schomburgk's reports. Among native Guyanese death is understood to be the result of human or spirit malevolence or maleficence. Poisoning is a standard form of explanation although it does not necessarily involve the administration of a physical substance; a soul can be poisoned by a curse.

[2] Carib.

[3] Also known as annato. A red dye made from the fruit of *Bixa orellana*.

was told the Pe-i-man[1] is put; in case of sickness or misery befalling any member of the family – here he performs his exhortation of the evil Spirits.

The Carabisce this side of the Falls are great potters; we saw at their settlement one hut which appeared to be their grand Store-room, it contained large jars, pots to boil Pepperpot[2] in, and various other articles. The clay is found on the shores of the Massaroony and Cayuni.

At the mouth of the Massaroony is the small Island Kyk over all, famed for the old fortifications which in earlier times, protected the settlers at Cartabo Point. The situation was well chosen and commanded any approach from the Essequibo and Massaroony. When the Colonists emigrated to Fort Island, part of the works were taken down and the building-materials carried to the Island for the raising of the Fort there. But still a great part of the Parapets and two arched entrances had remained, and bid defiance to time but not to the pick-axes of men.

These ruins were always considered as a relic until lately a Mr Armstrong the Missionary at Barteka Point has taken upon himself to pull down part of the Parapets &c in order to build himself a Kitchen and an oven. These ruins being the property of the Crown and Mr A having commenced the work of destruction upon his own authority, I am happy to say that His Excellency the Governor of the Colony, has given orders to stop his proceedings or the Coloured inhabitants in the vicinity when in want of building materials might have considered themselves equally authorized to pull down the walls in order to use the Bricks, and in a short time not a vestige would be left of this old monument. On the Key-Stone over the arched entrance from the West, which appears to have been the Chief Entrance, and fronted the settlement at Cartabo, there is a Cross. This circumstance has induced many to consider the Fort to have been built by Portuguese.

Next day we undertook an Expedition to the River Cayuni, our Corial efficiently manned, we crossed over to the right Bank of the Cayuni. I saw here some of the most splendid flowers and regretted most sincerely that I was not prepared to preserve them[. O]ne which belonged to the natural family of Combretaceae, our Indians of the Carabisce nation called Cauabahiracahrie;[3] not minor in beauty was another which I found at the mines[4] called by them Toucoushou-aheru very likely belonging to the Genus Brownea.[5]

The Banks of the Cayuni are higher than those of the Massaroony, and appear to be loamy; there is likewise a great difference in the colour of the water: that of the

---

[1] This is the native term for what is usually called a shaman in western writing. There is a vast literature on Native Amazonian shamans and shamanism, and there is not room here to provide more than a very summary account of the complex phenomenon. The Native Amazonian world is composed of a visible and an invisible component. The explanation of what happens in the visible quotidian world lies in the invisible world. The shaman has access, by various means, to this invisible world and is thus able to interpret mundane events. It is as a result of this ability that he is able to treat sickness.

[2] Pepperpot is an Amerindian stew consisting of meat, hot peppers and casareep. The last is the juice that is extracted from the cassava root, and then boiled to remove the poison. A pepperpot may be kept going for months with new ingredients being added as required.

[3] Appendix 2 (Volume II) consists of 'A glossary of vernacular plant names'. In this volume, at the first appearance of a particular vernacular plant name, it will be identified. In cases where no identification has been made, this will not be stated. In this case, although it is listed as 'unidentified', there is a remote possibility that it is *kwai*: *Terminalia amazonia*.

[4] See below, p. 42.

[5] Tukushuahiru: *Brownea latifolia*.

Massaroony is slightly coloured but as clear as crystal, that of the Cayuni is loamy and leaves a sediment after it has been for some time in the glass.

We halted at a Carabisce Settlement – Are-nai – the Captain appeared to have left it with his followers – we proceeded therefore further west. While turning round a projecting point, we met a Corial. In these solitary rivers, the meeting of another Corial causes the same interest as the meeting of a vessel on the open sea. It contained several Carabisce and a coloured Man, who has lately arrived at Kay-tan's settlement in order to instruct the Carabisce in religion, and attempt civilization.[1]

The view was beautiful at that point, the river appeared more like a lake, studded with small islands, which not being extensive enough to obstruct the view of both banks of the river, added a great deal to the effect of the scenery. The prospect was closed by a branch of the Tiger mountains. We landed at Kay-tan's settlement, who met us at the bank of the river; he spoke the Dutch Creole like most of the Indians settled in the neighbourhood of the Colony. He led us to a large hut, which is dedicated to their receiving instruction from the Missionary. A strange mistake occurred here, which I must not pass over; M[r]. T. having read in the Corial in a small edition of Shakespeare, had the Volume in his hands, and as it was bound very like an elegant Prayer-book, Kaytan drew the Conclusion that M[r]. T. had come to keep service; we were therefore astonished when one of the Indians blew a horn, and soon after we saw them assemble, and range themselves according to sex and age. They remained sitting with their hands crossed, and stared at M[r]. T. and myself who had taken place on the chair which I presume is only occupied by the Missionary; while we were considering what all this could be about, the mistake was unriddled by Kaytan full of impatience of the delay, calling out to commence to sing; it was some time before we could explain ourselves properly. The rain was descending in torrents, and many of the poor people having become wet, while obeying the call of the horn, a small glass of Gopie (Rum) could not hurt them, and tended to make them forget their mistake. The Measles raged to a great extent at Kaytan's settlement; we found in each hut one or two with that complaint. We met likewise "Arenai" whose settlement we visited in the morning, without finding him or any of his followers at home. M[r]. T who knew him before, scarcely recognized in the emaciated figure in the hammock his old acquaintance. In a conjugal strife one of his wives bit him severely in the hand. The hand was still very much swollen, though it had happened a month before, and it appeared to have had such effect upon him, that I scarcely think he will recover. The culprit was sitting below the hammock, looking sullen; when one of our companions up[b]raided her, she gave him such a look on his turning away, in which every malice was depicted.

We bartered several articles here, as hammocks[,] the fibres of the Silk-grass, which when prepared, are equal to any thread, I procured likewise a roll of Tobacco, which was manufactured by the Indians of that river. Kay-tan had been several times in Angustura,[2] which journey he undertook in his canoe upon the Cayuni and its confluences.

---

[1] This was almost certainly John Doyce, a single man and a baker by trade, who had been recruited by the missionary Thomas Youd in 1833 as an assistant. He accompanied Youd for much of the time the latter was in the interior, but was dismissed in 1841 for marrying a woman of doubtful reputation. He died in a miserable state in 1848. See Rivière, *Absent-minded Imperialism, passim*.

[2] Angostura, modern day Ciudad Bolívar.

He gave us a description of the rites of the Catholic Church, and dwelt particularly upon the custom of taking the holy water; according to his account he performed the journey in a month.

An attempt was made in the Colony to dig for Silver. In 1721, the Council of Ten[1] granted a privilege, whereby it was enacted that all persons disposed to work in mines might do so, and a M[r.] Hildebrand a Miner,[2] was sent from Holland for that purpose, but the little ore which was discovered was not worth the expenses connected with the labour. One of these attempts was made a little Coastwards of Kay-tan's settlement, we visited it. The Shaft is about 13 to 20 feet above the water, and goes firstly in a horizontal direction. I did not enter it for a great way, as some preparations are necessary to dislodge wild animals if any should have taken shelter there; I satisfied myself with taking several specimens of Granite away.

On our return we had a view of the first rapids in the Cayuni; the river took apparently a different course, and branched off W by N, and S.S.E. Our last days excursion extended to the mareska-Fall, up the Massaroony. Our Corial was manned with 14 Paddlers and a Steersman or Captain, five Carabisce Indians were placed on the larboard side, and I could not help to admire the regularity with which they paddled. Their arms formed under all movements of paddling almost a straight line, no one paddle was raised or depressed an inch higher than the other. The Paddlers kept regular time; changing the same in a quicker or slower mode. Their quick motion increased with every stroke until one more tired gave the signal by throwing up some water with the paddle, when the movement was changed again to a slow stroke.

We passed Caria Island,[3] where cultivation had been carried on by the first Dutch settlers. It was then low water and we observed some posts, the remnants of former wharfs – there are likewise a few Cocoa trees. The smaller Islands become more numerous the more one advances, and the silence which appears to reign over these retired regions was only interupted by the noise caused by the paddles of the Canoe, or our own voices; even the parrots appeared to be hushed in.

We approached the first rapids, called by the Indians Trou-trouba[4] – white flocks of foam which passed us rapidly, had given us the first information of our being near to the falls. They were rather insignificant and it wanted only additional strength to cross the current in a diagonal line, the same was repeated from left to right, and we were comparatively speaking in smoother water. The scenery is now beautiful, the number of Islands increases; the whole has a lake-like appearance, studded with Islands, and the comparisson with "the lake of thousand isles", I think is a very happy one.[5]

---

[1] The supreme directorate of the Dutch West India Company based in Amsterdam.

[2] Thomas Hildebrand. Schomburgk appears to have the date wrong. According to Rodway *History of British Guiana*, I, pp. 106–9, Hildebrand was sent out in 1740 and was banished from the colony for reason of cruelty to his labourers in 1744. Mining operations, which proved unprofitable, were discontinued in 1746.

[3] Karia Island.

[4] Probably Turtruba.

[5] Schomburgk, on a number of occasions, places phrases in inverted commas, without them evidentially being a quotation. This may be one such. Evan MacColl's (1808–98) poem, 'The Lake of the Thousand Isles', referring to stretch of the St Lawrence River downstream from Lake Ontario, is too late to be Schomburgk's source.

The second Rapid of any consequence is Percatabo; it was traversed in the same manner as the former. The river became afterwards more open and we were opposite the Maresca-falls. The rainy season, which was not over as yet, as we could certify from experience – the rain descending in torrents while coming near that fall, caused the river to be still swollen.

Though the Maresca-falls are rather insignificant during the dry season they offered a different aspect now at the foot of the falls – whirl-pools were formed which frightened our crew, and the delay connected with hauling our boat across the rocks would have tired out our patience – we resolved therefore to return to the Post, not without however taken a full view of the falls. The rocks which constitute the falls, are Granite traversed by some beds of Quartz; on that part of the Quartz rocks which are washed by the water, grows the Weycu a saline plant,*

*Podostemon ruppioides Humb.[1]

its leaves are thick and contain salty particles. The Pacou,[2] one of the finest river fishes, feeds on its leaves and seeds.

I think it took us four hours to ascend from the Post to the Maresca falls; we were not more than two in descending – it appeared indeed as if the banks, bushes and trees were flying away from us, with so much velocity went the boat through the water.

Next noon we returned to Wakenham highly delighted with our excursion, and our invalids much improved in health.

****

The manuscript breaks off at this point, but it is clear that the end of the excursion is imminent and all that is left to do is to return to Georgetown.

Prolonged rains delayed the departure of the first expedition from Georgetown to 21 September. A few days were then spent with the Essequibo Postholder at Cuyuni Mouth while waiting for the crew to assemble before the expedition finally set off on 1 October.[3] The story is taken up from this point by Schomburgk's first report. The manuscript of this consists of nineteen pages, all in Schomburgk's handwriting, plus no fewer than four later cover sheets. It is dated 29 October 1835, but there is no indication of when it was received by the Royal Geographical Society. The published version is significantly different from the manuscript, the latter having been almost entirely rewritten. On one of the cover sheets is written 'Mem: Some pages of original misplaced for preparation of abstract for publication'. This refers to the whole of JMS 6/13(a), but as previously mentioned, the original order has been restored in the present transcription.

---

[1] Schomburgk is almost certainly referring to 'weyra' (*Lacis fluviatilis*) which belongs to the family Podostemeae. *P. ruppioides*, now known as *Apinagia ruppioides*, is not found in Guyana but occurs in Colombia and Venezuela. This illustrates well the problems involved in identifying the plants referred to in Schomburgk's reports.

[2] The Indian name 'pacu' refers to three different species: *Myletes pacu*, *Colossoma bidens* and *C. oculus*. Schomburgk is probably referring to the first.

[3] RGS Corres 1834–40, Letter of Schomburgk to Maconochie, 29 October 1835.

FIRST REPORT TO THE ROYAL GEOGRAPHICAL SOCIETY OF LONDON DURING AN EXPEDITION IN THE INTERIOR OF BRITISH GUIANA – CONDUCTED BY ROBERT H. SCHOMBURGK C.M.R.G.S.

The Expedition consisting of Lieut[nt] Haining of the 65th Reg[t.] as Volunteer,[1] M[r.] Brotherson[2] of this Colony and myself, four coloured people variously employed,[3] and the Crew of the three boats[4] viz: 5 coloured people 5 Carabees, 3 Macoosies & 2 Accaways,[5] left the Post at the Cayuni on the first of October in the afternoon. Being under the particular direction of the Royal Geographical Society, aided by His Majesty's Government, we hoisted at our starting, Great Britain's proud union in our two principal boats, and under its auspices we flattered ourselves with hopes of the best success in our undertaking.

We met the first Cataracts that opposed difficulties to our progress at Aritaka[6] and Arissaro,[7] the latter in 6°11′4″N. Lat. Lieut[t.] Haining who had complained for some days previously here became so unwell, that we were obliged to halt for several days – we procured a better shelter for him, than our encampment would have afforded at an Accaway Settlement, the Captain of which assigned us one of his huts. Some active medicine there restored him, and enabled us to continue our voyage. On the 6[th.] October we passed the last cataracts of that series, of which Eitabally[8] was the

---

[1] James Haining of the 65th or the 2nd Yorkshire North Riding Regiment. He was promoted to Captain in 1841. In March 1843 he transferred to the 3rd West Indian Regiment with which he was serving in Sierra Leone when he died on 21 July 1844.

[2] Robert N. Brotherson. There had been various Brothersons in the colony since the 18th century. There is a J. Brotherson who was a planter in 1785 and a C. M. Brotherson who was a Burgher Captain in 1808. See Rodway, *History of British Guiana*, II, p. 55 and 188. There are three properties belonging to Brothersons on von Bouchenroeder's map of 1798. One of them was a property called Sandberg on the west bank of the Demerara River. This last suggests some relationship with Robert because Richard Schomburgk, during a journey up the Demerara River in 1844, stayed with a Brotherson, with whom he was already acquainted, at a place called Sandhills (R. Schomburgk, *Travels*, II, p. 390). It is more than likely that this is the same Brotherson who accompanied Schomburgk and had made previous ornithological expeditions into the interior, at least as far as the Rupununi River (see pp. 60–1). Hilhouse did not think much of Brotherson whom he described as a 'Bird stuffer ... who has no science or travel' (RGS Corres 1834–40, Postscript to Letter of Hilhouse to Maconochie, 10 October 1835).

[3] They were John Heraut to help Schomburgk with his botany and sketching; Peter Gerard, Schomburgk's servant; an assistant, John Wade, and a servant for Brotherson (RGS Corres 1834–40, Letter of Schomburgk to Maconochie, 19 September 1835). Hilhouse, who appears not to have had much time for anyone, called Heraut 'an execrable dauber' (RGS Corres 1834–40, Letter of Hilhouse to Maconochie, 12 April 1836).

[4] These were named the *Maconochie*, 35½ feet long, the *Bentham*, 21 feet long, and an unnamed light hunting canoe. Room is needed for surveying equipment, boxes for natural history collections and goods for trading with the Indians which included beads, knives, axes, cutlasses, fowling pieces, powder, shot, cloth, calico, scissors, fishhooks, combs, and looking-glasses. The cost of the expedition turned out to be much higher than originally estimated as the colony was a far more expensive place than had been appreciated. Schomburgk, who had so far received £300 and put his expenses at £400, sold his collection of sea shells to raise funds (RGS Corres 1834–40, Letters of Schomburgk to Maconochie, 19 September 1835, 25 September 1835).

[5] Carib, Macushi and Akawaio respectively.

[6] Aritaku River is marked on the reference map, but no cataract of that name.

[7] Arisaru.

[8] Itaballi.

Figure 2: Departure from the post on the Cuyuni River on 1 October 1835. The longer boat is the *Maconochie* and the shorter the *Bentham*. From the original watercolour by Robert Schomburgk. Included by permission of the Royal Geographical Society, London.

most considerable. They are generally called falls, but this is incorrect; they are nothing more than rapids, though large enough to prevent any navigation further up than Aritaka.

My mountain Barometer having suffered during our journey from Georgetown to the Post, I was deprived of the means of determining the heights of the cataracts above the sea level – It wanted re-filling, which I could not do 'en route'.[1]

Hills of inconsiderable height, approached the river from both sides – the vegetation of its banks was luxuriant and bore witness of the fertility of the soil. South of the Cataracts, the river assumed a new aspect; before this we had had proof that the level was falling; but here a number of sandbanks which rose above its surface were a new evidence of this. Our course led us along Glock,[2] or Great Island, the largest Island in the river. From time to time we observed a species of Palm, which is called by the natives Sawaray;[3] not being in flower I was unable to determine it specifically, but it appears to be peculiar to the Essequibo and Rupununy, and forms sometimes whole forests. The sandbanks obliged us often to cross and recross the river to avoid running

[1] At the time the only instrument for measuring atmospheric pressure, and thus altitude, was the mercury barometer. It was both a cumbersome and fragile instrument. On this occasion it appears to have lost all or some of its mercury which required replacing.

[2] Gluck Island.

[3] *Astrocaryum jauari*.

45

aground. Numerous Guanas (Iguana – Lacerta iguana)[1] had selected them as deposits for their eggs; our Indians were eager after these, and certainly when fresh, they are great delicacies. We collected several hundreds in a short space of time, and the animal itself, which the Indians are very desirous in securing was not less acceptable.

The banks of the river were about 10 to 12 feet high, clay mixed with sand and slightly covered with mould – we generally found behind the bank a natural ditch which had been formed by the receding waters after the annual inundation; on many places it was still partly filled with water and the abode of numerous fish with their natural enemy, the heron; our guns and arrows found therefore sufficient occupation. The brook Tiboroo[2] was the largest we had passed since we left the Cayuni; it is on the river's western or left bank. We landed on the 7th. on Houboucourou Island, where I measured on a Sandbank which was on the southern point of the Island, a baseline in order to determine the breadth of the river, which I found to be 1523 yards. The Arissaro mountains[3] bore then S.5°E. and their height determined from the same baseline was 640 feet. The heat on the sand was almost insupportable, the Thermometer in the sun stood at 120° and it was only with pain that one could walk upon the Sand without shoes and stockings; our people complained very much.

The most conspicuous among the trees that border the river is the Mora,[*4] Sawary[+5] Sirwabally[++6] and some Species of Wallaba.[+++7]

> * A Mimosa
> +Pekea tuberculosa of Aublet[8]
> ++Ocotea Spec?
> +++Dimorpha falcata and others.

On the 8th. October we landed opposite the Arissaro mountains; the appearance of high land was a novelty, which we had not enjoyed for a length of time. When we saw their bluish outline first, Carioero and some others of the Carabees, who had never been so high up before had to undergo a peculiar christening or initiatory rite, envied by none of us; Cabicoe the principal man of our Carabee followers, performed the office; he took some Tobacco, dipped it in the water and pressed the juice in the poor fellows' eyes; they kept as still as if the Operation had been connected with the most pleasant feelings – so far carries superstition.[9] Our halting place was a ledge of granitic rocks. I collected on the banks a number of specimens of Haiowa in blossom; this is the

[1] Probably the Common Iguana (*Iguana iguana*). Lacertidae are a family of Old World lizards.
[2] Tipuru River.
[3] Arisaru Mountains. These mountains have no connection with the Arisaru Falls referred to above.
[4] *Mora excelsa*.
[5] *Caryocar nuciferum*.
[6] Shiruaballi: *Aniba hypoglauca*; *Licaria canella*; *Ocotea canaliculata*.
[7] Wallaba: *Dicymbe altsonii*; *D. corymbosa*. Wallaba, Ituri: *Campsiandra comosa*; *Eperua grandiflora*; *E. jenmanii*. Wallaba, Soft: *Eperua falcata*.
[8] Fusée Aublet (1720–78), French botanist and author of *Histoire des plantes de la Guiane Françoise* (1775).
[9] The tobacco plant and its products are used in a large number of different ways across Lowland South America. See Johannes Wilbert, *Tobacco and Shamanism in South America*, New Haven and London, Yale University Press, 1987. Tobacco juice placed in the eyes results in an occlusion of them, in other words a change of vision in order to confront the visible representation of the invisible world. Mountains and rocks are closely associated with the spirit world.

Amyris ambrosiaca[1] the gum of which is used for pains in the Stomach while the bark is employed as a gentle emetic. It is highly recommended to persons with pulmonary complaints; the Indians also burn it instead of Candles.

It appears that the river makes from time to time inroads upon its banks; huge trunks of trees which lay now partly raised out of the surface of the water, in their fall had carried with them a portion of the bank and all that grew upon it – some were dry, others still clothed with verdure; they had evidently come to an untimely end in consequence of the river having undermined the bank upon which they stood. The general wall-like vegetation of the banks, was nevertheless, overtopped by many fine forest-trees. The Water-Guava (Psidium aromaticum)[2] which replaces the mangrove of the Sea-shore is considered an excellent simple; its aromatic leaves are used in dysentery and sore throat and are likewise a suduorific; the place next to them along the banks is occupied by Palms and the Trumpet-tree (Cecropia)[3] over which the Mora, the monarch of the forest, spreads its dark-leaved branches, and Flora as if anxious to perfect the groupe had arranged some of her choicest gifts, the Passion flowers, some white as snow (Passiflora albida?) others incarnate (P. coccinea),[4] intermixed with the Combretia racemosa,[5] several Species of Bignonia, in natural festoons. Numerous vines spread from tree to tree, some of the thickness of a thread, others vieing in diameter with the trunk of the tree, to the highest branches of which they climb throwing down roots into the soil; indeed they are often so numerous, that they appear like the stays and rigging of a mast.

The Yaya mountains[6] of less size and extent than the Arissaro, became next visible; Mariawa[7] a stream was on the left – a path partly by that stream, partly by land, leads from here to Demerara river; these streams and brooks of which there are several which afford communication with the Demerary river, will afford here after the means of an in-land navigation to avoid the falls; according to the information I have been able to collect, the portage is often a few miles.

I do not recollect but once that we were troubled by Musquitos in our encampment; in the region of 'the falls' the river appears to be quite free of them, but the 'bête rouge'[8] caused us increasing itching – this little animal eats itself into the flesh and causes a swelling, and a red spot, which remains sometime where ever one has been regaling itself.

From the preceding day (the 8[th.]) the river had taken a western course, on the morning of the 9[th.] it was more decided west and even north of west; the reason of the change

[1] The genus today is *Protium*. There are six species called 'haiawa' in Arawak and three of these are known in Creole as Incense tree.

[2] *Campomanesia aromatica*.

[3] *Cecropia angulata*; *C. sciadophylla*.

[4] *Passiflora albida* = *P. mucronata*; species is not native to Guyana, but twenty species, including *P. coccinea*, are.

[5] Schomburgk is probably referring to *Combretum racemosum*, but this species occurs only in Africa. There are seven species of *Combretum* reported from Guyana.

[6] The Yaya Mountains do not appear on the reference map but are shown on Schomburgk's map as lying on the right bank of the Essequibo, opposite the mouth of the Potaro River.

[7] Probably Mariwa River. It is a right-bank tributary of the Essequibo but Schomburgk is referring to his direction of travel.

[8] A small red insect *Eutrombicula alfreddugesi (Trombiculidae))* that burrows into the human skin, causing intense itching.

in its course was not visible; if we except the Yaya and Oumai[1] hills, which we estimated about 200 feet high, there were no impediments. At 9ʰ·45ᵐ· we observed the blueish outlines of the Twasinkie mountains,*[2]

> *Twasinkie and not Quasinkie is the general name, by which these mountains are known; the first is the pronunciation of our Indians and free-coloured people.

they bore at that time West.[3] At a point north of Oumai Creek our pilot pointed out to us a whole cluster of Lanah trees (Maripa?).[4] This tree is to be found along the banks of the Essequibo and Demerary and the fruit is used by the Arrowaaks and other tribes to paint their faces, it gives a blueish dye.

At Cumpoua Creek we found that the Character of the rocks had changed; they were more homogenous in their composition and the surface appeared as if they had been glazed. In their direction they do not differ from the grantic ledges we had met so often, but the dykes which crossed the river had at a short distance the deceiving appearance of a dry stone wall; they formed rapids which at Cumaka[5] and Acramalally we found some difficulties to pass; the fall of water was insignificant, but numberless detached rocks offered every where sharp edges to the bottom and sides of our boats.

No night's quarters had offered more discomfort than the present; our curtain for want of a better place having been spread over the sand, we came every where in contact with the sand, this might have been endured; but our quarters being disputed by the wood-ants, we were attacked by them even in our hammocks and it became difficult to obtain the shortest period of sleep. According to a meridian Altitude of Achernar, our resting place, formerly the site of a post, was in 5°20'7"N. Lat.

We commenced our journey next morning a little after 6 o'clock; on the rivers western bank rose the hills Courassik and Parissaecrou; to the South we observed the mountains of Pataro;[6] we passed the river of that name a little after seven; the mountains of Twasinkie bore then nearly South, and stretched in a western direction. We could trace the course of the Pataro river for a considerable distance running south-west towards the Peak Couranoucou;[7] according to our pilots, who had frequently travelled up and down the river, there is a communication between the rivers Pataro and Massaroony, but the first river is impassable for Canoes of larger size, in consequence of falls not far distant from its mouth.

White flocks of foam which came sailing down the river, gave us plainly to understand that we were approaching a new series of rapids and while turning round a sharp point of the river, a dyke presented itself, which apparently crossed its whole breadth and made every passage impossible. We considered how we should find a way through this impediment, but the calm look of our pilot, in whom we had full right to put every

---

[1] Omai.
[2] Twasinki Mountain.
[3] In the margin of the manuscript at this point someone has written '!!South'.
[4] More often known today as genipa (*Genipa americana*). Maripa is the Carib and Macushi word for the palm *Attalea regia*.
[5] Kumaka Falls. The kumaka is *Ceiba pentandra*, the Silk-Cotton or Kapok tree. This is a common place name as, according to Mennega et al., *Check-list*, p. 48, it is 'Frequently seen as a relic because of local prejudice in felling the tree'.
[6] Potaro River.
[7] Possibly Kurungiku.

confidence assured us of a passage with out being obliged to put wings to our boats. The dyke consisted of rocks thrown over each other in the greatest confusion and took a south-western direction towards the peak Couranoucou.

It was a lovely view, the dyke which afforded a passage to the turbulent river on three places, completely hid to us, when we first saw it, formed the foreground with its black rocks, while the Pataro mountains only a few miles distant with the peak towering over them and envelopped in fleecy clouds, formed the chief object in the landscape; the outlines of the Twasinkie mountains, just discernable through the morning mist, afforded as picturesque a background as would have satisfied a Claude Lorraine.[1] We had to haul the boats over the rapids formed in consequence of this dyke; they have got their name from the peak Couranoucou; the next rapids which were likewise formed by a dyke of similar origin and direction have the short name Benhouri-Boumoucou.[2] In a geological collection which I sent to Berlin, a rock similar in its composition will be observed, which I detached from boulders that lay on Bordeaux-Hill in the Island of St. John's. In a memorial which accompanied that collection, I observed that the granitic masses peculiar to the Virgin Islands might be found very likely on the South-American Continent, the Granite I found opposite the Arissaro Mountains is the same in appearance as that of Virgin Gorda and Tortola and a comparison of the rock from Bordeaux-hill with those I collected at the rapids of Couranoucou will prove that they are likewise of the same composition. I do not wish to enter here into arguments unde-sired by the most of my readers, but should my collection and memorial have safely arrived and the latter be thought worthy of publication I refer those who have an inter-est in such matters to the source.*

*The collection and memorial in question were despatched before my departure from St. Thomas' to Professor Weiss of Berlin;[3] while writing this I am entirely unconscious whether it has arrived – but I despatched one other series of geological specimens from the Virgin Islands to London in order to be presented by the Royal Geographical Society to the Geological Society.[4]

We halted at Bonhouri-boumoucou Island; it is of considerable extent and on its southern point a lateral branch of Captain James (or Macoosie James, by which cognomen he is generally known to the traders and fishermen of the river) have recently settled here; two temporary huts sheltered them against the immediate contact with the rain, to which trees only lately felled made the approach difficult. According to an observation of the sun when crossing the meridian and the river as horizon that island is in 5°14′20″N. Lat.

It was our intention to halt several days at Macoosie James' in order to procure Cassada[5] bread, his settlement was at some distance from the latter Island at the Cataract of Warapoota;[6] we arrived on the foot of it on the 10th. October at 2 o'clock in the afternoon. The number of rocks which oppose the advance is so great, that it causes

[1] Claude Lorraine (1600–82), the originator of the romantic tradition in French landscape painting.
[2] Benhori-bumoka.
[3] Possibly Christian Samuel Weiss (1780–1856), author of *Ende des Gebirgszuges von Brasilien*.
[4] The collection for the Geological Society did arrive and was entered in their list of donations for 23 June 1835. See *Transactions of the Geological Society of London*, 5 (2nd series), 1838.
[5] Cassava (*Manihot esculenta* spp.).
[6] Waraputa Falls.

not one rapid but five or six in succession; several passages not wider than six feet were attempted and when perhaps more than half way through a new impediment appeared which was not to be overcome and we had to relinquish the passage and chose an other – only after fatiguing work of several hours, where we did not advance more than a hundred yards, we arrived at Captain James', who with his seraglio, children, brothers sisters and other relatives had been passive spectators to our toil. When we landed Captain James who for the occasion had dressed himself with a shirt as a distinguishing mark and had put an additional quantity of Roucou on his forehead, tendered his hand and graciously permitted us to select a spot next to his palace for our camp. This palace consisted of a miserable hut, open on all sides and indifferently covered with palm-leaves. Camboree which was James' Indian name, was rather a good looking man, but through his connections in trade and his visits to Georgetown, he had lost his natural openness and acquired subtelty in return; indeed we discovered soon his political views in locating us near his residence; the approach to our Rum bottle was connected with less bodily exertions. His women of whom he had three were occupied in spinning cotton for hammocks; it was done in a most primitive way – a spindle and the forefingers were the means to perform it. Our arrival must have deranged the order of their domestic duties, it became necessary to do part of it by artificial light; for that purpose a piece of Haiowa Gum was lighted, which did not afford only a beautiful light but the odour of it perfumed the whole environs of the hut. Whether it was fancy or reality I know not, but I thought my chest felt twice as light when inhaling the steam which arose from it. They use likewise spun cotton, immersed in wild bee's wax instead of a Candle.

Capt James' young men were mostly absent; a party had gone to Georgetown and others were out hunting, and as I found our boat-crews too weak and wanted to engage some additional Indians, it became necessary to wait two days not only for their return, but likewise to allow the women time to make us Cassava-bread.

Our situation was most unfortunately selected for astronomical observations; trees from 80 to 100 feet high made it quite impossible to see any thing but the zenith; even where the ground had been partly cleared, none of those stars of minor elevation were visible, which would have enabled me to determine the latitude with a Sextant and artificial horizon. The danger of crossing over during night to one of the rocks were so great in consequence of the rapids, that none of the crew would attempt it; these were likewise the causes which prevented me to take Lunar distances.

Twenty seven Cassava-cakes were ready – their amount was to be paid in Knives and beads; and though the Cassava roots had been taken out of Capt James' field he told me that his women and children should have the benefit; they were therefore summoned to make their choice – some took Knives others beads, combs, pins and if I add the presents which I was obliged to make to Capt James I found our lodgings rather expensive. James' relations and followers which may consist of about 50 men, women & children, are not only Macoosies, but likewise Carabees, Accaways and Arowaaks; we even observed a Warpissano[1] and an Atorayi,[2] who distinguished themselves by having their faces painted fancyfully their feet were tied as far as the ankles with Cotton coloured

---

[1] Wapishiana.
[2] Atorai.

with Roucou, and on their calfs there were painted rings and strokes – they were taller than the Indians I had seen hithertho and uncommonly well made.

South of Warapoota the banks of the river became more abrupt, but the Vegetation was still as luxuriant as before. One of the most common trees in the region of the falls is the Kamarakata – satisfied with the sterile rock it reaches nevertheless a height of from 50 to 60 feet, an other tree called Warrakaro, the seeds of which resemble those of the Abrus, is very common between the small islands, the wood of both is not in use, but the bark of the first is considered a good remedy against tooth-ache – they were not in blossom in order to determine them; the wood of the Acouri broad-tree is used for framing houses and different Species of Wallaba (Dimorpha) so useful for building houses &c were seen in all directions.[1]

Scarcely was one rapid passed when an other came in view, and I do not think that in the whole course of the day, we made more than five miles; while the necessary preparations were made to haul the boats over the rapids the most expert of our bowmen went out to shoot the Pacou a Delicious fish which frequents the cataracts in order to feed upon the Weira, different Species of Lacis; we shot that day fourteen, each of 12 to 16lbs weight. It is a particular feature of the river in that region that the islands run mostly east and west, while further north they took the direction of the river. On the 13[th.] after 3 o'clock p.m. the Twasinkie mountains bore S27W distance 1½ mile; we had arrived at a rapid which it took us nearly 2 hours to cross, and the night had thus approached that we were obliged to chose a place at the rapid for our night quarter – we were rather favoured – our floor consisted of a solid piece of granite, shaded partly by trees, and when our curtain was fixed we declared unanimously that our bed chamber had never been better regulated. The cataract was not more than three yards from our hammocks; what delight to jump in one of the lateral channels, where our strength was able to stem the current and enjoy the delicious feeling of subjecting the body to the foaming stream and refreshing the limbs after having been exposed the whole day to the tropical sun.

The solitude of the river is certainly astonishing; since we had left the post, we had met only two corials; one below the first cataracts, the other at Houboucourou Island and from the Warapoota to Rapoo,[2] the last rapid before the junction of the Rupununy and the Essequibo, there was not one settlement.[3] Who would think it possible, when observing such evident proofs of the soil's fertility. I have seen Sugar Canes from the upper Macoosie Settlement at Warapoota, which were 2 inches in diameter and were 6 to 8 feet long before the leaves made it useless. I have seen the Coffee, the luxuriant leaves of which spoke of its satisfaction with the soil, covered with the red berries; in the immediate vicinity of the Settlement grew trees the heights and span of which astonished me, though I had botanized in Puerto Rico and seen the primitive productions of the Laquilla Mountains.

Our resting place was that night in 4°59'13"N. Lat. and within 2 miles north of the Twasinkie mountains. We breakfasted next morning opposite them; their greatest height was estimated 1100f. The most of the islands stretched with their shorter side to

---

[1] Kamarakata, *Acosmium nitens*; Warrakaro, *Tabebuia insignis*; Acouri, *Licania densiflora*.
[2] Rappu Falls.
[3] This is not correct. Schomburgk in the next paragraph refers to a Macushi settlement near the Akaiwanna River.

the south and with their longer to the east; at 4 o'clock p.m. (15th October) the Akai-wanne mountains[1] on the rivers right or eastern shore bore south-east, the river was here from east to west about 2 miles wide. We pitched our camp near a large rapid, the pleasure of ascending which we anticipated for next morning. They were the falls of Youcourit,[2] still more grand than those of Twasinkie, which we had passed the previous day. They are formed by granitic beds which from time to time show distinct stratifica-tion, running from N. to S. and form a connection with the Twasinkie mountains on the left and the Akaiwanne mountains on the eastern shore – we saw the latter hills rising at some distance, those of Taquiara or Commoutie[3] showing themselves only in an outline. The Twasinkie, their south branch the Commoutie and the Akaywanne, form a beautiful amphitheatre and the vulgar belief is that the Cataract of Youcourit receive tributaries from seven hills; it is not so much the height of the Cataract but the quantity of water, which by a previous series of rapids has received a strong impulse precipitates itself with the greatest vehemence towards Youcourit, where narrowed in, sharp pointed rocks throw new impediments in their way, and they cause that foaming and tossing of the waters, which make the Cataract at once so fearful & magnificent. Our Sketcher was employed at its foot while we others rambled about the small island on which our effects had been landed in order to haul the boats over. I found a beautiful orchideous plant, new to me, nor could I find its description in Sprengel's edition of Linné.[4] Its flower was an inch and a half in diameter; the sepals of a rich purple and a velvet like appearance; the helmet of the same colour and the labellum striated with yellow. After we had crossed Youcourit we [found] a little above the cataract a settle-ment of Macoosie Indians; their houses were of a better construction than those of Captain James' which stood as yet unparelled for want of comfort and durability; oppo-site to the settlement is Akaywanne Creek, a much frequented path to Demerary river. The Akaywanna mountains approached the eastern bank so much, that the river took quite a western and even for a short time a north of west direction; indeed it meandred through the hills of Akaywanna and Commoutie, which from both sides approached its shores. We breakfasted on a small island at the foot of some rapids; the number of Pacou were here so large, that in the course of half an hour, 21 fine fishes were shot and caught, none of less than 12 lbs weight. The rapids were difficult to ascend there being but little water on the rocks, and as those channels which possessed the most, turned in different directions, our labour was multiplied. We found against the rocks, the remnants of a Coorial, which on its descent, badly managed must have split against the rocks; or while ascending the rope might have given away, and destruction is then almost unavoidable if the river be full; broken arrows and bows, and other Indian implements had been found previously, almost a proof that the unfortunate occupants lost their lives. The boat appeared to have split on the upper rocks right in two; one half of it we found below, the other one half way up.

The river expanded and was less studded with islands the nearer we approached the ridge of the Commouti mountains; the highest south-eastern peak bore in the evening

---

[1] Akaiwanna Mountains

[2] Yukuriba Falls.

[3] Takwari or Kumuti Mountains.

[4] Kurt Polycarp Joachim Sprengel (1766–1833), Professor of Botany at Halle University and editor of *Caroli Linnaei ... systema vegetabilium*, 5 vols, Göttingen, 1825–28.

west, distant half a mile. My wish to ascertain the latitude was frustrated by heavy showers, which set in in the evening and made our lodgings most uncomfortable; the Indians found it the same and according to the superstitious belief, Lewis a Carabee, who appeared to have the next claim to the Piaimanship, when absent from the settlement commenced to piai the rain away;[1] a quick movement with the hands and a sound muttered between the teeth was the charm; but the spirit appeared to be immovable and after vain attempts the conjurer was the first who sought shelter under our curtain, which afforded but little protection against the tropical shower. At that period a tremendous crash startled us all; the rain had softened the earth and the ground under one of the large trees, which stood near the banks partly undermined by the river, had given away and fallen into the water. Before it reached the surface of the water, the bearing down of all the minor trees and branches was heard – then the plunge, and lastly the cry of frightened macaws, parrots, & baboons;[2] a moment after and every thing was hushed in silence, except the monotonous noise of the falling rain. 'A tree fallen into the water' was the first observation of those who were familiar with these occurrences, and the safety of our boats was now our next inquiry, but as near as it had sounded, we heard soon from the watchman that it had happened on the opposite shore.

Half an hour's paddling brought us next morning to the ridge of the mountains, which extend to the Water's edge. The highest peak is formed from some granitic boulders, overlying each other, and the upper one smooth and rounded, resembling in a striking manner a waterjar called in Arrowaak Commouti and in Carabees Taquiari from whence the mountains received their name; they are however much more known by the people of the Essequibo by the first name, that part having formerly been inhabited by Arrowaaks. Some of the coloured people who accompanied me had been on the top, which possesses a cavity and is partly covered by a square piece of granite laying across; they described the depth of the hole as considerable. I estimated the height of the peak 800 feet; those fanciful rocky masses are about 150 feet lower, perpendicular and at least 100 feet high. The Indians who had not seen them before had to drink Limejuice and Tobacco water was put in their eyes; I ascertained that this was done to prevent an awful head-ache which otherwise the spirit of the place would cause to those, who see them for the first time.

A little while after we passed the Creek Bourro-bourro[3] which according to our pilots, leads to Savannas and its banks are said to be inhabited by tribes of Macoosie Indians. What appears almost incredible, but what was asserted not only by the coloured people, but likewise by Basico[4] an intelligent Macoosie Indian, who lives

---

[1] One of the duties of the South American shaman is to prevent heavy rain and storms. See Johannes Wilbert, *Mindful of Famine. Religious Climatology of the Warao Indians*, Cambridge, Mass., Harvard University, Center for the Study of World Religions, 1996, in which he reviews many examples of this practice from all over Lowland South America.

[2] There are no baboons native to South America, but in Guyana the term is used to refer to monkeys, in particular the Howler monkey (*Alouatta* spp.).

[3] It is not clear which river this is but it could be the Muruwa. The Burro-burro joins the Siparuni before they flow together into the Essequibo. As will be seen below, the mouth of the Siparuni was passed later the same day.

[4] For a portrait of Basico see Plate 11 in Goodall, *Sketches of Amerindian Tribes*. Basico, sometimes spelt Basiko or Pasico, is mentioned on several occasions in Schomburgk's reports. As a reward for his help to the Boundary Commission, he accompanied Richard Schomburgk to Georgetown in June, 1843, in order to receive from the Governor 'a beautiful ornamented chieftain's staff, and a large printed patent of office' (R. Schomburgk, *Travels*, II, p. 315).

between the Rupununy and Tokoto[1] rivers, this Creek so small at its mouth is said to extend further than the Siperonie,[2] and the Macoosie Indians, South of the Itaka mountains, when bound to the Essequibo carry their woodskins (a small and light boat, made out of the bark of trees) to the head of that brook, and make their journey in a much shorter time than if they had descended the Rupununy.

We breakfasted (the 16th. October) on the eastern side of a large Island; the first plant I met with on landing was a Mikania (angulata) and in its vicinity grew likewise the famed Guaco (Mikania Guaco). The bitter extractive stuff, so peculiar to the tribe of Eupatorinae is prevailing in a striking manner in the Guaco; an opportunity was offered to me to compare the two species of Mikania both of which are medicinal. The young leaves possess the bitter much more than the old ones. The natives call it Erra-warang and use a decoction of it in siphilis; but its properties as a preventitive or antidote against the bite of poisonous snakes are not known here.[3]

Opposite to our halting place there was a path which leads to the great falls of Demerary river; [where] the path meets the Essequibo, there is a large [inlet], or as it is called by the natives the Kirahagh which stretches for a considerable distance NNE. and which must be crossed, being of considerable extent to go round it. We passed the mouth of the Siperonie on the 16th. at 2h. p.m.; several miles further South we met the re-junction of a branch of the Essequibo which came from the E.N.E., while the river itself came from W.S.W; we passed the point of division next day; the Island which is formed in consequence of it, is called Tambicabo,[4] in most of the Charts this branch has been stated as a river.

Our resting place was selected at Tambicabo in the vicinity of thousands of palm-trees, but as inviting as it appeared at a distance we found it by no means comfortable, the ground being overgrown by bushwood and covered with sharp prickles which had dropped from the Palm trees. Where-ever that Species of Palm is growing (Sawaray) it is indicative of a barren, sandy soil. The chattering of numerous monkeys, resounded from the interior of the wood, but we were too polite to interrupt their debates which to judge from the vehemence of their voices became from time to time quite hot. The night was beautifully clear and I had a fine observation of Fomalhaut; the Siperonie mountains on the rivers southern shore bore N61°W about 2½ miles distant and our resting place being in 4°45′20″N Lat. the mouth of the river is in 4°46′38″N Lat. We passed on the 18th. the Cataracts of Ouropocari[5] where we had to unload the boats entirely. They are by no means so grand as those of Youcourit, they ressemble much more a milldam on a grand scale, but as there were no lateral channels deep enough for our boats to pass, we had to haul them over where the water descended with great strength. On the eastern side of the Cataract is a small island called Ouropocary, here it is said was formerly a large Coffee Estate, where not many years ago fruits have been

---

[1] Takutu River.

[2] Siparuni River.

[3] *Mikania angulata* occurs in Mexico, not in Guyana, whereas *M. guaco* does. For a list of chemically active *Mikania* species found in French Guiana and their uses, see P. Grenand, C. Moretti and H. Jacquemin, *Pharmacopées traditionnelles en Guyane, Créoles, Palikur, Wayãpi*, Paris, ORSTOM, 1987, pp. 206–8. Interestingly enough, whereas the Creole population recognize it as a cure for snake bites, the Amerindians do not.

[4] Tambicubo. It is a large inlet, not an island.

[5] Kurupukari Falls.

gathered. It would have been planted at the time of the first settlement, when the Dutch Posts extended to Arinda. We landed and found the remnants of a dyke, several fruit-trees and ornamental plants not indigenous in Guiana, by all means proofs of former cultivation, but it was so overgrown with prickly mimosa, Solanum &c that we soon gave up our search after Coffee-plants.

On the 19[th.] in the morning we saw the Maccary Mountains[1] before us, they looked highly picturesque and appeared so abrupt that we considered the angle they formed to be from 50 to 60°. Our course was now E. & E.b.S., the river free of Islands and slightly meandring; I found a number of graceful little Palms (perhaps a Bactris), and what was my astonishment when Basico told me that his nation (Macoosies) made their celebrated blow pipes out of a similar Species. I cut several and certainly the pith inside is so soft, that it can be removed with the greatest ease[;] he told me that a species up at the Rupununy is still more qualified for it. In its vicinity grew an other palm, called by the natives Kirahagh-palm, who use it for fencing in the mouths of inlets (Kirahagh), to prevent the escaping of fish when the water has been poisoned.[2] It is knotted and the internodes are only 1½ to 2 inches in length and I consider it more elegant that the Rattan-cane.

In the afternoon at half-past four the Maccary mountains were to our left, bearing S.E., the distance not more than 2 miles and their highest elevation was seen under an angle of 8°22′; they are very abrupt, studded with whitish masses of rocks, often perpendicular – their western peak has quite the appearance of a gigantic roof or gable end. According to an observation of Fomalhaut they are in 4°27′30″N Lat.

At 8 o'clock next morning we met the first rapids South of the Maccary mountains and others followed in the course of the day; the river presents here a real Labyrinth of islands, and I wondered only how they could find their way through. The quantity of Pacou which we found here was numerous indeed; since we left the post we had at the interval of our halts caught 110 pacous which at an average of 12[lb] gave us 1320[lb] weight of fish, exclusive of other fish.

The granitic boulders which we had met from time to time in our last day's travel (20[th.] October) assumed now quite a new feature; they filled nearly the bed of the river were 40 feet high and from 50 to 150 feet long. They were mostly dome-shaped, but likewise singular and often split asunder, the fissure being wide enough to admit the passage of a person. Every feature of the singular scene reminded me of the granitic rocks in Virgin Gorda, with the difference, the landscape being here an inland river, the rocks of Virgin Gorda are bounded by the sea. There is likewise a modification in their composition. Where the scenery appeared to us wildest, the rocks were often 60 feet high, crowned with Cereae,[3] which by their decomposition had covered the surface with a slight vegetable mould[;] numerous pines spread an inviting perfume. I had been attracted to the rock by a beautiful orchideous plant, crowned with bright yellow flowers; the plant itself ressembled much the young plant of the Sugar-cane. The current where the rocks had left passages was strong indeed and we had to force our

[1] Makari Mountain.
[2] The Native peoples of Amazonia use various vegetable substances to poison stretches of rivers or ponds in order to catch fish. The poison acts to drive fish to the surface and large quantities are often taken in this manner.
[3] A genus of the Family Cactaceae.

way through these mighty floodgates by ropes and poles; the place is called Achramoucra.[1] On the 22[d.] at 8 o'clock in the morning we passed the last cataract north of the Rupununy; at that time we saw two canoes with Indians in the distance, a novel sight which we had only twice [seen] since we left the post and 13 days had elapsed since we had seen any one but those who composed the Expedition. The Indians were Macoosies from the Rupununy and on a visit to Demerary River – their boat was loaded with hammocks, large balls of spun cotton, bows of letter wood, Tobacco in leaves, parrots, maccaws &c – the Captain as a distinguishing sign wore a Crown of Maccaw feathers, and, as he had landed on a rocky islet in the river, we paddled there and landed; he returned to his boat and taking seat on one of the benches, he awaited us with great gravity. Our people bartered for several of their commodities and gave in exchange knives and scissors and after I handed him and his wife some trifling presents, he promised to take care of some letters to the Colony.

The river becomes free of Islands and widens to several hundred yards and tends mostly south-west and even north-west. Towards evening we saw the Makarapan mountains, the eastern peak bearing S.65°W. and next morning on the 23[d.] October at 9 o'clock in the morning, the mouth of the Rupununy bore S.35°W., we were then on the eastern bank of the Essequibo which river has blackish water and that of the Rupununy being of a turbid yellowish colour, the line of division was perceptible for a considerable extent beyond the junction. Cloudy sky, rain and the high woody banks of the Essequibo had prevented me the previous nights to take an observation; it was now my chief object to determine the geographical situation of the junction of the two rivers, I selected therefore a favourable place on the very western point of the Rupununy's mouth, along side of a small Kirahagh or inlet. On its banks we found a species of Haiari;[2] the wood of which the Indians use for poisoning the waters to catch fish. It is a ligneous twiner or bush-rope as they are called here, with pinnated leaves and papilionaceous and without doubt a new species of Piscidia.

How many times have I been disappointed by the uncertain state of the weather to take observations and a mischievous cloud has perhaps at the very moment I had so anxiously watched for, obscured the meridian passage of the star. On this night I was more fortunate and by satisfactory passages of Fomalhaut & Achernar, I determined the latitude of the junction as in 3°57′42″N Lat.

The people from the post at the Essequibo were only engaged to bring me to the first settlement of the Indians at the Rupununy, where it was my intention to make a halt and to collect every information with regard to the south-eastern course of the Essquibo, a terra incognita to our crew. A settlement of Carabees under Cap[t.] Jacobus had been recommended to me as best calculated for my purpose; the migratory habits of the Indians, often caused by sickness or death at their settlement, which are ascribed to the predominance of the evil genius of the place, had induced him to remove to the western side of the Macarapan mountains. We had been for the last six days without any Cassada-bread, not having been able to procure a quantity large enough at Warapoota and the consequences now, when nothing but fish was our daily food, became visible, half of the number of our crew were often incapable to paddle, the water and food having caused disentery and it was the more

[1] Akramukra Falls.
[2] Haiari, Black: *Lonchocarpus chrysophyllus*; Haiari, White: *Lonchocarpus martynii*.

necessary to hasten our departure; my first intention to determine the Longitude by a set of Lunar distances was therefore relinquished since two days would elapse before the moon was in a favourable position.

The next morning saw us therefore ascending the Rupununy. Its course is in the commencement winding between South and West; the width about 200 yards and often not more than 3 feet deep, though the river was not as yet on its lowest level, the banks a yellowish clay, which had received its light colour from the presence of large quantities of sand. The difference between the Rupununy and Essequibo exists not only in the colour but is likewise strikingly observable in the less luxuriant growth of its trees and shrubs. The banks are lined with the Mangrove of the upper Essequibo, the Water-Guave, with its light green leaves and snow-white blossoms and clusters of the Sawary-Palm are conspicuous among the trees that border the river but their very presence is a sign of a poor and sandy soil, and thus I found it as far as I had leisure to penetrate through the bushes; by no means very amusing since numerous dead branches of the prickly Sawaray made the advance difficult.

The banks are abrupt and show the different stages of the rivers stand, since it commenced to fall. Like the concentric rings of the aged oaktree, shows the springs it has passed, thus had the daily stand of the river from the period of its returning to its bed, left horizontal stripes of sand and detritus. At our halting place we had a fine view of the Makarapan mountains which were only a few miles distant from us. We lodged that night at Jacobus' abandoned place on the western bank of the stream Arrouimah, not far from its junction with the Rupununy. Not a hundred yards from its northern bank rose the Makarapan mountains, their greatest height has been estimated 4000 feet above the level of the Rupununy.

For several days past the Caymans[1] had been very frequent, but their audacity at our night's quarters exceeded description, one of them rich in age, possessed so much curiosity that he came quite near the shore and to judge from that part of the body which he raised above the surface of the water he must have measured from 15 to 16 feet. We fired with balls at him, saw them strike his body, without taking effect; when annoyed at it he gave a plunge and disappeared for a short period, but soon returned to continue his observations on the intruders. A meridian Altitude of Fomalhaut gave the situation of the north-eastern foot of the hills as in 3°55'14"N.Lat.

The morning was fresh, the wind blowing from the north of east, the Thermometer stood at half past five in the morning 69°F at 7 o'clock 71°. The river appeared under a new feature and meandres in short turns along the southern foot of the Makarapan mountains, we advanced therefore but slowly in a straight line and towards evening the highest peak bore N.13°E. The banks being abrupt and about 16 feet high, we had to scale them to find a place for a night's quarter, we were obliged to leave our effects in the boats. We had sent the small Coorial in the morning early before us to procure some Cassada-bread at a small settlement of Macoosies, it returned long after nightfall and unsuccessful; they had procured some plantains and Sugar-cane, the latter was of uncommon size and sweetness. Our disappointment was not great, we flattered ourselves to reach in the course of the next day Jacobus' settlement. At 9 o'clock we

---

[1] There are three species of caiman in the region: Spectacled Caiman (*Caiman crocodilus*); Broadnosed Caiman (*C. latirostris*); Black Caiman (*Melanosuchus niger*). The first two grow to some 2.5 metres in length, the last to over 4.4 metres.

passed the River Taraqua (Rewa and Quitaro[1] in the charts); at one o'clock the Annaih[2] mountains bore S.8°W, we landed a little while after on the river's left bank to take a view of the first Savannah we met in our journey. At the distance we met a great chain of mountains, stretching N.b.E. to S.b.W; a retrospective glance to the Makarapan gave us his situation as N.50°E. from the south-eastern edge of the Savannah. At half past three we halted at the mouth of the brook Courasawaka[3] to the banks of which at a short distance from the mouth, we had been informed Jacobus had removed. In order to reconnoitre and to see whether the place afforded us any opportunities to encamp for the next two or three months, Lieut. Haining and myself mounted the little Coorial, and taking some presents with us, we started. The brook was in the commencement narrow but widened while advancing; numerous aquatic birds and hawks, which having been disturbed at their resting places, flew from bush to bush; not less numerous were the Caymans, which raised their ugly heads above the water and did not appear to care much for our approach.

Some newly thatched houses came now in view; we landed and advanced towards them through a Cassada-field; we thought it strange that no human voice was heard; on approaching the first hut we found it empty, the second the same; we went to the Captain's house which distinguished itself by being of larger size, and what I had never observed before it was wattled and plastered over with clay. There were pots, balls of cotton and a new hammock not quite finished, but no human being. We made many conjectures and thought they might have been frightened away, we looked in every direction for them but in vain; observing that the posts and parts of the hut showed more or less the effects of fire, we thought that the settlement had been surprized perhaps by an inimical party. Our pilot recollected that there was formerly an other settlement somewhat higher up; we went there, but it gave evident proofs that it had been abandoned for the last twelve months; we had therefore to return and who can paint the disappointment of our crew when we came without bread. The riddle was soon solved, a Macoosie had arrived who belonged to Jacobus' settlement and who lived in a temporary hut at the banks of the Rupununy. One of Jacobus' wifes had died lately and the consequence was that though the settlement was quite new, the houses most comfortable and the Cassada still in the field, every one left it, and the Macoosie was to take care of the Cassada – but to dwell on the old settlement, this he would not have done on any account. Jacobus had removed to the mountains and thither we were obliged to proceed, though a whole day's journey further.

The Rupununy takes a far northern course, bounded on its left bank by the Savannahs, it widens to 200 yards and the Vegetation appears more fresh and luxuriant. We passed Haiowa point, and before us extended the Chain of mountains where we hoped to be more fortunate in procuring provision. A northern breeze accompanied us, which we had not experienced so strong since we left the coast; the Thermometer was in the morning 69° and at 9 o'clock exposed to the influence of the sun and breeze 89°. The river took a north-western direction and returning to a west by south course, it forms an elbow; at that

---

[1] On the reference map, the river is marked as the Rewa and the Kwitaro is shown as a tributary of it. The Rewa is also known as the Illiwa.

[2] Annai.

[3] It is referred to as Curassawaak hereafter. It is called Kurawa River on the reference map.

part we found the brook Anna-y,[1] and here is where according to the Charts the boundary line between British Guiana and the Portuguese territories joins the Rupununy. The brook Anna-y has received its name from a 'mountain', at the foot of which there are several Macoosie villages. We landed at the brook, in order to get information whether we could encamp in their vicinity and Mr Brotherson and our head pilot returned towards evening to inform us that we had the offer of a tolerable good hut and their good will – both of which were highly acceptable. The Captain of the Village and his wife and children paid us a visit, they were presented with looking glasses, knives, handkerchiefs &c and next morning we resolved to remove the first part of our effects. The latitude of the brook was in [blank] North according to observations of Fomalhaut & Canopus.

The walk to our hut was most fatiguing, having been cramped up in the boats for nearly a month, the distance though not more than perhaps 6 or 7 miles appeared to us more than double that sum. It gave us fever and those who had complained previous felt much more in consequence, indeed one of the servants became dangerously ill.

I conclude here my first report with the wish that my proceedings may meet with the approval, I am anxious for.
Anna-y 29[th.] October 1835.

****

Schomburgk arrived at Annai on 28 October and his party remained there until 1 December. Everyone was sick for at least part of the time and, although astronomical observations and scientific collections were undertaken, Schomburgk complained that he had been unable to do as much as he would had he been healthy. From here the coloured members of the boat crew who had been taken on only to accompany the expedition as far as the first Indian settlements on the Rupununi returned downstream.[2]

The Second Report is composed of thirty-seven pages, including the original cover sheet, in Schomburgk's handwriting, together with two more recent cover sheets. It is in fairly good condition and has not suffered to the same degree from editorial rewriting as the First Report. To the original title, an editorial hand has added 'dated Curassawaak Jan[y] 15 1836' but there is no note of when it was received by the Royal Geographical Society.

SECOND REPORT DURING THE FIRST EXPEDITION IN THE INTERIOR OF BRITISH GUIANA TO THE ROYAL GEOGRAPHICAL SOCIETY OF LONDON BY ROBERT SCHOMBURGK

The river Rupununy being generally marked from its northern elbow as boundary line between British Guiana & the Brazilian territory & finding it impossible to procure a crew to accompany me higher up the Essequibo, a terra incognita to all the Indians of this side, I resolved to ascend the Rupununy as far as circumstances would permit it.

[1] Annai.
[2] RGS Corres 1834–40, Letters of Schomburgk to Maconochie, 29 October 1835, 1 November 1835, 5 December 1835.

Capt. Jacobus (Yhrayee) was to accompany me with 14 Indians, partly Charibees,[1] and partly Macoosies. Our travelling effects were much curtailed, being well aware that the River was at low level & that we would have to meet many difficulties. Every arrangement was completed and M[r] Haining and myself went with the last transport to the river's bank. What a sight at our arrival there! Indian men, women & children – baskets with provisions, our trunks & cases – all were mixed in the greatest confusion. The red hammocks slung from tree to tree, fires with pots on them in various directions, all realized the picture of a Gipsy Camp.

The Indian does not like to leave his wife & children at home when he undertakes a journey of several weeks length. It is partly out of jealousy so common among them, partly out of indolence having all his wants provided to him by his wife. Though Jacobus had assured me that there would not be more than three women and his child, we found to our greatest astonishment that our whole number amounted to thirty three.

We started with the dawn of morning on the 1st of December in three Coorials. The River meanders along a lateral branch of the Parime[2] mountains, & takes so far a northern direction that at [times] we were only a few miles from Anna-y. The banks have the same uninteresting appearance as farther north: a light yellowish clay mixed with sand; trees, of moderate if not small size, skirt only the banks, & immediately behind them extend the Savannahs to the foot of the mountains. The River was so shallow that the Indians were obliged to push the Coorials forward by means of long poles, & only from time to time they were able to use their paddles. Sand-banks rose frequently out of the river & we had to look out for a channel to force our way through; however it must not be forgotten that we were then at the height of the dry season. We observed frequently the black porous rock lying free on the banks, or being embedded in the clay. The Sand banks change sometimes with gravel banks which consist mostly of small fragments of quartz & granite of angular form.

The Rupununy forms many inlets (kirahagh). We had passed several during the day of which only Assicouneh deserves to be mentioned. At its mouth it is wider than the river but M[r] Brotherson who had visited it during his ornithological excursions told us that further inwards it narrows to about ten feet then shortly after it expands to a small lake alive with fish & waterfowl. The Kingfisher (Alcedo), called by the Charibbees Sacka Sacka & by the Arrowaaks Saxicarlie is the most numerous bird in these regions. We observed four species one of the size of a sparrow with a fine orange breast (in Charibbee Sarrie-curou).[3] Divers or duckers were likewise very frequent. The Charibee call them Carara. We saw them sometimes dive into the water without making their reappearance for many minutes after; their nasal organs are peculiarly formed, a skin is drawn over them & no opening is visible.[4]

Our halting place was selected opposite the mountains which approached quite near the shore. The highest hill in that direction had attracted my attention for some time

[1] Carib.

[2] Pakaraima. This is a Carib word which can be translated literally as 'large basket'. A 'pakara' is a square shaped storage basket, and 'ima' is a suffix which means not simply large in a physical sense but implies some supernatural quality as well. Many of the mountains in the Pakaraima chain have the shape of huge baskets.

[3] There are six species of kingfisher to be found in Guyana. Sacka-sacka has not been identified, but the Sarrie-curou is possibly the Pygmy Kingfisher (*Chloroceryle aenea*).

[4] Probably the anhinga (*Anhinga anhinga*).

past. Jacobus had told me its name with some reluctance, but unfortunately it escaped me before I noted it down. When we approached the mountains' foot I enquired once more. "I scarcely wish to repeat its name," observed Jacobus, "because if said twice the Spirit of the mountains will send rains." However, I prevailed upon him & found its name was Sawacko-toonally or Rain Mountain.

It had been cloudy the whole morning but as if to strengthen their superstition a shower descended not many minutes after & they laughed now at our unbelief. The mountains are mostly only from time to time grown over by patches of wood. Boulders of granite, some of immense size, lay on their sides & became easily observable by the difference of colour between the scanty grass & the whitish rock.

We passed a small rapid in the afternoon formed by the porous rock which I have had occasion to mention before. The River continues its meandering course to the [south]. Vestiges of its late inundation were observable wherever it took a turn & in many places trees broken down by the current, or withered away, gave its banks the appearance as if a tropical hurricane had swept over them. The Mountain Apayabo Optayo (Macaw's Mother) approaches quite close to the shore. We were told that it possesses two remarkable caverns on its northern side. The mountains increase in height, we estimated them often 1500 feet. The rivers general breadth is about 120 feet but south of the Creek Bononi[1] it narrowed on a point to 30 feet widening to its former breadth almost immediately after. The vegetation appeared here more luxuriant than we had seen it for some time. We observed some Mora trees the height & fresh appearance of which was by no means insignificant. We passed the mouth of the Creek Simmony.[2] On its banks there live several Macoosies.

The Simmony is very narrow at its mouth but widens & forms several lake-like sheets of water. Its banks are, according to Mr. Brotherson, who had visited the same, low & appeared to him more fertile than those of the Rupununy.

While turning round a sand bank which extended into the river, we observed on the left bank at some distance from us, a number of rocks which had the appearance of men placed in a row. The Charibees have attached a tradition to it: they say that long ago some of their nation undertook an expedition to the Macoosies land for plunder & murder. While ascending the Rupununy heavy rains set in, & not being able to get forward or to return they were all turned into stone. The Rocks are called Karinampo[3] & like Sawacko-toonally the repetition of their name causes rain.

They are of the same porous formation as already noted. Their direction along the river N.60°E. Their stratum apparently N.60°W. They were then from 12 to 14 feet above the level of the water, but the depth being here considerable it may be supposed that they have much more perpendicular height. Towards evening we passed a sand bank of which the tradition is that the Charibees barbacued here a Macoosie called Moracoo-naima while at war with that nation; the sand bank is called therefore Moracoo-naima-nocabo that is Moracoo-naimas barbacue – though ages may have elapsed since that cruel act was committed tradition will for ever now perpetuate it.

I had brought a letter from the Colony with me to the Bishop of Grand Para which I was requested to forward to the Brasilian Fort San Joaquim in order to reach

[1] Benoni River.
[2] Simoni River.
[3] Karanambo.

from there its destination. Not understanding Portuguese I wrote my request to the Commandant in French, who laboured under the same disabilities with regard to that language & concluded that I wanted a Conveyance to the Fort. While still at Anna-y I received an answer from him informing me that his Sargiento & a number of horses were awaiting us at the Macoosie village of Pirarara.[1] We were then about to ascend the Rupununy & as M[r] Brotherson's health was very poorly we advised him to take advantage of that opportunity & to recruit at the Fort while we continued our investigation of the river.

On our arrival at the inlet Wy-y-poocari[2] we were informed that the Commandant himself was at the village & a messenger being sent there S[r.] Cordiero, a Captain in the Army,[3] came next day himself with peons & led horses. When the misunderstanding was explained he appeared very sorry that we could not accompany him but requested us to ride with him as far as Pirarara, a fine village of 14 houses & from 80 to 100 inhabitants, remarkable as laying on the border of the once famed Lake Amucu.[4]

After a days rest S[r.] Cordiero & M[r.] Brotherson proceeded to Fort S. Joaquim, and M[r.] Haining and myself returned to the Inlet.*

*The Inlet is in Lat 3°38'14"N.L. and West of Annay – 7'45['] (approx) in 58°44' W.L. Pirárárá in Lat. 3°33'59"NL & 58°53' ditto.

Next morning we continued our ascent of the Rupununy: the banks were wooded & exchanged occasionally with Savannahs which approached the river on its eastern side. We ascended one of the banks to take a view of the Savannahs. No Indians living near it the grass had not been burnt[5] & had its full growth. It was man's height. The Savannahs appeared to extend 4 to 5 miles to the East & were bounded by thick wood covering gently undulating ground. The mountain chain of Conuco[6] bore S.56°E.

We passed the mouth of the Creek Wariacourou.[7] During the rainy season it affords a passage to the brook Pirarara & thence to the River Branco. At present there was a sandbank at its mouth with scarcely two inches of water over it. On the streamlet Mourackiarou there is, at some distance from its mouth, a settlement of Macoosies under Cap[t] Arriance.

The streamlet runs S.E. through the savannahs and a path leads from the settlement to those at the Simmony. The Coucourite Palm here becomes very frequent along the rivers bank; its fruits afford a fine oil. We observed in its neighbourhood a Palm tree even more graceful than the Coucourite which the Charibees called Courába.

---

[1] Pirara.

[2] Yupukarri Inlet.

[3] José Valente Cordeiro. Nothing more is known about him, although see below, p. 375.

[4] The Golden City of El Dorado was said to be located on the shores of Lake Amuku. The failed quest for El Dorado from the 16th century onwards had gradually moved its possible site further east until it came to rest here on the Essequibo/Amazon watershed. For an account of the search for El Dorado, see Hemming, *The Search for El Dorado*.

[5] The burning of the savannah grass seems to have been a very old Amerindian practice. Today it is mainly done to encourage new shoots of grass for cattle. In the past the same reason may have applied with respect to deer, although other reasons such as ease of movement, elimination of snakes and other pests, or the fun of seeing the blaze, may have played their part.

[6] Kanuku Mountains.

[7] Awarikuru, marked on the reference map as Quatata River.

The nearer we approached the mountains, the more turnings made the river, & the shallower it became. Its banks have however a more lively appearance, & we singled out some noble trees; even some silk cotton trees (Bombax Globosum) (in Charib Maccau)[1] would have done honor to the banks of the Essequibo. The Heliconia (Bihai)[2] with its large green leaves; and the leafless Jacaranda[3] covered with numerous blossoms of the finest blue, changed in a great measure the former monotony of the vegetation along the River. A brook which has got its name from a chain of mountains called by the Indians Mapiríe[4] joins, at the entrance of the mountains, the Rupununy on its Eastern bank. It has fine black cool water, quite different from that of the river.

We had now a fine view of the mountains through which the River had forced its way. The Indians make a difference in the name of the mountain chains; those on the eastern bank are called the Maparíe or Mapirie Mountains while those on the westerns had on their northern angle the name of Touro & further South of Conocoo[5] (The Portuguese designate the whole chain under the name of Conocou).

We now entered the mountainous regions (11th Decr). They approached the river from right & left, some of them often from 2 to 3000 feet high well wooded and of rich appearance. We observed on the banks species of Palms which we had not seen before[;] one of small size but graceful grows in groves and is called by the Indians Maraniara. The other is slender often 50 feet high & has only a few leaves of a light blue colour – both were without flowers or fruits.

The River had been for the last two days so shallow that we had often been obliged to get out of the Coorials & to await on a sand bank until they were shoved over; the more we advanced the worse it became, & it often took us hours to cross a small space. I had not expected this where the mountains would have led me to believe that the current caused by rains, & the more rapid descent of the river itself might have carried the detritus farther towards its mouth. Indeed we found it impossible to continue our journey in the larger coorials & had therefore to come to the conclusion of forming an encampment, whereat to leave the women, children & effects, and to proceed with only a small Coorial & the most indispensable articles.

We selected the mouth of the Creek Arripai for that purpose, not far from a settlement of Warpeshanas.[6]

On our landing all hands set to to build temporary huts. It rained hard & every one was anxious to get under cover. We heard the ax, hatchet & cutlass resounding in all directions, & many a young tree or a graceful Palm came to an untimely end.

Soon were huts erected of all shapes. Two poles were generally planted firmly in the ground and another thinner one tied horizontally to them; these two were connected with a third likewise horizontally by thin poles so that the whole presents the figure of a horizontal triangle covered by long staves upon which were laid in every direction

---

[1] The examples that Schomburgk saw may have been *Bombax globosum* Aublet, but the Carib term Maccau [Makau] refers to *Ceiba pentandra* (L.) Gaertner.

[2] *Heliconia behai*, a wild plant of the banana family (Musaceae).

[3] Mennega et al., list two species of Jacaranda from Guyana: *J. copaia* and *J. obtusifolia*. It is probably the latter which is described as chiefly riparian and leaves very finely divided.

[4] Maparri Mountain and River. A little further upstream on the west bank lies Mapuri (Tapir) Mountain from which flows the Mapuro River.

[5] Kanuku Mountains.

[6] Wapishiana.

leaves of the Coucourite Palm.[1] Another & more simple form was as follows. Two poles are planted as under & connected by a horizontal one tied to their end. A number of the same leaves, which were often 30 feet long, were now placed in a sloping direction upon the horizontal pole & touching with their ends the next tree afforded sufficient shelter & accomplished the object of the builder.

The rain descended for several days in torrents. Since my departure from Pirarara I had been attacked every other day by severe fever & ague; my situation therefore in a hut covered only by a sort of wax cloth, open to the rain from all sides, with the Thermometer at 78° F. at noon, was certainly not to [be] envied. We left nevertheless on Tuesday the 5th Decr. in the small coorial with only 4 Indians and Capt Jacobus. Mr Haining was my only companion. We soon found that the rain had not extended far south. We had even to leave the small coorial, to ease her, & walk whole stretches upon sandbanks.

The banks of the river were, in the commencement, low, well wooded, & with high towering mountains sometimes at a distance, sometimes approaching the bank of the river. Serpent like flowed the latter through the chain, its course being often turned in quite a different direction by a dyke of Granitic rocks, or a projecting point of the mountains. At these sudden turns desolation appeared to have spread its empire. During the rainy season the current being so much increased encroaches upon the banks, carries away the earth & the trees next to the shore fall into the water; but it is not only that trees are uprooted, the neighbouring ones also perish, whether injured from the force of the water or what else I am unable to say. The River was therefore often so barricaded by trunks of trees & such as had lately fallen, that we had often to wait for hours until a passage was cleared. At some places we had to force our way literally through sandbanks by cutting channels, the width of the running water being only 3 to 6 feet though its bed extended to 120 feet & often more.

The form of the whole mountain chain is mostly conical, very seldom undulating. Its tops & sides show occasionally granitic walls of rugged appearance; nevertheless, they are much better wooded than the Parime mountains, & naked hills are quite a scarcity.

At a dyke called Peroupan (Dogs-ear) granitic veins of rich composition traversed the base of a Platform (it might be called). On the mountain opposite, called Macapoo by the Warpeshanas, there is a settlement of that tribe; indeed we had entered the territory or land of the Warpeshanas since the last two or three days.

The state of the River obliged us to discontinue our progress by water: it was now a small insignificant mountain stream. We landed therefore & had our Coorial unloaded & hauled up.

Since we had left Anna-y we had no reason to complain of the Mosquitos, there were few or none at our night quarters, but in lieu of them we had from sunrise until sunset to endure the painful bites of a small fly which were in thousands on the river. Whereever they alighted either on the face or hands they drew blood and a spot remained for weeks. The poor Indians, uncovered as they were, presented a pitiful appearance, their bodies resembled so many graters in consequence of the stings, & swellings which followed them. The Charibees call the insect Mapiré, the Portuguese Pio.[2]

Next morning early we took our sticks & wandered over the Savannahs, which,

[1] Kokorite: *Attalea regia.*
[2] Kabauro in Guyana, pium in Brazil (*Simulium* spp.).

approached here for the first time the eastern or right shore of the river since we had entered the mountains, and went to a small settlement of Warpeshanas where we purposed to provide ourselves with provender.

The distance was not great, on approaching the place we observed that it consisted of a dome-shaped house & two smaller open ones. A number of Warpeshanas had assembled from the neighbouring places; as we found hereafter to have a Piwarrie feast.[1] They were fine formed people & taller than any Indians I had seen before. In their dress they do not distinguish themselves from the other tribes, but their language is so different from the Caribe & Macoosie that they can not understand each other.[2] Many of the different tribes speak Macoosie by means of which they are able to converse with each other.

The men all came forward & greeted us in a manner similar to the Macoosies, namely waving the hand before our face; afterwards they retired to their place & a lively conversation, mixed with loud laughter, took place, the subject of which was doubtless our persons, dresses, &c.

I peeped a moment in one of the open houses where women & children were occupied in baking fresh Cassada bread for the feast. What an uproar when I made my appearance! The Children retreated screeching with the utmost speed, fowls & parrots followed & barking dogs, which, if their number only was regarded, would have done honour to the kennels of an Earl, had every intention to attack me, but remained at a respectable distance only increasing their barking the nearer I approached.

Though our Indian crew were as much strangers to the dogs & parrots as we were, the first never barked nor fled the latter screeching away when they approached but as soon as Mr Haining or I showed ourselves, the noise of birds & beasts was insupportable.

The round house was differently built from those of the Macoosies; there were no walls of clay, only the entrance was plastered, all the rest consisted of palm leaves plaited neatly together. The interior resembled entirely a Cupola of a dome supported by three beams & several oblique posts. Around it the hammocks were slung, & the different implements of the Kitchen & chase ranged against the walls. The middle was occupied by a wooden trough carved & painted after Indian fashion which on this occasion was filled with Piwarrie although it was so large that it might contain sixty gallons. The guests assembled for the drink had slung their hammocks partly in the round-house partly in one of the open huts, while others stood outside each party being attended by a person highly painted & ornamented for the occasion, to bring them the intoxicating drink when wanted.

Fever forced me to keep my hammock & I had thus opportunity to watch their proceedings.

On a signal given by the host or one of the guests, the Calabash was filled & handed to the person who desired it. If the Calabash was small, or he could manage it, the same was emptied, and another was given to his neighbour & thus they continue until it has made the round; but little rest was granted to the poor vessel, and before many hours had elapsed the large trough was emptied & refilled from immense earthen vessels which had been kept in reserve.

---

[1] Paiwari is beer, of fairly low alcoholic content, made from cassava.
[2] Wapishiana is an Arawak language, whereas the other two groups speak Carib.

The conversation became meanwhile most violent. Old feats of valour, when the tribes had still their wars, meeting with tigers &c. might be their subjects, but before the second trough was emptied one tongue after the other became silent & sickness appeared to have taken possession of almost every individual – we had oral & occular demonstrations of it. Thus is the beverage, uncleanly already in its preparation, misused, and man lowers himself to the beast.

The Indians have been accused of want of affection towards their children. I have seen frequent instances to the contrary – great injustice has been done to them in that regard. A Warpeshana returned from a few days journey and it was a pleasure to see his children flock around him, hang about his neck, & putting a thousand questions to him, very likely about his success, what he had brought them, &c. He took some Cashews out of his queck or basket, which caused them great joy, though they might have been got as good at a few yards distance. His wife brought him the youngest child – a baby. He caressed & kissed it with the same fondness as Europeans would do where their manners are unsophisticated & not constrained by etiquette or ceremony.

They show much more attention to their Wives than I would have expected after what I had read. I allude to the Charibees where the women appear to be considered more as companions than slaves. They certainly must do a deal of work – the men clear the ground and the women have to cultivate it, and to bring in the crop, but they are by no means the low slaves & drudges which some authors have represented them. There is one want which unfortunately appears to prevail among all the tribes – neglect of old persons and the sick; indeed they receive but little attention, are stowed away in a small corner of the house, neglected & left to themselves, & where weakness keeps them to their hammocks perhaps often without the necessaries of life.

Our journey across the savannahs was to commence next morning (the 19th Decr); trunks, and all other things which we could spare, were to be left behind, & our whole effects consisted therefore of a second suit of clothes, hammocks, Chronometer, Sextant, artificial horizon, Compass, &c, all of which were carried in quecks or baskets; our provision was calculated for 10 days. We had to make a detour in order to get some plantains at a place we had visited the day previous. Among other Indian curiosities I observed a large string of the lower jaws of the howling monkey[1] hung up as a trophy of the hosts prowess as huntsman. Our journey was today of short duration; the intermittent fever attacked me so violently on the way that we had to stop at the last Indian settlement (Warpeshanas) in that direction, at an early hour. The chain of mountains is here at a short distance from the house; one of the Indian boys brought me a beautiful piece of chrystallized quartz with lamina of mica. On my return from the Corona I inspected it; it rested upon gypsum in which the chrystals were partly imbedded, its direction N.W. and the place surrounded by numerous boulders of granite.

We continued our journey next morning accompanied by many Warpeshanas who intended to make it a trip of pleasure; three had been engaged on certain terms as carriers of provisions & guides. We followed the foot of the mountain-chain on our left rising to a height of 500 to 1000 feet mostly of a conical shape, & on our right were small hillocks bare of wood & covered with blocks of granite.

---

[1] Howler monkey (*Alouatta* spp.).

The expression of "Indian file" is well known but today I saw it in all its perfection. Our party consisted of 18 individuals & the path leading through the savannahs not being wider than 6 to 8 inches we had to follow close the footsteps of the person before us; sometimes the path was lost or became smaller than stated above; this is immaterial to the Indian, his peculiar method of walking with the toes inward enables him to walk the smallest path with comfort while it incommoded us. They ridicule our method of walking & observe that in a wood we take up too much bush-room.

We crossed the brook Akataurie (Cardouaur in Warpeshana) coming from the East. This brook winds itself through the mountain chain & from this place there was formerly a path to Mahanarwa, the late Cazique's settlement.[1] According to Capt Jacobus, his grandson from the daughters side, the distance is three days journey & from thence one day to the River Quitaro, we may therefore calculate that the river was about one degree E. from us (57°30′W.).

The Malpighia verbascifolium[2] was, here, only in blossom while at our leaving Anna-y, a flower of that plant was scarcely to be discovered. It spread over whole savannahs & its bright yellow flowers & light green leaves, silvery below, gave to this natural plantation quite an interesting view, it added to diversity, but the pleasure of the eye was entirely forgotten when we came to a tree loaded with fruit of the size & appearance of a black cherry, & of a most delicious taste, resembling custard; it is milky & contains one or two flat seeds. The leaves are bright green, entire & lanceolate. The Charibbees called the fruit "Parata", the Warpeshanas "Witchaway".[3]

We met several times large beds of Quartz which crossed the savannahs apparently in a N.E. and S.W. direction. From what I could observe they consisted of loose fragments being raised sometimes only one or two feet above the savannah. The quartz itself is milk white going over into rose colour – quartz is here one of the most prevailing rocks.

In the afternoon we reached the Southern angle of the mountain chain; they take now a far eastern direction. The Saeraerie[4] mountains on the rivers western shore are of most imposing character & undoubtedly the highest of the chain. They are conically rugged, but well wooded at the base. I do not hesitate to consider them as M. de Humboldts Sierra Vassari or Wassari; the Indian tribes however living in this neighbourhood call them Saeraerie.[5] North of them at perhaps 2 miles distant from the base rises a pyramidical mountain, the top consisting of granite; its shape is so peculiar that it can not fail to attract attention; it appears quite isolated; the Warpeshanas call the hill Ochlapan.

---

[1] Mahanarwa, Mahanarva or Manariwan was a Carib chief who appeared in Georgetown in 1810 demanding the gifts that the Amerindians had been accustomed to receive on a regular basis from the Dutch. Mahanarva boasted of his military might and an expedition was dispatched into the interior to assess what threat the natives of the interior might represent. An account of Mahanarva's visit to Georgetown is to be found in R. Schomburgk, *Travels*, II, p. 346; and Nádia Farage has recently provided an interesting interpretation of the event *As Muralhas dos Sertões. Os povos indígenas no rio Branco e a colonização*, Rio de Janeiro, Paz e Terra, ANPOCS, 1991, pp. 169–73.

[2] *Byrsonima verbascifolia*.

[3] The Carib and Wapishiana names are Barata and Wichabai respectively, but they are two different subspecies of *Manilkara bidentata*

[4] Shiriri Mountain.

[5] The Wassari Mountains are much further south, at approximately 1°35′N., near the sources of the Essequibo.

Our Indians pointed out to us a hill of moderate height which at the angle of the mountain-chain bore N.77°E. distance 10 to 12 miles. It is famed for wild plantains of large size (Musa paradisiaca) which they told us grew there in great quantities. They pretend that never Indian had been there, & that they had not been planted by human hands. The hill is called Vivie Mount.

We had for some time lost every vestige of a path & our guides conducted us according to land marks; our course was usually south. At 4ʰ·40ᵐ· we reached the brook Arraquay,[1] according to an observation of Achernar, in 2°44′54″N. Lat.

The milder attacks of my fever had led me to hope that after the seventh fit I should get rid of it – vain were my hopes, my ague was so severe next morning that we were obliged to give up our intentions of proceeding on our journey that day.

I found now that it had fixed itself, & that it would require peculiar attention to drive it out of my constitution. I would not have mentioned these circumstances as they can be of little interest to the reader, if they were not of importance to my further proceedings.

We broke up our encampment before daybreak, crossed the brook, & followed our guide through the Savannahs. We had to wade several Eta swamps by no means pleasant, & though I looked always with renewed pleasure on that majestic palm (Mauritia vinifera)[2] it was somewhat damped by being aware that we had to cross another swamp.

At 8 o'C. a.m. on the 22ᵈ· Decʳ· we reached the Corona the largest cataract of the Rupununy. It is formed by a granitic bed which crosses the river in an E.N.E. direction. At several places while crossing the Savannah I had observed isolated blocks of the same composition. The Granite which forms the Corona (called by the Indians Cartatan) shows often[3] circular holes as if chiselled by human hands; they are rather numerous, & if we consider the hardness of the rock, remarkable. The river was very low, and the cataract lost its grandeur. It was not to be compared with any of the Essequibo. A little below the Fall, the brook Maycar & a little above, the brook Fournacou[4] join the River, the latter being by far the larger of the two. In the afternoon we went to a hill which, at two miles distance from the Corona, rose out of the Savannah, & afforded us a most beautiful view. Far in the distant horizon at the distance of 50 to 60 miles from us, rose the Caraway-mee[5] mountains of less height than either the Parime or Conucou have. Our Warpeshanas pointed it out as being inhabited by many Indians of their tribe, while some mountains to the E.S.E. were told us to be the place of habitation of Atoroys.[6] The Rupununy took a south eastern direction widening in some places lake-like, in others narrowing. It went through several Eta swamps from which it received doubtless its river like appearance at a degrees distance from its sources, as, according to our Warpeshanas, two of whom pretended to have been there, it rises at the mountain chain we saw on the horizon.

According to the courses set by Schmalkalders Compass, & the distances estimated by time, our hill was 8½ miles South from the brook Arraquay or in 2°36′24″ N. Lat.

---

[1] Arakwai River.

[2] Ita or Ite palm, *Mauritia flexuosa*.

[3] The next two pages of the manuscript (19 & 20) are a redrafting by the editor and have not been included. The original pages are to be found in the Memoir, pp. 19 & 20, and have been restored here to their original place.

[4] These are probably the Makudud and Kunaruwau respectively.

[5] Probably the Marudi-Karawaimentau, although these are at the most only forty miles from Schomburgk's position.

[6] Atorai.

The sources of the Rupununy have been generally placed in from 2°30′ to 2°50′N. L.; from what I have mentioned above it is much more likely that they must be looked for in the Caraway-mee mountains in 1°30′N. Lat.[1] The chain took an eastern and western direction & formed the boundary of large Savannahs. I have not doubt it was the Sierra Acaray or Tumucuraque, but according to my belief it is entirely unconnected with the Saeraerie mountains.

Our Guides pointed out to us, to the south, the hills Pahaeteyou (Cassada-bread mountains) & towards the S.W. a small chain of mountains called Penngheatee, at their foot live Warpeshanas.

S.87°W. rose the Dororou[2] Mountains. N.84W. the Ursato[3] mountains all more or less connected with the Saeraerie. Numerous quartz rocks in large pieces and angular fragments were on the place of our observation; it was the same quartz of which I have spoken previously[;] milk white & some pieces tinged with rose.[*]

*This was the extent of the Expeditions southern advance (2°36′24″N. Lat.).

When I left Anna-y it was my intention to explore the Rupununy to its sources. The low state of the River opposed the first difficulties, & we had daily proofs that it was still falling.

On our arrival at the Corona we found that its sources were much farther south than we had supposed; Lieu[t.] Hainings leave of absence, who had[4] accompanied me, was nigh at an end, & my unfortunate fever, from which I could only travel one day out of two, would have lengthened our journey to three weeks. The question arose now: shall we advance further, or shall we return; the advantages of the first bore by no means the difficulties out in which such a delay might have placed us. There is no short or intermediate rainy season in these regions. There are small showers in January & February, but otherwise the year is divided only into two seasons – the rainy from April to the commencement of October, & the dry from October to April. We could not therefore expect that the river should rise; on the contrary it was more likely that it would fall more every day, & we would be cut off from the lower Rupununy. We resolved therefore to return next morning, & arrived the second day at the place where we left our effects which were found all in the same order as we delivered them to our host.

When I planned my ascent of the Rupununy River, it was one of my chief intentions to see the plant from which the Indians prepare their celebrated Ouralie or Wourari poison.[5] While at the lower Rupununy I had been always told that it grew on the

---

[1] In fact the Rupununi rises in approximately 2°5′N.

[2] Probably the present day Raad Mountain.

[3] Probably the present day Kusad Mountain.

[4] Page 21 of the manuscript starts here.

[5] The curare plant *Strychnos toxifera* and the poison from which it is made have held a perennial fascination for travellers into the interior of Guyana, and few have failed to give a description of its ingredients and manufacture. Charles Waterton, author of *Wanderings in South America*, brought a supply of it back to England and demonstrated its effectiveness on a bullock in front of an audience of scientists. For a full account of curare in South America, see Vellard, *Histoire du curare. Les poisons de chasse en Amérique du Sud*, Paris, Gallimard, 1965. Recently, Schomburgk's claim that the sole active ingredient was *Strychnos toxifera*, and that other things were little more than what might have delighted Macbeth's witches, has been questioned. See Conrad Gorinsky, 'Isolation and Characterisation of Biologically Active Constituents from Cissampelos ovalifolia, d.c. and Clibadium sylvestre (aubl.) Baill.', unpublished PhD thesis, University of London, 1974–5.

Conocou Mountains. I had ascertained now that a journey of one day & a half would bring us there. After our return guides were therefore engaged, & we started on the morning of the 25ᵗʰ Decʳ. Our way led us first to the south over pathless savannahs, until we met a place in the Rupununy where we could ford it. As the mountains stretched their foot to the rivers bank we expected that the ascending part would immediately commence, our guide led us however through a mountain pass & before us was a large arid savannah. We turned now to the North meeting with plains covered with wood, or low shrubs & coarse grass, bounded on both sides by the mountains. It was a wild road crossed frequently by streams the most of which were now dried out.

At last after we had walked more than 5 miles the extent of the valley from whence we entered it, the ascent commenced, it was by no means an easy matter – the path, Indian-like, led over fallen trees between boulders of granite, & was often so steep that we had to use hands & feet. I wondered only how the Indians with their burdens could climb up. At 3 o'Clock P.M., after a march of eight hours & a half we reached a settlement of Warpeshanas where we intended to rest for the night. The Thermometer which had ranged at the settlements on the savannahs 88°, stood here at 3 o'C 80° & next day at the same hour 79°.

We recognised in the chief person "Oronappy" one of the guests at the Piwarrie feast. He showed great joy at our coming, brought us a Calabash with the favourite drink & some ripe plantains.

He dispatched some person to his field who soon afterwards returned with a load of the finest sugar-cane I ever saw; indeed the fertility of the soil was astonishing although the height was between 2300 & 2500 feet; the size of the plantains & the sweetness of the banana surpassed by far those of the plain; the dark or purple Banana, so much esteemed at the Colony for culinary purposes grew to perfection.

The Cotton which had been collected around the house was likewise of good quality – nevertheless the fertility of the soil profited only a few; the difficulty of the ascent & the distance secludes them from those in the valleys and the productions of their fields rot on the ground & become useless to man.

The Thermometer stood at 6 o'C in the evening at 69°F., the sky clouded.

Our host purposed to accompany the Warpeshana who was to bring us to the place where the Ouralie grew; already the evening previous he attempted by signs to make us desist from our intention to go with them; he told us that the path was very bad & that it was so far that we would only reach the place at noon & that we could not return before nightfall. He repeated the same story in the morning and made a sour face when he observed that we were determined to go with them. Whether he thought we could not walk so far, or whether he wished us not to learn the place where the plant grew I know not. Enough of his stories – we found the first alone was true – an Indian only could have guided us, & they directed their course mostly after broken branches or marks cut in the trees, sometimes standing for several moments to consider which direction to turn; it was a path over hill & dale mostly in a N.N.W. & N.W. direction.

We passed a Maran-tree Copaifera officinalis.[1] It is a lofty tree with light grey bark, a fine branching head & pinnated leaves. The Indians cut a hole towards the base of the trunk to the very heart of the tree, the hole being semicircular & deepened at the base.

---

[1] Probably *Copaifera guianensis*.

At certain seasons of the year chiefly in Feb^y & March, the balsam flows abundantly & fills the hole in the course of a day, when next morning it is put into Calabashes & forms an article of barter.

We found a large quantity in the hole, it was of a yellowish colour & quite clear; our Indians eagerly anointed their bodies & hair with it. The medicinal qualities of the Balsam Cop[a]ivi are too well known to be repeated here.[1] Our guides stopt at last at one of the glens near a spring & going to one of the ligneous twiners which wound themselves snake-like from tree to tree, they called out "Ourari," the name of the plant in Warpeshana.

The Ouralie, as already observed, is a ligneous twiner; its stem often more than arms thickness & very crooked, its bark rough & of a dark greyish colour; the branches thin and inclined to climbing; the leaves dark green and opposite, ovate, acute, 5 nerved, veins; young branches & leaves hirsute; hairs brown; cirrhiferous, however not peculiar to every branch, fruit of the size of a large apple round, smooth, bluish green, seeds imbedded in a pulp & consist chiefly of a gummy matter which is intensely bitter.

We observed many heaps of the cut wood, covered with palm leaves which, as the Indians told us, had been left by the Macoosies. The plant grows only in two or three places which are resorted to by the Indians from all directions & often from a great distance.*

*A much fuller description of the plant & the mode of preparation I hope soon to lay before the Society.[2]

Before we left the place we cut us sticks, & returned at two o'Clock, after having been absent eight hours, highly delighted that, though we could not see the plant in all its stages, we had succeeded in collecting a few of its fruits.

We descended next morning to the Savannahs where every preparation was made to leave the following day for the encampment. We found that the river during our first days journey had fallen still more, & our difficulties were consequently multiplied. Fortunately after reaching the encampment & coming into the vicinity of the northern mountains late rains had swollen the brooks & increased the mass of water in the Rupununy, we made, therefore, in one day, with the assistance of the current, as much progress as in two days & a half while ascending.

We halted at a settlement of Warpeshanas who have built an oblong house a little above the rapids Coura-watoka; the settlement consisted of 4 men & about 12 women & children. A larger settlement, we were told, is at a short distance from the river. The women were occupied in cleaning cotton from the seeds, & large balls of spun cotton which were hung up in the hut showed of their industry.

---

[1] It was used for the treatment of venereal diseases.

[2] A paper by Schomburgk, entitled 'On the Wooraly or Ourary Poison of the Indo-Americans, with a Description of the Plant from which it is Extracted', was read before the Linnean Society on 1 November 1836 (LS, SP 996). In the paper Schomburgk recorded that, having run out of quinine, he took curare for malaria fever. He noted that it produced a slight headache but did not remove the fever. He stopped this usage through fear of open wounds in his mouth or gums.

He later published two article on the subject: 'On the Urari, the Arrow Poison of the Indians of Guiana; with a Description of the Plant from which it is Extracted', *The Annals and Magazine of Natural History, including Zoology, Botany, and Geology*, 7, 1841, pp. 407–27; and 'The Urari, or Arrow Poison of the Indians of Guiana', *Pharmaceutical Journal and Transactions*, 16, 1857, pp. 500–507.

It appears that this is the most northern settlement of the Warpeshanas. Further North, to the mouth of the Rupununy, & likewise west, the Country is occupied by Macoosies & a very few Charibees. On the evening of the 1ˢᵗ Janʸ 1836, we landed again at the Inlet Wy-a-poucarie and proceeded next morning towards Pirarara in order to await Mʳ Brotherson's return from Fort San Joachim.

Many of the Savannahs which we crossed are covered with the Fabrick of a species of Termites: their houses are most fantastic and from 5 to 10 feet high; they are formed of the ochreous clay of which the Savannahs mostly consist & of pyramidal shape. The animals themselves do not appear to be different from those which build large nests on the trees & which are known in the West India Islands by the name of wood-ants – if in any thing different they are somewhat smaller, they are called by the Indians Touk-ousiba. Another kind encrusted the trunks of trees from the base to the branches, giving them an appearance as if they were fringed.

In order to communicate with Mʳ Brotherson whom we still thought at Fort San Joaquim I requested Basico after our arrival at Pirarara to procure me a messenger. I afterwards found, to my greatest astonishment, that Basicos father, the Captain of the Village & a man of a least 70 years of age, had carried the letter himself. He is a single instance of longevity united with health & strength; the Indians meet generally with a premature death – during my present expedition I have seen but few old men & these sickly & helpless, mere shadows of life.

As we could not expect Mʳ Brotherson for several days Lieuᵗ Haining & myself planned an excursion to the mountain valley of the river Maou or Mahou[1] at the Parime Mountains.

We provided us therefore with provisions for several days, & started with Basico & other Indians as guides & carriers towards the mountains. The brook Pirarara, which has its source to the south of the village, flows through a lake which, although it was now the dry season, was of several miles in extent; it takes then an eastern course, crosses the lake for a second time & after having wound itself through the low savannah joins the Maou about 15 miles above the junction of that river with the Tocoto.[2] During the rainy season the Lake extends itself from Pirarara to the mountains & this is the site of the celebrated Lake Amucu.

Numerous flocks of ducks rose out of the rushes & flew around us in circles; they were mostly of that kind called Vicissi. The species peculiar to these regions is uncommonly pretty in appearance, the feathers variously coloured, their bill short, eyes black.[3] The musk-duck (Anas Moschatas) frequents likewise the lake in large flocks.[4]

We entered now dry savannahs. For some time we had already observed the mark of cattle feet & shortly afterwards we saw a large black bull not far from our path, very likely an outpost. He looked at us at first without changing his position but the more we approached the more impatient he appeared to become, with his horns & feet he tossed the earth high up in the air, accompanying that action with a low groan.

---

[1] Marked on the Guyana reference map as Ireng River and on the Brazil reference map as Mau or Ireng. It forms the boundary between the two countries.

[2] Takutu River. It forms the boundary between Brazil and Guyana upstream of its junction with the Ireng.

[3] The vicissi or wicissi is not a duck although it lives in swampy areas and has webbed feet. There are three species of *Dendrocygna* in Guyana.

[4] The Muscovy (*Cairina moschata*).

After a careful survey he must have considered us too strong for attack; he retreated a few steps, turned & took another look until he fairly trotted off. It was a noble animal & while trotting along his fat neck waved from side to side. We saw the whole herd returning from one of the pools where they had been for water – their number might amount to 40 or 50, black & red were the most prevailing colours.

In our further progress we met them frequently single & in numbers of two & four.

These herds of wild cattle appear to frequent only the Savannahs south of the Parime Mountains in the vicinity of the rivers Maou, Tocoto, and chiefly Branco and are undoubtedly of Portuguese origin. Though the savannahs at Anna-y are connected with those of the Maou they never descend so far north.[1]

We had to cross the Pirarara for the third time & saw the mouth of the valley from whence the Maou issues at a few hours walk before us, when I was so violently attacked by fever that for the time it became impossible for me to advance further; we were then in an open savannah without a tree to afford shelter – the nearest cluster which formed one of those spots called 'an Island' being several miles distant and out of our road.

As soon as my attack would permit me we set off to it. We had taken forcible possession of the abode of numerous birds which had selected this spot for their roosting place. What a noise when they returned in the evening & found us intruders. Pigeons arrived from all quarters & our Indians ready with their bows & arrows prevented many from seeking safety in a rapid retreat.

The mountains of the Parime chain have by no means the imposing character of those of the Conocou or Conokoo. They are seldom higher than from 1800 to 2000 feet & often only 5 to 600 feet. Many are bare of wood, overgrown with a short kind of grass, & covered with fragments of rock. What I have seen of their geological character they rested on a granitic base & boulders of the same nature covered their sides. Quartz by no means unfrequently passes into the granite or as often bounded by trappean rocks.[2]

The Indians brought me specimens of red rocks which they consider great curiosities and which, according to their account, they get five days journey from Pirarara at the western mountains of Parime. I consider it a cornean.[3] Rock-Chrystals are likewise said to be found there, & Mr. Brotherson was told by the Commandant of Fort San Joachim that the Indians from the Upper Branco had brought him at different times specimens of silver. Mr. Brotherson related likewise that he had been told that from one of the mountains on the South Western angle of the Parime Chain a detonation was heard from time to time without either flames or smoke being observed.

A bare & rugged mountain was our guide to the Maou. When we approached it I found that it was covered with quartzose fragments while large boulders of trappean

---

[1] The Portuguese established three cattle ranches on the banks of the Rio Branco, not far from its junction with the Takutu, during the final decades of the 18th century. The ranching was open range, and animals strayed and became wild. Herds of wild cattle still existed on the Rio Branco savannahs in the late 1960s. For an account of the introduction of cattle to the region, see John Hemming, 'How Brazil acquired Roraima', *The Hispanic American Historical Review*, 70:2, 1990, pp. 295–325. For an account of cattle ranching in the 1960s, see Peter Rivière, *The Forgotten Frontier. Ranchers of Northern Brazil*, New York, Holt, Rinehart & Winston, 1972.

[2] Trap-rock was used in the 19th century to describe igneous rocks other than those which are granitic or of recent volcanic origin.

[3] Cornea is also known as aphanite, a hornblende.

origin gave it a rugged appearance. We followed the brook Samaria being often obliged to climb over rocks & to use the sides of the hills to avoid the swampy ground. We passed a hill where confusion appeared to have selected her seat: thousands of rocks from the size of an egg to that of the immense block covered its side, & reminded me forcibly of the Hill St. Bernard's in the Island of Tortola; the rock itself had the same mineralogical character & strange to say, trees & bushes which grow among those rocks at Tortola, I observed here for the first time since my expedition commenced. I found the Bursera gummifera[1] or turpentine tree of the Islands; Croton balsamiferum;[2] Astroites;[3] betulinum;[4] Mimosa nudiflora;[5] Randia aculeata;[6] Cactus Royeni;[7] trigonus;[8] Agave, &c. &c. I flattered myself of discovering, every moment, the Exostemma Caribaeum[9] which I have generally observed to grow in the company of the above in the Virgin Islands, but I had hoped in vain.

A singular rock called by the Macoosies Toupanaghae from its resemblance to a hand, attracted our attention. It stood on the top of a mountain on our right side, was deeply furrowed & had for its base a rock of larger size. The Indians, as is generally the case with phenomena of nature, make it the seat of a Demon & pass it under fear and trembling.

Where the brook Samaria comes from the East a fine valley extends from East to West about 4 or 5 miles; it afforded us a beautiful prospective view of the western mountains – the Maou crosses it from North to South.

We passed from the valley of the brook Samaria to that of the Maou, our course being mostly North. The mountains had here a slaty texture, showing sometimes veins of quartz, their dip was low the direction S.W. by W.

We had entered, now, the valley of Maou which river flowed toward us from the North. Being at some distance from the River which was lined with trees its view was still hid from us, but we heard the noise of falling water, a bed of rocks forming a cataract. I imagined of finding a river of lesser volume, I was therefore surprized to see a large fine river before me, with black waters & a rapid current; from this I conclude that its sources must be in the [fourth] parallel of Latitude.[10]

We had entered a fine amphitheatre of mountains consisting partly of naked hills; the small brook Maviesie occupied its eastern, the Maou its western side.

Our Indians had shot a large rattlesnake[;] this was the second in the course of the day; gorged with its prey it was lying, inactive under the trunk of an old tree when it was discovered & killed with a poisoned arrow. The cups of its rattle amounted to seven.

---

[1] *Bursera simaruba*.

[2] *Croton flavens*. This species is not reported from Guiana.

[3] Search through botanical dictionaries has failed to reveal the use of this word in botany, The *OED*, however, mentions its use in relation to geology and zoology, to mean 'star-shaped'.

[4] A community of betulinum or birch-tree vegetation. In fact, the genus *Betula* is not found in tropical South America. It may be noted, however, that *Bursera simaruba* is known as the West Indian birch.

[5] *Acacia nudiflora*. This does not appear to be a South American species.

[6] The White Indigo berry (*Randia mitis*). This species does not appear to be present in Guiana.

[7] *Pilosocereus royeni*. This species does not appear to be present in Guiana.

[8] Trigonus refers to a three-angled plant.

[9] *Exostema caribaeum*, a Caribbean species, does not appear to be present in Guiana.

[10] In fact it rises north of the fifth parallel.

We had encamped at the brook Maviesie in a thicket of trees; our Indians had told us of a large cataract which the Maou forms a day and a half further north, & it was our intention to extend our journey so far, but Mr Haining being taken unwell (the prelude to an intermitting fever) we thought it advisable to return to the village as soon as he was strong enough for the pedestrian tour, the Corona as the Cataract was called remained therefore unvisited, & after a days rest we broke up our encampment and returned. The Indians had set, previously, the Savannahs on fire, & we found the path much more comfortable although the dust of the burnt grass raised by the wind, & our feet gave us the appearance of Coal-heavers.

To our great joy we found M^r. Brotherson on our return, in Pirarara, recovered in health & appearance. My letter had met him on his way to the village, where it was his intention to await us.

Next day there was to be a great Piwarrie feast in the village; extensive preparations were made for it – the trough filled, cassada-bread baked, fish & game barbecued. The guests arrived on the day appointed & the drinking commenced. It was however much more orderly conducted than the drinking match at the Warpeshanas.

In the afternoon they danced[;] the masters of ceremony of whom there were two were adorned with macaw feathers & had in their hands two large pieces of bamboo the cavities of which were filled with small pebbles & the outside surrounded by cotton-hanging & feathers. They walked at the head of the dancing column stamping at intervals with their bamboos on the ground by which a rattling noise was caused, women & men accompanying the same by a monotonous song.

They advanced & retreated from the Piwarrie-trough & went round it stamping with their feet; but as the hands & feet only were in motion & their faces showed neither expression of enjoyment or animation they appeared to me more like automatons than figures of life.

They continued their dance till two o'Clock in the morning, varying the song which guided their steps only once or twice.

We returned now towards Anna-y & landed at the mouth of that brook on the 15th. January after an absence of six weeks. All the effects which we had left at the settlement we found in the same state as we had disposed them there.

The difficulty of procuring water at our old residence at Anna-y & our having been so sickly there during our former stay, and not less the tedious labour of having our effects carried across the Savannah, had made us resolve not to return to Anna-y & to chuse a hut at Currassawak, Jacobus' old settlement, for our residence during the remainder of our stay in the Rupununy.

The entrance to our new domicile was disheartening enough – the house which had been burnt down & only partially rebuilt was open to wind & weather in all directions; and it was with some difficulty that we found a tenable place.

Robert H. Schomburgk C.M.R.G.S.

****

The Third Report consists of forty-four pages excluding the cover sheet added at a later date than the original manuscript; however, three of these pages (pp. 41–3) have been taken from the 'Geographical Memoir' and have been returned to their original position. The manuscript is in good condition and clearly legible. Much of it is not in

Schomburgk's handwriting but in that of one or more copyists. It is dated Georgetown, 1 April 1836 and, accordingly, was written after the expedition had returned to the coast.

THIRD REPORT TO THE ROYAL GEOGRAPHICAL SOCIETY OF LONDON DURING THE FIRST EXPEDITION IN THE INTERIOR OF BRITISH GUIANA

Our safe return to the lower Rupununy and entrance into the new domicile was not to be passed over without some celebration; a Piwarrie-feast was resolved upon, but the settlement was in want of one of the most indispensable articles, the large trough. The chief men of the little Colony went therefore 'in pleno' to the neighbouring wood, and after the proper choice had been made, all hands set to cut the selected tree down, and to dub it out; partly by the Axe and partly by Fire. The appointed day approached and the trough was not yet ready; and as the Piwarrie had to ferment, it ought to have been put into the Vessel at least two days before it was to be used – but an expedient was soon found – a small Corial was meanwhile substituted, and the whole Settlement, Men, Women, and Children, were seen occupied in chewing the burnt Cassada-bread and preparing it for use;[1] after having thus secured its fermenting in due measure and form, and the new trough having been completed on the morning the feast was to take place, the favourite drink was transferred from the Corial into the new Harlova or trough. I have already described the intemperance the Indian is guilty of at his drinking-bouts, and the scenes incident to the present, were not far different from those at the Warpeshanas and Macoosies.

Capt. Yhryee had shot, during one of his excursions on the Rupununy, with an arrow provided with a Spike poisoned by the Woorali, a young female Tapir or Mypourie (Sus rostratus, Tapir Americanus), and though the point of the arrow had only penetrated the skin and caused scarcely any loss of blood, the animal paid it with its life. I was glad to have an opportunity of inspecting this animal, which hitherto I knew only from description and drawings. It was, from the Nose to the short tail 5 feet long, and nearly three feet high; in its shape it resembled most the Hog with the exception that in proportion it had much shorter legs; on the fore feet it had four toes, and three behind; from the forehead projects a bone which is connected with the upper lip, forming with the nostrils a kind of proboscis, not unlike that of the Elephant – the Tapir makes in many respects a similar use of it. The skin is very thick and covered with short hair of a dusky grey colour, the ears are small and pointed. In the upper jaw I counted seven incisors on each side, four teeth in front and two tusks, in the under jaw six incisors and one tusk on each side. The three kinds of teeth formed an uninterrupted line.

We found its meat uncommonly good, resembling beef, and as it had been shot the day before the Piwarrie-feast, it was a most welcome gift to the assembled Indians.

---

[1] Fermentation of cassava beer is achieved by the chewing of bits of cassava which are then spat into a container of grated cassava matter. The chewing helps release starches which act with enzymes in the saliva to bring about the fermentation. Another method of inducing fermentation is to leave the cassava matter to grow mould.

Lieutenant Haining's departure drew near; the Macoosie Chieftain and his crew, who were to take him to Georgetown, had already arrived at Currassawaak. It pained me to see him depart; he had been my faithful Companion during all my excursions and I had received many kind attentions from him during my frequent indispositions: – but his leave of absence was nearly expired, and his duty bade him to return without waiting the time where the whole party would descend to the coast. Who could blame him if he should openly express the pleasure he felt in anticipating the early enjoyment of those comforts, which necessity had taught him to relinquish during the greatest part of our expedition. We miss an absent friend where the circle of our acquaintances is extensive, where we are surrounded by the comforts and enjoyment of civilized life, and where we may direct the course of our thoughts to many sources to divert us; it was different with us, hundreds of miles separated from any traces of civilization, one had to rely upon ourselves, our conversations were our resources when fatigued from the day's journey, we found ourselves at rest under some aged Mora-Tree; though impossible to describe my feelings they will be understood when I saw M[r.] Haining stepping into the boat – M[r.] Brotherson accompanied him to the Rupununy.

It had been my wish to see the Tree which produces the Caska preciosa (of the Brazilians)[1] or the Amapaima (of the Indians) – there were but few trees near Currassawaak, and those at a considerable distance.

I resolved however to accompany the Captain Yhryee there and following the course of the brook upwards in a western direction, we started on our expedition: it was a wild path, if path it could be called. We approached a thicket of wild Bamboo (Nastus)[2] and while we were still a few yards from it, a large Guana Snake (Scytale Spec.? perhaps catenatus)[3] came out of the jungle and ran towards the brook; it was shot by one of the attendants. Like the Guana, it had a pouch under the throat; the mouth was protected by large plates, the head covered with scales, and the belly and tail with shields, those on the belly being perfectly formed, while those on the tail were not entire; and there were four rows of small pointed scales which terminated the tail. Its colour was yellow, with black spots in the form of a lozenge, its length about 6½ feet. On our approach, it coiled its tail, and raised its head to the height of three feet, with a gently trembling motion; it then uncoiled itself, and repeated the same manoeuvre in the reverse manner, making its head the point d'appui and vibrating its elevated tail; it was in the act of renewing this singular feat, when it was shot through the head. It was impossible to induce one of the Indians to carry the Snake to our encampment; they evinced the greatest horror at it; and if we are to believe their accounts of frequent accidents, where human life is destroyed by their poisonous fangs, or where the individual survived the venomous bite that a life of misery was the consequence, we must not be astonished at the horror they display, even when their enemy is lifeless; the story is well known where the tooth of a Rattle-Snake, which was hid in a boat, caused the death of two men, and the Indians maintain that a wound inflicted with the tooth of any poisonous Snake is alike dangerous.

Our purpose to see the tree which produces the aromatic bark was a failure – after we had searched for hours, at the place where the tree was said to be, the Indians had to

---

[1] Casca-preciosa which is also the Guyana creole word for the tree *Aniba canelilla*, of which the bark and wood are cinnamon scented.

[2] There are nine species of *Nastus*, but they occur in Java and New Guinea.

[3] This was probably the Bushmaster, *Lachesis muta*, for which *Scytale catenatus* is a synonym.

acknowledge that they could not find it; I was subsequently fortunate enough to procure at least, the bark and leaves, though the tree was at the period in that state so uninteresting to Botanists, namely neither bearing blossom or fruit. The bark is highly aromatic, and is used by the Indians in Dysentery, fluxes and other similar diseases. I saw likewise the Varnish-tree, which possesses a milk, which after being boiled to a consistency is used to give to their Cassada-graters and other implements a gloss, and more durability; but in this instance I was not more fortunate than with the former; the tree was in its state of rest, and neither in blossom, nor covered with fruit; it is from 50 to 60 feet high, its bark rather grey, and the leaves resemble most, those of the Amyris.*[1]

*I have collected Specimens of leaves and of the bark from both trees – and send them, for inspection, with exception of the bark of the Varnish-tree, to Geo. Bentham Esquire. The Bark of the Varnish-tree formed part of the Collection lost at the falls.

While we followed our different pursuits, dissension had broken out amongst our Indian Community – the brother-in-law of the Chief Dabaero, a man already advanced in years and by no means an Apollo, was married to a young Indian, but her affections were so openly bestowed upon a younger lover, that her husband could not but take notice of her infidelities; the consequence was that he threatened to kill the lover, and the lover the husband. They never went out without their War-clubs and the Knife (with them an adopted weapon) in the girdle – even at night they wear their companions in the hammock. The fair one meanwhile had left her husband's hut, and went to a neighbouring one. Captain Jacobus succeeded however in reconciling the offended husband, and in order to quiet his jealousies, he married one of his servant maids to the young Lothario; peace was now again established, much to the regret of the gossiping women, who had no more tales to carry to the parties concerned – after all "tout comme chez nous".[2]

The greatest proprietor of Provision-grounds at the Currassawaak was an old Macoosie woman, who in consequence of having lost her husband at the settlement, did not reside permanently at Currassawaak, but came only from time to time, to convert the root of the Cassada into bread, and to carry the other ripe productions of her field to her present habitation at Anna-y.

While we were encamped at Currassawaak she came twice for that purpose, accompanied by her daughters, young women, and her grand-children. She commanded over the whole settlement; every one appeared to be subservient to her, and what was a riddle to us, the Caribees even submitted to her orders, in consequence of which, she was ycleped by us, "Dutchess" of Currassawaak. She possessed likewise a field planted with Sugar-cane, and as many months had elapsed since Sugar had sweetened our Coffee, we resolved to build an Indian Sugar-mill, and to buy from her the Canes then on the field. By the mechanical skill of M^r. Brotherson we soon had a Mill erected, and our

[1] The Varnish tree is probably *Symphonia globulifera*; mani in Arawak and karamanni in Macushi. Balata is also used for the same purpose.

[2] Among many Native Amazonian people, chiefs or leaders are provided with little power other than their personal authority which includes those of persuasion and tact. It is not clear what Schomburgk means when he refers to the chief's 'servant girl'. It may be a similar institution to that found among the Carib-speaking Trio of Surinam among whom there is a recognized social arrangement whereby an older man will adopt a young girl and bring her up, usually with the intention of making her a young wife in due course. See Peter Rivière, *Marriage among the Trio. A Principle of Social Organisation*, Oxford, Clarendon Press, 1969, pp. 161–2.

Indians were busily employed in pressing out the juice of the Cane, which was converted into Syrup, and next morning's Coffee was sweetened. Trifling as the circumstance may appear, it was to us a novelty, and we had only to regret that our Canes gave out so soon, nevertheless, we reserved a couple of bottles syrup to carry with us whenever we were to depart from Currassawaak.

Our Indians having procured themselves, during the period of the intercourse we had with them, all the necessities they stood in want of, they relapsed into their old indolence – neither knives, nor combs, nor scissors, for which they would have sold their birth-right when we first arrived, could now induce them to leave their hammocks. The neighbouring brook was full of fish, nevertheless they satisfied themselves with Cassada bread and Pepper-water[1] rather than give themselves the trouble to angle for fish – it need not be mentioned that our table was in consequence but poorly served, and we had to depend entirely upon our success in fishing and hunting; we learned however from our Dutchess a method of catching a number of fish without much trouble. The brook Currassawaak was on a low level, and we observed that she had her Corial drawn across the brook, and closed every opening still left, with rocks and dry branches – the place selected for that purpose was where the brook widened further upwards – the fish on their passage downwards, finding the communication stopped, attempted to jump over the impediment laid in their way, but failing, they fell into the Corial. We followed the same plan, and found generally in the morning, from 50 to 70 fish of different sizes in our boat, which we had barbecued and salted, to serve in days of want. The low state of the brook however soon put an end to our fishing on the Dutchess's plan.

Our departure from Currassawaak approached now daily; in every hut were preparations made for it; a new life appeared to reign throughout the Settlement – every one appeared to rejoice in the idea of visiting town, from morning to night cakes were baked out of the flour of the Cassada; or the flour prepared from the same root, packed into baskets to last for the journey. To us, the stay at Currassawaak became irksome; legions of Chigoes[2] and their next of kindred Fleas had taken possession of our hut, and the first plagued us to such a degree, that we really feared they would completely ruin our feet – not satisfied with penetrating between the nails of our feet, they attacked likewise our hands, and buried themselves during night under the finger-nails – indeed we enjoyed but little rest. The scarcity of provisions was an other reason why we hurried our departure.

From numerous inquiries which we had made among the Indians, we had to expect the rainy season in two Moons, we thought therefore if we departed towards the end of February, we should be in Georgetown by the period the rains commenced. On the 20th. of that Month, the wind became N.W. and was accompanied by distant thunder; the appearance of the sky was changed, and it was covered with heavy clouds of a dark greyish colour; the Thermometer was seldom more than 80° F. – however, there was no rain as yet, and the generality of our Indians maintained still, that two Moons would have to

[1] Water in which peppers have been boiled. Cassava bread becomes very hard and, if nothing better is available, it is dipped in pepper water to make it soft enough to chew.

[2] Also chigger and jigger (*Pulex penetrans* or *Tungs penetrans*). The chigoe is a blood-sucking flea, found in sandy soil. The female burrows into the human skin, usually the foot, to lay her eggs which if left can cause intense irritation and acute infection. They are relatively easily removed and most Indian women are skilled at doing so.

elapse before the rain set in; only an old Caribee was of a different opinion, he told us that we might soon expect it, and gave as a reason for his opinion, that the young turtles were so far advanced towards perfection that the rain might set in, in the course of a week. He was correct in his conjecture, and we had only to regret, that we did not consult him previously. How strange that instinct should have taught these animals, subordinate in animated nature to many classes and tribes to watch the seasons, to deposit their eggs time enough to enable the Sun to hatch them. There are chiefly two species of Turtle which frequent the Rupununy and upper Essequebo, the Emys tricarinata, called by the Indians Casseepan, and an other species perhaps of the same Genus which the Indians call Tarakayba; there is a third species of fresh-water turtle, which however is scarce in the Rupununy; it is the Matamata or Chelys fimbriata of authors, the latter is about 2 feet long, the nose terminates in a kind of proboscis, the feet are webbed, five toes before and four behind, are armed with claws, and the short tail is rather rounded.[1]

The large head and the elongated nose give to this species quite a peculiar appearance; its flesh is as delicate as that of the other fresh-water turtle. The eggs of the two first species are gathered by the Indians in large quantities, in the months of February and March; they are different in form; those of the first are almost perfectly round and the calcareous shell resembles parchment, while those of the second, smaller in size and of an oblong shape might be taken for Birds eggs. The eggs of the Tarakayba are more delicate than those of the Casseepare – they are deposited generally in holes, the number of eggs contained in them, amounting to, from 16 to 20. The Indians undertake large expeditions to the river Rewa, an affluent of the Rupununy, where they appear more numerous than either in the Rupununy or Essequebo. I witnessed the return of one of these expeditions; the boats were loaded with eggs, those collected during the last two days of their excursion were in a fresh state, the others barbacued. When barbacued, they lose the albumen, and it is only the Yolk which is rendered hard by this process; they are by no means to be rejected when in that state.

Several Indians in the neighbourhood purposed taking advantage of our departure for Demerary, and requested that they might be allowed to travel in our company.

The Indian always prefers to travel in large numbers, his dread of evil spirits is so great, that he will subject himself to great inconvenience rather than travel alone; we therefore left the mouth of the Currassawaak on the 26th. of February in eight Boats – their inmates amounting to upwards of eighty persons. The weather had been unfavourable for the three days previous, and we set out under rain; as long as the rain does not descend in torrents, the Caribee laughs at it and increases his "paddling". Should his riches amount to the possession of a Shirt and he wears the same on approaching rain, it is immediately pulled off, and secured in a dry place, unless perhaps his wife is sitting shivering next to him; when it is surrendered to her to put over her head and shoulders. She does not make further use of it, and must consider the wearing of a Shirt a pollution. I have never observed an Indian Woman from the regions South of the Confluence of the Rupununy with the Essequebo, wear that article of dress.

---

[1] The first two turtles referred to here cannot be identified with certainty, but are probably subspecies of *Rhinoclemmys punctularia*. The third is *Chelus fimbriatus*. See Marcos Freiburg, *Turtles of South America*, Neptune, New Jersey, TFH Publications, 1981.

It was my purpose to ascend the Essequebo for several days' journey from the point where it received the waters of the Rupununy. The Indians, with whom I had much intercourse, had told me frequently of a great Cataract, which they said stopped all further advance in boats. They had received those accounts from their fathers: all my endeavours to find a person who had been there, were in vain: the greatest extent of their advance was the inlet Primross[1] – from whence a path led to the river Courantine,[2] and which inlet is not more than two days' journey from the embouchure of the Rupununy – the latter of which we reached on the 27th February.

We formed here an encampment, where we left Women, Children, Dogs, Parrots – indeed of the animal kingdom almost a Menagerie. In the course of the following day, the necessary preparations were made for our further advance, the most effective crew selected for the swiftest of our Corials, and we put only such articles on board as were indispensable. While thus occupied a flock of Trumpeters (Psophea crepitans)[3] flew over the Essequibo; they must have had a far journey, three were unable to cross the river, and fell into the water – two corials were in chase of them immediately after, and they were soon secured by the Indians: they are beautiful birds, but too well known to deserve farther description. The Indians call them Waracaba. We proceeded on our further ascent on the 29th February, though the indications of the weather were by no means favourable; we became now well aware that the rainy season had set in; the sky was constantly covered and astronomical observations were out of the question. The black waters of the Essequibo were nevertheless a welcome sight; how much we did enjoy their freshness! indeed we were persuaded that they were more wholesome than those of the white Rupununy. The vegetation of its banks were more luxuriant; and upwards of three hundred yards wide; it took a much straighter course, and meandred by no means in such short turns as the Rupununy. The river upwards had almost an easterly course; not far from the junction with its affluent, there was formerly (according to Indian testimony) a post on the Essequebo's left blank, to prevent the Caribees from descending the river for the purpose of making or dealing in Slaves – though it stopped their proceedings for a short while, they soon found a way to avoid the post, and selected for that purpose the path at the inlet Primross; the Postholder was therefore recalled, and the buildings decayed.*

*The present inhabitants of Georgetown appear to be entirely unacquainted with the circumstance that the Dutch had extended their Posts so far south; but several Indians assured me that they recollected their fathers had told them of such having been the case, and adduced as further proof that Mahanarva's brother had taken away the Canons and carried them to his Settlement further South; we passed the site of that Settlement next morning: its former possessor appeared likewise to have been more advanced in civilization than the generality of his tribe. He had passed part of his life at the Colony, and possessed himself there of the English and Creole languages. As his nephew Jacobus or Yhryee assured us, one of the Canon was still to be seen – the others had sunk.

The streamlet Acoujou is the outflow of an inlet of some extent which runs parallel with the river; it is said to be inhabited by the Crocodile of the Orinoco.[4] Higher up we found the Essequibo impeded by rocks stratified, running N.W. and S.E.; a Caribee

[1] Primo's Inlet.
[2] Corentyne River.
[3] The Gray-winged Trumpeter.
[4] Orinoco Crocodile (*Crocodylus intermedius*).

settlement Musaro[1] was formerly here; but like many others, its inhabitants had mostly died and the rest removed.

One of the rocks in the river is called by the Indians Toumounae or White head, but we could not discover any claims to such an apellation. Wet through and through from the almost incessant rain, we took our night's quarters at the inlet Masaeta-yourou, what comforts we met there, with the rain descending the greatest part of the night, may be imagined; our journey was commenced under no better auspices next morning. We passed in the course of the day several abandoned settlements – the vegetation of these places being less dense and a number of Trumpet-trees (Cecropia peltata)[2] announced generally their having been inhabited. The frequency of these abandoned places, formerly inhabited by Caribees, prove how numerous their tribe must have been even at the close of the last Century. A path led formerly from the mouth of the inlet Primross to the river Courantine. Dabaero, whom the reader will recollect, told us that his Grandfather had been settled here. We found a lime-tree in bearing; a number of Coco-trees,[3] hog-plums,[4] &c., proved that its former possessor had unlike the Indian in general planted and raised useful trees, which spoke [much] of his character. We formed the plan of exploring this site more minutely on our return.

We reached next morning the island Pahumpo,[5] where Mahanarva, who appears to have been of most migratory habits, likewise resided for some time.

The Essequibo receives but seldom additional waters from tributaries of consequence in these regions, we were therefore rather surprised when we observed on its left bank, a river flowing into it, it was the largest we had seen since we left the Rupununy. Our Indians were entirely unacquainted with its existence and its name. I called it therefore Smyth's river,[6] in honour of Major General Sir James Carmichael Smyth, Bart., Lieutenant Governor of British Guiana who has taken great interest in advancing the present expedition. In the afternoon we arrived at a point where the river is narrowed on its right shore by a sand bank and on its left by rocks; it was here not more than 200 feet wide, while a little upwards it widened again to its general breadth of about 300 yards. The banks of the river had still the same luxuriant appearance as the lower Essequibo, so different from the Rupununy with its banks often dreary enough in aspect.

The Mora-trees were in blossom, and the white flowers formed a pretty contrast with the dark green leaves; the branching Ouboudi,[7] or Wild Cashew-tree vied in height with the Mora, and numerous Monkeys jumped from branch to branch and astonished at the uncommon visit accompanied us for considerable distances. Our Caribees called this [illegible] species Arieghi, or Yahriae – the male has straight long hair of a shining black, the head rather round, the forehead and part of the face and neck covered with short yellowish hair, part of the front, the nose and mouth black the latter slightly bearded, hands black, nails claw-like, except the thumb. The female is different in colour, and her fur resembles that of the European hare; her hands are likewise black,

[1] Possibly near present day Massara.
[2] *Cecropia metenis*.
[3] Probably the cocoa tree rather than the coconut palm.
[4] *Spondias mombin*.
[5] Paumbo Island.
[6] Smyths River.
[7] Ubudi: *Anacardium giganteum*.

and covered with short yellowish hair, from under the eyes to the chin extends hair of a similar colour, but somewhat larger than those of the front and cheek, the breast is nearly naked and the os hyoides visible. They jumped with great agility from tree to tree, the female and sometimes the male carrying the young ones upon the back. The length of the body is 16 inches, that of the tail 16 to 16½ inches, their height about 10½ to 11 inches. In their general aspect they resemble the Squirrel.[1]

On our further ascent of the river we observed rising ground and the smaller rapids became more frequent; the river presented here a strange feature, coming from S.18°W. and assumed N.51°W it formed at the bent a large basin which had the latter direction. Numerous rocks obstructed its course and toward the South we discovered a hill, the height of which we estimated 500 feet, bearing then S.18W. – opposite to an Island a number of rocks were peculiarly ranged; they fronted with their smaller sides the E.N.E., while the broader inclined toward the N.W. The river exhibited quite the appearance of its lower region, studded with small islands, consisting of a confused mass of rocks between which some soil had collected – the rock Guava, a species of Capparis and some grasses formed generally their vegetation. Between the rocks subjected to the flow of water, grew the smaller Weya, (Lacis dichotoma mihi)[2] and we were not long among them before the Indians shot the first Pacou. Every object reminded us of the lower falls, with which the present measured themselves in height and extent. The scenery around the cataracts was highly romantic, and the cheering cry of our Indians while drawing the boats over them, added life to it.

The existence of these Cataracts removed some of our doubts with regard to the larger Cataract. We were told by some of the Indians who had this information from Mahanarva that we would have to pass a series of smaller Cataracts before we reached the larger. Already the previous night, some of the fallen leaves on the ground appeared to be covered with a phosphoric light, their number had considerably increased during the present. I had never observed this phosphorescence before, and I ascribed it to a cryptogamous plant called forth by the incessant rains. The ground about our tent was quite illuminated, not only leaves but likewise smaller branches which lay on the ground, exhibited the whitish light.[3] But this was not the only wonderful production of the rain – the latter had loosened the tongues of all the frog-kind in the vicinity, and to judge from the variety of their cries, the species were numerous – the cry of some resembled the bleating of calves, others the chirping of birds, call of the Duck, and even the voice of men when hoarse to a considerable degree; but the most remarkable among the strange crew was "the paddler" whose quacking voice resembled so much the regular stroke of a paddle, that it deceived Mr. Haining entirely, when he heard it for the first time at the Essequibo Post. For several mornings he told us that he had heard a boat passing – the Post-holder was astonished that neither he nor his Watchman should have heard it, in order to stop the same and to inquire after the business which led it up the river, and the Watchman received a severe reprimand for neglect of duty; the frequency

---

[1] Despite Schomburgk's comparison of this monkey with the squirrel, it is not certain that it is the Squirrel Monkey (*Saimiri* spp.). Whereas the size and behaviour seem to fit, the colouring does not.

[2] Unidentified. 'Mihi' (to me) indicates that Schomburgk had named the plant.

[3] It is likely that this phosphorescent light is emitted from the mycelia of a basidiomycetic fungi (i.e., a mushroom). David Hammond, who provided me with this information, has observed the phenomenon in the Essequibo on various occasions and describes the light as 'violet-white'.

of boats passing however, cleared up the mistake. The paddler as we called the frog thereafter lives on the land, and as M$^{r.}$ Brotherson told me, is nearly the size of the Rana paradoxa,[1] it has long yellowish legs, a brown body spotted with black, and its abode is generally an old tree, until the night invites him to his ramble, and exercise of vocal power.

While we turned suddenly round a point next morning, we observed on the opposite shore on some large rocks a Jaguar (Felis onca); he was sitting on his hind legs like a dog and looked calmly at our approach until the foremost Corial was within the distance of about fifty feet, when he left slowly his seat and retired to the Woods; it was the first I had seen during my expedition. The rapids became more frequent, and the ascent fatiguing to our crew; hillocks of the height of about 200 feet, wooded at their base, and grown over with grass above, surrounded the rapids amphitheatre like – they were mostly of a conical form and showed on their sides walls of granite of at least fifty to sixty feet perpendicular height – two hillocks distinguished themselves by their great height – they were at some distance from the river's right bank, and perhaps five hundred feet high. Smaller hillocks stretched to the very edge of the water. While passing them quite a peculiar cry resounded from the high trees, it was almost startling, it arose from a species of Monkey, which the Indians called "Quatta," and which is related to the howlers.[2]

We breakfasted on an Island almost covered with the Corró-va palm; I admired again its beauty: in its leaves and general appearance resembling the Cocoanut-tree, which it surpasses in its growth & mighty pinions, to which the beautiful formed leaves might be compared. One was in fruit, and as there were so many, I did not hesitate to have it cut down, in order to procure some: they are not eatable, but they may serve to establish its scientific name if the species has been described before. I found likewise two or three Specimens of the "Oubatee" of the Warpeshanas, a proof that this Species of palm does not confine itself to the higher regions.

On the evening of the 4$^{th.}$ March we "bivouacqued" within a mile of the great Cataract. Dabaero, who was the only Indian, not only of our crew but of the whole neighbourhood of Annay, who pretended to have visited it in his boyhood, and to whom we had put a thousand questions; with regard to its distance and situation became at last quite confused and even now, as the ocular demonstration proved that some great fall was before us, he was not certain whether it really was the place we were in search of. Shortly after our landing, and having our temporary huts erected, a severe thunder storm commenced and the rain which set in with it, continued the whole night – my desire to take astronomical observations was therefore again frustrated – the rain continued till next morning, when we left our encampment.

The river contracted considerably; the hills approached each other from both sides, and the indentations of the opposite shores were so exactly matched, that the channel appeared to have been the work of art, and if it were possible to draw the banks

---

[1] *Pseudis paradoxa* is the current name. Two genera and several species of the family Pseudidae are found in the region. Most tree-living frogs belong to the Family Hylidae.

[2] It is not clear which species this is. The spider monkey (*Ateles* species) is variously called in Portuguese *cuatá*, *quatá* or *coatá* which are close phonetic approximations to 'quatta'. On the other hand, the howler monkey (*Alouatta* species) is *arawata* in Carib of which 'quatta' is also conceivably a version. The fact that the monkeys in question were noted for the noise they made might favour their identification as howler monkeys.

together, the angles would have fitted for miles of the river's course. The weather, as if to reward us for the sufferings it had caused us during the last few days, cleared partly up; the mist hovering still around the tops of the hills, and the sun venturing a few stray beams through the dark clouds, threw the landscape in such a light as to render it still more picturesque. A lovely prospect was now before us; the verdure of the hills which allowed the river scarcely a few hundred feet to pursue its course with the foaming waters in the back ground, bearing away everything opposed to its progress, combined so much beauty that I considered it among the finest scenery I had enjoyed during our Expedition.

We ventured with the boats as near to the Cataract as prudence would permit us. The water descends in two falls, the upper is the larger, and may amount to from 12 to 14 feet in height; the water precipitating itself over a ridge of jagged rocks, pursues its way foaming and tossing to the second fall; the perpendicular height of which we estimated at 7 feet – so that the falls from the upper to the lower cataract amount at least to 20 feet. The granite walls between which the river has forcibly worked its way, are opposite the falls entirely smooth and form an angle of about 45°. We climbed up some rocks at the lower falls – numerous Swallows, perhaps thousands, which had selected their night quarters on one of those walls, disturbed by our appearance, flew around us in circles until the larger party which they saw arrive caused them to continue their migratory flight.*

*It was the Species with a white ring around the neck (Hirundo melba?)[1] which I have seen frequently in North America. We met next morning another flock, which though they did not obscure the sky, was nevertheless, very numerous.

All the Indians who composed our crew, as well as those about Annay, concurred in declaring that never before had a White Man been at the Cataract. I considered myself authorized to give it a name; the greatest Cataract was therefore called after His Gracious Majesty,[2] the Patron of the Royal Geographical Society, and to go through this Ceremony in due form, we broke in our store of reserve, for one of the last bottles of wine, we had treasured up for months. Our Indians who saw that something uncommon was going on followed us, the women not excepted. In order to reach the head of the Cataract, we followed in the commencement, the river's course, but this became soon impossible in consequence of the smooth and steep sides which the granitic blocks presented towards the river; we climbed therefore the Hillock with feet and hands, and after an hour's tedious work, we had arrived at the upper part of the Cataract. From one of the higher rocks flow the red juice of the grape mingling with the white foaming torrent, and while naming it King William's Cataract, Great Britains Union was unfolded, and a salute fired according to our means. His Majesty's health was then drunk with "three times three", the Indians joining most heartily in the "Hurrah". I then penned our proceedings, and after having put the paper in a bottle and sealed the same, it was buried under the rocks to leave it to chance whether it will be found hereafter.*

*The contents of the paper were –
"Mr. Robert H Schomburgk, conductor of an Expedition in the interior of British Guiana for Scientific purposes, under the direction of the Royal Geographical Society of London,

[1] Seven genera of *Hirundinidae* have been reported from Guyana. This is possibly the White-banded Swallow (*Atticora fasciata*).
[2] King William IV.

KING WILLIAM IV.TH'S CATARACT.
River Essequibo, Lat 3°.14.35.N.

Figure 3: King William's Falls on the Essequibo River. From the *Journal of the Royal Geographical Society,* 1836, facing p. 267. Included by permission of the Leeds Library.

aided by His Majesty's Government; and M.r Robert N Brotherson, who accompanied the same as Ornithologist as well as their assistants John Haraut and John Wade visited this Cataract on the 5.th of March 1836, and as after every information, M.r Schomburgk and M.r Brotherson could collect, they were the first persons of White Colour, who visited the same – they called it after His Majesty William IV, King of Great Britain, &c, &c, &c – and Patron of the Royal Geographical Society –
KING WILLIAM'S CATARACT
The Indian crew of the three Corials was under the command of the Caribee Chief Yhryee."

We had our initials and the year of our visit engraved on a smooth rock, after which we returned to our Corials.

As far as we could see when at the head of the cataract, we observed a series of rapids, the valley of the Essequibo continued in its contracted state, and necessarily obliged us to leave it unexplored; it was impossible, provided as we were at that time to bring even the smallest corial over the Cataract, though the river was only a foot above its lowest level. The velocity with which its volume of water precipitated itself through the narrow, and the circumstance that neither rock could be reached to afford firm footing to the Indians, in order to force the Corial through the descending waters destroyed all hopes of overcoming by direct means this obstacle to the navigation. The only way of continuing the ascent of the Essequibo would be to form an encampment on the right bank at the foot of the Cataract, and to construct a path over the hillock, in order to carry the Luggage which must be put in small packages, to the head of the fall; meanwhile Woodskins*

> *Woodskins are small boats formed solely out of the bark of trees; according to their size they are able to take from three to four persons.

might be constructed on the other side to receive the necessary luggage and crew for the further continuation of the journey; this is the only way to overcome the difficulties at King Williams Cataract.

The river itself had considerably decreased in size; we observed this before we reached the Cataract. According to Indian information, it flows at some distance from the great Cataract through a lake, from which it receives chiefly its water, being before, only a large brook.

Marvellous stories are told of that lake, and it is made the seat of one of their evil spirits, which in former times was a large Camoudy Snake,[1] but conquered by a superior one, it was banished to this lake and turned into a large fish, resembling according to description our fabled mermaid, called Arkamally by the Caribees; when in bad humour, or incensed against mortals she disturbs the waters, sends squals, or calms the lake according to her pleasure, she has however a superior in the Mother of the finny tribe, called Okkolohmon.[2]

Mahanarva had a settlement at the Couyouweenee,[3] a branch of the Essequibo, and Jacobus observed that his grandfather had told him, he had been settled within a short distance of the mouth of the lake; as this information originates with him, it deserves credence. The night though clouded and the stars rather undefined, afforded me nevertheless an opportunity of taking the altitude of Canopus, when crossing the meridian, according to which King William's Cataract was in 3°14′35N. Lat. & 57°43′W. Long – it became impossible to determine the latter from Lunar distances; before the moon rose, the rain descended in torrents and the unfavourable weather made me resolve not to wait a third night; we returned therefore next day towards the mouth of the Rupununi. Our descent was much more rapid than our ascent, and we stood soon at the head of the series of the lesser Cataracts which were still nameless; they were therefore called after Sir George Murray, &c &c &c, to whom Geography owes so much, "the Murray's Cataracts."[4] We went nearly through the same ceremonies, and, had again to regret the deluge of rain which was falling.

There is a great deal of attention and presence of mind necessary in "Shooting a fall", as the descent in the boats is technically termed. The safety of the boat and its inmates depend almost entirely upon the man at the bow, called the foreman; by means of his paddle he directs the course of the boat, and it depends upon his look out, that she does

---

[1] Camoodi refers to two types of constrictors. The Land-camoodi (*Boa constrictor* spp.) and the Water-camoodi, better known as the Anaconda (*Eunectes murinus*). The latter features far more commonly in Amerindian mythology and is often the central character.

[2] No other version of this particular story has been found but many of the motifs are familiar, including the anaconda as the master or mother of the aquatic underworld. The term 'Okkolohmon' could conceivably be a version of the word for anaconda found in some Carib languages.

[3] Kuyuwini River.

[4] Murray's Fall. General Sir George Murray, FRS (1772–1846). He saw service in the West Indies 1795–96 and 1802–03, and in the Peninsula War. He was Governor of the Royal Military College at Sandhurst (1819–24) and Master-general of the Ordnance (1834–46).

not dash against a rock; the velocity with which she descends if once in the current and where the fall is considerable, would cause her to receive such a shock, that if she escaped splitting in two, she would be severely injured. Where several falls unite in one, the surge at the foot is considerable, and the danger by no means over; many a Corial has been swamped after she had passed safely the rocks, which threatened her destruction. Some of the "Murray Cataracts" were considerable, and while shooting through the foaming waters, they returned the compliment of christening in their own style, and gave us a complete wetting.

In consequence of the rains, the river had risen considerably. While ascending, we breakfasted at a place where a ledge of rocks connected with the shore stretched for a considerable distance into the river, we proposed making a similar use of it on our return, but found the rocks covered with water – upon a moderate estimate it must have risen 9 inches in 72 hours. We had a proof that the increased current also had commenced to undermine the banks; within a few hundred feet of us, we saw a tree tottering, and momently afterwards it fell with a tremendous crash into the river; all the minor branches broke into pieces as soon as the tree touched the surface of the water, and were immediately swept away by the current.

We encamped on the 7[th.] March at the inlet Primross in order to examine the path which was said to lead to the rivers Demerary and Courantine. The path was grown over by woods, and scarcely a vestige of it to be discovered, and after we had wandered about for several hours, we arrived at a Swamp, grown over with briers and prickly palm; our guides now acknowledged themselves to be at a loss, and the rain still descending in torrents we gladly traced our way back to the encampment.

Our guides had walked that path in their youth, when it was much frequented by the tribes then inhabiting the banks of both rivers; this intercourse had ceased gradually, and stopt entirely when the Caribees between the Rupununy and the Cataract of the Essequibo had most of them died, and the rest removed. We did not make any further attempt, the most unfavourable weather and the inefficiency of the crew, who like ourselves suffered from swelling of the feet, made every pedestrian tour precarious.

I understood from Poroussou, a Caribee and the Veteran of our Indians, that from the inlet it is a day's walk (about 15 miles) to the brook Tokoutou, on the banks of which the travelling parties formerly took their night-quarters, and reached next morning after three hours walk, the Demerary river, which is only a few yards wide where the path formerly crossed it, and which according to his information has its sources in a cluster of Wallaba bushes (Panzera & Dimorpha) – from this point the Indians pursued their way and reached the Courantine generally on the third day.[1]

While penetrating through the Woods in search of the path, we saw numerous Cocoa-trees (Theobroma cocoa)[2] loaded with fruit in all stages, they even extended more than a mile from the river's bank and though they were overshaded by larger trees they had reached nevertheless a height of 30 to 40 feet and the luxuriant growth and numerous fruit proved that the plant was satisfied with the soil. It is not to be doubted that the trees were originally planted by the Indians, but from their number and

---

[1] The following year Schomburgk made this journey in both directions, from the Berbice to the Essequibo and back. An important geographical feature he noted was the absence of any sign of the Demerara River during the crossing. See p. 211.

[2] Presumably the Wild Cocoa (*Theobroma bicolor*).

distance from the river, I judged that they were propagated by animals – when the fruit has reached its maturity it falls to the ground and is eagerly sought by the Peccary or Bush-hog (Dicotyles). The forest-trees consisted chiefly of Crab-wood (Aublet's Carapa Guianesis) the fruit of which covered the ground – the Indians press an oil out of the nut, which burns very well, but it is generally used for anointing the hair. The Indian Women so famed for the beauty of their hair and its peculiar gloss, make constant use of it; When setting out on a journey, a Gourd filled with Crab-oil is sure to form part of the baggage.

They have found means at the Colony, to deprive it of its peculiar smell, and it is now to be found on the Toilette of many a fair Creole or European. In our progress through the woods, we found a remarkable tree, called by the Caribees, Mussara;[1] its base like the Mora and Silk Cotton-tree, had not only excrescences, but, the whole tree, (5 to 6 feet in diameter) and perhaps 50 feet high before it divided in branches, was entirely fluted as if it consisted of the trunks of numerous more slender trees. A Passion-flower which slung itself around it attracted my attention; its ligneous stem was at the base twice the thickness of a man's arm, and its beautiful flowers, outside scarlet and inside dark blue, were arranged in clusters, and grew out of the stem but a short distance from the ground. Within twenty feet of its roots there were no leaves and being unable to climb the tree in consequence of my swollen feet, I was prevented examining them nearer, they were however ovate; appeared to be rough, and resembled most those of P. quadrangularis.

We returned now to our encampment at the mouth of the Rupununy, where we found everything in good order, and after we had taken our baggage on board of the different craft, we left the Rupununy on the 9th. of March for our final departure to the coast. A few hours afterwards we met a numerous party of Accaways in seven Corials and Woodskins; their Cassada crop being exhausted at home it was their purpose to pay a long visit to the Macoosies of the Parime Mountains, until such time as they thought their Cassada fields would be fit for crop. They had their boats loaded with Sugar cane, fish, and game; but they had neither a morsel of Cassada bread, nor a Yam, nor a sweet Potato. We had plenty of the first, and being in want of fish and game, we bartered for the latter, giving in exchange bread, knives and hooks.

We visited the abandoned Caribee Settlement Mourre-mourre-patee, famed on the high-road of the Essequibo for the large quantity of Sugar canes which grow there, it might be said almost wild.

The Settlement belonged formerly to our friend Jacobus, and as he told us his stay there was only for two years, being so unfortunate as to lose several of his people by sickness; and though more civilized than the rest, he could not divest himself of the superstitions of his tribe, which were planted in him from childhood – he left it therefore when the new settlement was just about to become productive. The Sugar cane had grown up without farther attention of human hands, and though many years had elapsed, we found it of a size equal to any in the Colony and of a particular sweetness; the spare places of our Corials were soon loaded with it. We found that the Accaways which we met the previous morning had been encamped here for several days – a newly dug grave under a shed told us that they had left one of their number in the place.

Many of the Indian tribes but chiefly the Caribees, Macoosies, and Accaways have the custom of burying their dead either in the hut where they lived, or if a case of death

---

[1] *Aspidosperma excelsum.*

89

should happen during a journey, a shed covered with palm-leaves is built over the grave to prevent the weather from incommoding the person who rests beneath.

We passed Achra-moucra the place of those piles of granitic-rocks on which in our ascent we looked with admiration, mixed with awe. In consequence of our visit to Mourre-mourre-patee, our Captain chose a different way, with the intention of gaining the common channel by one of the passages formed between two Islands; We found to our regret that one of those giants of the forest, a Mora tree had lately fallen across the passage and made every further advance in that direction impossible. It would have taken us half a day to return by the way we came, until we met the navigable channel – our Captain resolved therefore to force a passage through unfrequented channels – an undertaking most laborious, and threatening destruction to our Corials at once. We travelled thus more than three to four miles between numerous dykes of rocks, and Islands of every form and shape, the current being divided by them into numberless rapids. Many of the rocks were covered with lichen, parasitic plants, and a coarse grass; some of them exhibited, even more, bushes; or a Balsam-tree (Clusia Spec.)[1] covered with its beautiful wax-like flowers. We arrived at the fall of Ouropocary on the 11th. March; here we had again to unload our boats, and to carry the baggage across the small island, on which we observed the remarkable rock resembling gothic spires, and described at our ascent – all the boats reached safely the foot of the falls, but there were moments of deep anxiety while standing ashore, from the time I saw the boat swept forward by the upper current until it had reached the foot of the falls, winding itself through the sinuosities of the Cataract, and avoiding the dangers which pointed rocks opposed from both sides.

We observed some Mountains on the eastern shore of the river, which have received their name from a brook that flows at their foot, and which is of such a blackness that the Indians have named it Siroppa Creek, resembling the fluid in colour, but not in sweetness. The Indian is never at a loss for an appropriate name; it is likely that they only became acquainted with that brook after the first Settlers had arrived, and cultivated the Sugar-cane. They saw the Syrup, and finding that the sluggish waters of the brook had the same colour, they attached a vowel to the foreign word and Indianized it.[2]

Several of our utensils new to them, were thus named; the frying-pan, a most useful article in order to bake Cakes of the Pouroumoh or Cassada-flour, reminding them in its form of the Sting-ray received its name Ceepari. Our mugs were made into muggi and the Coffee pot into Coffie; to our family name one or other vowel was attached.

The contrary accounts which I had heard of the river Bourre-Bourre, an affluent of the Siporoonie, made me resolve to ascend the latter until I met the mouth of its tributary.

The weather became daily more disagreeable – the Thermometer stood generally at sun-rise at 72° F. and reached seldom 80° during the warmest part of the day; the rain fell in torrents and when it stopped for a short while it appeared only as if to collect new forces to descend with double its former strength. Our situation was rendered most unpleasant. Wet through and through, we had no Sun to dry our clothes; and our Stock not being on the largest scale towards the end of our pilgrimage, we saw ourselves often

---

[1] *Clusia amazonia.*

[2] Schomburgk's claim that the Native peoples were unaware of this brook before the arrival of the first settlers and their introduction to sugar-cane syrup is most improbable but reflects his poor view of the Amerindian.

obliged to make use of damp clothes – it was worse with regard to our night quarters – our curtains having sundry openings did not keep the rain out, and the Huts which our Indians built and covered with Palm-leaves stood very well a moderate shower, but no tropical torrent; and in spite of fires which we kindled under our hammocks we were not able to warm ourselves and we passed frequently the greater part of the night by walking up and down. The river swelled daily, and by the time we reached the Siporoonie, it grew from 8 to 9 inches every day. In consequence of its fullness our Indians failed in catching fish, and the rain preventing them from hunting, we had to live solely upon Cassada-bread from the time we passed the falls of Rappoo to our arrival among the coloured people of Essequibo.

We left the greater part of our crew at the mouth of the Siporoonie, and as the day was not yet far advanced we took one of the smaller Corials in order to reach the Bourre-Bourre. The waters of that river have a reddish colour – its banks are skirted by high trees, among which we distinguished the Timber Wallaba (Dimorpha Spec?) in large numbers; the soil appeared more fertile than even that of the Essequibo. The same granitic dyke which crosses the latter river at Ouropocary impedes likewise the Siporoonie, within a few miles of its mouth. We found them very difficult to ascend, and had to cut us a channel through the bushes, which overhung the river, which was full to overflowing – after an hours hard work, the rain descending in torrents all the time, we reached the head of the cataract.

The Solitude which prevailed here, caused almost an oppressive feeling; the narrowness of the river, which only 150 yards wide at its union, had become much narrower; the dense foliage of the trees and bushes which skirted its banks, and a temporary calm after the severe shower, all united to make us fancy nature was asleep: the tap of the Woodpecker, resounding like the heavy fall of the axe through the woods, was really a relief and gave new matter to conversation between my companion, Mr Brotherson and myself – indeed it is astonishing what a loud sound the larger species (Picus multicolor)[1] produces, one would think it impossible that it could come from a bird. The bird itself is elegant in appearance, the dark colours of its body contrast strongly with the orange of its head and neck. We reached the mouth of the Bourre Bourre next morning – the two rivers appear here of equal width and of similar colour – the Siporoonie coming from the West, the Bourre Bourre from the S.S.W. – their width amounting to about 200 feet; not far from their union they emerge from a chain of mountains and to judge from the information I was able to collect at Anna-y and Pirarara, they have their sources at the western angle of the Pacarayma or Parime Mountains; we followed the Bourre Bourre for some distance, but as there were rapids before us, which we did not wish to ascend, we returned towards our encampment. The junction of the two rivers is in approximately Lat.[blank]° North and Long^t·[blank]° ′ West.*

*They have been calculated according to courses steered and time elapsed.[2]

The acuteness of the Indians in discovering the Guana (Iguana delicatissima),[3]

---

[1] Possibly the Crimson-crested Woodpecker (*Phloeoceastes melanoleucos*).

[2] The figures are missing from the manuscript, and the sentence and footnote have been deleted from the published version, 'Report of an Expedition into the Interior of British Guayana, in 1835–36', p. 273.

[3] *Iguana delicatissima* is the West Indian Iguana, and Schomburgk presumably means the Common Iguana (*Iguana iguana*).

though hid partly among the thick foliage of the bushes, is really surprising. While following the course of the river the current carried us often with the greatest swiftness nevertheless our Caribees discovered the poor Guana while feeding on the leaves of a favourite tree, a species of Mimosa, or lurking for insects. The discovery of a Gold Mine could not have caused more joy to our crew; the bow-string was quickly fastened and the arrow, properly directed, seldom missed its aim; but it often happened that the animal with the arrow fixed in its body, dropped into the water and before the Indian had time to jump overboard vanished under it, and with it the hope of a delicate morsel, and the arrow to boot were lost; many were then the wailings of the disappointed. This Guana-hunting took away a good deal of time, and I had given strict orders that none but the hunting-boat should stop for the purpose of shooting them, however our scarcity made me repeal my former order, unfortunately without the desired effect – the Guanas appeared to be in league with the finny-tribe; all our endeavours to procure either the one or the other were in vain.

Towards the evening which followed our departure from the Siporoonie we observed some moving objects on a sandy beach at a good distance from us; every one in the boat was of opinion that they were Men, and from their being dressed in White, we concluded that they were coloured people from the Essequibo, on a fishing expedition. Though our long absence from the Colony might have served as a good excuse for the presence of sundry openings in our habiliments the hope of meeting in a few minutes beings several steps higher in civilization than our Indians, we pulled on our clothes with studied care, to hide their defects; the hair received an aditional adjusting, and we sat now full of expectation to meet our fellow creatures. The Accaways which the reader will recollect we met not far from the mouth of the Rupununy, had told us of an epidemic disease which had broken out in the Colony,[1] and was said to have committed great ravages among whites, coloured, and Indians; who can describe therefore the anxiety of my companion and our assistants who had the nearest relations at the Colony, and I though a perfect stranger on my arrival had formed many acquaintances who I had learned to esteem even during the short period of my stay in Demerary; our crew seemed to understand our feeling and with doubled swiftness resounded the stroke of the paddle – we approached the beach but who can depict our disappointment, when in lieu of human creatures, we found three Jabirus (Mycteria americanus)[2] pacing leisurely up and down – the disappointment was too severe to be laughed at, besides the information which we were so anxious to receive, we flattered ourselves that we should be able to procure some provisions from the new-comers. The Jabirus might have discovered our half starving faces and sinister purposes on their lives; they took to their wings before we came within Gun-shot, and thus another disappointment that of revenge and the hope of an excellent supper was added to the former. This large bird which is often 6 feet high resembles our Stork, however, its bill is bent upwards. We saw them in numerous flocks on the Savannahs near the Parime Mountains, and met them in threes and fours on the sandy beaches of the Rupununy and Essequibo. Their measured step and upright bearing had frequently amused our friend Haining who was forcibly reminded of the Parade, so that he could not refrain, while passing the beach,

[1] Yellow fever.
[2] *Mycteria americana* is the Wood Ibis. The Jabiru Stork, the bird in question here, is *Jabiru mycteria*.

from giving to these feathered recruits the word of command. Whenever we discovered them afterwards we cried out, "Look, there are some of Haining's Company".

We met next day two Woodskins with Macoosie Indians, on their return from a visit to Berbice. They had left the Demerary river the previous day and passed one night on the route, from which we may calculate that the Demerary river is about 20 Miles from the Essequibo, where the path, meets the latter river, opposite the Commouti Mountains. On their descent they hide their craft at that point and walk to one of the Indian settlements on the Demerary River, and thence to the Berbice, which journey is executed in three or four days from the time they leave the Essequibo.

We passed next day the Twasinkie Mountains and by means of a lateral channel avoided its large cataract Encourite or Cumaka-toto, the engulpher of our letters, newspapers, and provisions.[1] In order to avoid a dangerous cataract, called by the Caribees, Apou-coyahan, Jacobus chose one of the by-ways which the numerous Islands afforded – we soon observed that our Captain was a stranger to it, we, nevertheless, continued as we judged from the strong current, that there must be an outflow; we saw some rapids before us, but as the water did not present any dangerous appearance, we put the Corial in the Current, and with the rapidity of lightning we were carried towards the descent, which to our greatest surprise, we discovered now too late, to be at least six feet perpendicular – there was no redress, nothing in the world could have stopped the boat, and the next moment would decide her fate and ours; the silence of the grave reigned now in our Corial; the few orders necessary in such a case had been given by Jacobus in a decisive manner, and upon the ruler above depended the rest – we arrived at the brink; carried forward with still redoubled impulse she took the fall, and skipping over the void, buried her bow in the surge at its foot, and rising above the foaming waters, she obeyed again the steady hand of the helmsman; it was a simultaneous burst of joy which arose from the inmates of our Corial – the other crafts of which our squadron was composed did not think it expedient to follow the flag-ship, and thus we got separated for the day.

Among the Indians who requested to travel in our company when we left Currassawaak was James, the chief of the Macoosie settlements at Warapoota. Scarcity of provisions and still more the dreaded revenge of a tribe of Accaways to whom he had given provocation, induced him to make a trip to the "Macoosie country" as the district about the Parime Mountains is generally called. He returned now with his Wife and followers in a large Canoe and a Corial. While we ascended the Essequibo and Siporoonie, he had slowly proceeded, and at our arrival at the first settlement above Warapoota, we met with him, he having arrived the day previously. The rain prevented us from proceeding after mid-day, we were therefore glad of having an apology for stopping, the more so as the Indian hut promised us shelter against the pelting rain and a few hours sound sleep; how the latter was effected, remains a riddle to me, the combined crews of "Macoosie James" and our Corials amounted to upwards of 50 Men, and a numerous herd of quarrelling dogs and screeching parots, the latter of which always accompanied by their noisy cry that of the canine warriors, as if like the trumpet of War they purposed to encourage the Combatants to deeds of valour – then came the

---

[1] Schomburgk is referring to the letters, medicines and other goods which had been entrusted to a Macushi who was returning from the coast to the interior. The canoe upset in the rapids and the only thing saved was five bottles of brandy (RGS Corres 1834–40, Letter of Schomburgk to Maconochie, 5 February 1836).

cudgel of the enraged Indian distributing merciless stripes to the parties concerned, and howling at the unnecessary interference, they sought security in the adjacent woods – but scarcely had their masters retired to their hammocks when they returned to continue their undecided quarrel.

We parted next morning from "Macoosie James" who was to return to his settlement at Warapoota.

The rapids of that name were safely passed, and ordering the other Crafts to proceed, Mr Brotherson and myself went to the foot of the large Cataract, which we had avoided by a lateral channel.

It is not only famed for its own grandeur but likewise for a number of figures, which the Indians have cut into the rocks that form a small island at its foot. The rocks which bear inscriptions are very numerous – these rude figures resemble those which I had seen in St John's, one of the Virgin Isles, where there is no doubt that they proceed from the Carib, who formerly inhabited that Island. We had looked in vain for inscriptions, which, according to Baron d'Humboldt, Hortsman[1] had discovered on the banks of the Rupununy, and I was therefore happy to see those just alluded to. I was most anxious to carry part of one of the rocks which bore inscriptions and figures, with me – but weakened by fever the blows of a large axe were not sufficient to break the hard rock. Mr Brotherson's endeavours were not more successful, neither threats nor promises could induce any of our Indians to strike a blow against these Monuments of their ancestors skill and superiority. They ascribe them to the great Spirit, and their existence was known to all the tribes we met with. The greatest uneasiness was depicted upon the faces of our poor Crew – in the very abode of the Spirits, they momently expected to see fire descend to punish our temerity – the fire did not descend, but the Waters did, and that in large quantities – and as we did not succeed in breaking one of the rocks – I was obliged to satisfy myself with taking an accurate drawing of the most remarkable ones.[2]

We were rather astonished in looking back, to observe that "Macoosie James" was following us – he had expressly told us that he did not intend to proceed to town directly – but the mystery was soon cleared up, on arriving at his settlement he was told by an old Indian woman, whom he had left at the place, that during his absence, a strong party of Accaways had been at Warapoota in search of him, and being disappointed in meeting him, they had proceeded to Demerary River, to take revenge on the Arrawaak Chief, Simon, who some years ago, fell with his followers upon one

---

[1] Nicolas Horstman was a German surgeon from Hildesheim in the service of the Dutch who was sent on an expedition into the interior of Guiana in 1739. However, instead of returning to the Dutch colonies he travelled down the Rio Branco to the Portuguese settlements. In 1743 he met at Pará the French scientist Charles-Marie de La Condamine, who had journeyed down the Amazon from Quito. He gave to the Frenchman an account of his journey and a sketch map of his route. Back in Paris, La Condamine showed these documents to the cartographer Jean D'Anville, who incorporated the details in his 1748 map of South America. An important feature of this map was the absence of Lake Parima or Amucu, although this was only a temporary state of affairs as the lake reappeared in his 1760 map, and on numerous later maps made by others.

[2] Even if the spirits did not exact revenge, Schomburgk found himself the target of some editorial displeasure. In the published version (p. 276) the following editorial note has been inserted: 'It is truly to be wished that no one may be more successful, and that no civilized hand may ever again be raised to deface these monuments of the "untutored Indian." – ED.' What may have been more hurtful is that Humboldt ('Sur quelques points importans', pp. 178–9) also reprimanded Schomburgk for his attempt.

of their parties encamped peacefully on the Essequibo, and slew seven of their number.*

*Simon was tried for this cold-blooded murder executed by him under the influence of fanaticism and superstition, but the want of evidence, or rather the plea that the Witnesses could not be put upon Oath, as they were not aware of the nature of that solemn obligation, and finally, the circumstance that there was no certainty how far the boundary of British Guiana extended, and that consequently the act might have been committed out of its jurisdiction, saved him.

Macoosie James reasoned therefore that they would probably return, and considered it advisable to hasten his departure.

He hung close upon our heels as long as we had to pass the different paths, which communicate with Demerary river, and only after we were among the Series of the first rapids, he slackened his exertions and remained behind us.

The Potaro or black river, gives to the Essequibo its dark colour again, which after having received the white waters of the Rupununy, and the red ones of the Siporoonie, assumed a tint quite different from its colour above the Rupununy; the contrast is remarkable indeed.

We flattered ourselves that after we should have past the Arissaro Mountains, the weather might become a little more favourable, as it is well known that Mountains in general, but chiefly wooded Mountains attract the clouds charged with rain; We reasoned that after one should have past the last Mountainous Chain, we should meet with a change – but we were greatly disappointed, the quantity of rain which fell daily was more than I ever had experienced in a similar time. We were obliged to encamp at noon, at the foot of the Arissaro; the rain fell in torrents, and in order to keep us warm, we made several fires under and in the neighbourhood of our hammocks. The Thermometer stood in the afternoon at 3 °Clock 72° and our breath became plainly visible when we conversed with each other. An awful crash awoke me out of my first sleep, and the sound of many voices, the crying of a child startled my blood – only a tree in its fall had produced that sound, and I feared serious consequences – fortunately it was merely the outer branches, which fell upon the hut – the shock was however strong enough to throw it down, and it was more the fright than any serious injury which made the child cry; the escape was miraculous indeed; if the tree had turned a foot more aside, the inmates of the hut could not have escaped destruction. We passed next morning the mouth of the Brook Moucou-moucou,[1] one of the most frequented thoroughfares between the Essequibo and Demerary. By following the course of the Essequibo, the Indian on his way to town is obliged to pass the coast, and though not afraid of shooting the Cataracts of the inland rivers, more dangerous than the surge of the Sea along shore, the novelty of this navigation has something frightful for him; he prefers therefore leaving his Craft on the banks of the Essequibo and crossing over on foot to the Demerary river. The Moucou-moucou takes an eastern direction, the brook is therefore soon abandoned, the path then leading through heavy Woods; after penetrating for 10 or 12 Miles, it divides in three branches, the highest of which leads to Piawatanni, the second to the Post-Seba, and the third to a settlement further north; the journey is generally performed in one day and a half, and the ground being perfectly level, this

[1] Moko-moko River.

Portage may hereafter be of great advantage. A few miles south of the Moucou-Moucou is the brook Cortuaharo[1] from whence a path leads likewise to Demerary river.

The distance between river and river is scarcely more than 18 or 20 Miles, and a connecting canal might be easily constructed.

The weather was the same when we started in the morning – in the afternoon our large Coorial which besides the crew, Mr Brotherson and myself occupied, was the only one in sight; this did not alarm us, they might have chosen another channel or their zeal to keep up with us might have relaxed, for the first time since the commencement of our expedition we past one night separated from the others. Our huts were situated on the foot of the Cataract Etabaly Fall, the descent of which was much easier than I expected. We fired several times in the course of the Evening and likewise in the morning before we started, and as our signals remained unanswered we concluded that the boats might have preceeded us. The Cataract of Taminett or Arissaro was before us, we did not find it difficult to ascend it, what was therefore our astonishment, when the river, as far as our eyes could range, presented one foaming mass; torrent contending with torrent, foaming eddies and whirlpools. Our Captain in consequence of the success with which he had brought the Corial so far, became daring, and before we were aware what he was about, we were already in the midst of the Cataract, and the waves as if incensed at our temerity dashed violently against the boat, and the next moment one of them more forward than the others rose to a considerable height, curled its head and striking the bow, almost filled the boat and nearly sunk it. Jacobus received many reproaches for his foolhardiness, not only from those whose lives he had risked but likewise from the coloured people on the Essequibo, who thought we were jesting when we told them that we had descended Taminett. At 8ʰ·15ᵐ· on the 18ᵗʰ· of March we passed the last rapid and approached now the habitations of civilized persons.

How grateful were my feelings towards the Almighty who brought us safely through Dangers of a manifold nature, and "led us forth by the right way, that we might go to the City of habitation"!![2]

We landed at Mr. Bradford's; his house at a projecting point of the river, commands a fine view of those numbers of inlets and rocks, which fill the river and give the first indication while ascending, that the rapids are not far distant.

I threw many an anxious glance in that direction, to discover the missing boats, but in vain.

We proceeded to Hipya[3] where on our ascent we passed a night in the unfinished "house of prayer." The settlement consists of coloured people and Indians – the children of which are not only instructed in religion, but likewise receive the first rudiments of reading.

One of the Missionaries from Barteka-Point performs divine service here two or three time a month. The house of prayer, to which the neatly executed hut was dedicated, formed of Posts from the neighbouring wood, and covered with the leaves of the Trooly and other Palms, afforded us again shelter, and every hope of a night's comfortable rest – how we luxuriated in the idea of enjoying sleep, undisturbed by rain and wind. The wish to await the missing boats, and the weather made us stop so early as 11

---

[1] Kurtuahara River. It is to the north of the Moko-moko, as it is shown on the map.
[2] 'And he led them forth by the right way, that they might go to a city of habitation' (Psalms 107:7).
[3] Hipaia.

°'Clock, and we had thus an opportunity to dry our hammocks and clothes, by large fires, which the kindness of the inhabitants had kindled for us. We were less fortunate in procuring provisions – indeed it appeared that the settlement was also in want. The rain prevented the men from fishing or hunting and though many of them had still the Cassada-root in plenty, in their fields; it was difficult to get the roots to their huts – as the way to the field was overflowed.

We had comforted ourselves while on the Cassada-diet with the idea, that ere long, we should have the power of choosing of what our meals should consist and we drew in our imaginations an elegant picture of a pair of Fowls, a roasted Pig, a smoking hot Quarter of Deer, a fine Labba,[1] &c – vain hopes indeed! None of these desirables were to be procured; and some fresh Cassada-bread in lieu of our hard old stock, now several weeks old, was the only change on our Breakfast-table, but in the afternoon some kind soul sent us part of a Deer to the Settlement, which, prepared for dinner, was an excellent morceau.

In the course of the afternoon the missing boats arrived with the exception of one which was quite new and for the first time on the Essequibo; it had been put under the guidance of Hermanus a Caribee, and as it had passed our hunting-boat in the morning early, its non-appearance created uneasiness. Hermanus was however known to be steady and well acquainted with the Channels and Cataracts; we concluded therefore that he had preceded us to the Post; the Corial contained eleven Indians, Men, Women and Children, part of my Collections of Indian-Curiosities, the whole of my Geological Collections, the Barks of several remarkable trees, Gums and divers Seeds.

How did we hail the appearance of the Post, which during our absence in the Interior, had been removed to Ampa.[2] We had been the whole morning in a state of excitement; the people who inhabited the Western bank of the river left their huts and stood in groups on the shore, waving their hats and handkerchiefs – though we were perfect strangers to them and they to us, our expedition had excited thier interest – and the weak state in which our coloured crew left us at Annay, had made them fear that we had fallen victims to disease. The former Captains of the two Corials, the "Maconochie" and the "Bentham" showed so much delight at seeing us again, that we must have been hard-hearted indeed, if it had not touched us. The Postholder, M.r Richardson and his family received us with every demonstration of kindness and hospitality and the only damp thrown over our joy was the uncertainty of the fate of Hermanus and his crew – that day and the next elapsed, boats had been sent in different directions, as we had been informed that a Corial with Indians, had been seen passing; their return without further information caused wailings indeed among the relations of those who were missed; every one gave them up for lost; even M.r Brotherson, the stoutest in holding out hopes,

---

[1] Labba, paca or gibnut (*Agouti* spp.). Rather confusingly, the agouti, an animal very similar to the paca, belongs to a different genus (*Dasyprocta*). There is a well known colonial Guianese saying: 'if one eat labba and drink creek water, one must return to the colony'.

[2] It is interesting that Schomburgk at the time made no mention of visiting the Bartica Mission on this occasion (but see p. 404 below). That he did so was recorded by the missionary Thomas Youd; the visit turned out to be not unimportant as the Bishop of Barbados, William Hart Coleridge, was there on a tour of inspection. Youd recorded that Schomburgk enthusiastically supported, to the bishop, the plan to found a mission in the interior, among the Macushi. In August 1838 Schomburgk, in a letter to T. F. Buxton (1786–1845), Member of Parliament for Weymouth and President of the Aborigines Protection Society, referred to the occasion and noted his role in the founding of the mission (Rivière, *Absent-minded Imperialism*, pp. 18–19).

and relaxed – a boat was at last spied out on the third day – it approached the Post, and what relief it afforded us when we recognized the Crew of the missing Corial I need not describe; They were not in their own Craft, but in that of Macoosie James', the Corial with its cargo was entirely lost at the Cataract of Etabaly. Hermanus possessed a Woodskin, which was loaded with hammocks and other articles of trade – as she wanted two men to be navigated, of which he stood rather in need, we had several times requested him to put his effects in one of our Corials, and to abandon her, in which case I promised to pay him the full value of the Woodskin; but his Indian obstinacy was not to be overcome, and thus was incurred a very serious loss in the result of the expedition. The morning after our separation the Woodskin being in company with the Corial, shot the Cataract first, negligence or accident made her run against a rock, and she upset. Hermanus, who followed her close, in attempting to assist her ran too near the rocks, his Corial became unmanageable; she was carried forward by the current, and running against a rock partly hidden, she split right in two; the lives of the poor inmates were in the greatest danger; his wife disappeared twice under the water, and only to the presence of mind of one of the Macoosie Indians, who dived after her, she had to attribute her preservation. Fortunately for the crew thus saved, Macoosie James well aware that there was no danger of meeting the Accaways at the region of the lower Cataracts, took it much easier, and made slower progress than we did; and at his arrival at Etabaly, he discovered the poor beings, and took them in his boat. Grateful that all were saved, I forgot at first the loss of my geological & other collections; it nevertheless has left a chasm which cannot be so easily filled up; and a regret that so much labour was thrown away often intruded itself upon my feelings.

This is too frequently the lot of the Traveller, after having amassed treasures of natural science and having taken every pain to preserve them, weather, accident, negligence, and malice, often conspire to deprive him of them. How frequently was I obliged to use every persuasion to induce the Indian to carry the geological Specimens collected during our pedestrian tours! I might have loaded him with provisions, wearing apparel &c, and he would not have objected to it, but to increase his burden, by adding rocks, he thought could only be done out of mischief, therefore I had been more than once under the necessity to carry the Specimens myself assisted by Mr Haining when we traversed the Savannahs between the Parime Mountains and Pirarara; and almost the whole of them (eight Specimens only being saved) were doomed to be lost, after having passed the upper and more dangerous Cataracts. Nor was this my only loss; numerous were the Plants spoiled by rain, several members of my Menagerie[1] also died in consequence of the wet, and the lessened attention paid to them; and it wanted an additional portion of energy to induce me to attempt to save what could be saved, after we arrived at the Post.

Mr Brotherson, anxious to see his relations, left me at Ampa, and proceeded to Georgetown, while I unpacked boxes and chests, to expose to the air their contents. It was heart-rending to see the state they were in!! In spite of oil-cloth, palm-leaves, and other covers, if not the rain, the moisture had found its way into the packages – and for a second time during the first Expedition, the Mildew had committed the greatest ravages among the plants and Birdskins.

---

[1] Menagerie. Schomburgk had made a collection of live animals and birds, very few of which survived to reach Europe.

I left the Post on the 28th of March in my Corial, manned by 12 of the best and ablest men, most of them were for the first time on their way to town, I was therefore highly anxious to see what effect the aspect of our Ships, our Buildings &c would have upon them. Zeno himself could not have showed more unconcern than these Savages. I watched a boy of the Atoria-tribe, who occupied the bow, he threw a glance on the object which was new to him, but there was no change of feature, and the next moment the eye was directed again upon the head of the Corial – even the Ferry Steam-boat, which was plying between shore and shore, did not interest them. I was greatly disappointed. At my arrival in Georgetown, I received the greatest demonstrations of gladness at my safe return. I hastened to present myself to Sir James Carmichael Smyth, the Governor, who received me in the most obliging manner, and the interest thus displayed made me forget the sufferings of the previous six months.[1]

****

The fourth manuscript of part (a) constitutes a summary of the geography of the Essequibo and Rupununi area traversed by Schomburgk together with other comments. It originally consisted of twenty-four pages but, as already mentioned, some of these have been transferred physically to other sections of part (a). Some of its contents were included in the published version. The memoir, as transcribed here, has been returned to its original order and form. It is in Schomburgk's handwriting.

GEOGRAPHICAL MEMOIR TO ACCOMPANY THE MAP OF THE ESSEQUEBO AND ITS TRIBUTARY, THE RUPUNUNY, &c &c BY ROBERT H. SCHOMBURGK ADDRESSED TO THE PRESIDENT AND COUNCIL OF THE ROYAL GEOGRAPHICAL SOCIETY OF LONDON

The gradual melting of the Snow on those ice-covered summits, the Andes, is the first source of those immense rivers which enter the Continent of South America, and while the Streams which flow into the Pacific have but a short distance to run, the mountainous nature of the land obliges them to force their way through rugged Channels, to the vast recipient.

The waters which flow from the eastern acclivities to the Atlantic, have to overcome much less obstacles and meandring for three to four hundred leagues[2] through a country of varied aspect, form by their junction those rivers which are considered the first in the Western Hemisphere. A chain of Mountains in the 19th. parallel of South Latitude the Sas Seiada and Santa Martha[3] separates the rivers flowing into the Amazon from those which are tributaries to the Rio De la Plata.

---

[1] At this point in the manuscript (p. 40), three pages from 'Geographical Memoir' (pp. 21–3) are inserted and renumbered as pp. 41–3 of the 'Third Report on the First Expedition', and form pp. 281–3 of the published version. They are not included here but have been returned to their original place in that manuscript (see below p. 113, fn. 1).

[2] A league is about three miles and varies in length in different countries.

[3] Serra de Santa Marta or das Divisões lies to the west of the modern city of Goiánia. Serra Seiada, also known as Serra do Caiapó, is a little further west and the source of the River Araguaia.

99

The Cordillera de la Parime as it has been named by Baron de Humboldt, extends between the third and seventh degree of North Latitude, and one of its branches, the Pacaraima divides the waters of the Orinoco (if we except the Cassiquiari) from those of the Amazon; and its most eastern spur, those of the Rio Branco from the tributaries of the Essequibo.

It is this spur of the Parime which bounds the Savannahs of those regions, to which my researches in the expedition undertaken under your instructions and patronage were chiefly directed, and that forms the principal feature in the hydraulic system of the river Essequibo.

While the rainy season in 1836, was so far advanced, that we found it impossible to follow that river's course upwards further South than 3°·14″N. Lat. we ascended the Rupununy within twenty leagues of its sources, and the circumstance of having explored that river to a greater distance, induces me to conduct you in the first place to the Sources of the Rupununy.

Circumstances which I stated in my second Report to the Royal Geographical Society, and the low state of the Rupununy, combined to oblige us to retrace our steps, after we had reached the Cartatan or Corona,*

> *The Indians have borrowed that word, and bestow it upon the first or largest Cataract of the River; we have thus a Corona of the Rupununy, the Maou, the Tokoto &c &c.

the first and largest Cataract of the River. The night previous to our reaching the Corona, while on the banks of the brook Arracuay, I had a good observation of the Star Achernar, according to which our encampment was in 2°·44′.54″N. Lat. from which observation the position of the Corona was computed to be in 2°·38′.24″N. Lat. Two miles south of it rose a Solitary hill from the Savannahs, which I ascertained to be in the same Meridian with the Summit of the Southern angle of the Conocou Mountains, their respective distance being 13.2 miles from the Summit of the first. I had a perfect view of the Carawaymee Mountains, without doubt, the Sierra Arrary or Tumu-curaque of Geographers.[1]

Some intelligent Warpeshanas who had travelled in that direction, pointed out a hill where they said the Rupununy had its source, receiving from the East a tributary, which at their junction formed a large +Eta-Swamp.

> +The Eta-palm is Humboldt's Mauritia.

Where the river became visible to the armed eye, it meandred through the Savannahs, spreading itself into Lake-like sheets of water, or diminishing apparently into the breadth of a silvery thread. It passes East of the Pahaeteeyan or Cassada-bread Hills, and became from there under my immediate observation: Determined by corresponding angles from the above two elevations, the sources of the river and its course to the Pahaeteeyan are therefore by no means hypothetical, but rest upon the information I was able to collect from those which Humboldt considers 'the best Geographers of their own country.' The source of the Rupununy has been hitherto placed in 2°·30N. to 2.50N. Lat. almost a degree too far North; while according to my informants and trigonometrical operations it must be in 1°·49′N. Where the river issues from the

---

[1] Schomburgk is presumably referring here to the Serra Acarai and Tumuchumac. The latter range lies much further east, on the boundary between Brazil and French Guiana.

Carawaymee Mountains, it takes a North-western course through the Savannahs; there stretch no Mountains to its banks, until it meets the Pahaeteeyan on the left shore; a few miles further north it forces its way through a bed of Stratified Granite, which runs E.N.E. and W.S.W, and appears to be connected with the Ursato Mountains.

Seeking an outflow, it has spread into many Channels, and the extreme boundaries of its bed were about 1300 feet. Above the Cataract it receives the Waters of the brook Fournacou from the West; and below, those of the brook Maycar, which is said to have its sources in the Saeraerie Mountains.

The Savannahs which skirt immediately the banks of the river, formed of a whitish clay, from which it receives its white colour, are covered with numerous grasses and Plants.

The river meandring through these extensive plains, marks its course by a fringe of trees; similarly girded are all the small rills and brooks of which the Rupununy is the recipient, (forming a line of the greatest declivity between the 58th and 59th Meridian, and the second and third parallel) and thus the monotony of a Savannah is much relieved; numerous Deer, (two or three together but never in Herds,) graze here undisturbed, the nearest Indian huts at the foot of the surrounding Mountains being often 15 to 20 Miles distant. The distance of the Cataract is 160 Miles from the embouchure of the Rupununy. While there, I took the following thermometrical observations[:]

December 2nd. 1835.

Cataract of the Rupununy

Thermometer shaded in the open air, at 8h. A.M. 81°.F.*

*All Thermometical observations are according to Fahrenheit's Scale.

Water of the Rupununy below the falls 85°., above the same, 84°.F. at 2h. p.m. in the air 86°.5, the water 88°. the bulb applied to the Surface of the granitic Rocks, (coated with Oxide of Manganeese) 98°.5. ditto burried in the Sand along shore, 115°. At 6h. p.m. 83°. the Water 84.5.

December 3rd. – 6h. a.m. 72°. the Water 78°.

The river continues its North-Western course for a few miles more, and meeting the Saeraerie Mountains, turns suddenly to the North-east,+

+A path is said to lead from here, to the River Tokoto, which River (according to Humboldt) is reached in a three day's journey; I do not know whether it is the same which Dr. Hancock chose, when travelling from the Branco to the Quitaro.[1]

forming thus its most Western point, and flows towards its recipient, the Essequibo; the plane inclines to the North-East, as the upper Rupununy, according to its Situation would appear to belong to the basin of the Rio Branco. The Saerarie Mountains but a few miles distant from the banks of the Rupununy, rise solitary at the Savannahs, to a hight of about 2,500 feet – undulating hills stretch from there, certainly not in an uninterupted line, to the Southern angle of the Sierre Conocou.

The Rupununy forces its way through the chain of Mountains, which the Brazilians call collectively Sierra Conocou; though the Mountains which are thus named by the Indians, form only a part of the Chain which according to their Testimony, consist of

[1] This is the journey that Dr John Hancock and two companions made in 1810 to assess the strength of the Amerindians in the interior.

four chief Divisions, named Mapure, Conocoo, Tourou and Mapara; They are well wooded, and inhabited by a large tribe of Indians which call themselves Warpeshanas or Mapeshanas. The base of these Mountains is granitic and numerous dykes obstruct the river's course.[1]

We travelled at a period, where the river was at its minimum flow of Water, (December) and Sand-banks, formed by an accumulation during the time of the periodical rain so rendered our progress difficult, that even the smallest Corial could not float, and we would have found it easier, could we have walked, with occasional wading from Sandbank to Sand-bank. In one situation opposite the Mapure Mountains, the flowing water was contracted to six feet width, with scarcely a foot depth; the sand I have no doubt having engulphed the principal part of the water, which a little further North, without receiving visibly any additional Water, widens again considerably.

At the point where the Mountains approach the river from both sides (in 3°N. L) its bed is about 130 yards wide, it preserves the same width through the whole Mountain-chain, and even after having freed itself from the fetters of the Mountains, it does not increase in breadth. At its issue it turns once more to the North, and meeting in 3°.29 Lat. a granite Dyke, forms the Rapids of Curowotako. They may be considered the Key to the Country of the Warpeshanas; the first settlement of that tribe is to be found a little above the Cataract, on the river's right shore. After the Rupununy has received the Waters of the Brook Waaecourou[2] (the Tavicourou and Tauricuru of the Maps) it turns near the Inlet Weyipoucari to the N.E.

The inlet Weyipoucari, in Lat. 3°.38'14"N., is the Haven of the 'Imperial and golden City of Manoa', a path leads from here to the Macoosie village Pirara on the margin of the Amucu, 'the great Lake with auriferous banks.'[3] The distance, the sinuosities of the path included, is about 11 Miles, leading in the commencement over undulating ground, sparely wooded, and covered with short grass; it traverses then several Eta-Swamps, and at the foot of a small elevation, of scarcely more than 30 feet, flows the brook Pirarara, which must be crossed, before the Village of the same name can be reached. The brook, before it mingles its waters with the Lake Amucu, is scarcely more than 3 yards wide; that famous lake, the nucleus of the Parima or White Sea stretches E and W, and was at the time we visited it, in December and January, scarcely a league long, and almost covered with Rushes, showing only from time to time, sheets of water. Where the Pirarara issues from it (W.N.W. from the Village) it has considerably gained in breadth and depth; and meandring through the Savannah, it joins lastly the river Maou or Mahou.

[1] The manuscript is out of order at this point. The six misplaced pages are to be found at the end of the Memoir. The first four pages are numbered 27–30, although they are pp. 5–8 of the Memoir. The last two pages are also out of order; the penultimate is numbered 10 and the last, although unnumbered, is clearly p. 9. Much of the material contained in these pages was incorporated in the published version of the first expedition. In this transcription, all these pages have here been returned to their original place.

[2] Although not marked on the reference map, this is almost certainly the creek known today as Awarikuru.

[3] This phrase and the previous words in quotation marks are taken from Humboldt's *Personal Narrative of Travels to the Equinoctial Regions of the New Continent during 1799–1804*, transl. by Helen Maria Williams, 7 vols, London, Longman, Hursts, Rees, Orme and Brown; J. Murray; and H. Colburn, 1814–29. Humboldt's discussion of the myth of El Dorado appears in Volume 5, Part 2, pp. 773–99 of this edition, and the particular phrase on p. 783.

According to the information which I collected, the latter river has its sources on the Northern side of the Pacarayma-Mountains, on a table land, and forms a fine Cataract, called the Corona. We were on our way to visit it, when my Companion de Voyage, Lieut.t. Haining (of the 65th. Regt.) became, on the third day of our journey, so unwell, that we were obliged to relinquish our purpose and return to the Village.

While journeying thither, we had to cross the brook Pirarara three times, which only after having turned to all the Cardinal points of the Compass, joins the Maou.

The latter river has waters of a Coffee-brown colour, and in its current is more rapid than the Rupununy. Among the Mountains, between which it has forced its course, it is about 60 yards wide, and its Valley forms a peculiar Mountain-scenery, not void of the picturesque, but by no means fertile; It is inhabited by Macoosies. In the month of April the Savannahs are inundated, and present then the peculiar feature that the Waters of two Rivers belonging to two systems, are commingled, and the extent to which the inundation amounts, has given rise to the fable of the Lake Parime.

During this period, an inland-navigation, entirely by Water, may be carried on between Demerara and Para. Several groups of trees, which during the dry season, rise like oases out of the Savannah, form during the inundation small islands; two of those groups are not far from the borders of the lake, which doubtless are the 'Islas Ipomucena' described by Don Antonio Santos.[1] The groups or Islets consist of accumulated sand, mixed with vegetable earth; the drift matter of the Currents during the inundation.

The soil being richer than the surrounding arid Savannahs, some seeds may have sprung up; they survived the first overflowings and became able to withstand the force of the Currents, and assisted to a larger accumulation of detritus and seeds. These hillocks scarcely raised more than 10 to 12 feet above the Savannah, have its peculiar Flora: the Inga unquis cati,[2] several Cassiae, large Cacti which raise their limbs like gigantic Candelabras and a species of night-blooming Cereus,[3] interlacing the trees, formed the chief features. At one of these Oases we found several Cashew-trees, in full bearing (Anacardium occidentale) a most welcome discovery where the water is scarce, and has a pernicious influence besides on the constitution.

The Cana Pirarara has its source one mile east of the Village, and within two miles of a branch of the Waaecourou,*

*The Waaecourou is generally called Tavaricourou in the late Maps, but the first is the name which is given to this Brook by the Inhabitants of its banks; the Rupununy is called Rupunuwini, Rupunury, Reponoony; the Macoosies call it as stated by me; the Caribees, Opununy, as they find it difficult to pronounce the R.

a tributary of the Rupununy and ultimately of the Essequibo, while the waters of the former flow into the rivers Maou, Tokoto, Branco, Negro and lastly into the Amazon.

---

[1] Don Antonio Santos was a Spanish soldier who in 1775–80 travelled from Angostura on the Orinoco to the Rio Branco by way of the Caroni River. Humboldt makes frequent reference to him and stated that he had acquired the the manuscript journal of Don Nicolas Rodriguez who had accompanied Santos. The present whereabouts of this manuscript has not been traced. Santos and Rodriguez were members of the expedition sent by the governor of Angostura, Don Manuel Centurión, in 1775 to explore the upper reaches of the Rio Branco. There was a rapid response to this incursion on the part of the Portuguese who captured all its members.

[2] *Pithecolobium unguis-cati.*

[3] The genus *Cereus* belongs to the Family Cactaceae.

The plains between the Branco and Rupununy have their valleys and alternate slopes, the line of elevation being a few miles east of the Village Pirarara; and thus the division of the two basins is formed.

When we passed the Waaecourou in December, its mouth was almost choked with sand, and only a rill of water, scarcely a yard in width found its way to its recipient; but, during the rainy season, this brook affords the readiest means to reach Pirarara by boating. The site of the Macoosie Village is in 3°·33′50″N. Lat., and according to my Chronometer, 16′45″ West of Annay, or 58°·53′ West of Greenwich. The Northeasterly wind blows here with immense force, and we found the Thermometer in the morning of the 26th December as low as 66°· Fahr.[1]

A number of Thermometical Observations gives as means

before Sunrise*	at 8.h. A.M.	2.h. P.M.	6.h. P.M.
67°.3	75°.9	84°	80°.3

> *I have constantly observed that the Thermometer stands lowest half an hour before sunrise, thus at 5.h. A.M. it was generally ½ to 1 degree higher than at the period stated above, from whence it commenced gradually to rise. While at the Settlement of the Warpeshanas at the Conocou Mountains, 2500 feet above the Rupununy, the Thermometer stood on the 25th, 26 & 27th December 1835, –
>
> | before Sunrise | 8.h AM | 3.h PM | 6.h.PM. |
> |---|---|---|---|
> | 63°.5 | 78°.5 | 80° | 69° |
> | 63 | | 81. | 68.5. |

For several Thermometical observations, see the Apendix.[2]

The width of the Rupununy in the neighbourhood of the Inlet Weyipouccari is about 100 yards, its banks a reddish clay, sparely covered with mould or vegetable earth, and the bed in December and January so shallow that we were often obliged to drag the Corial over the sand. The river runs East, and receiving the brook Simmony in 3°·41′30N. Lat. it takes a northerly course, forming its most Northern point near the Mount Sawacko-Toonally; (in 3°·53′) it meanders from thence, for a few miles south, and takes afterwards, an eastern direction through the Savannahs which skirt its banks, and is joined in 3°·52′33″N. Lat. by the brook Annay, which has its rise on the Savannah, not far from the Mountain Annay. N.52°W., Distant 5½ Miles from its mouth, is the Caribee Settlement Annay, the Longt. of which was determined by a series of Luna Observations, and was found to be in 58°·36′15″ West of Greenwich and in 3°·56′1″ Lat. N.

I attach some importance to these observations, as according to the treaty of Utrecht (?)[3] the boundry line between now British Guiana, Columbia and Brazilian Guiana, meets at the most Northern point of the Rupununy and the Eastern Spur of the Pacarayma Mountains. The Pacarayma Mountains divide literally the Savannahs from the thick Forest of Guiana. The Savannahs here are covered with a short grass and sometimes even bare of all vegetation; indeed they afford a real picture of infertility; the trees which at intervals may be observed are stunted and what

---

[1] It is not clear to where Schomburgk is referring. On 26 December Schomburgk was in the Kanuku Mountains. See pp. 70–71 and Schomburgk's next footnote.

[2] No appendix has been found.

[3] The question mark is in the original. The Treaty of Utrecht (1713) concluded the War of the Spanish Succession, and confirmed Spain's Latin American territories to be as they were before the outbreak of the war.

may be called comparatively productive soil, is only to be found at the foot of the Mountains. The Indians are nevertheless obliged to change their fields after a few years' crops, as the Soil is soon exhausted.

The Deer is much more scarce here than at the Savannahs of Pirarara and Conocou, and though the plains of Annay are connected with those of Piarara, where numerous wild Cattle*

*These numerous herds of Cattle and Horses descend from several Brazilian Government cattle-farms, while the cattle during the public disturbances were allowed to go wild and have now increased in such such a manner that often hundreds may be counted grazing in company.

are to be found, none have[1] ever been seen to graze at Annay.+

+The Mount Annay has received its name from Maize (Annay in the Macoosie language) which was said to have been found here wild.

The brook Curassawaak joins from the South; we were here encamped at a Caribee Settlement about two miles South from the river in 3°.48′29″N. Lat.: the banks of that brook were formerly thickly peopled with Macoosies, and Caribees of which at present only one Settlement exists and that approaches rapidly to decay.

The river Rewa joins the Rupununy (approximate) in Lat. 3°.51′20″N. and Longt. 58°.25′40″W.

In laying down the river and its tributary the Quitaro, I have been obliged to rely entirely upon Indian information and a series of angles which I took on high elevations; it is sparely inhabited, but much frequented by the Indians who dwell at the Savannahs of the Pacarayma during the Season of the Turtle eggs, which are found on its Sandbanks in large quantities. The river Quitaro is famed for a mass of Granite which rises to a height of more than 700 feet, and forms a natural Pyramid; it is called Ataripoor[2] or Devils rock, and was pointed out to us when at the Conocou, bearing from their Southern Spur E.N.E. distant about 55 Miles.

These Mountains are well wooded and on their southern acclivities, I saw numerous walls of granite. The Inlet Aroumok extends to the foot of the higher hills.[*][3]

[*]The atmosphere was in the afternoon, thick, and the distance from the Mountains about 22 Miles; I do not therefore depend much on my own Observations, according to which the Peak was only 2700 feet high but I am almost certain, from comparison with other Mountains, the heights of which is accurately known, that it is not higher than 3000 feet.

The Rupununy joins ultimately the Essequibo in 3°.57′42″N. Lat. and 58°.3′W. Longt. as deduced from my observations at Annay, and is almost in the same meridian with its sources, describing in its course a semicircle. Numerous inlets or Kirahaghs, as they are called, and which are thus stocked with fish as to form literally natural reservoirs of the finny tribe, are an other peculiarity; though the Essequibo is not void of

[1] The unpaginated p. 9 of the Memoir, and the last page in the manuscript as currently ordered, starts here. The penultimate page of the Memoir, paginated p. 10, follows it.

[2] Ataraipu, but Kalishadaker on the reference map.

[3] There is on this page a footnote for which there is no corresponding indicator in the text. This seems an appropriate place for it, although it is not clear to what mountains or to which peak Schomburgk is referring, possibly Ataraipu.

them, they are by no means so numerous and extensive. What may have caused these inlets, is a riddle to me; if they were in the direction of the Current it might be explainable; but they are mostly against the Current, and the uninterrupted line of the River's banks, prevents my supposing them to be old beds; the only likelyhood is, that they have been formed during the inundations. They are at their mouth often wider than the river itself, and a stranger may easily suppose the Inlet to be a continuation of the River, if the currentless motion of the water does not prevent him from making the mistake.

The banks of the Rupunoony, with only a few exceptions, are as sterile as the adjacent Savannahs, they consist of an ochrous clay, and it appears that even the annual inundations do not better them. Before I left Demerara my attention was directed to the circumstances that wherever two Rivers, one of black, and the other of white Waters were found to join, the black water would be from one to two degrees warmer than the white water.

When at the Post Cayuni, I made the first experiment and repeated the same at the Rupununy.

September, 25th 1835
Temperature of the

Air	the black waters of the	the white Waters
7h A.M. 79°.	River Mazaroony – 84°.	of the river Cayuni – 83°.

October, 22d 1835

	The black Waters of the River Essequebo	The white Waters of the River Rupununy
6h. A.M. 75°.	82°.	80°.5
6 P.M. 80.	83°.	81°.

The different colour of water of these Rivers, makes at their[1] junction a perceptible division, and the bulb was put into the respective Waters about 30 Yards from the line.

I transport now the reader from the mouth of the Rupununy, at once to one of the most interesting Scenes I witnessed during my late Expedition. I allude to the great Cataract of the Essequibo, in 3°.14′35″N. Lat. and 57°43′ approximately W. Long[t], which, as its name was unknown to the Indians of the Savannahs, and those who accompanied me, I called King William's Cataract, in honour of His Majesty, the Patron of the Royal Geographical Society. The Scene is entirely Alpine; numerous conical hills, though of inconsiderable height, rising scarcely more than 300 feet above the river, composed of walls of Granite of a recent formation, narrow the Essequebo so much that the distance from bank to bank, is within 150 feet – the fall of the River in a distance of about 50 feet, amounting to not less than 25 feet. The mountains which form the Cataract belong to those of Taripona, their greatest hight where they gird the Essequibo, is 500 feet, being North of the Cataract. What contributes to embellish the Scenery, is the beautiful luxuriant Verdure, and the Vegetation with which the hills are clothed, leaving bare of trees only their summits, covered with a long grass. One mile

---

[1] The manuscript reverts at this point (p. 11) to its correct order.

N.28°E of the Cataract, I had a satisfactory Observation of Canopus, from which I deduced its geographical position.

The difference of the Vegetation between the banks of the Essequibo and the Rupununy is great indeed; if I except the Conocou-Mountains, the trees which skirted the banks of the latter river are smaller and less vivid in their colours; Greenheart,[1] one of the finest Timber-trees which Guiana possesses, has entirely vanished on the Rupununy, while we found it on the Essequibo as high as we ascended. Mora-trees as majestic in their growth as north of the Confluence of the Rupununy, give likewise here to the vegetable Walls of the river's banks, a peculiar feature, and the costly Letterwood,[2] the Bourra-Courra of the Indians, the Houcouya, or Ironwood,[3] the Crabwood[4] &c, all were found when penetrating a short distance from the river. Seven miles north from the great Cataract, numerous Dykes oppose themselves anew to the river's course, and though their perpendicular height is but a few feet, the numerous Islands and shelves through which the river has to path itself a way, form by their currents and counter currents, several Whirlpools: the Water itself dark from nature, by the resistance which it finds in its progress, presents now a sheet of foam, forming a strong contrast to the gloomy tint of the Rocks, coated by an Oxide of Manganeese. We called these Cataracts after Sir George Murray, who occupied the Presidential Chair of the Royal Geographical Society, when the plan of the present Expedition was finally determined upon. North of these Cataracts, hillocks approach from the West to the river's left bank, and undulating ground turns its course in 3°.30′ for a while to the West. In 3°.27′30″ the Essequibo receives from the West, its largest tributary south of the Rupununy; the Indians could not tell me its name, and I had thus an opportunity of calling it after His Excellency, Sir James Carmichael Smyth, who has taken the liveliest interest in the Expedition.

The Essequibo was here about 250 Yards wide. A large Island, called Paumbo, is crossed by several granitic Dykes, and a series of Rapids are formed in consequence. The Inlet Primoss in 3°18′N. Lat. is famed among the Indians, as there having led from here a path to the rivers Demerara Berbice and Courantine. From the information which I was able to collect, the path conducts in a N.E. direction in somewhat more than a day's march to the Demerara, which is here so small, that it can not be navigated, and its source was described to me, as being about 12 miles further South, and having its rise in a swampy bush of Wallaba (Dimorpha & Panzera).

Somewhat more than half way between the Essequibo and Demerara, the Brook Tokoto, which is a tributary to the first named river, must be crossed. The Inlet Primrose extends about 1½ Miles South. On its mouth there was formerly an Indian Settlement, the traces of which we still discovered. Numerous Cocao-trees, & a few Lime-trees appeared to thrive well in their wild state. The river is about 400 yards wide, and continues its Northern course, until it turns a little north of the Rock Toumounae in 3°.57′N. Lat. to the west, which direction it pursues to its junction with the Rupununy.

On the first glance, the Rupununy might be considered the continuation of the lower Essequibo, but the same features, the same vegetation peculiar to the lower Essequibo

---

[1] *Ocotea rodiaei.*

[2] *Brosimum guianensis.*

[3] *Dialium guianense; Mouriri huberi; M. sideroxylon; Swartzia leiocalycina; Tabebuia capitata; T. serratifolia.*

[4] *Carapa guianensis.*

are still to be met in the upper branch, while not only the colour, but likewise the aspect changes as soon as the Rupununy is entered. The upper Essequibo is besides this, more in the general direction of the lower and though its western course before it is joined by the Rupununy, causes a bend at a sharp angle, the latter river shows that the general slope of the ground, has an inclination from West to East. The Essequibo above the junction is wider than the Rupununy, where it joins; the opinion entertained by some of the Colonists that it is the upper Essequibo, may therefore be easily controverted on the above grounds.

The River resumes its Northern course, and presents for many miles one branch of about 500 yards breadth; the Banks are 12 to 15 feet high, and consist of a clear white clay, clothed to the Water's edge with Majestic trees. The river has here but little current. The Brook Tokootou enters from the East; it is the brook which must be crossed when going from Primoss to the Demerara river; about three miles further North, the river divides in two branches, the trunk continuing North-west, while the other forms the Channel, Youkoupato; on the main branch there is an Inlet of some extent and breadth called Tokoto or Arouan Inlet; it has been represented as a river, which it is not according to the information I gathered; it lay still and currentless, like an inland Lake. The Channel Youkoupato re-joins the river a short distance from the Inlet; here, commences the Rapids of Rappoo, which have received their name from a large quantity of Bamboo (Nastus latifolia)[1] that grows in their Vacinity.

Large blocks of granite, and bare shelves of the same substance, however apparently going over into Gneiss are the prevailing formation over which the river rolled turbulently its Waters. I did not observe the black coating, nor had the Rocks that vitrified appearance, of which I purpose to speak when reaching the other Cataracts.

The rocks of Achra-moucrou present a very interesting Scenery; enormous blocks of Granite from 30 to 40 feet high, and 10 to 15 in diameter obstruct the river's course for several miles; they are often piled together and crowned with numerous orchideous plants, pine-apples, small shrubs and a few stunted trees, and form a labyrinth of rocks and islands, with which one must be well acquainted, to find an outlet; the current between some of them was found to run 8 feet in a second. These Rocks have apparently a W.N.W. and E.S.E. direction, and are perceived to extend far from the Shore.

The depth in the intervening Channels was found 80 to 90 feet, a great difference with the shallowness of the river above and below the Scene where it amounted to only 12 feet. Many of the boulders are black and glossy.

A natural Channel called Amatopo, or, the great eastern Channel, less impeded by the rocks, dykes & boulders, is generally made use of in descending the Essequibo – it joins the main branch again a little above the Maccary Mountains, where the river becomes comparatively free of Islands, and may be from bank to bank, about 1400 Yards wide. The Maccary Mountains in 4°28N. Lat. approach the river on its eastern shore, they are steep rugged and sparely Wooded, but they form by no means the extensive chain which they represent in older Maps. The inclination of the highest peak was 60°; it resembled the Gable-end of a gigantic Building.

[1] *Bambusa latifolia*, but not a species reported from Guiana.
[2] Kuratoka Falls.

The falls of Korotoko[2] or golden falls, (called Carncoony-malally, by the Indians) in 4°25'47"N. Lat. consists of a series of rapids, not of a high perpendicular descent, but tedious in overcoming the difficulties, which they oppose: more formidable is a large Dyke a few miles further north, where the Canoes in descending are generally unloaded, and the packages carried across a small island to smoother water. It is called Ouropocary and there was formerly a Dutch Post here.

The Tambicabo Islands divide the river into two main branches; about 5 miles above the mouth of the Siperonie and on the western branch, there stood formerly the Dutch Post Arinda. The Tambicabo Islands, though of no great width, extend nevertheless 7 to 8 miles South, and are famed as the rendezvous for numerous River-turtle, which deposit their eggs into the vast Sandbanks.

The river Siperonie enters from the West; the union of the two rivers presents an interesting aspect; the Essequibo is nearly a Mile wide, skirted on both sides by a thick Forest, and as there was not much current, I felt disposed to consider it a Lake. The Siperonie has received its name from its Waters resembling the colour which is obtained from the bark of the tree Maparakuni, it is a brownish red. The river is, at its mouth, about 100 yards wide, its banks are fertile, and fine Timber-trees from 60 to 80 feet high, were numerous: at a mile and half from its mouth it is impeded by a large Cataract. It is joined in 4°42'20N. Lat. by the Bourre-bourre, likewise of red waters and equal in size to the Siperonie; both rivers, we were told (while at Piarara) have their sources on the northern acclivities of the Pacarayma Mountains. Our Indians were entirely unacquainted with regard to the Volcanic Mountain which figures already at the Sources of the Siperonie in the Caart van Guiana by Hartsinck,*

*See Beschryving van Guiana of de Wildekust in Zuid-America, door Ian Jacob Hartsinck. Amsterdam 1770. Vol 1 s.l.

nor could I hear any thing of its existence from the Macoosies at Pirarara.[1]

From the Inlet Ortuahar a path is said to lead to the River Demerara, in a North-eastern direction, and meets that river above the great Falls; it is however not much frequented by the Indians.

The brook Mourawa or Murya waters the southern foot of the Commoutie Mountains, and falls into the river opposite the rapid of Cooribiru.

The Mountains of Commoutie, by which name they are much more known than by that of Taquira have received their name from a pile of large granitic boulders, which resemble a Water-jar, called Commoutie by the Arrawaaks, and Taquiara by the Caribees.

They are in 4°52'30"N. Lat. and form with the Akaywanna Mountains, and those of Twasinkie a perfect Amphitheatre, famed for three Cataracts, namely, Elaboo, Cumaka-toto or Eucourite (in 4°58'30") and Apoucouyahaa.

These Mountains, the highest peak of which is about 900 feet, are well wooded, but scantily inhabited by a few Macoosies. A path leads by the brook Akaywanna to the Accaway Settlements above the great falls of the Demerara river. The river is so studded

[1] As Schomburgk states, J. J. Hartsinck, *Beschryving van Guiana of de Wildekust in Zuid-America*, 2 vols, Amsterdam, Gerrit Tielenburg, 1770, I, p. 265–6 (see also Map 1), refers to the existence of a volcano about forty miles up the Siparuni which had been discovered in 1749. It is not clear who discovered it, but presumably it was based on misunderstood hearsay, as certainly no volcano exists in the region nor anywhere in Guiana.

with Islands, that its banks are entirely unseen; this Islets show generally a luxuriant growth of trees and their banks are almost concealed by under-brush.

The Mountains on the East seemed to retire further back, but on the West shore they appeared to be connected with those of the Warapoota. The Scene at the head of the Cataract is very singular, and resembles most the rocks of Achra Moucra, it is however not so grand; the rocks are granite, passing into Gneiss, and have several circular holes filled with small pebbles.

The Cataract of Warapoota is formed by the resistance which the river finds in its course from a ridge of Mountains and Dykes that extend to the Demerara river, and form the Ororoo Malally[1] or great falls.

At the foot of the greater Cataract at Warapoota there are a number of pointed rocks. From the brook Warapoota leads a path in a N.E. direction to the Post Seba, but though the direct distance between Warapoota and the most western point of the Demerara river is within 9 miles, the Indians have to march more than a day before they reach the river, and nearly two before they meet the Post; a shorter path leads from the brook Yaya to Seba.

The Couranoucou Mountains about 1200 feet high and very rugged of appearance, extend between the river Potaro and the Essequibo; where these Mountains approach the latter river, the scene is extremely picturesque. A Dyke crosses the river in a S.W. and N.E. direction; it has at the distance, the deceiving appearance of a dry Stone Wall – it consisted of trappean rocks, thrown over each other in the greatest confusion, and covered with a thick crust of Manganeese; the Dykes which form the Rapids of Acra and Cumaka are of a similar structure. The Potaro enters from the South-West in 5°19 N. Lat., it has black Waters, as its name signifies, and is much impeded by rapids & Cataracts.

The first impediment, when ascending the river, is thrown in the way about 5 Miles from its Mouth; and is said to be a Cataract of such force that it proves a difficulty to bring even a small Corial over.[2] Its course is mostly North-easterly from its sources, which I was told were in a chain of Mountains in which rock crystals abound; its banks are inhabited by Accaways, who keep up a communication with those of the Maza-roony, by a short portage between two brooks, the tributaries of the respective rivers.

After the junction of the Potaro with the Essequibo the latter river receives the Colour of the Water, which it has before it is joined with the Rupununy; it takes now an eastern direction and the Dykes and rocks which we met, were more homogenous than at Warapoota. While we ascended the Essequibo the rocks at the brook Cumpara struck us first, in consequence of their coating, we observed it hereafter at Warapoota, Ouropocary, Korotoko, Achra-Moucra, King William's Cataract, &c. It is not peculiar only to the Granite, but we found it likewise upon Trappean rocks, which indeed, have a much more glassy appearance; and strange to say, the pebbles which cover the Savan-nahs of Pirarara and Annay, present the same peculiarity. Oxide of Manganeese is found in various places and collected by the Indians.*

*I had among my Geological collections (lost at the Cataract of Etabally) several tubes of Bamboo filled with the Oxide of Manganeese, which the Indians use for painting their

[1] Ororo Marali or Malali Falls.
[2] This seems too close to the Essequibo for it to be a reference to the Kaietur Falls, but it is noticeable that Schomburgk, even if he heard mention of them, nowhere alludes to them.

Skin. The pebbles above alluded to, are often brought to the Colony and eagerly sought after by Grooms, to clean the Steel-work on their Horses' bridles.

But it is not every Species of rock which possesses the affinities of attaching the crust when in chemical solution, nor is it peculiar to either the white or black waters; the rocks in the vicinity of King William's Cataract were as much coated as the Karinampo rocks at the Rupununy.

The Arissaro Mountains are the first of consequence south of the Mouth of the Essequebo; we found their greatest height 640 feet above the river – they extend E & W, and are connected with those at Post Seba at the Demerara river. A much frequented path leads from the brook Moucou-Moucou and Cortuaharo to Post Seba, Baywadan and Astfic island: it is generally walked in a day, and will be of much importance when Colonization extends further inland. The ligne de faite[1] runs parallel with the two rivers but the slope is more towards the Essequibo than the Demerara, nevertheless, a connecting Canal between the brooks Cortuaharo and Coreta would meet the Demerara river somewhat above Lucky-Spot, where a square-rigged Vessel has been known to load. The dangerous falls of Etaballly are thus avoided, and the Demerara river north of Lucky Spot offers no impediment for navigation. The Brook Moucou-Moucou is in 5°57′ – the Cortuharo somewhat more than a Mile further North.

The river is near Cortuaharo 1523 yards wide and preserves this width, until it is joined by the Brook Tipoorie; the Essequibo forms an inlet in which that Brook flows, having its source South of some Hillocks, which were pointed out to us.

N.E. from the mouth of the Inlet, is the southern point of Gluck or Great Island, called by the Carribees Aramisarey-Youpacou. It has received its name from a small species of Tiger-Cat, which was found formerly in large numbers on that Island. At its Northern end commence a new series of Cataracts, of which Etaballly is the largest: they are formed by a passage of a chain of Hillocks, scarcely 200 feet high. They present the same formation as the Cataracts further South, but I did not observe any Oxide on their surface. At Cumaka Sirama the river is narrowed in, and as it is the last Settlement below the Falls, and the Granite region commences here, it may be considered the ultima Tule of the Colonists. It has received its name from the Silk-Cotton tree, called in Arrawaak "Cumaka", and from "Serima" point, the Dutch called it Farlight. Small Schooners have thus far navigated the River. The river widens below Cumaka Serima to about 1800 yards; but a small chain of Hillocks narrow it, so that it is scarcely more than 250 feet across; here was formerly an Estate called Osterbooke, from which the Point received its name; the inhabitants of the region call it "Monkey's Waist". The view from the hills is the most picturesque of the lower Essequibo.

As soon as the Essequibo has released itself from the fetters of the Hillocks, it widens to its former extent and continues its Northern direction to P^t. Saccharo, where it turns to the West, until it receives the united Rivers, Mazaroony and Cayuni, turning then anew to the north. The point of confluence of the three rivers is called Barteka, where there is at present a Mission of the London Society, for the conversion of Indians, which, I am happy to say, has already made some progress. The astronomical determination of this Point, would be of geographical interest, but the unfavourable weather

---

[1] The watershed.

111

prevented me from effecting it; the rains being incessant at this point, both while ascending and descending the River.

The site of the Post has been changed to Ampa on the Eastern shore of the Essequibo.

The joined Waters of the Mazaroony and Cuyuni give at their confluence, an other tint to the Essequibo, which thus changes the colour of its water four times. At William's Cataract it has a dark brownish tint, which becomes much lighter after having received the Rupununy and further north the redish waters of the Siperonie.

The Potaro river restores its first tint which it preserves until it is joined by the Mazaroony and Cayuni, where it has the appearance of the water north of the Rupununy.

It was not my plan to investigate the River, further north than to its junction with the Mazaroony and Cayuni, besides this, the weather was in September 1835, and March 1836, of that nature, that often weeks elapsed without any of the heavenly bodies being visible. I have partly adopted therefore Major von Bouchenroeder's[1] survey of that part corrected by the best information I could procure.*

> *Since writing the above I have persuaded myself that the above survey of the lower Essequibo is not quite correct; I have changed it therefore and have laid down that part according to the best information I was able to procure, guided by a M.S. map of Capt. Kennedy's[2] of H.M. Steamer Spitfire.

I thought that it might prove of interest to be able to make comparisons between the Rivers Essequibo and Demerara on the East, and Mazaroony to the West, and while I have to place the positions and course of the Demerara to the credit of an inspection of Capt[n] Owen's[3] beautiful survey, which was kindly lent to me by His Excellency, Sir James Carmichael Smyth, I used M[r.] Hillhouse's Map of the Mazaroony, for the positions of that river, as far as it came in the field of my Map of the Essequibo. The Brazilian fort San Joaquim will be found further East than in any other Map; I have its Longitude taken from a Map, which is ascribed to D[r.] Hancock, and who, as I understand, deduced it from observations made with a good Chronometer.

---

[1] Major F. von Bouchenroeder. This is a reference to his 1798 map, 'Carte generale & particuliere de la Colonie d'Essequebo, & Demerarie située dans la Guiane, en Amerique redigée & dediée au Comité des Colonies & Possessions de la Republique Batave en Amerique, & a la Côte de Guinée'. The main map covers the coast from the Moruka River to the Abary River, the boundary with Berbice, and up the Essequibo, a little upstream of the junction with the Mazaruni and Cuyuni Rivers. The general map, which is an insert, covers the area from the Barima River (near the Orinoco Delta), marked as the boundary with the Spanish possessions, to the Berbice River, and inland as far as the junction of the Essequibo and Rupununi Rivers. The general map was also published separately in 1798. There is also an 1802 map by von Bouchenroeder, entitled 'Kaart van de Colonie de Berbice gelegen in Bat[e]. Guina in America tusschen de Colonien van Demerarie en van Surinamen'.

[2] Captain Andrew Kennedy RN. He was born in 1787 and entered the Royal Navy in 1808. He commanded the *Spitfire* in both the Mediterranean and West Indies in the 1830s. In this ship he demonstrated the ability of a steamer to resist the effects of a hurricane; something which had previously been doubted. The manuscript map to which Schomburgk refers has not been traced.

[3] Captain Richard Owen RN served in the Royal Navy from 1811 to 1837. As commander of the *Blossom* and later the *Thunder*, he was employed, from 1828 onwards, in surveying in the West Indies. The map of Demerara, to which Schomburgk refers, was surveyed in September and October 1833 and is to be found in the United Kingdom Hydrographic Office, Taunton (Shelfmark H766–70 TE).

As it regards my own observations, they were generally based upon the culmination of heavenly bodies, and a regular log, kept during our whole journey. The elements of the observations are in the possession of the Royal Geographical Society.

If I were asked 'is the country adjacent to the banks of the Rupununy favourable for Colonization?' I should unhesitating answer, No. Though the[1] landscape may please the eye, the soil consists mostly of arid sands, upon a clay sub-stratum, and is unproductive. Woods form only here and there, a fringe along the River, and its tributaries, and either disappear entirely, when retiring from the river's banks, or become quite stunted in growth. The only fertile soil is along the foot of Mountains, or on their ridges, but even here it is soon exhausted, and the Indians are obliged to change their Provision-grounds every three or four years. The Savannahs are mostly destitute of water, and where it is found it is but too frequently injurious to the constitution.*

*While we were encamped at Annay, in November 1835, we dug holes in the Savannahs, which were scantily filled with a whitish water, unpleasant of taste, and when exposed for some time to the Sun, we found it covered with a greenish Scum; we had to send therefore a distance of nearly 5 miles, to the brook Annay to get good water. Traversing the Savannahs of Pirarara, the heat of the Atmosphere caused almost an insupportable thirst, and we drank copiously of the brook Pirarara, and likewise of some pools – the consequence was that Dysentery to an alarming degree broke out; individually I was thus weakened in 24 hours, that the Indians were obliged to carry me in a Hammock from Piararara to the Rupunoony.

The Indians quench their thirst with Piwarie, for which purpose the water is boiled and loses perhaps its pernicious influence. The Grass which covers this arid Plain is diversified in its nature and not always fit for food for Cattle. The Savannahs of Annay produce thus grasses belonging to the Genus Elymus, Festuca, Cyperus,[2] and others; and are entirely unfit for grazing grounds; though these Savannahs are connected with those of Piarara, on which numerous herds of wild Cattle graze, none have ever been seen by the Indians about Annay.

The climate is by no means so healthy as it has been supposed. I do not infer from the circumstance that our whole party was more or less indisposed while sojourning in those regions, but the Indians themselves suffered from fever. We found whole families afflicted by fever, when we returned in January from the upper regions of the Rupununy. The Measles likewise committed great havock among these Aborigines, who, when covered with the disease, and warned by us not to expose themselves to cold, considered nevertheless the best remedy for allaying the insufferable heat was by plunging into the water. No family of those we visited but had to relate the loss of relations.

'What then' will be the question deduced from the above remarks, 'can have induced the Indians, those simple children of nature, to select such regions for their abode?' and often have I thus asked them myself without receiving a satisfactory answer. The love for the native soil may be the reason, which nevertheless is subjected to superstition; let

[1] The next two pages, numbered 17 and 18, are an editorial rewriting of pp. 17–20 of the Third Report, and have not been reproduced. The two after that, numbered 19 and 20, belong to the Second Report where its pp. 19–20 had been replaced by a version drafted by the editor. As noted in that place, these pages have been restored to their original position. Finally, pp. 41–3 of the Third Report are pp. 21–3 of the Memoir and are reproduced here, rather than there.

[2] The Genera Elymus and Festuca belong to the Family Gramineae, Cyperus to the Family Cyperaceae.

death have taken place among the more influential Members of the Settlement, and every individual will leave his hut – the fields may be ripe for Crop, or may just have been planted, nothing can conquer the fear that their further abode at that spot, is displeasing to Kanaima,[1] the arch-ennemy of the human race.

Nevertheless, the Savannahs may prove profitable to the enterprising Colonist. The herds of wild cattle and horses which graze on the Savannahs of the Rio Branco and its tributaries, the Tokoto and Maou, may be transported to the Colony of British Guiana, where ready purchasers will be found.

The Brazilian horse, though small, is swift and from youth accustomed to the tropics and hardships, [which] are great recommendations for the purchaser.

The best means of bringing them to the coast would be, to lead them across the Savannahs and Mountains to the foot of Makarapan; there are so far no difficulties to be surmounted – from thence it would be necessary to swim them across the Rupununy to its right shore, and swimming them for a second time across the Essequibo, from whence a path might be constructed to the vast Savannahs which extend between the rivers Demerara and Berbice.[2] The foot of the Makarapan Mountains might be reached from the Brazilian Fort, San Joaquim in eight days, without imposing much upon Men and horses. From the information I have gathered, I know that the plains between Berbice and Demerara are of great extent, but I am unable to point out the direction in which they will be most easily reached. On establishing such a communication, the Cattle, which are now sold at $6 to $8 per head, may prove likewise profitable to the Colony.

According to my opinion, the Regions south of the Islands at the Mouth of the Essequibo, to the second series of Cataracts, are the best calculated for colonization – the soil is divers and highly productive, the expenses connected with clearing the ground will be paid by the value of the Timber cut down. Barteka-point, at the confluence of the rivers will then become the nucleus of the Inland trade and Canals may connect it with the upper regions, while the latter by an intercourse with the Demerara river have the option to choose the Market for their productions.

My opinions thus advanced might have easily been proved by the Specimens of Soil which I collected from Barteka-Point to the Cartatan of the Rupununy, and King William's Cataract of the Essequibo; their loss at the falls of Etabally adds considerably to the regret I feel for my geological collections in general.

Robert H. Schomburgk

****

Back in Georgetown on 28 March, Schomburgk was upset by two letters from the Royal Geographical Society, of which unfortunately we have no copies. One

---

[1] A *kanaima* is a ritual killer found among the circum-Roraima Amerindians. For further discussion of *kanaima*, see Audrey Butt Colson, 'Itoto (Kanaima*) as Death and Anti-structure' in Laura M. Rival and Neil L. Whitehead, eds, *Beyond the Visible and the Material. The Amerindianization of Society in the Work of Peter Rivière*, Oxford, Oxford University Press, 2001, pp. 221–33; and Neil Whitehead, 'Kanaimà: Shamanism and Ritual Death in the Pakaraima Mountains, Guyana', ibid., pp. 235–45.

[2] The growth of ranching on the Rupununi savannahs in the second half of the 19th century led to the construction of a cattle trail which was first used in 1920. It crossed the Essequibo River at Kurupukari and the Demerara River at Canister Falls, and ended at Takama on the Berbice River, whence the cattle were shipped to the coast.

apparently contained Beaufort's criticism of Schomburgk's charts of Anegada and the Virgin Islands which, he complained, did not correspond. Schomburgk replied, regretting Beaufort's lack of goodwill, and tried to explain that although the charts were drawn on different principles, they did, in the main, correspond. Although he remained hurt by this criticism his confidence was bolstered when he heard that the survey ship *Lark* had checked the accuracy of Schomburgk's work and found that it did him 'infinite credit'.[1]

Another reason why Schomburgk was upset was because the letter had also contained the observation that 'there are others who doubt my [Schomburgk's] capacity of fully answering your [RGS's] expectations'. Who these 'others' are is by no means certain although Hilhouse is a possible candidate. Certainly the latter wrote immediately after Schomburgk's return from his first expedition, providing a solicited assessment of Schomburgk's performance which was not entirely favourable. Hilhouse stated that Schomburgk had left a month too late on his expedition and accordingly did not have enough time to complete the grand project of pursuing the Essequibo to its source. 'He has', wrote Hilhouse, 'been stopped he says by a fall of 20 feet! – 2000 feet would not have stopped me.' The expedition had not been sufficiently equipped, nothing new had been discovered geographically, although botanically much had been done. He added here that horticulturalists in Europe have no idea of the expense and trouble of making botanic collections in a region such as British Guiana. All-in-all, however, Hilhouse judges that Schomburgk had not acquitted himself badly on his first expedition and was competent to explore the *terra incognita* of central Guiana.[2] Hilhouse's judgement was not unfair and in many ways Schomburgk's first expedition cannot be rated a geographic success, although Schomburgk himself did so. The route via the Essequibo and Rupununi to Brazil was well travelled and had been by non-Amerindians for two hundred years, and despite what Indians might have said it is unlikely that the part of the Essequibo between the Rupununi mouth and King William's Falls was unknown, even if Schomburgk repeated his claim that it 'had never been visited by civilized person before'. The criticism of his failure to surmount the falls is perhaps unfair since it is not clear that his intention was to proceed any further. The important achievement was to have made the first accurate survey of these rivers and that part of the interior of the Colony. On the collecting front, the expedition did achieve something, and Schomburgk, when he described it as 'an entire blank', was referring to the financial rather than the scientific outcome. Collections were made and sent off to Europe and Schomburgk submitted papers to the Linnean and Geological Societies and the Society of Antiquaries.[3]

In the meantime Maconochie had resigned as Secretary of the Royal Geographical Society with effect from 1 June 1836 to become Secretary to Sir John Franklin, the

---

[1] RGS Corres 1834–40, Letters of Schomburgk to Maconochie, 15 April 1836, 20 April 1836.

[2] RGS Corres 1834–40, Letter of Schomburgk to Maconochie, 15 April 1836; Letter of Hilhouse to Maconochie, 12 April 1836.

[3] RGS Corres 1834–40, Letters of Schomburgk to Maconochie, 15 April 1836, 20 April 1836, 14 May 1836.

Governor of Tasmania, and had been replaced by Captain J. Washington RN[1] On learning this Schomburgk wrote to thank Maconochie for all he had done to help him but he is worried about who will look after his interests in future.[2] Washington, however, had already written to Schomburgk to tell him that he had taken over from Maconochie and to assure him that he was as keen as Maconochie to forward his success.[3]

Despite his resignation it is clear that Maconochie saw Hilhouse's letter of 12 April for he wrote to Washington about it on 1 July. 'I am extremely sorry that your accounts from Schomburgk are unfavourable – But I should be still more sorry if the Council were on that account to despair of his doing anything.' Lieutenant Barnet RN had checked his work on Anegada and found it 'very correct'; Captain Daniels spoke highly of him as did General Carmichael Smyth. Against these opinions you have an 'immediate want of success' and the views of Hilhouse, an 'ill-conditioned person' who was intolerant of anyone who disagreed with him.[4]

Schomburgk received in August a letter from Washington conveying the President's and Council's worry about the vagueness of his report and stating that the position that Schomburgk had given for King William's Fall did not put it on the Essequibo according to the existing maps. He also reminded Schomburgk that from the Society's point of view natural history collections are of secondary interest and these should be made only on return journeys after the geographical observations had been secured. Finally, he repeated yet again that the Royal Geographical Society would not provide more than the £900 originally offered.[5]

More hurtful for Schomburgk was to receive about the same time a letter from Maconochie, dated 15 July, which was also critical of his performance. While no copy of this letter has been found, Schomburgk's reaction to it in a letter to Washington gives some idea of its contents.

> After all the sacrifices, after all the exertions, and a severe shock to my constitution, I must read in Cap[t] Maconochie's letter 'On my return I learn with much concern that your late expedition has led to few satisfactory results !!' My conscience tells me that I have done my duty, it is acknowledged by the highest authority here, and when I expected that similar justice would have been done to me at home as an encouragement for approaching hardships every period in your letter expresses dissatisfaction without that one alludes to the particular point where I have failed.

In the same letter he also responded to some of the criticisms contained in Washington's letter of 2 July. He pointed out that to his financial detriment his botanical collecting had always come second and that he had put a lot of his own money into the first

---

[1] At the same time the practice of keeping a copy of outgoing letters was introduced, so that from now on we have both sides of most of the correspondence between Schomburgk and the Society.

[2] Schomburgk wrote to both Bentham and Hooker and expressed in agitated terms his concern at the loss of Maconochie's support within the Royal Geographical Society (RBGK, BC, Vol. IX, Letter of Schomburgk to Bentham, 28 June 1836; RBGK, DC, Vol. LXVII, Letter of Schomburgk to Hooker, 4 July 1836).

[3] RGS, Corres 1834–40, Letter of Schomburgk to Maconochie, 28 June 1836; RGS, Letter Book 1836–40, Letter of Washington to Schomburgk, 15 June 1836.

[4] RGS Corres 1834–40, Letter of Maconochie to Washington, 1 July 1836; Letter of Schomburgk to Washington, 20 August 1836.

[5] RGS Letter Book 1836–40, Letter of Washington to Schomburgk, 2 July 1836.

expedition as he would be into the second. He also confirmed that he was perfectly well aware that the Royal Geographical Society's funding was limited to £900 and had already agreed to this.[1] Washington in due course replied denying that his letters conveyed censure or implied that the first expedition had been a failure. They merely contained advice.[2]

---

[1] In fact Schomburgk was getting through his funds very rapidly. Within a year of arriving in the colony he had spent £715 of the £900 available (RGS Corres 1834–40, Letter of Schomburgk to Maconochie, 14 May 1836, see computations on back of this letter).

[2] RGS Corres 1834–40, Letter of Schomburgk to Washington, 20 August 1836; RGS Letter Book 1836–40, Letter of Washington to Schomburgk, 1 December 1836.

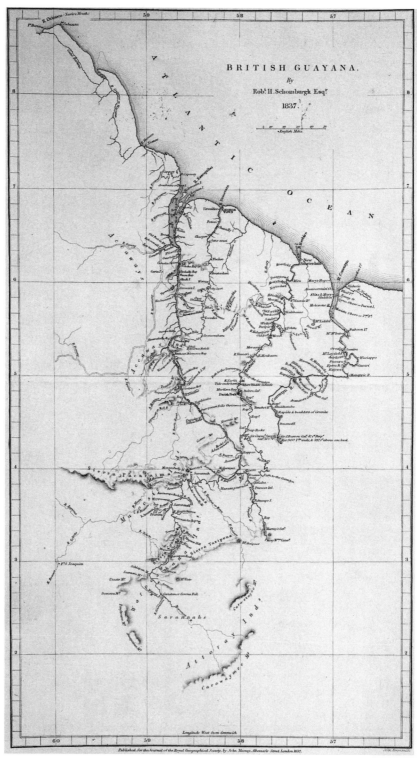

Map 2: 'British Guayana. By Rob^r. H. Schomburgk Esqr. 1837.' Proof copy, illustrating route of second expedition. Included by permission of the Royal Geographical Society, London.

CHAPTER 2

The Expeditions up the Rivers Corentyne and Berbice: 1836–1837

A period of ill health followed Schomburgk's return to Georgetown. In April he complained of rheumatic fever and stomach problems; in May he reported that an inflammation of the liver had left him unable to work for three weeks, and at the end of June that he had been so severely indisposed that he had been confined to his room for a further three weeks unable to read or write.[1]

When not ill, Schomburgk was busy preparing for his next expedition. The problem with this was where should he go. Schomburgk himself favoured the exploration of the Corentyne and he managed to obtain the Governor's support for this project. His plan was that it should get under way during the first week in September, but in the meantime he made a reconnaissance trip to Berbice where he learnt that little was known about the upper reaches of the Corentyne; some told him that a tribe of Amazons lived there and others that the river joined up with the Rio Negro.[2]

The Royal Geographical Society, on the other hand, was not so keen on the Corentyne expedition and refused to sanction it on the grounds that it did not fit with his instructions to explore the highlands between the Essequibo and the Amazon and then the divide between these rivers and the Orinoco. The exploration of the Corentyne, it claimed, was a minor objective as it had already been surveyed by the Dutch and was anyway probably of little interest as it rose and flowed through alluvial country. It is not difficult to trace the source of these objections as Hilhouse had written in almost exactly these words to the Society in April. Hilhouse, however, reserved his major criticisms for the Society and the Governor of British Guiana. The former, in Hilhouse's view, had made the mistake of allowing the latter to control Schomburgk's funds. The Governor, for his part, had sent Schomburgk to the Corentyne with 'more an eye to his own merit in dictating the journey of a boundary river – than to the general interests of scientific discovery'. Schomburgk for his part made, on 22 August, a strong defence of the proposed exploration; he rejected the claim that the river had been surveyed by the Dutch and that it flows through an alluvial plain. He argued that like the Essequibo and Rupununi the Corentyne rose in the Serra Acarai and its investigation was thus in accordance with his instructions.[3] Furthermore the plan had the

---

[1] RGS Corres 1834–40, Letters of Schomburgk to Maconochie, 20 April 1836, 14 May 1836, 28 June 1836.

[2] RGS Corres 1834–40, Letters of Schomburgk to Maconochie and Washington, 15 April 1836, 14 May 1836, 28 June 1836, 1 July 1836, 15 July 1836.

[3] Interestingly Maconochie was of the view that the exploration of the Corentyne was clearly within Schomburgk's original instructions whatever the opinion of Hilhouse (RGS Corres 1834–40, Letter of Maconochie to Washington, 1 July 1836).

approval of the Governor and if the Society continued to disagree would it please inform the Governor, but it would be pleasant to undertake the expedition, whatever its outcome, with the Society's approval. Schomburgk left for the Corentyne on 2 September and three months later (by which time the expedition was over) Washington wrote saying that the Council had not been able to sanction the expedition to the Corentyne when it had not been given reasons for it. Now the reasons were known it was satisfied.[1]

The manuscript of the report of the second expedition is held by the Royal Geographical Society as JMS 6/18. It is in three parts, (a), (b), and (c). Part (a) is the account of the expedition up the River Corentyne and Part (b) of that up the Berbice River. They were published consecutively, in abbreviated form, in Volume 7 (1837) of the *Journal of the Royal Geographical Society*.[2] Part (c), entitled 'Rough Notes on the Courantyne and Berbice Expedition 1837', was not published, but has been reproduced here as it contains a lot of additional interesting information, particularly of an ethnographic nature. Because, despite its title, it is exclusively about the Corentyne, it has been placed after the report on the Corentyne expedition.

Part (a) consists of thirty pages together with no fewer than five cover sheets, each dating from a different time. It is not in Schomburgk's handwriting, and there is some evidence to suggest that at least parts of it were dictated. On a concluding page it is wrongly stated that it is dated Berbice, 24 November 1836 (it is 25 November). It was received at the Royal Geographical Society on 8 February 1837 and read at a meeting on 13 February.

FIRST REPORT TO THE ROYAL GEOGRAPHICAL SOCIETY OF LONDON DURING THE SECOND EXPEDITION IN THE INTERIOR OF BRITISH GUIANA BY ROBERT H. SCHOMBURGK

Agreeable to a plan laid before His Excellency Sir James Carmichael Smyth, Lieu[t] Governor of British Guiana, the River Corentyne was selected for the field of my investigations during the season of 1836 & 37. The little knowledge which the Colonists had of this River and the Reports of those who had visited its lower regions occasionally, painted its adaptness for Colonization, in such favourable Colours, that a further examination appeared to be a desirable object. His Excellency had attracted previously my attention to this River, and my plan met therefore with his approval. Lieutenant Losack of the 69th Reg[t.] & Messrs Cameron & Reiss offered to accompany me as Volunteers; in order to be able to dedicate my attention uninterrupted to the chief object of the Expedition, I had engaged M[r] Vieth as Ornithologist and

---

[1] RGS Letter Book 1836–40, Letters of Washington to Schomburgk, 2 July 1836, 1 December 1836; RGS Corres 1834–40, Letters of Hilhouse to Washington, 12 April 1836, 10 October 1836; RGS Corres 1834–40, Letter of Schomburgk to Washington, 22 August 1836.

[2] See Schomburgk, 'Diary of an Ascent of the River Corentyn in British Guayana, in October, 1836', *JRGS*, 7, 1837, pp. 285–301, and 'Diary of an Ascent of the River Berbice in British Guayana, in 1836–37', ibid., pp. 302–50.

M[r] Heraut who accompanied me already during my former Expedition in similar capacity as draughtsman.[1]

We left Demerara on the 2[d] September in the Schooner the Lady D'Urban which I had chartered to take the Expedition to Berbice; so little is the Navigation of the Corentyne known, that I found it impossible to get a Conveyance direct for the Corentyne. I was therefore obliged to charter another Schooner in Berbice to convey us to Plantation Skeldon on the Western bank of the River Corentyne where we arrived on the 9th September and were received with every Kindness and Hospitality by the Proprietor M[r.] Ross. According to the arrangements I had made with the Post Holder M[r] de Wolff,[2] I expected to find a sufficient number of Indians at the Plantation Mary's hope to convey me to the Post. Mary's hope is situated on the mouth of the river; and as I was anxious to determine its Geographical position, I proceeded thither next Morning. I found to my regret only a few Indians of the Caribee tribe, and that number by no means sufficient to man the Corials. A Clouded Sky was unfavourable for my Astronomical observations and I succeeded only after the lapse of some days, according to which Mary's Hope was in Lat 5°58'51"N., and Long[t] 57°1'17"W.[3] The insufficient number of Indians obliged me to make this stay as I purposed to take advantage of an opportunity by a Schooner which was to proceed to the Post, meanwhile I despatched such of the Corials as could be manned. We arrived at the Post on the Morning of the 19th September; the Banks of the Corentyn are generally low, but uncommonly fertile and well calculated for the Cultivation of the Staple Commodities, at present they are almost uninhabited; with the exception of two Wood Cutting Establishments on the British side of the River no Inhabitants are to be traced from Plantation Skeldon to within a few miles of the Post. Whole tracts of the most fertile land are left uncultivated and are the sole and undisputed haunt of the Jaguar and the fleet Deer. It is not only the fertility of the Soil that recommends that tract for cultivation, the easy communication which might be established between the River Corentyne and Canje[4] is an object of the greatest consideration.

The Course of the River is almost due South in ascending, until, in the vicinity of the Post, it takes a somewhat Eastern bend, here the soil changes, and a chain of hillocks are observed on the Rivers left shore, which in consequence of their appearance have received the name of Chalk-hills. On one of these hillocks, the general height of which

[1] George Losack of the 69th or South Lincolnshire Regiment of Foot was promoted to Captain in 1846 and transferred to the 1st West India Regiment in the same year. He died serving with that regiment on the Cape Coast on 20 March 1848.

Cameron may be the Lewis Cameron referred to by Rodway, *History of British Guiana*, III, p. 174, as a woodcutter involved in searching for gold on the Demerara River around 1837.

We know very little about William Vieth other than that he was a resident of British Guiana and an ornithologist. Vieth also accompanied Schomburgk on his third expedition but died in December 1839, six months after returning from that expedition, from a snake bite received many years before (Schomburgk, *Fishes of Guiana*, I, 1841, p. 83).

Nor has anything been discovered about Charles Reiss other than that he drowned on the Berbice expedition (see p. 215).

[2] N. J. de Wolff. In 1843 he became Superintendent of Rivers and Creeks for the Corentyne. A journal of his is to be found in the National Archives of Guyana (Menezes, *British Policy Towards the Amerindians*, p. 114).

[3] In the published version (p. 286), the coordinates are given as 6°2'15"N., 57°1'47"W.

[4] The Canje River flows to the west of the Corentyne and almost parallel to it, joining the Berbice just below New Amsterdam.

may amount from 50 to 60 feet, is at present the site of the Post,[1] where we intended to sojourn for a few days in order to recruit a Crew sufficiently strong for manning our Corials. I found the greatest difficulties to effect this, sickness prevailed to an alarming degree among the Indian settlements, and a general dislike was shown to Venture on such an undertaking as the ascent of the Upper Corentyn, which according their superstition is believed to be inhabited by evil spirits, besides the apprehension of coming in contact with the Caribees, a nation dreaded by every other tribe, many an artifice was therefore necessary to induce them to enroll on our list.

There are several Settlements of Arawaaks and Warrows in the Vicinity of the Post, their whole number may amount to [400] souls;[2] like the generality of the Indians they cultivate provisions and live from hunting and fishing, while the most of their time is spent in the hammock. It is only lately they have commenced assisting Wood Cutters to fell timber or to split staves, for which they receive Monthly Wages or a stipulated sum for a certain quantity of staves or squared Timber. It is a pity that the Credulous Indian should be imposed upon by many of the unconscientious Woodcutters, who under value his Work, or pay him in articles with an enormous profit[;] if he discover hereafter that he has been imposed upon, his natural indolence finds a ready excuse for his return to the Hammock, and more injury is done to the Cause of Civilization than can be remedied by the promoters and Friends of such a desirable object. Would it not be possible to guard the Indian against the imposition of the Colonists?

The situation of the Post is in Lat. 5°16′38″N. and Long^t 56°53′31″W. by Chronometer. I paid a Visit next day to one of the Cliffs, which have received the name of 'Chalk Hills' and on one of which the Post Holders House is erected, the Hills are called by the Arawaaks Oreálá, by the Warows Alivavara. I descended by a hollow which had been formed by freshet, and after having gained the River I had a view of a section of the formation; It was composed of Horizontal Beds of little continuity of a silicious conglomerate intermixed with red sand stone, with small grains of slightly rounded quartz, a calcareous and often schistose bluish clay, beds of loose sand, and beds of a substance which by the diminution or loss of the calcareous ingredient, resemble shale. The unctuous and blue schistose clays are however predominate. I did not discover any organic remains, but they could have been scarcely expected where I could dedicate only a superficial investigation to the formation; there were however many pisiform and remiform cavaties, filled with nodules of indurated clay at other times with sand and silex; these cliffs extended North & South, for about three Miles; in the rear extend Savannahs for a considerable distance, they are clothed with short grass and the soil is here infertile and soon exhausted.

While I was at the Post the period approached which Sir John Hershel[3] had set apart for Meteorological observations at the Autumnal equinox and I took a regular set of observations, which I had the honor to transmit previously to the Royal Geographical Society.

Our arrangements were at last completed, and we left the Post on the 25th September, but a contrary tide obliged us to come earlier to a halt than it was our wish, and

---

[1] The post was at Orealla, still the site of an Arawak settlement.

[2] The original figure is obscured by '400' written over it. In the published version (p. 286), the figure is given as 'may be 650', and is broken down into 300 Arawak, 250 Warao, and 90 Caribs.

[3] Sir John Frederick Herschel (1792–1871), FRS, astronomer. President of the Royal Astronomical Society, 1827–33.

we awaited the turn of the tide at M.ʳ Layfield's. I measured here a baseline to determine the Width of the River, and found it to be from highwater mark to highwater mark on the opposite side 1230 Yards, the average rise of the tide is 6 feet, the velocity of the Current increased by the ebb tide 5.3 f.ᵗ in a second, the temperature of water was 82°.5 Fah.ʳ. [A] short distance from M.ʳ Layfield's, there are two Islands, the smaller is called Bungabanabú, the larger Kirekaghe; from the southern end of the latter extends a considerable sand-bank towards the left bank of the River; but on the right shore is a channel deep enough for Vessels of 50 to 60 tons. While approaching Serikan or Long Island,[1] we observed that all at once the Corials before us changed their Course, and steered towards the Western shore; a huge wave rose suddenly to more than three feet height, and advancing rapidly with a thundering noise, it vanished in undulating masses, dashing violently against the shore; this was repeated thrice. M.ʳ Cameron & M.ʳ Reiss who were in the Boat furthest in advance, described it to me as having had in the commencement, the appearance of a high sand Bank, from whence the Water rushed violently, and under this Idea they changed suddenly their course and bore about. The Island is famed for the Wave, which is known by the name of "the bore", and occurs at the first setting in of the flood tide; it is highest at the equinoxes; the Indians call it Abapouri.

The River, though there are two Islands is by no means narrowed in, but it takes further North a sudden bend, which may cause an increase in the force of the Young tide. I observed distinctly two Currents, one setting for several hundred Yards along shore up the River, produced by concealed sand Banks, while the other decended more rapidly in the Centre; this Current resists the advance of the tide and combined with the other may cause in some respect the formation of the sudden swell. We observed the Abapouri at 4ʰ45ᵐ p.m. off Serikan, when according to calculation the flood tide must have set in at the Mouth of the Corentyne at 11ʰ50ᵐ a.m., if the rise of the wave was therefore the indication of the changing water, it travels almost five hours a distance of 60 Miles, the Windings included. I did not hear the Corentyne below Serikan offers a similar instance, though a bore of 5 feet rise is said to occur opposite the Indian settlement Washap.[2] We reached before Night-fall the second range of clay hills, called by the Indians Siprouta, they are of less height than the former and their formation made me almost suppose when on my return from the Cataracts, I examined them more closely, that they might contain Coal[3] – other features strengthened me in my supposition, and as I do not doubt that this geological feature extends to Berbice, its formation may be more developed and indicative of a discovery which would be of the most vital interest to the Colony. The composition of the Beds consisting in alternating substances, as clay, shale, and sand, as described before is analogical to the coal measures of Poland and scattered portions of a bituminous substance I found on Sand Banks in the River drew first my attention to the possibility. My present Report is not of a nature to admit a detailed geological description, which shall be submitted at the end of the present expedition.

---

[1] This is not the same Long Island as marked on modern maps near the mouth of the Corentyne.

[2] Probably near Wassiabo River, a right bank tributary of the Corentyne.

[3] Coal, in the 19th century, held the position that oil did in the 20th. The location of its deposits was of major geopolitical importance.

The River is some what hemmed in by the hillocks of Siprouta, and takes a far North eastern, and afterwards Southern & South Western Course,*

> *It must be understood that these Courses refer to persons ascending the River, as with the current or descending it is just the contrary.

indeed it describes almost a Circle, and a due Southern Course across the land leads from Siprouta in three quarters of an hour to Paerourou,[1] the opposite [point] or the Commencement of the almost Circular Course, while six hours are required to follow the River's proper course; The luxuriant Vegetation of the River appeared to increase the further we advanced. I readily recognised all the useful Timber Trees for which Guiana is so much famed; the soil is equal if not Superior to that of the Essequibo and rests upon a clayey substratum. The Banks in the Vicinity of Paerourou consist of ochrous clay, this substance is frequently met with. The River now takes a decided Western Course, somewhat more than a Mile West of Paerourou is the brook Epira, inhabited by many Arawaak Indians. We visited them on our return, but were obliged to wade through swamps and to cross several times the brook Epira, before we reached their settlement. The Manicole Palm[2] is almost the only Tree which delights in the morassy soil, which extended between the River and the settlements. The latter are built upon sandy hillocks, perhaps not more than from 15 to 20 feet high, and stretching in a South Western direction. I consider them a spur of those at Kayiwa. The number of Indians that live here may amount to 150, and by paths across the Savannahs, they keep up a regular intercourse with those at the Post. At the first Caribee settlement, where we resolved to stay until the turn of the tide, we found that high water was at 11^h5^m. Consequently at 10^h39^m at full and change and 5 hours later than at the Mouth of the River, the rise amounted to somewhat more than thirty inches. From the Bank of the River rises a sand hill to the height of about 100 feet on the top of which the Caribee settlement is located; it is called Kayiwa, which signifies indurated or hard sand. I determined its latitude to be 5°4'10"N. These hillocks extend farther inland in a South Western direction; about a mile from Kayiwa we saw another cliff where clay and a peat like earth were the most prevailing substances. The clay is of the finest quality, and resembles pipe-clay. We estimated the height of these cliffs from fifty to sixty feet. The Indians have a tradition that they are inhabited by a tremendous snake, which from time to time goes to drink the water of the Corentyne, and its passage thither has deprived the Cliffs of every Vegetation. They end by a sudden escarpment and the River's banks have now their former height of about 12 feet; at the Stream Manarobi we met a coarse crystalline and micaceous sand stone; the direction was N.85°E, the dip South, the angle 80°. The rivulet Matappie[3] joins from the East, and is said to be connected with the River Copename,[4] the Maroon Negroes[5] keep up a communication between the latter River, and the Corentyne. We observed now rocks *in situ* in the

---

[1] Piruru River.

[2] *Euterpe oleracea*.

[3] Matappi River. It is the word in many Carib languages for the cassava-squeezer, a woven instrument used in the preparation of cassava flour.

[4] Coppename River, but Schomburgk probably meant the Nickerie River which lies between the Corentyne and Coppename.

[5] The Maroons or Bush Negroes were and are the descendants of groups of former African slaves who escaped to live free on the middle reaches of the rivers of Surinam.

River, and passed a little afterwards several rocky islets; on the right or dutch shore joined the River Cabalaba[1] which I ascended a few days as far as the Cataract.[2] This River which is about 100 yards wide at its mouth exhibited all the luxuriance of a rich soil, numerous shrubs of the wild Arnotto margined its banks, and the splendid flowers of the Cassia Calyantha[3] towered over them. The observation made so frequently that generally one of the Banks of the River is considerably higher than the other, holds out likewise here, but the height changed alternately more frequently than I had observed before. The river is very winding, and is considerable wider at 6 Miles distance from the mouth; the Water is of the same colour as the Corentyne namely Ochrey and apparently muddy though when it is put in a Glass, it is clear. The average of the depth is 12 feet. It is a circumstance worthy of remark that I have generally found the Water of the Cabalaba and the Corentyne to be of a much higher temperature than the outer air; the difference amounted often from 5 to 10°F. The Cabalaba reminded me much of the upper Rupununy, its Water of similar appearance, it flows in short turns, and its sandy beaches encroach likewise here during the dry season upon the River's Dominion. We found the River peopled by similar fishes, and the stingray so common in the Rupununy, was likewise frequently speared by our Indians. We met with some hillocks in lat 4°51' – they were inconsiderable, scarcely more that 60 feet high, but erratic blocks became much more frequent. We met sometimes a rocky islet, and its concomitant, the Aromatic Guava[4] growing luxuriantly upon it. Numerous Sacki Winkis (Hapale Spec.?)[5] jumped with agility from branch to branch, the Waterhare a species of Cavia,[6] appeared likewise frequently on the Banks of the River, and plunged in the River as soon as they had espied us. The Rush of a Cataract attracted our attention, and discovering the mouth of a stream, we forced a way through the branches which almost hid the Entrance. The Cataract is about 20 feet in height, the rock consists of sand stone in which I found vestiges of feldspar. Where the stream had formed a lip the Rocks are obscurely stratified, their dip being S.20°W. the angle about 40°. I was astonished to find a number of blocks of a whitish sandstone, which I could not trace to the Parent rock, they were fine grained and are used by the Indians as Grindstones, their quality is so Superior that they need only to be known to be adopted by the Colonists. This interesting Cataract is called Iraffé by the Indians.

We slept that night on a sandy spit. While we were occupied to construct our Tents, we heard a report of a Gun to the East which our Indians ascribed to the Maroon Negroes, a signal which the Outposts generally adopt to inform the Camps of the presence of strangers. Our Indians told us that these Maroons visit frequently the Cabalaba on fishing Expeditions; indeed by means of the Cabalaba and its tributaries, as well as

---

[1] Kabalebo River.

[2] The account here is not in strictly chronological order. The expedition ascended the river to a Carib village, upstream of the mouth of the Kabalebo, to which the expedition subsequently returned in order to explore it.

[3] *Senna multijuga*.

[4] *Campomanesia aromatica*.

[5] Sakiwinki. According to Allsopp, *Dictionary of Caribbean English Usage*, Oxford University Press, 1996 (hereafter *DCEU*), this is the Guyanese vernacular for the Squirrel Monkey (*Saimiri sciureus*), although it seems also to be used for other small arboreal animals such as marmosets and tamarins.

[6] From the Dutch 'waterhaas'. It is better known as the capybara (*Hydrochacris hydrochacris*), an amphibious rodent which looks like a huge guinea-pig weighing up to 100 lb.

those of the River Copenama and Saramaca, they are said to keep up communications with the Corentyne. In order to show that we were equally awake, we fired a small Cannon, and we were not a little astonished when Mr Vieth who had remained with the rest of our party at Tomatai[1] told us on our return, that the Report of our cannon had been heard at that settlement, the direct distance of the two Places is according to my calculation nearly 11 Miles, and the charge amounting to scarcely more than 2½ ounces of Powder, it will give an Idea how far the sound travels through the Woods hushed at that part of the day's perfect silence. We started next morning early in order to reach in time the Cataract of Avanavero,[2] the aim of our present excursion; the Morning was Misty, and we could scarcely see more than 20 yards before us. The Thermometer stood at 6^h 77°F. while the surface of the Water had a temperature of 82°. We passed numerous rocky islets, showing sometimes stratified rocks, their dip being South the angle about 65° and their direction E.N.E. and W.S.W. No where had I seen the black crust of oxide of Manganese in such thick layers upon the Rocks as here; they belonged to the trappean formation. Sandy beaches extending in the bed of the River, are always the first indication of approaching Rocks and islets. These beaches explain to a great measure the formation of pegas, as the half decayed Vegetable mould from leaves and grass is called; during the inundation the fallen leaves of Trees are swept from the land, and being thus carried away by the Current they are deposited on these sandy points, where the course of the River changes often at right angles; there they form layers of from one to two feet deep. The River still increasing in height deposits in lieu of the leaves a layer of sand and fixes them for the present to that situation and while the River retires and decreases in size, the decomposition of the Vegetable matter takes place; and having become now so light, that even a breath of air may disturb it, it is carried away at the first swelling of the River, and floats in consequence of its lightness on the surface of the River, until some obstacle is thrown in its course, when it is newly deposited. We find therefore this Vegetable mould so frequently in estuaries where a contrary tide obliges the River to deposit it.[3]

We saw a chain of Hillocks stretching East & West, through which the River has forced itself a Passage; they consist of boulders piled upon each other, and their interstices being filled with soil, a luxuriant vegetation and fine Timber Trees cover now these granitic heaps; their height was estimated at 300 feet; at their foot rushes the Cabalaba over a granitic barrier, and forms the Cataract of Aranavaro, the perpendicular height of which was estimated 25 feet. The tract of granite is of inconsiderable width, and amounts to scarcely a Mile, when the River flows again uninterrupted, its breadth is about 200 Yards – according to observation which I took on the sandy spit the night previous Aranavaro is in Lat. 4°47′13″N. & Long^t 57°12′48″W.

On our return to Tomatai every possible difficulty was thrown in our way to prevent our departure. The difficulty with which luggage can be conveyed, had obliged me to curtail the stock of provisions, expecting that the Indians would furnish me with Casada bread. Before I left Tomatai they had given me their promise to have a large quantity ready on my return from Cabalaba; they advanced numerous excuses for not having

---

[1] Presumably in the vicinity of the Tomotai River.
[2] Avanavero Falls which are today the site of the Davis Dam which contains the Kabalebo Reservoir.
[3] Pegasse. The *DCEU* defines it as 'A dark, loose, spongy, peat-like surface layer of soil, sometimes several feet deep, formed from decomposed flora and found behind the coastal front-land clays of Guyana'.

complied with their promise, and desired me to wait three days longer, at the expiration of which, eight or ten Cakes were handed in, a quantity which was not sufficient for one days sustenance and neither threats nor promises could induce them to sell us more; those whom the Post holder had engaged to accompany me in my Expedition did not refuse to do so, but the provisions they took with them were by no means sufficient for a lengthened period; towards the other Indians the Caribees were overbearing and refused them any of the provision which they had in superfluity. This may have been the reason that four[1] of my Arawaak Crew took a Corial and ran away, and consequently I was the more obliged to depend upon our uncivilized Caribees. Their number is by no means great, the settlement Kayiwa, on the British side, does not muster beyond thirty Men, Women and Children included, while the population of the three settlements Tomatai, Pacouima[2] and Mayari on the Dutch side, may amount to 100 souls, many of them belong to the mixed race, the descendants of a Caribee Father and a Negress as mother; they keep up a constant intercourse with the Caribees on the rivers Copenama and Wayomba.[3] The old Maps represent generally a connection between the River Corentyne and Nickerie by the river Maratica.[4] I was not able to receive the slightest information on the subject, and as the Caribees who purpose of visiting the settlements on the Corentyne use always that River as high road, it proves that they are not acquainted with any other, or they would have chosen the shortest. We found at Tomatai three Macoosie Women kept in bondage by the Caribees, and it was only a short time ago, that one had attempted to make her escape, and swearing Revenge they had pursued her; the unfortunate Woman was recaptured, but it was beyond my power to ascertain her fate; on enquiry I was told she had been sent to Copenama. This nefarious trade is therefore still carried on and from several observations, which fell from them we suspected that a new Expedition to the Macoosies was in contemplation, and further circumstances, as will be seen in the sequel, proved that our suspicions had been too well founded.

We left Tomatai the latitude and Longitude of which is 4°59'23"N. & 57°15'45"W., on the 11th October. I was rather surprised to find that three Corials with Caribees, which were entirely unattached to my Expedition, followed us; though in the commencement keeping behind us, we saw them the next day in our Company. I saw clearly through their policy, the Caribees were thus by far the more numerous party, and while I could not prevent it, I adopted every precaution to render any bad intentions from their side harmless; our Corials were chained and locked every night, and my own manned with Warrows, kept always the rear when en route; our whole party thus encreased by unwelcome guests amounted to 58 souls. From the Geographical position of Tomatai, it will be observed that the Corentyne comes further from the West than it has been represented; its Western Course upwards continues from Tomatai; above that settlement, the River is studded with Rocks. We met some hillocks on the River's left bank, but their generally height was scarcely more than 150 feet. I consider them a spur of the Twasinkie Mountains in the River Essequibo; their Geological Character was equivalent to those Hills. A small stream which the Indians called

[1] This figure is three in 'Rough Notes'. See below p. 150.
[2] Presumably in the vicinity of the Pakuima River.
[3] Wayambo River. On some maps this river is shown to connect the Nickerie and Coppename Rivers.
[4] Maratakka River.

Assiproua[1] ran parallel with these hills. South of the Island Alapalissa[2] the rocks appeared to have a North and South direction, and in their Gigantic forms resembled much those of Achra Moucra in the Essequibo; there is no doubt they are a continuation of that tract; the Banks of the River in the Vicinity of Alavarlae Island are 10 to 12 feet high and consist of a species of clay which the Indians call Alina or Acourou, they use it for the manufacture of Pottery. The substratum was an ochrous clay covered with rich mould in which trees and plants appeared to thrive most luxuriantly. The Wild Cotton which I found here is of a superior texture and the samples which I brought with me were much admired. We experienced on the night of the 11th a severe thunder storm, the rain decended in torrents with the noise of a Cataract and I found that the rain fallen in 11 hours amounted to the enormous quantity of 5.7 inches. We met next morning the first rapid of consequence, in the Vicinity of the Island Bacac-ai; after we had passed the Island our course lay towards high ground, but before we reached it, the River represented another of those scenes of Confusion which are met so frequently in the Rivers of Guiana; the boulders were often 40 feet high and a large decayed trunk which the Current during the inundation had swept across two or three boulders, where it might have served in lieu of a Bridge, proved that the Corentyne in that place, is during the rainy season, at least 20 feet above its present level. The nearer we approached the hillocks we had seen in the distance, the stronger we found the Current, narrowed in by the hillocks, which we estimated 120 feet high, a slight bend of the River increases the Velocity and almost an hour elapsed before we could overcome its influence, though the distance we had past during that Period amounted to scarcely more than half a Mile, that Current ran at the rate of 4.5 Knots. We stopped for Breakfast at the foot of the hillocks; the rocks appeared to be obscurely stratified, and were highly ferruginous; the hillocks had a N.W.bN. & S.E.bS. direction. I was told by some of the Caribees that from here a path leads alternately over Savannah and Woodlands, to the River Berbice which they reached in a day and half easy walking. We passed many Islands, from their points extended spits of whitish sand in the River, during our ascent we selected sandy spits for our Night's Camp. The sand heated during the day keeps up a high temperature long after the sun has retired, at 8[h.] in the Evening the outer air was generally 77°, the Thermometer put in the sand rose to 85°.3. I have frequently repeated this Experiment and found always a difference of from 5 to 8°F. this difference amounted in the afternoon often to 40° and while at Tomatai, I observed that the white sand at 3[h] P.M. had a temperature of 128°, when the atmosphere was only 85°. On a point where the River was hemmed in on one side by numerous boulders of sandstone, on the other by a sandbank, we halted to examine the nature of the Rocks, they were of the same description as those I had seen at Itaffé and in the Cabalaba, and in consequence of their close structure and fine grain peculiarly qualified for Grind stones. The boulders are often 10 to 12 feet high & sometimes that size in Circumference; if hereafter Building stones should become desireable, this tract will afford material for the most extensive Buildings. These rocks are in Lat. 4°43′. Long[t] 57°40′ at nearly the most Western point of the Corentyne as far as I have had an opportunity to visit it.

---

[1] Possibly Assipoya River.
[2] Presumably in the neighbourhood of the Alapaliso River.

Our progress was next day quite slow, rocks and Islands were so numerous that our scout had often to visit several passages before we could venture to attempt one with our Corials. These Gigantic boulders are a most remarkable feature, and though they astonished me while ascending the Essequebo, they are in the Corentyne more numerous and not less in height and size. Only a few are angular, the most of them being spheroids, or dome shaped – all are more or less coated with the Metallic lustre, which is ascribed to arise from a coating of Oxide of Manganeese. Where we found several smaller blocks accumulated, the place between each was filled up with that strange vitreous matter already noticed while ascending the Essequibo, which I am much inclined to consider as having been under fusion. The scene is here very interesting, the Chaos of Rocks, the Rushing of the Waters, the numerous Islands which make the total width of the River to upwards of one Mile; each has its particular attraction, but the most striking feature was, I might say a Forest of Lacis these beautiful aquatic Plants were in full blossom, the light brownish scape, the thickly set flowers naked and of lilac colour, formed a strong contrast to the otherwise barren Granitic Rocks, thousands were in flower, and their luxuriance showed how much they were delighted with the spot. I measured one of the lacerated leaves which I found 3 feet 2 inches long and 2 feet wide. Our Camp was selected at a rocky islet, called by the Caribee Akalikatabo in Lat. 4°40′30″N. 57°39′17″W.

We passed next Morning a remarkable Rock, called by the Caribees Timehri,[1] It is not only distinguished for its size, but there are a number of Gigantic figures engraved on it, one of which measures more than ten feet.[+]

[+]Drawings and a particular description of these Figures I shall have much pleasure to forward to the Society on my return from the second Expedition.[2]

After we had passed on the 17th October a turn which the River makes, we observed several hillocks approaching to Banks on both sides; half an hour further progress and we found ourselves in apparently a large Basin formed by Hillocks from 60 to 100 feet high. The River broken up in torrents, the white flakes of foam, which came sailing down as if to give us a welcome; the thundering noise of falling Waters, and a cloud which like perpetual mist hung over the southern hillocks, spoke in an intelligible Voice, that some great scene of Nature was before us. Without further examination of the terrain, I observed that we would have to make a stay here, and I gave consequently the necessary orders for erecting our tents; while thus occupied, the Caribees told us that we would find it impossible to get on further, and though it was true, that there was a path existing, it was only passable during the rainy season, when the River's Bed was full and the impediments much less. It struck me as peculiar that I heard for the first

[1] According to Everard Im Thurn, the word is Carib and an alternative form is Timeneeri. He gives its meaning as 'Signifying certain marks or figures which like our letters and words, express ideas'. He wrote this in 'An Editor's Prologue' to the first issue of *Timehri Being the Journal of the Royal Agricultural and Commercial Society of British Guiana* (1, 1882, p. 4), of which he was editor. This seems very likely as a very similar word appears in the Trio language. It is *timenure* which means 'painted, designed'. There is a cognate word *imenuhtë*, 'to make designs' (literally to provide with marks), which was adopted by the missionaries to mean 'to write'. *Imenu* is the word for black genipa dye, also used as a body paint. Today the word Timehri is probably best known as being the name of Guyana's International Airport.

[2] An editorial footnote in the published version (p. 294) states that these had not yet arrived. No trace of them has been found in the Royal Geographical Society.

time of the impracticability of passing the falls before us, the hints that had been thrown out for the last two days had not specified in what the difficulties consisted, and as I had been frequently threatened in a similar way during my former Expedition, and had safely passed them by perseverance, I entertained the same hopes at present. We reconoitred therefore the terrain next morning, after the Corial had been hauled over a Bed of Rocks, we crossed a rapid in oblique direction, and stood shortly after before a Pile of Rocks, which when the river is full, are the Bed of a Cataract, at present only a small stream rippled over their blackened surface. It had appeared to me from our Encampment, as if this place would afford me the possibility of drawing the Corials over, my hopes fell with every step I advanced, enormous piles of Rocks, grouped together, opposed even obstacles for the further advance by us pedestrians; at other times we saw chasms at our feet, and a courageous leap was necessary to land on the other side, or we had to wade through a stream, which pushed its way meandring through rocks, and disappeared as if by magic and the subterraneous noise told us that it was rolling below our feet, and made perhaps it[s] reappearance where we least expected it, and were wondering from whence it came. Some of the rocks are shelfy;[1] many exhibit circular holes, partly filled with Quartz pebbles. I measured one of the larger cavities and found it 3 feet deep and 10 Inches in diameter. Many of the Rocks were clothed with numerous plants, a species of Orchidea*

> *Possibly Brossia Lanceana,[2] that species having been found near the Great Falls of the Essequibo under circumstance similar to those here described.

and an Agave were the most remarkable among them; clusters of bright Yellow flowers distinguished the first, while the long and slender scape of the latter, adorned with thousands of flowers, gave a Picture of luxuriance even to sterile Rock. At my right I heard the thundering noise of a Cataract, over which a dense cloud of mist was hovering; thousands of swallows were skipping through this Cloud, falling and rising as if delighted by the constant moisture the spray of the Cataract kept their plumes.

We visited that Cataract afterwards, which in grandeur surpassed any I had seen before in Guiana; the mass of Water, the velocity with which it precipitates over the ledge of Rocks, to a depth of upwards of thirty feet perpendicular, causes the spray to form the cloud we had observed, when the cause was not known to us as yet.

Previous to my Visit to the great Cataract which is the most Western, I had followed a party of Indians, and after some labour and wading reached a branch of the River, which divided itself in two Channels, the Western formed a fall, and the opening prospect at my arrival on its head was beautiful indeed; the Water rushed at an angle of 60° into a Valley formed by Gigantic piles of rocks, which we had taken the previous day for hillocks, in which belief we had been strengthened by seeing them covered with large Trees, at our feet foamed the disturbed water, dashing its spray against the Rocks that impeded its course, but the most lovely object was a Cascade on the opposite side of the Chasm, the rocks over which the water fell were of scalar nature and clothed with a lacis, the pendulous branches of which are often 5 to 6 feet long and the tout ensemble resembled a rich Carpet; the endless Modifications of its green, the strong contrast of its flowers, and the foam of the Water which rushed

---

[1] Shelfy is defined in the *OED* as 'Full of slaty rock'.
[2] *Brossia lanceana* is a species of Vandoid orchid.

over it, made the prospect exceedingly beautiful. I estimated the height of that Cascade 25 feet, the one on the top of which I stood 30 feet, they are almost opposite each other, but the commotion of the Waters where they met, the silvery whiteness of the foam, and the Wave which from the conflict rose to a considerable height, made me suppose that there was a third which was hid from my View, by an intervening island; unacquainted with swimming, I would not venture to cross the Channel, where even an Expert Swimmer would have hesitated to stem the Current, and I was for some time at a loss how to come there; but by great circuits and dint of wading, I succeeded at last, and I was richly rewarded; three branches of the River unite at the head of the Cataract, and seek one and the same outlet at their junction their further progress is contested by huge blocks of granite through which they have forced a passage, and as if now anxious, which Water of the three branches should reach first the foot of the Cataract, they precipitated in a Chasm which the Water had groved in the Granitic Rocks; it falls thus upwards of Forty feet perpendicular, representing one Sheet of Foam. A large rock stands out as in relieve and has been resembled to a human thigh bone. The most Western Cataract is on a grander Scale, and its View has something overpowering which I find it impossible to describe; this is not the case with those just now described, and what they want in grandeur is fully compensated by the lovely prospect they afford, when viewed from the foot of the Valley-like Chasm, and while we named the former General Sir James Carmichael Smyths Cataract, we bestowed the name of Sir John Barrow upon the latter.[1] There is a third Cataract further East, which under any other circumstance we would have considered grand, if we had not viewed the former previously.

The River above the Cataracts is divided into numerous branches which form the three series of falls in a lateral line. As much as we had been delighted with the romantic scenery we witnessed at the Cataracts, the circumstance that it appeared to us impossible to cross the rocks in our Corials, lessened in a great measure our Enjoyment, nevertheless the hope remained that there might be a path by which they could be avoided. I summoned the Caribees who composed part of my Crew, and which I had selected as Guides, as they were the only Nation acquainted with the upper Corentyne and questioned them closely on a subject so important to me, but to no purpose; they did not deny that they passed these impediments during the rainy season in order to cross by a path, which was two days journey above the Cataract, over to the Essequibo; but that at present we could not pass. In order to serve as a Stimulus for exertions, I offered now a reward to any Indian who should discover a place where we might be able to cut a path for the transport of Boats and luggage, and a still higher reward was held out to the Coloured people, who made part of my Crew; in consequence of which Expeditions were undertaken every day, but the more I inspected the terrian, the more I was persuaded that it was impossible to construct a path with willing hands in a shorter period than 6 to 8 weeks; and that our Indians were not willing we had now daily proofs, the Caribees, by far the most numerous of my Crew, threatened to depart, they had from the commencement behaved in a manner which I could not explain; they demanded to receive provisions like the other Indians, though their Cassava fields if they had been willing would have afforded us sustenance for six

---

[1] The lower falls are still called Barrow's Fall, and of the upstream complex of falls, the western is Smyth's Fall and the eastern is today known as Governor Lights Fall or Wonotobo Fall.

131

Months, and as policy directed me not to spoil it entirely with them, I was obliged to give them allowances in Rice and other provisions, and the inroad which was consequently made in my stores, caused the well found apprehension, that even if I dismissed the Caribees my provisions would have given out in less than three weeks.[1] My Companions urged therefore to return and as in my own mind I knew the perilous situation we were placed in, I consented with a heavy heart: at a long consultation which we had on the subject, I expressed the hope that the ascent of the River Berbice which is more inhabited by friendly Indians might lead us perhaps to the accomplishment of our design of crossing the impediment of the Cataracts and of penetrating to the Chain of Mountains in the second parallel of Latitude. I occupied myself the following days with surveying the lower basin, and to extend the operations to that point where the River meets the first impediments. The Result of this Survey was that this tract of Rocks extends 5.3 Miles North & South, and is doubtless connected with the boulders in the Essequebo. In order to continue the Survey from Gen.l Sir James Carmichaels Cataract, I had carried the small canons I possessed to the head of the Cataract. M.r Vieth was left in charge of the Canons and directed to Fire two Guns in succession every half hour, having compared our Watches, I noted the time I heard the Report and its direction, and adopting the Velocity of sound at 1130 [ft] per second, I received a check against any irregularity, the unequal progress and delay in our march would have caused otherwise. Through the whole defile, Cataract followed upon Cataract, and we had at one time four Cataracts in view following each other in succession. We reached after 12 o'Clock the point where the River flowed smooth and uninterrupted. I placed here Englefield's Barometer,[2] and found that spot 100 feet above our Encampment, which I had previously ascertained to be 430 feet above the level of the Sea. This was the last Barometrical observation I was able to take; Troughton's Mountain Barometer met with an accident while it was landed at the Mouth of the Corentyne, and on my return on the present occasion, though Englefield's was entrusted to the most careful man of the party, the bearer slipped from a Rock and fell with his charge to the ground, and the Bag of the Instrument burst. I met the fate of other Travellers in that regard, but few have been successful to carry this delicate instrument to the end of their Travels[.][3] [T]he Fruits of my prolonged survey were not only a knowledge of the Country above the Cataracts, but likewise the discovery of several new Orchideae and some Cacti which I had not seen before. I had certainly to regret the accident which befell the Barometer, but I consoled myself for its loss by the knowledge of the extensive tract of boulders I had reaped, and the firm persuasion whatever may have been the Cause of disturbances which produced such a Chaotic Appearance they reaped Original Strength at the spot, and in this I was confirmed by the exact resemblance to igneous substances which occur in the paste in which many angular pieces of a porphyritic nature were imbedded, indeed it resembled a scoriform lava, but the Cells were rounded, and the paste glazed by a Vitreous Varnish; these appearances occurred very frequently

---

[1] At this point an unknown hand has written in the margin 'only 3 weeks from the post at Oreala!'.

[2] A Mountain Barometer designed by Sir Henry Englefield in 1806.

[3] Schomburgk was entirely correct. The mercurial barometer (the aneroid barometer was not yet invented), with its three foot long glass tube, was a notoriously fragile instrument. An 1850s manual on Indian surveying stated 'Those only who have had any practical experience with such delicate and expensive instruments as Mercurial Mountain Barometers can be fully aware of the disappointments met with in a country like this' (quoted by John Keay, *The Great Arc. The Dramatic Tale of How India was Mapped and Everest was Named*, London, *Publisher*, 2000, p. 119).

between the granitic boulders which often rested upon this formation. It does not belong to my Plan to enter here in details on that subject otherwise so interesting to Geologists.[1]

The means of several observations gave me as Latitude of our Encampment 4°21′31″N. 57°35′32″W.

On the morning of the 23ᵈ October, we returned towards the North. At our arrival at Tomatai the Caribee Settlement, the most of the Caribees absented themselves and it was only a few with their Captain Smith, who accompanied us to the Post. After our arrival there, a large Corial (about 40 feet long) with Caribees from the River Wayombo landed there, and exhibited a pass from the Authorities at Nickery, a dutch settlement on the Mouth of the Corentyne. We heard to our greatest astonishment, that they purposed ascending the Corentyne, in order to cross over by land to the Essequibo, and from thence to proceed to the Macoosis with the object of Trading for Slaves; they most openly asserted that this was their object, and showed us Guns and other Articles of Trade for that purpose, but they likewise assured us, that the Caribees of the Corentyne were to accompany them, and that Captain Smith had been for that purpose, a few Months ago at their Settlement in order to arrange matters. Our suspicions were thus verified, and their behaviour fully explained; under the Idea that we were bound for the same direction, they had supposed that our presence would interfere with their design, and every ruse was used to prevent our crossing the Cataracts. We discovered likewise that they had with held from us the knowledge of a path, where by means of a Creek, the Cataracts might have been passed, and that even large Corials might have been brought to the point of re-embarkation. In reconsidering on the feasibility whether we should return to the Cataracts and force them to show us the passage, it became evident, that now, the more they would use every means to prevent our executing this design, and being so near the Coast, I adhered by my former plan to ascend the Berbice, thus another river of British Guiana would be explored, and its ultimate object of penetrating to the Sierra Accaray might be rendered easier.

Though the expedition failed in that regard up the Corentyne, the Knowledge of this River, the adaptness of its banks for Colonization, the peculiar formation in its Vicinity with regard to Mineralogy and the hope that Guiana may possess Coal measures are of some importance. The River represented in the Map as one of inferior size, I have found almost equal to the Essequebo, and its course laid down from Lat 5° in supposition, is ascertained to adopt just the Contrary Course, and where it is represented to have its Sources it is found 900 Yards wide. Indeed if I consider every Circumstance, I come to the Conclusion, that the three Chief Rivers of British Guiana have their source in the same Chain of Mountains within a short distance of each other, or should they arise out of a lake, of the existence of which I received new information from the Indians; their Report however is too vague and contradictory to deserve credence.

New Amsterdam
Berbice 25ᵗʰ· November 1836
Robert H. Schomburgk C.M.R.G.S.

****

---

[1] An editorial note in the margin reads 'quite unintelligible', with which sentiment one can barely disagree.

It would be difficult to regard Schomburgk's exploration of the Corentyne a success, and in a letter to the Royal Geographical Society he identified two reasons for this: the uncooperative behaviour of his Indian crew and the barrier to further advance presented by the falls.[1] In fact Schomburgk should have foreseen both these possibilities. The Indians' behaviour was by no means out of the normal and he should have been prepared for it. As far as his failure to surmount the falls is concerned, unless he had been convinced by popular belief that the river flowed through an alluvial plain, he should have expected to meet falls and also to have appreciated that at that season of the year it might prove very difficult to surmount them.

Schomburgk returned to New Amsterdam and, either before he got there or soon after he arrived, wrote on 7 November to the Governor of British Guiana, telling him, because of the treachery of the Indians he had failed to reach the Serra Acarai by means of the Corentyne, and sought permission to try via the Berbice River. The Secretary to the Government replied on behalf of the Governor, giving permission, but referring to it as the 'next best thing'.[2]

****

The part of the manuscript catalogued JMS 6/18(c) is entitled 'Rough Notes on the Courantyn & Berbice Expedition', but, as already mentioned, it is exclusively concerned with the Corentyne expedition, and contains nothing about the Berbice expedition. The manuscript was received by the Royal Geographical Society on 25 September 1837. It was never published and there are no editorial marks on the manuscript. Some of the material contained in this manuscript duplicates, and on occasion differs from that to be found in the report on the Corentyne expedition. It represents a rather fuller account of many aspects of the Corentyne expedition than the 'Report' does. Accordingly it contains more than enough new and interesting information on a variety of topics to warrant its inclusion in this volume. Furthermore it has been decided to place the document here so that the two accounts of the Corentyne expedition are brought together.

There are two cover sheets, one of which is part of the original manuscript and the other similar in form to those on other Schomburgk manuscripts and clearly provided by someone at the Royal Geographical Society. The former gives the length of the manuscript as 61 pages, the latter as 63, which is correct if the original cover sheet, which is unnumbered, is included as part of the manuscript. There are also two sets of pagination; in one the first page, excluding the cover sheet, is marked 0 and the second 1, and thus runs from 0–61. The other set of pages numbers runs from 1–62, and it is this set which is used when reference is made to the manuscript. On both cover sheets it is noted that pp. 45–9 are missing, when, in fact they are not; nor is there any obvious gap in the manuscript at this point. The manuscript is not in Schomburgk's own handwriting. This fits with the fact that he reported that during a bout of rheumatic fever after the Berbice expedition he had employed a 'Copist' (and he may well have taken to dictating some of his account of these journeys as well).[1] Of all Schomburgk's documents this has been the most difficult to read; the writing is extremely poor and often

---

[1] RGS Corres 1834–40, Letter of Schomburgk to Washington, 24 November 1836.
[2] RGS Corres 1834–40, Letter of Young to Schomburgk, 12 November 1836.

very faint. Furthermore there has been a great deal of scratching out and writing over the top of existing sentences. Regrettably it has been necessary in places to reconstruct the sense rather than transcribe the text, but where this has been done is clearly indicated. At one point a passage has been omitted because it was found impossible to reconstruct it.

ROUGH NOTES ON THE COURANTYN & BERBICE EXPEDITION

Data
To be filled up hereafter
Our leaving Demerara in the Schr. the Lady d'Urban on Septbr 2ᵈ., our arrival at Berbice on Monday 5ᵗʰ., chartered the John Eliza to convey us to the Plantation Skeld[on] on the western bank of the Courantyne on Wednesday 7ᵗʰ arrived there on the 9ᵗʰ proceeded next Day to the Plantation Mary's hope, which is generally considered to be situated on the mouth of the Courantyne, had the most unfavorable weather for observation determined however to be situated in Lat 5°58′51N Longt 57°1′30″W. In lieu of 15 to 20 Indians which I expected to find at Mary's hope there were only 10 among which number 2 were invalids and 2 small boys, I despatched therefore the Corials almost empty and took the remainder of our Luggage in the Schr of Mr Robertson. Great kindness and assistance of Dr Taits, Mr Ross.

We left Skeldon on Sunday 18ᵗʰ after we had attended divine service and heard a good sermon of the Revᵈ Mr Stuart, an ordained clergyman of the Skotch[2] whom Mr Ross pays a salary in order to perform divine service and teach the children of his apprenticed labourers. Soon after we hove anchor night set in and we saw but little of the beauty of the river, the scenery at its mouth studded with Islands promised fair. We arrived off the Post of the river Courantyne the same day after 11 oᶜˡ at night;[3] the appearance of the Sandhills being white forming a strong contrast to the dark colours in which the banks of the river appeared to be envelopped.

19ᵗʰ The appearance of the high banks of the river had deceived me. When I first saw them during night I would have considered them much higher, while I estimated their hight at daybreak only 80 to 100 feet. They are called the Chalkhills from their whitish appearance and are known to the Indians by the name of Ohreala. On one of this banks is the habitation of the Postholder of the Courantyne, at present a Mr de Wolff, where we intended to sojourn for a few days in order to recruit a crew sufficient for manning

---

[1] RGS Corres 1834–40, Letter of Schomburgk to Washington, 11 May 1837.

[2] The Church of St Margaret at Skeldon was erected at the expense of the owners of the Skeldon estates, Eliza and Mary, who contributed £800 towards the first chapel and £200 annually for the salary of the clergyman. The Revd Mr Stuart belonged to the Church of Scotland. Mr Ross was the owner of one of the Skeldon estates but nothing is known of Dr Tait. See T. Farrar, *Notes on the History of the Church in Guiana*, British Guiana, Wm. Macdonald, "Gazette" Office, Berbice, [1892].

[3] The time of arrival was originally written as 'on Monday the 19ᵗʰ', but these words have been crossed out and replaced with 'the same day after'. In the Report (see above p. 121), the arrival is stated as 'on the morning of 19th September'. The discussion in the following paragraph about overestimating the height of the banks in the dark supports the time of arrival as being at night.

the Corials. The house in which the Postholder lived did not deviate in appearance much from the better class of houses of the Indians and the younger part of his family, from the constant intercourse they had with the Indians had adopted many of their manners; his second daughter might be called another Diana. She was as skilled with her bow and arrow as an Indian hunter, and disdaining the customary viands of civilized people, preferred the fruits of the woods and provision fields. We have here an example how readily nature recalls man from adopted habits and the constraint custom has laid him under.

There are several settlements of Arrowaaks and Warrows in the vicinity of the Post; it struck me as peculiar that the generality of them could express themselves in English, though they live adjacent to Surinam, while in the Essequibo the knowledge of the Indians does not extend further than the Creole a mixture of Dutch French and English.

Among the settlements which I visited during my stay at the Post, sickness prevailed to a high degree, and many deaths had occurred. At a Warrow-village at the post I found the greater part of the inhabitants more or less indisposed, and a child died the second day after our arrival. Scarcely had it breathed its last when three shots anonnced the death, and the Captain of the Settlement came to Mr de Wolff to buy several flasks with Rum, for those who intended to attend the wake. We went there in the evening[;] the hut only lighted by a [blank][1] which had been dipped in a mixture of beeswax and the Gum of the Amyris (Haiowa) scarcely allowed us to discern the objects; five or six old crows were sitting in a circle, one of them had the dead child adorned with numerous beads in her lap while she or the others broke out from time to time in the greatest lamentations; the grief of the mother appeared to be the most violent and she rended almost the air with Katinama, Katinama 'my daughter is dead' her mother breaking out in a similar complaint that her grand child was gone and imploring the spirits that they might receive her well. The body was then taken in the lap of an other woman and the old lamentations commenced, for a few minutes silence would prevail only interrupted by the groans of the mother, until some circumstance or the other, perhaps the former playfulness of the child, what it had said reminded them of their loss and the wailings broke then out anew with redoubled strength. Thus they continued the whole night, the sound following us to our camp, and though some distance from the Indian village we could plainly discern the mothers voice from the others. The father of the Child a fine looking Indian, perhaps not more than 20 to 24 years old was lying in his hammock, where the women were sitting mostly hiding his face until the feelings of a father directed perhaps unvoluntarily the glances to his first child now a corpse and then the pride of not shedding a tear in the presence of strangers was forgotten and he allowed nature her full right. We returned next morning to the place, the Cap[t] or Chieftain was engaged in preparing a rough Coffin out of the bark of the tree, otherwise the scene represented the same differences[,] the women were sitting in a circle, weeping and crying and the father laying motionless in his hammock. The Coffin was finished, and the body wrapped in a piece of Salempore[2] was deposited in it, one of the women put a bracelet made of Palm[wood] round its little arm; the mother put

---

[1] Amerindians fashion lamps out of cotton threads and other vegetable fibres coated in beeswax or natural gums.

[2] A blue cotton cloth made in Madras, India.

afterwards a Sackie-Sackie[1] in its coffin some strings of beads and the lid was nailed down. The Coffin was then put in the grave, which had been made in the hut at the place where its little hammock was slung formerly and the earth put over it; there was no further ceremony connected with the interring but scarcely was the grave finished when the mother who with her husband had taken no part in the interment, loosened her hammock from the former place and hung it over the grave. Her face was swollen from weeping and it appeared that from the period the child became dangerously sick she had not washed herself. [I]n the evening we found that she had lighted a fire over the grave, which she kept constantly burning. The Cry of Katianama resounded still day and night. I met her the following day while on a botanical excursion, collecting wood, she did not observe me but fixing her eye on one spot she threw at once the collected wood on the ground and breaking out in a flood of tears, the wailings were repeated.

We found the greatest difficulty in procuring a Crew and when we had fairly removed one excuse given as reason for not being able to accompany us new ones were started. The Courantyne is but little known even to the native tribes and their superstition paints monsters which are said to devour the daring Indian who should venture to enter its dominions; they fancy likewise that the upper Courantyne is inhabited by hostile tribes. Though the Postholder had received the Government's orders to have a crew ready, I found that he had made no progress in accomplishing this desideratum; I tried next morning a conversation with two Arrawaak Captain who promised me their assistance.

Or Mathias as he is generally called was a disciple of the Moravians when they had a settlement at the Courantyne[2] and was baptized, his manners, his readiness in conversing in English, proclaimed that he had passed more than the first step of civilisation. Hector the other could express himself likewise in the english but a victim of that bane, rum, his very looks bespoke its effect, and while Mathias had full command over his followers Hector's authority appeared to be but trifling. Each of them promised to accompany me with 8 men, Mathias kept word, but Hector could only muster two at the day of starting. The Postholders lose daily their influence and it is scarcely otherwise to be expected where such mismanagement is carried on; the generality of them, contrary to their instruction induce the Indians by dread to work for them and in return they receive knives, cutlasses and hatchets at enormous prices – should the Indian refuse he is marked by the Postholder as a malcontent and no oportunity is neglected to let him feel his displeasure. Many of the Indians have lately commenced to cut timber in their own nati[ve] forest, their property by natural right – by this they avoided the avidity and imposition of their soi-dissant friends and procured themselves the few necessar[ies] of life they wanted – this they are now prevented to as according to a late regulation a licence must be taken out for wood cutting, and while I was at the Post a rafter with forty logs of wood, the fruits of many a months labour were seized; if the Indian wishes therefore to be industrious he is forced to fall in the hands of men, who firstly undervalue his labour and pay him afterwards in articles at 300 pC advantage, can

---

[1] Several species of Tanager are called 'sackie', as are two species of monkey (*Chiropotes satanas* and *Pithecia piethecia*), but it remains unclear what the 'sackie-sackie' referred to here may have been.

[2] There were Moravian missionaries on the Berbice and Corentyne throughout the second half of the 18th century.

this induce him to put confidence in the Colonists or to adopt civilization. The Indians received formerly triennial presents[1] – this [w]as done away with as being too expensive, but what item would it make in the Colony's expenses to provide the Postholder with the most necessary medicines to allay the more frequent diseases[.] It is evident that the Indian population is rapidly decreasing, their intercourse with Europeans has caused them to adopt their vices and with it, diseases are introduced which produce a steady decrease in their number, as already observed. I found several Warrows suffer under fever and the Indians apathy prevented them to have recourse to such medicine as nature offers. I took pity of a little girl who suffered under a severe bilious fever, and though I had been told that it would be in vain to induce any of them to take medicines, I found not the slightest difficulty in inducing the patient to take it, and whenever she felt averse to it, as children will do, the other inmates of the hut encouraged her to take it – I had the pleasure to see her recovered before I left the Post – it is much to be regretted that the generality consider the poor Indian not much better than a being scarcely removed a step from the animal creation[;] he is beaten, cursed, and scarcely a friendly word is addressed to him. How little are they acquainted with the Character of those who live to far removed to be spoiled by our vices.

I paid next day a visit to one of the Cliffs which have received the name of Chalk-hills (in Arawaak Oreálá in Warrow Alivávárá – these two Indians tribes inhabiting the region where the Post is situated). I descended by a hollow which had been formed by rain waters, and after having gained the river I had a complete view of the formation, it was composed of horizontal beds of little continuity of a siliceous conglomerate, intermixed with red Sandstone with small grains of slightly rounded quartz a slightly calcareous and often s[c]histose bluish clay, of beds of lose sand and beds of marl; the unctuous and blue s[c]histose clays are however predominant – the superficial investigation I was able to dedicate to it, did not let me discover any organic remains, but there were numerous pisiform and remi-form cavities. I estimated the height of the highest of these cliffs between 80 and ninety feet, they extend N & S for about 3 miles.

The Moravians or United bretheren had formerly a mission on the Courantyne for the conversion of Indians, but circumstances combined to induce them to give it up, among them was the wandering habits of the Indians predominant[.] The site of their mission was once opposite the Post on the Dutch Side, but they lived on the British Side, now occupied by Mr Leighfield[2] a Wood-cutter. I went there with some of my companions and received a friendly welcome. The place itself showed of that zeal so predominant among Germans and chiefly followed by Moravians, whereever they sojourn to plant useful trees – numerous Orange, Mangro, Lime-trees &c the former loaded with fruit delighted us now by their freshness.

During the whole period I was delayed at the post, we had the most unfavourable weather for observations – the sky was constantly cloudy and as anxious as I was to

---

[1] Although with some reluctance, the British had continued the Dutch policy of giving regular presents to Amerindians. The Dutch had employed the Amerindians as protection against escaped African slaves and the presents were in recognition of this alliance. Various British Governors of the Colony made attempts to bring the system to an end, and although 'allowances and rations' were given intermittently to Amerindians after 1837, the presents appear to have come to an end in that year. See Menezes, *British Policy Towards the Amerindians*, Chapter 2.

[2] Layfield in the 'Report'.

determine the Latitude I was obliged to leave without having succeeded; it was about the equinox and blue sky only visible for a few minutes. While there the period approached which Sir John Hershel had set apart for [meteoro]logical observations for the autumnal equinox and I took a regular set of observations. While watching the 22^d Septb I observed two white circles round the moon, the outer one of which was 22°55′50″ distan[t] from the centre of the moon; at 10^{h}2^m when I took a sketch of it the Barom. stood 29.950; the external Therm. 76°; a cumulus approaching from the East covered the circles and the moon, but when it had vanished at 11^{h}15^m I observed still the outlines. The phenomenon had altogether a very pretty appearance. Our arrangements were now completed and we left the Post in four Corials on the 25th. Septbr, but a contrary tide obliged us to come earlier to a halt than it was our wish[;] we found likewise that our Corials were overloaded and we awaited the turn of the tide at Mr Leighfield. I measured here a Baseline to determine the breadth of the river and found it to be from high-water mark to high-water mark 1230 yards – the tide rises here 6 feet, the velocity of the Current increased by the ebb-tide is 5.3 ft in a second, the Temperature of the water was 82°.5.

Mr Leighfield had the goodness to offer us one of his Corials to escort us as far as the Caribee Settlements and volunteered to accompany us thither[.] Mr Leighfield's is the ultima Thule of civilized life in that direction, with it we bade adieu to comforts and an unexplored interior lay before us. We directed our course towards a small Island which occupied apparently the middle of the river though what I took first for the river's left Bank, I found afterwards to be an Island. The first starting presents a most animating scene – the Indian wants only encouragement and his eyes otherwise sharpedly fixed on one and the same spot, are able to be kindled not only by the passion of revenge but are likewise enlivened by nobler feelings and wakened out of their apathy. The Corials entered on a race and the cheering cry of their crew repeated by the echo of the woods became almost deafening. The Caribees distinguished themselves by their body bent forward and taking a full sweep with the paddle it descended quick in the agitated water and giving it a quick turn its broader part formed a feather edge; the Warrows and Arawaaks might have used more bodily force, but their stiff upright posture, formed a less interesting picture and prevented them to be the quicker or winning boat, though in the long run they would have been the gainer.

The smaller Island is called Bunjábánáboo, the larger Kíríkághé; from its southern end extends a considerable Sandbank towards the main shore but on the right shore there is a Channel deep enough for vessels of 50 to 60 Tons – the larger Corial in which Mr Losack and myself were grounded, and it took us a considerable time before we could get of the Sand bank and we fell back consequently. While approaching Serikan or Long Island, we observed that all at once the Corials before us changed their course and steered towards the western shore[.] A huge wave rose suddenly to 3 feet height, and advancing rapidly with a thundering noise it vanished in undulating masses dashing violently against the shore, this was repeated[.] Mr Cameron & Mr Reiss who were in the boat furthest in advance described it to me as having had the appearance of a high Sandbank from whence the water rushed violently down and under this idea they changed suddenly their course and bore away. This bore, for which the Island is famed occurs at the first setting in of the flood tide and is highest at the Equinoxes; the Indians call it Abápourí. The river though there are two islands, is by no means narrowed in, but it takes further north a sudden bend, in consequence of which the young tide being increased in force[;] it has besides this to contend with two currents which I plainly observed, one setting along shore up the river for several hundred yards the effect of concealed sandbanks[;] while the other descends more rapidly in the centre; heavy punts*

> * A punt is a flat bottomed boat employed by the Colonists for conveying produce along the sea-shore rivers, canals &c.

have been known to have been sunk by the swell. We observed the Abápourí at 4^h 43^m pm off Serikan when according to Calculation the flood tide must have set in at the mouth of the Courantyne at 11^h 50^m am, if the rise of the wave was therefore the first indication of the changing water it travelled almost 5 hours a distance of [blank].[1] I did not hear that the Courantyne lower than Séríkán offers a similar instance, though a bore of 5 feet rise is said to be opposite the Indian Settlement of Washap. We reached before nightfall the second range of marly hills called by the Indians Siprouta – they are of less height than the former and the river is somewhat hemmed in by them. The Courantyne takes from here a far northeastern and afterwards north-western course; a peninsula is thus formed which it takes more than a day to circum-navigate while by land the cord[2] is scarcely more than [blank] miles.[3] The tide being in our favour we continued our course even after nightfall. There was something peculiar in the appearance of our Corials partly lighted up and the first burst of joy having evaporated long before this; those of our own colour had taken up the broken thread and songs and glees resounded. We were at 8 o'clock opposite the Cabouri, an affluent of the Courantyne; the river is here wide and the glimpse of a light showed us, who heavier laden than the other boats were the last, from time to time the position of the boats; though a full moon had risen, a cloudy sky obscured her light. We landed at ten o'clock at Washap, an Indian Settlement, the landing place was miserable and I succeeded only after a good deal of wading to reach the terra firma with my instruments; the village, which we found to consist of a few miserable huts, was about 1 mile distant and thither I proceeded, merely for the purpose of taking observations. The Indians were not a little astonished to see us arrive at so late an hour, many of them suffered from fever[.] I had not succeeded at 11 o'clock to get the altitude of a culminating star, when I received the information that the largest Corial had gone adrift. My servant offered to watch in her and there was no doubt that he had dropt asleep when the Corial got lose of her morings & that the ebb had swept him downward the river. I manned immediately one of the smaller Corials with 8 of the best paddlers and accompanied by Messrs Losack, Leighfield, Cameron & we rowed swiftly down the river – after the elapse of an hour we found her between two islands, her Captain Cornelius a man who accompanied me on my former expedition had started alone in a small skiff and overtook her a little further down. The servant told us that he had dropt asleep and when awakened he found himself separated from the others and the Corial going swiftly down the river, all his outcries were naturally in vain and impossible to manage even a paddle he recollected that he was fastly approaching the place where he had seen the bore and he considered

---

[1] The distance has been left blank here but in the 'Report' it is given as 60 miles, see above p. 123.
[2] Presumably 'chord'.
[3] In the 'Report', it is said to take three-quarters of an hour to walk across, in other words the distance would have been under three miles, see above p. 124.

himself for lost – when the Corial was boarded he [Cornelius] found him laying on the bench weeping like a Child. We returned to Washap before day light and started an hour after. The luxuriant vegetation of the river appeared to increase the further we advanced. I readily recognized all the useful timbertrees of the Colony and if I could have conjured the vegetable walls of the river to the metropolis of Great Britain, this curiosity would have occupied the inhabitants for a few months. The soil is equal if not superior to that of the Essequibo and rests upon a clayey sub-stratum, but what struck me as peculiar was that the soil appeared to be diversified. Somewhat after 9 o'clock we arrived opposite to several Islands which give the river a most interesting appearance – after we had passed them, we discerned on the river's left shore or the British side a high bank, called Paerourou – it consists of ochrous clay and its whole length may amount to a mile – behind it is a fine Savannah, across these Savannahs a path leads from Ohreala the Post. The river is rather narrow, as if the high bank had encroached on its domin-ion, two hours afterwards we landed at the first Caribee Settlement commanded by Capt William. We found that high Water was at 11^h5^m consequently at 10^h39^m at full and change and 5^h later than at the mouth of the river; the rise amounts to somewhat more than 20 inches. From the bank of the river rises a sand hill to the height of ab^t 120 feet on the top of which the Caribee Settlement is located. It is called Kie-éwa,[1] which signifies endurated or hard Sand.

A severe thunderstorm approached from the North-west and prevented us to proceed further, we went therefore to the Settlement which we found tenantless. As inmates having proceeded on a visit higher up the river to the other Caribee Settle-ment, while others composed part of our crew, we took possession of one of the empty huts and were scarcely located when one of my assistants came and told me that one of the Children of a Caribee who made one of my crew was very sick and that the Pí-ie-man[2] was just about to go to work. We heard shortly afterwards a rattling noise, produced by a large Calabash filled with Mountain Crystalls the teeth of Snakes &c, this was accompanied by a song firstly rather murmured and increasing in strength, without profany it resembled the Catholic mass; our curiosity was now so much raised that we approached the place where the conjuration took place. It was a hut with the upper story which was concealed by mats plaited of palm-leaves. The Pí-ie man had an assistant a boy who was to learn the great art, his business was to shake the rattle accord-ing to the incantation; when the voice sunk we heard only a single stone making the round in the calabash and with it died the singing away, some cadences of which ressembled the national song of the Caribees.[3] The mother approached now the hut with the Child in her arms and ascended part of the rude steps which led to the apart-ment which was occupied by the Pí-ie man; here she remained for some time, her mother or the Grandmother of the child accompanied her – at last she was addressed by the Pí-ie man who put several questions to her which she answered. She was however not yet admitted and returned with the child to her hut. An other series of incantations commenced now and he changed frequently his voice by speaking through a reed, at other periods the voice and the rattling of the Maracca encreased and by a species of

---

[1] Spelt Kayiwa in the 'Report'.
[2] The shaman.
[3] By 'national song' Schomburgk can mean little more than a song common among the Caribs.

ventriloquism he made it appear as if the evil Spirit in consequence of his powerful conjuration was approaching[;] he spoke with him and the mother and child were now admitted; we saw smoke coming out of the hut and smelt it to arise from Tobacco and the suffocating voice of the child told us that he was blowing the stupifying smoke on the poor little sufferer – the child cried in the commencement vehemently until the Tobacco smoke took affect and lulled it to an unnatural sleep. The ceremonies were however not quite finished as yet and after the woman and child had left, singing through the nose was continued while the assistant beat a drum, firstly rapid and loud and by degrees dying away.[1]

I succeeded that night in getting an altitude of Fomalhaut when culminating according to which it was situated in 5°4'10"N Lat. We left next morning at an early hour, the Therm. stood a 6 oclock 76° the Water was 85° – the tide was strong against us and we resolved therefore to have a hunt after Labas (Cavia). Mr Leighfield had a couple of dogs trained for that purpose and in a short time we had several of these animals which are deservedly considered a great delicacy. The banks of the river are about 12 to 15 feet high and consist of red clay; at 9 o'clock we were opposite the rivulet Matappie which takes an eastern course and must have its source in the vicinity of Surinam River, as the Maroon Negros keep up a Communication between the latter river and the Courantyne.[2] Rocks made now their first appearance and a little afterwards we passed several rocky islets. At the right or Dutch shore joined the river Cabalaba which as I purposed to investigate the lower region I pass it over for the present. We breakfasted opposite a sandy Island and reached with a favourable tide Capt Smith's settlement that evening. The river adopts here a romantic appearance, margined on either side by lofty trees & walls of flowering vines it is studded with rocks some of which are pyramidical and 12 to 15 feet high. The river receives the waters of two rivulets almost opposite to each other, and in the vicinity of the one which joins the Courantyne from the right, there are the three Caribee Settlements, commanded by Capt Smith, Thomas & Christian. After we had landed Capt Smith came to meet us; he was of small stature being only 5ft 2 and his face had such a resemblance to the Simiadae that it wanted to see the whole man to become persuaded that he belonged to the bimana.[3] His father was an Arawaak but being maltreated by his tribe he run away and associated with the Caribees where he acquired influence enough to be elected Captain. His better half, as she had full right to be called was entirely his counterpart and outweighed him twice – in each of her ears there was a piece of Bamboo almost an inch in diameter and her calfs in consequence of garters which acted as ligatures, not having been removed since her child[hood] exhibited much more the form of oranges than the line of beauty – with one word she was a perfect Caribbean beauty. Her frequent visits to the Coast had made her acquainted with the title given to married women and she delighted in hearing herself styled Mrs Sarah.

---

[1] There is a striking continuity in many features of the shamanistic seance as described by Schomburgk. Pierre Barrère, *Nouvelle relation de la France Equinoxiale*, Paris, Chez Piget, Damonneville, Durand, 1743, in the first half of the 18th century, described many similar practices, and they could equally be observed in the second half of the 20th.

[2] In fact its source is some 150 miles from the Surinam River. In the 'Report' Schomburgk wrote that the communication was with the Coppename River (see p. 124 above).

[3] Literally 'two-handed'. A term coined by Cuvier for an order of Mammalia, of which humans are the only members.

Smith's followers were by no means numerous, his whole settlement did not consist of more than 30 people, children included, many of them were Capoucres, the mixed race of the Indian and the Maroon negro – they are generally finer formed men, but by no means superior in morals to the pure Indians – on the contrary they have inherited with the blood the vices of the African race; the mongrel race is more crafty and [illegible] the property of others if he only possesses ingenuity enough to appropriate it. Their colour approaches most a Zambo[1] and the hair resembles more the African than the Indian.

Mr Leighfield was to leave us here and as it became consequently necessary to purchase an other Corial I bargained with Cap[t] Smith for one which he had bought lately at the river Copenan.[2] Our agreement was that I was to pay him a Gun, [6lbs] Powder, 1 bag shot 1 Cutlass, 1 piece of Calicoe, this was considered a high price though I had paid in the Colony more than twice the amount for a similar Corial.

In consequence of the high trees and the steep banks of the river, I found it impossible to take observations at our encampment and I was therefore obliged to sleep at the Caribee Settlement. Capt Smith had given up part of his hut where we slung our hammocks, it proved certainly inconvenient as the greater [number] of the party were obliged to remain at the encampment – the wish however of having a place well determined by astronomical observations made me overlook the incommodities. The Caribees of the river Courantyne are by no means so hospitable and willing as those I met on the Essequibo and Rupununy. The last year we had not to complain of any rudeness or [illegible]. Mr L had a musical box and one of those dolls which being managed by threads exhibit the skill of an Indian juggler, with which we purposed to surprize the natives for the first time. At the appointed night they collected in our hut and the tricks of the juggler, combined with the music of the box moved even their otherwise apathic features – they were persuaded that the little black man possessed life and expressed their astonishment that they had never seen him yet – as with regard to the musical box, they could not form any idea whatever, all were delighted with it and long after we had finished our exhibition they remained crouching on the ground, in expectation that we should commence anew.

The[3] little child which we had seen pe-ied[4] at Kayewa was taken sick anew immediately after our exhibition and a man from Copanan acted as Pe-ie man. The Sacerdotum of the acting Priest was a small pyramidical hut affording room for only two persons – the sick child was brought before it and after the Pe-ie man had lighted a Cigar he enhaled the smoke and afterwards blew it upon the Child – his assistance a boy keeping all the time the Maracca going – the action was now changed and after having blown a puff of Tobacco smoke on the child, he put his lips to the breast of the child and commenced to suck there; this he continued alternately until he made them belief that the poison he had thus extracted overcame him and he retired to the pyramidical

---

[1] *The Dictionary of Latin American Racial and Ethnic Terminology*, Thomas Stephens, Gainesville, University Press of Florida, 1999, has six pages devoted to the meaning of 'zambo' in Spanish America and a further one page of Brazilian Portuguese meanings. The term is mainly applied to someone of African and Native American descent in various degrees.

[2] Presumably Coppename River.

[3] At the top of p. 16, a direction indicates that the passage in the lower half of the page should come first. This direction has been followed here.

[4] That is shamanized.

hut, where he fained to vomit severely[1] – he commenced now to sing in that nasal way already described, and after he had put several questions to the mother he regaled the sick child with an other puff of Tobacco and allowed the mother to carry her away – by this time the child was stupefied and quiet as a lamb.

While I was at the Post I had heard a great deal of Cabálábá which was described to me as a creek, but which I found to be a river when we passed it the [other] day; my crew being entirely incomplete and many of the Caribees being absent on a fishing expedition, and a delay not to be avoided I purposed of visiting it as far as the Cataract which makes further progress without much trouble impossible – we manned therefore the smaller Corials and left Tomatai on the 1ˢᵗ October – we reached the mouth of the river after a few hours paddling – ascending in its course it exhibited all the characters of a tropical river and high fertile soil, indeed I formed a higher idea of the fertility of that river than of any I had seen previous. Numerous shrubs of a species of Rucou or Arnatto margined the river and the splendid flowers of the Cassia Calyanthis towered over them. The observation made so frequently that generally one of the banks of the river is high, while the other is flat, held out likewise here; it changed more frequently that I had seen it before. The banks were generally from 8 to 10 feet high, the substratum consisting of a red Clay overlaying a blue Clay soil[;] 8 to 12 inches vegetable soil or mould this on the top was every where observable. We had not yet finished our temporary tent, when with the rapidness so common to thunderstorm in the tropics, electric clouds approached and the rain descended in torrents – we were most uncomfortably situated and our endeavours to kindle a fire in order to protect ourselves against that chilly sensation which is so easily produced even by a high degree of temperature, were baffled by the wood being wet for almost an hour. The Thermometer fell from 83° to 74° and the Barometer stood during the storm at 29.649 and rose afterwards to 29.[8]50.

The Sun rose cloudy and misty, the Therm. stood at 76° while I found the water to be 84°. It is a Circumstance worthy of remark that I have generally found the water of the Corantyne, Cabalaba &c to be of a lower temperature than the outer air.

How often have I seen the Manicole and Coucourite palms nevertheless I can not but admire their stately appearance. The former reaches with its slender stem the height of 60 feet before it spreads out its pinions delicate of growth it can not resist the rude winds and gives way like the small man of the north to the mightier[;][2] its stem is generally found to bend to the opposite direction from which the wind generally blows. Its delicate leaves of a bluish tinge form a perfect arch, only the middle one not developed entirely rises perpendicular. The Coucourite is built more substantial and it bids defiance to Boreas and his disciples. We soon discovered in their company an other acquaintance of our last expedition, the prickly Sawarai, much dreaded by the barefoot Indian, who when coming in their vicinity steps softly and with caution less one of the prickles often 3 to 4 inches long black as ebony and hard should enter his foot. The

---

[1] One cause of sickness widely recognized among Native Amazonians is that the victim or patient is shot with an invisible weapon or dart. This object can be seen by the shaman whose task it is to remove it, usually by sucking it out.

[2] The reference, two sentences below, to Boreas, the God of the North Wind in Greek mythology, suggests that 'the small man of the north' belongs within the same corpus of myths, but the reference has not been traced.

Vegetation resembles much that of the Essequebo, the splendid flowers of the Cassia Calyanthis and the rose coloured blossom of the Roucu form a distinctive feature in the Flora of the river Cabalaba – [a few pithairis][1] of a white colour yellowish breast and blue Cere at the base of the beak [were] flying before us – Mr Vieth had shot a similar one a few days ago which was entirely unknown to our party, it recommended itself by its large [blank] which adorned the head and we were therefore anxious to procure more of them – however they baffled all our attempts and after they had tantalized us for several hours we desisted. By this time we had arrived at a sudden turn of the river, where in consequence of the peculiar formation of its banks, the current was sweeping with redoubled force – as if to protect itself against the onset[;] the left bank was high formed of ochrous clay, blue clay and sand alternately – the high bank had for all the appearance of an enscarpment and formed a strong contrast to the flat shore of the opposite side which exhibited only low bushes and the winding Convolvulus, while the former was crowned with flowering Heliconiae and Clusters of Mora trees.

We met a tree which had fallen in the water was loaded with flowers – it was a species which I had seen last year in the Essequebo, but my attempts to collect it were feelingly punished in breaking the branches, I found them hollow and filled with a Species of ant, the bites of which caused severe pain and swelling and they spread over the Corial in such a short time that in self defence we were obliged to pull away. The plant belonged to Iriandica bignonia[2] but did not come in my collection as the few specimens were lost – I was therefore happy to have an other opportunity to collect them but without thinking in my eagerness on the visitation which befell us last year or rather considering it local – a general outcry rose at once in the boat and we found ourselves covered with the same Species of ant which punished us most unmercifully, they bit us on our neck, face, hands, and those parts were soon red with inflammation. I though it strange that our Indians did not assist in breaking specimens, but they were too well aware what would be the consequence, as this peculiar species of ants frequents always that kind of tree which the Arrawaaks call [blank] and the ant which inhabits it [blank]. According to the resources I am able to consult the tree is undescribed. It lasted several days before the swelling was entirely removed – the ant is of a light brown colour, long and thin in proportion.[3]

I went a little while afterwards on shore to break some geological specimens of some variegated marls of a wine red and bluish colour mixed, above the section was vegetable mould 8 to 10 inches thick, an [illegible] green clay 2 feet, Nodules of feldspar and quartz 6 inches, yellow sand 3 to 4 inches, variegated marl 2½ feet, ochreous clay, the thickness of which the water prevented us to trace. The slight endeavours I made to look for organic remains proved fruitless and for minute investigations I had no time, the more since I was instructed not to loiter on the lower Courantyne – not far distant from the spot but on the opposite shore we found a clay which I considered to be Caolin or Wavellite.[4] Soon after we arrived at the first indications of rocks, some of them were embedded in the marl noted above. We saw some objects moving on shore and on

[1] Possibly *Pithys albifrons*, the white-plumed antbird.
[2] Unidentified.
[3] In South America ants live in the hollow thorns of some species of *Acacia*, the hollow stems of some species of *Cecropia*, and the inflated leaf bases of some species of *Clidemia*.
[4] Caolin is presumably kaolin or china clay. Wavellite is a hydrous phosphate of aluminium.

approaching we found them to be Waterhaas (Cavia), there were three or four, and we saw them delighting in the mud as much as the domestic hog would have done; they allowed us to come quite near them and only after Mr Losack fired the contents of his gun after them they scampered in the water – the shots were not large enough to take effect.

The Cabalaba reminds me much the upper Rupuny, water of similar appearance, those short turns, the sandy shores encroaching during the dry season on the river's bed are features which are so frequent in the Rupununy. Our crew caught a Sting-ray (Trygon)[1] the [illegible] body was 3 feet 2 inches long the tail 2 feet 6 inches below reddish white above almost black with orange spots, the sting this formidable weapon was nearly 5 inches long. The Indians have the utmost dread of them and consider a wound inflicted by them next to incurable. After having cut off the sting and wounded it in several places with a Cutlass they took it in the boat when out of its mouth came 4 to 5 perfect young ones – their sting was not hardened though a cartilaginous mass showed which would be hereafter their weapon of defence. In the afternoon some hillocks hove in sight, and the erratic blocks, noticed above, became more frequent; we met sometimes a rocky islet and as its concomitant the aromatic Guave growing luxuriantly upon it – numerous Sacki-winkies (Hapale) jumped in the trees which margined the river, from branch to branch – from one of the Corials a shot was fired at them and was so well directed that several fell victim to their Curiosity – in the agony of death one had grasped a overhanging branch and kept itself balanced for some time – at last he dropt in the water and was joined to the others who were to serve as breakfast to the Caribees. Next to the Alligator and the Guana the Caribees consider a monkey the most delicate morsel. They are by no means choice in the selection of their food; we have seen them eating snakes, frogs and a few days ago they brought a porcupine rat (Illus spinosus – Espinosa)[2] and as anxious as I was to get it for my collection they would not part with it and it was thrown into the pot.

In spite of the splashing of our boats I heard the rushing of a Cataract[;] we observed on the rivers right bank the mouth of a stream and forcing ourselves a way through the opposing branches which almost [blocked] it up by means of Cutlasses and Knives, we stood soon before a pretty cataract of about 20 feet perpendicular height. The water is dark coloured and the white foam of the descending water forms a strong contrast with its original Colour – this scene is gloomy – high trees margin the course of the stream above the cataract and arriving at its fall it has formed itself a basin large enough to admit the light from above. The rock consists of sandstone – in which I found vestiges of feldspar; where the stream has formed a lip the rocks are obscurely stratified – their dip being S20W. the $\angle$ about 40°. I was astonished at the numerous blocks of a white sandstone which I could not find in place. They are fine grained used by the Indians as Grindstones – their quality so superior that they need only to be known to be likewise adopted by the Colonists in lieu of the European Grindstones. This interesting Cataract is called Itáfé by the Indians. We slept that night on a sandy Island formed by the retiring waters. While we were engaged to pitch our tents, we heard the report of a

---

[1] The freshwater stingrays of South America belong to the Family Potamotrygonidae of which there are fourteen species divided between two genera, *Disceus* and *Potamotrygon*.

[2] This is probably one of the species of the genus *Coendou*, and perhaps the reason why Schomburgk refers to it as a 'rat' is because the South American porcupine belongs to the Order Rodentia.

Gun to the East, which our Indians ascribed to the Marron Negros, who they said often visit the Cabalaba in order to fish. Indeed by means of the Cabalaba, its tributaries, & those of the Rivers Copaname and Saramacca, they are said to visit the Courantyne. We fired a small Canon which we had with us and we were not a little astonished when Mr Vieth told us on our return that he and the Indians had heard the report at Tomatai, the direct distance of which two places is [blank][1] and the charge amounting to scarcely more than 1½ ounce of powder; it will give an idea how far the sound travells through the woods hushed at that part of the day in perfect silence.

We started next morning early towards the Cataract which was the aim of our present expedition; the morning was foggy and we could scarcely see more than 20 yards before us. The Thermometer stood at 6^h 77° while in the water it rose to 82°, we passed numerous rocky islets, showing sometimes stratified rocks, their dip being South, the ∠ abt 65 and their direction ENE & WSW – now where[2] had I seen the black crust in such thick layers as upon these rocks, which belonged to the Trappean formation. The morning dull enough in appearance seemed likewise to have a gloomy influence upon the feathered tribe with the exception of some humming birds, which in excentric[3] flight hunted after small insects, no other bird was to be seen. Sandy beaches extending in the bed of the river, are always the first indication of approaching rocks and islets – these beaches the formation of pegass – so much valued by the economist for manure – the inundation sweeps the fallen leaves of trees from the land and being carried by the current, they are deposited on the sandy points where the course of the river changes often at right angles, others form often layers of from 1 to 2 feet, covered by a layer of sand – when the river commences to swell the next season the leaves are rotten and form a vegetable earth which being swept away by the stream, in consequence of its lightness floats on the surface and is frequently anewly deposited on the coast where as already observed it is called Pegass.

We saw a chain of hills stretching East and West through which the river has forced itself a passage, they consist of boulders heaved upon each other, their interstices being filled with soil and thus a luxuriant vegetation covers these heaps of granite, which might afford timber of a large size. At their foot rushes the Cabalaba over a granite barrier and forms the beautiful Cataract Avánavero. We halted at a small island on its foot and after having unloaded one of the lightest Corials that we might be able to force it through the rush of water we paid then the Cataract the first visit. It forms almost a half circle and is divided from the other by a small Island. The pretty Lacis fluviatalis[4] covered the rocks; As large risps[5] of lilac flowers formed a tract in the landscape which was not to be overlooked my friends who saw the plant for the first time could not admire it enough. I discovered growing in its company a species of that strange family of plants which I had not seen before.

By means of the little Island we crossed over to the other Cataract; the Island itself was a vivid picture of a luxuriant vegetation, it appeared as if the plants on this little spot

[1] The figure is eleven miles in the 'Report' (see above p. 126).
[2] Presumably 'nowhere'.
[3] That is, eccentric.
[4] *Mourera fluviatilis*.
[5] Schomburgk has apparently slipped into German at this point; 'rispe' is the German for panicle or compound inflorescence.

strove to outdo each other in growth. The representatives of the tribe Bromeliacea distinguished themselves and I saw a Tureraea[1] the outer leaves of which were 9 feet long the greatest circumference of the plant was 14 feet, the spike not yet developped measured 5 feet[;] even the decayed trunks and branches of trees were ornamented with numerous Orchideae which adhering by their tortuous roots to the lifeless trunk made them appear anew as if in the full vigour of vegetation. Several Oncidium among them the beautiful O. lanceanum[2] the gigantic O. altissimum[3] were found in company with Aroideae,[4] Cacti and Tillandsea ferns and mosses.[5] A three angular Cactus, trailed from tree to tree and formed festoons, which certainly were better to be admired in the distance, the long spines with which it was armed were sufficient warning without further Noli me tangere.

A short distance above the Cataract, the perpendicular height of which I estimated 20 feet, the river has its former breadth; the hillocks in the vicinity of the Cataract were not more than 200 feet high, nevertheless we were obliged to relinquish our attempt from reaching their top and high trees allowed us not to foresee any likelihood of a fair prospect. We discovered on the foot of the larger Cataract a rock with some picture writing; it was the first I saw on my present expedition and being in the vicinity of a Cataract, the more interesting to me. More regular in its configuration, the distinct one distinguished itself besides by its size, the others were partly erased by the influence of the air and water.

Highly delighted with our excursion and the beautiful scenery in the vicinity of the Cataract we left Avanevro and returned to the sandy Island where we had camped the night before. From what I had seen of the Cabalaba I formed the Conclusion that it has its sources not far from those of the Courantyne, it resembles so much its recipient that I would not be astonished if it were a branch of the Courantyne. The high fertility of its bank recommends it for cultivation, which to British Colonists can be of less interest as it belongs to the Dutch Colony of Surinam. We left next morning at an early hour; the morning was ushered in by a strong fog and a chilliness which though the Thermometer was 74° made us almost shiver. We could not pass the Cataract Itafé without paying it an other visit, the misty weather threw an additional gloom over the Scenery, at 7^h30^m the temperature of the air was 75°, the water above the Cataract 75°.5 but though I tried repeatedly whether there was a difference in the temperature of the Water above the Cataract and where after having precipitated itself over the rocks, it was foaming and tossing the most, I could not discover the slightest. The ground at the bottom of the Cascade is very deceitful; a great deal of water finds its way through the fissures formed by the heaped up boulders and the Cataract bringing a great deal of fallen leaves, which by the assistance of the water have decayed and though the soil has now the appearance of terra firma, Mr Cameron found much to his annoyance, that it was not; in his eagerness to be the first at the Cataract, he jumped out of the boat and sunk as quick in the mire, his re-appearance coated by the mire was so ludicrous that in spite of his misfortune we could not prevent our bursting out in laughter – we others prefered to make a detour over hard rocks, &c than to walk upon the soft ground.

[1] This is possibly a mistake for *Turnera*.
[2] *Lophiaris lanceana*.
[3] *Oncidium baueri*.
[4] Family Araceae.
[5] For example, *Tillandsia usneoides* is Spanish Moss.

It remained cloudy the whole day, it was therefore useless to stay at the mouth of the river in order to take observations; more especial as its banks did not offer a place for our tents, we reached toward evening a place where the Indians had camped while on fishing-expeditions. An aromatic smell attracted my attention; it arose from the aerial root of an Aroideae which our Indians used in lieu of ropes. The plant grows on high trees and sends the aerial roots to the ground; some have the thickness of a finger, others that of a thread, and frequently appear like the stays of a ship. The Indians call it Ikanna and Akoukoua.[1] Its leaves are cordate sagitate, about 2 feet long, its aerial roots often above 50 knotted and are of a stronger aromatic smell than any other part of the plant, it possesses a slight acrid principle and is stimulant nevertheless the Indians could not inform me of any further medicinal use as that they used it in cases of rheumatic pains and they say after the leave has been put over slow coals they put it upon the painful part and it greatly alleviates the pain.

After my return to Tomatai my departure was delayed for several days, there were thousand excuses for it – they told me they could not make Cassada bread in a shorter time and that Capt Thomas was to have a Piewarie feast and the long & short of it was that they would not go earlier – how many times have I been similarly situated, and not being able to do without the Indians, I have been obliged to endure whenever the sternest resolution and most determined proceedings would have been of no avail as at the first appearance of such measures they would have fled in the woods. The programme for the festivities having been communicated to us we were invited to assist in the celebrations[;] the day previous to the Piewarie feast, the women were to have a dance; we went there in the evening; their efforts were then already at an ebb, however in honour of our visit those who had already retired to their hammocks reappeared – the women, the men were not to dance that day, formed a column, and having a bundle of arrows in their hand with which they beat the [time] by stamping it on the ground accompanying it by a song which resembled more a dirth[2] than the accompaniment to a dance – thus are all the songs of the Caribee nation; they are the object of the death of their relations and the wailing for the decay of their nation. The dancers would go sometimes to several figures and if the mournful song and the stamping of the arrows as well as the apathy so much depicted on their face, had not spoke to the contrary, I might have compared the dance to one of our monotonous Polonaise – the song was for sometimes interrupted and a general conversation took place when as if hired for that purpose and they were to go through it as an undesired labour, they recommenced the male part and those not employed in dancing were not a little astonished at a pair of masks which we had brought with us and which we put before our faces, but it had not the slightest effect upon the dancers, they continued their laborious task without interruption. It struck one as particular that the women carried their children round with them while dancing and those who had none had puppies; even the canine race appeared to participate in the general apathy; they submitted silently to be thus carried for hours.[3]

Mr Losack & Mr Cameron paid in the morning a visit to the drinking bout of the men, they returned disgusted with the scene they witnessed[;] men and women

[1] Possibly *Philodendron* sp.

[2] Presumably 'dirge'.

[3] In the manuscript the next two pages, 26 and 27, are in the wrong order. They have been returned to their correct sequence here.

indulged alike – I had given a promise to come thither in the evening and so we went. The stupid look of the Indians present showed to what excess the drinking had been carried, indeed we found that a Corial 22 feet by four wide and 2 feet and a half deep had been emptied by not more than 60 Individuals women included[,] upon a moderate calculation containing [blank] Gallons of Piwarie.[1] They recommenced dancing, with their hands slung round each others neck, they moved towards the corial and round it, while others gave the measure of the step by beating an Indian drum and playing the Quama or flute;[2] I was astonished to find that the women joined in the dance, which I had not observed while among the Caribees of the Rupununy. My Companions had joined before me in the dance, and I was obliged to do the same after the old Captain had requested me several times to do so. Our friend Cameron cut the most grotesque figure, a Dutch pipe in his mouth and the Indian drum slung round him, he had taken upon himself the office of time-beater – so much enamoured with the harmonious sound thus produced his feet could not resist their influence and raised not a little our risible nerves firstly in a Solo and afterwards engaging a Capoucre[3] in a Duet. We were obliged to admire that latter man's agility and from his regular motions and balancing of his body by means of his stretched out arms, we came to the conclusion that he would make a good opera-dancer. The Piwarie perhaps still acting upon him, and part of the coloured men who accompanied him, indulging him in his jokes he challenged them to wrestling and threw them down without any effort – with the exception of the Ornithologists assistant who though weaker in appearance threw the Indian at every onset, much to his and the other Indians' annoyance; to prevent mischief I had at last to stop the wrestling and thought it best to give orders for our return.[4]

The disagreeable news was brought to me next morning that three of our Arrawaak Crew, had taken away a small Caribee Corial and had absconded – their defection was discovered too late for pursuit and as disagreeable as it was otherwise to me as I had now the more to depend upon the Caribees in whom I had no confidence. We left however on the 11th October accompanied by many of the Indians their women & children, thus swell the number of the Individuals to fifty eight – all opposition from my side was rendered useless by their observation if they shall not go, we wo'nt go either. Above Tomatie the river is studded with rocks; we met some hillocks on the river's left side, but their general height was scarcely more than 150 feet. I consider them a spur of the Twasinkie Mountains; their geological Character was equivalent to those hills; a small brook which the Indians called Assiproua runs almost parallel with the Hills. A small group of Islands attracted next our attention, their beautiful verdure and fine sandy beaches gave them a very pretty

---

[1] These are presumably external dimensions, because if internal the total capacity is 220 cubic feet which converts into approximately 1,370 imperial gallons (10,960 pints). Even if we reduce this total to a quarter on the grounds that the internal measurements were smaller and the canoe was not filled to the brim, it still adds up to 2,740 pints or 45 pints a head. Although Amerindians do consume vast quantities of the weak beer, vomiting as necessary in order to make room for more, this figure is extraordinarily high.

[2] Quama is a species of bamboo. It is common in Carib for an object and the material out of which it is made to have the same name.

[3] Indian/Maroon mix (see p. 143 above).

[4] Wrestling is a common Native Amazonian activity that often forms part of welcoming ceremonies or other rituals.

appearance and if there had not been something high sounding in their Indian name Alapalissa we should have felt much inclined to bestow some poetical name upon them. The rocks which we saw [in] their neighbourhood appeared to have a N. & S direction and in their gigantic forms resembled much those of Achra moucra in the Essequibo. The Courantyne trends far west in ascending, its banks at that time 10 to 12 feet high consisted of that species of clay which I had already observed at Tomatai and which the Indians called Acourou or Alina – they use it for the manufacture of pottery – the sub-stratum was an ochrous clay covered with mould in which trees and plants appeared to drive[1] most luxuriantly. We stopt in the afternoon at rather an early period, dark clouds predicted rain and anxious to get under some shelter, our afternoon's progress was but trifling. The expected storm approached by no means so rapidly as I had expected but the atmosphere became so sultry and oppressive that even breathing became difficulter than generally, animation appeared suspended and even the Pera-piea,[2] the earliest and the latest of the feathered tribe was hushed in silence. The Thermometer was at 6 o'clock in the afternoon 83° the Barometer 29.650.

We had scarcely retired to our hammocks when the grand scene of a tropical storm commenced, it broke lose with great fury and the thunder-cloud passing over our head went first towards the East, but being driven back [by] a Counter-current, it passed our Zenith for a second time and appeared to discharge itself by one of the brightest flashes of lightning, I ever witnessed, a severe thunderclap followed immediately after it, the reverberations of which lasted for 45 seconds and resembled the discharge of a park of artillery – this appeared to have been the signal for torrents of rain falling with the noise of a cataract, and which with little abatement continued until 7 o clock next morning – the quantity of rain during the night amounted to 7.5 inches.

We met next morning the first rapid of consequence, in the vicinity of the Island Bacaeai; after we had passed the Island our course lay towards the high Ground, but before we reached it the river represented an other of those scenes of desolation and confusion so frequent in the rivers of Guiana – the boulders were often 40 feet high and a large decayed trunk which we saw laying across the rocks, and which had been drifted there that the river was high, proved that it is during the rainy season at least 20 feet above its present level. the more we approached towards the hillocks we had seen at the distance, the stronger we found the current – narrowed in by the hillocks, which we estimated 120 feet high, a slight bend of the river materially increases the velocity and almost an hour elapsed before we could overcome its influence though the distance we laid back during that time amounted to scarcely more than half a mile – that current ran at the rate of 4.5 knots. An abandoned Caribee settlement was pointed out to us on the Dutch side – some of the Indians went there to gather Plantains and Bananas – which now grow almost wild. We stopt for breakfast at the foot of the hillocks; the rocks appeared to be obscurely stratified and were highly ferruginous. The hillocks had a N.W.bN & SEbS direction; I was told by some of the Caribees that from their foot a path leads alternately over Savannahs and Woodland to the river Berbice, and that they

---

[1] Presumably 'thrive'.

[2] Probably the Screaming Piha or Piea (*Lipaugus vociferans*), although there are other possibilities such as the Powis or Maroodie (both Cracidae) which call at dawn and dusk, or the Maam (a Tinamou) which whistles at any hour of night.

reached the latter river in a day and a half easy walking. Before we reached our camp which we pitched on the Island Oubali;[1] we met a group of rocks which distinguished themselves by their spheroidical form, they were often piled one upon the other and appeared to keep themselves on their exalted situation by their own gravity; the circumstance was so inviting to hurl some down into the deep that we could not resist from landing, but in spite of their apparent unsure situation a steam engine of so many horsepower would have been required to change the situation which they may have occupied for thousands of years. The depth of the river in the vicinity of these rocks amounted often from 20 to 30 fathoms, their being piled up extends therefore deep below the level of the water.

My Corial was the first which landed on the Island Oubali; we saw something moving rapidly through the mud and the low brush which formed a separation between the Island and the Sandbank – it raised itself and the ungainly head of a large Boa[2] made its appearance – but scarcely had it taken a survey of our party when it rushed toward the river and sunk under the surface; we saw it moving for some time until in consequence of the disturbed state of the water it had received quite a muddy appearance. A young Coloured man who accompanied Mr Vieth as assistant rushed after it with a knife in its hand, but too late to come up with the Snake; all the while the Indians appeared petrified; they abhor not only the snake which by their poison prove dangerous, but likewise those which are innocent. The Sandbank which extended from the northern point of the Island had quite a lively appearance in the evening – temporary huts had been erected in all directions and as our party amounted to upwards of fifty the numerous fires looked quite cheering – the hunters had been fortunate the pepperpots were filled and while I took a stroll through the Camp, I saw the men stretched with the greatest complacency in their Silk Grass hammocks,[3] each having a long cigar in his mouth – how little is necessary to make this people happy, they do not care for the present, nor do they fear to morrow – if scarcity forces them to satisfy the calling of their stomach with the portions of a child, no complaints escape their mouth, and neither joy or delight is depicted upon their faces when plenty transforms them to gluttons.

The different tribes were likewise today divided the Arawaaks and Warrows had erected their panaps or huts[4] in one neighbourhood; while a small rill of water divided them from the Caribees, though this distinction was always strictly adhered to, there were instances where the Arawaak would mix with the Caribee in the course of the day, but the Warrows kept themselves always separate. The heated sand keeps a high temperature long after the sun has sunk below the horizon, at 8^h in the evening, when the temperature of the outer air was 77° the thermometer put in the sand rose to 85°.5; I have frequently repeated this experiment and found always a difference of from 5 to 8°F – this difference amounted in the afternoon often to 40° and even found when at

[1] Possibly Iwaballi Island.

[2] Given that it made for the water, presumably it was an anaconda.

[3] These are hammocks made from vegetable fibres of a Bromelia. Most of the Native Guianese people make both cotton and silk grass hammocks. It is often the case that the silk grass hammocks are made by men, the cotton by women although their use is not so divided. Although the silk grass hammock is not as comfortable as the cotton version, it is much lighter to carry when travelling and has the great advantage of drying out quickly if it gets wet.

[4] A simple temporary shelter would be a better description of a panap.

Tomatai that the white sand possessed a temperature of 128° when the atmosphere was only 85°F.

We started next morning from the Island Oubali along its northern shore. I observed an opening in the afternoon along the river's left bank and concluded that it might be Savannahs, we directed our course therefore towards it, but after we had penetrated the woods which were between the opening and the river, we found it to be a large Swamp that ran parallel with the river; in the morning we had noted the mouth of a brook that has its origin in this Swamp – I saw a small palm which appeared to be very frequent and pleased with the situation it occupied; the mocko-mocko (Caladium astorycum)[1] grew likewise in large quantities, but as we did not observe any thing further interesting in the vicinity we retraced our steps to the Corials. The river continues a breadth of 900 yards, whenever it is not impeded by rocks or islands. We saw at the distance the hillocks on the foot of which we had breakfasted the preceeding day, they extended further than I had supposed when we were in their vicinity, and the particular state of the atmosphere, wrapped them in a bluish tint and gave them a higher appearance than they possess in reality. This is frequently the case in the tropics and was most surprizing a few days ago when we came in view of Mavarlae Island at a distance of about 2 miles, all of us were attracted by the immense size of a tree which occupied the southern point of the Island, it appeared to tower high over every other object and anxious to see this curiosity at a less distance we hurried our Indians to encrease the rate of paddling, the nearer we approached the more vanished the uncommon size until on landing we found that it was a Balsam tree (Clusia) which had taken root on a rock and in consequence of this circumstance raised over the other objects, the atmospheric illusion had made it appear so large; in reality it was scarcely fifty feet high. The blueish hue which surrounds distant objects gives an additional attraction to a tropical landscape; the outlines on the horizon are rendered less hard and it appears as if almost a union took place between the object and the horizon itself – it is different during the momentary dwilight if so it can be called – the green changes in black and while the reflection of the Sun though below the horizon plays still on the western Sky, it renders the contrast the stronger; I have frequently observed this phenomenon and always with renewed delight.

Octbr 14ᵗʰ

We slept last night at the mouth of a small stream on the British Side of the river; the visit of what we considered to be a lake had belated us and we were glad to find in any way a place suited for a camp. Smith came in the evening and told me that one of his people was sick – I found him suffering under a severe fit of ague, the first Indian I saw thus afflicted. The next morning was very cloudy and a temperature of the Water was again a fraction lower than the outer air. In consequence of our Commissary having neglected to draw Rum the preceding evening we had not been able to share the general allowance and they were promised to get a double share this morning – so presented us new proves of their love for ardent Spirits – the signal for sharing rum was hailed with loud acclamations and not satisfied with a double quantity it was curious to see the ingenious claims brought forward to get a still larger quantity. It is disheartening to see the hold this destroyer takes even on the Savage and I fear much in our case our small

---

[1] Moka-moka (*Montrichardia arborescens*).

stock having given out, the Indians will have no further inducement to accompany us and leave us to our fate and the best means to reach the Colony again.

The river is more than 1000 yards wide and keeps to western or rather eastern course – opposite to the Creek commenced a Sandbank which extended for several miles, being sparely covered with the [illegible]-like plant I mentioned before and a few Guava-bushes – I saw one or two palm-seedlings on the southern end and a few shrubs of the common Solanum – a few years hence and it will be an Island – at present it is only frequented by a few Gulls and numerous Guanas which our Indians did not neglect to hunt out. We are told that we shall reach to night a large cataract. We passed two Creeks, one on the British Side, the other on the opposite bank[;] we heard here the rushing of falling water, but as it appeared insignificant we thought it not worth while to enter the brook – the river narrows and we observed numerous rocks that obstructed its course[;] on the little sandy spots that had only lately risen out of the water were numerous Gulls. It was the Rindrops nigra[1] with a depressed and truncated bill of which the upper mandible, much shorter than the lower fits in the latter like a clasp knife; it is black, the front and belly white, the roof of the beak red. Their peculiar formation gives them a ridic[ulous look] when standing, but scarcely are they on the wing when they show their agility and soaring over the water, slightly dipping their wings in that element they slay the fishs in its gamboles and carry it away as prey – their cry is peculiar as the bird's formation, shrill and disagreeable. We indulged occasionally in tea at breakfast, our Indians judging from the colour considered it to be Grog and threw the most longing glances at it – but scarcely had we satisfied their desire when they did not hesitate to spit it out, wondering how Paneghiries[2] could find pleasure in drinking such stuff – I had succeeded however in my intention to deprive them of their erroneous idea, that we were indulging so largely in a liquor, the evil effects of which I took every opportunity to tell them – circumstances and customs forced me to have ardent spirits with me but I had made it a firm rule that never an extra [illegible] should be shared out. We were astonished to find the Waters of the Courantyne suddenly changed in black or rather the Coffee-brown colour of the Aguas negras – indeed they were so dark that objects comparatively near the surface became invisible[.] a sudden shock which made the whole boat tremble told us that we had run on a rock, the next corials met with the same accident. At such occasions it is best to sit quite still, the slightest movement may cause the corial to upset – at the same instance some of the paddlers jump in the waters and pull her by mainforce of her perilous situation; a third boat which followed upon the same rock, she was however light and easily got off. We passed two creeks with waters as black as ink and the Courantyne having afterwards its former colour, we naturally concluded that the discharge of the two creeks had given it the Coffee-brown colour mentioned above. The Current was very strong and it costed some effort to our boatmen to make progress – the cause became soon visible, a second Achra moucra, a labyrinth of rocks was before us, besides this the river was hemmed in on one side by porphyric rocks on the other by a sandbank which stretched over to the other side – we landed on the Sandbank where it was partly our intention to encamp for the night but numerous tracks of tigers which must have selected this island for their rendez-vous

---

[1] *Rynchops nigra*, the black skimmer.
[2] Europeans, but usually excluding Brazilians of European extraction.

made them fear of receiving a visit from these unwelcome guests, that they rather preferred to paddle on longer. The rocks are here different in composition. I considered them trappean, though their stratification was not quite clear, I considered their direction N.E. & S.W. their dip SSE. – they are very rugged, of a coppery appearance, almost lustre and sloped generally towards the north. It was remarkable to see the different sets of the currents after we were fairly among these rocks, some of them formed in their course a perfect circle and as if enraged at the difficulties which they found constantly thrown in their way they foamed and tossed and formed whirlpools on a minor scale. I landed at one of these rocks to take observations for determining the Longitude of our situation by Chronometer it was in [blank]°[blank]'[blank]"[1] the most western point I had taken observations in during my present expedition and [blank] miles westward from the most western point the river has been laid down in Arrowsmith late Chart of Columbia (London 1834).

One of our boats had met with an old Waterhaas (Waterhair) and her young ones and had succeeded in catching one – it was about 1½ foot long, its hind feet were somewhat shorter than the forefeet, there were three toes on each of the hind-feet and four fingers, the upper lip was split and I observed four grinders on each side in both jaws; its Colour was brown, the hair rather long and the tail only 2 inches long. I must however repeat that my description is taken from a young one – they are excellent swimmers but appear to be attacked in the water by the Perie or Carib-fish[2] – the present was deprived of its parts and the account so current that this fish makes those parts the particular point of its attack gained credit with me; it had lost likewise on one of its hindlegs its toes. The Perie or Carib fish is here very frequent and our fishermen have caught some which measured 16 inches in length and 7 inches in breadth – they are of good taste but the certainty that they prefer flesh as bait to any other causes many to hesitate in eating them – necessity forced us to have no such scruples. They bite very easily but their teeth are so sharp that they bite often through the smaller hooks, and with large ones they are not easily caught.

Our progress was the next day quite slow, rocks and Islands were so numerous that our scout had often to visit several passages before he could select one which we could pass with our Corials – these rocks are a most remarkable feature in these regions and though they astonished me while ascending the Essequebo, they are in the Courantyne more numerous and not less in size and length – very few are angular the most of them being spheroids or domeshaped, all are more or less coated with that metallic lustre – where we found several smaller blocks accumulated, the place between each was filled up with that strange vitreous matter so frequently noticed – which I am much inclined to consider as having been under fusion.

The scene is here very interesting, the Chaos of rocks, the rushing of the waters, the numerous islands which make the total width of the river to upwards of two miles, each has its peculiar attraction but the most striking feature was a forest of Lacis (fluvialalis) all in flower, the light brown scape, the thickly set flowers naked & of a lilac colour formed a strong contrast to the otherwise barren granitic rock, thousands were in flower and their luxuriance showed how much they were delighted with this spot. I

---

[1] 57°40′W. See above p. 128.
[2] Pirai or Piranha (*Serrasulmus* spp.).

measured one of the lacerated leaves which I found 3 feet 2 inches long and 2 feet wide. Its peculiar formation deserves notice. [...][1]

Our camp was this night selected upon a rocky islet, called by the Caribees Akalikatabo in Lat 4°40′N. The more we advanced the next day the more we found our way obstructed by rapids or narrow passages and all the agility and bodily strength of our crew was called forth, to force a passage for our Corials – the perpendicular fall of the river is insignificant but the length the water continues to run over shallows, beset with dangers is tiresome enough and threatens at every step destruction to the boats. The Indians told me I would not be able to advance much further in Corials, a circumstance so little foreseen that it is a great disappointment to me. We passed at nine o'clock the rock Tíméré[2] distinguished for its size – on the top there are said to be Indian picture-writing but the current run so strong that our attempts to come near them proved in vain. After having paddled a whole day without little intermission we had after all not made more than three miles in a direct course. The night proved stormy, thunder clouds collected in all quarters and we expected a most uncomfortable night – however it proved better. Our huts were erected in one line and there being but little place afforded to each the noise and din of 54 souls was by no means conducive to a refreshing sleep – our whole party must have found it so, the Indians commenced their accustomed conversation an hour earlier, that is at three o'clock and even the canine race seemed to share in the general restlessness and gamboling under our hammocks awoke even those who had shut their ears against the noise caused by the conversative powers of our Indian gentry out of the sleep which they purposed to steal upon the morning hour.

October 16th

Helas the river's nature has not changed as yet rocks and Islands in all directions – we passed in the morning early a remarkable rock, scored out by the action of the atmosphere it astonished us by its gigantic size. One of those cavities represented a couching tiger without much stress of imagination – a proper emblematic coat of arms for these regions.

The rock was about 30 feet high and 12 wide and consisted of a solid piece.

The river after having run for some time to the East*

*It must be understood that I mean its natural course to be west which to us in ascending or against the stream became east, and like wise North, South.

turned and came from the South; at that point we had to pass some rapids, and the middle one being too shallow we tried several lateral channels before we succeeded – the numerous Islands gave the river a total width of nearly three miles, above the rapid I estimated it 1000 yards.

Our Corial was somewhat behind, when I saw a great commotion among those which preceded us, they pulled towards the shore and with their bows ready we saw the

---

[1] Most of the next fifteen lines of handwriting on p. 34 of the manuscript, in which the Lacis is described, are illegible. Rather than providing a very incomplete and incomprehensible text, it has been decided to leave out the passage in its entirety including a related footnote which refers to John Lindley's *An Introduction to the Natural System of Botany: or, a Systematic View of the Organisation, Natural Affinities, and Geographical Distribution, of the Whole Vegetable Kingdom*, London, Longman, Rees, Orme, Brown, & Green, 1830.

[2] Timehri.

Figure 4: Robert Schomburgk's sketch of a weather-carved rock in the Corentyne River. Included by permission of the Royal Geographical Society, London.

Indians firing after an object – it was a large Tapiba or Waterhaas.[1] – it had received already three arrows in its head and still it dived under the water for minutes before it made its appearance again, only after having received the charges of two guns, we were able to secure it – it had quite a strange appearance to see, first the arrows make their appearance when the animal came to the surface of the water to take a gasp of fresh air, then came the unshapen head, the arrow heads sticking in an oblique direction between the head and neck.

It is astonishing what numbers of Perie or Carib-fish are in these parts – our crew catch frequently in half an hour more than they can consume in a day – but their

[1] This creature is clearly a capybara, but I have been unable to find any confirmation that this animal was ever called a 'tapiba'. This word is suspiciously close to tapir, but it would be difficult to confuse the two animals.

ferociousness [knows] no bounds[. W]ill it be believed that this morning something came floating down the river which it puzzled us to make out what it was[1] – numerous Peries were floating around it – we put our boat about to satisfy our curiosity and a large Luganani[2] was drawn out of the water, the hinder half of which was eaten up by the Peries, the poor animal being still alive – to judge from the stump the Luganani must have weighed at least twenty pounds. By our interference it escaped certainly the slow death of being eaten piece-meal by the Peries but only to be prepared as an addition to our breakfast. The Luganani assailed by a numerous host succumbed, and while the conquerors divided the prey without congress or stipulations, according to the right of the strongest a new and more powerful claimant appeared, and without hesitation took possession of the fruits of their victory.

We camped that night at the Island Paumatil in Lat 4°28′35″N. We found next morning that the river had taken a different aspect; not with regard to the numerous rocks, with which it was studded, to this we were accustomed but along shore we found a number of detached blocks which extended far inland. I found that the strength of the current had increased and our progress became much slower the wind blew fresh and in gusts, the Thermometer stood at 8 o'clock 75° the surface of the water was 83°. At 11 o'clock we saw rising ground before us, and the river was hemmed in by piles of granitic blocks, between the crevices of which fertile soil has been collected and large forest trees have sprung up. We had become callous to the beauty of such scenes and were anxiously looking out for a place where we might land to take breakfast – our eyes were searching in every direction, no where presented itself a place to push our corials ashore, the numberless granitic rocks rendered every attempt fruitless; the river took a turn, and the hillocks which we observed previously only on its left shore approached it now from both sides, half an hour's further progress and we found ourselves in apparently a large basin formed by hillocks of 60 to 100 feet high, the river broken up in torrents, the white flocks of foam which came sailing down as if to meet us, the thundering noise of falling waters, and a cloud which like perpetual mist hung over the southern hillocks spoke in an intelligible voice that some great scene of nature was before us. We selected a sandy bay, skirted by large forest trees for our camp and with regard to romantic scenery we could not have made a better selection. Without further examination of the terrain I observed that we would have to make a stay here and I gave consequently orders for the erection of our tents while thus occupied the Caribees observed that we would find it impossible to get further, there was not enough water in the river and that they only succeeded during the rainy season to cross the falls when the river was full and they were able to select a lateral channel for the transport of their canoes. This was distressing news and though I had been prepared by the hints they had thrown out a few days previous, I had no idea that the difficulties should be so formidable. I had still hopes, I recollected how frequently I had been threatened in a sinister way during my last expedition and I had not seen as yet with my own eyes the difficulties which we were told to find insurmountable. It was almost dark when I selected one of the small Corials and proceeded towards the Cataract, we were obliged to draw the Corial over a bar of rocks but arrived on the other side we found that the evening was

---

[1] There is more than one possible reading of these words and this one has been selected.

[2] Lukanani (*Cichla ocellaris*), a freshwater fish that grows to 45cm in length and is exceptionally good eating.

too far advanced to proceed further. To the South we heard the rush of the Cataract, we saw as yet nothing of it and judged only of the foam and high waves with which the water was passing us, that the fall must be considerable. On our return to the Camp we made the necessary arrangements for an exploratory tour. The night of 17ᵗʰ October was beautiful, and I succeeded in getting two observations by culminating Stars.*

*The means of my observations give me Lat. of the encampment at the Cataract 4°21′31″N. & Longᵗ 57°35′32″W., the great Cataract bore from there S.

While watching for this [blank] and surrounded by the stillness of night, I heard the rush of Cataracts plainly in two directions and I became now persuaded that it was not one fall but a series of falls at the foot of which we were encamped; full of expectations and fear what the examination of these barriers would bring us at day-light, I could not close my eyes during the few hours which remained between the last observation and the appearance of day, and happy when the Hamiequa[1] announced the approach of the morning clouds I left my hammock and awoke my companions to make themselves ready. We took some of the most able of our crew with us and the two Caribees, Smith and Accouritch were appointed guides, as we had gleaned from them that they had been here before. We followed the same course as last evening and having hauled the corial over the rocks, crossed the lower rapid in oblique direction and stood shortly after before a pile of rocks, which during the rainy season are the bed of a cataract, at present only a small stream of water rippled over their blackened surface. From the encampment it had appeared to me as if this place would afford me the possibility of drawing the corials over; my hope fell with every step I advanced, enormous piles of rocks grouped together to a height of 90 to 40 feet opposed obstacles in every direction even to us pedestrians, at other times we saw chasms at our feet and a courageous leap was necessary to land on the other side – we had to wade through a stream which pathed its way meandring through the rocks and disappeared as if by magic, and the subterranean noise told us that it had found a way through some cavities. The space which is occupied by the waters during the inundations is smooth and possesses the peculiar black coating. These rocks exhibited a great many circular holes partly filled with quartz pebbles – I measured one of the larger and found it 3 feet deep and 10 inches in diameter. Adjacent to the former had rose piles of rocks often to 40 feet high, they are clothed with numerous plants, a species of Orchidea and an Agave were the most remarkable among them, clusters of bright yellow flowers distinguished the first, while the long and slender scape of the latter adorned with thousands of flowers gave a picture of luxuriance even to the sterile rocks. At my right I heard the thundering noise of a Cataract over which a dense cloud of mist, thousands of Swallows were skipping through the [air,] falling and rising as if delighted by the constant moisture which surrounded them. I followed the party who left the large fall for the present unvisitted and after some labour and wading got to a branch of the river which divided itself in two channels, the western formed a fall and the opening prospect at my arrival on its head was beautiful indeed, the water rushed at an angle of 60° into a valley formed by gigantic piles of rocks which we had taken the previous day for hillocks, the more so since they were clothed with large trees; at our feet foamed the disturbed waters, dashing their spray against the rocks that impeded

[1] This is possibly the Little Chachalaca (*Ortalis motmot*). The Indians call it 'Hannaquoi' after the sound of its cry which is commonly heard at dawn and dusk.

their course, but the most lively object was a cascade on the oposite side of the chasm, the rocks over which the water falls is of scalar nature and clothed with a Lacis the pendulous branches of which are often 5 to 6 feet long and resemble a rich carpet, and the endless modifications of its green, the strong contrast of its pink flowers and the foam of the water which rushed over the scalar like rocks and fell in three divisions, made the prospect exceedingly beautiful. I estimated the height of the Cataract 20 feet, the one on the top of which I stood 30 feet – they are almost opposite each other and I need not to observe that at the junction of the falling waters of the two cataracts, the greatest commotion prevails which is more encreased by the [furious] rush of the water of a third cataract which was hid from my view by an Island but the silvery whiteness of the foam and the waves which form the conflict rose to a considerable height made me suppose that it was the larger of the three; But how to come there was an other question, unacquainted with swimming I could not venture to cross the channel, where even an expert swimmer would have hesitated to stem the current, however by great circuits & dint of wading climbing and crawling I succeeded at last and I was richly rewarded for my trouble. Three different branches of the river are here united and seek one and the same outway, at their junction their further progress is contested by huge blocks of granite through which they have forced a passage and as if now anxious which water of the three branches should reach first the foot of the Cataract, they precipitate perpendicular in a chasm which the waters have grooved in the granitic rock, it falls thus upwards of forty feet perpendicular, representing one sheet of foam. A large rock stands out as in relieve and has been resembled to a human thigh-bone the Indians have given therefore that fall the name [blank]. I descended to the foot of the Cataract and succeeded to reach the place of the first Cataract by climbing up the opposite side, one of the Caribees served me as a guide and I freely acknowledge that I was glad to find an other path than the circuitous one I had chosen on the former occasion. I found Mr Reiss sketching the view I had so much admired. Mr Cameron joined us soon afterwards with Cornelius, they had visited the most eastern fall and Mr C. was quite enthusiastic in its description. They brought with them several Swallows alive, while passing a Cavern at the eastern fall, formed by boulders, overlying each other, they found them climbing against the rock and disturbed by their appearance they rushed in large numbers out of their abode, and so numerous were they that they knocked down several with their hands. We immediately resolved to proceed thither, though all of us were fatigued and after climbing over and crawling round numerous boulders we stood at the head of the largest fall I had seen in Guiana. It is a grand sight indeed, the mass of water, the velocity with which it precipitates over the ledge of rocks to a depth of upwards of seventy feet perpendicular cause the spray to form a cloud of dense mist which rises in height with the stately palm trees that rose out of the crevices of clusters of rocks. The vivid green of the foliage of the trees, numerous parasitical plants which even covered the trunks and branches of trees added to the luxuriance and diversity of the picture. I stood surprized and [delighted] on a rock from whence I had a full view of the foaming bed at my feet combined with the unceasing noise of the Cataract, which drowned every attempt to converse with my companions or to communicate the impression this scene must cause to the observer, the silence to which one is condemned renders the impression of so much grandeur more powerful, even to oppression. I became giddy and retired quickly to prevent my joining the dance of the whirling white crested billows below. I have stood on much more perilious situation in the mountains of the

Hartz without ever feeling the slightest sensation of vertigo, and I ascribe it to those masses of water unceasingly rolling in the abyss below which produced the sensation as if urging to follow them. Mr Reiss felt a similar effect at a later point. I was anxious to see the fall from below, I left therefore the party with Cornelius and seeked to reach the bed of the river at the foot of the Cataract. Cornelius who had been there in the morning led the way over immense boulders, the trunk of a fallen tree served us frequently as a bridge, while at other times we were obliged to let us down to the next ledge of rocks by means of a bush rope – under our feet we heard rolling of water which pathed itself with a hollow noise a course through numerous cavities. I had sometimes a glance of the water by means of a chasm, formed by two boulders not lying quite close to each other – these chasms were sometimes grown over with a vine and partly covered, it was therefore necessary to step with the greatest caution – like the drops of a heavy summer shower, thus descended the spray which was driven in the air by the fall, and the constant moisture thus produced covered rocks and trunks of trees with numerous lichens. Before I reached the foot of the fall all my clothes were wet as if I had been exposed to rain, but the view of the fall from that situation fully recompensed for the trifling inconvenience; the sun being to the west I saw large spots adorned with all colours of the rainbow forming itself in the spray and vanishing in order to reappear the next moment. I followed now the course of the river by climbing over the rocks which confined its bed and joined soon after my companions.

The evening was rapidly approaching when we returned. We found our little Camp in some commotion; the sickly child which had been under the hand of the Peieman repeatedly appeared to be near his solution and a temporary hut had been erected to cast out the evil Spirit – his imposition went so far that after having applied his lips to the child's chest he produced a large piece of charcoal, which he said had been the cause of the disease and he had sucked through bone flesh and skin. We considered the patient on death's door, nevertheless the little boy recovered, which did not elate a little the consequence of the Peie-man.[1]

As much as we had been delighted with the romantic Scenery we witnessed at the Cataracts, it appeared to us impossible to cross the rocks with our Corials – and only the hope remained to us that there might be a path by which they could be avoided.[2] I summoned therefore the Caribees who made part of my expedition as they were the only nation acquainted with the upper Courantyne and questioned them closely on that subject so important to me, but to no purpose; they repeated that we might pass during the rainy season, at present however where the river was so low I would find it impossible. In order to serve as a stimulant for exertions I offered now a reward to any Indian who should discover a place where we might be able to cut a path for the transport of our boats, and a still higher reward was held out to the coloured individuals of my crew and consequence of which expeditions were undertaken every day. I had not inspected as yet the eastern side of the Cataracts; we found here a fall which we would have

---

[1] The Amerindian shaman and his patients are not as incredulous as Schomburgk and most travellers have assumed. The spirit dart or weapon that causes an illness is non-material and invisible except to shamanic sight. What the shaman is doing when he produces a piece of wood, charcoal or other substance is giving visible and material representation to an invisible cause.

[2] This sentence is much scored out and written over, but the version reproduced here accurately follows one reading although it is impossible to tell if it is the final one intended.

considered interesting, if we had not seen the others before – the velocity and height of the water was similar to the others and there was no more likelihood of a passage than in the former case. I left my companions sketching and climbed over rocks and other impediments to get at the head of the fall; as far as my eye could reach I saw a continuation of rapids and a chaos of boulders, objects but little calculated for the hope of a passage.

There were but few of these rocky soils which did not present a varied and even rich vegetation, some supported trees while others only barely covered with soil were adorned with beautiful orchideous plants, Cacti and Rhizomates.[1] An erect Cereus four angled and of a greyish-green colour distinguished itself by the height which it reached while an other with weaker stems that could not support themselves seeked that support from trees trailing from branch to branch. Two Orchideae, the one with the bright yellow flower, the other of less outer beauty but of an odour which perfumed the atmosphere in its vicinity were the gems of flora's empire in the granite rocks. I went in different directions accompanied by Cornelius and some swift Indians, and more than once I thought of having succeeded to find a path through this labyrinth until a chasm of 30 to 40 feet depth opened at our feet and destroyed our hopes. I returned unsuccessful to my companions, persuaded in my mind, that it would be impossible to cross the Cataracts unless we constructed a circuitous path, which it would have taken us 6 to 8 weeks to accomplish. The Gentlemen who accompanied me as Volunteers undertook several expeditions hereafter and only after their report of the impracticability of crossing the rocks under present circumstances unless a path were constructed for that purpose the last spark of hope vanished for accomplishing this object. The Caribees by far the most numerous of my crew threatened to depart – they had from the commencement behaved in a manner which I could not explain; though their fields were covered with Cassada, they refused to supply me with any and on their leaving the Settlements they had taken only enough for 10 days maintenance – after the elapse of that time, they depended entirely upon my stores, and though I was strong enough to resist any open force, policy and the hope that a passage might be discovered obliged me to spoil it not entirely with them, and I was therefore necessitated to give them allowances in rice and other provisions, and the inroad which consequently was made, caused the well-founded apprehension that in less than three weeks we would have to subsist upon game and fish [and] long before this be abandoned by our treacherous friends.

My companions urged therefore to return and with a heavy heart I was obliged to consent to it at a long consultation we had on the subject. I proposed that the ascent of the river Berbice which is more populated might lead us perhaps to the accomplishment of our design of crossing the impediments of the Cataracts and penetrating to the chain of mountains in the second parallel of Latitude. I resolved to stay three days more at the Cataract partly for surveying the lower basin and to carry the plan to that point where the river meets with the first impediments, and partly from the desire to commemorate the first visit of Europeans[2] by giving the two principal cataracts the

---

[1] Whereas this is a fairly secure reading, what is probably intended is Rhizophora, i.e., mangroves.

[2] This claim is wrong. In 1718 a Dutch trader, Gerrit Jacobs, travelled up the Corentyne and crossed to the Essequibo by the path that leads via the Berbice River. Jacobs repeated his journey in 1720. Similar journeys may have been made in the 17th century. See G. Bos, 'Atorai, Trio, Tunayana and Wai Wai in Early Eighteenth Century Records', *Folk*, 27, 1985, pp. 6–8.

name of General Sir J^s Carmichael Smyth and Sir John Barrow; the latter distinguished as promoter of Geography and the President of the Royal Geographical Society while Sir James had taken from all commencement a lively and active interest in the Guiana Expedition. It would be tedious to go through the details connected with the Survey, but after we had reached the great Cataract we made the necessary preparations to christen it with the normal honours, and after it had received the name of General Sir James Carmichael Smyth's Cataract we drank his Excellency's health and fired a salute the proceedings being then deposited in a bottle it was placed on the highest rock in the vicinity. I had purposely brought the small canons which we possessed in order to continue my survey by means of the velocity of sound which I had taken at 1130 feet pr second and according to which the tract of boulders extended to five miles N. & S. Mr Vieth was left in charge of the canons and was directed to fire two guns in succession every half an hour. Having compared our watches I noted the time the report was heard and its direction and thus I received a check against any irregularities the unequal progress and delays in our march would have caused otherwise. Through the whole defile, cataract followed cataract and we had at one time four cataracts in view following each other in succession.

We reached after 12 o'clock the point where the river flowed smooth and uninterrupted. I placed here Englefield's Barometer and found that spot to be 102 feet above our encampment; I had previously ascertained that our camp was 432 feet above the level of the sea. This was the last barometrical observation I was able to take; Troughton's Mountain Barometer met with an accident while it was landed at the mouth of the Courantyne and on my return on the present occasion, though Englefield was entrusted to Cornelius, whom I considered the most careful person and one who was perfectly accustomed to such rocky paths, he slipped from a rock and fell with its charge to the ground and the bag of the Instrument burst. I met the fate of other travellers in that regard, but few have been successful to carry this delicate instrument to the end of their journey. Mr. Losack and Mr. Reiss investigated the rocks to the east until they arrived at the end of a chain of hillocks similar formed to those we had investigated before. While swimming across one of the branches of the river Mr Reiss had nearly lost his life; a less expert swimmer than he supposed to be he sunk and if it had not been for the timely interference of Lt Losack, we would have had to regret the loss of a Companion and a friend.

The fruits of our excursion were not only a knowledge of the country beyond the great cataract but likewise the acquaintance of several new Orchideae and some Cacti which I had not seen before – we had certainly to regret the accident which befell Mr Reiss and the loss of my Barometer, but as the first had no further bad consequences, I consoled myself with the loss of the latter by the knowledge of the extensive tract of boulders I had reaped and the firm persuasion that whatever may have been the original cause of disturbances which produced them, they reaped original strength at the spot, and in this I was born out on account of the exact resemblance which occurs in the paste in which many angular pieces of a porphyritic nature were embedded – indeed it ressembled a scoriform lava, but the cells were rounded and the paste glazed by a vitreous varnish. It does not belong to my plan to enter here in details on that subject which in every other respect must be interesting to Geologists.

We were accustomed to send out hunts men every morning they were frequently most successful and brought a rich harvest for the larder and collection. At different occasions they brought several Specimens of the Pisa a monkey most interesting for its appearance.[1] At an other time a pair of those singular birds, the Cock of the rock or rock mamakin (Piper expicula)[2] were shot by a Caribee which we considered the gem of our collection. What a difference between the male and female, while the first glows in a bright orange colour, the female appears only in a dusky olive only. They are peculiar to granite ridges and apparently delight after the resplendent luminary has retired to its watery couch, as if too modest to exhibit its aurora-like colours after the goddess has opened her gates. They were the only pair I had procured during my expeditions in Guiana and therefore the more valued.

On an expedition which my companions undertook for the investigation of the ground they discovered some picture writings in the vicinity of the great Cataract. I took an early opportunity to view them. They were engraved on a large boulder and resembled in the general outlines those we saw at Cabalaba. In comparing them with the picture writings I saw at Warapoota in the Essequebo, those at the Courantyne distinguished themselves by their larger size or the greater regularity with which the outlines were executed. We found only two on this rock while a third had suffered so much by the influence of the water that it was nearly erased. A few more were discovered later on the eastern Cataract.

We returned on the morning of the [blank]; we halted our Corials several times to listen to the distant sound of the Cataracts until it became fainter and fainter and lost itself among the [voice] of the rustling leaves. We heard the most eastern cataract longest, its distance might have been then upwards of 2 miles. The frequent rains which we had had lately, had caused the river to swell, many of the lower rapids where we found difficulties in ascending were passed without the least obstruction. We halted at the rock Timehri and saw the Indian Hyeroglyphs for which the river is famed among the tribes of the Corentyne – they were more gigantic than any I had seen before, the largest measured 12½ feet and was in its widest part 64 inches across – in the general outlines it resembled those of the Cabalaba and of the Corentyne at the great Cataracts. It appeared that the rock had been once covered with it on its eastern side – at present there are only six visible, many parts of which are injured by the atmosphere. The rock is granitic and perfectly smooth and its eastern side is inclined towards the horizon at an angle of about 50° – it is therefore to be wondered at, in what posture these figures were executed which from the hardness of the stone it is to be conjectured must have required a great deal of bodily strength to execute. The present Caribees of the river know nothing of their origin they hold the rock in awe and have attached the superstition to it, that if its name be repeated it will cause rain. I could not learn what the name 'Timehri' signifies.[3]

We took up our Camp at one of our old Camps in the vicinity of a small brook – we had had daily rains and observed that the river commenced to swell – that evening ([blank]) we found it uncommon sultry however there were no signs of the severe thunderstorm which commenced at 11 o'clock when we retired to our hammocks, the whirlwinds which accompanied it, unroofed our temporary huts, and if it should have happened that we had camped that night unprotected by trees, but little would have

---

[1] Pisa, also spelt bisa, is the black saki (*Chiropotes satanas*).

[2] *Rupicola rupicola*.

[3] See p. 129, fn. 1 for comment on this.

remained of our oil-sheets – during the period this [storm] lasted I stood constantly in fear that it might unroot one of the trees in our neighbourhood and in its fall endanger our lives. It continued to rain until the morning. A great deal of noise and lively talking awoke me at dawn. I heard several angry voices from some and laughter from others; what was my astonishment to find the huts which were occupied by the Caribees under water – the river had risen so rapidly that the lower huts which were at some distance from its banks stood 2 feet under water. The discovery had been only made by some when not expecting that they might commodiously step out of their hammocks in the Corials they had jumped right in the water – old Thomas had profited by the misfortune of the others and it looked certainly ludicrous to see him order his corial and go out of his hammock into it. The first alarm had been given by Christian and his wife, who were disagreeably awakened by the water [reaching] to their hammocks. The rains [which had persisted] for some time past had caused the river to swell at such an unusual time. The fine sandbank at the Island Oubali where we camped when we ascended the river was completely under water and it reached to the eves of the frames of our former huts, it had risen therefore upwards of 10 feet.

The increased current carried us swiftly to Tomatai where we arrived on [blank] at dusk. When I engaged the Caribees it was stipulated that they were to accompany me for the time the expedition lasted – however their treacherous conduct did not make me wish to have their Company further than the Coast where I could procure a vessel to convey the expedition to Berbice. Full conscious of their behaviour and supposing perhaps that now we might be [intimidated] by their number, they demanded to be paid at Tomatai and refused to go further with me. Smith considered this likewise an excellent opportunity to get again possession of the Corial for which I had paid him before we left Tomatai – we discovered next morning that it had been carried away during night – to prevent their pilfering us which certainly they would have done if we had tamely submitted to their demands our arms were put ready for use and Smith was told that if the Corial was not returned before dusk, I should take reprisals and as with regard to their payment I was ready to give it to them as soon as we arrived at the Coast – they were likewise told that I was to leave next morning and who was not there an hour after the Signal had been fired might consider himself paid for the services rendered. Smith arrived next morning with seven Caribbees four however did not make their appearance – I wondered even that Smith had come – his cupidity had outmastered all fear.

We breakfasted in our descent at the brook Hanaubi here was formerly a settlement which is now entirely abandoned – some of the Indians knew however the former Provision grounds and they returned soon with some fine bunches of plantains. I observed at the mouth of the Creek a coarse Sand-stone with small particles of mica, its direction appeared to N85°E its dip N and as far as I was able to judge its angle almost 80°, this may be considered the first indication of rock in the river Corentyne if we except in a wider sense the Clays and Marls. In the vicinity of Kayeewa a beautiful section of the latter formation is exhibited.

Kayeewa is the most northern Settlement of the Caribees from thence commence the Settlements of the Arawaak. We landed next morning at the mouth of the Creek Epira to visit some Arawaak settlements; they live at a distance of several miles from the Corentyne – the path thither led us through a swamp grown over with Manicole, a pretty species of Palm, the brook Epira with water as dark as ink meandres through it and we had to cross it several times – roads and bridges do not receive the Indian's attention and while the first obliged us to wade knee-deep through the mud the latter appeared to be an unknown commodity to the inhabitants of Epira, we had therefore to ford the brook 4 or 5 times. The settlement is built on the sandy ridge which stretches towards Kayeewa and rises there to a considerable height. In a distance of about three miles and parallel with the river there are four settlements each composing of five or six huts and about 30 inhabitants. At one of these settlements the fruits of the Bastard bullet-tree[1] were handed to us, they were of a delicious taste and to judge from the fruit I believe the tree belongs to the Sapodilla tribe – it is of the size of a Damson and beautiful purple – the inside greenish there are four or five flat seeds in it. We returned about noon to the banks of the Corentyne, several of the Arawaaks followed us with Yams, sweet Patatas and other vegetables which they offered us for barter. When among the Caribees I had been obliged to pay for six small yams to the value of 1fl (1/6^d) here almost a bushel were offered to me for the same prize – we bought whatever they brought to us, it was really a luxury to taste vegetables again, after our friends at Tomatai would not furnish any from their rich field, either for money or barter; those who were still with me appeared rather ashamed of their conduct when they saw how different we were treated by the Arawaaks.

I bought an Indian Dog of the Macoosy tribe – there is no doubt that they descend from those introduced by the Spaniards but by many cross breeds they have formed a Variety different from our European dogs – those of the Macoosies are highly esteemed and well paid by the Colonists – they are generally good hunters and trained to chase the Laba out of its burrow and to stay the deer in its course until the native huntsman comes up to shoot the barbed arrow in its neck. The quality of a good hunting dog are judged from the scars which his body shows as a mark that he will boldly attack the Laba or wild hog – many have like a film over their eyes – this is an other recommending quality and is the consequence of the dog's fleetness – when brushing through the underwood, eager to seize his game their eyes get injured by the sticks and small brambles. Many of the dogs are only trained to hunt quite particular game, while one hunts down the deer an other would not even follow it, but let him scent a Capibara or a herd of Peccaries and his shrill barking is able to tell in which direction he is following. I have a dog which is trained to hunt different game is therefore the more valuable.

The head of the Macoosie dog is more elongated and in consequence of the parietal bones approaching each other only slightly its head appears rather small[,] the ears are rather short[,] its tail is short haired and rather long in proportion – its size about [blank] feet long and [blank] inches high[;] they are teachable but ferocious towards strangers, but chiefly to whites – whenever we approached an Indian hut we were assaulted by the canine race in every direction and it appeared to us to be the duty of the women to appease them or to tie them to prevent mischief. An Indian is fond of his dog – he allows him to sleep in his hammock or has a hammock made for him. When the dog is to be trained he has to undergo a sort of peie-ing he receives Capiscum in his food and the juice of it mixed with that of some herbs is inoculated in several parts of his body. When they appear to answer for the purpose they are intended for, they receive the liver and heart of the game they are taught to hunt. They have the strange superstition that if the dog is beaten with a fan

[1] Unidentified, perhaps *Chrysophyllum* spp.

(which they use for fanning the fire and which the Caribees call Wari-wari) it loses all his good qualities and becomes useless – it is therefore the greatest offence which could be offered to the Caribee to beat his dog with a Wari-wari. I am not aware that the other nations have the same superstition.

The dog which was offered to me for sale was to possess all good qualities. I took him more from his good appearance than from the ipse dixit of the Indians – he had the high-sounding name Caniando, worth to be of grecian origin. These dogs are all taught to occupy the very front of the Corial; and the bustle in the morning or at any time of starting is to them at once a call to be at their place. I have seen sometimes four or five huddled together in the bow. Caniando appeared to have received a good education and gave us little trouble – he was always to be found on his place.

I observed previously when ascending that the river circumscribes almost a circle in the vicinity of the small second range of marly hills called Siprouta – we had heard much of a passage over land across a savannah and I was anxious to visit it – we arrived shortly after we left Epira at the place where the Savannah borders the river, here near the small brook Paerourou leads the path to Siprouta – the Gentlemen who accompanied me as Volunteers, myself and a spare Indian to carry our luggage landed at 4 o'clock in the afternoon; while the Corials were to continue their course as a favourable tide was expected to set in about 7 o'clock we calculated that they might be with us at day break. [We] emerged from a small thicket and [a savannah of] one miles and a half extent lay before us[1] – it was a miniature of those I had seen in the vicinity of the Pacarayma Mountains. I recognised many of the Plants I had collected there and a fine breeze blowing from the North and the heat of the Sun being much modified by that luminary approaching the horizon, the walking across the savannah though not shaded was less fatiguing and the new scene much enjoyed by us all. The path went north over undulating ground, we entered afterwards a thicket and had to cross the Stream Maypoure, which has received its Caribbee name from the number of tapirs which live in its vicinity – we ascended afterwards one of the sandhills which are a continuation of those at Epira and Kayeewa and stood at the settlement Maypoure – the Arawaaks who live here were abroad – when we ascended the Corantyne, we met Wellington the Captain of the Settlement at Skeldon – they had not returned as yet. Wellington is one of the finest formed Arawaaks I have ever seen – he is taller and fairer than the generality of his tribe and every limb is in proportion to the whole figure. I do not know [who has] bestowed upon him the name of the hero of Waterloo but since it has been given to one of the redmen, I think it could not have been bestowed upon a handsomer individual[;] he is austere and uncommon distant with new acquaintances, but it appears where he is well acquainted it melts away and he is ready to do any service. I was anxious to buy a large Corial from one of his men, ycleped Cochrane, he did not wish to part with it, but upon Mr Ross speaking to Wellington, he soon managed it that it was in my possession – though I paid a very high prize for it, the Corial was roomily upward of 35 feet long and suited exceedingly well for my purpose. We took possession of one of the empty huts and slung our hammocks, but little rest was in store for us, the mosquitos were so numerous, but we could not shut an eye and we found hands, face and feet

---

[1] This is not an entirely secure reading as the part of two sentences are here written over the top of one another, obscuring both.

resembled more a [grater], so thickly they were set with bumps caused by the bites of these merciless tormentors. According to an unsatisfactory observation of α Gruis, Maypure was 5°11'10"N Lat. The sky was covered and to increase our misfortune, it commenced shortly after 8 o'clock to thunder and to rain.

Maypoura is a few hundred yards from the river's side and here are the marly hills called Siprouta, a scene which must be allways interesting to Geologist.

We heard the approach of our Corials with the first dawn – they had rested for an hour and a half and paddled with a favourable tide through the whole night – while thus ten hours had been necessary to bring them around by the circuitous path which the course of the river forms we had walked it across in three quarters of an hour's easy walking. We did not lose any time to re-embark and approached rapidly the Post Oreala – though the river being swollen where the tide had but trifling influence, nothing of its rise was to be observed along the banks below Maypure, but the tide ebbed stronger and upwards of two hours longer than when the Corentyne is low. I need not observe how astonished our new acquaintances were at Mr Layfield's and at Post Oreala to see us return at such an early periode. The most ridiculous reports had been afloat – the Arawaaks, who the reader will remember run away while at Tomatai had in order to veil their desertion spread most absurd accounts, which were most eagerly believed by the Indians and the superstitious. Among other fables they had told that while ascending the Cabalabo, and we had arrived at the Cataract Anavero, large streams of boiling water had spouted out of the earth and the trees had commenced to groan and where ever we had cut or broken a branch blood had flown out of it. These accounts had been expounded by the Warrows as a sure sign that their relations who accompanied us had or were to perish, and their wailings and weepings had been carried to such an extent that Mr de Wollf the Postholder, saw himself obliged to interfere.

We remained some days at Oreala and occupied our old quarters at Mr de Wolffs – the second day after our arrival a large Canoe upwards of forty feet long arrived filled with Caribees mostly of the mixed race; they landed at the Post and produced a passport from the Landdrost[1] or chief civil authority at Nickerie in the Dutch colony Surinam. They stated that they purposed to visit their brethren at the Corentyne of which several had joined in my expedition. The new-comers had a large supply of rum, and it was freely shared – and they were soon in a talkative mood. Some observations of theirs made me soon suspect that their visit was only a pretense and by a little mannoeuvring we found out that their real purpose was to proceed to the Macoosie country to trade for slaves, in which undertaking they were to be joined by our friends the Caribees in the Corentyne and an other Canoe was expected from the Woyombo a tributary to the Copenaam. Having been detected so far they threw over all reserve, showed us the guns for which they purposed to barter slaves while others possessed Dollars, which we were told were intended for the same purpose. I was rather astonished that they should have arrived at such an early period, where according to the testimony of the Caribees of Tomatai no Corial could cross the great Cataract. I expressed myself to that effect to one who could speak some broken English and how was my astonishment increased when I was told that there was a path where the largest Corial could cross and that it would be an easy matter to bring their own, which surpassed in size any of mine, over

---

[1] A bailiff or sheriff.

the impediments which according to the Caribee of Tomatai was only possible during the time the river was much swollen – and which it appeared to us like impracticable. I could scarcely believe it; one of the women who spoke the Creole language was next examined, and I received the same assurance – our interpreters of the Arawaak tribe were set to work and they brought the same information so that there remained now [not] the slightest doubt that we had been the dupes of the Caribees. I confronted now Smith with the Caribees from Woyombo and he could not bring forward a single word in his defence he stood there stubborn and motionless. We were now told by the Arawaaks Mathias and Nathaniel that the Caribees from Tomatai had told them a few days previous before we could have had an idea to meet those of Woyombo, that they could have brought us very easily over the Cataract, but that they did not wish to show us the path which lead over the Cataracts and that they wanted to prevent us to go to the Macoosy-country, which they thought it was our intention to visit, in order that we might not interfere with their projects – being well aware that I had expressed myself in the strongest terms about the nefarious trade in human beings, when I found the Macoosies from Annay held in bondage at Tomatai. We were further told that they had been nearly over-ruled by the women who accompanied our party when ascending – as they are generally left at home when such expeditions are to be executed, they thought they had now a fair opportunity to see that much spoken off Macoosy-country. The dread which every other tribe has for the Caribees had prevented the Arawaaks to communicate this to me, but as they found it was discovered by some other means they came now forward. On receiving this information, it was first my intention to send to Berbice for Provisions, and to return, but on re-considering, the impracticability of such a plan was quite obvious without endangering the lives of those who composed the expedition – it was naturally to expect that they would forcibly resist our advance when passing Tomatai or follow us clandestinely until they could execute their design, and though we might have mastered them before they received the re-inforcement, it might have been now doubtful since they were joined by the Party from Woyombo, this plan was therefore perfectly relinquished and I adhered still on my former one to ascend the river Berbice.

It would have been only a just punishment to the Caribees to refuse them payment in consequence of their treachery and I was even adviced by the Postholder to do so – however I resolved to act according to my engagement and to pay them as soon as we arrived at the Coast.

It appeared from the information which we received that the path leads round the most eastern Cataract partly by a Creek or brook – this must have been in the vicinity of the rocks where we discovered Indian Hieroglyphs[;] the investigation of this spot had been particularly entrusted to Cornelius, on whom I thought I could have trusted as he accompanied me on my former Expedition and proved himself then useful and trust-worthy – the former disappointment was [materially] encreased by this information – but I could not [blank] against the combined forces of nature and man.

While we were at Oreala having promised the Indians a few days rest and stay with their families before we set out again on our new expedition, Mr. Layfield with his usual readiness to oblige promised us the spectacle of a Warrow-dance – information was therefore given to the settlements in the neighbourhood that at such a day a dance was to take place at his abode. A place was for that purpose cleared under some shady Tamarind-trees planted many years ago by the Moravian Missionaries and the hour fixed for the commencement of the festivities. When leaving the house of Mr de Wolff's in the evening previous and about to retire to my tent I was forcibly struck by a peculiar sound which made me believe in the commencement I heard a russian horn-band – the sounds being carried by a gentle breeze swelled and died away until they burst fully upon my ear again; there was something wild in it but [the cadence softened it and reproduced harmony, the sounds were too full and too varied for an Aeolian harp.][1] I stood and at last I recollected the dance which was to take place the following evening and that I had been told every settlement of Warrows of any [size] had their band-master, Music-director, or Hoo-ho-hoo[2] who regularly trained his pupils, I gave immediately information to my Companions of what I had heard and though quite dark and the path to the Settlement leading partly through a wood we lost no time to scamper of.

We found the young men all collected round old Marose under whose guidance those sounds were produced which so much astonished me. The instrument (Wanna) is a piece of bamboo in which a smaller is introduced the one end of which is slit, on the principle of the mouth piece of a Clarinet or to make it more familiar to those who will allow their imagination to carry them back to their childhood and well remember the whistles made of quills[;] according to the size of the slit the reed produces a higher or deeper sound, this is powerfully increased by the hollow Bamboo, and its size while the deep note of a Bassoon is produced by a reed upwards of 5 feet long called Wanna Walie.[3] Marose sat on one side his disciples were placed in groupes round him and stamping time, a wave with his hand, foot, a nod with his head or instrument were the different signals to those around him to fall in with their instruments which naturally gave only one tune. Who are now the inventors of that peculiar and mechanical music which a few years ago made so much noise in Europe and delighted thousands of those who heard it? The musical sounds which the Warrow produces with his bamboo pipe are conducted on the same principle as those of a russian horn-band. There is much more melody in the Warrow-music than either in that of the Caribees or Arawaaks.

The next day proved fair and we left Oreala at three o'clock in the afternoon. On our arrival at Mr Layfields we found a great number of Indians but mostly Warrows, the women were handsomely dressed according to their fashion, loose garments of flowery Calicoe or Salempores went to their waist where they were fixed, or partly slung round their left or right shoulder – the neck, arms, wrists and angles were richly adorned by red and white beads while some had by means of a gum fixed the white downs of some bird in patches to their face & arms; others wore pieces of silver or metal in their noses which covered the upper lip – many of them had a line dividing towards its end in the figure of an anchor extending from the corners of the mouth – this must have been done on a similar manner as sailors imprint figures on their arms – some had their eyebrows shaved and a similar line of a blueish colour was imprinted at the place which they occupy.

---

[1] Various changes and over-writings make it difficult to be certain of the correct reading, but that provided is reliable as far as the general sense is concerned.

[2] It has not been possible to identify the term 'Hoo-ho-hoo', but the a similar office to band master is found among the modern Warao. He is the 'Isimoi arotu' or 'owner of the sacred flute' (D. Heinen, personal communication).

[3] The term 'wana' is still used among the modern Warao of the Orinoco Delta for a type of bamboo and the flute made from it. However, it is a flute, not a clarinet-type instrument which they also have, but made from the Moriche palm. It has not been possible to identify the term 'Walie' (D. Heinen, personal communication).

A little while after our arrival we got the information that the band was to make its appearance – they issued out of a neighbouring thicket, all cowerd and carrying their instruments grasped in the middle horizontally in their left hand – on their head was the band-master, on his head he wore a long cap called by the Warrows Passie[1] made of two rows off feathers of the white heron, the quills meeting in the middle, where they were neatly fastened by basket work, consequently the feathers turned up and down, from the middle of the upper part rose an upright on which like a balance, carved on its ends to imitate a bird's head and painted a horizontal piece of wood was fixed – each end held a square piece of basketwork, covered completely with cottonthread while from its margin hundreds of wings of the beautiful Camey'orek[2] were suspended, from the corners of these squares being likewise strings with parrot feathers, over the whole towered four of the largest Macaw-feathers, while two smaller ones were fixed to the ends of the horizontal piece of wood – several others had similar caps but by no means so richly embellished.[3] Many of the men had tied round their angles long strings with shells of a triangular nut, which made a rattling noise whenever the foot was put to the ground, and which is called Sae-wae.[4] They approached slowly the place where they were to dance, all still cowered, their movements being directed by a small whistle of the band-master which imitated the cry of a monkey, thus they formed a circle round the dancing place, on an other sound of the whistle the instruments were laid down – they remained there for a little while the band-master muttering incomprehensible things[+5]

> [+]This is done to appropriate the place for the amusement and to pe-ie away all mischievous spirits – except the most mischievous one – rum.

until on an other sound of the Whistle all rose with their instruments and the band struck up. Dancing commenced now, but their etiquette is somewhat reversed to our notions; the Warrow does not ask the felicity to dance with miss so and so – he places himself in the dancing circle, when the Warrow fair one who feels inclined to dance approaches him and places her hand loosely upon his shoulder, he takes no further notice as that he returns the compliment in the same manner; two or three steps are now put forward and next an equal number aside – at a certain point of the music the stepping forward is repeated and then all step for some time aside again; when the dance is about to end the Warrow does not lead his fair dancer to a chair, the sign pour prendre conge is that the men shake distinctly three times the foot on which the shells are tied – is his dancer an intimate acquaintance, a sweetheart, wife or sister, she will patiently await the third rattle, but if only superficial acquainted or a stranger, she will leave with the swiftness of a deer at the second signal.

Not like the Caribees, Waccaways and Macoosies, the dances of the Warrows are diversified and numerous; they have a bird-dance, a monkey-dance and many others,

[1] It has not been possible to identify the term 'Passie', but the use of caps or headdresses made from feathers is common throughout Lowland South America.

[2] It has not been possible to identify the 'Camey'orek', but presumably it is a small bird, perhaps the hummingbird.

[3] There is an asterisk at this point indicating a sentence included at the foot of the page with the instruction for it to be included here. This instruction has been obeyed.

[4] The seed of the *Thevetia nereifolia*, alternatively known as *Thevetia peruviana*.

[5] There is a sentence at the foot of the page marked by a + but there is no equivalent symbol in the text. This seems the most likely position and it has been inserted here as a footnote.

where they try to imitate the voice or movements of the animals, but the most interesting is the Macoosie-dance or Najabo maho which deserves a description as it reminded me of the Cotillons of the Continent; it represents the slaving among the Macoosies. As soon as the dance is to commence all the women hide themselves, they have sufficient time for it as the men move firstly round in a circle – after a signal of the band-master the search commences, the men look in all directions the house, no room is excepted; as soon as one has been laid hold of she is conducted to the dancing place where she must cower down; here they are put in rows and for their life they would leave the place assigned to them; after the men think that they have found them all they commence to dance round them and at an other signal the women are at liberty to run of, but the men are as quick after the one they have selected and if fortunate to capture her, she is led back to the circle and all dance the usual step. It is a most animating scene to see how swiftness is expected from both sides[,] from the one to escape which if executed is much applauded by the women, from the other to capture a Macoosie-slave. We joined in this dance and were much applauded by the Indians for doing so.

As long as the rum does not sway its power and influence, every thing is conducted with the strictest propriety; the manner in which the dancers hold each other could not be more delicate; the hand of the girl rests lightly upon her dancer and the same is the case on the other side – with sisters and wives an exception may be made but even this I observed only in a few instances. The Indian girl is from nature coy and I have never seen a forward girl among them, even where longer acquaintance might have warranted a less reserved manner. This does not arise from being schooled or having been scolded or punished for having been the contrary, it is the consequence of example. The little girl sees the reservedness of her mother and older sisters indeed of every female, perhaps with the exception of the Captain's favourite wife[,] and if she should possess from nature vivacity it is killed in its bud. The boy learns to shoot with bow and arrow; it is not taught to him he only imitates, and being applauded by his play fellows if he hit the mark it is incitement enough to surpass his former feats – while being able to smoke a Tampipo or vinah (Cigarr)[1] stamps him as having stepped out of the control of women – he wrestles, lays smoking in his hammock and assists perhaps his father in fishing or lends a hand when the provisions for the ensuing season are planted.

It is impossible to prevent that at such occasions not one or the other individual should drink more than is good for him; the consequence is that they get quarrelsome. It amused us much to see the plan which the careful wifes followed to prevent mischief. As soon as they observed that their dread lords and husbands were in that state, where they became unmangeable by words and prayers, the co-operation of others were called in, the individual was secured and forcibly put in the hammock, the open sides of which were strongly laced, so that he could not move and became thus harmless; there he remained until he has slept out his drunkeness and his reason was comperatively restored. It reminded me much of a plan which the Police in Leipsic followed with

---

[1] John Bennett, *Arawak-English Dictionary*, Georgetown, Walter Roth Museum, 1989, gives the meaning of 'Wina' as 'cigarette paper made from the inner bark of the wina kakarali tree'. There are numerous species called kakaralli by the Arawaks (*Lecythis alutacea*; *L. chartacea*; *Eschweilera alata*; *E. coriacea*; *E. decolorans*; *E. grata*; *E. longpipes*; *E. parviflora*; *E. sagotiana*; *E. schomburgkii*; *E. subglandulosa*; *E. wachenheimii*) and wina is *Lecythis corrugata*.

unruly drunkards or such which were found upon the streets – the malefactor was put in a small vehicle with four wheels amply provided with straps and firmly laced down and to the delight of the street-boys and the waggon drawn by two servants of the Police rapidly over the pavement to the lock-up house.

Lieut Losack and Mr Cameron accompanied Mr Layfield next morning on a fishing Expedition – they had provided themselves amply with Haiary, the juice of which is intoxicating to fish – they promised themselves boat loads-full – however after three days absence they returned only with a few. I remained at home as I expected next day already several of my Indians to return from their home; in the meanwhile I visited with Mr de Wolff and of which that Gentleman had been told many wonderful things. The Indians consider it to be the habitation of one of their Spirits (the mother of the Salamander tribe) called by the Arawaaks Maranika mama. We had to go there partly by water and afterwards along a small brook after an hours good walking we stood on the head of the famed cavern the Palace of the Maranika Mama. The waters of a rill had percolated through a coarse sandstone. In consequence of the declivity the water in its progress had carried away firstly the mould, the coarse sand had lost its support and was so gradually worn away that it did not form exactly a cavern but more a grotto of which the most remarkable point was that the rill or Streamlet has cut itself a circular hole through the upper [illegible] and falls about 30 feet into a basin which it has excavated at its foot.

We observed in the sandstone near some rubbish, the consequence of the mechanical destruction of the water; two holes there the Indians say are the entrance to the Manicro Mama – those who accompanied us and among whom was Nathaniel who prides himself upon his superior education having been on board a Schooner trading between the Islands, stood at respectable distance, and the greatest horror was depicted on their faces when I told them to cut me a pole as I wanted to drive the Spirit out of its abode. I got one at last with some difficulty but I could induce none of them to assist me in shoving the pole in the cavities – they made rather broad faces when they found that nothing made its appearance and that these celebrated holes which they said extended for miles

Figure 5: Robert Schomburgk's sketch of the entrance to the palace of Maranika Mama, the spiritual mother of the Salamander tribe. Included by permission of the Royal Geographical Society, London.

underground as the Manicro Mama herself was upwards of 4 miles long, namely from Look-out Island to Oreala, were scarcely so many yards deep. Being then in the neighbourhood of some Arawaak Settlements, we visited them, they consisted of a few houses – many of the inmates were sick and others absent. I observed in one of the hut a number of baskets with Sawarro nuts (Caryocar tuberculosa)[1] certainly a delicious species of the nutkind but by no means the Brazil nut of the Shops as stated by various authors which are the seeds of the Bertholletia excelsa. For my part I prefere the Souari nut when a few weeks taken from the tree, fresh picked they are too watery, which they lose in a week or two. They are very numerous in the forests of the Corentyne – the Indian receives seldom more than 2 to 3 bits (about 8 to 10d) for a basket containing more than hundred nuts. A Species of Lecythideae is likewise eatable and much esteemed, it is called Tasoka.[2] This comes much nearer in taste to the Brazil nut, indeed the latter belongs to the tribe of Lecythidaea. An other tree of the same tribe is a most indispensable commodity to the Tobacco loving Indian – it is the Lecythis ollaria the bark of which is so separable that it may be split from the base of the tree to its first branches often 40 to 50 feet high. When first split it is about [4] lines[3] thick nevertheless by beating it with a piece of a wood systematically along its length the layers divide in the thickness of tissue paper and if properly dried they remain pliable for a length of time. They are then cut to a proper length and used as wrappers for Cigarrs (Caribee Tampipo, Arawaak Vinah). The bark of several Species of Lecythis are used for that purpose but the L. ollaria is the most preferable. I brought from my first Expedition several Cigarrs prepared in that way from Tobacco grown by the Macoosies, and the greatest praise was bestowed upon them by connoisseurs in the smoking line. My Companions, who are moderate smokers use now constantly these wrappers and they tell me that they add greatly to the flavour of the Tobacco. It has happened that we have not met a Cackarally tree[4] for some time and I need scarcely say that the first which was discovered had to make up for the deprivation endured – it stood there completely stripped of its bark in an incredible short time.

Mr. Reiss had surprized on one of his excursions Abraham, one of the Arawaaks who run away from us while at Tomatai; he brought him a close prisoner to the Post, and as certainly his crime was aggravating enough and served as a bad example to others, it was necessary that some punishment should be inflicted – I consulted with the Post-holder and came to the conclusion to be satisfied with inflicting three lashes upon him. His wife, a good-looking young woman was standing next to him when I told him what was to take place and scarcely was the first lash inflicted, when off she run like a deer – the Indian stood the three lashes without changing a feature – and walked afterwards away. I was certainly astonished when Mathias their Captain came next day to me and asked me whether I would not forgive Abraham and that he was most anxious to go with me. Every one of my companions advised me not to take him, as they were sure he did it only under the pretext

---

[1] 'Ouari' has been written under Sawarro in a different handwriting. Presumably Souari is intended as the nut is known both as Sawari and Souari in Guyana, and is so called four lines below in the text. The modern taxonomic name for the tree is *Caryocar nuciferum*.

[2] This is probably the Sapucaia nut which is the fruit of *Lecythis ollaria*.

[3] A line is the twelfth part of an inch.

[4] Kakaralli. There are several species of *Lecythis*, *Eschweilera* and *Couratari* whose bark is suitable for making cigar wrappers (see p. 172, fn. 1).

to find an opportunity to revenge himself. I thought different of the man and considered him only to have been led away by the others and engaged him anew. His faithful wife who run so swiftly away when she observed that there was danger, was to accompany him. Poor Abraham had certainly no claim to beauty – having lost by accident the use of one of his eyes. He could console himself with the better half of the Warrow Christians, she presented one of the strangest objects I ever saw – there was no pupil visible in either of her eyes and she presented thus, when she stood motionless an antique bust – I was told that she was born in that manner – nevertheless she had the use of her eyes, but her aspect was really frightful and if by the motion of her head or the direction of her face it was not discovered it was impossible to say at whom or at what she looked.

The day of departure from the Post was one of great trouble – but four of the Indians had arrived at the appointed time. I had to go to the neighbouring Settlements myself and hunt them out. We started at last in the afternoon at 5 o'clock and having the tide with us rowed until 2 o'clock in the morning. Only two Corials had kept up with mine in one of them I observed several women the wives of different Individuals of my crew, who with the assistance of a little boy had managed it to keep up with the Corial. At enquiry I was told that they were only to go to the Coast and then to return to the settlement. I observed the woman (without pupils) among them[;] she had a baby of about 6 to 8 months with her. Two Corials had not come up at the time we continued our journey next morning. That as Mr Cameron and Mr Reiss were in one of them I did not think any thing about and concluded they might have rested at one of the habitations we passed at night. The nearer we approached Skeldon the rougher we found the river, the Indians not acquainted with such navigation shipped constantly waves and we had to exert ourselves to pail the Corial to keep her from swamping. We landed in the afternoon of Sunday the 6th November at Skeldon much to the astonishment of Mr and Mrs Ross who certainly did not expect us to return so early.

The Corial with Messr Reiss and Cameron did not arrive that day and I stood under apprehension that something had occurred – as nothing had been heard of them on Monday afternoon, orders had been given to start with the next favourable tide in search of them, when they hove in sight. The Corial had been swamped through carelessness of the Indians, and books, cloths and the greater part of the provisions which remained from the Corentyne trip were lost and spoiled.

Mr Ross continued to show us the kindest attention and the greatest hospitality – for my part I was however anxious to proceed without delay to Berbice, his invitation to recruit from our fatigues I could not accept; it was different with the Gentlemen who had accompanied me as volunteers – they were aware that His Excellency the Governor's pleasure with regard to the Expedition up the river Berbice could not arrive under less than eight days from Demerara – they resolved therefore to stay a few days more at Skeldon and to pay a few days' visit to the Dutch Settlement Niekkery on the eastern Point of the river Corentyne. I proceeded on Tuesday morning with part of my Indian Crew and Luggage to New Amsterdam. The Navigation from the river Corentyne to that latter place is decidedly intricate, but a Captain and crew who are repeatedly sailing between the two places are to be acquainted with every shoal and bank – it was therefore vexatious when the Schooner run at the mouth of the river on a mudbank and grounded – the attempts to get her of were so unseaman like that just the contrary was produced and we got faster – by that time night had broken in and the water was ebbing and as uncomfortable as it might have proved on board of a small craft stacked with Luggage and

Indians, I would have passed it over if the accident had not proved injurious to the Chronometer. With the change of the water a strong N.E. breeze set in and drove a high surge before it – every wave with struck the little vessel made her shiver like an asp-leave – the attempts at midnight to get her of at midnight at High water failed likewise and I had to submit as it would have been madness to attempt to leave in the Corials with Indians unacquainted with the river and a high surge running. I had the Corials launched with day light and proceeded to New Amsterdam where I found but too soon that what the hauling of our Corials over Cataracts and carrying the Chronometer over rocks had not been effected had been done by the beating of the surge against the Schooner[;] the first observation showed me that the Chronometer had lost its rate and run wild.

I had despatched with the first opportunity a report to his Excellency relating to the Corentyne Expedition and the causes of our return and proposed since according to my Instructions it was the wish of the Royal Geographical Society that I should dedicate the first eighteen months to the investigation of British Guiana, it might be perhaps advisable to explore the river Berbice – besides that upper regions of the river being entirely unknown to the Colonists it might lead to the mountainous region. I received His Excellency's approbation to this place and having fitted myself out for a second time during this year – Mr Cameron and Mr Vieth left Berbice on Monday 21st November in advance – while I had to await the arrival of orders from the Governor.

****

The original manuscript of Schomburgk's report on the Berbice expedition, of which the transcription follows, is held by the Royal Geographical Society archives, catalogue number JMS 6/18(b). It is dated Berbice, May 1837 and was received by the Royal Geographical Society on 18 July 1837. It is partly in Schomburgk's handwriting and partly in that of another, presumably a copyist. Excluding two cover sheets added at a later date, the manuscript consists of eighty pages, although the pagination runs from 1–78; p. 72 being followed by pp. 71A and 72A. Certain pages in the manuscript occur in the wrong order and these have been returned here to their original positions. Where this has been done, it has been duly noted. The same difficulties were encountered in transcribing the manuscript of this report as were experienced with his other manuscripts, and similar remedies have been applied. The published version (*Journal of the Royal Geographical Society*, 7, 1837, pp. 302–50), is some 10,000 words shorter than the original manuscript. There is no title to the original manuscript, but an editorial hand has added one similar to that used for the published version.

DIARY OF AN ASCENT OF THE RIVER BERBICE IN BRITISH GUAYANA IN 1836–1837 BY ROBERT H. SCHOMBURGK, Esq Corr. Mem. R.G.S.

It will be remembered that short of Provisions and deceived by the Caribees the expedition up the River Corentyne was under the necessity to return to Berbice early in November. At my arrival at New Amsterdam I lost no time to inform his Excellency, Sir Jas Carmichael Smyth, of the circumstance that led to our return, and proposed, as the season was too far advanced to undertake any thing of import, I might be permitted to ascend the river Berbice, as little known to the Colonists as the Corentyne or upper Essequibo. His Excellency gave his approbation, and I made the necessary arrangements, and in order to be better guarded and less dependent from the Indians, increased my stock provision in double ratio I had provided myself with in former occasions. It is a point of the greatest difficulty to store a sufficient quantity of provisions to last for the greater part of the journey thus undertaken; the difficulties connected with travelling in the interior of British Guiana are fearfully increased by the circumstance, that weeks, nay months elapse sometimes before a human habitation is met with, where the stock of provision might be replenished; and if the traveller has been so fortunate, it depends from the humour of the inhabitant whether he feels inclined to furnish it, though he may have the means of doing so in abundance. Whether the Berbice expedition was more successful in that regard, will be seen in the sequel, enough the behaviour of the Caribbees of the Corentyne had imposed, the necessity upon me, to man the same number of Corials, I had during the Corentyne expedition. Three of them, under the command of Mr Cameron, had preceded me, while I awaited another communication from His Excellency the Governor. Mr Reiss was to join my own Corial, while Lieut Losack of the 69th under the plea of the approaching rainy season declined to accompany me any further. The Indian crew consisted of the Arawaaks and Warrows, and three of the Caribbees, who went with me up the Corentyne. (I left ultimately on Novbr 25th 1836.)

We were once more en route and though badly manned, the large Corial having not more than three paddlers and a Steersman, a favourable tide carried us rapidly along. When the tide changed we were at some distance from any habitation, and the night setting in, we had to use all our bodily strength to make some progress; we reached the Plantation Yuydwik at a late hour, and satisfied with two hours sleep; at the coming in the of the flood tide at three o'clock in the morning, we occupied again our Corials. When the morning dawned the river presented a continued line of cultivation; the sun rose and clearing away the fogg which surrounded the different objects like a veil[;] we were opposite a Sugar Estate (Herstelling); there was no stir as yet among the inhabitants but thousands of mocking birds (*Oriolus Perisis*)[1] rose from an aged Orinok-tree *Erythrina* Spec.?),[2] and flew across the river. It appeared they had selected that wide branching tree for their night quarters, and dispersed with the dawn of the day in various directions; they did not leave their night's abode in masses as by the uncommon number confusion might have arisen, but as if directed by a wise Commander, detachment followed detachment from the time we observed the tree first, until it was hid from our view by a turn of the river – how many thousands might have been quartered on that tree? I have seen Swallows collected in a numerous body, but I was not aware that the Oriole roosts in such numbers.

The cultivation continued on the Eastern bank but on the opposing shore man had surrendered the soil and nature reclaimed her seat. What a difference there must be at present in the appearances of the banks of the river when compared with the pleasing aspect they must have presented towards the end of the last Century!! Plantation

---

[1] Today New World mocking-birds belong to the Family Mimidae. Two species are reported from Guyana: the Tropical Mocking-bird (*Mimus gilvus*) and the Black-capped Mocking-bird (*Donacobius atricapillus*). Orioles of the species *Icterus* are also found in Guyana.

[2] Oronoque: *Erythrina fusca*.

followed Plantation to the Savonette, the last Estate of the Dutch West India Company in about 5°25N. Lat.; of the greater number not a vestige is now to be discovered and they figure only in old Maps. Slavery, that bane, was the originating cause; having reached towards the middle of the last century its acme, many adventurers calculated upon the sweat of their brethren, and while without the help of the African bondsmen, the cultivation of the Colony left to its natural course, could have been made only slow progress; the banks of the river represented, as if by enchantment, the picture of industry. It was a phantom. If left to its natural course, though slow, it would have been built upon a firm foundation; while the mode pursued, its inhumanity set apart and the millions of human lives it cost, was sure to fail, as soon as the artificial state which caused the fabric was removed, and it tottered to its very foundation. When Europe conceded the African human right, the Slave trade was declared abolished, labour rose in value, and those adventurers who had speculated upon the sweat of thousands of their Brethren found their inhuman reign at an end; and only the Capitalist was able to stem the tide, produced by the change, and the withdrawnment of the cultivation of land of the Dutch West India Company[1] at a great distance from the coast followed this humane act. A new day has dawned, and though the effects may not be visible for some time, the fertility of the soil will form the solid ground upon which the cultivation of British Guiana is hereafter to be founded; and these shores may in some tens of years offer the lively and pleasing picture of an industrious and happy population.[2]

We passed in the Afternoon Daageraad;[3] formerly an Estate of the Dutch West Indian Company, now a Wilderness. It is famed in the river navigation for the height and strength of the Abapouri which is said to rise from 12 to 15 feet here, and has caused on several occasions the loss of life and property. As I observed on a previous occasion (see first report during the second Expedition) the Abapouri sets in with a young spring tide, and is formed so suddenly, that if a craft should be near shore, or if even in the middle of the river should turn its broad side to the approaching wave, it is unavoidably swamped. There are generally three waves in quick succession, after which the tide continues to flow uninterrupted. A large mud bank stretches from the eastern bank at Daagaraad towards the western, leaving a small but comparitively deep channel; (with 20 to 25 feet water) above Daageraad the river has a western turn, below it, an eastern, which localities, connected with the mud bank, render the Abapouri here so powerful and distructive. The river in the vicinity of Daageraad and Vigilantia[4] is most subjected to this strange Phenomenon. We observed a short distance above Daageraad,

---

[1] In the manuscript (p. 3), a change in the word order has been marked. This change has been adopted here. The original reads 'and the withdrawnment of, of the Dutch West Indian Company, the cultivation of the land'.

[2] At the foot of this page (p. 3) an unknown hand has written 'The last 3 fourths of this page, very unhappily worded, is no doubt justly intended to anathematise the system of African Slavery'. Schomburgk held strong abolitionist views. In fact two important turning points in his life resulted from his disgust at acts of slavery (see Rivière, 'From Science to Imperialism').

[3] On the reference map, there are two places called Dageraad marked, Old Dageraad and New Dageraad. The position of New Dageraad is where Schomburgk locates 'Daaggerad' on his map. Old Dageraad is some fifteen miles further south in a direct line.

[4] A place called Vigilantie is marked on the reference map a few miles upstream from Old Dageraad. Either the bore occurred at two sites some twenty miles apart, or there was another place called Vigilantia near the modern New Dageraad, or some mistake has been made.

on the rivers left bank, the mouth of a stream; on our return when I had engaged Indian guides, acquainted with the localities, I was informed that this stream spreads out considerably and is directly connected with the Abary;[1] it is therefore called Abary-itabou; Itabou denoting a lake-like and currentless expansion of water, the kirahagh of the Caribbees on the Essequibo.[2] A small cottage hove in sight towards nightfall, and we were glad to take advantage of its shelter, as the horizon was covered with dark clouds, and vivid lightening told of an approaching storm; the name of the place was Noytgedazt (not expected), and to us thus it proved. As far as the tide has influence on the river the Banks are low, and if not overflowed during High water, it is generally very muddy; places fit for encampment are only found at some distance from the banks, and the danger boats are subjected to during the rise and fall of the water, is so imminent, that it would not have been prudent to camp at some distance from the shore, and we had the prospect to weather the storm in the small Corial; we considered it therefore particularly fortunate, when we discovered the cottage. We were scarcely housed, when the storm broke loose with fury, and raged until day light. The owner or resident cultivates rice with much success, and he observed that if he only could procure labourers he would be able to carry it on on a larger scale, and he was quite sanguine with great advantage. The sample which I saw was very fair. [During] our further progress up the river, whenever the contrary tide forced us to halt, we received great civilities from the inhabitants; they are distinguished for this trait, every stranger journeying up and down this River is welcomed, and should an unfavourable tide force him to await the morning, room is readily offered to sling the hammock and to partake of what the house can offer. We passed the site of Fort Nassau[3] during night; the river narrows from here considerably but it keeps its general depth of 20 to 40 feet and on our return we ascertained the current to be 2.5 Knots in an hour. The anchorage before the old Capital of Berbice is particularly favoured, the river forms a basin. We met the first hillocks formed by heaped up sand the boundary line of the gradual receding sea of a former era on Latitude 5°50′. The Indians call the hillocks the heights of which amount to about 50 feet Hitia; it was the site of a Post, now some Arawaak Indians live there; a few miles south of these sandy barriers join the brook Kaderbiecie which is said to be connected with the Stream Abary, by a short portage, while the Herounie unites the Abary with the river Maicony.[4] From Kaderbiecie leads a short path across Savannahs to the River W-ieronie.[5]

The contrary tide brought us to the mouth of the stream Moshieba; bell birds or the daras (Ampelis carunculata)[6] were tolling in all directions – with the exception of the Conocou mountains I had never met with them so numerous. Several Arawaak Indians

---

[1] The Abari flows to the sea parallel with the Berbice on the latter's west bank.

[2] 'Itabo' is defined in Bennett's *Arawak-English Dictionary* as 'waterway, a small stream or channel used to avoid dangers in a bigger body of water, e.g. the sea or waterfalls in a river'.

[3] The construction of Fort Nassau followed closely on the founding of the first Dutch trading post on the Berbice River in 1627. It remained the main Dutch centre on the river until 1785 when it was resolved to move to New Amsterdam at the mouth of the river. The move did not take place until some five years later, waiting on the completion of Fort St Andries which defended New Amsterdam.

[4] Mahaicony River.

[5] Wiruni River, a left-bank tributary of the Berbice.

[6] The two species of Bellbird reported from Guyana are the White Bellbird (*Procnias alba*) and the Bearded Bellbird (*P. averano*).

live in the vicinity of this Brook, and a path leads from here to the mouth of the Wieronie which may be walked in an hour, while it took us nearly five hours to follow the river's course. We met the Corials which had preceded us at Peereboom, the residence of Mr Duggen, an industrious wood cutter, from him we received a great many civilities and every assistance to forward my crews. The hillocks of sand approach again the River at Peereboom, and the extensive Savannah stretches from the sand hills west and is said to extend to the River Demerara; as it belonged to my plan to visit that river from the Berbice on my return, I made only a short stay at Peereboom and proceeded to Wickie.[1] It became necessary to inspect the rate of the Chronometer, and to determine the latitude of a place with correctness and precision, in order to use it as a point of departure. I had selected before my departure from New Amsterdam, Mr McCullum's residence, opposite the mouth of the river Wickie, for that purpose. M[r] McCullum was absent on our arrival, but a Corial was immediately despatched to Moracco,[2] where his woodcutting Establishment is mostly carried on, in order to inform him of our arrival; the boat left that day at three oclock in the afternoon. At Wickie a marsh extends aback for 2 miles; I walked in that direction next morning in order to reach the Savannahs. The line of division between the Savannahs and the bog, are those sand hills, which I have already noted, and which are here about 110 feet high; they consist of a fine white sand with particles of quartz, some angular some pounded by atrition. Though there can be little doubt that they were formed by a receding sea, it has astonished me that no organic remains have been found in it. Was animal or organic life not existing when they were formed? or is it preserved to closer investigations to discover fossil accumulation? The abrupt nature of these sand hills prevents us from supposing them to be a deposit of a current; if such were the case, the sand would not have arranged itself in high inclined beds, but would have been gradually pushed forward, and represent now horizontal strata – be then that we suppose the fall of the sea to have been most sudden and violent. In the absence of data, they remind me much more of the sand hills formed by breakers, along the north western part of the Island of Anegada*

> *See Journal of the Royal Geographical Society Vol V, p1 & 28. The subject is of such interest that I preserve its discussion until I have formed a mature opinion borne out by facts, for which place and opportunity do not offer at present the desiderata.

which rise often to a height of 40 feet, from which those under discussion differ only by their colour and the particles of quartz mixed with it. The contrast of the snow white sand with the black mould which covered the Sand hills or sand reefs, as they are generally styled here, chiefly where a Colony of Ants had settled and thrown up the white sand or where a rabbit has burrowed, was strong indeed. The Wallaba (Dimorpha Spec.?) one of the most useful trees for posts, shingles, and staves, occupies the soil almost exclusively. When I issued from the wood, a large Savannah undulating and partly grown over with grass, partly covered with woods was lying before me. On the edge of the wood I discovered an Indian settlement, it consisted of five or six huts, and curiosity urged me to visit it. They were Arawaaks; the men were all absent and employed in wood cutting; the women appeared rather frightened at my appearance; I

[1] Wikki.
[2] Possibly Moroka River.

asked for some water which was readily presented to me in a gourd, but this done the woman retired to the corner which she had previously occupied. After having given some small presents to the terrified children, I continued my walk across the Savannah, until the brook Etounie stopped my further progress. I found some very interesting Savannah plants, and returned home almost loaded. While absent, some of the Indians had killed a Conocoushie or Bush Master,[1] the most dangerous snake which Guiana possesses; it measured a little more than 6 feet and its formidable fangs were nearly half an inch long. Mr McCullum arrived while we were inspecting it; it was then two O'clock and the distance of Moracco from Wickie being the windings of the river included, about 26 miles, it may be seen what can be done in a corial where dispatch is required, and where there are no impediments. The Conocushi became the subject of our Conversation, and as the Caribbee Acouritah nearly escaped being bitten by it, I was anxious to hear whether there were any antidotes. Mr McCallum told me that though the bite proved fatal, if there were none resorted to, he had saved several Individuals. In the first instance, he makes a cross cut in the wound, in order to be the better enabled to extract the teeth which generally break off when the wound is inflicted; a little spirit or brandy is then put in a wine glass & set in flame, and put, when burning with the mouth of the Glass downwards upon the wound, it acts then as a powerful cupping machine; and he has told me where the situation of the wound allowed this remedy, the glass has been in a shorte time full of matter; the patient receives meanwhile large quantities of sweet oil, and strong purgatives are administered; should the wound be inflicted on a part where this remedy cannot be applied, gunpowder is put upon the wound and ignited which naturally causes suppuration. Mr McCallum has a large wood cutting Establishment where often 200 Indians and upwards of 50 negroes are employed and such accidents are not uncommon.

Since Mr McCallum has settled in the Berbice River, he has collected a great number of Indians who, with the exception of the time they are absent to put their provision fields in order, are employed by him in cutting and squaring timber. As head of the firm under which the business is carried on, he has been for many years back residing there, and he has had sufficient opportunities to form an idea of their respective value as labourers; I lay therefore particular weight upon his observations on this subject. "Of later years, he said, I have introduced task work, and as part of my labourers consist of Indians of different tribes, but chiefly Arawaaks, and the other part of Negroes, I am able to form a correct Idea respectively of their industry. I have invariably found that the Indian sets with good heart at once to his work, and remains at it until it is finished; it is generally the case that they have finished their task work two or three hours earlier than the Negroes – but not satisfied with this, he continues to work in his own hours, and I know many an Indian, who besides his regular wages, earns from two to three dollars a week. The most fatigueing of my work is squaring timber, and to haul it from the place where it has been felled to the banks of the river, and for that occupation I readily prefer one Indian to two Negroes. With regard to their honesty, the balance is likewise on the side of the Indian, I most con-scientiously assert that I not aware that I have been deprived of any thing of value, except that opportunity has afforded to purloin a Dram or a mouthful of provisions, while my black labourers have frequently broken open my stores and deprived me of numerous

---

[1] *Lachesis muta*. This snake is reputed to grow to twenty-five feet in length and to be the largest poisonous snake in the world.

other articles. I advance frequently money & goods to Indians, if they particularly desire me to do so, and I have generally received the amount in labour or in timber; nay, I have known many instances that where an individual has died in my debt, the relations have come forward and offered to settle the debt by labour. I am sure, he concluded, if the Indians were treated in a proper way he would prove a most valuable labourer." And that M^r McCallum treats them in that manner, is proved [by] the number which he has collected around him; unfortunately this is not the case with every individual by whom they are employed. To secure an Indian labourer foul and fair means have been resorted to: they give him a quantity of Articles, sometimes to a large amount; and this Credit is extended to any one who will accept it, provided he be able to work, being aware that the Indian considers himself in duty bound to work for his Creditor until the debt is paid; but many woodcutters use every means to prevent his getting out of debt by constantly supplying him with more articles and large quantities of that bane, Rum, thus the poor Indian is always kept in a state of bondage. This unjust traffic is the fruitful source of misunderstanding between those who employ Indian labourers; if thus an Indian has received money or articles from two or more Settlers, which are often put in his hands when intoxicated, it causes quarrels among them, and the Indian's confidence must be shaken; he finds himself harrassed, & when least expected his huts and fields are abandoned, and he emigrates to another district, if not to another Colony. The spirit of Emigration has lately much increased, and is particularly directed to Surinam. M^r McCullum observed to me: – "give me a few thousand Guilders to spend in presents, and I would entice every Indian, in the upper river Berbice, if it were my object, to follow me to Surinam." I am as well aware as M^r McCallum that little will induce the Indian to leave his residence. He is less tied to his birth place than many other uncivilized nations, and possessed with a roaming disposition, he leaves his fields to the brutes of the forest, and plants his four posts where he has to contend with nature for the occupancy and production of his food. I mentioned the Indian habits for wandering in my former reports; while at M^r McCullums, I received another proof. He told me that lately Kanaima,[1] chieftain of the Macoosie tribe had come to settle in his vicinity. I left Kanaima comfortably settled in a substantial Macoosie house at Annay, and he had then no idea to leave his residence & his rich provision fields, at the foot of the Pacaraima mountains. At present he is felling trees and toils to put but a small spot of woodland in Cultivation. If no means are taken to cultivate the Indian's good will, the Colony runs the risk to loose many individuals who may prove in different regards valuable. M^r McCullum has always most liberally paid his Indians and has made several spirited attempts to expose and put a stop to those disgraceful transactions. If the Indian population is of sufficient interest to the Colonist, my humble opinion is, that a protector of Indians ought to be appointed with sufficient power to do justice, regular contracts ought to be entered into with those who employ the Indian before the Protector, and the latter should be prohibited from employing any Indian in any other capacity, but as a domestic, and the practice of a regular traffic between the Protector and an Indian should be strictly prohibited. The Indian of British Guiana is a heathen. The Caffre, the Hottentot and the Esquimaux, the poor benighted beings of the East, the aborigines of Australia, all have had their missions & instruction in our religion has been offered to them, the Indian of British Guiana alone is neglected in that regard; except the mission

---

[1] Here the word Kanaima is used as a personal name and not to identify a ritual killer. See p. 114, fn. 1.

at Barteka point established not for the sake of the Indians, the Crown Colonies of Guiana have not a single institute for the conversion of the Indian. The difference of the Indian of Columbia the former Colony of Spain, is strikingly exhibited, their advance in civilization is only to be ascribed to the exertions of the Catholic missionaries, and proved that the Indian is capable to receive religious instructions if they are tendered to him.

The weather was very unfavourable during my stay in Wickie for celestial observations, the means of six observations gave me as Latitude, 5°33′47″N. and the Longitude 3ʰ50ᵐ01ˢW in time by Chronometer. The width of the river was ascertained to be 429 feet with an average depth of 53 feet, the tide rose here during the Springs 5½ feet. We left Wickie on the 4ᵗʰ December. At Paripi[1] the same reefs approach again the river's banks, on their top is an Arawaak settlement. We bivouqued at the mouth of the stream Kabiribirie,[2] famed for its cold waters. I found however the difference not so great as I would have expected; the air was at 5ʰ a.m. 80°F., the water of the Berbice 80°·2 the water of the stream 77°. We stopt next day at an early hour at Moracco, where Mʳ McCullum carries on his wood cutting Establishment. We had started that morning at 5 oclock, when I found the thermometer so low as 68°, the water of the river was then 11° warmer, namely 79°. The trees in the vicinity of Moracco consist chiefly of different species of Wallaba, some Green heart, Mora, yabirou or paddle wood,[3] Kakarally and Wamara.[4] At the distance of two miles from the River commence the savannahs, extending towards Demerara river. They are said to be inhabited by Indian tribes, who never visit the abodes of Colonists; by means of barter they procure Powder, shot, knives, Salempores &c from those Indians who keep up Communication with the coast; and give them hammocks, spun Cotton, and crab oil in return. My informants could not give me an estimate of the number of these Savanah Indians but to conclude from their expressions, they must amount to upwards of thirty settlements, and I should say to about 500 individuals. A few miles from Moracco, we came to a strange feature of the river, narrowed in from both sides, patches of a coarse long grass (Panicum),[5] and Mocco-moccos (Caladium arborescens) make it appear as if there was no out[let]; the river turns at a sharp angle and the distance from shore to shore is not more than 100 feet – its width became so variable, sometimes it narrowed considerable while at the next turn, it represented a lake. After ten O'clock we met the first inlet called Itabou in general by the Indians, its entrance presented a silvan appearance, a small island occupied the middle of the inlet, and on it capricious nature had planted a number of trumpet trees (Cecropia Peltata) in regular rows; they were clothed from their base to the top with a species of Convolvulus, while some under shrubs similarly clothed, might be compared to theatrical Scenery, so regularly they were formed. After we had passed an Indian Settlement on the river's right bank, called Manbakka, we saw some hillocks a head and on our approach we found they were formed of sand; they were by far the highest I had seen of that formation; I estimated them 100 feet; where they approach the river they are very steep; we halted however and I scrambled up them[.] I was richly rewarded. The prospect over undulating ground extended to the South-East upwards of 15 miles & the number of Hills of the same formation as that

[1] Paripi River.
[2] Possibly the Kibilibiri River.
[3] *Aspidosperma excelsum*; *A. oblongum*.
[4] *Swartzia leiocalycina*.
[5] Genus of the Family Poaceae.

I stood upon, covered with dense wood, formed one of the finest views of woodland imaginable. Immediately below our feet, the placid river spread lakelike & the magnificent woods that margined its banks reflect their image in the glossy stream; beyond an immense extent of wood of every tint & hue, from the bright yellow blossomed Hakea[1] to the dark lucid Green of the Gigantic Mora. The view in the distance was closed by these parallel ranges of thickly wooded hills; behind us was an extensive Savannah with beautiful slopes, covered with verdure and clusters of trees. The hillocks run suddenly south, by which the river is narrowed in to 80 feet, and its Current materially increased, the river again widens above, and forms several small Islands. We passed the brook Youacari,[2] a path leads from here to the River Demerara which is frequently made use of by the Indians. They follow for two days the windings of the brook, and go one day over land.

I had engaged whilst at M^r McCullums an Accaway family to accompany me, consisting of Andres who was considered the chieftain, two men & four boys, besides three females – the men were divided among the Corials, while the women and three of the boys conducted their own crafts, one being a small Corial, the other a Woodskin. The Arawaaks and Accaways of the upper River Berbice use generally Woodskins in lieu of Corials; they are made of a single piece of the tough bark of the Mourianara tree,[3] which grows to a very large size. After the tree is felled, and the length of the Craft is determined upon, an incision is made to that extent in the bark, which is removed by driving in wedges of wood; after it is loosened from on the wood, it is now kept open by cross pieces of wood, and rests free upon two beams of wood, in order to raise therefore parts of the woodskin; the other part of the bark is partly cut to the inner layer, at about two feet distance from each other, and fastened afterwards by folding that part in; it remains for several days exposed to the sun before it is used. Though the woodskin is so crank that the slightest motion, when once seated, renders it liable to be upset, I have seen frequently three men in it besides their baggage. The advantage is, they will go where a common Corial of the smallest description cannot pass, being almost flat on the bottom, and so light that at crossing Cataracts, one man can easily carry a woodskin on his head. If only one man propels the woodskin, he sits or rather squats in the middle and paddles on either side, as circumstance demand. Great care must be taken in stepping in or out of them, as they easily swamp and sink almost instantly, the specific gravity of the wood or bark being so much heavier. The two boys who conducted the Woodskin on the present occasion, were perhaps not more than eight years old, and we were highly delighted to see how ably they conducted it; it appeared as if it were flying through the water, and the juvenile steersman directed its course so well, that it never grounded, though it went over places where there was not more than 8 or 9 inches water. They were proficient in the use of the bow & arrow, and where ever they thought their well directed arrow might procure an addition to their meal, the Woodskin was halted, the bow

---

[1] Hakia: *Tabebuia capitata*; *T. serratifolia*; *T. subtilis*.

[2] Possibly the Yawakuri River.

[3] W. E. Roth, 'An Introductory Study of the Arts, Crafts, and Customs of the Guiana Indians', *38th Annual Report of the Bureau of American Ethnology*, 1916–17, pp. 25–745 (pp. 615–17), says that the best and most long-lasting tree from which to make a woodskin is the purpleheart, and gives the native term for this tree as *marianara*. This word is not given for the purpleheart by Mennega et al., *Check-list*. Roth mentions four other trees whose bark is suitable for the manufacture of woodskins. They are Mararen (Maran: *Copaifera guianensis*; *C. langsdorfii*; *C. publiflora*); Simiri, both the Arawak and Carib term for *Hymenaea oblongifolia*; the Bullet tree (*Chrysophyllum* spp.) for which Roth gives the native term makaratalli, a term that does not appear in Mennega et al.; and baramalli (Baromalli: *Catostemma altsonii*; *C. commune*; *C. fragans. Scleronema guianense*).

strung, and off flew the pointed arrow; when it was taken out of the sand which the water covered but sparely, we observed generally one of the finny tribe pierced by the sharp arrow head, and grapling for liberty. In spite of these occasional detentions, they were always in the van when we were to come too for breakfast, or night quarters.

We halted next morning (Decb. 3rd)[1] for a few moments at a new settlement, just commenced by a Waccaway family. I was not a little astonished to recognise in the head of the Settlement, an old acquaintance of mine, called Phillander, who accompanied me on my expedition up the Essequibo; I left him settled with the Macoosies at Warapoota, and now I found him at the bank of the river Berbice. This is another exemplification of the unsettled habits of the Indian and the want of attachment to localities. His fields had been only lately prepared, the trunks & branches of felled trees were lying about in great confusion, however he had planted Indian corn, pumpkins &c and though the first was only a few months old, it would vie with that I had seen in Virginia; he expected to reap his first crop in about three weeks. We found him occupied in planting Cassada and Sugar cane; one is as indispensable in an Indian Settlement as the other.

We were all much disappointed, when we arrived at the Accaway Settlement, of which Andres was the Chieftain and found only a few miserable huts; indeed they were in worse condition than I had ever seen any before. The Accaways or as they call themselves, the Waccaways, are a tribe of peddlars or the Jews of the Indian Nations, they are constantly wandering and they carry on a trade of Barter, and are well known to make the hardest bargains. I was only able to engage Andres under the condition, that I would permit him to stay a couple of days at his place, in order to prepare Cassada bread for himself & for us. His settlement however did not present any facilities for celestial observations, and I preferred to proceed half a mile further, to a large sand bank, where I had every advantage for observations but the glare of the sun & the heat reflected from the sand more than outbalanced this good quality and the partial shade which we could procure, arose from our tents. The mornings and evenings were generally clouded and even rainy, but about 10 o'clock the clouds dispersed and the sun shone in all its force.*

*I give the following extracts from my meteorological observations during that period.

Barometer			Att Therm[2]	Det. Therm	surface of the River
Decembr					
9th	3h. p m	29. 820	91°	90°.5	84°
	6. ” ”	” 830	85.	85.	82
10th	6. a m	” 890	73.5	73	78
	9. ” ”	” 920	82.	81	81
	2. p m	” 890	91.5	92°.5	81
	12. p m	” 910	88.	86.	84
	3. ” ”	” 880	91.	91.	84
					84[3]

Thermometer: exposed to the sun	98°.
The bulb buried in the sand	115°.

[1] This date must be wrong as the expedition had left Mr McCullum's on 4 December. In the published version (p. 306), it is given as 8 December.

[2] An Attached Thermometer is one whose bulb is within the metal tube surrounding a mercury barometer, and is used for making any corrections for temperature of the barometric reading.

[3] This column contains eight readings, as compared with only seven in all the others.

Hammocks form the chief article of Trade between the Waccaways and the more industrious Macoosies. They are generally made of cotton, twisted into thick thread-like cords; a great number of these threads are passed at regular intervals round two stakes, planted up right in the ground, and according to the length the hammock is to receive, the distance between them is gaged. After the threads have been fixed horizontally similar threads are woven by the hand across the former, in a ordered position at equal distance from each other, which form the bands. These cross threads are generally 5 to 6 inches apart, but much closer in the better sort of hammocks. Cotton cords or strings made of the silk grass or the palmated leaf of the Eta (Mauritia) are then passed through separate bundles of the double Cotton threads at each end of the hammock, which cords being passed at their other end, the hammock is finished; the Arawaaks & Warrows prepare their hammocks entirely out of the cord prepared from the Eta, which thread or cord they call Eta vissieri. The Caribbees & Waccaways paint their hammocks red with the Arnatto which is mixed with Crabnut-Oil, (prepared of the seed of Carrapua Guianensis) in order to fix the colour. I have seen an industrious Indian woman finish a common cotton Hammock in a day.

The time had elapsed which I had granted the Accaways to make the necessary preparations to accompany us, and in consequence of the unfavourable weather for observations, my further stay was of no advantage, though I wished most anxiously to inspect the rate of the Chronometer, which from comparison with other watches, I found to fluctuate. The observed altitudes gave 5°2'48"N. as latitude, and 57°58'25"W. as longitude by Chronometer. Andres arrived with two men less than he had promised, when we enquired for the stores of Cassada bread which we expected from him, and which he had promised, he tried every excuse. Warned by the example of Caribbees, I had sent daily to their place in order to ascertain whether their women were busy, and they were always found to prepare Cassada bread and large piles of Cakes were seen in different directions; his excuse therefore that a number of Macoosies who were with him, had taken it away was therefore not believed; and we returned to the Settlement, to pursue ourselves [the truth] – no person was to be seen but a sickly woman[;] all the woodskins were removed, and the woman told us that the Macoosies and some of Andres' own men had left that night on their way to Demerara River. We were therefore outwitted. We started about 8 o'clock; in one of their own Corials there were women and two boys who followed us, certainly an undesired addition, but I was obliged to [consent] at it.

We had already observed at the Waccaway settlement some blocks of indurated clay; this morning we met the first rocks, being of Trappean origin; the rocks were only a few in number, and were observed on the river's left bank. The river itself was shallow and impeded by numerous trunks of trees, which had been torn down from the river's banks, and stretched now almost across the river. The further we ascended, the more frequent became the inlets; they expanded in the direction of the river when ascending; where the river turned suddenly, sometimes almost at right angles, the greatest attention was therefore required to prevent the inlet to be mistaken for the river. Some of the decayed trees stretched across the river and obstructed our advance – we were therefore under the necessity to cut them through to procure a passage. How many years may have elapsed since they occupied this situation; entirely deprived of vegetation, their naked branches reminded me, if their gigantic size were set aside, of the antlers of some stalk.[1]

---

[1] Presumably 'stag' is intended.

We passed next morning the Brook Yariki, its waters are ochreous, and of much lighter colour than the river, the muddy appearance of which forms a strong contrast to the bright yellow of the stream. The sound of rushing waters made us halt a little further south, we followed the noise, and stood before a small cascade, not unlike that of Itafé in the Corentyne, but the nature of the ledge of rocks over which it falls 10 to 12 feet perpendicular was different; the Waccaways called it Idoué-wadde or Tivourouade. The influence of tide is not more felt here; it was but trifling at our camp near the Waccaway Settlement; its extent, the windings of the river included amounts therefore to 160 Miles. The river is navigable to this point for flat-bottomed canoes, drawing 2 feet water without meeting any impediments. The river now becomes less winding and has a breadth of about [240] feet[;][1] we met further south a ledge of granitic rocks on which we observed a great number of Indian picture writings. They resemble those I observed at Warapoota in the river Essequibo but they were neither so regular nor on such a large scale as those we had seen on the river Cabalaba and Corentyne. The Granite is here red, the surface smooth and covered with a thicker crust of that black substance, repeatedly noted, that I have observed it before. I am of opinion that the process which produced it, does not go on at present. In many places, in consequence of the influence of the weather or perhaps other circumstances, the outer side has split and thus the black coating has been removed; this must have taken place a long time ago, we found a great many lichens and mosses, and in some instances bushes to grow on such parts, but there was no vestige of the coating. Boulders which were at present lying at some distance from the banks of the river, and which at the utmost are only subjected to the flood during the inundations, possess the coating as much as those which are constantly exposed to the waters. The conclusion presses easily itself therefore upon the mind that the formation of that crust of Oxide of manganeese was concomitant with the cause that deposited them.[2] We passed soon after the first rapid called by the Waccaways Marlissae,[3] and several others followed in the course of the morning; at 11 Oclock we saw some hills before us, where it was evident that the river had caused a break, it turned almost at right angles and the point from whence the river issued was so completely hid, that we were almost persuaded the river's course was here at an end. The Indians from the Corentyne appeared to be of the same opinion, they set up a shout and stared. The Waccaways smiled, they had been here before and knew that it turned between two hills; rapid followed rapid[;] in the afternoon we arrived at a point where the contracted river forms an entrance to a natural basin, bordered by hills; it is followed by a second, the entrance to which through barriers of rocks is only 43 feet wide; the basin spreads in the form of a curved lozenge, and is upwards of 1600 feet long and 900 feet wide; [at] its northern [arc] the river rushes violently over a dyke of rocks, and forms the Cataract Itabrou.[4] I saw the impossibility of getting the Corials loaded over the Cataract and orders were consequently given to unload them, and to carry the baggage over the Rocks to the head of the Cataract; the difficulties connected with such

---

[1] The original figure has been scored out and replaced with 80 yards. It is clear that the original figure contained '2' and '0' as the first and third digits but the second is illegible. The figure of 240 assumes that the conversion has been done on the normal basis of three feet to the yard.

[2] That is, the boulders.

[3] Marlissa Falls.

[4] Itabru Falls.

an undertaking were various, we had to sling our chests, barrels, &c. to poles, and raise them over heaps of boulders, some of which were ten feet high, and their surfaces smooth as glass. After the baggage had been transported to the head of the Cataract, the question arose: how shall I get the Corials over? The most eligible way appeared to be to force them through the rush of water; we made the attempt with the "Maconochie" next morning; she was lashed to a rope about 20 yards long and an inch thick, and after the most courageous of our crew, Henry a half Indian, or Cobb,[1] had gained by trial one of the rocks in the middle of the Cataract, the end of the rope was thrown to him; he carried it then to a less dangerous place which the expert swimmers of my Indian crew had reached meanwhile, and now they drew the Corial by main force through the opposing waters, the steersman occupying his seat, having lashed himself for security sake to the corial, by means of a large paddle, he attributed to direct her course. We were occupied the following day to transport the baggage of the other corials, and succeeded so well that by evening there was only one corial this side of it. The situation which we occupied as Camp, was very pretty; it afforded a prospect over the basin to the hills, which encompassed it; one of these hills rose at the distance of one mile to a height of 511 feet, according to a trigonometrical measurement, while those contiguous to the basin were about 150 to 250 feet high. The weather continued unfavourable for celestial observations and I did not succeed to ascertain the altitude of a star when culminating, but from a series of observations of the Sun when near the meridian, I calculated the Latitude to be 4°49′N.; rather an unsatisfactory observation gave me as Longitude 3^{h}52^m West of Greenwich.

Our crew had exerted themselves to transport the Corials and baggage to the head of the cataract, I had therefore no tangible reason, to refuse Andres the Chieftain of the Accaways, the permission to dance; it was rather an extraordinary request and as he told me that evening, that the women and children who accompanied him were next morning to return, I did not trust entirely their intentions and while I granted their request and ordered extra allowances to be shared out, I ordered at the same time that the only Corial which remained this side of the Cataract, as well as their own should be hauled up and secured by chains and lock. The dance of the Waccaways resembles much that of the Caribbees, the same monotonous and dirge-like song accompanies it; the motions are almost the same; they move sideways forward, by stepping with the right foot; the right hand is placed upon the neighbour's shoulder, and the left hangs motionless on the body; they describe generally a circle in their movements, and when the dance is finished, the leader of the column sets up a shout, which is echoed by the dancers. Next morning early (December 15th) we conveyed the last Corial over the Cataract; Hendrick whom I mentioned before,[2] as having selected the most dangerous situation, in the middle of the Cataract, in order that the rope might be thrown to him to which the Corial was fastened, lost in the attempt his footing and was immediately swept away: Mr Cameron & myself stood on the shore while the accident happened and I acknowledge that it were moments of the greatest anxiety, from the time we saw him carried away, until he grasped the rope and was drawn ashore, one foot further and he would have been carried with the greatest violence against a large boulder, which rises its head upwards of ten feet out of the water, and against which the water dashes with

---

[1] Cob, a person of brown skin (*DCEU*).
[2] As Henry.

the greatest fury. This cataract has been visited several times by some of the most enterprising Colonists, we found their names and initials cut in trees, but they did not extend their explorations many miles further. After we had passed a second and a third Cataract of less height, we observed mountains a head, higher than any we had seen in the Corentyne; they formed a ridge running South-East and North-West. The ridge resembled a gigantic wall and ended in a Peak the height of which we estimated 8 to 900 feet, they were thickly-wooded and approached in slopes. The river is so much impeded, that we met continually rapids and Cataracts. The progress of our ascent was therefore slow and after two days of the most fatigueing labour, we were only 5 miles distant from Itabrou. It took us frequently two hours to travel over the distance of 100 yards, and the Combined Crews met with the greatest difficulties to put the Corials over. My crew consisted of Individuals of the five Chief tribes of British Guiana, namely Arawaaks, Warrows, Caribbees, Wacouways, and Macoosies. I was certainly astonished to see how well they agreed together; while we journied on, the service for which they were employed, obliged them to mix with each other, but scarcely were orders given to halt for that day, when the different tribes separated and made their own night quarters. The Macoosies and Waccaways slept and messed together, there was something peculiar in their manner towards us, which I did not like and I determined to watch them. As we advanced the Kaymen or large Alligators[1] became very numerous; we met them frequently in the middle of Cataracts with the upper part of their head above water, and fronting the current, their jaws partly open; for the purpose we concluded, to procure any fish which by chance might be swept down by the current and directed towards their jaws; otherwise what might be their reason to remain in that situation for hours without moving.[2] They allowed us to come quite near, and we could not desist to direct a ball through their eyes, by far the most tangible part of the monster, otherwise armee Cap a Pie.[3] Their tenacity of life is most astonishing, we fired at one thus situated, and the ball took off the further end of the snout, it received immediately afterwards another ball in the hinder part of the skull and being a rifle ball, it appeared to have taken effect; nevertheless the Indians were not sparing in their blows, and after there was not much likelihood of its possessing a spark of life, it was deposited in the bow of one of the Corials. Whilst the Corial was drawn across the rapids, it was found to be in the way, and as it had remained motionless, since it had been put in, two of the Arawaaks got courage, and took it up in order to lay it in some other place; they had just effected this, when in one action, it jumped out of the Corial into the river, and disappeared, the two Indians I need scarcely observe, looked quite stupid, and ever hereafter could not be persuaded to touch a Kayman again. The next day afforded us another instance of a similar description, the first Ball fired at a Kayman fell short, it dived under beating violently with its tail, it reappeared almost instantly, when it was shot in the head; it raised itself almost perpendicular out of the water & lashed the water with great force; however two of the smaller Corials were immediately up with it, and it was killed with Cutlasses and blows. Though it appeared perfectly dead we recollected our yesterday's adventure; Hendrick cut therefore its throat open and cut out of the wind pipe a piece of upwards of three inches, and we considered ourselves now secure. As it was

[1] The caiman belongs to the Family Alligatoridae.
[2] It is more likely to do with keeping cool.
[3] 'Armed head to foot'.

intended to be skinned, Mr Reiss took the Reptile in his Corial; who can describe our Astonishment, when an hour after, it was alive again and if it had not been for some ropes, with which it was lashed, it would have escaped. A strong knife was driven by main force in its head and brain, before it expired. These facts would have appeared to me incredible, if I had not seen them myself. We toiled through the rapids and Cataracts, one following the [other; the] mountains continued on our right; those on the Eastern bank of the river were of less height. These regions appeared to be the favourite abode of the reptile tribe; the Guanas were so numerous that, awakened out of their revery by the approach of our corials, when lurking on a tree at the bank of the river, we saw sometimes three jumping at once from a height of 15 to 20 feet into the water, and disappear almost instantly; the splash thus produced was heard at a great distance, and produced always a cry of grief and disappointment from our Indians, the consequence of having lost now every chance to procure them for their pot. Mr Vieth shot one 5 feet 9 inches long, including the tail which measured 4 feet 2 inches. Several of our Indians caught them while swimming in the water. Two of the lighter corials had preceded us over a rapid, while our larger required more time and strength to be hauled over; they had discovered a Commoudie Snake (Boa Draco Gigas);[1] it was lying inert in a kind a of jungle, and had just slipped its skin. When we came up Mr. Reiss had fired a ball at it without having taken effect, and it was slowly retreating towards the water, at this moment Hendrick jumped ashore, and slipped dexterously a noose round its head and was on the point of lashing it, when the snake turned round and made a motion as if to dart at him; at this attack all his former courage gave way, and he retreated with the greatest precipitation, over bushes and rocks into the water. The Indians stood all as if petrified, they could not be induced to put even a hand to the rope to draw the snake out of the jungle, and we ran a fair chance to lose our ropes to boot, when Mr Cameron fired a timely ball somewhat behind the head in the neck, and Mr Vieth succeeded to catch the head in a noose; it was now quickly despatched and secured in the boat; it measured 16 feet 4 inches in length and 28 inches in circumference; while skinning it 40 to 50 eggs were discovered, which had not yet come to maturity.

The flora of the river's banks was not much diversified. [I obser]ved however some plants which hitherto I knew only from description and which were highly interesting, in consequence of their peculiar formation; among them were the Marcgraavia umbellata[2] and Norantea guianensis (Aublet)[;] the Marcgraavia was very numerous along the banks of the rivers; it may be called a ligneous twiner, though its branches are pendulous, but they are it more in consequence of the inflorescence which too weighty increased by the peculiar bractea causes the slender branches to hang down. It is frequently parasitical, and I have found it in such various shapes, that at first glance I have taken the young branches for a Lygodium. The flexible branches are thickly set with alternate leaves of a lanceolate form, and are terminated by flowering umbels, which with the singular form of the bractea, resemble a chandelier, the flowers are insignificant but remarkable for the Calyptra with which the receptacle is covered; as soon as it falls off the stamens drop shortly after. The most curious organs of the plant are however the pitcher-shaped bractea of which there are generally four or five fixed to the flowering stem, and surrounded by the flowers in long peduncles. The bractea is

[1] Presumably the Land boa (*Boa constrictor*).
[2] *Marcgravia umbellata*.

190

fleshy cucullate, and hollow; the opening is wide on the top, and decreases in size; it contains a moist substance; the fluid contained in one amounts to a teaspoonful; it was tasteless. Equally curious and more splendid in appearance is Aublet's Norantea (Ascium Aubletii (Schreber)).[1] Its branches are likewise flexible and in common with many of the Guttiferae[2] to which the Genus is nearly allied, it has sub-parasitical habits; the leaves are alternate and so coriaceous that the upper skin, like a cuticle, may be removed; it flowers in endrisps and the peduncles have an appendage of a deep orange colour which is clubshaped and hollow, the risp is from 10 to 24 inches long. The flowers are 5 petaled, of a deep crimson, but so small that they are entirely eclipsed by the brightness of the orange coloured bractea; each flower has one of the bractea appended to its peduncle, and I counted on one of the risps 325; an idea may be therefore formed of the appearance where the climbing shrub overrunning partly some huge tree, many hundred flowering risps may be seen. It forms one of the greatest ornaments of the Flora of British Guiana. Since speaking of plants and the highly interesting Botany of these rivers, I must not omit a species of Capparis, which grew alongside the banks of the River; it was a tree of moderate size and every afternoon about 4 Oclock it was so much covered with its snow white flowers distinguished by its indefinite number of stamens, that it afforded really a pretty sight. With the rise of sun next morning, the flower detaches itself from the disk and drops into the water, and is carried along by the stream; we met therefore thousands in the morning early floating downwards and took it generally as a sign, that no rapids or cataracts were in the vicinity, as we but seldom found the tree in such situations. We started next morning early; our advance however was of short duration; while turning round a sudden bend of the river, a series of formidable Cataracts was before us. I took a survey of them, accompanied by the most experienced of our Crew, and the result was that they extended in an eastern direction for upwards of a mile & a half, and that we would have to pass besides five large Cataracts, several rapids before we came to still water, & that every circumstance favorably calculated, it would take up 5 or 6 days to transport corials & baggage over the dyke. I became therefore apprehensive that our provisions might give out, and I resolved to send a Corial back to Mr McCullum's wood cutting Establishment for a fresh supply of provisions; Mr Reiss kindly offered to command it, he left us next morning the 19th December.

It was first my intention to have a road cut along the river's bank for the transport of our effects, but I found it impracticable, the rising ground consisted of numerous boulders, heaped upon each other, and the crevices were only partially filled out with mould; it would have been therefore impossible to place rollers for the conveyance of the Corials; I preferred therefore to have the baggage carried over the different ledges of rocks which constitute these Cataracts, and to haul the Corials after. The Cataracts are formed by a continuation of the hills which we met in 4°50′ lat., their direction is evidently South East and their system was found regular as far as it has been under my immediate inspection; indeed here the valleys kept to nearly the same course as the

---

[1] Johann Christian Daniel von Schreber (1739–1810), German botanist. Presumably Schomburgk is here describing *Norantea guianesis* (Aublet) mentioned a few lines above.

[2] Today the Family Guttiferae are commonly classed as Clusiaceae, which family includes Bonnetiaceae. For example, Mennega et al., employ Guttiferae and Bonnetiaceae, whereas the NMNH Check-list uses Clusiaceae.

main range of mountains, namely South-East, with but little variation on either side, and if we continue the direction in a North western line we will be lead to the Twasinkie and Commoudie Mountains of the Essequibo, which are a north eastern offset of the Sierra Pacaraima; the line continued to the S.E. along its natural range meets the Marowinie Mountains[1] in 3[d] parallel; accordingly the Sierra Acaray would be therefore connected by aid of the Marowinie Mountains with these on the river Berbice and the Twasinkie mountains of the Essequibo, from the whence the system takes a north eastern direction towards the Sierra Pacaraima in the 4th parallel of latitude & between the 60 & 64th Meridian.[2] The nature of the rocks at Twasinkie and the Cataracts of the Berbice is however different, while the former consists of Granite and its modifications, these of the Berbice are more of Trappean origin; their stratification is N35°E, their dip West 10° by North; the strata have been disturbed after their deposition; various examples of cross-currents are evident and the beds are sometimes contorted & cut off by faults, which are filled with a species of wacke[3] of a red colour: the angle of the regular beds amounts to upwards of 80°. The beds like those at the lower cataracts, are remarkable for large holes, entirely smooth inside and often 2 to 3 feet in diameter, indeed they might be called cavernous. Where the current during inundations has cut out beds, I observed numerous boulders of about 3 to 4 feet in diameter, decidedly of the same formation, but much more covered with the black coating & exhibiting ripple marks. Our transport over these ledges of rocks advanced but slowly, we had to unload and reload the Corials four times & as in consequence of the shallow water at the rapids, we could only take half a load, an idea of the harassing work may be formed. Three Corials were thus at the head of the Cataract in the evening of the 21st, when next morning at the time the rations were generally distributed, the information was brought to me that the Macoosies and Waccaways with Andres at their head had decamped and were no where to be found. We had been accustomed to their freak of having their camp further removed from ours, than any other of the tribes, who were with me, & it was not considered singular when we found that the same was the case when at these Cataracts; there were no signs that they had had fire that night, an indispensable article to an Indian during night and there was no doubt left that they had escaped already the previous evening. No Colonist had ever been able to induce them to go higher up the Berbice, than the Cataract Itabrou, & when they saw that it did not offer an insurmountable obstacle to our progress, they expressed their astonishment & they fell upon the Plan to try whether horrible stories of mountain spirits, gigantic snakes, & thousands of Kaymans, which were said to [illegible] in the river, and were able to digest a corial with its crew & baggage before breakfast, might have the desired effect, they were

---

[1] The Marowinie Mountains have not been identified, but one would assume that a mountain range of this name would be found much further east, towards the sources of the Marowini or Maroni River, the frontier between French Guiana and Surinam.

[2] There are numerous corrections to this passage, some of them by Schomburgk himself and others by an editor. The published version reads: 'a continuation in a north-western line leads to the Twasinkie and Coomootie mountains of the Essequibo, which are a north-eastern off-set of the Sierra Pacaraima: a line continued to the S.E. along this range would strike the Marawini mountains in the 3rd parallel; so that the Sierra Acaray would be connected with these hills on the Berbice and the Twasinkie mountains on the Essequibo, which are again joined to the Sierra Pacaraima about the 4th parallel of latitude' ('Diary of an Ascent of the River Berbice', p. 316).

[3] 'A sandstone-like rock, resulting from the decomposition of basaltic rocks *in situ*' (*OED*).

mistaken; then came the demand that they might be allowed to dance. I allowed it – took however the precaution to haul up their Corial as well as the one, which had remained at the foot of the Cataract; the first thing which I heard the previous morning was that the women, who had accompanied them hitherto, were to return to the settlement, & from that moment they must have resolved to leave us secretly as soon as an opportunity offered, and they effected it on the night from the 21st to the 22nd, after they had broken open our stores of biscuit & wine. Our crew being already weakened by Mr Reiss's absence with one Corial, and many of those who remained with me being sick, I relinquished all ideas of pursuing them. I took on the 21st and 22nd of December the hourly observations recommended by Sir John Hershel; celestial observations were very precarious, I had been up three nights in succession, to procure a set of Lunar distances, but in vain. The means of the meteorological hourly observations on the appointed days were:

> Barometer 29.758, Attached Thermometer 76°5′F, External Thermometer 75°7′, Wet Thermometer 73°8′, Surface of the river 79°.7. The height of the Cataract above the level of the sea was ascertained to be 245 feet, the Lat 4°41′45″N the Longt 57°53′45″. The variation of the needle amounted to 6°57 East for Schmalcalder's compass. The night from the 20 to the 21 was one of the coldest I ever experienced at a low situation in Guiana; at 2 oclock in the morning of the 21st the Thermometer stood 64°.5, the wet Thermometer 64°, the surface of the water of the river was 72°. The Barometer 29.740.

Christmas day approached when we were at the Cataracts, though but few of our Indians were aware of the occasion and origin of this joyful day, and equally unable to understand what I told them of the birth of our blessed Saviour. I wished that they should participate in some regard in the better fare which we enjoyed on that day. Several pieces of salt beef were shared among them, & though not every one of the Indians would eat it, I found them not so strict as those I met during the former Expedition in the Rupununy; they received otherwise additional allowances and every four men a bottle of rum and some sugar. We enjoyed therefore Christmas in our own way, and the proposal that as we could not learn whether these Cataracts had any name, they might be called "Christmas Cataracts"[1] was gladly adopted.

Mr Reiss could scarcely be expected before 3 or 4 days more had elapsed. I gave orders to break up the Camp. On the morning of the 27th we transported the last Corial, which in case of necessity had been kept at the lower Cataract, over the rocks. The river was falling, and Diarrhoea and severe colds were much prevailing among the Indians. I thought to conquer it by giving them occupation. I had come to the conclusion to abandon one of the Corials, the desertion of the Accaways, six in number, had much reduced the number of my crew & I had not sufficient Indians to man them; we hauled the Corial therefore up and divided her load among the others. The night proved a sleepless one for us; we were but a short time in our hammocks when we discovered that our tents were visited by Coushi ant or yagerman, by which name the Creoles denominate the Atta cephalotes or migratoria;[2] they distributed most merciless bites, and those who

---

[1] They are still known as Christmas Falls.

[2] Acoushi ant (*Atta cephalotes* or *Atta sexdens* or *Acromyrmex octospinosus*). They are also known as Parasol, Umbrella or Leaf-cutting ants. The names derive from their practice of cutting pieces out of leaves and carrying them back to the nest above their heads. However, it is possible from the description that these were Army or Driver ants (*Eciton* spp.).

attempted to get out of their Hammocks, were soon obliged to seek their way back, our poor dogs suffered the most; they had no place to get out of their reach and they ran about the whole night like mad, howling in consequence of the severe bites which they received. One of the Columns of marching ants had moved up a tree and whether it was in consequence of the immense numbers, enough we heard them dropping from the tree upon our tents, as if it were drops of rain from the leaves, after a heavy shower.

Decebʳ 28ᵗʰ Our progress was quite slow; we turned round a sudden bend of the river when a most obnoxious effluvia greeted our noses, and we observed a flock of that curious bird, the King of the Vultures,[1] rising from a dead Kayman; we did not succeed to shoot a full grown one, a young one was however procured; the feathers of which were just about to turn from black into white; this is certainly a curious change, peculiar to several birds and appears to reverse the nature of things. There were upwards from fifteen to twenty assembled round the carrion; they flew with the noise of heavy wings from branch to branch, until scared by the first shot, they flew deeper into the woods. The opportunity of glutting themselves was too inviting to be abandoned by a rapid flight. We were not very successful in procuring game, but we were indemnified by a large number of fish, which were as acceptable at the period as they had been scarce for some time past; our Crew procured fourteen large Haimouras[2] one of the most delicate of the finny tribe in these rivers; their average weight is about 15 lbs. In order to procure the Haimoura, spring hooks are set in the evening, and when the fish allured by the bait takes it, it is drawn by the elasticity of the rod out of the water, and there it hangs until it is secured by the fisherman; but there are not only bipeds who are anxious to secure the entrapped fish, among the foremost in that regard stands the Kayman, which attracted by the noise which the fish makes when caught by being partly drawn out of the water, and slapping it with its tail, considers to have as much right towards it as the one who set the Hooks; in that piratical system, it is assisted by the Pi-rie, called by the Arawaaks Houma, which slashes piece after piece from the poor Captive, and when the fisherman takes his round, he finds nothing but the head attached to the rod. It is therefore necessary that those who set the Hooks should be constantly on the alert. December 30ᵗʰ. The Kaymen are very numerous, I had one, which measured 14 feet the tail included, which was 4 feet 8 inches. It is astonishing how far foolhardiness carries sometimes the Indians, while at other periods, he shows the greatest cowardice; he acts on impulse. The Kayman lay motionless and apparently dead along the banks of the river; Salomon the chief man of my Warrows, jumped ashore, and after having given him a few blows with the Cutlass across the head, attempted to force its jaws open with his hands, he desisted only by my commands; scarcely had he allowed the Kayman's head to drop to its former position, when the monster snapped most violently at the Indian; it missed him but got hold of an old stump of a tree, where we had to use the axe to get him loose. Mʳ Cameron had shot another with a ball through the head, just under the eye: after having beaten violently the water with its tail, it rose to the surface of the river, its white shining belly turned upwards and we considered it for dead; one of the Corials was sent to secure the head, but on the approach of the Corial, new life appeared to start in its veins; it turned itself round, and rushed violently through the water; we could not give up the idea of despatching it and the foreman

[1] Presumably the King Vulture (*Sarcoramphus papa*).

[2] The Haimara (*Macrodon trahira* or *Hoplias macrophthalmus*), a large fish, famed for its excellent eating but also renowned for its ferocity.

of the smaller Corial, Hendrick, stood ready with the Cutlass; it turned now its attack towards the assailant, and with its formidable jaws open, it rushed towards the bow. Hendrick got so much frightened at this unexpected display of teeth, that he even allowed his paddle which he had in the other hand, to drop in the water and fell back without directing a single blow. I ordered instantly my large Corial to be drawn across to hem the monster in, but it did not await our arrival, and with open mouth came violently towards our broadside, as if it intended to join the party inside, not a little to the consternation of its inmates, chiefly of those, who were occupying that side, it literally ran against the side of the Corial, sunk under it but not until it had given a lash with its tail wetting us all over, and vanished in the deep water, the ruffle of it on the surface showed us for some time its course.

Jany 1st 1837. We made but slow progress; the river narrowed considerably and numerous trees which in consequence of age or the undermining effects of the current, had fallen across, disputed our advance; we were obliged to cut a passage through them. Nine out of ten were Mora trees, one of the hardest woods which Guiana possesses & which by being immersed in water had increased in hardness; it took us two to three hours to cut through one of these trees, and there were sometimes three to four in succession; we had therefore to spell the Cutter and none but Women were excepted from using the axe. In order to increase the difficulties many of our Indians were unfit for any work in consequence of indisposition; the entrance of the new Year was therefore well calculated to enhance the feeling of disappointment, that we should at that advanced period be within so short a distance from the coast: a succession of adverse circumstances had almost taken place since we undertook the Corentyne Expedition, difficulties beset us from the onset, and though I battled most resolutely to overcome them, and was determined to advance as long as there was any possibility of making progress, and famine did not threaten us, I could not feel but doubly the mortification on the first day of the year. Such thoughts crossed my mind when we arrived at a point where the river expanded and formed on its eastern Bank a smooth basin, the current of the river directing its course along the rivers western or right bank.[1] Some object on the southern point of the basin attracted my attention, it was impossible to see to form any idea of what it could be, and I hurried the crew to increase the rate of their paddles, and in a short time, we were opposite the object of our curiosity, a vegetable wonder! all calamities were forgotten, I felt as botanist, & felt myself rewarded. A gigantic leaf from 5 to 6 feet in diameter, salver shaped, with a broad rim of a light green above, and a vivid crimson below, rested upon the water; quite in character with the wonderful leaf was the luxuriant flower consisting of many hundred petals passing in alternate tints from pure white to rose and pink. The smooth water was covered with them, and I rowed from one to the other and observed always something new to be admired. The leaf is on the surface of a bright green, in form almost orbiculate, with the exceptions opposite its axis, where it is slightly bent in; its diameter measured from 5 to 6 feet; around the whole margin extends a rim about 3 to 5 inches high, at the inside of a light green like the surface of the leaf, on the outside like the leafs lower part of a bright crimson. The ribs are very prominent almost an inch high and radiate from a common centre and consist of eight principal ones, with a great many others branching off from

---

[1] The western side of the Berbice is its left bank. This is a further example of Schomburgk's tendency to orient himself on the basis of his own direction of travel.

them; these are crossed again by raised membranes or bands at right angles, which give the whole the appearance of a spiders web, and are beset with prickles; the veins contain air cells like the petiole and flowerstem. The divisions of the ribs and bands are visible on the upper surface of the leaf, by which it appears aerolated. The stem of the flower is an inch thick near the calix, and is studded with sharp elastic prickles about ¾ of an inch in length. The calix is four-leaved, each upwards of 7 inches in length and 3 inches in breadth; at the base they are thick – white inside and reddish brown and prickly outside; the diameter of the calix is 12 to 13 inches; on it rests the magnificent flower which when fully developed covers completely the calix with its hundred petals. When it first opens, it is white with pink in the middle, which spreads over the whole flower the more it advances in age, and is generally found the next day of a pink colour; as if to enhance its beauty, it is sweet scented. Like others of the tribe, it possesses a fleshy disk and the petals and stamens pass gradually in each other, and many petaloid leaves may be observed which have vestiges of an another. The petals next to the leaves of the calix are fleshy and possess air cells, which certainly must contribute to the buoyancy of the flower. The seeds of the many celled fruit are numerous, and embedded in a spongy substance. We met them hereafter frequently, and the higher we advanced, the more gigantic they became; we measured a leaf which was 6 feet 5 inches in diameter its rim 5½ inches high and the flower across 15 inches. The flower is much injured by a beetle (Trichius Spec.?)[1] which destroys completely the inner part of the disk; we have accounted sometimes from 20 to 30 in one flower.[2]

[1] Ghillean Prance and Jorge Arias who made an extended study of the lily near Manaus found four species of Dynastid beetles, three of the genus *Cyclocephala* and one of the genus *Ligyrus*, in 90 per cent of the flowers examined. See 'A Study of the Floral Biology of *Victoria amazonica* (Poepp.) Sowerby (Nymphaeaceae)', *Acta Amazonica*, 5, 1975, pp. 109–39.

[2] Although its official name today is *Victoria amazonica*, it was originally called *Victoria regia*. This name was given because Schomburgk, on reporting his find, asked that Queen Victoria be humbly requested if it might be dedicated to her, to which she consented.

Schomburgk's claim to have discovered it was wrong. It emerged that the German botanist Thaddäus Hänke (1761–1817) had found it on the Rio Mamoré (a tributary of the Rio Madeira) in 1801, but that he had lost his collections and news of it only emerged when the French botanist, Alcide Dessalines D'Orbigny (1802–57), heard about it from a priest, Father Cueva, who had been with Hänke at the time. D'Orbigny himself found the plant at Corrientes, near the junction of the Parana and Paraguay Rivers in 1827, but had been forestalled in this area by Aimé Bonpland (1773–1858), Humboldt's former travelling companion, in 1820. D'Orbigny also found the lily on the Rio Mamoré in 1834, but in the meantime the German Eduard Friedrich Pöppig (1798–1868) had found examples on the Amazon in 1832. History has credited Poeppig, rather than Schomburgk, with authorship, and its full taxonomic name is now *Victoria amazonica* (Pöppig) Sowerby. Also today it seems generally accepted that the plants found in Paraguay and Northern Argentina are a second species of the genus (*V. cruziana*).

Even if Schomburgk is no longer credited with being the lily's discoverer, he certainly was at the time. Furthermore the plant aroused much public interest. Various attempts to grow it in England did not succeed until 1849 at Kew, whence plants were distributed to other gardens. There was then considerable excitement about when the first plant would flower. This was to happen the same year at Chatsworth where Joseph Paxton (1801–65) had prepared a special lily house with a large heated tank. The structure of the lily inspired Paxton's design of the Crystal Palace.

There are two similar contemporary accounts of all this, although neither, unfortunately, is very accessible. They are: W. Fitch & W. Hooker, *Victoria Regia or Illustrations of the Royal Water-lily, in a Series of Figures Chiefly Made From Specimens Flowering at Syon and at Kew*, London, Reeve & Benham, 1851, and George Lawson, *The Royal Water-lily of South America, and the Water-lilies of our own Land: Their History and Cultivation*, Edinburgh, James Hogg, 1851.

Our advance amounted next day scarcely to 2 miles, the trees which barricaded our passage were so numerous – while the men were employed to cut through a large Mora tree, the information was brought that a herd of Kairounies or Carouns, the large Peccary or Indian hog (Sus cystiferous major),[1] was feeding at a short distance from the river; all our guns were put immediately in requisition, and off we started; Acouritch the Caribbee armed with bows and Ironheaded arrows in the van; I came first up with them and found them in a pool of water where they wallowed in the mire like our domestic hog; one appeared to stand watch while the rest enjoyed the muddy bath, the young ones of several sizes keeping the middle. When I was at a distance of 15 yards the sentinel observed me, the bristles on the back rose and it turned towards me, chattering formidably with its teeth; in the next moment it lay prostrate in the mud by a rifle ball, but how can I describe the bustle, the rush, and the chattering of the tusks of upwards of two hundred, which immediately after were seeing to seek their security in rapid flight in the opposite direction; an Indian, who had come up by this time fired after them and shot another, and the retreat was now perfect; I had loaded again but hesitated a moment to wade through the swamp, the Arawaak Mathias observed it, and he requested me to give him my rifle and ammunition: I gave it to him, and off he started and I found myself quite alone. I heard four or five shots fall shortly after at some distance on my right, and while yet calculating how many of them might have told, I heard a rushing noise coming like a whirlwind through the bushes, the peculiar growl, and that awful clapping of the teeth caused me not long to conjecture what it was; I concluded that part of the herd had divided, and they were coming directly towards the place which I occupied. I stood alone unarmed and I had even not a knife to defend myself. I do not know yet how I had come up the lower part of a mora tree, when by they rushed, their muzzles sweeping almost the ground and their rough bristles on the back standing almost erect; they might have numbered fifty; they approached and passed like a whirlwind, while I had not yet recovered from my astonishment, I heard them already plunge into the river and swim over to the opposite bank. The other hunters had not been so fortunate as I expected; excitement or fear made them miss where it would have appeared almost impossible. The one I had shot included, three had been shot with guns, and one by Acouritch with an arrow; they were a most welcome addition to our stock, as I was already then obliged to economize and our endeavours to procure fish were not so successful.

The Kairounie has been so well described that it is superfluous to dwell further on it, but there is an anatomical difference in the internal structure of the skull which I do not find noted in the works on Natural History, which form part of my travelling library; it possesses only a small quantity of brain which is protected by a double bone. Naturalists observe, that it does not love to wallow in the mire. I found the whole herd almost buried in it, & we discovered later another pool of water where the marks of their having wallowed were evident enough. The liquor which flows out of the gland is highly offensive, and peculiar to male and female – the latter produces only two young ones frequently only one; the cry of the Kairounie, when grown up is a grunt but the cry of the younger ones resembles much the bleating of a goat.

January 2nd.[2] The indisposition of the Crew had so much increased that I had not sufficient hands to paddle, I was therefore obliged to encamp until the health of my party

---

[1] Commonly known as the White-lipped peccary (*Tayassu pecari*).

[2] This date is wrong since 'next day', i.e., that after 1 January, is referred to in the first line of this page.

was reestablished. Jany 4th. The report of two guns had been heard while I was absent on a hunting excursion & they had formed the Conclusion that it was Mr Reiss returning from the foraging Expedition; our surmises proved correct and Mr Reiss was with us an hour after. M^r McCullum, from whom the Expedition received so many attentions and assistance, had most readily come forward to advance the desired for quantity of rice salt-fish &c and the Corial had succeeded to pass the Cataracts without accident. We had a severe thunderstorm in the afternoon, while I was occupied to observe the changes of the Barometer & Thermometers[;] during its approach the lightning struck a tree just on the opposite side of the River. The clap followed the lightning instantly, and the reverbera-tion was so severe that man and beast appeared startled. The Barometer did not show any fluctuations, the Thermometer had fallen however since its commencement; it stood at 2^h15^m p.m. 81° & at 2^h55^m when the rain fell in torrents 75°, there it remained until 3^h35^m, when it rose again to 75°.8 and at 4^h it had risen to 76°.5; the thunder was then still heard; indeed it continued the whole night. We could not flatter ourselves of being particularly favoured by the weather, but it had not come to extremes as yet. I augured nothing good from its present appearance, the atmosphere was heavy and constantly clouded in the North West; we were then so near to the change of the moon, which generally has an undenied influence upon the weather, that I apprehended the setting in of the rainy sea-son, and my surmises proved unfortunately correct. Active Medicines had partially restored so many of the Indians that I was able to continue our Journey on Jany 6th. We met occasionally detached badges[1] of rocks, of the same nature, dip, and direction, as those at the Christmas Cataracts; the river narrowed considerably, and we were again under the necessity of having recourse to axes and cutlasses; its width amounted fre-quently to scarcely more than 30 feet, while its current sweeping over a sandy bottom & partly covered with pebbles, was almost too much for my weakened crew; they had to take to account every particle of strength left in their sinews in order not to retrogate;[2] the Current run at the rate of 2 knots. The river formed frequently inlets which spread from its banks, & were studded with islets of different shapes, covered with numerous palms, that bade defiance to any intruder by their sharp prickles which were often 3 to 4 inches long, indeed the river was bordered by a dense forest of Palms, they scarcely allow any other plant to grow up and usurp humidity, air, and light. The under strata of the soil for the succeeding 10 miles (N & S lat. 4°20′ to 4°10′) is highly retentive; while on the surface it consists of a chalky marl, mixed with mould; it is particularly qualified for the cultivation of rice, the more so since it is annually inundated & enriched by the deposi-tion of mud. If these extensive lands were put under partial drainage, I am almost per-suaded in my own mind, that they would answer exceedingly well, the Soil itself is so springy, and the periodical inundations would be connected with the deposition of mud which would make any manure unnecessary. I really think that two crops would be obtained in one year, if the first favourable moment after the waters of the inundations have withdrawn, was taken advantage of; this occurs generally towards the end of August, and by the time the rainy season commences in May, a second crop would be ripe with sufficient time to bring it in.*

*Mr. Bilstein of Essequibo got 2 crops of rice & three of Guinea corn pr. ann.

[1] This is a secure reading of the manuscript; it appears as ledges in the published version (p. 323).
[2] An editorial hand has amended this to 'retrograde'.

The current was now frequently our only guide to find out the river & with the greatest attention we appeared sometimes at a loss what direction we had to take, when after a strict examination, we found perhaps that the course of the River was perfectly covered with Bushes and jungle and therefore no wonder that we mistook the large inlet for the river until we found out our mistake, as not the slightest ripple moved the mass of water. The beautiful waterlilly covered whole stretches with its singular leaves; we saw some Muscovy ducks nibbling on its leaves; while numerous spurwings – Sultana hens,[1] and other aquatic birds were walking on the surface of the leaf in search of insects.

Many might have been satisfied that they had now reached the sources of the River, and would have returned to the Colony with information, that it arises in a lake, where at its issue it is not more than 16 feet wide; how astonished would they have been, if they had been told that a few miles further south, the river widens again to 450 feet! As already observed the perfect smoothness of the water induced me to look for another out[way], and, after some delay we had cut a path for our Corials and were once more on a fine stream unimpeded by jungle. We found here the Iron-wood-tree and a new species of dipterix, the flower of which has a beatiful perfume resembling Violets – it is called by the Indians Itikieri-bouri-bally; the wood is speckled like a Tiger's skin and is sometimes brought to the Colony, where it commands a prize of 4 fl (5/9[d]) per foot.[2] At the first acquaintance which our axes made with the Iron wood, a tree laying across the river, they revolted; after a few blows, the smooth axe resembled almost a saw and if we had not possessed some American axes we would have been obliged to haul the Corials over land. As if to form a strong contrast in the vicinity of the sweet scented dipterix and the hard Iron-wood, grew a tree superior in size to either the one or the other and when we applied the axe to it, it diffused a most unpleasant smell, it was very soft & white and the outer bark grey.

Janr[y] 8th We met at noon numerous boulders of granite of the same composition as those at Achramoucra, in the river Essequibo in 4°20′N. Lat. and at the Cataracts of the River Corentyne (4°21′[3]″N. Lat.) according to the observations which I took at that period we were then in 4°19′51″ N. Lat[;] the tract preserves therefore its eastern direction; the boulders were much rounded, often spherical and gigantic in size.

Our pleasure at the open river did not last long – it narrowed again, and dwindled in width to about thirty feet – the islets and Palms of the former tract were wanting; but they were amply replaced by lianas, chiefly Mikania, Convolvulaceæ and a spreading bush which I might call the Mangrove of the fresh waters. Our progress was now connected with constant toil; with the most harassing labour, we laid often scarcely two miles back in a day, and, in order to avoid to cut through trees which it would have taken us a day to accomplish, we preferred to unload the Corials and to draw them overland. I resolved now to halt every alternate day, and to send parties forward to clear partly our path. As if to render our progress to the South still slower, the river meandred in short turns and the constant rains which had set in at the change of the moon, had caused its banks to overflow. Five weeks had now elapsed since we had left the last

---

[1] This term refers to birds belonging to the genus *Porphyrula*, of which two species have been reported from Guyana.
[2] There are two species of *Dipteryx* reported for Guyana by Mennega et al., both of them are known as Tonka bean in Creole. Itikiboroballi, in Arawak, refers to various species of *Swartzia*.

human habitation, and as we had not been able to increase our stock of provisions, I was under the necessity to curtail the allowances, the river had swollen rapidly and game and fish was now a scarcity, while the difficulties increased with every step we advanced, I observed dissatisfaction among the crew, they were tired of proceeding further and I had to use energetic measures, to have my orders enforced.

While some of the Indians were hunting, they met a pack of wild dogs, our own dogs secured one, and as Indians are generally fond to cross their breed, Acouritch had tied it to a tree, in order to take it with him when he returned from the chase; but the dog had gnawed his rope and was off before our prudent huntsman could execute his design. Hendrick who had accompanied Accouritch, told me that the pack might have accounted to thirty or more; in figure he likened them to the bull-terrier the ears rounded and hanging, and the colour reddish brown. I was sorry that by the Indians negligence I lost the opportunity to see one of these animals, of which I had heard so much, and which I conclude, belong to the Subgenus Fox; they are sometimes met with near the coast, and hunt always in packs.[1]

January 22nd. Our difficulties appeared to encrease with every hour, and every step grew more painful; the river is quite narrow and winds its course through a real wilderness; margined by prickly palms, it is almost entirely grown over by a species of Solanum. We were now obliged to man one of the smaller Corials with some of the ablest men, with cutlasses and axes in their hands, to clear the greatest obstacles out of the way, while we followed with the other corials which were forced forward by long poles. We came constantly in contact with the bushes on either side and were frequently molested by ants centipedes, spiders, and scorpions, which secreted themselves in the rubbish, left on the bushes by the last inundations, and which inflicted the severest bites on us – or we received a brush over our face and hands by one of the prickly palm-leaves, which never failed to leave marks of its passage, the Indian Crew fared worse in that regard, we were partly protected by our clothes, but their stock had given out long before this, and they had no protection whatever. The banks originally low, were under water in consequence of the continued rains, and it proved frequently precarious to find a place, where we could sling our hammocks. It was late in the Afternoon when we were still on the look out to find a dry spot, we had sent one of the Indians of the mixed race, up a high tree he gave us information that so far as the eye could reach, the swamps continued, a bad comfort for us weary travellers. Acouritch was hallowing out most lustily, in order to try in what direction his voice resounded, to serve as an indication of dry land, but in vain. After sunset, and when we had made up our minds to remain in the corials, a small spot which the water had not reached as yet, was discovered. It rained severely and as the water was growing, we were really glad, when we could leave next morning, without having been dislodged & not further molested as that we had to wade to the place, where we had landed on dry ground the previous evening; indeed we had looked forward with sad forbodings to this night's rest.

Jany 24 I received this evening a most unpleasant information; A Warrow Indian, who was rather a favourite, informed me that mischief was going on in the Camp. For some days past I had discovered rebellious conduct. I had previously observed

---

[1] This is probably the Bush Dog (*Speothos venaticus*).

disobedience to my orders, and I had been under the necessity to inflict punishment[1] but they never showed it so openly as during the last two days. I was well aware that the generality of the Indian were disaffected to the further progress of the Expedition, and I had even proof that the Coloured people were equally to be distrusted. All endeavours to procure game or fish proved in vain, and the dreary prospect, that during the continuance of the rainy weather, no better success awaited us, had laid me under the necessity to curtail still more our daily allowances, and to reduce it to little more than six ozs of rice for a man and five for a woman. The hard and continued labour to which they were exposed, the absence of rum, and the impossibility of procuring game as a relish to their scanty rice-diet, were certainly not encouraging. I was now informed that the Caribbees with Acouritch at their head, had instigated the others to take the corials away and to leave us during the night; and if we should show resistance to tie us with hammock ropes to the trees. I do not know, how far Acouritch might have succeeded with the Arawaaks, however I was aware that my own boat crew, the Warrows, would not suffer their fidelity to be tampered with; our Mems as we called the young Warrow was therefore sent to give me information. The intelligence of this treachery caused me great uneasiness, I did not know how far the disaffection might have spread; I knew there was no individual in the camp who did not loath to proceed farther. I informed Mr Reiss of the circumstance, and as it had been my intention to take hold of the ringleader at once, and to hand cuff him, on mature deliberation I disproved of this plan, as we were perfectly ignorant how far he had succeeded and such a step might have produced the catastrophe; it was therefore resolved upon to conceal all knowledge of their treachery, and to be vigilant and have a strict guard upon the corials and ammunitions. Acouritch must have had knowledge of his plot being discovered; they had their camp that night not far from my tent, I saw their fires burning through the night, and was therefore not a little astonished to find next morning that they had deserted about midnight; we had heard the barking of one of our dogs at some distance of the Camp, Mr Reiss reconnoitered, but discovering nothing unusual, he retired to his hammock; misled by the fires, he supposed the Caribbees in their hammocks. They had taken with them some of our best Cutlasses, iron pots, Camp Kettles, &c and as Acouritch was particularly attached to the dog which we heard barking during night, we concluded afterwards that he had attempted to take the animal with him, but the dog having found an opportunity to get loose, it returned by morning to our Camp. We found no traces, which direction they had taken; but I concluded then, that they might have attempted to reach the Corentyne by pursuing an eastern direction. The forests which we had passed during the latter week, were full with a species of mountain cabbage tree,[2] he might have therefore calculated that as soon as he had cleared the swamps, they might partly live on it, and the seeds of another palm were then ripe, which the Arawaaks call Caria, and the Caribs

---

[1] One can only speculate on what form the punishment took, although, as we have already seen (p. 174), Schomburgk had an Indian whipped on the Corentyne expedition. However, as many other travellers have discovered, attempts to discipline Amerindians are often counterproductive. The Amerindian will frequently prefer to desert rather than put up with harsh treatment.

[2] The Cabbage Palm (*Euterpe oleracea* and spp.). The edible part is more commonly known today as palmito.

Mouro Mouro,[1] and of which the Indians were very fond. Though they might save themselves from starvation, the adventure was perilous enough, and proves the daring spirit of that tribe. Their natural indolence and the fatigues to contend with nature, for a passage through regions, where it was impossible, that the human voice had ever been heard before, overcame all idea of dangers connected with their returning, prompted now by the knowledge that their treasonable schemes had been revealed to me.

My situation became more critical every day, I was now reduced to 11 effective men which were to be distributed among four corials – I was still bent, however, on pushing forward. The party which I had sent forward to clear the greatest obstacles in our road, returned in the evening of the 25th January with the information that at the point where at the approaching fall of the day, they had obliged to return, the river widened again.

Jan[y] 26th In the course of the day we found the river widening lake-like, bordered by low bush and partly grown over with the beautiful nymphea, the pride of my botanical discoveries, and which grew here so luxuriant that some of the leaves measured here 6 feet 5 inches in diameter. A species of Polygonum[2] and numerous grasses of different tints, covered the river so completely, that only a small space where the current was strongest, was left open. The Sun favoured us then with a transient glance, and the white water reflecting its rays, I might have resembled it to a green drapery of various tints, with a silvery ribbon woven through it – it was certainly a beautiful sight and I commenced to breath more free – helas! our joy did not last long, it narrowed and we had to cut again through Prickly palms and numerous Solanums, with prickles as sharp as those of the rose bush, and so rank in growth, that at some places we had the corial to drag by main force over it; we were really worn out, when we came too at three o'clock, and these difficulties connected with last day's discovery, my anxiety may be imagined. It was doubly increased by the circumstance that the good understanding between those who ought to have gone forward with a good example to the untutored Indian was at that time impaired, and cross purposes commenced to show their pernicious influence.

Jan[y] 27. I had not been able to procure any celestial observations since Jany 22nd, when I had found, by meridian Altitude of the Sun, that we were in 4°0'59"N Lat consequently nearly in a parallel with the junction of the Rupununy and Essequibo[. A]fter a night of sleepless meditations I concluded to advance for three days more, during which time I hoped to be able to make from 6 to 10 miles southing, when it was my intention to encamp, and cross over by foot to the Essequibo. I communicated my resolution to my companions, and it spread quickly among the Indians who received it with the greatest demonstrations of joy. Aback of our encampment, our Indians had found many of the Palms mentioned previously, in seed, and they indulged to a full extent, in order to indemnify themselves for the past sufferings. The Caria grows in bunches of from 12 to 20 inches in length and 9 to 10 inches in diameter, each nut is about an inch and a half long, round at the top and pointed towards the end, where the fruit is sessile; the outer rind is provided with prickles; the kernel is eaten and tastes somewhat like coconut if young; it is also roasted on the fire. The Caudex is low, the leaves or fronds are provided with long

---

[1] The Arawak 'Karia' and the Carib 'Murumuru' are different species of the same genus, *Astrocaryum*.
[2] Knotweed. Polygonum is a genus of the Family Polygonaceae.

prickles, and it is remarkable, that I do not recollect of having met this palm previously, either in the Corentyne or Essequibo – I think it is Astrocaryon muru muru* (Mart.).[1]

> *I have found frequently the seeds of this palm on the low shores of the Island Anegada (one of the virgin isles) where it has been drifted by the current; it is vulgarly called Sea coconut, though quite different from the Coco de Mar (Lodoicea Sechellarum).[2] During inundations the seeds are swept from the land, and carried by the rivers to the estuaries and there taken up by the currents.

We observed in the vicinity of our Camp some gigantic Ant-hills, they are conical in form, and are constructed from the soil on which they rise; it was here a mixture of sand and Clay upon a marly substratum. We opened one of these hills, and found the inner apartments to be constructed of particles of wood, leaves, and flowers; the Ant is of a reddish brown colour; the body about four to five eighth of an inch in length, and is called by the Arawaaks Haracorlie. They increase these hills continually in height, by throwing up the fresh ground. When it becomes necessary to enlarge the appartments in consequence of an increased population, and new passes & galleries are constructed. The passages near the entrance were found to be from 3 to 4 inches in diameter, and decrease in width the nearer they approach the royal appartments & it was curious to observe the indefatigable miners, as they issued from their tunnels each with a load of the soil of which their fabric was constructed perhaps as big as a pea in their mouth which was deposited at some distance from the entrance to the galleries while others were busily engaged to remove what in hurried instances might have been deposited too near the opening, and now in consequence of its accumulation, threatened to fall in again, or likely would have been washed in by the rain; as a protection against the rain we found several dry leaves thrown over the entrance which for better security sake had been cemented with clay & the glutinous substance peculiar to ants; it is thus rendered waterproof, well aware perhaps from experience, that the soft newly excavated marl would not withstand a shower; during rain, we found they ceased to work, but returned to it, as soon as it was over. Several parties were similarly employed at the same time, in different places, and it was surprising how rapidly they ejected the earth, forming a number of small cones upon a common base, the hill which I particularly inspected was 10 feet elevated above the surrounding ground. The working Ant or labourer has four prickly points on the back, and two on the head, and resembles much the Coushi ant (Atta) being only smaller.[3]

Our party of pioneers returned in the evening, the information which they brought was by no means consoling, they had met with various difficulties and had not been able to clear much before us, we expected therefore only slow progress on the succeeding day. Jany 29th[4] We wound slowly our way through the meandring river, margined by

[1] This species is not found in Guyana, but *Astrocaryum vulgare*, which is, is called 'murumuru' in Carib. 'Mart.' is Carl Friedrich Philipp Von Martius, a Bavarian botantist, who explored the Amazon between 1817 and 1820 in the company of Johan Baptist von Spix. Their best known work is Johann Baptist von Spix, and Karl Friedrich Phil. von Martius, *Reise in Brasilien auf Befehl Sr. Majestät Maximilian Joseph I, Königs von Baiern in den Jahren 1817 bis 1820*, 3 vols, Munich, Lindauar, 1823–31.

[2] *Lodoicea maldivica*.

[3] Bennett (*Arawak-English Dictionary*) gives the meaning of *harakuli* as 'the smaller kind of acoushi ant'. The acoushi ant is the umbrella, parasol or leaf-cutting ant (*Atta* spp.).

[4] Probably 28th, as the next day is also given as 29th, see below, p. 204.

prickly palms and encroached upon by numerous Marantaceae; soon after we had passed the point, where our pioners had returned the preceeding day, we found that the river gradually widened, and showed a fine sheet of water upwards of 150 yards wide – the river was covered similarly with those plants which I mentioned on another occasion; their number was however increased by a very pretty Pontederea[1] and an other plant*

  Marsilea quadrifolia probably.[2]

which was highly interesting to us in consequence of its leaves resembling the rare four leaved Clover, which though a monstrosity according to Botanical Conception, is considered a lucky omen according to popular belief, if picked up by accident, and not sought after. I saw neither blossoms or seeds to become acquainted with the name.

The River continued to keep its width of about 150 yards for several miles, and I could almost fancy, we had entered a different river; as this sudden expansion extended likewise to the east, where we issued from the jungles, I had pursued its course in that direction for some miles until I found myself arrested by thick jungle, and the current-less water had long before this announced itself as an Inlet. We observed some granitic boulders in the river; and as there was some likeliehood of procuring observations, we halted half an hour before noon. I was successful and determined the Latitude to be 3°58′5″N. our progress south had been therefore since Jan[y] 22nd scarcely 3 miles. Where the River narrowed again, the Current was very strong (2 knots) and as it required afterwards some time to cut through two trees we were rather rejoiced to find the river spreading to about 30 yards after we had passed the impediment & from its high banks both sides, I concluded for some time; we took therefore advantage of the favourable opportunity to make every progress. It was nearly evening when while paddling along, I saw what I considered to be five or six land turtles, ranged one by one on an old prostrated trunk on the rivers left bank; such an opportunity for a good meal was in our narrow circumstances not to be neglected; I ordered the corial might be halted. While stepping ashore, the Indians drew my attention to some bushes which had been recently cut with a knife; we approached now cautious the tree on which I had observed the turtles, but to our astonishment we found that they were only the shells & that the meat had been removed. We found now the remnants of former fires, and I was not slow in the conclusion that I had found by accident the path which leads to the Essequibo – some of the Indians discovered now a raft on the other side of the river, made of mocco-moccos. [T]he other Corials had come up meanwhile and we referred[3] from it that the Expedition contemplated by the Caribbees had been executed; we concluded from several circumstances that not many weeks could have elapsed, since a party of men had encamped here, but there were likewise tokens of a longer standing of the visit of men on different occasions; an hour after our arrival our tents stood upon the same spot.

The succeeding day January 29th was the day of rest, appointed by our Lord; we remained therefore the more readily in our Camp, as Circumstances had not always allowed us to rest on the Sabbath. I had appointed the following day to commence our

---

[1] The Family Pontederiaceae belongs to the Order Liliales.
[2] The Water Clover or Shamrock, but not reported from Guyana.
[3] Presumably 'inferred' was intended.

tour from the Berbice to the Essequibo; Mr Reiss was anxious to accompany me; an injury which Mr Cameron had suffered on one of his feet, had obliged him since Christmas to guard his Hammock. We heard in the evening a sound, which resembled much the report of a Gun, though it was merely conjecture, it gave me opportunity to arrange in case our speedy return to the Camp should be necessary, three guns should be fired in succession as a signal.

Jany 30th. Many arrangements which had to be completed on Monday morning, prevented us from starting before nine oclock, besides Mr Reiss, I took Cornelious and five Indians with me, to carry our hammocks and the necessary provisions. The path was small, and numerous trees having fallen across it our limbs which had been confined in the corials for the last two months, were called to exercise not without pain, the consequence of the novelty of the thing. It was evident that lately, when clearing the path, by whatever party it might have been, early recollections of trees and marks had conducted them, and according to the Indian fashions it was scarcely 12 inches wide; the soil over which we travelled was fertile to the extreme, and generally speaking, the ground preserved the same level – we crossed several swamps in which the manicole Palm grew most luxuriantly; I met likewise that strange species of Palm, which I had seen on a former occasion in the Conocou Mountains, (Geonoma W. Spec.?).[1] It is called by the Arawaaks Bouba;[2] it reaches here a very great height, but few leaves and obtuse as if they had been torn off at the end; single specimens of it, are to be found in the Colony very likely transplanted thither, but they are very scarce. After an hours walk from our Camp we passed a large tree with a smooth bark; several marks had been cut in it by Indians, and the bark having completely grown over it, I concluded that at least 6 to eight years had elapsed since it had been done – the circumstance that the present path, only lately cut, passed that tree, proves how accurate and observant the Indian must be, where he has neither track or guide, and where a European would be completely lost without compass. We ascertained afterwards that the Caribbees call the tree Okheri-puima. The woods which we traversed, consisted of magnificent trees, and the soil springy, and of a rich vegetable mould, mixed with sand, would produce any thing. We saw the stately Crab wood tree[,] the Souari famed for its delicious nuts, which we only regretted were not then in season; the Yarourie or paddle wood which is a curious tree; the trunk appears as if it consisted of a number of small flute-shaped trees, grown together. The bark is dark coloured with a few light greyish spots, the seed is flat-shaped and rugose and I conceive the tree to belong to the trumpet flower Tribe (Bignoniaceæ), the wood is very elastic, and in consequence of the peculiar construction of its trunk, it is much esteemed by the Indians for paddles. I have frequently seen the Indians split one of the flutes off, and finish a paddle in the course of a few hours, having no other tool but a Cutlass and common knife; it was then handed to the woman, who painted it with Roucou and Lana. We observed likewise the Amara or Wamarra* tree,

*Bannia of the Arawaaks?[3]

of which the Indians make their war-clubs. The wood is very hard and dark coloured.

---

[1] The 'W' is not a secure reading; nor is it known what it might signify.
[2] Boba: *Iriartea exorrhiza*.
[3] The Banya of the Arawak is *Swartzia bannia*, and Wamara is *Swartzia leiocalycina*.

The Warada[1] is a species of Lecythis; its seed-capsules are shaped like an extinguisher. It is a large tree with a light coloured bark: and there were also many others which astonished us by their size and of which the Indians make their Corials & Canoes. After we had walked for about an hour and an half we found rising ground and observed numerous rocks, from the size of a Pigeon's egg to that of a large boulder; they were crystalline, weighty, and appeared to be impregnated with Iron. A tree had been thrown down by the wind and unrooted; the lower stratum was therefore exposed to view – it consisted of ochreous Clay mixed with fragments of quartz, rounded by attrition, and of the same nature, as those we had seen to cover for miles the Savannahs of the Pacaraima Mountains; the perpendicular height of the sloping hillock might have amounted to ab[t] 40 feet, its direction NW & SE.*

*On my return I found rocks of a similar composition at the Christmas Cataracts, the tract appears therefore to be N & S.

M[r] Reiss who followed with some of the Indians in the rear, had fallen in with a herd of Kairounies and killed two, but as our men were already loaded enough, only one could be quarted and shared out, in order to be taken with us. I had just been joined by that party and we were about to continue our march, when we heard the report of a gun, a second followed and at the regular interval a third, the direction of the sound was NE; there could be no doubt that it was the preconcerted signal for our speedy return; only an urgency case would have induced M[r] Cameron to fire the signal and though M[r] Reiss would have fain persuaded me to the contrary, I retraced my steps. I headed the party and we had not far advanced, when I saw the herd of Kairounis before us, they did not observe me, and were in regular line of march, one by one with a third one aside of two single ones, the young walked under the belly of the mother; we shot two more, as there was no time to be lost, they were cleaned and hung up on a tree, to be sent for in case circumstances permitted it. I and Salomon, one of my faithful Warrows, took now the van guard – hundred causes passed my imagination, what might have given reasons to M[r] Cameron to fire the signals, should Acouritch after his desertion, have met with some men of his tribe, and have come back to pilfer? should we have been mistaken, when we supposed the Copenaam party to have recrossed the Berbice? or what accident can have happened? I coupled the report, which we heard the previous night, with these vague surmises, and the first conjecture gained ground. It actuated on our haste, and by the time I crossed the dry bed of a streamlet, I knew that I was only a few hundred yards from our Camp. I had out distanced every one of the party except Salomon; I heard the hum of voices and cautioning the Indian to go softly, we came nearer. "They are Caribbees," he whispered in my ear; I told him to harken again: "Caribbees" was again his reply. I stole somewhat nearer and had a survey of a number of red hammocks. It is then correct, I thought by myself, your camp has been surprised[,] M[r] Cameron and M[r] Vieth have been most likely murdered, or are perhaps lashed to the next tree, and your life is in their hands, what does it matter now whether you lose it a few hours earlier or later. With this resolution I went forward, my Pistol however cocked for the first assailant, as soon as I came up with them I asked, whether they came here as friends or as enemies? I received no answer, my next inquiry was

[1] Possibly Warapa: *Macoubea guianensis*.

"who was their chieftain? 'Smittee' (Smith), he is at Praneghieries (white mans)[1] tent". I immediately proceeded there and found my friend Smith of Corentyne recollection and the Copenaam chieftain, whom we met in the Oreála, with Mr Cameron in conversation. All my apprehensions melted like snow, and I ascertained now that the Macoosie Expedition had in reality only arrived a few hours ago. When they were approaching the Eastern bank of the Berbice, a musket had been fired by accident in our Camp, and the Caribbees supposing that some of their friends from the Rupununy were awaiting them, had set up a hue and cry which had given Mr Cameron the first notice of their approach. But what must have been their astonishment, when coming in sight of the river, they observed my Corials? When I formerly reasoned with them while in Oreála, on the injustice of their intentions to enslave Macoosies, and I found that it made no impression I threatened them with the vengeance of the big Governor*

> *This expression wants an explanation. The Indian is well aware of the different degrees of authority which are exercised by the Postholder, Protector, Fiscal or Sheriff, and Governor and the equal situations and authorities under these names in the Dutch Colonies. He connects with the idea of "big Governor" every thing that is great and commands obedience and respect.

and that I should be before them at the path which crosses the Berbice to the Rupununy. They smiled at my assertions and classed them among the impossibilities. I had resolved though unprotected and alone, to use every means which policy allowed me to prevent them from executing their designs, but the difficulties, and detentions which I met with, while ascending the Berbice, made me despair of reaching the path in time; however it had been decreed otherwise. In the course of the day we learned that after Smith had returned from Skeldon, whither it will be recollected he accompanied me, to receive his payment, every preparation was made for the contemplated trip. Before they set out 'old Thomas' died, a pi-ai man of great renown; he had planned this expedition and was to accompany it. He belonged to my Crew, when ascending the Corentyne, and when I attempted whilst in Oreála, to persuade them not to undertake the Expedition for slaving, I found my intentions always counteracted by his interference and threats; he laboured under pulmonary complaints and was greatly emaciated by the time he left us in Skeldon, it was natural therefore to suppose that not many months would elapse, before he was a corpse, and I told this to Smith before we parted. It had so happened what any man might have predicted: but upon the superstitious Indian, it had great effect; they paused in their designs, long consultations were going on, and they relinquished their original plan of the expedition, and having once hesitated and become apprehensive, they were now afraid to go even on a trading expedition without even having sent first a deputation to the Macoosie country to sound the way. They had selected a Macoosie named Sakourra who had been brought up from childhood among them, and his two sons, for that purpose. There had been every inclination to receive them as traders, and meeting the Caribbee chieftain Yhrayee (my faithful friend during the Essequibo Expedition) in Curassawaak, the deputies induced him to lend them his corial. They proceeded now to the Inlet Primoss, hauled the corial up, and crossed the Berbice by means of a raft; they found their woodskin on the banks of the Corentyne

[1] Although an unusual spelling this word is recognizably cognate with the term widely used for 'white man' in Guianese native languages.

207

and hastened to give the necessary information to the party at Tomatai.[1] Thus had the delay arisen and favourable circumstances had assisted me, that my prediction in this regard proved likewise true. We had been therefore quite correct when we concluded from the marks of the fresh cut bushes, that a party had crossed and recrossed. Smith took the earliest opportunity, after I had arrived in the Camp, to inform me that they had given up all idea of enslaving, and that they were merely going to barter for hammocks, cotton, dogs, &c &c[.] I was well aware of this, as soon as I had opportunity to look about, from the number of women and children in their train; there were 26 men and two grown up boys, 6 women and 6 children. If the Caribbees undertake a warlike expedition, women and children are left behind; however Smith kept the reason which had induced him to that change wisely for himself and it was only ascertained by degrees, when they became unguarded. It was to be expected that I took the greatest advantage of the ascendancy, I had got over them, increased by the truth of my prediction, that I would be before them at the path, and as I did not tell them what were my future intentions, it was a moment of pride and exultation, when I considered, that I had been the means of sparing many an innocent Indian bondage, and their being torn from their families and country. As the procuring of slaves, could not have been executed without bloody contests, the idea that I have been the indirect means to prevent it, recompenses me for the fatigues & the anxiety, I suffered, when I saw that the difficulties of making any progress, were of quite a new description, and nature and man it appeared were in league against reaching the high mountains by this road. Lately my mind had really undergone torture; to other apprehensions was added the horrible presentiment that we would have to starve. Nevertheless it was my lot to preserve a cheerful mien in order to encourage others and to make easy with the apprehensions which arose in the mind of my companions. Twenty four hours, I had stipulated, on the morning before I discovered the path, when I had promised to advance no further.

The Caribbees were in as grave a plight as we with regard to Provisions; having been extravagant in the commencement, they now suffered from want; our short stock of provisions did not allow us to assist them. According to their information, it was twelve days, since they had left Tomatai. They had passed the Corentyne falls by hauling the corials over land to the left, behind the large Cataract, called Marisappa Youma, from whence they had reached, by water, the path which leads to the Berbice in two days and a half. Here they had hauled up their Corials, to remain until their return, and had accomplished their journey from the Corentyne to the Berbice in another 2 day and a half easy march. Most of them were painted with roucou and lana (Tabou-seba in Caribbee). I observed a boy, who had painted on his limbs, representations of some of the figures, which we had observed cut in the rock Timehrie and in some of the boulders near the great Cataracts.

In the course of the evening Smith communicated his desire, to go with us next morning, to which I could have no objection.

---

[1] There must be some doubts about this version of events. The date is 30 January and it had only been during the last week in October that Smith and Schomburgk parted at Orealla. Accordingly, within a space of three months, the shaman Old Thomas had to die, a decision had to be reached to send deputies to the Macushi. The latter then had to travel to Curassawaak and back, and after that the expedition had to be mounted and travel to the Berbice. This seems barely possible and highly unlikely given the normal Amerindian speed of decision-making and travel.

Jany 31st. We rose rather early and were soon en route; much to my regret I had previously observed, that since we had been encamped, the river had fallen 10 inches, I planned therefore to return with all despatch, as I was well aware, should it fall 12 inches more, we would have been blocked up for the present until the rainy season should set in, in the mountains, which it was not to be effected before March; while the middle of February was the best time to cross the lower Cataracts, partly swollen by the rainy season of the coast regions. Should I find on my return from the Essequibo that the Berbice had not fallen materially, I contemplated to visit likewise the Corentyne.

Our line of March presented a strange sight; Indians with baskets, containing the articles, to carry on their barter, large bundles of bows and arrows; women with children, or when the husband had taken the pleasing duty of carrying the offspring it was sitting astride his shoulders; others with luggage and the remnant of their provisions, and little girls, as if anxious to perform a part in this important affair, and perhaps not entrusted with any thing of great value, carried a squalling puppy in their arms;*

*The Indians girls great and small, are uncommonly fond of a puppy – I have seldom met an Indian settlement, where there had not been four or five of those plagues under the particular protectionship of some of the Indian fair ones. I do not recollect any of my Expeditions, where girls when among our Crew, that they had not brought puppies with them in spite of all the precautions from my side to prevent it. In order to get rid of the annoyance, I have often offered what may be considered a large price for the dog, but in vain, the puppy was not to be parted with, and I have now come fairly to the conclusion, that puppidom is all over the world alike admired.

thus we trod the path man for man. I stood still several times and allowed them to pass in defile. When we arrived at the place where we had killed the bush hogs on the previous day, we halted as I had promised Smith and his people one, and some Indians had accompanied me for purpose of carrying the other to the Camp; but no bush hog was to be seen, they had vanished from the trees on which we had tied them, and there were evident marks that they had been carried away by a tiger – while we scoured the bush, a little Arawaak boy from our Camp, discovered my Indian dog Caniantho,[1] stretched out dead, and a triangular wound on each side of the neck, proved that it had been killed likely by the same tiger which carried away the Kairounies, [those] of the latter [were] discovered; they had been dragged some distance from the place, where we had hung them up, and laid side by side to serve for the brutes next night's repast. Caniantho, though an excellent hunting dog with bow and arrow, had the greatest aversion for a Gun; it appeared therefore that on firing the three Guns in succession, he must have started in the woods, and having found afterwards my track, he must have followed it, and at the place where we diverted from the path, to hunt the Kairounies, he likely fell in with the tiger; there were sufficient proofs that he had fought with him. The tiger must have been satiated with other food, as he had not touched the dog. I acknowledge I could not help to feel regret at his loss; the dog had shown much attachment to me, and being of the Macoosie breed, with all the marks of that variety, I bought him with the intention of sending him after my return to the Zoological Gardens.

We reached the spot where we had been called back by Signal, in two hours walking from the Camp; the path got narrower, and more intricate; at half past nine in the

---

[1] Previously called Caniando, see p. 167.

morning we arrived at swampy ground, which I immediately recognized as the one, which had set a boundary to our exploring tour from Primoss last year; at that time we sunk to our knees in the mud, at present it was almost dry. Sometime after, we met the first Cocoa-trees and fifteen minutes after the broad Essequibo was before us; the sight was hailed with much transport. We had walked from our camp at the Berbice to the Primoss at the eastern Bank of the Essequibo, in 3ʰ·20ᵐ· I found still the hut which we had erected almost twelve months ago, and in which Mʳ Brotherson and myself passed a most uncomfortable night, the rain falling in torrents. Mʳ Reiss followed 25 minutes after me, he was quite enthusiastic when he saw the fine broad Essequibo for the first time. As soon as the whole party was up, the Caribbees made immediate preparations to leave us, though they had intended to camp that night at Primoss, they had now resolved to proceed to the abandoned Settlement Cumaka. Mʳ Reiss was anxious to see something more of the Essequibo and was desirous to go with them as far as Cumaka; I considered it therefore best to keep Smith as hostage until Mʳ Reiss had safely returned. Smith consented and the others proceeded on – Mʳ Reiss returned in the afternoon and Smith departed. I had desired, when I left the Camp, that a Gun might be fired at 6 oclock in the evening, we heard it at that time quite distinctly, the direction was N55°E. the direct distance was according to the traverse tables 9.5 miles. In consequence of the unfavourable weather I had not burthened myself with any of my instruments except the compass; and observations were the less of consequence in Primoss since I had been here and deduced its situation from observations at the mouth of the Rupununy, according to these computations Primoss is in Lat 3°50′N. Longt 57°51′48″W while the situation at the River Berbice, where the Path crosses the River, is in 3°55′24″N Lat. & 57°50′45″W Longt. The traverse table of our courses from the Berbice to the Essequibo exhibits Southing 5.[1] miles & Westing 7.7 miles, the difference therefore in Lat is ³/₁₀ of a mile, while in Longt it is 6.6 miles. It must be recollected that the difference in Longitude may arise from the circumstance that the Longitude of the Essequibo is deduced from dead reckonings and lunar distances at Annay.[1]

Feby 1ˢᵗ· We left the Essequibo rather early; nothing remarkable occurred and after a walk of three hours and 20m I entered our camp; as I know now from experience that I do walk 3 Stat miles in an hour the distance and windings of the path included is 10 miles. The result of my crossing from the Berbice to the Essequibo will prove of importance to Geography, the short period which is required to cross from river to river, establishes most undeniably the far western course of the river Berbice. In Arrowsmith's late map of Columbia (London, 1834)[2] the sources of the River Berbice are laid down in

---

[1] There is at this point in the published version (pp. 333–4) an editorial footnote which is worth reproducing:

'The difference in longitude is trifling; and when we consider that the former position of Primoss was determined by dead reckoning, worked up from lunar distances at Annay to the west, and the latter by meridian distance carried from New Amsterdam, on the east, during two months, and up a series of cataracts, it may be considered as surprisingly accurate: the determination of the relative position of the two rivers Berbice and Essequibo at this point, by walking across the intervening land, is highly important. Mr. Scomburgk's [sic] indefatigable zeal in obtaining celestial observations whenever practicable must strike the most cursory reader of this Report, and his candour in honestly stating this slight discrepancy is well worthy of imitation by all travellers. – ED.'

[2] John Arrowsmith's 1834 map of Colombia, it should be noted, is on a scale of approximately one inch to eighty miles.

Lat 4°30′N Longt 57°14′W[;] from three observations of stars, when culminating, I have deduced the Latitude of that part where the path from the Corentyne to the Essequibo crosses the Berbice to be 3°55′2″N and Longt 57°50′45″W, or 35 miles south of its assumed sources. The River was here from Bank to Bank 99 feet wide, with a depth from 8 to 10 feet and appeared to continue so as far as it was visited by us.

The next point of consequence is the non-existence of the River Demerara, where I walked a cross from the Berbice to the Essequibo. With the exception of a dry bed of a streamlet, which flowing during the rainy season, discharges itself a little beyond our Camp, we did not meet any appearance of other stream, brook or River between the Berbice and Essequibo. In the maps, already alluded to, the sources of the river Demerara are placed in the fourth parallel of Latitude, and about 30 miles south of those of the Berbice of the maps, while it is my opinion that it has its sources in the mountain chain between Lat 4°40 to 4°30N. We observed a small river which emptied its black waters into the river Berbice in Lat 4°21N. In consequence of the dark colour of its waters I called it "Black water river". It was across its mouth about 50 feet wide; as far as pressure of time allowed to investigate it, its course became WbS after we had entered it; it does not exist more, where I crossed over to the Essequibo and we may therefore infer that it has its sources between the parallels 4°20 & 4° Lat and very likely in the vicinity of the Essequibo, for which its black water speaks. I consider the Berbice lower than either the Essequibo or Corentyne, and from this may arise the circumstance that Black water river becomes the tributary of the Berbice. It is not likely that the sources of the Demerara are south of this river; and this leads us again to the more than probability that it has its sources in the mountains range in 4°40 Lat. From strict observations, but without actual measurement, I consider the Essequibo about 20 feet higher than the Berbice; indeed the Berbice forms a valley, which drains the natural ground of the two great rivers of British Guiana, the Essequibo and the Corentyne; it is therefore not to be wondered that these two magnificent rivers receive no large tributaries; the first from the East, the latter from the West; and the numerous lakes and swamps of the Berbice, which make it now appear in size of a brook, while one or two miles further, it represents a width of 200 yards and ranges in that latitude with a river of the first size. The Barometer showed at our Camp a height of 333 feet above the level of the sea; the Cataracts of the Corentyne are therefore considerably higher; this becomes apparent from the stronger Current of the Corentyne.

The soil which we found between the two rivers appears to be particularly calculated for the cultivation of Cocoa, an article which ere long will be of importance, as affording to the lower classes a wholesome and nutritive diet. That plant delights in a rich and springy soil or in a situation where irrigation may be admitted; a vertical sun is injurious to it, the shade which ombrageous trees afford must be therefore courted. The Chocolate Trees,[1] which we found in the vicinity of Primoss are the best witnesses of a congenial soil, and though they are left to nature if originally they should have been planted by human hands, they certainly astonished me by their size. The fruits are of a delicate yellow or lemon colour, while those I have seen cultivated in the Islands approach to purple. On my return the river had fallen 8 to 10 inches in the two days of our absence, and I really apprehended our return would be completely cut off. On a

[1] *Theobroma bicolor*, the cocoa tree.

211

close inspection of our provisions I found that with the strictest economy, and still more curtailed allowances (it must be recollected that we were then reduced to five ounces of rice per diem) they would not last longer than a fortnight. Preservation of life made it therefore a peremptory duty to lose no time to return, and my former plan to visit the Corentyne overland, was reinquished; it would have required five days to execute this design, and what a precious time would then have been lost under such circumstances; as stated above, when I was at Primoss and before Smith left me, it was my intention to cross overland to the Corentyne, and I procured every information on the path; from what I heard of him, the ground is similar to that between the Berbice and the Essequibo and there is only a small brook to be crossed, which was the only water that they passed; they had performed the distance in two days and a half, rather slow walking, as there were many children in their train; from which I concluded the distance is not more than 24 miles. [T]here are therefore no difficulties to connect the upper Essequibo with the Corentyne, an object of the greatest importance, if the Colony should continue to prosper and henceforth the population increased by Immigration, make it easier to procure labourers. The navigation of the Corentyne, by flat bottomed boats, offers less impediments, with the exception of the great Cataracts, than the Essequibo; and the Interior from the Coast to the Equator would thus be laid open to the enterprising Colonist. And I hope yet to see a direct overland communication between the Coast regions of British Guiana, and the mightiest river of the world the Amazon, carried on.

We know from Humboldt's observations that a Colonel Barata went from Para to Surinam with despatches in the year 1793;*

*vide likewise Journ of the Royal Geog Society Vol VI part 1 s16.[1]

there is no doubt that he descended the Rupununy, and reached the Corentyne by the path just described. This path exists in the recollection of the oldest Caribbees, who remember at the time of their youth, when the Essequibo and Corentyne were thickly inhabited, that a constant communication was kept up, between the Caribbees of the Pacaraima mountains and those of Surinam while the low Swamps of the Berbice were only the abode of beasts of prey, and noxious reptiles – we were the first I dare to pretend who ever ascended the River Berbice from its mouth to 3°55N. Lat; and the difficulties connected with the undertaking will be remembered as long as recollection is able to carry me to the past; the alternated state of ourselves and crew were the best proofs of what we had suffered, while individually I must assert that my mind was on the

---

[1] Francisco José Rodrigues Barata. The year was 1798 and Barata travelled from Belém to Paramaribo via the Rio Branco, Takutu, Sauriwau, Rupununi, and Essequibo. He returned the following year by the same route except that he crossed from the Rupununi to the Takutu via the Pirara and Mahu rivers. The article in the *JRGS* to which Schomburgk refers is Lieutenant [William H.] Smyth RN, 'Account of the Rivers Amazon and Negro, from recent Observations', *JRGS*, 6, 1836, pp. 11–23. This article includes the translation of parts of a manuscript in the possession of Padre André Fernandes de Sousa. The full manuscript, under the title 'Diario da Viagem que fez á Colonia Hollandeza de Surinam o Porta Bandeira da Setima Compania do Regimento da Cidade do Pará, pelos Sertões e Rios d'este Estado, em diligencia do Real Serviço', was published in *Revista Trimensal de Historia e Geographia* 8, 1846, pp. 1–53, 157–204. Smyth's full account of his journey down the Amazon is to be found in Smyth & Lowe, *Narrative of a Journey from Lima to Para*, London, John Murray, 1836. Captain Smyth, as he was to become, was President of the Royal Geographical Society in 1849–50.

rack from the time the first desertion occurred among my Crew, and every day offered new difficulties to our progress.

Feby 2ᵈ· This morning our return commenced; as I had expected we met the greatest difficulties, it was really distressing, when we crossed the first jungle and our Crew had to haul by main force the Corials through the water, scarcely 12 inches deep, to observe how frequently they were wounded by the sharp and long Prickles of the Sawarie palm (Astrocaryon) but they did not complain, though we had weeks to journey, every step brought them nearer to the coast. The delays which we found therefore the first day alarmed my companions so much that one of them was deputed to advise the abandonment of three of the Corials and to direct those of the Crew who could not find place in my own, to seek their way by land. I could not for a moment harbour such an Idea, and I [scorned] it. If it were decreed, that we had no other alternative, I would have shared the difficulties willingly, however I hoped better, we were near the change of the moon and with it, I expected rain: I was correct in my suppositions, it commenced to rain in the afternoon of the fourth and with such good intentions, that the river was considerably swollen by the 6ᵗʰ Feby· and we made now rapid progress in our descent.

Feby 7ᵗʰ· We passed today black water river, just a month after we had seen it for the first time. I should have been glad to procure observations here (its computed Lat being 4°21'51) but the rain had descended in torrents since day light and the highest stand of the detached Thermometer 78° Fahrenheit during the day.

Nothing of interest happened, the constant rains it appeared induced even the animal creation to hide and protect themselves against the tropical torrents. [O]ccasionally a Carara (Plotus Spec.) was seen to fly along the rivers course stretching its long neck, at the unusual appearance of our Corials. It is a drowsy bird, after its meal it takes its Siesta as if it belonged to the Aristocracy of the feathered tribe, one of that gentry paid that indulgence with its liberty and life; having fallen asleep on the branch of a tree, which overhung the river the noise of the paddles and voices might have awaked it out of its rosy dreams; it found itself surprised, attempted to save itself by precipitation in the water, however it mistook the distance, and fell in the middle of the Corial and stunned by the fall, it was immediately secured. When surprised, the Darter does not seek its security in flight, but precipitates itself into the water and dives; the peculiar formation of its beak chiefly with regard to the nasal organs, allow the bird to remain to 15 minutes underwater. After having landed, I put the prisoner in my tent – our dogs were anxious to make its acquaintance, but paid the attempts with bleeding noses; its neck is so pliable in consequence of an additional joint; and the straight bill is so pointed that it is able to take an accurate aim and its attack is generally directed towards the eye; they dart with it forward, while the neck is contracted like the body of a serpent; it is from 2 feet 6 inches to 3 feet long.

Feby 9ᵗʰ· We arrived in the afternoon at 2 Oclock at the uppermost, of that series of Cataracts which we had called for want of an Indian name 'the Christmas Cataracts'. [A]s it will be recollected, I had here hauled up the Corial, which the desertion of the Waccaways obliged me to abandon – nothing of it was to be seen, and there were evident marks, that it had been taken away by Indians; our suspicions fell immediately upon the Caribbees under Acouritch; we had met with marks as if men had lately passed, and our suspicion gained in strength, when we arrived at places where we had deposited the heads of Kaymen, in order to take the skulls with us on our return; we found invariably that the large teeth had been broken out to which the Caribbees and almost every Indian ascribe talismanic powers and which they are prone to carry round their neck; our premiss received now full force by the absence of the Corial. In consequence of the river having swollen, the rocks which we found bare, when we ascended, were now mostly covered with water, and the Cataracts in consequence of the increased volume of water, more powerful; nevertheless Cornelius thought he might venture to slide the Cataract, and as I knew that he had great experience in these matters, I did not countersay his opinion. I took however the precaution to remove the Chronometer, Barometer and every other valuable Instrument. It was fortunate that I had done so the heavy surge at the Cataract filled almost the Corial, and it was with difficulty that she could be brought afloat to the next Island; with the exception that some of the books were wet and some of the dried plants completely spoiled, no further injury was done to her cargo; the other Corials were brought by a more laborious, but safer road to the foot of the first cataract. In order to pass the other Cataracts, which form the 'Christmas Cataracts', I ordered the Corials to be unloaded, and the baggage to be carried over land from the head to the foot of the succeeding Cataracts; while we were still under the necessity to hazard our Corials, which we could not bring to the foot in any other way but by conducting them through the Cataracts, which is technically called to slide or shoot the Cataract. It is an exciting scene to see the Corial when once put in the current, shooting along with the swiftness of lightning; she arrives at the edge of the cataract, and balancing for the shortest space of time between the surge at the foot and the edge, she plunges her head into the foam, white as snow, the spray dashing from both sides against the rocks that narrow in the passage, and if her descent should prove fortunate, she rises and is carried forward by the increased velocity of the current. The large Corial, which carried generally our provisions, was thus on the point of descending; those who were not employed in conducting her went to the foot of the Cataract to see her descent. Mr Reiss & myself were among the number; the river makes a sudden bend & and the enraged stream descends rather in a crooked way; we saw therefore scarcely the corial coming round the point when she was already in the current and flew towards the fall; the steersman and foreman (the one who occupies the bow of the corial and from whose steering and look out in a great measure depends the safety of the craft) perhaps not acting in concert, it appeared, she took the direct course towards the Rocks, and when I expected that she would strike and split in pieces, the back currents of the rocks drove her off, and she escaped with taking an extra portion of water in. The descent of the Corial became the lengthened theme of a conversation between Mr Reiss and myself, and it was my wish that my Corial, which was by far the most expensive, should not be hazarded if there were any other method of lowering it.

We were now within a 5 days journey from the first settlement; and as I had most scrupulously preserved a present of wine, from his Excellency Sir Jas. C. Smyth, in case of sickness, I relaxed my economical scruples and a bottle of Rhenish was taken out of its recess. Our conversation after our scanty meal was more lengthened, and we were rather astonished when Mr Reiss indulged rather in a melancholy strain, and observed 'he knew he should die young'. We ridiculed him and as the sky was more favourable than generally in the evening I left the Gentlemen to their conversations in order to observe the Meridian Altitude of a Star (Canopus) in which I was assisted by Mr Reiss.

Feby 12th Cornelius reported this morning that he had inspected the Cataract and he thought it impossible that the Coorial could be lowered down by ropes, since it did not afford footing to the Indians. Mr Reiss, who was standing next to me [thought I was too] apprehensive, and he considered there was less danger for my Corial, than the one which decended the preceding evening. The Corial was therefore to slide the Cataract, and I saw that the necessary arrangements were made for her descent. I was certainly astonished when Mr Reiss expressed his intention to go in the Corial in order to see better how she would go down. I remonstrated with him, as he was not an experienced swimmer; and being called away by some other business I thought it was a mere whim which would be given up by a second reflection. I was yet in conversation with Mr Vieth, when the information was brought to me, that the corial was just on the point of starting; I proceeded direct to the foot of the Cataract: when the Corial hove in sight the first object that struck me, was Mr Reiss standing on one of the benches in the Corial, where common prudence would have commanded him to sit down; from that moment to the catastrophe not two seconds elapsed; they intended perhaps to avoid the danger of yesterday and descended at a different point where it was more precipitous; the shock when her bow struck the surf, caused Mr Reiss to lose his balance, in falling over, he grasped one of the iron stanchions of the tent, the corial was upset, and in the next moment her inmates, thirteen in number, were seen to struggle with the current, and not able to stem it were carried with rapidity towards the next Cataract. My eyes were fixed on poor Reiss, he kept himself above the water but a short time, sunk and reappeared, and when I had hopes he might reach one of the rocks, the Current of the next Rapid seized him and I fear he came in contact with a sunken rock, he was turned completely round, and he sunk in the whirlpool at the foot of that rapid – his cap was taken up by the first Indian (old Mathias) who was able to stem the current and attempted to swim to his assistance, he mistook the cap for poor Mr Reiss. As soon as I was able to muster one of those, who were at the same time precipitated in the water, to assist me in guiding a Corial, we commenced a most diligent search, in which we were assisted by those who had in the meanwhile manned the second Corial; for the two next hours all our endeavours were fruitless, we found his body in a direction where we least would have expected it, and where an under current must have drifted him – all life was extinguished, nevertheless the usual means for recovering drowned persons, were resorted to, but naturally in vain.

It became now my painful duty to make arrangements for his interment and the following morning was determined upon, to bring him to his last home. I had selected for that purpose a romantic spot, opposite to the place where he was drowned, on a rising ground which the water, even when at its highest, during inundations, does not reach; two aged trees margin the river, from whence I ordered a path to be cleared to his future resting place.

Feby 13. This morning we carried our poor friend to his grave. In absence of materials for a coffin, we wrapped him in his hammock as a shroud and after he had been put in that Corial, by the upsetting of which, he lost his life, we conveyed him to the opposite shore and from thence he was carried by the young men who professed Christianity to the level spot on the hill, which we had prepared for his resting place, and while I was doomed to read the expressive and beautiful service for the burial of the dead, there was not an eye dry of those, who call themselves Christians, and even the Indians, decently apparelled, stood with down cast eyes round his grave and over many a rude cheek stole a tear. On a level ground round which mora trees & Palms – the latter the emblem of the Christian faith – form an almost perfect circle, there rises now a pile of tufty stones, under which he rests, to await his makers call. A small tablet which he himself brought, in order to engrave his name, and to leave it as a remembrance in case we should reach the Acaray mountains, bears now this inscription

Drowned.

12 Feb^y

1837

CHARLES F. REISS

Aged

22 Y. 8 D

and is firmly fixed to one of the trees that form the Circle.

February 15th. With what feelings we left our Camp may be imagined; in the morning of the 14th. my Corial was repaired, and in the course of the day we accomplished to transport the last of the baggage to the foot of the lower of the Christmas Cataracts. We continued our journey on the morning of the 15th. The cataracts and the rapids, we had to pass were very numerous. I think there are 48 to the Christmas Cataracts; the very necessity of crossing some of the Cataracts, dismayed many of the Crew, in their present enfeebled and dejected state; and the remembrance of the late accident and loss stood yet too vivid before their eyes; we did not pass therefore some of the larger Cataracts without getting the Corials filled with water, and we had twice to unload in order to pail the crafts. We halted at noon of the 15th at the foot of the mountains, which are apparently the highest adjacent to the Berbice, and I commenced to observe the Barometer hourly, in order to procure the necessary data for computing the height of the mountains. I found that the height of the river Berbice was here in Lat 4°46′42″N. 160 feet above the level of the sea.

February 16th. Accompanied by some Indians, I left the morning early; in consequence of some Injury which Mr Cameron had suffered on his foot he was inable to join me. The morning was chilly, the sky covered, and the Thermometer stood at 6 oclock 70°F. Our path led for some time along the river upwards, until it turned northerly over undulating ground. I never saw such a variety of Ferns, assembled in such a small area as I found here, there were upwards of 15 species, some very interesting. A mountain stream which meandred through the gradually rising ground, forming glens in miniature. We had to cross it repeatedly. Half an hour's walk brought us to the cone, in that shape represented itself the most eastern mountain. The mountain stream we crossed previously, has pathed itself a way through numerous fragments of rocks – sometimes of considerable size. In ascending we found many of the same description until the peak rises almost perpendicular, and the rock contains large fragments of rounded quartz. We scrambled up the best way we could, the greater part of my Indians had never seen such a large hill before, and they were not a little amused when the fragile hold of a rotten stick or a brittle rock, on which the climber had placed his dependence, gave way, & he came down by the run. I trembled for the fate of the Barometer; however the Arawaak, to whom it was entrusted, seemed to be as sure-footed as a Goat, and I saw it soon safe on the top of the first peak. The sky was clouded, and a thick fogg hovered over the wooded valley, the view was besides obstructed by gigantic trees, and though I had mounted one of the boulders, I could not succeed to get an extensive view. I adjusted the Barometer and found that the first peak was 828 feet above the level of the sea; the detached Thermometer stood at 8^h15^m am 72°. A higher peak bore from here N25°W, in order to reach it, we went for some time along the ridge, and after having proceeded in that direction for about a mile and a half, we were, what I considered, on the highest part of these mountains. A chance stray of the sun found its way sometimes through the thick coat of clouds, and a strong easterly wind dispersed the fog, which had dispersed over the valleys. In order to be the better enabled to take advantage of such a favorable moment, I selected a tree which partly over hung the perpendicular wall of rocks, of which the ridge was formed. The peak on which I stood formed the north western angle of the valley, and afforded me therefore a fine view over extensive wood-land, most extensive towards the South-east; the peak next highest to the one I stood on, bore north and was about 1 mile distant, indeed it was the hill I measured while at the Cataract Itabrou. The valleys run in the direction of the mountain chain, their sides generally covered with lofty trees, their heights broken pieces of rocks, or perpendicular walls. Many of the rocks appeared marly, and I was not a little astonished to find as well the ridge as the sides of the mountains covered with similar angular and rounded quartz-pebbles which I had seen previously at the savannahs of the Pacaraima, at the Caribbee path, the Christmas Cataracts, and now on the top of the highest mountain of the River Berbice, as far as I have visited it. The boulders which we found in such large quantities on the sides of the South Eastern peak, contained rounded and angular fragments of quartz, sometimes several inches in diameter, which displayed proof of transportation or long continued friction. I did not observe any intervening element[,] on the contrary where I dislodged the foreign substance, the excavation was perfectly smooth.

I remained above two hours on this spot, observing the Barometer & Thermometer every fifteen numbers & received as result, that this Peak which I called Parishs Peak, in honour of (now[)] Sir Woodbine Parish,[1] was 909.8 feet above the level of the sea and 744.[illegible] feet above the River Berbice, where that river meanders along its foot. After having engraved in the Bark of a Tree PARISH's PEAK as a memento I left it highly delighted with my excursion and pondering whether it might be probable that the peak had been visited before by a human being, some rocks attracted my attention, which I went to inspect. I got thus separated from my party; after I had satisfied my curiosity, I thought of being sure to have taken the right direction; after half an hours search looking in vain for the marks which we had made on our ascent, I was now persuaded that I had mistaken the direction and I found myself a short while after, for a second time at Parish's Peak and I took heed not to fall in a similar mistake again and observed more attentively the marks. My party awaited me at the foot of the mountain. Mr Vieth fared that evening much worse, I had told him of some plants, I had seen at the foot of the mountains, & which I had no time to collect; he went in search of them after my return, accompanied by one of his assistants, being on his return so near the Camp, that he could hear the hum of voices, he sent therefore the assistant to the Camp and went in search of more plants; all his endeavours to discover about nightfall, the tract to the Camp, were in vain; meanwhile his absence alarmed us, & I ordered every quarter of an hour a Gun to be fired, and sent some of the Indians in search of him. It was however nearly 9 oclock before he could come up with the Camp, following the report of the Guns; he found himself just walking in the opposite direction when he heard the first report.

The adaptness of this hilly tract for the cultivation of Coffee, and in consequence of

[1] Sir Woodbine Parish, FRS (1796–1882), diplomatist, was Vice-President of the Royal Geographical Society for many years. He was knighted in 1837.

its gravelly and clayey nature, for the cultivation of the vine and olive, is surprising; the springy soil in the valleys would produce almost anything, but the sides of the hills, I am sure as far as my experience goes, are particularly qualified for the production of the finest grapes, no doubt they would prove equal to those of the Madeiras without much labour and expense, these fertile regions, being not subjected to the draughts, prevailing in the African Isles. What an area might therefore be claimed from nature, and made subservient to the wants of man?

The mountain chain which is connected with the Twasinkie and the Sierra Pacaraima, I am inclined to consider the old boundary of the Atlantic, the geological features of the main are conducive to such a supposition; further north commence the hillocks of sands, the consequence of a receding sea.

Feb[y] 17[th.] We arrived in the afternoon at the Cataract Itabrou. As I was anxious to send M[r] Vieth with the melancholy information of Mr Reiss' death to M[r] M[c]Cullum's wood cutting Establishment, I had given orders that the swiftest corial should be lowered by Ropes to the foot of the Cataract that evening; the baggage had been carried overland, though every precaution was taken, to insure her descent, the rope snapped, and carried with full force against a rock, she split at the head. We had now no other alternative but to transport the Corial over the hill, and as it was very steep, the path we constructed for that purpose was by no means an easy undertaking; the hope of being able to enjoy a full and substantial meal, and to indulge in a dram, as we were then within two days and a half from M[r] M[c]Cullum's, acted as an impulse and on the following day the corials were at the foot of the Cataract, and reloaded. M[r] Vieth had left in another corial the preceding noon.

Jan[yl] 19 All arrangements were completed at 12 o'clock today, and we left the last Cataract where danger might be apprehended under great demonstrations of joy from our Indians who appeared to have received additional strength in their sinews to propel the Corials. We arrived in the morning of the 20th Feby at the Waccaway Settlement, the first human abode we had seen since we left it accompanied by the Chieftain Andres and his men, who it will be recollected, deserted us while ascending the Christmas Cataracts. It was naturally to be expected, that none of those who deserted us, would be found at the Settlement. That Settlement may be considered a half way house, there are always strange Indians to be met here – the vicinity of the upper path from the Berbice to the Demerara makes it convenient as a resting-place. At the present occasion, we found some Waccaways and Macoosies who had been working for some months, at one of the wood cutters. As fruits of their labours, each a Gun & some pieces of Calico were ostentatiously exhibited, and it appeared there was not the slightest thought that by exposing them, they might be perloined by a third person if they left the hut several times, without removing their property, though our whole crew were strangers to them. It shews the extent of confidence these unsophisticated Savages put one in the other.

The Corial which I occupied was in the evening as generally, far a head of the others, and while we were just turning round a point, which the River forms in the vicinity of a newly settled place, I saw some woodskins with Indians coming from the opposite direction, but scarcely had they observed my Corial, when they paddled with all their

---

[1] February.

might towards the shore and arrived there, they jumped out of it, leaving the woodskins and their cargo to their fate. I was not long in conjecturing that they were some of the runaway Waccaways. One of the woodskins with two women paddled towards the Settlement, the younger one ran, after having landed with the swiftness of a gazelle towards the woods; we recognized Andres' wife; he himself must have been in the woodskin, we saw his Gun and shot belt in it. Since I did not succeed in apprehending him, I did not feel any desire to hunt after the others, or to frighten the women, we continued therefore our journey.

February 21 We arrived at noon at Mr McCullum's; where we were received with the same hospitality, we had experienced when we ascended the river. Mr McCullum came readily forward to provide us with the needful, and my poor Indians were after six weeks' scarcity and deprivation of the most distressing nature, once more allowed to indulge in the luxury of a meal, unrestricted by principles of provident care and economy.

Many of them were swollen to a frightful degree, while others, and we among them were so attenuated, that our acquaintances broke out in a cry of surprise & though we had suffered much and yet all might have been forgotten had we not had to bewail the untimely death of Mr Reiss.

We received new certainty, that Acouritch, the Caribbee had passed with his companions in the stolen Corials. He had landed at Mr McCullum's, and told, when that gentleman uttered his surprize of their return, without us, that I had desired him to proceed with every haste to the Colony as he was so unwell that the art of a Physician was necessary to restore him. And it had been believed as he and his Crew resembled more Skeletons than human beings, he more perhaps than we, had to fight against starvation.

I allowed the Indians the following day to rest, and, accompanied by Mr McCullum proceeded on the 23d. Feby to Wickie, where I renewed my astronomical observations.

During my stay at Wickie, I found that the weather was more favourable in the Coast regions, than the advanced season would have led me to expect. I resolved therefore to take a tour to the River Demerara partly by means of the River Wieronie, a tributary of the Berbice & partly by land over the Savannahs. I selected from my Indians those whom I considered best qualified for pedestrian tours and having provided myself only with the most necessary articles, which found place in my Corial, we started on Monday the 27th Feby, we reached that day Peereboom, Mr Duggin's residence, who vied with Mr McCullum to show us every attention, and readiness to forward my designs. Mr Duggin has a wood cutting establishment in the Wieronie, and as I proposed to ascend the river as far as I could, to judge of its adaptness for being navigated by punts and other river crafts, I thankfully accepted his offer of a letter to his superintendent to give me an Arawaak Chieftain Moses by name as a guide across the Savannahs, if I should find the navigation too intricate to be followed up further. Mr Duggin advanced me most readily the necessary provisions for the contemplated journey.

Feby 28th. We arrived at 8 o'clock at the mouth of the Wieronie. The Berbice River expands here considerably and forms almost a basin, the Wieronie joins it from the N.E.;[1] its waters are black as ink, but perfectly clear; its width is about 150 feet, its depth

---

[1] While it is possible that the final stretch of the Wiruni before it joins the Berbice is from the north-east, the general direction of its final stretch is from the north-west.

27 feet. At the entrance of the Wieronie, there was formerly a redoubt and a Reformed Church, of which the remains are to be seen. The minister's house was on the river's opposite side. We found the current uncommonly strong, and as the river is influenced by the tides, the ebb obliged us to come to. There had been formerly several plantations along the banks of the river, and we observed the remnants of a wharf, trenches, &c. The soil appeared to be very fertile; the river is meandring and keeps an average depth of 18 feet. The Savannahs approach frequently the river, at other times its banks were margined with trees & bush. I ascended a small hillock on the right and had an extensive view over savanahs – which stretch to the Rivers Maicony and Mahaica, and a lively intercourse is carried on between the Indian of these respective rivers across these Savannahs.

March 1st. The scenery of the river became very interesting, it expanded occasionally like the upper River Berbice, but the lake like expansions were generally encompassed by higher land, and studded with little Islands from which numbers of the majestic Eta trees rose. Their lofty stem supports numerous fan-shaped leaves, and the gigantic cluster of seeds might have served as an emblem of Caleb's bunch of grapes;[1] the seeds are almost round, and 2 and a half inches in diameter and marked like the Cone of a Pine; this Palm is as much revered and of equal use among the Indians as the Cocoanut tree is to the Natives of its indigenous Country.

A path leads from one of these inlets, called Catacabura across the Savannahs to the River Demerara, but as I had no guide I preferred to proceed to Yucabura where Mr Duggin's settlement was, in order to procure a guide, where we arrived in the afternoon. The river becomes shallow, wherever it expands, and though it is scarcely in such places more than 4 to 5 feet deep, punts loaded with wood navigate it freely. On consulting on the mode of my further progress I found that it would be advisable to leave the Corial at Yucabura, and to proceed on foot over the Savannahs.

March 2d. Our baggage was reduced to indispensable things, and with Moses as guide, we commenced our pedestrian tour. Moses was accompanied by his wife, a young Arawaak, while her dread Lord and husband might have double outnumbered her years, he burthened her with his share of the baggage, and now fully equipped we followed for almost three miles the rivers course through woods, which border its banks; the rich vegetable soil was here several feet in depth, and while walking over it appeared as if we were moving upon elastic springs. We issued from the wood and entered low bush, which to one unacquainted with the vegetation of these tracts, would cause the inquiry; how does it happen, that they appear to luxuriate in a loose sandy soil, as white and sterile as the sand of the sea Shore or the Downs? The riddle is easily explained, as in digging it will be found that the sand is mixed at a certain depth with rich mould. Nevertheless the Flora is quite peculiar and the flowers of these bushes, generally of an average height of about 12 feet, distinguished by their fragrance. The Arawaak Indian names these spots of undergrowth 'Moro', they are the transition from the wood to the naked Savannah. We entered the Savannah shortly after; I was agreeably surprised to see the Savannah alternate with woodland and hillocks; the prospect

---

[1] Caleb was the representative of the tribe of Judah, whom Moses sent with representatives of the other eleven tribes to spy out the land of Canaan. The bunch of grapes they found there was so large and heavy that it required two men to carry it on a pole between them. See Numbers 13.

was therefore by no means so monotonous as in the Savannahs of the Pacaraima mountains; some of our Indians gave out and we halted at the margin of some wood near a spring, to await the weary. The spring originated in the Savannah not far from our resting place and meandred as a sprightly streamlet through the wood towards the Wieronie; my guide called it Catchie Cabura. After we had refreshed ourselves, we continued our journey exchanging the hot Savannah with the shady Forest, or the plain with a Glen. The eye was never wearied by monotony; from time to time it swept over the plain to the dense forest which bounded the prospect to the West or it was arrested by a ridge of copse over which the Eta towered its fan shaped head, and which marks the course of a Brook on its way to its recipient. We observed the Wieronie on our right, it was not to be mistaken by the number of Eta trees. At 4 o'clock in the afternoon, it was not more than a mile from us. I did not lose the opportunity to ascertain its course by compass bearings. We passed some abandoned huts in the passage of a wood; we were told that the owner in a quarrel slew another Indian and as the Crime was committed in the jurisdiction of the Colony the justice had taken cognizance of it, and he had fled carrying Cains mark on his forehead, though several parties had been sent out to apprehend him, he had always eluded them.

After a march of 24 miles, we arrived at some huts in the Savannahs; they were tenantless. Moses, our guide, who presided here as chieftain, assisted with his people at M[r] Duggin's woodcutting establishment. Hundreds of Chigoes were anxious to give us their welcome as soon as I entered the abandoned Huts, and I saw myself obliged to have a temporary hut constructed. I succeeded to ascertain the Altitude of Canopus when on the Meridian according to which we were in Lat. 5°40'10″N.

March 3rd. We crossed at an early hour the brook Aroma[;] it had pathed itself a course through a glen about 40 feet deep; it was therefore to be supposed that the water had cut by degrees perpendicularly downwards and had left a steep wall on either side.*

*See Researches in Geology by H T de la Beche p198.[1]

This propensity was peculiar to all the running waters we met with. When we came out of the wood we saw some Indian huts before us – they were abandoned; our guide recollected however the former provision fields, and off started the whole train to cut Sugar Canes. After nearly an hour's delay, they returned almost loaded with Canes and Pine Apples. Our march continued over Savannahs and through woods; we arrived at 10 o'clock at the brook Yawarie with light brown water; it joined the Wieronie at a short distance from the place where we crossed the Yawarie. We ascended a hillock of about 60 feet and continued our march along its brow; below us flew the Wieronie; half an hour afterwards we descended and had to wade through a swamp before we reached that river, it was almost darker than at its mouth, but scarcely more than 25 feet wide and 9 feet deep its current was strong; arrived at the opposite bank we had to wade for some distance through a swamp, we sank often to our waist in the mud and were really rejoiced, when we had anew to ascend. We stopped fatigued by our march and drenched by torrents of rain, at 5 o'clock in the afternoon at the edge of a wood, where some temporary huts proved that it had been used as a halting place before us, a few

[1] Sir Henry Thomas de La Beche FRS (1796–1855) was one of the foremost geologists of the second quarter of the 19th century. The work to which Schomburgk refers is *Researches in Theoretical Geology*, London, Charles Knight, 1834.

steps from our Camp flew the brook Etissau.[1] The unsettled weather did not permit me to procure observations. My Guide told me that the next day's march would lead us through woods, and that we might expect to reach the Demerara river at 3 Oclock in the afternoon. About nightfall a party of Indians arrived from the river Demerara, they had left in the morning early, but the rain had much detained them[.] They were on the way to their settlement in the Savannahs, within 2 miles from the Etounie.[2] They gave us a distressing picture of the scarcity of Provisions among the Indians of the Demerara River and as it was not much out of our road to pass their Settlement on our return, I took the opportunity to order a supply of Cassada bread as they told us that they had plenty of Cassada in their fields, and the object of their return now was to prepare large quantities and to carry it to their suffering brethren.

March 4th. We resumed our course through the woods, it was now mostly west; the Brook Wannoka, with Black waters, was almost as large as the Wieronie, where we crossed it. The soil mostly fertile woodland, the Trees consisted mostly of Tederma, Wamara, Kakerally, Manaribally, Kakerabally, Pourouck or Bullet tree, &c. &c. The weather was not more favourable than the preceding day, and several swamps which we had to cross did not assist by any means to make our journey agreeable. It is difficult walking through one of these swamps, they are generally overgrown with the manicole Palm, and as soon as some substantial soil has collected around their base, that graceful tree appears to rise from a hillock. If the traveller succeed to step from one of these hillocks to the next, he is sure to sink not much above his ancles in the black mud, but should he miss his aim or should the distance be too great to reach it by a single step, he may prepare himself to sink to his waist in the soft mudd, and he rises, not as a swan, but bedaubed with a solution of the boggy ground. We passed several brooks which sent their waters to the north, very likely Tributaries to the Maiconie and Mahaica. At one o'clock we arrived at the brook Alissaro; previously we had followed along the ridge of a hillock about 50 feet high, we descended anew and crossed the Alissaro, a brook with white water and the first which is in a Southern direction or contrary to those we had passed previously. After we had ascended a steep hillock, higher than any (abt 80 feet) we had hitherto yet, we passed two streamlets and passed the vestiges of a former timber path.*

> *The wood cutters examine generally the trees which they consider worth to be felled and after they have been deprived of the useless branches and squared, they are perhaps a distance of three to four miles hauled through the woods to the Rivers banks, and from thence shipped to the coast. In order to ease the labour connected with the hauling, round pieces of wood are laid at certain distances from each other, over which the heavy timber is drawn by main force, a road thus prepared is called a timber path. It may be imagined what work it wants, to haul a heavy piece of timber perhaps for miles through woods to the River's banks.

An hour afterwards we passed some new fields, the trees had been cut down and set afire and the soil had been planted in Cassada, pumpkins, and other necessaries for the sustenance of the Indian. The path descended from here gradually, but I should say that these fields were upwards of 200 feet above the Demerara river. When we came out of

---

[1] In both the published version (p. 343) and on the accompanying map this is spelt Elissa.
[2] Ituni River. A left bank tributary of the Berbice, which joins the latter river a few miles above the Wikki. Today there is a mining town of the same name near its source.

the wood we were at an abandoned Settlement and in sight of the River Demerara, which we hailed with delight. It is here dark coloured, and quite different in appearance, from the muddy river it is at Georgetown. The place where we met the Demerara was called Ajakwa. We followed the Rivers Course northward for about a mile and a half, and arrived 15 minutes to four, at the Post Seba where Mr. Spencer[1] the Postholder gave us a most hearty welcome.

We crossed the Wieronie in Lat 5°39′30″ & Long^t. 58°3′W., from whence it appeared to take a far southern direction; the direct distance from that point to the river Demerara is therefore about 21½ miles, and there is no doubt in my mind, that the Wieronie is ample enough to be rendered navigable for Canoes and punts to the point where we crossed it; the trees which have fallen across it need only to be removed to make it already now navigable for corials and light Canoes. The whole distance which we had walked according to the circuitous road which we had been led amounted to 50 miles. The Savannahs which we had traversed are plentifully watered by beautiful streams, tributaries to the Wieronie and Berbice, and abound in wholesome and nutritious grasses. They are therefore particularly qualified for the grazing ground of many thousand heads of Cattle and horses. The favorable circumstance that these Savannahs are so well watered and interspersed by woodland, to afford shade, enhances the value and if it want an experiment whether the grass be wholesome, I need only to refer the querist to Mr Duggin, who has lately commenced to raise cattle and is highly satisfied with the results.

It was my intention when circumstances else should permit it to pay a visit to the great Fall of the River Demerara, I had heard much of it, and was anxious to make a comparison with those I had passed in the Essequibo, Corentyne & Berbice. The weather was unfavorable, but this did not prevent me to execute my design. Through the kindness of a Mr Hebberd, I was provided with a batteau or build canoe,[2] and I left the morning after my arrival at Seba. I was fortunate enough to procure the great Arawaak chieftain Simon as a guide and he performed most faithfully and attentively his duty. A relation of this excursion is beyond the limits of this report, sufficient to say we arrived on the 7th of March at the great fall and I lost no time to visit it next morning. I was disappointed, it has neither the grandeur nor the volume of water of King William 4th's Cataract in the Essequibo, and can by no means measure itself with Genl Carmichael Smyth's Cataract in the Corentyne. As with regard to the difficulties which it might have opposed to me, in case I wished to pass it with my Corials, I can assert that I would not have hesitated a moment to transport baggage and Corials over and with less trouble, than at the Cataract Itabrou. At the great fall (as it is called 'par excellence') of the Demerara, the road has been cleared and the necessary rollers are laid by Indians, who have transported their corials and woodskins over; while in every instance where such a transport became necessary in the River Berbice, we had to make the

[1] John Spencer, the postholder on the Demarara River, became involved in 1839–41 in a notorious law case. He was accused, along with his wife, an Arawak, of enslaving Amerindians. See Menezes, *British Policy Towards the Amerindians*, pp. 185–9.

[2] This type of craft is one constructed from planks, in other words not a dugout.

For no obvious reason the manuscript continues at this point, in the middle of p. 72, with Schomburgk's description of his later, overland journey from the Berbice towards the Corentyne. The account of the Demerara journey continues on the next two consecutive pages, numbered 71A and 72A. These are followed by p. 73. The chronological order rather than the page order is followed here.

preparations ourselves, and with regard to our difficulties at the Christmas Cataracts they far, far, outbalanced those which the great fall could have offered us.

Among the Indians of the upper river Demerara, the greatest scarcity was prevailing; in consequence of severe rains the Casada roots rotted in the ground and in order to secure themselves against starvation they had to resort to the seeds of the Green heart tree, which contains a substance as bitter as Quinine. The seeds were grated and put in fresh water, and a matter precipitates similar in appearance to starch, it is repeatedly washed to lessen its bitterness, which it never loses entirely; it is then mixed with rotten wood pounded previously and sifted, and those who have it in their power mix a little cassada flour with it. The substitute of bread is not only quite black but likewise as bitter as wormwood and cannot be wholesome in consequence of the admixture of rotten wood. The Indians will have to subsist for months on this kind of bread as that time will elapse before they are able to reap their new crop of Cassada.

We returned now to Seba which we left on the 7th March[1] after having rested a day. We retraced our steps towards the Wieronie but after we had crossed that river, we took a different path, to pay our promised visit to the Indian settlement and to buy Cassada bread. The settlement was larger than the generality of the Arawaak villages I had seen along the River Berbice. It might consist of about 60 souls in 10 huts. After the Indians in my train had taken place the Chieftain of the Settlement came forward and said three short sentences to him whom he considered the first among my crew. Those sentences expressed in an increased ratio his welcome, and are literally translated "Sit down, sit well down, sit very well down." The man thus addressed said to each sentence, "wang" "I thank you"[;] he went then to the next guest and so in rotation, until all had received his welcome; then came his sons and all the men of the Settlement, one by one, and repeated the same; the whole ceremony lasted upwards of half an hour. I was excluded from the welcome. As soon as I had procured the supply of bread we left the Settlement – accompanied by two young men which I had hired to carry it to the Banks of the Wieronie. We slept that night in an open Savannah, drenched by the rain, and arrived in a similar state next day (March 13th) at Youcabura, where we had left our Corials[.] As tedious as our ascent of the Wieronie was, the Current bore us now along at a rapid rate and we made in 7 hours 34 miles[;] on our ascent we had found the Current to run from 4 to 5 knots. We landed on the 15th. at Wickie where we found those whom we had left behind in perfect health and all recovered from their late fatigues and deprivations.[2]

One other Pedestrian tour stood before me, I was anxious to visit the Corentyne by means of the Wickie and Canje, and as many of my Indians from Oreála and its neighbourhood had their wives and children with them, which it would have proved inconvenient to take to New Amsterdam, I resolved to accompany the Supernumeraries to their home; this would at the same time enable them to send Corials at their arrival for their husbands, to the mouth of the Corentyne, to await their return. We entered

---

[1] There is a mistake in the date here. Schomburgk stated that he arrived at the Great Falls of the Demarara River on March 7th and visited them next day. It is not possible to reconstruct his movements exactly, but he refers to reaching Yucabura on the 13th, having spent the night of the 12th on the savannah. This suggests that he arrived back at Seba on the 10th, where he had a day's rest (11th) and sets out on his return journey to the Berbice on the 12th.

[2] The two inserted pages, marked 71A and 72A, end here, and the narrative takes up again from the middle of p. 72.

therefore the River Wickie on the 20th, where it is about 120 feet wide and 12 feet deep, its waters are whitish and turbulent, in other respects it resembles much the Wieronie, as well with regard to Scenery as Soil. Numerous Orchideous Plants were seen attached to the branches which over hung the River & the curious Coryanthus, the yellow Oncidium[,] Gongora,[1] and others were in blossom, and distributed a beautiful fragrance. One was remarkable in consequence of its growing on the lofty stem of the Eta palms, and its narrow pendulous leaves are often 6 to 7 feet long.

We arrived at half past four in the afternoon at the Brook Pototo,[2] the course of which we followed, as we had understood that a short distance from its embouchure some Arawaaks were living. The Pototo resembles an Itabou (the Arawaak call the lake like basins or expansions of their Rivers). It spreads about 4 to 500 yards and is partly covered with Rushes and other water plants.

We ascended the Pototo for about 20 minutes, when we halted at the landing place of the Arawaak Settlement; we received shortly after a visit from some of the men they were very friendly and informed us that the nearest path led from their settlement to the Canje and Corentyne, there was another higher up, but it was not more frequented as the Indians who lived formerly there had removed. I resolved therefore to engage one as Guide to accompany us next morning.

March 21st. I was astonished to see what burdens the women of those, who returned now to their home, had loaded themselves with. They had carried on a lively barter with such articles as they had demanded from me in part of their payment, and calculated on a second profit on those which they had procured in return for knives, looking glasses, &c. The Savannahs which we traversed were not much different from those between the Wieronie and Demerara. They appeared to be more wooded, and possessed more Slopes. After we had crossed the stream Tourie-cabura, we had to ascend a hillock ab[t] 80 feet high, and as it was [illegible] convenient station, the view from here was very handsome. We had crossed a brook with a rapid current and black water and emerged from the wood, where we found ourselves on the border of an extensive swamp, on the other side of which we observed several Indian huts. It was really tantalizing to think that we would have to cross the formidable swamps, the difficulties of crossing which, were manifold increased by the circumstance, that the rushes and grasses which might have covered it, had been lately set on fire and burnt to the ground[,] the sharpe stumps remained sticking out. We set too with good heart and shortly after we were to the arm in the mire. What an aspect when we issued from the swamp, and there was no pure water by hand to perform the act of ablution, we had to content ourselves to make our appearance as we were, uncleaned and unbrushed, a matter of little consequence to the Indians. [T]he huts consisted of three or four, the owner entered them just from the other side with an Apouje (lesser Peccary)[3] over his shoulders which he had shot a little while ago; it was an inviting sight, and I bought half of it for some trifling articles to which a present of powder and shot was added.

We left the settlement half past three and continued our road through dense wood; the Indian had told us that he had a large Corial on the Banks of the Canje to the use of

---

[1] Three genera of orchid.

[2] Possibly the Bududa River of the reference map. This a case where the closeness of 'b' and 'p', and 'd' and 't', and the 'long o' and 'u' in the local Amerindian languages has resulted in a variant orthography.

[3] The collared peccary (*Tayassu tayacu*).

which we were welcome; he informed us likewise that some Arawaaks were living on the banks of the Canje, and that I would be able to procure a guide there; he would have accompanied us but being then the only male in the Settlement, he was prevented from doing so. His corial, he said, was quite new, he had made it only lately out of a fine tree, which he had felled in the neighbourhood of his Settlement, and after he had hollowed it out, he had transported the corial for miles through the woods to the banks of the Canje. I found the vestiges of the path in our further progress. An hour's walk through the dense wood, abounding in useful timber trees, chiefly Bulletwood and wallaba, brought us to the settlement, it had been only lately established. We found the Chieftain occupied in making baskets from the slender branches of a Species of Bignonia; when he rose, he presented a frightful picture, he suffered under far advanced Dropsy and his yellow cheeks, the skin flapping almost round it, formed a strong contrast to the preternatural swelling of the body. He offered however his service to accompany us to the Corentyne as he was well acquainted with the road. My plan of accompanying them was frustrated, being likely heated when we had to cross the swamps, the quick transition from heat to cold occasioned severe Rheumatic pains[;] we had likewise to contend with most unfavourable weather. The Canje was in the vicinity of the Settlement about 100 feet wide, the water dark coloured its current rapid. The party of Indians embarked next morning in three small corials, the larger, which we had expected to find, had been used a few days ago, to convey some Indians to a wood-cutting Establishment on the Canje, and as there were even no paddles by hand, the Corentyne Indians were obliged to use any substitute they could lay hold of. Their journey to the mouth of the brook Ikuruwa[1] where the Postholder of the Canje has his residence, is accomplished in one day, they follow the course of the Ikuruwa upwards to the Brae or Broad water, a small lake, through which the Ikuruwa flows and from thence the path leads over Savannahs to Oreála, the distance being about 12 miles.

With great exertions I reached the Settlement of Pototo next day, and we did not lose any time to return to Wickie, which we ultimately left on March 25th. It was the day before Easter Sunday and on our arrival at Mr Duggin's we found his house filled with Indians, who dressed in their best attire amused themselves in dancing. What a display of beads of all sizes and colours! the men had all new Camisaros or Hiatos, fringed with different coloured Cotton hangings, and divers figures cut out of white linen intended to represent tigers &c were fixed to the laps.[2] Their Chieftain Jandje, was one of the mixed race, who at a former time possessed the greatest influence over the Indians in his neighbourhood; he could at a short notice assemble 2 to 3 hundred armed Indians, and his will was undisputed law. He used to drill his Indians regularly, he himself, at occasions, where a display was to take place, dressed out in a costly uniform with Sword in hand, a present, I understand, from the late governor Baird.[3] His power was arbitrary and he adjusted every punishment, without court martial, on the spot the culprit was generally tied to a tree & soundly flogged. However he protected the Indians against

---

[1] The locality of the junction of the Canje and Ikuruwa is marked as Richmond Hill on the reference map.

[2] A lap is the usual term for the garment worn by Amerindian men. It consists of a length of cloth that is passed through a waistband at the front, then between the legs and through the waistband at the back. A length of the cloth is left hanging down at the front and rear. The editor of the *JRGS* changed 'laps' to 'caps' (p. 348).

[3] Probably Henry Beard, Governor of Berbice 1821–31.

the indispositions of the settlers who employed them, and thus preserved his sway. He himself worked very hard but naturally for high wages which were gladly given to him in order to secure his influence in procuring Indian labourers. Since the Colony has stopped the presents, which were formerly given to the Indians, he has entirely retired, and contents himself in superintending the affairs of his own relations and those who are under him at his Settlement, which for neatness and comfort surpasses any I have ever seen before, and vies with that of many Settlers. In his own Settlement he acts as Lord supreme, nothing must be done without his knowledge and consent. He is known for his gallantry and indulges in polygamy like the plurality of his tribe. He has lately taken unto himself a young Sultana, distinguished for her Indian charms and which on the present occasion was dressed as a European. She was certainly handsome, and he watched her as the apple of his eye. His feats of valour and villainy, when on the intent to replenish his Harem are the topics of the country.

We bid adieu to Mr Duggin's on the 28th March and having selected a guide among Jandje's subjects, to inform me of the names of streams and brooks in our descent of the Berbice from the Wieronie to the Coast, we were now obliged to suit our progress according to the tides. I was anxious to procure as accurate a survey of the lower River Berbice as circumstances and time would permit me, I used with great advantage the mode of surveying by signal fireing; for this purpose one of the Corials was sent forward and having been directed to fire three guns according to signals made for that purpose, the interval between flash and report were strictly observed and the means multiplied by the distance the sound was considered to have travelled, according to the state of the Barometer (which varied from 1010 to 1040 feet per second). The difference, where I made comparisons by the reel & log line, amounted seldom to more than 30 to 50 feet. We paid a visit to site of the old Fort Nassau and Old Amsterdam, the former capital of Berbice; the Streets of the latter are yet to be traced, by brick pavements, which even time has not been able to destroy; there is little to be seen of the fortifications, which are covered with bush and grass and we did not feel very anxious to enter in close investigations, as we had been warned to beware of Labari[1] and other poisonous Snakes, which frequent the old walls. As a mockery to the change of times rises, once the sumptuous dwelling of a rich Proprietor out of the present wilderness which surrounds it. It will soon be numbered among the ruins of this environs. The glazed and richly ornamented windows are shattered in by accident and wilful mischief, and the name of Buse which in ornamental letters and flourishes, decorates the entrance, will now be attacked by the same wanton hands.

March 30th. At the plantation Mara on the river's right banks, I measured a baseline to determine the [wi]dth[2] and found it 2509 feet wide its average depth is the[re 20 to] 25 feet the current 4 knots in an hour.*

*I had thus procured myself a number of accurate data which checked by astronomical observations may prove useful for the construction of a topographical map of the river on a large scale. I have a high idea of the mode of carrying on a running survey in that manner.

---

[1] Labaria, *Bothrops atrox*.
[2] There is a narrow tear in the manuscript here (p. 77) that extends over six lines of handwriting. The missing words or parts of words have been supplied partly by intuition and partly by reference to the published version, p. 349.

We succeeded to re[ach th]e Plantation Rossfield on the Rivers left Bank that [night] and were most Hospitably received by Mr Mackenzie. [I wa]s engaged in taking observations for time and latitude and computed the Geographical Situation of the managers house to be in Lat 6°10′5″N. Long^t. 57°26′30″W by Ch^r.

March 31st. After an absence of four months and several days, we arrived this afternoon at New Amsterdam. The crowd of feelings which oppressed my heart at my return, were very different from those with which we set out. On casting back an eye to the events which had occurred since the bow of my Corial was turned in the contrary direction and we were gradually passing the precincts of the little town, much had happened since to depress my spirits, a succession of adverse circumstances assailed me during the whole Expedition and though I battled resolutely against their influence, they undermined my intentions and caused the failure of my plans; the opportunity was well calculated to bring them in renewed Colours before my memory, to which the sad Catastrophe that now prevented one of our number to return, added a Chill, harsh enough to produce despondency, and yet at that moment I could say in my own heart: "I have done my duty!
New Amsterdam,
Berbice May 1837,
Robert H Schomburgk

****

In some ways the Berbice expedition had proved a success even if it had still not reached the mountains of the interior. Quite a lot had been added to the knowledge of the interior of British Guiana, and important natural history collections had been made. Unfortunately some 400 specimens of birds were lost at sea, but nearly 8,000 specimens of plants, representing 400 different species were collected, of which the star exhibit was *Victoria amazonica*. For Schomburgk, however, the death of Reiss overshadowed all other events and vicissitudes, and he was worried about the state of the collections because of the adverse conditions under which they had been collected and kept.[1]

Towards the end of the Berbice expedition Schomburgk started making plans for his next journey. On 4 March while at Post Seba on the Demerara River he wrote a long letter to the Royal Geographical Society reporting on the Berbice expedition but also setting out plans for his next expedition. He was convinced that there were two ways to the Serra Acarai, by either the Rupununi or the Essequibo. His first choice is by the former as the way is relatively easy and inhabited. As he now believed the sources of the Rupununi and the Essequibo to be close together he would descend by the latter. The problem with the Essequibo was not the King William's Falls, which he no longer considered much of an obstacle and had been stopped by them previously only because of fever, hunger and the rainy season, but the fact that the river's upper reaches were uninhabited. He pointed out that it was impossible to carry five or six months' supply of provisions and even if fish and game were plentiful the Indians would not put up with lack of bread and would desert. If the Royal Geographical Society wished him to ascend the Essequibo it would be necessary to set up a depot in the charge of a trustworthy

[1] RBGK, DC, Vol. LXVII, Letter of Schomburgk to Hooker, 7 April 1837.

man. After he had completed the exploration of the Rupununi and Essequibo he would turn his attention to the Sierra Pacaraima and the source of the Orinoco. He suggested using Fort São Joaquim as a base where he could spend the 1839 rainy season before setting out. However, if he was to do that he would need the Royal Geographical Society to arrange the necessary permission as the commandant of the fort was not allowed to let people in without a passport from Pará.[1]

However, whilst in New Amsterdam, Schomburgk suddenly found himself faced with the possibility that there would be no further explorations, at least under the patronage of the Royal Geographical Society. On news of Schomburgk's failure to ascend the Corentyne, the Society's Committee on the Guiana Expeditions[2] met on 14 February 1837 and considered all Schomburgk's correspondence and reports since November 1834.[3] The committee agreed that Schomburgk had failed to make a contribution of 'the least importance' to geography and of little, if any, benefit to the colony. In his pursuit of natural history Schomburgk had lost sight of the Royal Geographical Society's principal interest – geography – giving it secondary rather than primary consideration. His expeditions had been on too large a scale, fewer and smaller canoes should have been used and less baggage carried. Schomburgk's interests were too directed towards topography instead of ascertaining, as directed, the striking geographical features of the colony. The committee's recommendations were that Schomburgk be immediately suspended from service of the Society, that no further outlay be made until the result of the Berbice expedition be known, until the opinion of the Governor of British Guiana had been obtained and until it could be ascertained that it was practicable to fulfil that part of the original instructions concerning the connexion with Humboldt's observations on the Orinoco. A rather toned-down version of these criticisms was sent the following day, expressing Council's great disappointment and its decision to suspend temporarily Schomburgk's future proceedings and to defer any further expenses in outfitting the next expedition until a plan had been submitted and approved.[4]

---

[1] RGS Corres 1834–40, Letter of Schomburgk to Washington, 4 March 1837.

[2] The members of this committee were Captain Beaufort, Mr W. Parish and the Secretary, Captain Washington.

[3] Because of their location among the manuscripts next to the minutes of the committee it seems very possible that the committee also took into account two letters from Sir John Barrow at the Admiralty of which the dates are uncertain but which probably belong to November 1836, following the end of the first expedition. The contents are firm.

'This person should be clearly and definitely apprized that he is not proceeding according to instructions received from the Geog Society – that the Society takes no interest in the boundary of the colony, and that he must not expect to receive a farthing more than was originally appropriated for the solution of an interesting geographical problem which he has done nothing toward the solution of it. ... he is to consider himself no longer connected with the Society.'

A postscript reads 'He is too fond of working to accomplish much.' It seems as though Schomburgk had some sense of Barrow's views as he wrote in May 1837 to ask Washington 'Is Sir John Barrow friendly to my labours?' (RGS Corres 1834–40, Letters of Barrow to RGS, no dates; Letter of Schomburgk to Washington, 12 May 1837).

[4] RGS Corres 1834–40, Minutes of Committee on the Guayana Expeditions, 14 February 1837; RGS Letter Book (hereafter RGS LB) 1836–40, Letter of Washington to Schomburgk, 15 February 1837. Schomburgk first received news of the Council's displeasure in a letter dated 25 February of which no copy has been found. That letter reached Schomburgk in mid-April whereas he did not receive that of the 15 February until June.

The criticisms continued over the following months. On 15 May, in response to a letter Schomburgk sent from New Amsterdam on 1 April, immediately after his return from the Berbice expedition and written in haste as the ship was about to sail,[1] Washington complained that the contents of the letter were so general that he had been unable to make out what Schomburgk had been doing and cannot believe that he has spent four months reaching a point on the Demerara River first reached many years ago. Schomburgk was even upbraided for his failure to take soundings at the mouth of the Corentyne when there the previous September. They should have been taken under 'any circumstances', and Washington cannot believe the weather was too bad for a fortnight to have made it impossible. The only glimpse of commendation in the letter is the testimony to the accuracy of his surveying, even with imperfect instruments. Two weeks later, in response to the letter from Seba, Schomburgk is told 'I cannot refrain from expressing my regret that so much time & money have been spent on so unimportant (as it appears to us) a tract of country as that between Berbice & Essequibo'. It is pointed out that he has left only £25 of the £900 he was allotted for three years and he 'must not be surprised if it should be very unfavourably looked upon [by Council]'. There were other criticisms – four canoes instead of five would have saved time and expense; why had he not connected the Essequibo and Corentyne by land? and there is even a rather sarcastic jibe about whether Schomburgk actually made it to the Essequibo – 'but I hope you did not leave a doubt on your mind as to the fact of the water you saw being the river Essequibo.' But this same letter oddly contained some more positive indications and referred to plans for the future and mentioned that a letter was about to be despatched to the Brazilian authorities concerning them.[2]

Schomburgk responded to the Royal Geographical Society's letter of 25 February with some spirit.[3] He expressed his surprise at the decision to suspend him as he had adhered strictly to the instructions he had received. Furthermore his journey up the Corentyne had been made at the repeated insistence of the Governor of the Colony and had received Council's approval. Indeed it is his adherence to instructions that has contributed to his failure to achieve what Council thinks he should have done. On the advice about how he has conducted his expeditions, he comments acerbically that 'unacquainted as you must be with the actual state of travelling in these uninhabited regions', canoes are essential and it is out of the question to trek overland with a couple of Indians. He repeated much of what he had written in March about his plans for reaching the Serra Acarai, either by way of the Essequibo or Rupununi, and then wintering at Fort São Joaquim before heading for Esmeralda on the Orinoco. He did not expect further financial support from the Royal Geographical Society for this expedition which he would fund from private means and the sale of plants. On the other hand, although his duty to the Royal Geographical Society continued only until September 1838, he would be happy to extend it to February or March 1839 in return for its non-financial patronage. He was worried that the £150 he had recently drawn on the Society would not be honoured as he may have overshot his £900 grant.[4]

---

[1] This letter reached London before the much fuller letter sent from Seba on 4 March.
[2] RGS LB 1836–40, Letters of Washington to Schomburgk, 15 May 1837, 1 June 1837.
[3] As has already been pointed out, no letter dated 25 February has been found, but it is fairly clear that its contents were very similar to those of 15 February.
[4] RGS Corres 1834–40, Letter of Schomburgk to Washington, 22 April 1837.

Schomburgk remained in New Amsterdam, preparing his report on the Berbice expedition, which was delayed by a severe attack of rheumatic fever. He complained that he had always suffered from the painful disease after returning to the coast from the interior. He formally reported the finding of *Victoria amazonica* which he described as a reward for the 'disastrous trip up the Berbice', by which words he was probably referring to the death of Reiss rather than any other aspect. He was persuaded that the lily is a new species of *Nymphaea* 'and the Most Distinguished of its Tribe'. He proposed that the find be dedicated to Princess Victoria, whom he believed to be patron of the Botanical Society. He enclosed a description and drawing of the plant. When the Royal Geographical Society received the drawing it was decided not to pass it to the Botanical Society but to present it direct to the new Queen in Schomburgk's name. Queen Victoria graciously accepted the dedication and granted permission for it to be named *Victoria Regia*.[1]

At this time Schomburgk, although he knew about it, had still not received the Royal Geographical Society's letter of 15 February and it was causing him much anxiety. He was still at New Amsterdam waiting to chart the mouth of the Corentyne but delayed by his health, bad weather and the lack of a letter from the Governor to the Dutch authorities. When armed with the last he undertook the survey, not without some hindrance from the Dutch colonists, at the end of May. After that he returned to Georgetown in early June. This survey pleased those back in London, especially Captain Beaufort, and Schomburgk was congratulated on it as an important service to the hydrography and commerce of British Guiana. Furthermore Council showed its appreciation by paying for the expenses involved, despite its stated intention to cut off Schomburgk's funding.[2]

The second day after his return to Georgetown, Schomburgk was struck down by yellow fever which was raging in the town at the time. Saved by his 'good constitution' when most died, he was strong enough to write to the Royal Geographical Society in early July. He had by that time received the Society's letters of 15 February and 15 May but felt too weak to give them a proper answer. He felt, however, that much of the problem was the result of misunderstanding caused by the slowness of communication. He complained that 'reproaches appear to be my only reward for *all* exertions and sacrifices of health and means – I feel it is undeserved'. This same theme emerged later in the month when he turned to answering the Society's letters. He had covered many of the points in his earlier letters and here he mainly concentrated on financial matters. He argued that he had been greatly underfunded, everyone in the colony knew that and the governor had even written to Maconochie to say so. He had put a great deal of his own money into the first two expeditions which together cost £1,121.4s and this figure did not include personal expenses nor the wages for his assistant. Furthermore he would

---

[1] RGS Corres 1834–40, Letters of Schomburgk to Washington, 11 May 1837, 12 May 1837; RGS LB 1836–40, Letter of Washington to Schomburgk, 1 August 1837. The name *Victoria regia* was given by John Lindley who recognized the lily as a belonging to new genus and provided the authoritative description of it (see Lindley, *Victoria regia*). As already noted (p. 196, fn. 2 above), the official botanical designation today is *Victoria amazonica* (Poeppig) Sowerby, which name reflects the fact that the plant was found on the Amazon in 1832 by the German botanist Eduard Pöppig who, thinking it a member of the genus *Euryale*, called it *E. amazonica*..

[2] A report of this survey, composed by the editor of the *JRGS*, is to be found as an addendum to 'Ascent of the River Corentyn', pp. 299–301. RGS Corres 1834–40, Letter of Schomburgk to Washington, 11 May 1837; RGS LB 1836–40, Letters of Washington to Schomburgk, 1 September 1837, 1 October 1837.

have to meet the cost of the next entirely out of his own resources. Even if the next expedition was a success, the Royal Geographical Society would not recompense him. He had heard that some members of Council thought he had been well paid by the colony and it was for this reason that he had concentrated his explorations on the colony. In fact he had not received a penny, 'for the Colony ... have not taken the slightest interest in my Expeditions, nor have I courted it'. He had done his accounts which he was sending to the Royal Geographical Society and they show that he was over £400 poorer as a result of his efforts. However, his immediate and great concern was the absence of any firm instructions on what to do next because if the proposal he had made is to be executed, then he must leave for the interior by the end of August.[1]

Although the Royal Geographical Society's letter of 1 June hinted that Schomburgk would be allowed to proceed on a further expedition by referring to a letter being sent to the Brazilian authorities and to the shipment to him of a compass, it did not give specific permission to proceed. The letter, however, did contain further criticisms to which Schomburgk replied. For example, he was certain that he had reached the Essequibo because he had found the site of a hut that had been erected by the expedition the year before. As to a query about why he had overlooked so important a subject as the native languages, he replied sharply, 'You certainly could not suppose that so important a point as the languages of the Indians should be overlooked by me?' He had collected a vocabulary of 500 words and phrases.[2]

It would appear that soon after he replied to the Royal Geographical Society's letter of 1 June, that of 1 July reached Schomburgk. This letter gave him permission to proceed according to his plan and enclosed a passport. He was to explore the Serra Acarai and it was hoped that he would reach the source of the Maroni and even that of the Oyapock.[3]

His plan to winter at São Joaquim was welcomed for the time it would save and if he connected his observations with those of Humboldt he 'will fully realize the hopes of the Council in first engaging [him] to travel under their directions ... [and] will afford much gratification to every member of the Council'. Schomburgk replied that he would travel under the patronage of the Royal Geographical Society but expected no more funds from it. As there was little time he had immediately put preparations in hand and had sent Vieth to recruit crews for the canoes, of which, on the advice of the Society, he was taking only two.[4]

---

[1] RGS Corres 1834–40, Letters of Schomburgk to Washington, 4 July 1837, 20 July 1837; RGS JMS 6/13(d).

[2] RGS Corres 1834–40, Letter of Schomburgk to Washington, 8 August 1837; RGS LB 1836–40, Letter of Washington to Schomburgk, 1 June 1837.

No trace has been found of these vocabularies, but there is evidence of their existence through three of his publications. They are 'Contributions to the Philological Ethnography of South America', *Proceedings of the Philological Society*, 3, 1848, pp. 228–37; 'Remarks to Accompany a Comparative Vocabulary of Eighteen Languages and Dialects of Indian tribes Inhabiting Guiana', *Simmonds's Colonial Magazine*, 15, 1848, pp. 46–64; and 'A Vocabulary of the Maiongkong Language', *Proceedings of the Philological Society*, 4, 1850, pp. 217–22.

[3] The grandiose but completely impractical suggestion that Schomburgk might travel eastward from the source of Essequibo to join his survey up with that of the French on the Maroni and Oyapock Rivers, before returning along the southern slopes of the Serra Acarai to Fort São Joaquim for the wet season, merely illustrates the total ignorance of the members of the Royal Geographical Society about the geography and nature of the area.

[4] RGS Corres 1834–40, Letters of Schomburgk to Washington, 8 August 1837, 13 August 1837, 14 August 1837; RGS LB 1836–40, Letter of Washington to Schomburgk, 1 July 1837.

It is difficult to know whether it was because Schomburgk chose to stand up for himself but the Royal Geographical Society's tone became far more conciliatory and supportive from August onwards. It acknowledged that even if it had not intended Schomburgk to spend so much time and effort on so minor an object of geographical discovery as the topography and capabilities of British Guiana, doubtless the colonial government would be pleased. The report on the second expedition was even said to contain 'much interesting detail'. Perhaps the major volte-face on the part of the Society's Council was its acceptance that the cost of travel in British Guiana was very much greater than was ever expected. Washington also apologised that his letters had added to Schomburgk's suffering while ill, but it was done with the best intentions so as not to conceal Council's honest opinions. No reproach was meant and it must have been Schomburgk's ill health that made him think there was. On another occasion when Schomburgk mentioned that he was expecting another reprimand for his silence while suffering from yellow fever, Washington wrote back:

> I am willing to believe you are not exactly aware of the force of these terms in the English language (however well you write it and for which I give you credit) but I beg to assure you that in no letter of mine has any reprimand or reproach been expressed, nor was such a thing ever contemplated by me; I did express the *regret* of the Council at the result of your late expedition and you cannot be surprized that we share the feeling of disappointment which you must certainly have had on that occasion.[1]

However willing Council was to criticise Schomburgk privately, it was not willing to admit anything other than success publicly. In its Annual Report for 1837 it reported that Schomburgk's labours:

> claim especial notice, for the perseverance he has manifested, in spite of an unhealthy climate, in exploring the rivers Essequibo, Berbice, and Corentyn – in obtaining much topographical information – and for having very materially added to our knowledge of the natural productions of that rich and fertile country.[2]

Did Schomburgk deserve all of the private criticism that was heaped on him? Certainly some of it is justified in so far as he failed in his main objective which was to investigate 'the physical character and resources of that portion of the central ridge traversing this part of South America, which furnishes tributaries to the Demerara, Essequibo and other rivers flowing into the Atlantic, within, or immediately contiguous to the British colony of Guiana'. In other words he did not manage to reach and explore the Serra Acarai. On the other hand, Maconochie was of the view that what Schomburgk had done during his first expedition mainly fitted with his instructions and the British government's interest had primarily been in a description of the physical features of the colony, and if he produced a scientific report of these, his failure would not be as great as it at first appeared. In fact Schomburgk had achieved a lot and it prepared him to achieve even more.[3]

---

[1] RGS Corres 1834–40, Letter of Schomburgk to Washington, 20 July 1837; RGS LB 1836–40, Letters of Washington to Schomburgk, 1 August 1837, 1 September 1837, 1 October 1837.

[2] Royal Geographical Society, 'Annual Report for 1837', *JRGS*, 8, 1838, p. vi.

[3] RGS Corres 1834–40, Letter of Maconochie to Washington, 1 July 1836.

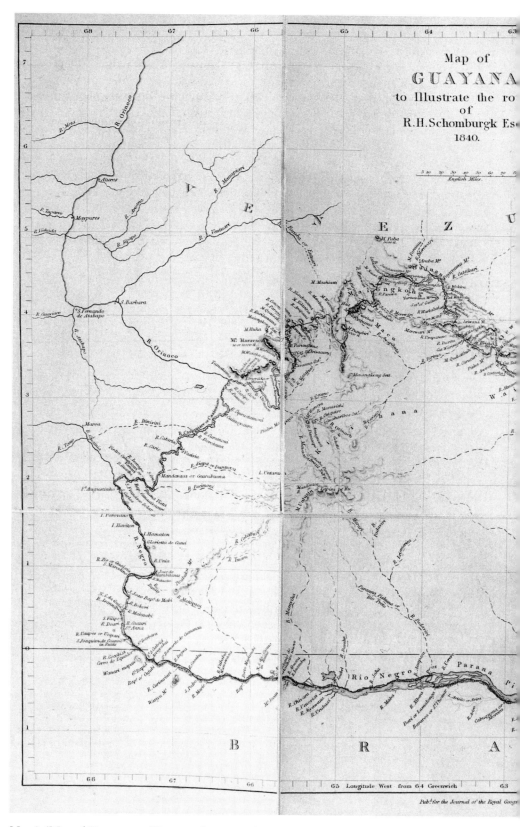

Map 3: 'Map of Guayana, to Illustrate the route of R. H. Schomburgk Esqʳ. 1840.' From the *Journal of*

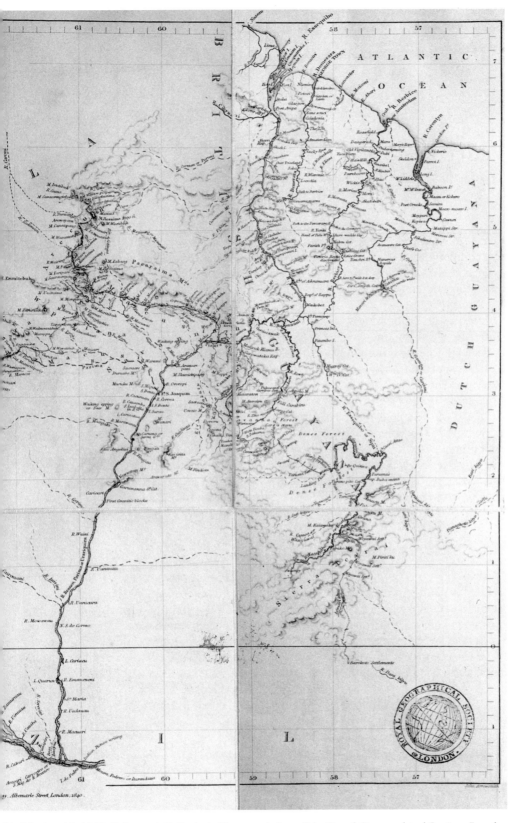

hical Society, 10, 1841, facing p. 160. Included by permission of the Royal Geographical Society, London.

CHAPTER 3

The Journeys to the Sources of the Essequibo and to Esmeralda on the Orinoco: 1837–1839

The manuscript of Robert Schomburgk's third expedition into the interior of British Guiana and beyond is held by the Royal Geographical Society, catalogued as JMS 6/29. It is composed of seven parts, labelled (a) to (g), which are uneven in their content and detail and not all in Schomburgk's handwriting. Part (g), which consists of the financial accounts of the third expedition between 11 September 1837 and 11 September 1838, is not reproduced here.

The Royal Geographical Society published three reports of the third expedition consecutively in Volume 10 of its *Journal*. In total they occupy 108 pages of the *Journal*, but even these represent barely half the length of the original manuscript.

The first of these articles, entitled: 'Report of the Third Expedition into the Interior of Guayana, comprising the Journey to the Sources of the Essequibo, to the Carumá Mountains, and to Fort San Joaquim, on the Rio Branco, in 1837–8'[1] is constituted from parts a–d of the manuscript. Part (a), which lacks a title, covers the period from 12 September 1837 when the third expedition left Georgetown to the 18 November when it was encamped at the Wapishiana village of Watu Ticaba. This report is rather thin, it consists of a mere twelve pages, and bears only passing resemblance to the published version which contains far more material and detail. We must assume that the additional detail was obtained from Schomburgk's lost journal, discussed in the Introduction (see above, p. 27).

TO THE SOURCES OF THE ESSEQUIBO

I had scarcely recovered from an attack of the yellow fever, which dangerous disease after an interval of fifteen years, had shown itself again in Georgetown and committed ravages, when I made every preparation for leaving the Colony – on my third Expedition; the object of which was to ascend, if possible the river Essequibo to its source, and to connect my researches with those of the celebrated Humboldt, at Esmeralda on the upper Orinoco. The necessary preparations were concluded and Mr Vieth who accompanied me already as assistant naturalist and whose services I found so valuable on my former journey, had been re-engaged for this Expedition. Mr Morrison a native from Glasgow was engaged as Draughtsman; and to M^r Le Breton was entrusted our Commissariat.[2]

---

[1] *JRGS*, 10, 1841, pp. 159–90.

[2] Little is known about John Morrison. He received little recognition from Schomburgk and for the *Twelve Views in the Interior of Guiana*, London, Ackermann & Co., 1841. Schomburgk got Charles Bentley to rework Morrison's original sketches. No information has been found on Le Breton.

We left Georgetown on the Sept 12th.[1] My kind friend Mr Arrindell[2] had left orders that his Schooner should convey us to Post Ampa from whence we intended to continue our tour by Corials. Several of my faithful Warraw Indians had joined me again from the Corentyn, and I had engaged others from the river Wai-inee[3] to accompany me; nevertheless their number was not sufficient to navigate our Corials and in the hope of procuring the complement of our Crew, I was detained several days at Post Ampa. I was however fortunate to engage Hermanus van Peterson as Coxswain who accompanied me during the first Expedition up the river Essequibo and Rupununy, and with whose Character I was well acquainted.

I can not praise enough the valuable assistance of Mr. Crichton[4] then post holder at Ampa and his unremitted attention during that period. We started from the Post on the 21st Septr and had past the first series of Falls on the 25th when the first mishap occurred; one of the Corials was upset in almost smooth water by the inattention of the steersman and its inmates eleven in number among them several small children, were put in the greatest jeopardy of life, we were however fortunate to save them all but her whole cargo was lost – we were yet deploring the loss suffered by this accident when on the 27th Septr an equal lot befel the corial which contained the provision and articles for Barter with the Indians – the articles which were saved had so much suffered by the water, that they were of little use and we had now to depend in a great measure upon Providence for our Sustenance. The attempt which we made to procure a supply of Cassada bread, at the settlements at Waraputa failed. There was scarcity prevailing among the Indians, and we had as our only resource the little rice which had been saved from a watery grave.

I do not repeat the description of the road we passed over, as this has been done already in the report of the first Expedition, inserted in the journal of the Royal Geographical society Vol. [blank][5]. The inland rivers are monotonous in their environs and it are only the mountains which gives Character to the Landscape[;] however I cannot pass without mentioning a short excursion which I undertook to see those granitic piles which have given to the Commuti and Taquiari chain of mountains their name. I was there suffering under a severe rheumatic attack but the desire to see the remarkable objects in the vicinity made me entirely forget my laments, and up I scrambled the mountains using for that purpose more the hands than the feet. I was rewarded with a splendid prospect over the valley of the Essequibo, which river meandered in branches at my feet through the woodland, sometimes smooth at other times foaming, where a rocky dyke contested its further progress towards the vast ocean. The mountains of Maccari and Makarapan

---

[1] An unidentified hand has included here '1838'. The year is 1837.

[2] This is probably William Arrindell, later Sir William. He was a barrister in Georgetown and became the Colony's Chief Justice. He owned the estate of Zeelandia on Wakenaam Island (see Farrar, *History of the Church in Guiana*, pp. 86, 158).

[3] Waini River.

[4] William Crichton later became Superintendent of Rivers and Creeks in the Essequibo and then Inspector General of Police.

[5] Volume 6.

Figure 6: 'Indian "picture writing" at Cumuti, on the Essequibo'. From the *Journal of the Royal Geographical Society*, 10, 1841, p. 160. Included by permission of the Leeds Library.

closed the view. Before me rose those granitic piles to upwards of a height of 150 feet.* [1]

*The ledge on which we stood measured 147 feet; see page [blank].

The Commuti or Taquiare consists of three huge boulders, one poised upon the other, and has been resembled to a waterjar, as the Indian name denotes. The two other Masses are not less remarkable, and the question passes itself involuntarily upon the mind, how they have been heaped one upon the other. Was it in consequence of a convulsion of nature, or has the Earth been washed away? I returned in the Evening highly delighted with my excursion to our Camp and we continued our journey the

[1] In the published version (p. 159), the passage here reads '[I] found the height of these masses of granite by measurement to be 160 feet, thus fully confirming my estimate of them on my first ascent of the Essequibo, which had been doubted.*' See also p. 404.

The accompanying footnote reads:

'*Journal, vol.vi p. 231., Editor's note.' This note reads '*Dr. Hancock ascended these hills, whose sides are covered with red argillaceous earth and ochres. The boulders consist of three huge blocks of blue granite; the second seated upon the lower one by only three points of support; and a third, rather smaller, poised or inclined to the eastward. "I measured their height", says Dr. Hancock, "and sketched this curious natural monument with the red stone of the place, having lost my pencil. The height of the column is not so great as it appears from the river; it measured only fifty feet, and is nearly perpendicular. Both the top and sides are covered with luxuriant vegetation; trees of malpighia; the great kofa, or scandent clusia; the boroway; barta-bally, and other species of sapota were noticed, and a multitude of the humbler plants; of arums; alpinias; several species of smilax (sarsaparilla); and the wild plantain, one of which grew on the upper edge of this pile of granite, and in its form, and size of the leaves, appeared very like the cultivated plant, the banana, or Musa paradisiaca.

'I spent the whole of Christmas Day with four Indians upon the hills, and could have remained a week with great pleasure. I saw several gullies and cavities on the slope of the hills, and observed some pebbles of red jasper, and those hard crystals known under the name of marawoony diamonds."'

This granitic column is alluded to by Mr Waterton in his attractive, yet faithful 'Wanderings' as the 'Giant of the Hills'.

following day.[1] We reached the Rupununy on the 16th Oct.; by this time more than half of the Crew were on the sick list, and our advance might be resembled to the progress of a snail. For some days past fever had broken out among them, which spread rapidly. I formed a camp at the mouth of the Rewa or Roiwa a tributary to the Rupununy and pushed on day and night to the settlement at Annai where I succeeded to procure a supply of cassada bread. On my return we commenced the ascent of the Roiwa, entered its tributary the Guidaru or Quitaro[2] in Lat 3°18′N. and rested for a couple of days at the Caribbee settlement Poukassanti[3] (Lat 3° 4′N) in order to recruit.

In the huts of the Indians I saw several baskets with Juva or Brazil nuts. The tree which produces them is of high interest to Botanists, its flowers being unknown. After a few hours walk through forests and swamps we reached the spot where they grew in great numbers. It is a beautiful tree and rises straight as an arrow to a height of 60 to 80 feet before it gives out in branches; the bark is rugged and resembles much that of our Oak the leaves dark green and smooth but helas! the trees had just been bearing and there were no flowers, however I procured some of the nuts.[4]

When in this vicinity in 1835–6 I had been told frequently of an immense pile of rocks called Ataraipu[5] or Devils rock by the Indians. The reports I had heard of it were so contradictory that I was glad I had now the opportunity of seeing it myself[;] on our further ascent of the Guidaru we passed it within a few hours walk, and headed by some Indians with cutlasses we pathed ourselves a way towards it. When we emerged from the wood a mountain formed of granite was before us – rising to a height of about 900 feet at an angle of 45° degrees. Here and there a few patches of Parasitic plants which got their scanty nourishment from the vegetable soil accumulated in the crevices of the rocks relieved the dreary grey of the granit. We scrambled up as well as we could and reaching a spot where the view opened to the West, a pyramid, not formed by the labours of man but one of nature's phenomena rose from the bosom of the wood, surpassing in height any of Egypts famous monuments, the base was thickly wooded for about 350 feet high but the rocks rose unencumbered for about 550 feet more, making its whole height 900 feet above the plain. The sun then near the Western horizon it appeared, had singled out that remarkable mass, to throw his parting rays on the solid figure while the other objects were thrown in shade; really it appeared there

> 'like giants stand,
> To sentinel enchanted land.'[6]

---

[1] In the published version, there are at this point (pp. 159–60) two paragraphs on 'picture writing' and a sketch of an example seen at Cumuti, which is reproduced here (see Fig. 6). It is not clear whence it comes as the original has not been found among any of Schomburgk's papers. It is clear that the passage in question was added after the end of the third expedition since it refers to other pictographs found later during the expedition of which Schomburgk had also made sketches.

[2] Kwitaro River.

[3] Pukasanta.

[4] The Brazil nut tree is *Bertholletia excelsa*. The name Juva is almost certainly taken from Humboldt (*Personal Narrative*, II, pp. 390–91).

[5] On the reference map it is called Kalishadaker Mountain.

[6] Walter Scott, 'Lady of the Lake', 1, 14, ll. 268–9. In the published version (p. 165), the editor has erroneously changed it to 'like a giant stands / to sentinel enchanted lands', but in the *Twelve Views* it is correctly cited again. Burnett (*Masters of All They Surveyed*, pp. 136–7), who seems to have overlooked the manuscript, makes much of the fact that Schomburgk got the quotation wrong in the *Journal*.

Figure 7: 'The Mountains of Ataraïpu, in Guayana'. From the *Journal of the Royal Geographical Society*, 10, 1841, p. 163. Included by permission of the Leeds Library.

Mountains surrounded the Ataraipu like an Amphitheatre, in the distance I observed the blueish outlines of the Sierra Conocou, the peaked tops of the Saeraeri and to the South the undulating Carawaimi Mountains the former had been the field of my investigation at a former time, towards the latter my steps were now to be directed. It was dark before we returned to the Camp. The Latitude of Ataraipu is 2°55′N.*

*In former maps it had been laid down according to Dr Hancock's map of these regions;

from 3 meridian Altitudes of Stars, of North & South Declinations, I have deduced the above result which is about 22 miles further south than the situation Dr Hancock assigned to it.

The further we advanced the following days the more difficulties were thrown in our way. The river became quite shallow and forced its way through beds of rocks which in the morning of the 10th Nov[r] prevented all further progress in Corials. We encamped for a few days on the left bank of the Guidaru as it was my plan to continue now my journey over land and to send the Corials to the Rupununy from where the people from the Essequibo were to return to the Coast.

We left the Camp on the Guidaru on the morning of the 16th, our path led through forest and we had to cross several brooks which flow in a North Eastern direction towards the Guidaru. In the afternoon we entered Savannahs, in the commencement interspersed with brushwood, but the further we advanced the more open they became. The Savannahs consisted of undulating ground but towards the latter end of our day's march, they were crossed by those bare granitic hills which I have already described. At 5 oclock in the afternoon we reached the Camp of our advanced party. It was situated near a spring, the first water which we had seen since we had left the woods. From the hillocks which rose about 200 feet above the Savannahs we had a splendid view – the Cannucu[1] mountains enveloped in a blueish vapour and high among them that strange object, the Ataraipu were the distinguishing features. To the South the Savannahs, their monotonous prospect relieved by hillocks and natural avenues of Eta Palms.

The sky was overcast, and the chief object why I mounted the hill, namely to take observations were frustrated. I got a few angles at the suns (doubtful) setting of the most remarkable objects.[2] I staid next morning until 7 Oclock but with no better success.

Nov 17th. We started after 7 Oclock, the dew had been very heavy during the night, and made the walking through the long grass of the Savannahs uncomfortable. We passed at 8[h].20 an abandoned place, Ataraipu bore NNE, it towered high above the forest, and as its wooded base being entirely hid, the bare granit looked the more strange (In my former letter I have made a mistatement – the granitic column is at least 550 feet high, the wooded base 350, making a total of 900 feet.)[3] It became frequently very painful to walk over Savannahs in consequence of tracts of angular pieces of quartz which crossed the Savannahs. These tracts were generally about 150 to 200 yards in width, and the quartz so regularly deposited, as if they had been laid piece by piece by human hands for the purpose of paving. I observed them likewise in 1835 when crossing the Savannahs their direction was WbN. shortly after we reached huge tracts of boulders of the same direction, their sharp sides were all turned E & W. These boulders were frequently of such a length that in the distance they had the appearance of fortifications, at other times they were heaped upon each other. Near one of those strange boulders, of which the form was very singular the late Chieftain Mahanarva had his residence; it was called Sei-ai. No vestiges of the place were now to be discovered. We met at two oclock two Wapisanas who had been sent by our advanced party to show us

---

[1] Kanuku Mountains.

[2] There is no doubt that this is the correct reading, but it is not clear whether the 'objects' are celestial or terrestrial features on which he wanted to take bearings.

[3] The contents of the brackets have been scored out on the manuscript. The correspondence referred to is RGS Corres 1834–40, Letter of Schomburgk to Washington, 13 November 1837.

the way, which became rather intricate. A fine spring of water which we then met was too inviting to be passed over without resting. We followed our guides partly through woods, partly through Savannahs but at 4 Oclock no vestage of our carriers were to be discovered, they were far behind us. I left therefore M[r] Morison to collect them and to encamp for the night while I continued my march, and reached half past five sadly tired the settlement of Wapisianas which consisted of six round huts and about 60 Souls.[1] The Captain was absent, he was one of those whom I had met while in Annai and from whom I had bought a dog. All who had feet to walk were assembled, round the strangers hut, we were greeted in their particular mode and the bowl of welcome, a huge gourd full of Paiworri was handed. We met several strange Indians here, who like us were travelling in different directions, namely a family from the Rio Branco[,] an other from the Conocou Mountains.

We were for a length of time the objects of their curiosity every thing was examined and the crowd round the Strangers house continued until dark.

Nov[r] 18th The fatigued crew arrived one by one to day their burden had been too much, unaccustomed as they were for carrying burdens, upon a slight calculation we had made about 55 miles during the preceeding two days, a great distance after having been for two months cooped up in Corials. The Indians are allowed to rest to day, and return to the Guidaru tomorrow.

****

Part (a) of the manuscript ends at this point (p. 12) and the second part, marked (b), continues using the same pagination, and consists of eighteen pages, numbered 13–30. It is composed of a letter written on 20 February 1838 from Curassawaka on the Rupununi River and addressed to Captain John Washington, Secretary of the Royal Geographical Society. It was received on 5 June 1838 and read at a meeting of the Society on 25 June. It is in Schomburgk's own handwriting, is remarkably clean and almost free of editorial over-writing. It covers the period from 24 November 1837 until 20 February 1838. At the beginning and end of the letter Schomburgk refers to his journal, and the fact that he has not had time to write it up, and is sending the letter instead. The letter is more detailed than Part (a) and is clearly the basis for the next part of the published account.

Currassawaka
lower Rupununy
Febr[y] 20th 1838

My dear Sir
It is with particular pleasure that I take the pen to inform you of my success with regard to the first object of the present Expedition; the Essequibo has been traced to its sources, and the Sierra Acaray has been followed from the Ouangouwai,*

*The sound of the vowels in father, there, ravine, mole, lunar have been adopted, to which has been added the diphthong au pronounced like ou in house.

[1] This was the village of Watu Ticaba.

or Mountain of the Sun,[1] to twelve miles South of the Equator in a southern direction, and to the Sources of the Essequibo in a south-western direction. I have only to regret that after my return to headquarters, so short a time is left to me that it falls out of question to arrange my Journal, while on the other hand, I should not wish to lose the present opportunity without giving you a summary Account of our proceedings since I had the pleasure to write you last from Watou Ticaba on the 18th November.[2]

Our departure was delayed until the 24th Novbr; it was only with great difficulty, and under high promises, that I could induce a Wapisiana Captain or Taroneni, to guide us to the Woyawais;[3] (not Woih Woyas as written in my former letter) we procured likewise three carriers for our baggage and provisions, and thus our party was increased to nine Individuals, my Assistant Draughtsman and my Coxswain included. We started from the Taroneni's place on the 25th Novbr and followed the Chain of Mountains which were connected with the Carawaimi in an eastern direction; the highest peak of the latter mountains was our guide. We crossed in the afternoon of the same day, the boundary between Woods and Savannahs. Our path was almost untrodden and frequently barricaded by fallen trees; indeed its tract was only observable to an Indian eye or one accustomed to travel in these regions; the path led us over the highest peak of the Carawaimi, the height of which I estimated 2500 feet above the Savannahs, its Latitude by account 2°21′N. and 14.7 miles East of Watou Ticaba. We descended and camped that night at the foot of the mountains near the River Quitaro or Guidaru; here only a mountain stream, it has its sources in an offset of the Carawaimi mountains. We entered at an early hour next day an Indian Settlement, inhabited by Atorais or Atoroyas. They are of a fairer hue than the Wapisianas, but not so muscular, nor so regular in features. Surrounded by woods, and bounded to the S.E. by extensive Swamps, it was no wonder that they suffered much from intermitting fever, and my small stock of medecin was set in requisition. The position of this Settlement is 2°24′4″N., and about 24.4 miles East of Watou Ticaba. Our road led next morning through the Swamps already mentioned, and as it rained mostly during the two following days, we found our journey very fatiguing. The woods abounded in Lecythideae, and among these were numerous trees of the Bertholletia excelsa. The small brooks which we crossed had all a northern direction, and are tributaries to the Guidaru. Towards Evening of the succeeding day we met a brook flowing south-eastward, and soon afterwards we entered the first Taruma Settlement. As already stated, our march during the previous two days had led us through dense Woods and Swamps, the latter abounded in Manico Palms;[4] the ground was sometimes undulating; chiefly after we had passed a Swamp. I observed in these regions, several tracts of brown Iron Ore. The Taruma Settlement was situated in the woods, and according to my observations its Lat. was 2°6′0″N. and 49.2 miles East of Watou Ticaba. The number of its inhabitants amounted to sixty two, of which two third were women and girls. At the distance of Seven miles, in a south eastern direction, flows the River Cuyuwini,[5] a tributary to the

---

[1] On the map that accompanied the published version, it is spelt Wanguwai and is located on the east bank of the Essequibo, downstream from a west bank tributary called 'Wanguwai or Camoa', the present Kamoa.
[2] RGS Corres 1834–40, Letter of Schomburgk to Washington, 18 November 1837.
[3] Waiwai Indians.
[4] Presumably Manicole (*Euterpe oleracea*).
[5] Kuyuwini River.

Essequibo. We were told that we had to descend that river for three days and a half before we met its junction with the Essequibo. Our arrangements were completed on the 4th Decbr and we proceeded through woods to its banks. At the sight of the Crafts which were to carry us for weeks, I asked myself, whether it would be prudent to enter them. The one which I was to occupy, afforded only place to myself, two paddlers and my Coxswain; it was worm eaten, and crank, and when we entered it, our weight sunk it to the Gunwales; it was only 2½ feet wide and 9 inches deep, and though I am small of stature, I had to adopt the Indian fashion of squatting; it did not afford me room for sitting – the others were placed two and two in Pakasses or Woodskins. No other Crafts were to be had, and we trusted to Providence, that we might safely pass the Cataracts in our way.

Where we entered our boats, the Cuyuwini was 150 feet wide, its water of a dirty yellow, and the Current so insignificant that it did not carry the Current log more than half a knot. (At our return in January, when it was swollen from heavy rains, we found the Current two knots). The Tarumas call it Cuyuni, merely an abbreviation of Cuyuwini; Cuyu is the name of the white headed Maroudi, (Penelope Pipile)[1] which once must have been very frequent here, and wuini is water or river. The Tarumas told me that it had its sources near those of the Rupununy or Oupunury, in mountains which connect with the Carawaimi on one side, are likely an offset of the Acaray Mountains; if now my Guide has informed me rightly, the sources of the Rupununy are according to my Calculations in Lat. 1°46'N., and are inhabited, as I am told, by the Takail tribe.[2] The basin of the Rupununy extends therefore from 1°46'N. Lat. to 4°N. Lat., and is bounded to the East by the Carawaimi and its offsets and to the West by the Sierras Conocou and Pacaraima; its meridian length is of little extend, its furthest Eastern Point being about 58°W. the most western 59°W., its chief tributary is the Roiwa.

After this digression, I return to the Cuyuwini; in our descent we found it obstructed by numerous boulders; in two situations I found Indian picture writing; when I asked the Tarumas who had done it, they told me that women had made them long, long time ago.[3] The Cuyuwini meandres E.N.E. I observed in no instance hillocks either on its right or left bank, until we came near its mouth, where some hillocks of about 150 feet height rose on the left side, but these belonged properly to the Essequibo. We entered the Essequibo on Decbr 8th in Lat 2°16'N. and 94.9 miles East of Watou Ticaba. Fifty one days had elapsed since we deviated from its course at the mouth of the Rupununy and our direct distance from that point was only 70 miles; nevertheless it was fortunate that circumstances obliged me to relinquish my former plan of ascending via Willm IVth's Cataract; the unfortunate descent of Mahanarva from the Cuyuwini down the Essequibo to the Rupununy is still lively in the recollection of the Tarumas and Atorais. I met an old Atorai, who said, he belonged to the party, and from him I have the following account. "A few days' journey north of the Cuyuwini, the rapids and Cataracts commenced and followed so closely upon each other, and were of such a nature, that three months elapsed before they reached the Rupununy. During that time, they suffered every kind of deprivation, as the whole tract was uninhabited; and had the

---

[1] White-headed Piping-Guan (*Pipile cumanensis*).

[2] This Amerindian group has not been identified.

[3] It seems quite likely that it was here that Schomburgk made the model of a young woman and then sacrificed it to the spirits in order to overcome native beliefs (see p. 37, fn. 1 above).

misfortune to lose a Corial in the falls, and every soul in it perished, besides others, who were lost in descending the Cataracts." How much of this tale belongs to exaggeration, I know not, enough no person has since attempted the descent, and the road which we came, is always selected. If only a part of it be true, the difficulties of the ascent, would have by far surpassed those of the descent, and after having toiled perhaps for weeks, we would have been obliged to return without success; while by chosing the other road, I saw my little bark now floating on the Essequibo, and had every hope to surmount the other difficulties.

The Cuyuwini is at its mouth (actually measured) 280 feet wide, the Essequibo where it receives the former river 533 feet; the average depth of the Essequibo was found to be along its breadth 22 feet, that of the Cuyuwini 16 feet. The water of the Essequibo was of a dark Colour, its Current (in December). 7 knots; its banks are wooded, but by no means with the luxuriance which is so striking in that river in the 5th parallel; hills from about 4 to 500 feet high, approach the river occasionally from both sides, and force it in some instances to adopt quite a retrograde course. It is studded with boulders, some of fantastical shape, to which the Indians have attached superstitious traditions. These boulders are equal in size to those of the lower Essequibo (North of the Rupununy), but they are more oblong, and their shape, and the manner in which they are grouped, are not uninteresting.

We passed Decbr 9th the brook Kuitiva, its general course being N.E. its last reach where it joins the Essequibo is north-west, and its upper banks are inhabited by Tarumas, who have communication by land with the Settlements at the Cuyuwini, and Youawauri.[1] We reached towards evening the first Settlement of Tarumas in the Essequibo; it was on the river's right bank, and consisted of thirty souls, men women and children; here were also the females prevailing, and were as three to five. I fixed its Latitude in 2°2'22"N. We had to ascend a rapid next morning, in the vicinity of which there were some figures cut in the rocks, they were however nearly effaced; the Rapid was called Boubamanna;[2] above it, the river, which had been very variable in its widths, adopts a breadth of 650 feet; it is much extended by boulders. At 11 o'clock, a chain of mountains bore S.43°E.; we had then only an imperfect view, but two hours after, we saw the range more distinct; the highest peak bore then S.35°E.; I estimated its height 3000 feet, and it is called by the Tarumas Ouangouwai, that is Mountain of the Sun; the mountains further west, which are rounded in their outline, are called Amucu, and I was informed by the Indians, that one of the chief branches of the Corentyne, the River Pani, has its sources there[3] – according to corresponding observations, N. & S. of

---

[1] Kassikaityu River.

[2] Bubamana Falls.

[3] Amuku Mountains. The Pani is almost certainly the New River which has its source in the Amuku Mountains. The New River is the largest tributary of the Corentyne, and sufficiently large for Surinam to claim that it is the mainstream. Schomburgk failed to note the mouth of the New River on his descent of the Corentyne in 1843, and it was left to Barrington Brown to report its existence in October 1871. It has been argued that Schomburgk deliberately did not report the existence of the New River so that the Guyana/Surinam frontier which follows the mainstream of the Corentyne was located much further east. However, it would have been very easy for Schomburgk to have missed its mouth as the river is dotted with islands at this point and C. Barrington Brown only found it because he was following the Corentyne's most westerly channels (*Canoe and Camp Life in British Guiana*, London, Edward Stanford, pp. 328–9). The large triangle of land between the Corentyne and the New River is currently disputed territory.

Ouangouwai, its Latitude is 1°41'30"N. The Amucu Mountains are of less height – the signification of the word, I could not learn. The detached hillocks which we had traced in our ascent, are the connecting links between the Ouangouwai and the mountains of the Essequibo, while the mountains Kaia-wacko, Macourua, Pakuke,[1] connect that offset closer with the Sierra Acaray. Our Latitude was that evening 1°55'24"N. We had to pass several rapids and Cataracts next day which were caused by small detached hillocks, mostly of a N.N.W. & S.S.E. direction. We reached the junction of the River Youawauri with the Essequibo an hour before noon (Decbr 11th). Where it joins the Essequibo it comes from the W.N.W. but its general course is W.S.W., and has its sources according to Indian information, in high mountains a day's journey (15 miles in a direct line) from those of the Cuyuwini; the Cuyuwini has however yellowish water, while that of the Youawauri is of a dark colour. It is somewhat smaller than the Cuyuwini. The Tarumas call it Cassi Kityou,[2] 'River of the Dead'; the tradition is, that it was formerly thickly inhabited, but having offended the evil Spirits, they all died in a short time; there is at present only one Settlement in that river. A little beyond the junction of the Youawauri, the brook Capidiri joins the Essequibo. I have deduced the Latitiude of the Youawauri from observations N. & S. of it. The Essequibo is much lighter of colour before it is joined by the former river; and is much reduced in width; it amounts some times to only 220 feet.

We arrived in the afternoon at two Taruma Settlements, one on the right the other on the left bank of the river Essequibo; we had here to replenish our provisions, as the small size of our boats did not allow us to provide for more than from 4 to 5 days. We were very friendly received, and they gladly entered in barter for knives, Salempores, Calicos, combs &c giving us Cassada bread, Plantains and Yams in return. At this period great sickness prevailed among our small party, the cause of the exposure, now to a pelting rain, and then to a burning Sun of 110° to 115° F., where the size of our Corials did not allow us to erect any protection, and having been under the necessity to limit our clothes to only one spare suit, we could not manage it to exchange always our wet clothes with dry ones. We were therefore obliged to stay two days longer than I intended; they were unprofitable days, as it rained almost constantly, every astronomical observation was put out of question. The more I approached the mountains, the more precarious became the opportunities for observations; indeed on the 15th Decbr. commenced the setting in of the rainy Season and from thence to our return to the Carawaimi mountains, we had every day more or less rain. During that period, dry weather had prevailed at the Savannahs.

The Tarumas who had never seen white men or Parannaghiri*

*The word is common among all Indians tribes.

(Paranna 'the Sea or Ocean' ghiri people) were much astonished at the implements of our Cookery; the forks underwent particularly their scrutinizing looks, and they laughed loud out, when I showed them their use. My compass amused them much, and when I made them understand, that by it, I could at any time, and at any place, find out

---

[1] Kaia-wacko is presumably Kaiawaka Mountain as it is called on Schomburgk's map and on the reference map. Macourua cannot be identified and does not appear on Schomburgk's map. There is a fall called Pakaku on the reference map in the same vicinity as the Pakuku Mountain is located on Schomburgk's map.
[2] Kassikaityu River.

where the Sun rises or sets, they considered it very wonderful. As the Indian divides his time, and calculates his distances by the Course of the Sun, the point of its rising is always of great interest to them. They have names for the four Cardinal points; the Taruma calls the Chief-point, which with them is

East	Natjiki
West	Nataki
North	Nanjiki
South	Nantaki

They call the Essequibo or Sipou (by the latter name of which, it is generally known to the Indians of the Savannahs and the Caribes) Koatjang Kityou (Kityou is river and Koatjang the Coati (Naswa).[1]

We left the Tarumas on the 12th Decbr, and continued the ascent of the Essequibo, and passed in the course of the day the mountains Macouroua and Pakouka; both from 1000 to 1100 feet high, and on the river's right bank. The Essequibo meandred between small and detached hillocks, which skirted its banks and narrowed it often to 50 feet. We passed on the 14th the small river Camoa or Ouangou (River of the Sun) which joins the Essequibo from the N.W.;[2] it is at its mouth about 80 feet wide. The large brook Wapouau[3] joins the Essequibo from the South-east, it has dark water; we passed it in the morning of the 17th Decbr,[4] and discovered in the afternoon some high mountains (Pirítikou)[5] which bore then S.24E and showed themselves under an angle of 2°37'; their distance was estimated 25 miles. We entered at two o'clock the small river Caner-ouau, which joins the Essequibo from the south-east.[6] We had fully ascertained that the Essequibo south of its junction with the Canerouau, is uninhabited; it was therefore my aim to gather information, and to replenish our provisions at the first settlement which we could reach. We had to march next day about 16 miles through swampy ground, and waded the Canerouau several times, which river divided itself in numerous branches. We ascended a hill, and entered shortly afterwards a settlement, inhabited by Woyawais. A sufficient number of Forest-trees had been cleared away, to allow an open view from the N.W. to the S. and I had now for the first time a view of the chief range of the Sierra Acaray; the Atmosphere was not clear, and the higher mountains were wrapt in clouds, but towards Sunset the moment was more favorable, and mounting with a Taruma Indian, who was acquainted with the different names of the mountains, a high stump of a tree, I indulged in the prolonged view of the picturesque mountain Scenery. As far as the eye could reach mountain rose behind mountain, some rounded in their outlines, but the most were peaked; all densely covered with wood. Their ridges are sharp, and the valleys are mostly longitudinal, namely S.W. & N.E. It is naturally to be expected that I saw only part of the Chain, and that part by no means extensive, but it

---

[1] The coati is a raccoon-like animal of the genus *Nasua*.

[2] An unidentified hand has written in the margin 'S.W.?', which seems the more probable direction.

[3] Wapuau River.

[4] There is some doubt about this date. Someone has written in the margin '16th?', whereas the published version (p. 169) has 15th.

[5] Presumably part of the Acarai Mountains.

[6] The Canerouau is not marked on the reference map but it is probably the stream that joins the Essequibo at the point where the latter river turns from flowing east to north. The eastward-flowing stretch of the river is called Sipu on the reference map, the Amerindian name for the Essequibo. This all fits with Schomburgk's map.

was distinguished by some high mountains, chiefly to the West, and the Indians informed me that Kaia-wacko was the highest in their neighbourhood; when I asked in which direction it were they pointed to the North (N.28°E) and gave me to understand, that it were a two days' journey distant. I estimated the height of those which I saw 3 to 4000 feet. We continued our march to the Southward, partly from the wish to see more of the Sierra Acaray, partly to cross that imaginary line, the Equator. We followed for some time the valley of the Canerouau, it turned however to the South-east, and fell consequently out of observation; the highest mountain then in view was Piritikou, it bore in the Evening N.70E. by Compass; its height was estimated 3000 feet. Piritikou forms a sharp ridge, ending to the eastward by a peaked mountain; I might compare the ridge to a gigantic wall; it was however plainly to be seen, that not withstanding its abrupt nature, it was thickly wooded. I considered the distance 25 miles from my station.

We arrived next day (Decbr 18th) at the line of separation of waters between the basins of the Essequibo and the gigantic Amazon, the river Assimari flows southward; this is according to my surmise the Ijatapu of Charts;[1] the Indians say that it flows in the Parasimomi, a very large river which flows from Southwest in a half circle in the Paranna or Ocean; there is no doubt that they designate the Amazon by that name. Where we saw the Assimari for the first time, it was as large as the Essequibo, where it is joined by the Canerouau, namely about 120 feet wide, and according to the Woyawais who inhabit it, it has its sources in the mountain Yiniko. Our Latitude was the preceeding night 0°53′15″ from which must be subtracted our progress South, we observed it therefore first in 0°46′N. Lat.

The Valleys which we crossed hitherto, have been of considerable extent; their direction run frequently with the range of mountains E.N.E. & W.S.W., however there are exceptions to it, as our course led us through several which were due S. The Indians have avoided as much as possible, to lead their path over the mountains, and have chosen one of the transverse valleys, though it caused a detour; where they found it impracticable, and necessity led to the ascent, the mountains were so well wooded that they never afforded an open prospect. The rocks which we have met with, were granite quartz, Diallage, Clinkstone and Greenstone[2] as well as others of the Trappean rocks; the latter are found on the highest peaks and in Fragments at the foot of mountains, in the bed of brooks &c. I must however confess that very little opportunity was afforded to me to study the Geological character of the parts which we passed – constant rains made every progress desirable.

We entered late in the evening of the 19th December a Barokoto Settlement;[3] the three or four Indian villages, which we had met in our path had been inhabited by Woyawais. The Barokoto resembles more the Wapisiana than the Woyawai, at least those which I had opportunity to see; they are stout and well made, their forehead high and the features are otherwise regular; the nose is slightly arched; the latter feature is

---

[1] Rio Jatapu.

[2] Diallage, 'a grass-green variety of pyroxene, of lamellar or foliated structure' (*SOED*). Clinkstone, 'a compact greyish-blue felspathic rock' (*SOED*). Greenstone, 'a wide term, usually comprising the greenish coloured eruptive rocks containing feldspar and hornblende (or augite)' (*SOED*).

[3] A relatively small Carib-speaking group who have now disappeared as a separate entity, having been absorbed into the Waiwai during the 20th century.

equally common among the Tarumas. They paint with Chica or Carivaerou, (the faecula of Bignonia Chica)[1] and a large patch of that stuff is put at the division of the front and hair; it is frequently ornamented with the down of the Eagle (Harpyia Spec?)[2] which inhabits the mountains. Their heads were adorned with Feather caps, made from the feathers at the breast and abdomen of the Eagle, intermixed with those from the pendant crest of the Egret, the inner ring is formed of Macaw and Parrot feathers. Their bows were upwards of six and a half feet high; I saw likewise some spears. My stay among them amounting to only a few hours, and the number of inhabitants at the Settlement amounting to thirty or fourty, I had naturally no opportunity to observe their manners closer. The night was favorable for observations, and I procured five Meridian Altitudes of Stars, according to which the Settlement was 0°12′9″S., we had passed the Equator about noontide.[3]

I had now realized my object; it was unfortunately too late to extend my journey to the East or West, the rainy season, which had set in, and which had caused the rivers and brooks to swell, made our tour to the present point one of the greatest toils, fatigues and even danger. I returned without delay, (regretting that my intentions of starting in August from Demerara had been prevented) and at our arrival at the Canerouau, we entered our boats, in order to trace the Essequibo to its Sources. However it remains me to state the information, which I was able to procure from the natives, about the Country which they inhabit. The river Dara, which flows in the Parasimoni has its sources about 15 miles E. from the Settlement, it is inhabited by Barocotos. The mountain Camouaa is the highest in that direction; the land becomes South of that mountain soon level. The mountains continue W.S.W., and when I asked, how far they extended in that direction, it was given me to understand, by showing me their fingers and toes, that twenty days were not sufficient to bring me there, indeed they did not know where it ended.[4] Their next neighbours to the North are the Woyawais, to the East a tribe of Maopityans, to the South their own tribe, which according to their account is the most numerous, and to the West the Harakoutjabo, a savage tribe, which they told me, would not allow any stranger to cross their boundary.[5]

---

[1] *Arrabideae chica.*

[2] The Harpy eagle (*Harpia harpyja*). Its down and feathers are frequently used as ornaments by Native Amazonians.

[3] This sentence has been underlined by some one other than Schomburgk and is almost certainly the subject of a marginal comment, probably by Washington, on the previous page (p. 21). It reads: 'Read attentively – more than suspicion rests upon these latitudes. The route from those he obs[d] on the 20th is circuitous, woody, & the course difficult – yet in one day (21st) he gives a space of 65 geog. miles direct distance – ab[t] 80 five miles by route!!!'.' These suspicions are very well grounded and it is unlikely that Schomburgk was as far south as he claimed. The current boundary between Brazil and Guyana follows the watershed between the rivers that flow north and south (i.e., into the Essequibo and Amazon river systems respectively). The whole length of the boundary lies north of 1° North latitude. It is not clear what went wrong with Schomburgk's survey at this point, but clearly something did. His actual location in the headwaters of the Jatapu was probably nearer to 1° North latitude than the Equator. Despite the doubts expressed, Schomburgk's claim to have crossed the Equator appeared in the published version (p. 170).

[4] It is not possible to identify any of these geographical features. A sarcastic marginal note at this point reads '20 days travelling at the rate which M[r] S. had on the 21st would nearly reach the Pacific'.

[5] The Maopityans, Mapidians or Mawayena, commonly referred to as the Frog People, are an Arawak-speaking people. The few remaining Mawayana Indians are to be found today living either among the Waiwai or the Trio. It has not been possible to identify the Harakoutjabo.

The filthiness of the Waccawai is proverbial among the Indians, but surely what I have seen of the huts of the Woyawais, surpasses in sluttishness those of the former. The number of inhabitants of that tribe, whom I saw in my journey, amounted to about 150, but a great number live in the upper Assimari, and to judge from their expressions, there can not be less than from three to four hundred Woyawais. The men were from 5f^t to 5f^t 6 inch^s high; they are of a lighter Colour than the Tarumas; indeed in their general appearance they resemble much the Macousis; like that tribe they allow the hair of the head to grow, which hangs round their shoulders. Their persons looked as neglected as their huts; they wore the general Indian dress, a girdle of cotton and a waistcloth consisting of a few ells of Salempores, or one manufactured of cotton by their own hands. The latter is very neat, and ornamented with hangings and fringes – it appears however that they prefer Salempores, and only a few of the former are to be met with. Their face was clumsily painted, frequently the Arnatto or Chica covered half the face, while the other side did not exhibit any painting. I can offer no better picture of the women; they looked equally dirty, and only necessity could induce me to eat any thing, what had been prepared by their hands. The Woyawais are a tribe of Nomads, they hunt in the mountains which surround them; the lesser game with bow and arrow, the Tapir with the Spear. They are famed for raising and training of dogs, and by their sale they procure themselves, through intercourse with the Wapisianas, the few necessities of life, which they do not manufacture themselves, namely Salempores, cutlasses, axes, knives, and for their wives the only article which composes their dress, Glassbeads, of which they work their waistlaps. The men practise polygamy like the other Indian tribes; though I have no reason to think, that the Custom is very general. While among them, I procured a few words in their language; like their appearance, it has some resemblance to the Macousi.[1]

Immediately after our arrival at the Canerouau, we started for the Essequibo. We had not been able to procure any information of its course south of the Canerouau, and I had resolved to follow its windings. Within half a mile from the junction of the Canerouau the Essequibo narrows to a brook, being only 45 feet wide. It meandres through a rich mountain Valley in a S.W. direction (ascending). As its banks are entirely uninhabited, and the river is not visited either by Tarumas or Woyawais, we had to surmount many difficulties, which trees fallen across it, put frequently in our way. Our crafts were however light, and were soon conveyed across them. During the two first days, we found the Current 2.5 knots; the water rushed over a bottom of pebbles and sand, and the average depth was about 3 feet. We found on the third day of our ascent, that we could not make further progress in the boats; they were therefore fastened to some trees, and leaving all our luggage behind, with the exception of the hammocks, we followed the banks of the river by land. Overcoming all difficulties which an exuberant Vegetation, or the jungle of marshy ground, put in our way, we stood in the afternoon of the 27th Decb^r at the Sources of the Essequibo. Our temporary hut was erected, where the rill pathed itself slowly a way over the sandy bottom, beyond it, it ceased to flow, the water was sluggish, and collected itself in small pools. A peculiarity of the rivers which flow through these rich valleys is, that they branch off, and having been separated for the course of a mile or two, they join again. We followed always the main branch, and

---

[1] This is a curiously prejudiced and inaccurate description of the Waiwai which, unfortunately, has been repeated many times over during the following century by other authors who had been nowhere near them.

having previously observed that it narrowed to ten feet, our attention was doubled, to prevent our mistaking a branch, or one of the numerous streamlets, which fell in the Essequibo from the surrounding mountains, for the recipient. Surrounded by high trees, interwoven with Lianas, it proved impossible to procure observations, but deducing it from my last observations and a carefully kept traverse-table, the Sources of the Essequibo are in 0°41'7"N. Lat. and 24 miles West of Watou Ticaba.[1]

We hoisted the British Union, and lashed it firmly to one of the trees which surround the Sources, there to remain until time destroys it, and after we had drunk Her Majesty's health, in a bumper of the pure unadulterated water of the Essequibo (we had nothing else), we returned towards our Corials.

We had but seldom opportunity to see the mountains through which the Essequibo flows; in two of three instances they approached within its banks; but the Character which is peculiar to the river within 20 miles of its embouchure, of being studded with boulders, it possesses already near its sources. The Current is variable, now running swiftly over pebbles, it appears a few hundred yards further sluggish; the water is of a yellowish colour, but perfectly clear in the glass. The additional waters which it receives from the surrounding mountains is astonishing, and its sudden swelling after rains, of only one or two days' duration, is easily explained by this circumstance. We forded sometimes in the course of an hour three or four. I have never seen a mountain chain so densely wooded, as the Sierra Acaray and I did not see a single naked mountain among them. The river is well stocked with fish in the mountainous regions; on our return we caught several Haimoura, from 12 to 16lbs weight, and the splashing at night and after rain, proved that the finny tribe was numerous. I have already mentioned the exuberance of Vegetation in the Valley of the Essequibo; it is rich in timber trees, chiefly of the tribes Laurineae[2] Lecythideae &c. There is certainly a marked difference in the Flora when compared with that of the 4th & 5th parallel. The Mora, Yarura,[3] several Laurineae and Mimosae, among the former Laurus Surinamensis[4] Sw.,[5] which almost lines the banks of rivers in that Latitude, are here entirely wanting; the Psidium aromaticum, Aubl. and its kindred will be likewise missed, and are replaced by an arborescent Myrtus, and a highly odoriferous Eugenia.[6] We were astonished at the scarcity of animals which we met in this sequestered spot – we met with no instance to show that human foot had ever trod here before, the brutes of the forest were therefore not disturbed, either by man or dog, nevertheless if I except the smaller birds & from time to time a single heron, or the Eagle soaring high in the air, one might as well have imagined to cross the sandy deserts of Africa, in lieu of the fertile valley of the Essequibo; even the prattling parrot or the noisy macaw were silent.

---

[1] It is difficult to work out where exactly Schomburgk had reached, as no part of the Essequibo is south of 1 degree north latitude. If he had reached the source of the Essequibo, or Sipu as marked on the reference map, he would have been at approximately 1°20'N, 59°15'W. There is on this page of the manuscript (p. 24) a further sceptical note in the margin concerning the distance that Schomburgk claimed to have covered each day – between the 21 and 27 December, 180 miles in total or 30 miles a day.

[2] Family Lauraceae.

[3] Paddlewood: *Aspidosperma excelsum*; *A. oblongum*.

[4] *Aniba megaphylla*.

[5] Sw. is Olof Peter Swartz (1760–1818), a Swedish botanist.

[6] Both *Myrtus* and *Eugenia* are genera of the Family Myrtaceae.

251

I fear that the fertility of these valleys will be entirely lost to man, we found marks that during the inundations the water reaches a height of 29 feet above its present level, and it was then growing rapidly. After we had once reached the Corials, our return was much accelerated; we were at the 30ᵗʰ Decbr at the Tarumas. The Captain of one of the Settlements, who had been absent, when we first visited them, had returned; he was a very intelligent man, and had travelled much among the mountains: I procured from him a great deal of information about the rivers which have their rise in the Acaray mountains. He drew a large map on the ground, which was remarkable in several respects, and I am consequently induced to send herewith a reduced, but exact Copy of the map which he drew, to which I have added the names of the rivers and tribes, who inhabit them, which I received from him at the same time.[1] It is much to be regretted that every tribe has its own name for rivers, mountains &c and if a Wapisiana were asked for the Koatjang Kitjou (Essequibo), he would be ignorant what was meant by it, while if he had been asked for the Sipou, he would have given the information which he possessed of that river. They have no collective names for a chain of mountains, and the Indian of these regions is as ignorant, where the Sierra Acaray or Pacarayma is situated, as if he were asked in what direction the Alps or Pyrenees are. Every mountain has its own name, if such it deserves either by its size, or any other remarkable circumstance.

The first point deserving notice when contemplating the rough Sketch of the savage Indian, is the knowledge which they possess of the round figure of the earth, surrounded by the Ocean or Paranna, the next is the proper position which has been assigned to the Cardinal points; their designating them by words of their own language, prepared us for such a knowledge. It is not a single circumstance that they have fixed their own country in the centre of the surface of the Earth; that honour has been claimed by several nations, and has caused controversy among Europeans. The Course of the Essequibo needs no comment; this point has been settled by my present journey; it appears however that the Youawauri of the Wapisianas or Cassi Kityou of the Tarumas, takes its rise in an offset of the Acaray Mountains which connect the Carawaimi with the former; west of it and in the same mountains are the Sources of the Uanau or Humble-bee River;[2] its course is west, and there is no doubt that it is the Anauau or Guanahau which joins the Rio Branco in about 0°56′N. Lat. I could not trace the slightest knowledge of the Rio Branco among the Tarumas as they make the Uanau flow into the Ocean. The distance of its sources is six days' journey from the mouth of the Youawauri; allowing therefore a direct progress by water of 12 miles p. diem its assumed Latitude will be 1°25′N. The Assimari Kityou or Haimoura River of the Tarumas, is the next one which attracts our attention; it has its sources at Mount Yiniko in the assumed Lat. of 1°1′N. and after having continued its course for 32 miles to the south, it turns south-westerly; I conceive it to be a tributary or the main branch of the Ijatapu which joins the Amazon in 2°13′S. Lat & 55°30′W. Longt. The Indians say that the Assimari flows into the Parasimoni, by which name they designate the Amazon. South-east of the Barocoto Settlement flows the river Dara; (Calabash river) near its banks rises the mountain Camouau, higher than Yiniko according to their account. The tradition goes that once Portuguese came up by this river, but when they entered the territory of the Barocotos, that tribe murdered every one. I consider the Dara

---

[1] Unfortunately no trace of this map has been found.
[2] Rio Anauá.

to be the river Jamuda.[1] All intercourse with the Amazon, by any of these rivers, is at present broken up, and it appears to me that the existing generation have no Knowledge that there ever was one.

We approach now the East, and in the native map arrests us the river Cassourou, it is [blank] days' journey from the first Woyawai Settlement (1°18′N L.) and according to their account it is inhabited by Negros; this circumstance and its flowing northward directly into the Ocean makes me not doubt that it is the Marowini, though its sources are placed in the maps in 54°34′ Longt and 1°47′N. Lat., however no person ever penetrated so far. It appears the next river, the Kaffou or Apine is the river Surinam; its chief Tributaries are the Pianoghotte or Couparu, (inhabited by Maopitians) and the River Tschae-Tschae. The Basi which flows between the Kaffou and the Corentyne, is likely the Saramacca. The Couritani Kityou or Corentyne divides according to my informant, in two branches, the eastern branch is called Youni, the western Pani by the Tarumas. The latter has it sources in the Amucu mountains. As far as the travels of the Captain had extended to the eastward, the mountains continued; he said however, they lessened in height, and there was none as high as Mt Yiniko (estim. 4000ft).[2]

We reached on the 6th Janr^y the mouth of the Cuyuwini, and on the 10th the landing place of the Tarumas, where with a joyful heart, I bid the Corials adieu; I had been cooped up in mine for many weeks. We recrossed the Carawaimi Mountains under the same unfavorable weather, which had accompanied us since the middle of December, and it was only after we entered the Savannahs (Janr^y 16th) that the weather improved. Fifty three days of toils, fatigues and deprivations had elapsed, since we left the Savannahs. We were obliged to stop at the first Settlement which we met, in consequence of the indisposition of several of the party, and eight days elapsed before we could continue our journey. Our road led us for three days over the Savannahs to the Rupununy, where we hoped to find corials to convey us to our appointed headquarters at Curassawaka. We were however sadly disappointed, there was neither Corial nor Woodskin to be had at the upper Rupununy, and I had no other alternative, but to send for one of my own Corials, though it caused a delay of 15 days. The interval proved most tedious; our blank paper had given out, or I might have occupied myself with arranging my notes, and my wardrobe was in such a state, that I was ashamed to show myself to the Indians; my shoes (the only remaining pair) gave open demonstration that they wanted to part company with their owner, and I was consequently confined to the hut. The corial arrived on the 14th Febr^y and we left next morning, and arrived at Curassawaka on the 20th Febr^y, after an absence of 3 months and 4 days from the rest of the party.

We have returned in a most languid state, but now, as some rest stands before us, and the necessary medecins to assist nature, are in our reach, I hope that the Invalids will soon be restored.

In order to carry a more extensive and detailed investigation of the Sierra Acaray into effect, the traveller should pass the rainy Season at one of the Settlements at the

---

[1] Rio Nhamundá.

[2] In a marginal note the opinion is expressed that it is 'quite impossible' that the Cassourou is the Marowini, the frontier River between Surinam and French Guiana. Rather, it is stated, there is 'scarcely a doubt of … [it] being the Trombetas'. Indeed it is unlikely that any of the identifications that Schomburgk made are correct. For example, Pianoghotto is the name of a group of Amerindians. The Kaffu is probably the Cafuine, which flows east and then south, not north. The Couritari Kityou is probably the Kutari, as the extreme upper reaches of the Corentyne are known, and, as already mentioned, the Pani is almost certainly the New River.

Savannahs, and with the setting in of the dry season, advance over land to the Cuyuwini, which would enable him to be about the middle of September at the first Woyawai Settlement. In the woody and mountainous regions of the Equator the rainy season commences about the middle of December, and continues until March; during this period dry weather prevails at the Savannahs, where the rain does not commence until April – and while the Essequibo overflows its banks, the Rupununy, a Savannah river is on its lowest level; the months of June, July to the middle of August, appear to be equally wet at the Savannahs as in the woody and mountainous regions.

Referring to the rough Sketch map of my journey, which accompanies this letter, I have to observe 'imprimis',[1] that the Longitude assumed, is that of my former map, though I am well aware that it is too far East. I have taken Lunar Distances at six places during my journey, but only returned since yesterday to headquarters, where the necessary tables for their calculation are at my command, it remained me no time to calculate any of the Sets. Cp[t] Maconochie, when Secretary, desired me to send even with my brief accounts a Sketch of the road; 'let it be ever so rough' were his words and on the strength of this the Sketch has been hastily executed. The distances East and West, are deduced from a careful Traverse table kept during my journey, and checked by the Chronometer as long as I had reason to put confidence in it.

I am sorry to say my Instruments have suffered much; the roughness of our wild path, and the necessity to carry the Sextant and other indispensable instruments merely in a waterproof bag, over the Shoulders, exposed them not only to collision with trunks of trees, but likewise to the powerful effect of the sun, which acted upon the graduated arch. These instruments were carried by my Coxswain, a careful person, while I carried the Chronometer in a girdle, which had been constructed for the purpose. It is to be supposed that its rate changed, and I found that its rate fluctuated between mean Time and 5 seconds gaining p. diem.

As soon as my health permits, it shall be my first occupation to arrange my Journal, to lay off the map and to copy my Astronomical observations. In consequence of the unfortunate accident, that during my ascent of the Essequibo, two of the Corials were upset, and the cargo of one completely lost, & that of the other partly lost, partly damaged, I have neither the necessary articles to continue my journey at the setting in of the dry season, nor have we any provisions to subsist during the dreary rainy weather. At my starting from Demerara I was provided for 19 months, at my return to headquarters, and after having paid off the strange Indians, who accompanied me, almost nothing remains. I have written therefore by the present opportunity for an other supply, which I expect towards the end of April, when the above mentioned papers shall be ready for despatch.

It is impossible for me to say at present any thing of my future plans, and it will be difficult for me to come to a conclusion, until I have gathered information at Fort San Joa[m].

Believe me with every esteem and regard.

My dear Sir,

your most obed[t] Serv[t]

Robert H Schomburgk

P. S. I have added some enclosures which I beg to forward. The Council can surely have no objection to the delivery of the papers to the Botanical & Linnaean Society.

---

[1] 'in the first place'.

****

Part (c) is entitled 'From our departure at Curassawaka to our arrival at Sao Joaquim do Rio Branco'. If this time period were strictly adhered to, it would only cover the period from 13 March to 30 June 1838, but in fact it also refers to some of the time after that which was spent at Fort São Joaquim during the rainy season of 1838. It was not received by the Royal Geographical Society until April 1840, and the reason for this is likely to be that the original was one of the documents that Schomburgk refers to as having been given to a Macushi to take to Georgetown but which never arrived (see below p. 273). In other words it is possible that this manuscript was not written in the form we have it until Schomburgk arrived back in Georgetown, or even in London, after the completion of the third expedition, and he learnt that the earlier version had gone astray.

Part of the manuscript is in Schomburgk's hand, part in that of someone else. It consists of twenty-two folio pages, but the pagination is not straightforward. The difficulties are best explained at the relevant points in the text. The first eighteen folios were received by the Royal Geographical Society on 11 April 1840. On the sheet numbered 19, it is noted that it (and presumably the remainder) was received on 14 April. It is this that suggests that Schomburgk was delivering the manuscript himself as he was in London at the time.

FROM OUR DEPARTURE AT CURASSAWAKA TO OUR ARRIVAL AT SÃO JOAQUIM DO RIO BRANCO[1]

The losses which we had suffered by the upsetting of the two corials on ascending the Essequibo, and the journey to the upper Essequibo had reduced our stock of merchandize to so low an ebb, that we were under the necessity to send for a new supply to the coast. My Coxswain Peterson and a Caribi crew from Curassawaka under their chief Irai[2] were selected for that purpose, while we intended to await their return at Pirara. The rainy season was expected to set in, in a few weeks, and the great change in the weather would at any rate have prevented us to journey during that period.

The morning of the 13th March approached before we left Curassawaka; the brook had fallen so much that we found some difficulty in reaching the Rupununi. We were so weakened that after reaching the Annai, we had to return the crew to Curassawaka for the remainder of our baggage, which delayed us an other day at our camp at Annai. I resolved therefore to ramble over familiar ground; my steps were first directed towards Mount Annai; the hut where we had passed a month in 1835 and where Lieut. Gullifer and Mr Smith, and Mr. Waterton, the author of the Wanderings[3] had sojourned was not more in existence – sedges and rank vegetation occupied its place; the wells were dried up, and I had to direct my steps to the south-east where I observed at a distance of two miles two huts which had been built since we sojourned here in 1835. When I

---

[1] The pagination starts folio-style.
[2] This is probably the same person whose name has previously been spelt Yhryee.
[3] Waterton, *Wanderings in South America.*

approached, neither the sound of barking dogs greeted me, nor did I see the smoke issuing from their roofs hovering over them; bad forebodings for finding them inhabited! I found them abandoned by man, but occupied by a multitude of Tshigoes. The former inmates had therefore built, and abandoned them in the course of two years. I proceeded now towards the mountain Monoshuballi where there were in 1836, a settlement at its southern and an other at its northern side. I found the doors of the first barricaded by huge pieces of Bamboo, and I was just about to return to our camp, when a poor cripple, a Caribi, whose acquaintance I had made during our former stay, crawled forth from a miserable hovel, and recognising me instantly, he appeared overjoyed. He pressed my hands repeatedly and gave me to understand that the inhabitants of the huts were all gone towards the mountains to pay visits to their friends, as at home they had nothing to live upon; and as he could not journey in consequence of his crippled state, he had been left at home, to take charge of the settlement, there being just enough provisions left at the field to give him sustenance. He went in the hut and returned with a tame bird, which he offered me as a present. I would have considered it sacrilege to deprive him of the only companion which he possessed, and after having made him a present, I went to the northern side of the hill, where he told me that a family of Macusis had just returned from a journey. Great changes had taken place at this settlement which at my visit in 1835 consisted of six huts; only one was now standing. I found a Macusi family consisting of a husband, his wife and five children; they were strangers to me. The woman brought me a Calabash with Cassiri, a beverage prepared of sweet potatos, and to me a most welcome refreshment.[1] Fatigued and disappointed of having found only one of the numerous acquaintances which I had made here during my former sojourn, I returned late to our camp.

March 16th/17th We continued this morning our journey ascending the Rupununi with slow progress. We had just halted on a gravely bank in the Rupununi to take our breakfast when we heard the sound of paddles and observed soon afterwards three corials coming the river downwards, manned with Macusis. They were from the village Pirara and among them were two young men, one a Macusi, the other a Caribi, who had been brought up at the mission at Bartika point, and who were now returning from Pirara accompanied by twenty eight Macusis to convey the Revd Mr. Youde, the first Protestant Missionary to the Indians in the Interior, from Bartika Point to that village.[2]

March 18/20th The Rupununi was so shallow that even as small as our crafts were, we found some difficulty to ascend it. We reached the inlet Wai-ipocari at noon of the 20th. I left next morning (March 21st) for Pirara, in order to make the necessary arrangements to procure the assistance of the inhabitants in carrying our baggage from our camp at the Rupununi to Pirara. In expectation of the missionary settling in Pirara, the village had greatly increased and I accounted thirty huts besides a house intended for the missionary and they were just about finishing an other building which is to be used as the house of prayer, at which the inhabitants, men, women and children, work in rotation. I found no difficulty to procure a number of men to go for our baggage and every article would have been at Pirara on the 26th of March had it not been for the serious

---

[1] According to Bennett (*Arawak-English Dictionary*) Kashiri is the name of a purple potato out of which the drink is made. The drink often also contains manioc and the potato acts as little more than a colouring agent.

[2] For an account of the events leading up to the founding of the mission in the interior, see Rivière, *Absent-minded Imperialism*, Chapters 2 & 3.

indisposition of Mr. Vieth who suffered under an attack of the spurious Pleurisy, and was consequently obliged to remain at the camp at the Rupununi.[1]

The Macusis appear to be a kind and hospitable tribe and are less indolent than the generality of Indians. The females rise early and attend to their domestic concerns; after having prepared the breakfast for their husbands, they go to their provision fields to put them in order for the ensuing season, to weed or to carry the ripe provisions to their homes in order to prepare the Cassada root into their substitute for our bread. Much has been complained by travellers that the Indian women were the mere drudges of their husbands. If attending to their domestic work, renders them drudges, they are it; but I put the question, is it different with the lower classes in Europe? Look at the peasant's wife; has she not to prepare her husband's meal, and to look after her children? And where their possessions amount to a small piece of provision ground, it falls to her share to plant it and keep it in order. Or has the wife of the lower class of farmers a less laborious life? With regard to Germany I say she has not. Equally ill founded is the outcry of tyranny of the Indian against his wife; during my intercourse with the Indians in the interior – I do not allude to those miserable beings near the coast who are contaminated by our vices and lowered to the brute creation by the use of that bane to the Indian races, rum – I have never witnessed a quarrel between husband and wife, much less where it came from words to blows. It would be desirable if a similar evidence could be offered by an Indian after three years residence among the lower classes in Europe. They pay us frequent visits, and if a bunch of plantains or a few cakes of cassada are brought to us for barter, the whole family, relations and friends included come to be present at the exchange of our respective commodities. At our arrival in Pirara a hut, the owner of which was then residing at the Canucu mountains, had been given up to us as residence. It was domeshaped, at the base 33 feet in diameter ending in a point which is 25 feet above the ground. It is thatched with palm leaves to the ground, with an opening which serves as entrance and for the admittance of light. The entrance fronts the east, the quarter from whence generally the breeze blows although two hundred miles distant from the sea. The hut is supported in the middle by a long pole which reaches to the point; six poles each 8 feet high support the sides of the hut; at the height of 6½ feet from the ground stretches a large beam from one side of the hut to the other, which rests upon uprights made of forked branches of trees; cross beams support the upper part of the house, and the whole displays an architectural skill which we are obliged to admire in these savages, as rude as it is in execution. The hut is comfortable enough, and I would be quite satisfied with my residence if there were not legions of Tshigoes and fleas, which we have vainly endeavoured to destroy either by cold or by boiling water. They withstand even mercury. The generality of houses in the village are of the same description. When paying us a visit they range themselves round the sides of the house; there they watch silently sometimes for hours our proceedings, but scarcely have

[1] This paragraph ends with a further sentence, which looks as though it had been scored out by Schomburgk himself. It reads: 'I was soon afterwards attacked, and our stay at Pirara was a melancholic one.' It is not clear what 'spurious pleurisy' might be, but it has been suggested to me by Dr Elisabeth Hsu, whose mother tongue is German, that Schomburgk had assumed that the English word spurious had the same general sense as the German word 'Spur'. In other words, what Schomburgk was trying to say was 'a trace of pleurisy'. Dr Hsu's suggestion carries that much more weight as she admits that she once laboured under a similar misapprehension about the meaning of 'spurious'.

they withdrawn and left the precincts of our hut when the most lively conversation ensues. They take great interest in our drawings, and when they are invited to look at them, and they recognise the object which they are to represent, it is with the greatest delight, and the words "Seni waquibé," this here is good, is frequently repeated pointing at the same time with the finger at the object of their recognition. They have observed that we collect plants, insects and birds, and they come frequently with such objects to us, and although they are seldom in a state fit for preserving, we acknowledge these little attentions by some presents.[1]

They bring us frequently fruits such as Cashews (Anacardium occidentale) Pine Apples and the fruit of the Coucourit Palm (Maximiliana regia).[2] The pine apples are of conical shape from 12 to 13 inches high, below 14 to 20 inches in circumference above 10 to 11. The species is very well tasted and would doubtless improve if cultivated. We have engaged a Huntsman to provide us with meat for our table, and seldom a day elapses without that he brings some Ducks or a Deer. We provide him with a Gun, powder and shot, and he receives articles to the Colonial value of Six dollars for his monthly wages. Wild Hogs appear to be scarce; the woods around the place are not extensive enough to afford a retreat for these animals. Fish can only be had at the distance of 6 or 7 miles; at a less distance the Pirara is too insignificant for the larger sort of the finny tribe. A species of Cicada is very numerous here about; it is of a larger size than the species which the Colonists call the Razor Grinder, and the sound which it produces resembles that which is caused by conducting the moistened finger over the edge of a tumbler. It is without doubt the Cicada tibicen. The Razor Grinder is quite a different insect from the Fulgora laternaria, though it has been asserted by Travellers, and copied in several natural Histories that the lantern fly produces the sound so similar to the sharpening of a Razor. The insect belongs to the same Genus as the preceeding but larger and different in its markings. The sound which the tibicen produces is very pleasing, and as the song of one invites the other to join it is frequently so strong that it may be heard at a considerable distance. The Macausis call the insect Caarta. It produces its musical note not by the proboscis, as it has been supposed, but by the means of the strangely constructed tympanum which occupies almost half of the abdomen.[3]

It is frequently heard by daytime but more generally towards sunset. The Razor Grinder, it may be said has stated hours; it is generally heard at Noon, at three oclock, and six oclock in the Evening. The sounds of insects and animals which we hear during night, are not equally diverting. The bellowing of the wild Bulls, which at that time approach the village is heard for miles, next comes the almost screaming voice of the frog kind, which inhabit the lake, or the hideous note of the owl, the call of courtship of this ill omened bird; mixed with their terrifying call is the note of the different Goatsuckers;[4] indeed Father Kircher[5] who set the voices of Birds to music, would have found it a very difficult task, to do the like with the numerous notes, which we hear at Pirara during a sleepless night. A species of Goatsuckers has a note which sounds like

---

[1] F. 3r, which ends here, is followed by f. 4r.
[2] *Maximiliana regia* is a synonym for *Attalea regia*.
[3] *Tibicen* is a genus of the Family Cicada; *Fulgora* of the Family Lantern flies.
[4] Nightjar (*Caprimulgus* spp.).
[5] Athanasius Kircher (1601/2–1680), Jesuit and polymath.

"Kukurukuku" and is so unlike the voice of a bird, that one unacquainted with it doubts whether it belongs to a bird or a quadruped. While I was in Demerara in August 1837, some acquaintances of mine arranged a visit to the Sandhills up the River Demerara. I was invited but, being pressed for time, declined it. The master of one of the Merchant Vessels there in the harbour furnished the boat and crew, and well provisioned they started with a favourable tide. Whether at their arrival at their journeys end their expectations might not have been realized, or what else might have been the cause, is of no object, enough they resolved to return immediately though night was then setting in. The tide was partly favorable and the hour of midnight approached when they found it rather chilly and would have been glad to find somewhere a comfortable quarter. One of the party recollected that there was a settler's house in the Vicinity and as they thought they observed an open place, like a landing place, they steered for it – as soon as the boat touched, two of the sailors jumped out. At that moment the cry Kukuruku-ku sounded from a tree which partly overhung the water; the sailors started but one took courage, and called out in rather an emphatic manner Who the D-l are you; Kukuruku-ku was answered from above and repeated by a similar note just above their heads. This was too much for Jack, they retreated to their boat with the greatest haste, and the panic had even stricken the valiant Captain who ordered the boat to withdraw without delay. The Sailor is the slave of superstition; any danger known, he meets dauntless and with courage, but when he thinks that any thing supernatural is in the play, he is a mere child, frightened by nursery tales. The bird was not known to any of the Company and as the strange noise was not unriddled, the Kukuruku-ku will be doubtless the object of many a tale during the nights watch.

The weather has been for the last week very sultry. The Thermometer which is entirely protected against the direct or intermediate rays of the sun and exposed in an airy passage to the breeze, stood on the 6th of April at 4 Oclock p.m. 93.5 F., it was lowest, on the 4th at 6 oclock in the Morning, when it stood at 72.8 F. The highest stand of the Barometer was 29.450 on the 2nd April at nine oclock in the Morning, and its lowest 29.316 on the 6th April at 6 oclock in the Evening. The difference amounted therefore between the highest and lowest in the course of the week to .144 of an inch. It must be stated however that the regular hours for the inspection of the instruments are 6h & 9h a.m., Noon and 3h & 6h p.m. Barometer or Thermometer may have been therefore higher or lower in the intervening hours. The 6th April was remarkable for the low state of the Barometer. It stood at:

6h a.m.	29.350	.362
12	.410	.419
3 p.m.	.318	.357
6	.316	.339

while at the same hours during the past week the means have been as stated in the annexed numbers.

The wind was from the N.E., the sky clouded, otherwise the means of the Barometer have been for the past week /1st–7th/ April 29.3807 and for the Thermometer 84.30. The prevailing wind was East.

Some Wapishanas who had been here for some days were on their way to the Fortoleza San Joaquim, and I availed myself of the opportunity to inform the Commandant of my arrival, and my wish if it proved convenient to him to pass the rainy season with my party at the Fortoleza. I have been sorry to learn that Captain Cordeiro who was Commandant when I was here in 1835 has been recalled as his time was over. His Gentlemanly and accommodating behaviour would have warranted his taking interest in the object of the Expedition.

The weather which had been very changeable dissolved on the 14th in rain and it continued through the succeeding night. When I rose in the morning of the 15th the whole air appeared to swarm with winged ants; unable to resist the wind they were driven before it but where a tree by its thick foliage afforded them protection, the[y] collected in prodigious numbers. They issued from the ground, and came out of the huts, indeed the ground of my residence was almost covered with them, crawling in columns towards the entrance, the only place from whence light was admitted. If they arrived safely there they rose in the Air, and joined the great mass. Many were however prevented to use their wings – numerous ants of a large and smaller size were awaiting them at the entrance, and attacked them without mercy. If the winged insects proved too large, the ant with admirable dexterity, deprived it of its wings, and carried it rapidly towards its nest – the large ants carried the whole insects with ease[;] they did not offer the least resistance and submitted to their fate. Before their flight had commenced and with the wings perfect they were seen in chase of each other, the male after the female. When the rain had ceased in some measure I walked out towards a small tuft of trees, which is at a short distance from the Village. Here the slaughter was immense; numbers of birds a species of Shrike and a Roller,[1] were in chase of them. Lizards awaited them on branches, spring-spiders on the ground and of the ant kind there were a whole legion of all sizes, and where one was not powerful enough to carry the poor victim to its nest, it was assisted by three or four, some dragging, some pushing. The length of the body of the insect was three lines*

*Ten lines to an inch [is the] measure, which I have adopted whenever I speak of lines.

it wing between 6 and 7 lines. The latter are of the finest tissues and detach themselves so easily that the slightest injury will cause it. I found the whole ground covered in the afternoon with their wings and a few of the animals running about without that appendage. It is only once in their life that they enjoy the privilege of winging themselves for a short period through the air and pay it generally with their lives, but few escape their enemies and are fortunate enough to be elected King and Queen of a new Empire. The tarsi had three joints, and are cylindrical, the feet are short, the antennae 13 to 15 jointed with strong triangular dentated mandibles. I conceive it to be the perfect insect of the Termes destructor,[2] or common wood-louse, as it is vulgarly called in the West Indies.

When Mr Vieth came to our Customary prayers on the Sabbath, he mentioned that round the village there were numerous fires, and wondering for what purpose they might be, I went with him after prayers and certainly the sight was magnificent. Not only at the foot of the hill, but likewise along the heights, a line of fires were observable each perhaps 10 to 15 yards apart. We saw the dusky figures of the Indians moving round them, and I thought they were executing some superstitious rites – we lost therefore no time to descend the hill, and when we came near the first fire, I observed that I

[1] Four genera of Shrike have been reported from Guyana, but Rollers do not occur in the New World.
[2] Termites, for which species *Termes fatalis* appears to be the more common synonym.

had been quite mistaken in my conjectures, and that they were collecting an other species of the winged Ant, each individual was provided with two or three torches which they put in the spot where they supposed the Ants might have their nests. Whether the warmth produced by the branches or the light, or whether they would have naturally issued from the ground, I do not venture to decide, but they came out of the ground in large numbers and were collected by the Indians in Calabashes. They were roasted and boiled and considered a great delicacy. Thus even Man is arraigned amongst the enemies of this unfortunate tribe. They are quite different from the preceeding, the length of their body is 7 lines, that of the upper wing 13 lines, the lower wings are scarcely a line less in size, while those in the former species are considerably shorter. Their antennae which are fixed at the anterior part of the head have twenty joints. I conceive them to be the perfect insect of that species which erect such wonderful buildings from 5 to 12 feet high, and to which I shall again as soon as my health permits me to undertake a lengthened walk in order to inspect minutely their fabric.

Next Evening (April 16th) my attention was attracted by the shout of all the little urchins in the Village. I left the Hammock to ascertain the reason and found them provided with sticks and the upper part of the Palm leaves, carrying on a War of extermination towards some winged insects. On inspection I found it was another species of the unfortunate tribe, much larger than any of the preceeding, indeed it was the perfect insect of the Atta or Cushi Ant of the colonists; the Antennae consists of 10 to 11 joints, the length of the whole body is 1 inch, that of the upper wing 13 lines, the lower 8 lines, the head, appears as if it were formed of two globes and is 15 lines large; the breast which just above the fore legs is armed with two small spines, and behind, below the insertion of the wing, with two larger ones, is 4 lines long, the peduncle of the abdomen has 2 rings. The head is of a brownish colour, the eyes black, the mandibles strong, dentated and cross each other. Contrary to the custom of the preceeding, they have kept part of the courage which they possessed in their wingless state, and known to defend themselves with their sharp mandibles; I found several who had shed their wings occupied the next day to dig themselves holes in the ground, for which purpose they used their mandibles. The abdomen is very thick (abt 3 to 4 lines) and is considered equal in delicacy to the Grugru worm, the grub of the Calandra palmarum.[1] The appearance of these winged insects announces sufficiently the weather, during the week (ending on the 15th April) indeed we have had days of rain and frequent showers and thunder[.] The distant mountains appeared occasionally as if they were only a few miles from us and this phenomenon is a sure prognostication of approaching rain.

From our elevated situation we see often whole herds of the Jabirus (Mycteria Americana) wading with great gravity in the swamps below, such a heard amounts sometimes to several hundred; they are very shy and are not easily approached within gun shot, one was however winged and brought in alive. The Bill measured 13 inches it was laterally compressed, thick at its base, and at its end rather sharp, the upper mandible is straight and triangular, the lower more thickened and slightly turned up. The nostrils are narrow as the bird seeks its food in the water, the feet with three anterior toes, slightly united by a membrane, the hallus or little toe, is high up on the tarsus. From the

---

[1] Grugru, groo-groo or grou-grou is the name of two species of the palm genus *Acrocomia* found in the West Indies. The worm or grub is probably the larva of a species of *Rhynchophorus* which inhabits the rotten palm wood.

point of the bill to the toes it was 6½ feet, from the tip to the insertion of the tail 4 feet 4 inches and to its end 4 feet 11 inches; from the end of the toes to the knee joint 1 foot 6 inches, from D° to the thigh joint 2 feet 10 inches. The extent of its wings were 8 feet and a half; the Jabiru has therefore next to the Condor the greatest extent of wings. Its plumes are white, the bill, head, and upper part of the neck is black and masked with the exception of a few scattered downy feathers, of a whitish colour, the lower part of the neck is red, and set with a few scattered downy feathers, the neck measured 21 inches in a full grown individual – they feed on fish, crabs, frogs, and that species of Ampullaria (A. Guyanensis)[1] which is to be found in prodigious numbers in Lakes, and swamps as well as in the rivulets which meander through the Savannahs. In spite of their mishapen beaks, they know to remove the operculum most admirably and to draw the animal out of the shell[.] Their flesh resembles beef most strikingly and when prepared as steaks, the generality would eat it as such[;] their young ones are Grey, and not roseate as stated by some Authors. While in Demerara a pair was brought to me from the Marocco coast.[2] They stood about 5 feet high when keeping their neck erect and were so tame that I allowed them to run about. They were considered a great curiosity and had constantly Visitors from old and young. They extended their walk frequently to the street, and I shall never forget the effect which their sight produced upon a Coloured woman. The Jabiru was leisurely stalking out at the gate, whe[n] she got first sight of the Gigantic bird. She stared with half open mouth at what she must have conceived a monster, but at that moment the bird spread its wings to their full extent, and changed its leisurely step in a hop when indeed the sight of the evil one could not have produced more fright to the poor woman and she ran as quick as her limbs would carry her in the next shop to seek protection throwing her arms over her head – together the ridiculousness of the scene cannot be described, it must have been seen.

While I was there, I fed them on Butchers meat and the Offals from the Kitchen. The first exploit of the larger when they were landed was to go near a cage where a Yawari (Didelphis murina)[3] was kept, and to draw the poor animal out of its recess and to swallow it alive. When the food was thrown to them, they catched it with great skill, they were very voracious and would frequently quarrel with each other for the food. When irritated they made a clattering noise with their beaks like a stork. Against dogs they would defend themselves most valiantly with their beaks and the clattering noise frightened the dog generally away. They are fierce in their wild state and if even deadly wounded, they will still defend themselves. They soar high and in circles. If they are disturbed at their feeding grounds, they hop twice or three times before they rise and flying in large circles round it, observe the intruders; if they apprehend danger they rise high in the air. The Macousis at Pirarara do not appear to be fond of their meat, though there are sufficient opportunities to kill them, they remain unmolested. They are called by the Macousis Tararumou, by the Brazilians Tuju, by the Arawaaks Mora Coyasipou, which signifies Spirit of the Moratree.

A few days after, our huntsman shot an American Stork (Ardea Maguvia Ciconia Maguari).[4] It was the first which we had met in our peregrinations and therefore

---

[1] The Applesnail (*Pomacea urceus guyanensis*).
[2] The stretch of coast around the mouth of the Moraka River, between the Essquibo and the Orinoco.
[3] An opossum. There are several species of *Didelphis* in South America.
[4] Probably the Maguari stork (*Euxenura galeata*).

interesting. I cannot say anything of its mode of living as it appeared to be only an occasional visitor at the Lake, I add however its description though mere words must convey but a poor idea of objects of nature so various in their vesture and attitudes, that even the best attempts of the painters brush, leave reality far behind. What pencil will be able to depict the gravity, with which the object of our description stalked between the rushes, now showing its long snake like neck forward to stay the unsightly frog in its hop or to draw the Ampullaria from that house, which it thought would render it an ample protection against all attacks of enemies. Now it throws its head aback to cleanse itself from the moisture which like dew drops hangs on the snow white feathers. At that moment the fowlers gun was levelled and his aim was too sure, the poor bird made its last efforts to rise, it spread its wings, and in the attempt fell prostrate among the rushes. We watched the progress on the hill above, with anxiety and exulted in the fowlers success. Having espied that it was a strange guest, the desire of adding it to our collection surpassed every other feeling. Its bill was strong, sharp edged, and notched at the tip; the upper part of a horn colour, darker near the point. The tip of the lower mandible was reddish, the skin round the region of the eyes was scarlet, and warty, the gullet bare and scarlet the head and neck light greyish, lightening to white, as it came nearer the body and ended in a tuft of long white feathers. The Bastard wings primaries, secondaries and tertials, as well as the tail were deep black, the latter forked, the outer feathers 8 inches long, the vent-feathers are longer than those of the tail. The legs were red and reticulated, the second and third quill feathers were the longest. Its dimensions were otherwise

> The wings from tip to tip – 6 feet 3 inches
> From the point of the bill to the insertion of the tail – 3 feet 3 inches
> D° D° to the end of the toes 4 feet 10 inches
> Middle toe 4 inches Bill 8³⁄₁₀ inches.[1]

Thus approached the month of May, and we had no tidings as yet of the Canoe which we had despatched to the coast regions. An Indian family which passed Pirara the other day informed us that they had been told my Coxswain was on his way up, and would have reached by this time Curassawaka. But the middle of May passed without any further tidings and we got alarmed for his safety. The rains had set in with little interruption and the Rupununi had grown upwards of twenty feet, since we camped at its banks.

In the course of the last days we have been rather alarmed at the visit of several rattlesnakes, which the chilly air that accompanies the rains, appears to have driven from the Savannah to the Settlements. A middle sized one, about five and a half feet long was killed in our neighbour's hut, who found it coiled up under the thatch of his house, and an other six and a quarter feet long was killed under some rubbish. The latter was by far the largest I have seen in Guiana; it was arm's thick and its rattles amounted to nine. What a blessing that this dangerous snake is so sluggish in its nature, or who could venture to live on a Savannah where there are so many! We have to walk with precaution on our botanical excursions, as they do not pass the daytime in holes

---

[1] Inserted in the manuscript at this point (after f. 13r – there is no verso) is a sheet of rough paper on which is written 'Pages from among (e) (and d). Correct place for insertion not found'. This statement dates from 1973 or later as it is on the back of a book review proof, and one of the books concerned was published in that year. However, it is not clear what the remark refers to as there are no such pages here. The manuscript continues without chronological break with f. 14r.

like many other snakes, and issue only at night, but coil themselves up under bushes, rubbish, and even under long grass. The sound of its rattle is dull, and would pass unnoticed in the greater number of cases, even if it were given on the approach of man, the more since the noise caused by walking through the grass is louder than the noise caused by the rattle. I assert this from my own experience, and it may serve to caution future travellers not to depend too much upon this sign of warning. The organs of smell serve the Indians much better to point out the danger. A musky smell which many of the reptiles possess in common with some Saurians and Mammalia, is a better guide than the feeble sound of the rattle. I fancied that I had acquired a greater acuteness of my nasal organs during three years wanderings, than I possessed when I commenced my expeditions; nor is it to be wondered as the Indian never fails to attract the attention of those who are in his company when he thinks he smells the musky exhalations of a snake; and the frequent repetition made me acquainted what the peculiar smell was which informed the Indian of the presence of a reptile.

The Rev^d Mr Youde was now daily expected at Pirara; tidings of his arrival at Curassawaka had been received, and the whole village is thrown in a bustle; all our hoes and spades have been put in requisition, and old and young are occupied to clear the open place before the missionary's intended house and chapel. He arrived in the afternoon of the 15th of May, and we attempted as much as it was in our power, to give evidence of our joy at the arrival of the first missionary whose intentions are to settle permanently among the Indians of the Savannahs. It is an epoch of great moment to these untutored beings; and it is to be hoped that the first step towards civilizing and instructing these poor benighted beings in our religion may be connected with prosperity. Their zeal stands perhaps unparalleled in the history of the missions for the propagation of the gospel; not only that the missionary was invited to come and settle among them, but long before it was decided whether the Church Missionary Society intended to maintain a mission among the Macusis,[1] they built not only a Chapel but likewise a house for the missionary, and twenty eight of their chief men undertook a journey of nearly three months to convey the missionary to their village. It is of great import that three coloured families who accompanied Mr. Youde from his former mission, intend to settle at Pirara, their example in religious worship and manner of living will have great influence upon the Indians and spurn[2] them to do the like.

Helas! that the joy of his arrival should have been damped by communicating to us the melancholic news of the sudden death of His Excellency Sir James Carmichael Smyth the Governor of British Guiana! This information was the more painful as it came unexpected and in him I lose not only a kind patron, but the Expedition a true and powerful friend. From my first arrival in Demerara to the period when I presented myself to take leave at the eve of my departure for the third expedition, the same urbanity, the same wish and will to promote the objects of these expeditions distinguished the late Governor. It does not become me to write a panegyric upon him whose public

---

[1] The Church Missionary Society did not intend to form a mission in the interior, at least not immediately, and had given Youd strict instructions that his journey into the interior was to be purely exploratory. Youd ignored these instructions. See Rivière, *Absent-minded Imperialism*, pp. 25–7.

[2] Presumably 'spur' was the word intended.

actions are recorded in the history of the colony, and under whose Government, British Guiana prospered unparalleled with any former period.[1]

May 20th We attended divine service this evening. In the course of the day, the Macusis of whom a great many had arrived from the neighbouring Settlements, were made acquainted by means of the interpreter with the object of Mr. Youde's mission, and the junior part received in the afternoon the first instructions in the alphabet. In the evening Mr Youde read the appointed Service of the church and spoke of the singular circumstance of our small party having assembled in the wilderness in a house erected by the hands of heathens for the purpose that it might be consecrated to the service of God and that they might receive instructions of that good Being.

May 23d, I am acquainted with a Species of European caterpillar (Bombyx processionea) which provided with hairs use their pubescence as a defensive armour. I had been told that some of these hairy caterpillars of Guiana produce severer pain than the European Bombyces and today when botanizing, my hand came in contact with one of those living nettles and it will be some time before the pains which I suffered in consequence will be forgotten. A pretty Rhexia[2] had attracted my attention, and while plucking it, I did not observe the hairy monster, until its sharp pointed bristles had already caused the mischief, and a stream of fire appeared to move from the palm of the hand to the shoulder. The pains were intense; firstly the palm of the hand and afterwards the whole arm commenced to swell, and the pain became more severe at the arm pit than at the spot of the hand which had come in contact with the caterpillar. As soon as I had reached home, I rubbed the arm with oil and volatile Alkali, which much lessened the pain, and after a feverish night, I felt released the next day. I have been stung repeatedly by scorpions, by wasps of all descriptions, but none caused the intensity of pain which followed the touch of that caterpillar. It was about an inch long of a whitish yellow colour, thickly set with hair of about half an inch in length. It was a Bombyx, but writhing under pain as I did, it escaped and with it the opportunity of ascertaining what butterfly would rise from it.[3]

The 24th of May approached, a day too dear to a British heart or to those who stood so closely connected with Great Britain, as I did, to allow it to pass without rejoicing.[4] It rained severely in the morning but it cleared partly towards noon, and firing at one o clock a salute the British Union waved likely for the first time at Pirara. Our Indian residence was otherwise decorated with every piece of coloured bunting which we could lay hold off. Mr. Youde the Missionary did us the pleasure of partaking of our simple fare, and the couple of bottles of wine which we discovered at the deepest recesses of our commissariat were properly employed to drink the health of Britain's Virgin Queen. Bang! went our little battery, much to the delight of the naked red-skins which in large numbers had assembled round our hut, and who accompanied with a warhoop, a substitute for a European huzah, every report according to their heart's desire.

---

[1] Smyth's successor was Sir Henry Light (1783–1870) who had served as a Captain in the Royal Artillery. He had been Lieutenant-Governor of Antigua. He was Governor of British Guiana from June 1838 to May 1848.

[2] A genus of the Family Melastomataceae.

[3] Many of the Family Bombycoidea have a defensive mechanism of this sort. For example, the caterpillar of the Venezuelan Emperor Moth (*Lonomia achelous*) can inject through its hairs an anti-coagulant which may result in a serious haemorrhage.

[4] Queen Victoria's birthday, 24 May 1819.

We could not omit to remember the illustrious man, who produced a revolution in the Sciences of Natural History, and who firstly pointed out the utility and advantage of some system by which nature could be studied, the great Linnaeus, who 131 years ago, was born on the same day of the month as Queen Victoria, in the obscure village of Raschult in the Province of Smaland.[1]

I projected a trip to the Canucu Mountains, anxious to enjoy the aspect of the Savannahs under water. I started therefore on the 28th of May, accompanied by some of my crew. I intended to reach the chain by the division of waters between the Rupununi and Mahu, and to follow it to the Southward to the banks of the Takutu. We started from Pirara in a South by west direction and reached a few hours afterwards the highest point of the Savannahs being not less than hundred and twenty feet above Lake Amucu. The prospect was from here very picturesque, the ground broken forming valleys which were intersected by numerous streamlets, the course of which we could trace by the more luxuriant vegetation along its banks or by the number of tufted Mauritia palms. We passed the streamlet Moroca, in the dry season very likely without water, but as it contributes its waters to the Avaricuru[2] it became remarkable; about a mile to the west of it, flows the Caribonota to the Pirara, our path led us therefore along the very position of the division of the waters between the Rupununi and Mahu. We ascended and descended hillocks, the ground was indeed remarkably undulating as if torn up by great bodies of water. Where rocky masses showed themselves they proved to be of the same nature and direction as those at Pirara which have given its Macusi name to that village, nor were the rounded and angular pebbles wanting now shining as if polished, now of a dull and dirty whitish colour, which in the vicinity of Pirara cover the Savannahs for a miles in a north and south direction.[+]

> [+]Clay Ironstone in small detached nodules, sometimes piriform with black shining surface sometimes aggregated with small quartz pebbles.

We passed at ten the Macusi village of Awarau or Tacuma. Our course had been SW.bS from the high point in the Savannah to the village, it was from thence S.S.W. Our path continued over the partly elevated Savannah, bordered by trees and low bushes, which although they were not planted in quincunx had nevertheless the appearance of a vast Orchard. We stood at one o clock at the brook Quayé;[3] it had overflowed its banks and a sheet of water a mile and half in breadth was before us. There was no other alternative but to strip, the water reaching us to the shoulder while crossings its regular bed, but otherwise it reached seldom further than the knee; the greatest discomforts arose from the thousands of mosquitoes which disturbed by our march, revenged themselves by most unmercifully bites, against which we could the less protect ourselves as we were in pura naturalibus.

The pretty Ampullaria Guyanensis prevailed here in large numbers, but as common as the shell showed it to be we found it seldom perfect, aquatic birds of the Genera Ardea, Tantalus,[4] Ibis[,] Platalea, Mycteria and others, are constantly on the watch to

---

[1] Carl Linnaeus (1707–78) was born at Stenbrohult, Småland, Southern Sweden on 23 May 1707.

[2] Awarikuru Creek which in turns flows into the Quatata River, that joins the Rupununi at the the Yupukarri Inlet, the eastern end of the Pirara portage.

[3] Possibly the Kwaye River. A tributary of the Nappi which, in turn is a tributary of the Pirara.

[4] The Genus *Tantalus* has not been reported from Guyana but many of its species have been reclassified as *Ibis*.

entrap the poor Mollusca. We reached in the afternoon, the Macusis Settlement Napi-Ipiwiraké, situated at a spot where the small river Napi, a tributary of the Pirara forms a large expansion of water (Ipiwiraké).

It afforded a fine prospect to the mountains among which the Napi (the Macusi name of the sweet Potato Convolvulus Batatta)[1] and Curassawaka distinguished themselves by their perpendicular walls of granitic rock.

May 29th Started at seven o clock after a severe shower of rain, and commenced to cross a branch of the stream Napi, which has its source in the mountain of the same name. Since we had crossed the Quayé, the soil took a different appearance, it had lost the admixture of ochre, which in the vicinity of Pirara gives it a red colour. The more we advanced towards the woods the blacker an appearance from vegetable matter did it adopt, and while the clayey soil prevented our sinking kneedeep in the mud when wading over the inundated Savannahs, we had now to contend for every step. That splendid species of Orchidea (an undescribed Vandeae perhaps Galeandra)[2] which I discovered first at the Savannahs of the Berbice river, appeared to delight here in the inundated and swampy soil; its luxuriant scape bore frequently from six to ten flowers, while at the Savannahs of the Berbice I accounted seldom more than four flowers. This abundance of flowers was likewise observable in some Habenariae[3] which round Pirara had generally only two flowers, while here they exhibited frequently five.

We entered five miles southeast from our last night's quarter the wood, which were likewise under water, and our progress was not only slow but fatiguing to the extreme; we had been wading since we started this morning and although prickly Mimosae and sedges scratched frequently our bare legs, when passing the inundated Savannahs, it was much worse in the woods where it was impossible to observe the numerous stumps and the trees which had fallen across, or to avoid the leaves of the numerous prickly palms, and we got all more or less wounded. I commenced to repent of having undertaken the excursion at the present unfavorable time, but I could not congratulate myself enough, that with the exception of a Kater's[4] compass I had left all other instruments at home. The poor Indians with their loads slipped so frequently that not an article of clothing or of provision escaped being wet through. Indeed two of the Indians wounded their feet so badly that I had to leave them in the next village. We rested at noon at a hut on a provision ground which belonged to some people in Pirara. Many of the inhabitants cultivate at that distance although it is twenty four miles from Pirara in consequence of the soil being more fertile. I observed numerous trees of a species of Amyris, different from that which yields the fragrant resin Haiowa. The tree in question was considerable higher, and its exudations were even more fragrant than those of the Haiowa tree; the Macusis call the tree Curukaiya.[5] We issued from the wood and continued for a short distance over Savannahs; having passed an abandoned hut, which still exhibited the neatness with which the former inhabitants had thatched it, our path led again through inundated forest. The yellow Hog plum, Spondias Myrobalanus,[6] was in season and we

---

[1] *Ipomea batatas.*
[2] *Galeandra* is a genus of Vandoid orchid.
[3] *Habenaria* is a genus of Orchidoid orchid.
[4] Henry Kater FRS (1777–1835). Best known for his pioneering work on precision instruments.
[5] Possibly Kurokai: *Protium crenatum*; *P. decandrum*; *P. sagotianum.*
[6] *Spondias mombin.*

found great numbers floating on the water. They would be an agreeable fruit, if they were not apt to make use of a common expression, "to set the teeth on the edge". The fruit is very aromatic, in consequence of which it has been resembled to the fruit which Dioscorides called *Myrobalanus*, and though it grows perfectly wild, there is nevertheless a great difference in the quality of the fruit.[1] After having crossed the Napi an other time, we entered a Macusi village of six houses, situated at the foot of Mount Napi, where we received every hospitality from the inhabitants. I found in the vicinity of the village several species of the Cimex, Cassida and Erotylus,[2] but one of the most remarkable insects which inhabits the Canucu Mountains is the Prionus cervicarius,[3] and I am happy that as eyewitness I can confirm the statement of other travellers of their peculiar habit to seize a branch of a tree or shrub between their powerful and serrated mandibles, and to fly round them, until they have succeeded of sawing it perfectly through. The branch thus divided by the insect has the appearance as if it were done with the sharpest tool, and it showed that the weight of the branch had caused it to break ultimately, when it had been reduced to the thickness of a goose's quill. The noise which is caused by the sawing and the quick motion of the insect while it performs this feat is most remarkable and audible at some distance. The little boys at the village had met the insect in full labour, and they came to give us information. We followed their steps and found the indefatigable insect still at work. It was flying round with the velocity of a Windmill, having selected that part of the branch which was free from branchlets. How long it might have worked before we came to witness this interesting fact, I know not, nor could I judge what progress it made, as the branch was upwards of twenty feet above the ground. Our presence did however not disturb it, and after we had watched it for about fifteen minutes the branch broke, and the insect fell with it to the ground; a simultaneous rush of the little urchins to capture it, frustrated their own wish and prevented me to observe what would be its next proceedings after having succeeded in sawing the branch through for which laborious undertaking it must have some reason. The length of the insect is from three and a half to five inches, and its breadth from one and a half to two inches. The body is depressed and the elytra or wing covers are of a dark brown colour variegated with stripes of a reddish-yellow and of unequal length and direction. The thorax is edged and provided with three strong and acute spines on each side, the margin between which is of unequal length and dentated; head and thorax are of a ferrugineous colour. The most remarkable part are however the mandibles, which surpass in size the head and thorax, and which in the insect from which I take the description are nearly one inch long. They are strong and bend towards each other and close firmly at the tip. Their inside edge is serrated and one of the teeth which occupies the middle of the mandible is considerable larger than the rest. The outer side of the mandible exhibit at about a third of its length an other tooth bent outwards. The antennae are about an inch and a half long. The Larva is frequently found in the Silk cotton trees (Bombax Spec) and in diverse species of Palms.

---

[1] Dioscorides (fl. c. 40–80 A.D.), physician from Anazarbus in Cilicia (in modern Turkey), and author of *De materia medica* (c. 50–70 A.D.). The myrobalan is the astringent plum-like fruit of the species *Terminalia*.

[2] Cimex is a genus of bugs, and Cassida and Erotylus both genera of beetles.

[3] I am very grateful to Martin Brendell of the Natural History Museum, who identified this as the Sawyer Beetle (*Macrodontia cervicornis*).

May 30th[1] We crossed the small brook Curassawaka and continued our path along the foot of the mountain chain, and entered a small settlement of five houses. After we had refreshed ourselves and were on the point of departing, a good looking woman with a child on her breast came to me and gave me to understand that I should blow the child in the face. I readily complied with the mother's wish, after which she carried it to the eldest of my guides who repeated the blowing. The child looked sickly and it is their belief that if thus blown on by a stranger, the child recovers and prospers.

Continued our march and passed the stream Rhinaouté and a mile further the Napi. Before we crossed the latter stream we had a prospect of the mountains Curassawaka and Napi; we stood at the foot of the former and admired a huge block of granite, which stood out from its side like a salient angle; it was of immense size and could not be less than fifty feet in height.

Left the Wood & entered Savannahs which we followed in a W. by S. direction. However wherever we crossed a stream we found the banks for three to four hundred yards on each side densely bordered by Palms trees and shrubs. In the vicinity of the stream Yatani I noted an extensive ledge of [blank][2] it resembled that of Pirara and had the same direction. The conglomerate was still better exhibited where the stream Yatani had greatly deepened its bed. The strata is horizontal and exhibits many fissures which no doubt has arisen from the undermining power of the stream.

Heavy rain obliged us to take shelter and nightquarters at a solitary hut inhabited by a man, his wife and four children. It was a riddle to me how the inhabitants of the solitary settlement could live where myriads of sand flies subjected them to a continual torture.

A tremendous storm raged from eight o'clock in the evening until two o'clock in the morning. The uproar was so great that we could only judge of the thunderstorm by the continued sheets of lightning, the reverberations of the thunder were entirely lost among the general uproar.

May 31. We were up and on our march by six o'clock. The low savannahs were over-floated, and the path completely torn up on the higher grounds and every hollow presented a little river; but the greatest effect of last night's storm had been the disloca-tion of an immense mass of rock near the brook Carusa, which in its fall from the mountain had overwhelmed hundreds of the noblest trees; the debris had almost filled the bed of the Carusa and presented a picture of desolation.

The mountain chain became more interesting the more we advanced to the South. We crossed the stream Muckee-muckee[3] a tributary to the Takutu. We had entered the basin of the latter river about a mile and a half east of our last nights quarter when we crossed the Cavauru. At the foot of Mount Quariwaka is a settlement of ten houses of Macusis. The hut of the Toyeputori[4] was differently formed from those I had generally seen; it was round like the generality of Macusi houses but its walls in lieu of being of clay or thatched with palm leaves were formed of the bark of trees and the entrance had a kind of Portiko.

The stream Quariwaka has its sources on the mountain of that name and forms in its descent a cataract, the thundering noise of which we heard quite plain in the village.

---

[1] It is at the page starting here that the note 'rec^d 14 April 40' is to be found.
[2] In the published version (p. 177) the missing words are 'conglomerate rock'.
[3] Moco-moco River.
[4] Toyeputori is the Macusi for village leader.

We crossed a little after noon the stream Ilamicklivauté which has its sources on Mount Ilamickipang. At the foot of that mountain is the Macusi settlement Cumuméru which for the present was to be the extent of our journey. In consequence of the extensive inundations we found it impracticable to continue our journey further westward; however the ascent of Mount Ilamickipang, partly in order to enjoy the splendid prospect which it promised, partly to see whether I would find the Urari plant in blossom, was resolved upon for the following day.

June 1st We commenced the ascent this morning. The mountain is steep and covered with blocks of granite, but the most remarkable feature is an immense mass of solid rock, which partly overhangs the summit and rises afterwards perpendicular to upwards of fifty feet. In the vicinity of that rocky mass, the stream Ilamicka has its source and paths itself tumpling[1] over large ledges of rock a way to the savannahs below. After having ascended for about 500 feet, we observed the first Urari plant in a glen and met subsequently several, but strange to say, although I found it in fruits when I saw this plant for the first time in January 1836, this was the case again in June, and I was disappointed in procuring flowers of it. I conclude therefore that it blossoms twice a year, likely in March and August, which gives three months for the fruit to ripen.

The nearer we approached the Summit the more numerous became that singular and magnificient bird the Rock Manakin[2] or Cabanaru of the Indian, and *Rupicola elegans* of Ornithologists. They were flirting round us and came so near that in one instance our guide had nearly knocked one down with the cutlass. The vegetation was peculiar amidst the thousands of granitic blocks by which we approached the rocky mass – several new species of Myrtaceae, the handsome Clusia rosea, several species of Epidendrum, Pleurothalis, Brassevole, Maxillaria[3] covered the aged trunks of trees, and a species of Tillandsia had selected the intermediate spaces between the blocks and the water which had collected at the base of the leaves, forming as it were a cistern, was so copious that our feet got quite wet while walking through it. We reached now the solid mass of rock, the Ilamickipang or overlying rock, as it might be translated. Its top is an inclined platform partly covered with Pitcairniae, Tillandsiae,[4] a new Epidendrum with bright scarlet flowers, resembling in its leaves that species which I discovered at an earlier period at the Ataraipu. I accounted four different species of Pleurothalis and Stelis.[5] The platform was quite moist and where the Pitcairniae and Tillandsiae did not usurp the ground, it was covered by a [pretty] running gramineae. But while the little area astonished us by the variety and luxuriance of its vegetation, the prospect which opened before us was unrivalled. Hitherto I had seen the Savannahs only from moderate elevations; but now they presented themselves from a height of nearly three thousand feet, and the eye swept unobstructed by any object from the isolated Makarapan to the boundless savannahs of the Rio Branco. Cleft into misshapen masses reared themselves on our right the rocky summits of the neighbouring mountains; a glance below

---

[1] Presumably 'tumbling' is the word intended.
[2] Another name for the Cock of the Rock. At this point, at the end of f. 20r, the pagination changes, and the last five pages are numbered 15–19.
[3] *Epidendrum*, *Brassavola* and *Pleurothallis* are Epidendroid orchids and *Maxillaria* a Vandoid.
[4] These are both genera of the Family Bromeliaceae.
[5] These are both genera of Epidendroid Orchids.

and the eye measured the abyss which extended at our feet, but the momentary shudder at the thought of a wrong step or slip of the foot, vanished at the enjoyment of the splendid view. The Makarapan mountain visible to the E.N.E., presented itself almost in a line with the northern side of the Canucu mountains; from thence reigned the forest triumphant and the boundary line between the forest and the Savannahs was well defined. The eye was arrested to the north by the Pacaraima mountains; a thick fringe of wood denoted the course of the Mahu; lake like expansions of water showed the extent of the inundation, while the river Takutu, where kept by high banks in its boundary, appeared like a silvery thread woven through a rich carpet. Some peaked mountains, which appeared to rise solitary from the Savannahs closed the view to the northwest.

We did not enjoy the prospect for a long time; clouds of mist which approached from the East enveloped the landscape in an impenetrable veil, and we returned towards evening to the Indian Settlement.

Aiyoukante, my Macusi guide, had injured his foot, and we could only commence our return to Pirara on the 3ᵈ of June, and reached that village by a more direct route in the afternoon of the 4ᵗʰ.

The canoes which we had despatched to the coast in quest of Provisions and merchandize, and which we commenced to give up for lost in consequence of their long delay, arrived at last on the 6ᵗʰ of June. I did not lose time to despatch a messenger to Fort Sao Joaquim informing the Commandant, of our readiness of removing from Pirara to the Fortolezza where we intended to pass the rest of the rainy season. My object was to have during that period at least an opportunity of determining astronomically the position of that place, which hitherto had been always considered the eastern boundary of the Brazilian Guiana. Our messenger had met the Commandant on his way to Pirara, being the bearer of letters from the Commander of the Military and Civil Affairs of the upper Amazon, Captain Ambrosio P. Ayres conveying in the most flattering terms his permission to reside during the rainy season at Fort São Joaquim, and that he had ordered the commandant of the Fortolezza to give us every assistance, and that he had despatched his brother Senhor Pedro Ayres as his representative to receive our expedition at the Brazilian frontier.[1]

The Revᵈ Mr. Youde intended to accompany us to the Fortolezza and we left Pirara in his company and under the escort of the Commandant Senhor Cato,[2] on the 27ᵗʰ of June, and arrived in the afternoon of the 30ᵗʰ of June at São Joaquim. Senhor Pedro Ayres received us with every civility and tendered his services to further our objects. Two comfortable houses outside of the Fort were given up to us as long as we might think it convenient, for our quarters.

This reception from a Government which we knew to be at that period in difficulties to suppress an insurrection,[3] which had lasted for more than five years and occupied

---

[1] For more about the brothers Ambrosio Pedro and Pedro Joaquim Ayres, see Rivière, *Absent-minded Imperialism, passim.*

[2] Lieutenant Manoel Affonço Gatto. His tour of duty at Fort São Joaquim was short-lived.

[3] This is what is known as the *cabanagem*, an uprising of those of Amerindian and mixed descent against those of more immediate European, mainly Portuguese, origin. It was characterized by bloody massacres on both sides and estimates put the total dead as thirty thousand, about a fifth of the population of the Province of Pará. It was at its height in 1836–7, but continued until the end of the decade.

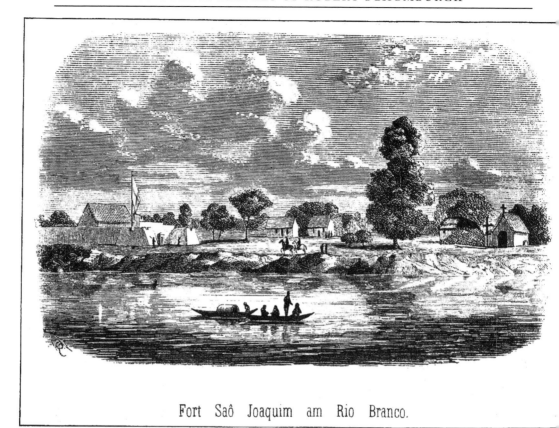

Fort Saô Joaquim am Rio Branco.

Figure 8: The Brazilian Fort São Joaquim located at the confluence of the Rio Branco and the River Takutu. was built in the 1770s to prevent Spanish or Dutch intrusion into the area. Most visitors in the first half of th nineteenth century described the fort as being in bad condition. From Richard Schomburgk, *Travels in Briti Guiana*, II, p. 270. Reproduced from editor's copy.

their whole attention, and had therefore little leisure to pay attention to scientific objects, was more than I could have expected in my most sanguine hopes, and was so diametrically opposite to the proceeding of the authorities in a neighbouring European Colony who though I had previously written to these authorities and enclosed a letter of Sir James Carmichael-Smyth the late Governor of British Guiana, explaining that my object of coming there was to survey the mouth of the Corentyn, intended never-theless to fire on us, when approaching in a sailing vessel with the British Ensign flying & unacquainted with the entrance of the river Nickeri, we had come too far to the windward of the proper channel, and which was only prevented by the interference of an English resident, and who after we had landed and I made our object known, forbid me to take any astronomical observations on their shore at my peril.[1]

The Fort São Joaquim is situated on the eastern shore of the river Takutu, a short

---

[1] This occurrence took place when Schomburgk was surveying the mouth of the Corentyne in September 1836. See above p. 231.

distance from its confluence with the Rio Branco, Parima, or Uraricoera. A detachment of Spaniards from Nueva Guayana arrived in 1775 by the Caroni and the Uraricapara at the Uraricoera or the present Rio Branco, and fortified themselves in the vicinity of the confluence of the river Yurumé. They were dispersed by the Portuguese, who erected now as well against the incursions of the Spaniards as against the Dutch the boundary fort São Joaquim. It is constructed of red sand stone which is found in the vicinity, and possesses fourteen embrasures, mounted with eight nine pounders in tolerable condition. It is garrisoned with a commandant and ten privates of the Provincial Militia. A small chapel and five houses constitute the village; and a priest visits every two or three years the fortress to administer to the spiritual want of the inhabitants.[1] In 1796 two individuals Antonio Amorim and Evora, commenced farming in the vicinity of the fort with fifty head of Cattle, which cattle rapidly encreased, but in consequence of mismanagement the owners fell in debt to the Government, who took the farms over and they have since remained in possession.[2]

The commandant of the place united formerly with his military post that of the Superintendent of the Cattle farms. At present the two offices have been divided and the commandant's authority refers only to the district of the fort, the discipline and order of his garrison and the integrity of the frontier. The farms São José, São Bento, and São Marco in the vicinity of the confluence of the rivers Takutu and Branco are under an Administrator who receives one fourth of all the cattle which he brands with the Government stamp.[3] The number of cattle was stated to me to consist of 3000 heads penned and 5000 heads wild cattle, and 500 horses. I conceive these however overrated. Twenty two cattle minders who are enlisted among the Indians and are said to have pay and rations equal to a private soldier have the care of the cattle. These cattle minders were formerly deported soldiers from Para.

The dreary time of the tropical winter was spent in São Joaquim with arranging the notes of our former Expedition and with constructing the map of the upper Essequibo. These papers which I had afterwards opportunity to despatch to the Colony by a Macusi Captain, never arrived in Demerara, and the three months which their construction cost me, were consequently lost time. Every opportunity which the changeable weather offered for astronomical observations was eagerly seized, nevertheless during a stay of nearly three months these opportunities were very scarce. The results of my astronomical observations give me 3°1′46″N. Lat., and 60°3′ West Long^t for the position of Fort São Joaquim.*

*The latitude is the mean of fourteen observations of the stars α Scorpi[oni]s, α Lyrae β Draconis, α Pavonis, α Cygni, α Pisc Austr. α Cassiopeae, α Eridani; eight observations are stars of northern Declination, six of southern. I am less satisfied with my observations of Longitude during the long interval of our sojourn, I had only once an opportunity to take Lunar Distances west, the others are all east of the moon.

[1] Schomburgk's description of the condition of the fort is probably too glowing. It was in poor condition when Waterton visited it in 1812 and was when Richard Schomburgk was there in 1843. The remains of the fort were still just visible in the late 1960s.

[2] For a recent account of the Portuguese occupation of the region, see John Hemming, 'How Brazil Acquired Roraima', *The Hispanic American Historical Review*, 70, 2, 1990, pp. 295–325.

[3] This method of payment was quite common on the cattle frontiers of Brazil. In the Rio Branco area it was known as *sorte* (luck), and was still in use, although dying out, in 1968 when I did field research there. For a description of it see Rivière, *Forgotten Frontier*, pp. 87–9.

During the dry season an East wind generally prevails and blows almost with the fury of a gale; a change to the west or northwest is at once an indication of approaching rain. We had frequent thunderstorms and scarcely once perfect clear sky and fine weather; it was only in September, when the wind turned to the E.N.E. that we had hopes for the setting in of the dry season.

****

Part (d) of the manuscript JMS 6/29 was received by the Royal Geographical Society on 1 February 1839, over fourteen months before part (c). It was given the title 'Account of the ascent of the Carumá or Serra grande on the Eastern bank of the Rio Branco in Brazil, in Aug. 1838'. It consists of thirty-seven pages and the pagination is straightforward. It was published, greatly abbreviated, as part of the first article (pp. 181–90) covering the third expedition. Most of manuscript is in a copyist's handwriting; there are numerous changes and deletions made by an unknown editor and a few amendments in Schomburgk's hand. Wherever Schomburgk's amendments can be identified with certainty they have been adopted. There are the usual problems of the original text being hidden by overwriting and heavy scoring out.

ACCOUNT OF THE ASCENT OF THE CARUMÁ OR SERRA GRANDE ON THE EASTERN BANK OF THE RIO BRANCO IN BRAZIL, IN AUG. 1838

The most vague accounts of the Serra Grande or Carumá[1] of the Indians, which is situated about 31 Geogrl miles below Fort San Joaquim, had long ago awakened the desire in me to visit it, and I planned with Senhor Pedro Ayres an excursion thither. They told us of a large lake, with black water, in which Porpoises were as common as in the Rio Branco, & it wanted only large ships, sailing on its surface, to make it another lake Parime.

An observation of M de Humboldt in "Sur quelques points Importans de la Géographie de la Guyane" p. 36*[2]

> *Nouvelles Annales des Voyages "J'ai trouvé dans les manuscrits de d'Anville, dont les héritiers m'ont obligeamment permis l'examen, que le Chirurgien Hortsmann de Hildesheim, qui a décrit ces contrées avec tant de soin, a connu un autre lac Alpin, quil place a deux journées de distance au-dessous du confluent du Mahu, avec le Rio Parime (le Takatu?). C'est un lac à eaux noires, situé sur la cime d'une Montagne."

that Hortsmann[3] was acquainted with an Alpine lake, on the summit of a mountain,

---

[1] Serra Grande or Carauna. It appears as Carauma on some maps.

[2] See Humboldt, 'Sur quelques points importans'. The quotation in Schomburgk's footnote is on p. 172.

[3] Nicholas Horstmann was a German surgeon employed by the Dutch. In 1739 he made an expedition up the Essequibo, crossed to the Rio Branco the following year and descended it to the Rio Negro where he was arrested by the Portuguese. Some years later, he handed his journal and map to the French scientist Charles-Marie de la Condamine. It is often claimed that Horstmann was the first European to cross from the Essequibo to Amazon river systems, but there must be some doubt about that. G. Bos, in an unpublished paper 'Some Notes on the History of the Pirara Portage', suggests that the first Dutch crossing of the portage may have been as early as 1660.

distant two days' journey from the confluence of the Mahu (Takatu) with the River Parime (R Branco), made me the more anxious to visit that mountain.

We left Fort San Joaquim on the 16th August shortly after 11 OClock in the morning, favoured by good weather & as our canoe was well manned, we made rapid progress. The first reach of the Rio Branco, after it has received the waters of the Takatu, is S.19½° W., following the course of the river. It is here about 1200 yards wide, & bordered by shady trees and with the mountains Wanari in the background, it affords a fine prospect.

Beyond the border of trees, extend vast Savannahs. One of the mountains, which form the small chain, is completely rounded towards its summit, and as the lower part is hid by trees in the foreground, its outlines have a very pretty affect, and it appears like a Gigantic Cupola or Dome.

The Banks of the first reach are covered by huge boulders of a red sandstone, lying upon stratified masses of the same description; the ground is somewhat raised, and where the water has washed away the earth, and the stratification becomes visible, it is ENE or more nearly N69½°E. It loses itself under the bed of the Rio Branco, & becomes visible again at Fort San Joaquim, bearing ENE. The fort is constructed of this stone, which sometimes contains particles of Iron.

The River turns at this course a point more to the west, & the Serra Carumá comes now in view, and remained to the end of our journey our loadstar. On the River's left bank, is the Island Sobradinho, which commands a fine view of the river, downwards & upwards, & may have received its name from a watchhouse which formerly stood here; It is low & sandy & about [blank] long. Opposite its southern end, the brook or Igarapé dos Gentios, falls in the Rio Branco from the East. It takes its rise in the Savannahs, & is called by the Indians Corova; it is very likely the River Ararau of the former maps.[1]

At the point where the river takes a more westerly course, the summit of Carumá or Serra Grande, bore S25½W., and we paddled now along the Island "San José". I estimated here the width of the river increased by Islands, about a mile, & the small channels which are produced between Island & Island, where they approach each other, or where the Island is situated more towards one shore than another, are called in the Lingua Geral[2] "Paranna-miri," or 'small waters'; the Island in succession is the Ilha de Retiró.*

> *A Retiró is a temporary hut where the salting & drying of meat is carried on, when wild cattle are slaughtered in the Savannahs, or as a protection against unfavourable weather for the Vaqueiris when camping on the Savannahs.

In the vicinity of these Islands, but on the main shore, we observed numerous trees of the Parica. This is a species of Mimosa, the seeds of which numerous tribes of Indians along Rios Amazon & Negro, as the Gaupes & Puros,[3] & use in the same way as the Otomacs & Guajibos the bean of the Acacia Niopo: they are pounded to powder and are then smoked or the smoke is inhaled by the nose, or the powder is put in the eyes,

---

[1] Rio Ararau is not marked on modern maps, but on J. Arrowsmith's 1834 map of Colombia a river of this name is shown as a left-bank tributary of the Rio Branco, flowing into that river from the east, a little to the north of the site of the modern city of Bôa Vista.

[2] The common or trade language over large areas of Amazonia. It is based mainly on the Tupi language.

[3] Rio Uaupés or Vaupés, and Rio Purus.

nose, ears, & even the Anus, as Senhor Ayres assured me; the effect is that they are thrown in a state of madness, which lasts for hours, & during which time they have not the slightest command of themselves, and their passions; they commit in that state the most obscene actions, and it is but too frequently the case that quarreling or murder follow in the train. A general stupour succeeds, and the Individual who has partaken in these orgies, appears to be deprived of sensibility for whole days. From these effects it may be concluded, how injurious this practice proves to their health.[1]

The Tree appeared to me to belong to the Genus Mimosa*

> *It is very unfortunate, that the only systematic work which I have at my command at present, namely Linnaei Systema Vegetabilioni. Edito 16, by Sprengel,[2] the sheet IV of the 2nd Volume, containing the Genus mimosa, is wanting – I cannot decide therefore, whether it is described, but its suberose bark is a good distinguishing mark.

and its bark is completely suberose. The leaves possess a bitter taste, & are considered an excellent remedy for internal bleedings and injuries. The Administrator of the Cattle farms told me a remarkable circumstance. A young calf had been gored by a bull, & though he gave it up for lost, he recollected this reputation which the Parica leaves enjoyed, & fed the calf for a week or so, entirely upon them; it recovered, & he killed it sometime after for his own use, on opening it, he found in its stomach a large ball, consisting of Parica leaves & coagulated blood. Senhor Ayres told me, he had used it after a severe fall from the horse, and as he thought with great success. The Bark & leaves are likewise used for tanning & it resembles in its principles the Algarobas & Prosopeses[3] of South America. We had a very pretty view of the Wanari & Coitáu mountains, which showed themselves between the Ilhas de Retiro & San Bento. Opposite the latter Island, & on the river's right bank, was formerly the old farm San Bento, which at a later period, was removed to the immediate neighbourhood of Fort San Joaquim.

The Houses being merely constructed of clay, no vestige of it is more discernable. It appears to have been favourably situated, as a fine clear brook, with blue & well tasted water, fell in its vicinity into the Rio Branco. The Indians call the brook Cacuruau, while the Creoles call these kinds of running streams "Agua boa", and they have the idea that they are more wholesome than the whitish waters, and the Cacuruau has blueish waters, which at some distance from the mouth are so clear that the smallest object becomes visible, though the depth may be from 20 to 50 feet. It runs for a considerable distance parallel with the Rio Branco, having its source very likely near the Muruku hills, which bear from fort San Joaquim N.[W. by W.] distant [18] miles.

The River Cauambé (the Gaume of maps)[4] is more considerable, than the former; it may be about 50 Yards wide, where it falls in the Rio Branco, and its last reach is N.33°W. From its mouth, the prospect down the Rio Branco is very lovely; the islands Boa Vista and Caricatua, assist to enhance the beauty, and the broad stream,

---

[1] Parika is an hallucinogenic substance. The name is applied to two Guyanese species: *Anadenanthera peregrina* (formerly classified as a species of Mimosa), and *Mimosa schomburgkii*. The use of hallucinogenic substances is very widespread among native Amazonian people and many different kinds are found. Its importance is that it provides access to the invisible world where the principles of causation lie.

[2] Sprengel, *Caroli Linnaei ... Systema Vegetabilium*.

[3] Algarobas are now classified as *Prosopis*.

[4] Rio Cauamé.

ʒure 9: The view of the Serra Grande or Carumá looking south down the Rio Branco from the site of Bôa
ʒta, the state capital of Roraima. Photograph taken by John H. Moore in December 1957. It has not been
ʒssible to trace Mr Moore to ask his permission to reproduce this photograph.

appears to wash the western foot of the Serra Grande, which presents itself here to
its best advantage.

Three naked hills from 250 to 300 feet in height occupied the foreground, they are
called "Serra pelada" by the Creoles & Matitikur by the Indians; a small settlement
called Santa Isabel was formerly a little to the south of the Cauambé mouth; it has been
long before this abandoned,[1] but Senhora Liberada, a woman of colour, has lately
commenced farming here.

The Senhora received us with great hospitality, & could not regret enough, that we
had not informed her of our intended visit, in order that she might have been prepared
for us. All what comes under the category of chairs, is not discernable in their houses,
but it is the custom of the country, to sling for each guest a Hammock, of which he takes
possession in lieu of a chair, and the Hammock is, without doubt the more comfortable
way of resting from fatigues.

While Senhor Ayres was close questioned of all, what in shape of novelty had
occurred at Fort San Joaquim, since the last Correo[2] had communicated the leading

[1] Santa Isabel was one of a number of villages in which the Portuguese settled the local Amerindian population in the mid-1770s. It was shortlived; its inhabitants revolted and abandoned the place in 1780.

[2] Correio, the Portuguese for messenger, postman, the carrier of news, etc., is probably the intended word.

articles of fashionable chit chat, Senhora had attended to the filling of a tobacco pipe, (Secundum artem)[1] having ordered one of her handmaidens to apply the match, a huge fire stick from the kitchen, she, with the most important air set it duely a going, and handed it lastly, with an undescribable grace to Senhor Ayres. She had been informed, that I did not smoke, but if this should have been the case, politeness would have required that after a few puffs, Senhor Ayres should have returned it to our hostess, who after having enjoyed the balsamic weed, would have handed it with the same grace to me.

It does not appear, that they consider it indelicate, as we Europeans would do, to pass the pipe or Cigar from the mouth of one person to that of an other. The tube of their pipes is generally formed of a species of wood, & is very tastily ornamented by the Indians. They give it a fine gloss with a fruit called Makuku,[2] and the head is made of Clay, & afterwards hardened in the fire, having been coloured previously. The tubes resemble those of Weichsel,[3] so much esteemed by the true Tobacco smokers on the continent. The Indians call the pipe Taquiari which word refers more to the head, as the word signifies any thing hollowed out.

The House of our hostess consisted of a large building, wattled, & plastered over with the soil in its vicinity. The roof was thatched with Eta leaves, & open to the roof in the manner of a barn. It had been only lately built & it was intended to have been divided by a partition. In one of the corners was fixed a hand loom, which, though of rude construction, answered every purpose; of which we had ocular proofs, a young Indian girl used the shuttle with dexterity, and as the cloth which is worn by the people in general is of a coarse and open structure, she made rapid progress. It goes by the general name of panno & is of the same texture as the Spanish [blank] which may be considered the current money along the Upper Amazon.[4] There are few families, where the women do not manufacture as much as is wanted for family use. In trade or barter its value is a dollar p Varas,[5] which is at least 1000 pCent above what it is really worth. They say it lasts them better than Salempores, Oznaburghs,[6] or any of our manufactures.

Many of the females are skilled in the manufacture of hammocks. For that purpose the loom consists of two upright & two horizontal pieces, to keep them together, it is fixed either in some corner of the hut, or frequently under trees. The thread is then laid of the whole length, & wound round two Cylinders, which are moveable. I ought to have observed that the loom is of the width of the hammock which is intended to be made, & that the cylinders are fixed Horizontally & not upright. Every thread of the woof is constructed with their fingers & many of divers coloured cottons are [illegible[7]]. These cottons are coloured with the diverse clays & ochres of the country, as well as with the juice of plants, as Chica, Roucou, the juice of a Bignonia which colours blue. A

---

[1] 'In accordance with the rules of the art'.

[2] Macucu is the vernacular Brazilian name for various genera of the Family Rosaceae.

[3] Weichsel is the wooden stem of a porcelain or meerschaum pipe.

[4] *Pano* is the general term for cloth in Portuguese. The Spanish equivalent is *paño* but it is not clear whether this is the word missing from the manuscript.

[5] An ancient measurement equivalent to 1.1 metres.

[6] Osnaburg is a kind of coarse linen made from flax and tow which came from the sovereign bishopric of that name in Northern Germany.

[7] Two, perhaps three, words are illegible, but 'incorporated in it' is a possible reading.

species of Salicornia, called Poluyo, is used as a mordant for all dyes. The Guapés, & other Indian tribes along the Rio Negro, prepare salt of the Poluyo.[1]

As the afternoon was far advanced, we had consented to take our night quarters at Senhora Liberada's house; meanwhile a clean mat had been spread on the ground, on which a white embroidered napkin was placed, upon which, the dishes intended for our refreshment were put; we sat down with our hostess, our right hands turned towards the dishes & resting on the left, rather an incommodious posture for those who are unaccustomed to it.

On my plate were a knife & fork, but Senhor Ayres & Senhora Liberada followed the general custom & used their fingers in lieu thereof. Before each plate, stood a small saucer of Farinha[2] which was used in company with the meats. After a piece of fish or meat had been torn in pieces, & conveyed to the mouth, the fingers were dipped in the Farinha, & so much as they take hold of between the fingers, was thrown into the mouth with such dexterity, that not a grain missed its destination. Xibé[3] is a favourite drink, & consists of Farinha, upon which water is poured which communicates to the water a pleasant and slightly acid taste. When nothing else is to be procured, the Farinha thus prepared, serves them as food, & in lieu of a spoon, they use a small calabash. A servant attended with a basin of water, to wash hands after the meal, which, by their mode of eating is indispensable.

Their customs at dinner, reminded me strongly of oriental manners, even the Café a la Sultane was not wanting, & the ceremonies of 'Madame' to prepare the Hookah for Senhor Ayres, followed.

We had taken a walk after dinner to the adjacent savannah, & had firstly to pass a fringe of wood. I observed here the largest Cereus or Cactus I had ever seen, & it deserved the name of a Cactus tree, if its construction admitted such a term. It measured upwards of six feet in circumference and its trunk, straight as an arrow, rose to ten feet before it divided into numerous erect limbs, some of them 40 feet high. Indeed it represented a perfect picture of a huge candelabra; the Symmetry of this gigantic herbaceous plant was in every respect perfect.

The savannah did not exhibit any novelties; numerous Parica trees, Curatella Americana,[4] & a species of Plumeria which appears to be common to all the savannahs of Guiana formed the chief features of the vegetation. The Plumeria, which is perhaps P. Bicolor of Ruiz & Pavon,[5] is called by the Brazilians Xucuba, and the milk is considered an excellent remedy against liver complaints.

Our hostess did not permit any of our servants to sling our hammocks when we were desirous to retire; she did it with her own hands which is a great compliment paid to the Guest.

August 17th. We left the house where we had been so hospitably treated, after a cup of coffee, and our attention having been drawn to large flocks of birds, which had been seen

---

[1] Salt was traditionally made by burning various plants, including aquatic specimens; the residue ash had a salty flavour.

[2] This almost certainly refers to *farinha de mandioca* which is a granular substance, a coarse flour, made from manioc.

[3] Chibé is the modern spelling.

[4] Popularly known in Guyana as the Sandpaper tree.

[5] *Plumeria rubra*. Hipólite Ruíz Lopez (1754–1815) and José Antonio Pavón (1754–1844), Spanish botanists.

stalking along a sandbank which rose out of the river, we directed our course thither; they consisted of Spurwing-plovers,[1] Roseate Spoonbills,[2] & the American Stork,[3] the two first did not await our coming within shot, but the Longlegs were more accomodating & permitted Sehnor Ayres, to fire three times at them, posessing a great deal of Phlegm in their constitution, no doubt the consequence of their mode of living in marshes & shallow rivers, they did not heed one small fire, & hopped merely after the report a few feet further. Such little exertion did not tire them, while it appeared that our Nimrod considered Priming & loading more troublesome, and the expense of Powder & Shot being also of weighty consideration in these distant regions, we resolved nem. con. to leave the storks to their leisure & grave strides, and to continue our course.

We passed the Island of Boa Vista which likely has received its name from the fine prospect, that opens at its southern point towards the Serra Grande and the naked mountains in the foreground. What a contrast, if the latter are compared with the luxuriant vegetation and gorgeous hues so peculiar to a tropical climate. Scarcely covered with a spare grass, sharp ridged & exhibiting numerous blocks of a dark colour, the sides of the hill torn by torrents into crevices, it appeared as if they had been called forth from the gloomy empire of Pluto, to serve as abode to some spirit, condemned to inhabit desolated hills, while spreading around it are rich valleys watered by clear springs, Mountains clothed with forest, exhibiting rocky surfaces enamelled with the splendid tribes of Cassiae, Mimoseae, Orchideae and a whole world of the prettiest ferns.

The Ilha Carricatua[4] is one of the largest in that part of the river. It is about six miles long, but of inconsiderable width. Its name signifies in the Lingua Geral, 'left Island'; I could not ascertain the origin of that name, it is not nearer situated to the left side of the river, than any other in its vicinity, & can scarcely have received its name from that circumstance. Having reached its southern point, we stood for the brook da Serra Grande. All our endeavours to procure a guide had proved fruitless. The person who accompanied Mr Smith was dead, & there is pretty much the idea among the people still prevalent that, whoever ascends Mountain Carumá will soon after fall into the hands of grim Death.

This is quite sufficient amongst the superstitious, to deter them from any attempt, the difficulties connected with the ascent entirely set aside; We had however ascertained that old Andrés Miguel, had been lately there in search of some strayed Cattle and as his hut was up the brook just mentioned, we intended to proceed thither.

When we entered the brook we found three fine Canoes, secured to its banks, which we soon recognised as those belonging to the Pressgang, a most villainous looking body, lately sent by the Brazilian Authorities, to press Indians for the navy. It appears they had landed here, in order to continue their way overland.[5]

---

[1] The Spur-winged Plover (*Hoploterus spinosus*) has been renamed the Spur-winged Lapwing (*Vanellus spinosus*). It has not been reported from the region.

[2] *Ajaia ajaja*.

[3] *Euxenura galeata*.

[4] Ilha de São Lourenço.

[5] Schomburgk had already met this party when they arrived at Fort São Joaquim on 1 August. He claimed that he persuaded Pedro Ayres to stop their raiding the mission at Pirara which he suspected was their target (TNA, CO111/162, Letter Schomburgk to Buxton, 25 August 1838). Service in the navy meant acting as paddlers for official canoes. As will be seen, the appearance of this pressgang – Schomburgk normally uses the word 'slavers' – had considerable consequences.

Our canoe was too large, to push up the brook, chiefly in consequence of the Tolda or Tent,[1] and we unloaded therefore our baggage into a smaller one. The brook was winding & much overgrown, & it was with some difficulty that we made progress. The Serra Grande is generally called 'the father & mother of rain', & it is generally said that if nowhere else it rains it is sure to pour in its vicinity. As if to prove the truth of the Adage, it sent it to us in bucketfulls. After a couple of hours' strong paddling, we landed at Andrés Miguel's. His house did not offer anything prepossessing in its appearance; it was worse constructed than many of the Indian houses. Our arrival scared a number of females, who fled in dark corners, or in the outhouses; but the old Dame slung a couple of Hammocks which it appeared to me, were suffering under Hydrophobia; they could not have seen water, (soap set entirely apart) for months. Andrés Miguel was not at home, but one of the girls was sent in search of him, and we saw him soon after arrive, hugging Senhor Ayres as soon as he came up with us, & greeting me respectfully. He was a good looking old man with grissly curled hair, hanging down his side & back part of his head & leaving a bald & open front; his nose was decidedly Roman, & if it had not been for that arched nose, I should have liked to say, his bust might serve as the 'beau Ideal' of that of an Indian Homerius. He is considered the Patriarch of the race of 'the Vaqueiros' or herdsmen; to him they flock if they want advice, on him the rising generation look with respect, & father Andres Miguel's name is in every mans mouth. The repeated experience of years, have fitted him for the adviser of the younger part of those, who have followed his calling; and I think I may state that all the present Vaqueiros of the farms of the Rio Branco, have grown up under him.

Many of his daughters, & I think I saw five, (he has no son) are married to Cattle minders, the youngest was a girl of not more than thirteen years, nevertheless she had been married when the visiting priest had been lately at the Fort San Joaquim. His visits – helas! there is nothing of the Angelic connected with them & the important part, is the wish for grasping fees – are few & far between and the cautious parents, observing the budding love of their daughter, secured her from sin in time, and she was married at that early age to her lover.

There are several small properties in the vicinity of his, the proprietors of which are either Cattle drivers, or serve to garrison the fort. They take from time to time furlough, in order to put their provision grounds in order, & the rest of the Year, they are at Fort San Joaquim or any of the farms, with the promise of receiving pay, like a soldier, namely four vintems p day,*

*A vintem is about 1½ᵈ Sterl.

living in the hope of getting their long arrears, one of these days – Poor fellows! if they reached the age of Methusselah, that day is not likely to arrive.

I measured a baseline from Miguel's house, in order to ascertain roughly the height of Mount Carumá, nice operations were out of the question, the day & atmosphere were unfavourable, and the ground was much broken up; the result gave me a height for the highest summit of Carumá, above Miguel's house 2082 feet, to which must be added, for the height of the house & instrument 50 feet, which would make the summit of Carumá 2132 feet above the Rio Branco.

[1] This is the awning over part of the canoe, for protection from sun and rain.

It commenced so severely to rain, that we gave up all further preparations for starting that day, and we accepted Miguel's offer of a night quarter. In a conversation with him, we had ascertained, that he attempted once to ascend the mountain, but that he had never reached the top, nor had Mr. Smith been more successful, as he had been told by his compadre[1] who served him as guide,*

> *Through the kindness of Lieut. Gullifer's brother, I possess his manuscript of the journey, & I well recollect that there were some obstacles, which prevented the travellers from reaching the summit, but I cannot recall the particulars to my memory, having left the manuscript in the Colony.[2]

that they only reached the fall or Cascade. Miguel was however willing to guide us to the best of his abilities. In a council which we convoked for that purpose, and in which the old dame received a vote, it was resolved to ascend the mountain from its western side, & to follow it along the whole ridge. I had been told, while at Fort San Joaquim that sometimes heavy detonations, are heard from the mountains; Miguel not only confirmed it, but asserted that one had taken place the previous day, at about four oclock in the afternoon. They are very frequent, and there is scarcely an individual who lives near the mountain who does not pretend of having heard them frequently. These sounds are not uncommon, and are generally ascribed to Gasses, nevertheless I fear that those of the Carumá have been mistaken for the reverberation, which the fall of a tree, perhaps many ages old, would cause, if falling down the steep precipices, that are along the sides of the mountains may have produced the report. How many times have we been awakened out of our slumber during our former expeditions when one of those Giants of the forest fell, even on level ground, and the sound started animated nature. How much more must this sound be increased by falling several hundred feet, & bearing in its fall whatever opposition it finds.

Our hammocks had been slung in an outhouse, we found it well cleaned, & lighted by a lamp with Manteiga oil,[3] which gave not a great lustre, but a very pleasing light. After the old man had seen it trimmed, he bade us good night & left us to our slumbers, rather a difficult task, where millions of Mosquitoes attempted to delight us by their music & smarted us by their stings.

August 18th, We were up very early, but the weather looked so threatening, that we preferred to await the result. It proved only a passing shower, and we embarked immediately after, the old man accompanying us in a smaller canoe. Our embarkation was attended with an unfortunate accident. One of the Indians, who was carrying my instruments to the Canoe, allowed the box which contained the artificial Horizon with a plane speculum, the one adapted best for measuring the height of mountains, to fall to the ground; the box split to pieces & one of the adjusting screws was broken – a sad accident in a place where it is impossible to have such things repaired. The strong current carried our vessel rapidly forward, & it required great dexterity, to prevent her from getting foul of the numerous stumps & trees which impeded the brook's course, we had however safely passed the

---

[1] A 'compadre' is a person who is your child's godfather or your godchild's father. Accordingly between men the term is used reciprocally. The female equivalent is 'comadre'. However, it is common for the terms to be used between close friends without a godparent relationship being involved.

[2] As mentioned above (see p. 19, fn. 3), if it still exists, this manuscript has not been located.

[3] Manteiga is the Portuguese word for butter, but in the north of Brazil it is also used for any animal or vegetable oil.

worst places, & calculated being soon at the Rio Branco, when at a sudden turn the stern of the canoe got foul of a protruding stump, & the violence with which she descended, caused her to split; she filled immediately, & if it had not been for the presence of mind of one Indian, who jumped immediately in the water, which was only about five feet deep, in order to keep her stern up & to push her bow inshore, she would have sunk, & we would have had the annoyance to see all our baggage sunk with her; as it was, we got many of our things completely soaked, and as old Miguel had proceeded before us, in order to fish, we had to devise means to reach our canoe at the mouth of the creek. It was therefore noon before we reached the Rio Branco.

The Brook Marawani joins the Rio Branco from the western side; it has fine clear waters likewise of a blueish tint as those of the Cacuruau. Mount Carumá bore from here S.7°E. On a sandbank, which extended opposite the brook, we saw Old Miguel busily employed in a destructive war with the finny tribes; one fish after the other was aimed at, shot, & drawn struggling into the boat. As we had not been able to procure provisions, those signs for a good dinner, were hailed with delight. We were now so near the mountain, that we plainly observed its structure, the prominent features of which were highly inclined planes of Gneiss, resembling in many instances perpendicular walls. A streamlet which rushed over one of those naked planes, formed a small cascade; while further south another was observed, which was considerable enough to afford a picturesque aspect. We intended to encamp at the foot of the first and to direct our further proceedings according to circumstances. Our tent was soon pitched, and as old Miguel had arrived with his treasure, the happy results of his exertions in the fishing way, we selected some of that delicate species of Siluridae, the yacima, or Tiger fish,[1] & handed them over to our cook to have them washed, smoked & stewed. Under these pleasing auspices for a stomach, sharpened by appetite since the morning's standing, our wreck and its consequences would have been buried in oblivion, if the remembrance of it had not been awakened by a new misfortune. The sun shone in full force, & Senhor Ayres intended to take the necessary advantage of it, in order to dry part of his luggage. The tent of the canoe offered a good place for it, on which they had been scarcely spread, when some mischievous [illegible] of a mountain spirit sent such a blast down the hill that it carried the tent, which exhibited much the appearance of a pawn-brokers counter, with all its paraphernalia in the Rio Branco, & before assistance could be given, the whole stock in trade sunk to the bottom.

We had despatched an exploring party to the heights above the camp where we had seen the smaller cascade; they returned towards dusk & reported that the mountain ended in a sharp ridge, & that the water collected from the rocky planes, on which it was running down in gentle streams. As there could be no lake in that direction, we resolved now to commence our ascent from the mountain's most SSW side, & after having fallen in with the larger brook which we saw precipitating itself from the rocks, it was our plan to follow its course. The day was too far advanced to attempt the ascent, & we delayed it until the following morning. The night was clouded & the air fresh & the state of the Atmosphere did not permit any astronomical observations. The Therm. stood at 6^h – 80°, the water of the Rio Branco was 3 degrees warmer viz 83° Far. At 9^h p.m. the air was 79° the water 80°.5.

---

[1] The Order Siluriformes, the catfish, has thirty-one Families. The Family Siluridae is confined to Europe and Asia. There are some 1,300 species of Catfish found in the New World.

August 19th We broke up our camp with dawn of day, & continued along the foot of the mountain until we reached its south western angle. We had now a full view of the larger cascade, which must be very splendid after severe rains; its fall cannot be less than 300 feet. We were told that Mr Smith attempted the ascent in this direction, however we preferred to proceed further to the south west to a place where the Rio Branco forms a small rapid.

Armed with a cutlass our marching column was opened by Andrés Miguel, the others followed in indian file, & the path led first over a rugged elevation of vitrified boulders and continued for a short distance over level ground. We observed a small elevated Savannah on our right, and commenced soon after the proper ascent. Here appeared to reign the greatest confusion; huge boulders of a coarse grained granite covered the acclivity of the mountain, some of the boulders formed caves by resting upon each other, & were so roomy that they would have afforded shelter to our whole party in case of Rain. Numerous smaller rocks lay scattered among them, some weathered & grown over with mosses, others appeared to have but lately rolled downwards, and as a rolling stone does not gather any grass, they formed a strong contrast with the surrounding rocks.

The nature of the soil did not allow any underbrush, but there were many gigantic trees which overshadowed the large blocks & their roots grasped in many instances immense boulders & kept them fast to the side of the mountain. Should age cause the decay of the tree, & its falls, the large block must roll down the mountain. We arrived at a rocky plane, inclined at the high angle of about 40° & quite smooth – it offered us however, the hopes of a fine prospect, & leaving the shoes behind, we attempted to climb up, & soon reached its top. The mist was still hovering over the valley, & only the summits of the Mocajahi[1] mountains looking like Islands raising their heads above the billowed ocean, were visible.

Other rocks of a similar description presented insurmountable obstacles to our present course, we could get no footing, & were obliged to change its direction. The vegetation was so strong & dense, that we were obliged to cut a passage through it and to follow the leader in a sloping direction, much to the detriment of our clothing. We had now ascended for a couple of hours & anxious to know where about we were, we sent one of our people to a high tree: he reported that in consequence of the thick forest, he could not see forward, but that he observed to our left another of those naked rocks, towards which we proceeded. The prospect from here to the southwest was beautiful, the mountains of Mocajahi, along the northern foot of which the river of the same name meanders, with the high mountains of Caritarimani[2] to the southwest, raising their elevated summits upwards of 4 to 5000 feet above the plains, were the principal features. To the northwest extended unbounded Savannahs, the dense woods of the Mokajahi forming the boundary line to the Southwest. A small pointed hillock, the most northern of the Serra Mocajahi, round which the river wound itself, bore N.72W., distant about 12 miles; the river takes from here a more southern turn, and falls 7 miles below the mountain Carumá into the Rio Branco.

Our lips were by this time considerably parched, & we despatched a party in search of water, but our patience outrun their return, and we preferred to follow them. We had

---

[1] Mucajaí. On the west bank of the Rio Branco and to the south of the river of the same name.
[2] Catrimani. This is presumably the Serra Tabatinga on the east bank of the Rio Catrimani.

reached another platform when we saw our party returning, who had found the small brook, which ultimately forms the cataract at but a small distance from the plane where we there were, & we resolved to proceed thither in order to partake of our breakfast.

The descent was steep, but after a few 'faux pas', & their consequences, we reached the limpid rill, turmoiling over numerous boulders, now disappearing among the broken fragments of rocks, and at its appearance forming cataracts in miniature. Boughs of trees overhung it & formed an arch, which even the rays of the sun could not penetrate, & the coolness was so delicious that it needed no further invitation to select it for our resting place.

After we had refreshed ourselves, we continued our march, preferring to follow the brook upwards. It divided soon after in two branches and we followed the lateral one to its end. It issued from a number of scattered rocks, through which it percolated, & gathered strength from the sides of the mountain, indeed the whole soil abounded in moisture.

We returned now again to the north in order to fall in again with the mainbranch, which itself was only of short duration, as half an hours walk eastward, brought us to its end. A steep mountain closed here the valley, and at its foot we found, comparatively speaking, the only level ground which we had seen hitherto, though its whole extent was scarcely 50 feet, & here the brook had its sources, receiving its waters from the surrounding mountains which rose about 250 feet higher on each side. We ascended the mountain which closed the valley, it was uncommonly steep; the ascent proved at an angle of 33° & numerous loose rocks, made it dangerous for those who followed. The leader of our train had first to try every rock whether it would sustain a man's weight.

Arrived at the top of this hill we were again on one of the rocky planes but much more extensive than any of those which we had traversed before[:] the present was remarkable for a profusion of beautiful plants & shrubs with tortuous branches. Spots had been left naked, & at their limits the manner in which these otherwise sterile planes are covered with the most luxuriant vegetation might be observed. Lichens, Ferns, & among them a species of Hemionitis and a pretty Adiantum,[1] as well as Graninae[2] had settled in crevices where a sufficient moisture insured their growth; this is the first step towards vegetation, & vegetable soil being swept from the higher mountains by each torrent of rain it is here arrested & accumulates with time. The gorgeous tribes of Orchideae, satisfied with little soil for their sustenance, follow next; of similar nature are the Bromeliaceae, & the decomposition of these thickly interwoven plants, produces already sufficient soil to afford nourishment to shrubs. The Orchideae which I found here consisted of three species of Epidendrum, one of them with long stalks & large umbels of crimson flowers, the splendid Zygopetalum rostratum,[3] with flowers two inches & a half in diameter, and an Epidendrae which I discovered first at the Cataracts of the Corentyne, & which another traveller during his subsequent ascent of the river Cuyuni characterizes as exclusively granitic, & pronounces to be an Oncidium, "much resembling the Oncidium Altissimum,"*[4]

*I do not think that the traveller (Mʳ Hillhouse) pretended to botanical knowledge, or such a faux pas as pronouncing an Epidendrea to be an Oncidium could not have occurred, nor

[1] Both genera of the Family Pteridaceae.
[2] Gramineae
[3] *Zygosepalum labiosum.*
[4] *Oncidium baueri.*

was the plant a novelty as I had collected & pictured it six months previously. It is not exclusively granitic[.] I have found it frequently on the banks of the upper Essequibo on trees, it might well be styled an Epiphite though its favourite situation appears to be granitic ledges.

occupied here whole acres, & diffused its fragrant smell.[1]

A Bromelia with small fruit contested with the Orchideae for the ground; among other herbaceous plants, I observed an Oxalis, a Verbena, with flowers of a vivid Cyan blue, and a Cardamine awakened many a recollection of boyish pleasure, when the appearance of the Cuckoo flower (Cardamine pratenas)[2] was hailed as the forerunner of delicious spring.

A Mimosa with tortuous branches, a Cassia with bright yellow flowers, and a Malpighia, with uncommonly small flowers, were equally new to me but the most distinguished shrub was an Eugenia, with linear aromatic leaves, & tortuous branches – it reigned paramount, & we had literally to cut ourselves a passage through its crooked branches, & to continue our march in a stooping posture. We were at a loss in what direction we should further proceed, the thick vegetation did not permit us to look forward & we had again to send a scout to one of the trees, in order to look for the summit. He communicated the unpleasing news, that we were yet far off, and it would take us three days before we could reach it.[3]

Our scout who tired like all of us, wished perhaps that his information should induce us to encamp or to give up the further ascent. It was then three OClock, & the thermometer stood at 87°.5, our height may have been about 1600 feet, & although the height was but trifling, the necessity of ascending & descending several mountains, before we reached the spot, where we now stood, had made us weary. I managed to mount one of the trees, & soon observed that a three days journey was not required to come to the summit, however there was no hope that we could reach it today. Where the mountain arises anew in a conical form, it makes a saddle, & there I proposed we should rest. We had to descend several hundred feet, & to walk along a sharp ridge, connected with the body of the mountain, our party got divided – we followed along the ridge, passing numerous walls of granite in our way, out of which the water oozed in large drops – we applied our lips, & quenched by this measure our thirst. These Rocks were clothed with the pretty Gesneria aggregata[4] & tomentosa,[5] also Alstroemeria salsilla,[6] so famed for its diaphoretic and diuretic qualities & several amarylliaceous plants.[7] The Erythrina Corallodendrum[8] grew spontaneously in the vicinity of the rocks, & the brilliant scarlet colour of its flowers, contributed much to enrich the floral display.

[1] See Hilhouse, 'Journal of an Expedition up the River Cuyuny, in British Guayana, in March, 1837', *JRGS*, 7, 1837, pp. 446–54, p 452.

[2] The Cuckoo Flower (*Cardamine pratensis*).

[3] Page 23 of the manuscript is blank except for the following in Schomburgk's handwriting: '(Note. Left blank by mistake of the Copist, and every apology is herewith rendered for the oversight. RHS.).' It is not clear why this apology was made since there does not appear to be any text missing; p. 24 carries on naturally from p. 22.

[4] *Sinningia aggregata*.

[5] *Gesneria tomentosa*, depending on author, is now classified as three different species of *Rhytidophyllum*.

[6] The genus *Alstroemeria* is now known as *Bomarea*, a member of the Family Liliaceae, but is not reported from Guiana.

[7] Possibly members of the Family Amaryllidaceae, although Schomburgk may simply have meant plants with a bulbous root.

[8] *Erythrina corallodendron* is reported from Brazil but apparently not from Guiana.

I was walking the fourth in succession, when on looking on the ground, I observed a Labari Snake coiled up, gorged with its prey; three persons had stepped therefore unaware of the danger, over it without fortunately touching it. Owing to its sluggishness after its meal we can only ascribe that this otherwise so venomous snake, had not injured any one; we killed it & found a frog inside.

We arrived at half-past 5 at the saddle & selected it the readier for our night quarter, [as] a small rill promised us sufficient water for cooking & quenching our thirst with a calabash of Xibé. The Thermometer stood at 6 o clock p.m. 78°, when at that time it stands generally from 83° to 85° at Fort San Joaquim[;] the water of the small rill was 80°.2. The evening was beautiful, but the branches of high trees hid completely the starry heavens from us and prevented observations.

August 20th We continued our march at six o'clock, and after half an hours ascent, we arrived at the northern side of the mountain, where we had a pretty prospect of the valley below, enlivened by the small cottages of the Vaqueiros, & herds of grazing cattle. A grove of Coucourite Palms, through which we directed now our course, formed a striking contrast with the Eugenias & Mimosas which we had left behind us, & though the acclivity proved steeper, not being covered by underbrush, we made rapid progress, & were at 8 OClock at the western summit. Further eastward is another, about 50 feet higher than the Western, & the depression between the two forms a saddle. We reached the eastern, or highest summit at nine OClock, where we observed with much regret that high trees & bushes, did not afford an open prospect. I mounted however one of the trees Kater's compass in my hand, & having made myself as comfortable as circumstances would permit, I commenced to scan the surrounding country, & Sororeng, my Indian interpreter, a Pauxian of birth,[1] who is well acquainted hereabouts, pointed out the different mountains to me. The Eye commanded a vast range of country. To the north east, it was arrested by the dim outlines of the Canucku mountains, the Rock Imanlickipang bearing N.54½E; further eastward we observed the three peaked Saereri & the Ursato or Cussato mountains,[2] at the western foot of which the Takatu flows which river is called by the Attoroys & Wapishanas Butu-au-urú, and is said to have its sources at the mountains Vindiau,[3] six days journey from the Ursato. The Takatu receives about 12 miles south of the mountains Ursato the river Quitavau, which has its

[1] The Pauxian, Pauixana or Paushiana, as Sororeng is described elsewhere (Schomburgk, *Twelve Views*, p. 37), used to inhabit the country between the Takutu and Rio Branco and the Catrimani River. Sororeng is said to have spoken a language similar to Wapishana (see Vol. II, chap. 3), which would indicate that the Paushiana are an Arawakan group. However this group, spelt Pauishiana, is listed by Çestmír Loukotka, *Classification of South American Indian Languages*, Los Angeles, Latin American Center, University of Los Angeles, 1968, pp. 207–8, as Carib, although the appellation sounds very much like a nickname, the Powis or Bush turkey People. There was also another group living in the same region, the Paravilhana, who spoke, according to Loukotka (p. 209), a different dialect of Carib. Schomburgk (see below, p. 288) refers to the Paravilhana as having migrated to the Amazon. We have quite a lot of information on the Paravilhana, who were the main tribe of the Rio Branco, from the mid-18th century until their virtual disappearance, by death, migration and absorption, in the following century. See Peter Rivière, *An Ethnographic Survey of the Indians on the Divide of the Guianese and Amazonian River Systems*, unpublished B. Litt. thesis, University of Oxford, 1963, pp. 198–204. It is not possible to sort out this ethnographic confusion, but that Sororeng spoke both Carib and Arawak is quite likely and this could be a good reason why he continued as Schomburgk's interpreter during his others expeditions.

[2] Shiriri Mountains and Kusad Mountains.

[3] Serra Vindaua.

sources in the Arawasute mountains, about 40 miles S.S.E. of the mountain Carumá, and approaches the Rio Branco in the vicinity of the latter mountain within 8 miles, but in lieu of continuing its course westerly, and to fall into the Rio Branco south of Carumá, it makes a sweep to the southeast, flows along the mountains Kie-i-rita & falls ultimately in the Takatu, as already mentioned.[1] It forms therefore with the Takatu a peninsula of about 90 miles in length, and its waters cross, united with those of the Branco, the parallel of the Serra Carumá again after a circuit of 200 miles. Next to the Canucku, the Kie-i-rita, or Kie-iwa is the most extensive mountain chain. Kie-i-rita signifies in the language of the Wapishanas 'the mountains of the moon'.[2] They extended, observed from Carumá from S24°E to S79½E or 55½° and as the distance was about [blank[3]] miles, we may calculate that they extended about [blank] miles. Several detached groups occupied the ground between the Kieirita (which the creoles call Serra da lua) and the Carumá, keeping up the link between the Serras Mokajahi & Karitarimani, west of the Rio Branco, & form at their passage through the river, the falls or Cachoêiras.

The collective name of these detatched groups appears to be in former maps the Serra Yauina, however as such it is not more known, and as the tribes, who formerly inhabited these regions, the Paravilhanes[4] & several sister-tribes of the Wapishanas, have wandered out, the former to the Amazon, the latter farther east, its origin would prove difficult of explanation.

To the far north, we observed the summit of the Tapaghé mountains, inhabited by the extensive tribe of Arécunas[5] & a large column of smoke pointed out the situation of the Fortaleza, where we knew that the Vaqueiros had intended to set the Savannahs on fire. The hills Maruckú[6] were just visible. The country farther west was concealed by the Western summit; a panoramic view was therefore out of question, nevertheless the interesting spectacle which the vast savannas afford through which the Rio Branco flows, forming a number of Islands, pays for the trouble connected with the ascent of the mountain. An Alpine Lake is out of question, and the water, which during torrents of rain, gushes down in vast Volumes, must have given rise to the fable.

We mounted Trees in all directions, but nowhere did we discover a level spot, of sufficient extent to warrant even a mere pond, much less a sheet of water, in which fishes, & the fresh water porpoise of the Rio Branco, amuse themselves in Gambols. Old Andrés Miguel observed already to us, that he had never known a white or coloured man, who pretended of having ascended the hill, or given a report of the famed lake, and it was his opinion, that the tradition had descended from the Indians, who formerly lived near the Caruma. I am not aware whether Hortsmann's manuscript observes, that he himself ascended the mountain & saw the lake, or whether he only reports what was told him. M De Humboldt in the paragraph cited above, does not express himself distinctly, & I am inclined to beleive that Hortsmann only related the common

---

[1] On Schomburgk's map the river Quitavau is called Guidirau, and is the modern Quitauau. He was later to discover that it does flow directly into the Rio Branco (see below Vol. II, chap. 2).

[2] Serra da Lua.

[3] Thirty miles in published version (p. 187).

[4] See discussion above (p. 287, fn. 1) concerning the Paravilhana.

[5] The Arecuna are a Carib-speaking people closely related to the Macushi and are part of a wider grouping called the Pemon.

[6] Murku M. is marked on Schomburgk's map in approximately the position of the modern Serra da Moça.

report.[1] An examination of the mountain from the savannah caused already doubts of the existence of the lake, I could not be therefore much disappointed, while on the other side, the extensive view which I enjoyed from its summit & the number of bearings of objects of great importance to a Geographical survey, more than recompensed me for the ascent. Andrés Miguel had visited the mountains in a SSE direction, which he described as extensive & inhabited by a nation called Arrowacca. If this be founded in fact, it would be an interesting instance of the distribution of tribes, as there could be no doubt that the Arawaaks, who at present inhabit the coast regions of Berbice, Demerara & Essequibo wandered from the South to the North. M De Humboldt in his enumeration of the Indian races, who inhabit the former province of New Andelusia, observes that the Pariagotos or Parias, formerly occupied the Coasts of Berbice & Essequibo. They have advanced therefore further west, while the Arawaaks from the South, & the Guaraounos or Warows from the WSW occupy at present their former place. The few Caribis, who at present inhabit British Guiana, say that their ancestors came from the Orinoco. A sister tribe of theirs, the Caripunas, inhabit the right bank of the River Amazon. The object of these wanderings is too important in the history of the Indian tribes, to be dismissed in a superficial manner, and I hope to be enabled to put it before the reader in a more detailed manner hereafter.[2]

We remained about two hours at the summit. The Thermometer stood at 9 am 72°, while at that time it ranges generally at Fort San Joaquim 79° to 83°. A fog passed about 10 OClock over the mountain & the Thermometer sunk to 71°·5 F. I cut with a cutlass, three notches in one of the trees which crown the summit,[3] & as from a survey of the declivity Southeast of the summit we observed that it did not offer any level spot, but sunk at a considerable angle, we did not follow our investigations in that direction. To the SSW the mountain formed deep hollows, & exhibited about 800 feet below the summitt, rocky plains inclined at an angle of 20° over which the water must rush with furious impetuosity during heavy rains; in that direction spread a little Savannah at its foot.

Our descent was rapid. Senhor Ayres wished to set those Eugenias & Mimosas on fire, which covered the rocky plane, nearest to the summit; dry wood was collected from all sides, & when we saw the pile fairly on flames, we left the mountain with the hope of seeing it in a blaze when we should reach that part of Serra from whence we had the first perfect view of the summit on our ascent; but the hatching mountain of Rain, would not have been true to the character which it enjoyed if it had allowed us to reach the foot without sending us its blessing. We got pretty well soaked, & with it the conflagration, with which Senhor Ayres had intended to astonish the surrounding country, was quenched in its infancy.

We broke up our camp of the previous night, & as we had shared the last of our provender, it appeared our crew was determined to prevent our camping another night on the hill, & run with a speed as if all the Hobgoblins of the Serra were at their heels; we did not lag behind them, not minding bushes or Briars which disputed our progress;

[1] Horstmann did not climb, or at least does not mention climbing, the Serra Grande.

[2] It is very difficult to sort out the movements of native groups in the region, but for a recent attempt, see G. Bos, *Some Recoveries in Guiana Indian History*, Amsterdam, VU Uitgeverij, 1998.

[3] It is not clear what the purpose of these notches may have been, but it may simply mean an opening was made in order to obtain a view.

we represented therefore at our arrival at the Canoe, any thing but a decent appearance. Indeed the most enterprizing of the "Jewish Cloth merchants," would have hesitated to offer a sixpence for Senhor Ayres "whole suit," & with the misfortune of losing the greater part of his stock, the other day, it became now a serious question in what to dress to prevent scandal.

Our descent from the summit, all stoppages included, had taken us three hours & three quarters.

In referring to Arrowsmith's six sheet map of South America,[1] I find a Serra Carumani in 2°.20N Lat on the right bank of the Rio Branco & in the second parallel of Latitude, one of the same name on the right, & one on the left shore; of those noted in the above map, exists only the mountain Carumá Caruman, or Serra Grande, which is situated in Lat [blank] on the western[2] or left bank of the river Branco and its north-western foot is washed by that river.

From the relation of our excursion, the reader will be informed that no lake exists at present nor is there any ground to beleive that one ever existed. Hortsmann as already stated, must have been misinformed by the Indians, from whom the tradition emanated. On close questioning those whom we were told, relate at present the story of the lake with its fishes – they confessed of having received the account from the Wapishana Indians.

Before we reached our canoes, the savoury odour of frying fish greeted already our nose, and we found that the young Indian, whom we had left in charge of the Canoes, had not been idle; he had caught a number of fish, which were highly welcome to our sharpened appetite.

During our repast, we were watched by a number of Turkey Buzzards (Cathartes Aura).[3] They were perched on the high branches of trees which fronted the river & looked most curiously at our enjoying the good things that were before us. We had to use every precaution that they did not act like those winged monsters, the Harpies, towards us, & Senhor Ayres told me that, while ascending the Rio Branco, they really spoiled by their filth a delicious dish of fish which had been just put on the green turf before him.

Every preparation for our departure being finished, & we having entered the canoe, this was the signal for a simultaneous attack of those which were next the place, where we had taken our dinner; they quarrelled & fought for the bones & refuse, & even from the other side of the river, we saw them hastening to the spoil. What a sharp eye & quick sight did those display which at a distance of a mile & a half, observed by the great commotion among their sable brothers, that an opportunity of glutting themselves was at hand.

We had now to toil against the current, & made but little progress; the night broke upon us and with it complete darkness; large fireflies, not with the pale Phosphoric light, which those near the coast display, but of a dark red luminous appearance, starred the dark mantle of the night, & formed a strong contrast. We paddled until 11 OClock at night, & as our crew appeared worn out, we halted for some hours at the mouth of the Igarapé da Serra Grande.

---

[1] This is A. Arrowsmith's map of South America in six sheets, first published in London in 1811; it was republished with additions in 1816, 1819 and 1840.

[2] Schomburgk meant 'eastern'.

[3] More commonly known as Turkey Vulture.

We missed the canoes of the pressgang; they had therefore returned, and a howling dog which hovered about the landing place, told the tale. Only those who have travelled for years amongst Indians know what value the red man places on his dog – he would wait for days, to secure him if he strayed, but here it was apparent, that force had driven the owner to abandon the dog, which had perhaps accompanied him for years on his hunting excursions. The circumstance fell harshly on me, and I conjectured from it, that they had been but too fortunate in their business. We departed at about four oclock in the morning, and with dawn of day, we discovered fires on a sandbank before us, and the conclusion was natural that the sandbank had served for night quarter to the Slaving Expedition. They started before we reached the sandbank, and howling dogs spoke of further abandonment. They kept the river's left bank, but we continued on the right. When the sun was high enough to permit us to discern objects at some distance, I counted three Canoes filled with people. We arrived at about 11 OClock in the morning at Senhora Liberada's where we had promised Andrés Miguel, our former guide, who had some business to attend at his home, to await him in order to accompany us to the Fort. We had lent him two men of our crew in order to hasten himself.

While we were at Liberada's the canoes arrived, & who can describe my disgust & horror at these descents,[1] when I counted only nine men, three of which approached in age the great Climacteric[,] the others consisted of thirteen women & eighteen children under twelve years, six of them were sucking babies? The object of the expedition was then at once explained, it was the basest of Kidnapping, yet I will not say that the higher authorities of the district had given orders for such misdoings; how is it possible to think that sucking babies, girls, women, & old men, are fit subjects to serve in the Brazilian navy? The whole blame falls on the inferior officers of the District, as Duardo, who commanded the gang, excuses himself that his orders were to seize old & young.

I made the strictest inquiry whether the gang had crossed the Rupununy, & carried their blasting march to the British Possessions; but I ascertained through my interpreter, that they were Wapishanas and Atoroyas from the Ursato Mountains at the eastern or right bank of the Takutu.

They remained only a short period at Senhora Liberadas; some of those who composed the gang, were relations of our hostess.

August 22nd Andres Miguel not having arrived this morning, we set off after a very severe storm & rain, & arrived at 5 OClock in the evening safely at Fort San Joaquim, where only an hour before us, the slaving expedition had arrived.

They had been quartered at the fort, & every pains were taken to make us beleive, that the poor Indians had abandoned their huts & fields & had followed them voluntarily. However we found opportunity soon to ascertain the contrary. Some were allowed to walk about, whilst the others were kept in the fort.

They paid us a visit, having ascertained that our party did not belong to those who had so greviously wronged them. With the assistance of my vocabulary I showed them that I knew a few words in their language, which caused them inexpressible joy.

They assailed me now with a volume of words, but alas! my knowledge did not reach so far, to understand what they had to say, however I understood sufficient to

---

[1] Schomburgk is making a literal translation of the Portuguese word 'descimento'; the term used to describe the rounding up of Indians for forced labour.

ascertain, that they had been surprised at night, had been fired at, two huts set on fire & who had not been able to make his escape had been led away with their hands tied to their back. The conduct of the ruffians towards their women & children incensed them most; they brought their little children of five & six years old, & showed us that even they had been tied with their hands to their back, for which purpose they used the children's own laps, with which their nakedness is partly covered, & fixed it in such a way that the lap which served as a rope, went around the neck & fixed the hands on the back. An old woman the mother of one of the young men, & grandmother of six children, had given likely offence by her vociferous tongue, & she had been treated still more harshly. The eyes of her son, a handsome young Indian, kindled fire at the relation of the treatment towards his mother. They told Sororeng, our interpreter, who had been summoned meanwhile, that six men, with several women, & some children, had made their escape in the bustle. The Attack had been made about midnight, but as their huts had been scattered, there had not been a sufficient number to surround them. After they had secured their victims, they rifled the huts, and carried away what they considered of value, Parrots, spun cotton, Dogs, &c. There being a number of children, the march towards the canoes proved slow, & their provisions gave out, nevertheless they were driven forward like a herd of cattle, flanked by these ruffians with their musquits loaded & primed, & reached the sixth day the canoes at the Igarapé de Serra Grande.

I communicated these facts to Senhor Ayres, who as he told me had, since the arrival of the expedition neither taken directly nor indirectly any interest in it; he would scarcely credit the relation of these atrocities. I summoned however my interpreter, & he put several questions, the answers to which showed him the truth. It was his opinion that the inferior officers wished to use the pressing of Indians for the navy, as an excuse to procure young & old, in order to sell those who were not fit for that purpose to their Allies.

He promised to report these proceedings to his brother the Commander of Civil & Military affairs of the Comarca (district), and he expressed his persuasion, that only those who could really serve in the navy, would be selected, while the Aged, women & children would be returned; by all means his report of the number who, have been secured, will prevent underlings to dispose of them.

If we picture to ourselves the Indian village a few days before the descent, their avocations carried on in peace & quietness, & we throw a glance at it after the blasting visit; the mother crying for her children or husband, the husband bewailing his wife, the Father his son, the children their parents; the picture is dismal, & does not belong to our enlightened times, it carries us back to the barbarous ages or tyrannical Government.

To the traveller, who should pass from the present village of Pirara to the place of embarkation, on the Rivulet Pirara, his guides will point out a place, which evidently shows, that it was once the site of human habitations. Posts, on which the vestiges of fire are observable, a few Cashew & Arnatto Trees (Anacardium & Bixa) as well as some straggling shrubs of Cotton, is all what remains of this once happy Macusi settlement.

His guides will tell him, that on one dark night, a lawless band of Kidnappers, arrived from the Rio Branco, surprized the poor inmates, & after having set their huts on fire, carried old & young away to die far from their native land in bondage & slavery. Such a fate threatened the young mission at Pirara, how far it has been my good fortune to prevent it, I leave the reader to judge. To Senhor Ayres' humane disposition much is due, & though the thunderbolt fell in another direction, the young mission was saved, and it will teach the Indian, that milder laws are prevailing where Britannia's Queen sways her sceptre.[1] May the moment soon arrive when the boundaries of the flourishing colony of British Guiana are made a Government question; only then can peace & happiness be insured to those, who settle on the British side; as long as these are not insured, the most populous settlement of these regions, is the one which is most exposed to these diabolical attacks.

After the Corials had been provided with washboards, to make them somewhat more roomy, the Brazilians left the fort with their spoil of human merchandize, on the 25th of August.

How distressing it was to my feelings, when previous to their departure, many of the poor beings came to me, & implored that I might prevent them from being carried away. Alas! my hands were tied in that regard as much as theirs when led from their burning huts! Happy for those who could wash their hands clean of the slightest participation in these iniquitous proceedings. The wailings of the parent, the cries of the innocent children & those deep drawn sighs of the manly breast, are registered by the 'avenging angel.'
Fort San Joaquim do Rio Branco,
September 1838.

****

The incidence of forced abduction of Amerindians that Schomburgk observed was to have considerable consequences, not only for Schomburgk's own career but for the history of Guyana up to the present day. Accordingly, before continuing with the next part of Schomburgk's journey, it is appropriate briefly to sketch out what happened.[2]

Schomburgk was shocked by what he saw as the enslaving of the Amerindians by the Brazilians and considered what might be done to prevent it. One obvious way was to claim that they were British subjects and we have just seen that he enquired where the village which was raided lay. When he learnt that it was located between the Rupununi and the Takutu Rivers, he accepted that it was outside British jurisdiction, or, in other words, the former river constituted the frontier. Although he reiterated this when he wrote about the incident to Thomas Buxton, President of the Aborigines Protection Society on 25 August 1838, he was also beginning to question it. He stated. that the Brazilians themselves did not know where the boundary lay and even claimed that the savannahs between the Takutu and the Rupununi had never been in Portuguese possession. He made the point that it was vital that the boundary be determined and proposed that it should follow the line of the watershed between the waters of the Amazon and Essequibo river systems. However, he soon came to see this as unsatisfactory in several

---

[1] The last part of this sentence has been deleted and replaced in the published version (p. 190), with the following lines from William Cooper, 'The Task' (Book II, 1784, ll. 46–7):
> 'Where Britain's power is felt,
> Mankind will feel her blessings too.'

[2] This account is summarized from Rivière, 'From Science to Imperialism', p. 6.

ways. The watershed here is flat and ill defined, it would leave Pirara on Brazilian soil and would not give Great Britain a foothold within the Amazon basin. Accordingly, in November 1838, after his visit to Mount Roraima, he proposed an even more westerly line for the frontier, the courses of the Rivers Takutu, Surumu and Cotingo.

Schomburgk's involvement with these geopolitical matters was to lead to his appointment as boundary commissioner for British Guiana and in due course to his later diplomatic career. His work, however, left modern Guyana with question marks hanging over her boundaries, and continuing disputes with her neighbours.

Part (e) of manuscript JMS 6/29 has been given the title 'Journey from San Joaquim to Esmeralda'. On the cover sheet there is a note stating that it is composed of 'c.162+ pages'. In fact there are 180 pages in the manuscript excluding two pages at the end which are from JMS 6/13, the account of the first expedition, and the last four pages which are the last four pages from JMS 6/29(f) and which have been returned to their rightful place (see p. 403, fn. 2). The pagination is in a mess, pages have been inserted and some are out of order. Rather than go into details here, explanatory notes will be found at the appropriate points. Furthermore, as the manuscript is composed of more than one document, a degree of repetition has crept in; this has been avoided in this transcription and once again it has been made clear at the relevant point what has been done. Some of the manuscript is in Schomburgk's own handwriting, but many pages are in the hands of others. Since it was not received by the Royal Geographical Society until 18 January 1840, it could have been prepared after Schomburgk's arrival in London in September 1839. However, part of it, if not all of it, was clearly written during the course of the expedition and then extensively amended by Schomburgk at a later date, probably in London. The changes mainly consist of deletions and in the following transcript these have been restored. There are also the familiar problems of editorial corrections overwritten on the original. An abbreviated version, about half the length of the original, was published in the *Journal of the Royal Geographical Society*, 10, 1841, pp. 191–247, as 'Journey from Fort San Joaquim, on the Rio Branco, to Roraima, and thence by the Rivers Parima and Merewari to Esmeralda, on the Orinoco, in 1838-9'.

JOURNEY FROM SAN JOAQUIM TO ESMERALDA

The[1] most unfavorable weather had delayed our departure to the 20th September. Through the assistance of Senhor Pedro Ayres, we had meanwhile succeeded to procure six Macusi Indians from the Molocca[2] over which Cosmo as To-je-putori or Chieftain presided. Their number was increased by a Soldier from Fort São Joaquim, and under a salute of seven Guns from the Fort, and the best wishes of our friend Ayres and the Commandant, we left the Fort at noon and against a strong Current commenced our ascent of the river Takutu. We pitched our camp that night on a large Sand bank about 6 miles N.E. from the Fort; the distance which we had been able to accomplish in the course of the afternoon. The afternoon had been fair, and towards evening we observed a great deal of heat lightning around the horizon; but after

---

[1] The pagination of the manuscript for the first 44 pages is straightforward.
[2] 'Maloca' is the *lingua geral* term for a native house, settlement or village.

midnight one of those severe thunder-storms, which are so frequent at the commencement and close of the rainy season, broke lose with such violence, that our fragile tents were soon blown down, and every one who could fled towards the canoe. It abated with daylight, and we were glad to recover at least our tents. The canoe had been sheltered by the Island and escaped the merciless fury of the storm.

September 21ˢᵗ A ledge of rocks which jut out from both banks narrow the river here to about 300 feet; about 200 yards from here a fine broad brook with blue water joins the river on its left bank. Our Indians called it Ororopi.[1] A large Tapir approached the opposite bank of the Takutu; it surveyed the surrounding objects, but did not notice our canoe, and plunged in the river to swim across. Our Indians were in a moment alive to the probability of getting within reach before it might have reached the opposite bank. Powerful but noiseless stroke the paddle the water, and we were within a few hundred yards, before the largest of the South American quadrupeds observed the approaching danger, and increasing its power of swimming to reach the thickly wooded bank, the efforts of our crew were redoubled. Now it came near the woody shore, and thrusting its powerful forefeet on the stony ridge which jutted in the river, it raised its huge body above the water and stood for a few moments panting and shaking the water from its short-haired coat. This was the moment for our hunters. Remiso had seized the rifle and stood at the bow of the Canoe, he touched the trigger, but only the insignificant report of the percussion cap followed, and the rustling of the animal through the bushes which in its precipitate flight opposed themselves, and which were crushed down with cracking noise told us that our game was out of reach. In the eagerness of the chase, and as we fancied the almost certainty of securing the Tapir, we had forgotten last night's storm and the effect which it had exercised on our guns; the powder had got damp. An exclamation of regret broke from our Indians at the failure, and they wistfully looked at their bows and arrows, as if to intimate this would not have occurred if you had left it to our management. The isolated mounts Muruku and Duruara bore in the afternoon S59W[,] the Warami mountains near the mouth of the Xuruma[2] in the evening from our camp N36E.

Septbr 22ᵈ We ascertained the current and found it 1.2 Knots, our progress was 2.3 Knots by the log, which after we deduct the current, left only for our active progress, a trifle more than a mile p hour. We reached the junction of the Xuruma with the Takutu at noon, and stopt as I was anxious to ascertain the breadth of the two rivers before and after their junction. A baseline was soon measured and I received the following results

Breadth of the Takutu before it receives the Xuruma .... 293.3 yards
D° of Xuruma at its mouth .... 289.7   „
D° after their junction .... 377.8   „

which is a greater breadth than the Thames possesses at London Bridge. Observations of culminating stars*

* Stars α Cygni, α Cephei & α Gruis.

gave me 3°22′N. Lat. for the point of the junction of these rivers; the distance east of São Joaquim was 7.3′.

---

[1] Possibly the Igarapé Garrafa.
[2] Rio Surumu.

The[1] river Xuruma is called by the Arecuna and Macusi Indians Cotingo, and has its sources according to Indian information at the eastern end of Mount Roraima; and receives the Xuruma or Xurung of the natives, as its tributary, while in Maps the Xuruma is the recipient of the Rio Cristaes (Coting of the natives). Whether modern Geography will adopt the opinion of the Indians, as the sounder when it regards their own country, or continue to misname the Xuruma a recipient of the Cristaes, must be left to the future.[2]

September 23ᵈ. We continued to toil against the current and passed the stream Aramure-panni in the afternoon.

September 24ᵗʰ. We started shortly after four o'clock in the morning, and halted at six o'clock where the river turns sharply and masses of indurated clay narrow it in. The banks were more than twelve feet above its present level; nevertheless the rocks showed evident marks that the flood reaches this height during inundations. We enjoyed a pretty prospect. The Pacaraima mountains, at a distance of 30 miles, stretched from their Southwestern angle as far as visible to us from N.N.W. to N.N.E., the Chain of Hillocks, which occupied the foreground were named by our Macusi Indians as the Watuta; the Warami near the mouth of the Xuruma bore W.bS. and a singular pointed hill, called Waiking-Epping or Deer Mountain was scarcely more than three miles from us. Towards the South, we observed the Cannucku Mountains and among them that singular rock Ilamickipang. We halted that night at a sandy Spit, from which the mouth of the river Virua[3] bore N56°E distant 1.2 mile. We find the Virua under the name of Manucuropa in maps, this is no doubt a corruption of *Manu igarapé*, the latter word signifying a small river or brook. The Indians call the river as stated above, Virua, and say it have its sources in the Pacaraima mountains.

September 24ᵗʰ[4] I was disappointed in procuring observations for Latitude; the Sky remained cloudy and although a few altitudes of α Persei were procured after three o clock in the morning, they were not satisfactory. I had been watching the whole night for a favorable moment, and not inclined to enjoy rest at so late or rather early an hour, I roused the camp, and we were by four o'clock under way, and reached by six o'clock in the morning the mouth of the Mahu, which according to last nights unsatisfactory observation would be in 3°30'50"N. Lat. and 28 miles East of S. Joaquim. We ascertained that the breadth of the Takutu before it receives the Mahu is only 192 yards, while its tributary is 263 yards wide; after their junction the increase of the river's breadth is merely 4 yards, namely 267. The Wapishanas and Atoraias, who inhabit the Takutu call it Butuauuru. The Macusis name the Mahu, Ireng. The course of the Takutu is eccentric, it describes a half circle, and appears more like a tributary of the Mahu. We entered the latter river; strata of indurated clay impeded its course and increased its current which at a distance of three miles from its mouth we found 2.5 miles.

September 25ᵗʰ[5] The Mahu winds considerably, in consequence of which its current is often powerfully increased. I conceived that it was then on its medium stand,

---

[1] A date, 'Septbr 24ᵗʰ', is in the manuscript at this point and has been scored out. The date which starts the next paragraph is the correct one.

[2] The reference maps mark the Cotingo as a left-bank tributary of the Surumu with its sources near Mount Roraima. The source of the Surumu is located further west in the Serra Pacaraima.

[3] Rio Viruaquim.

[4] An unknown hand has correctly changed it to 25ᵗʰ on the manuscript.

[5] This date is wrong and an unidentified hand has scored it out on the manuscript.

how much more that current must be when its bed is full may be supposed. During the dry season it forms several rapids a few miles southwest from where it is joined by the River Pirara; the Portuguese called them Pizaza.[1] I have not been able to discover the origin of that name; it was foreign to our Indians. Our progress up the Pirara, which deserves only the name of a rivulet during the dry season, was only of short duration[;] we had to come too, and to make the necessary arrangements for unloading our craft, and to carry from thence our luggage over land to the Macusi village Pirara.

Night had already approached, when the sound of paddles astonished us at such a late hour. We recognized one of our small hunting crafts, and two of our Indians, whom we had left with Mr. Vieth at São Joaquim.[2] Shortly after our departure from there, the distressing news had arrived from Manaos that the military Commandant of the upper Amazon, Senhor Ambrozio Ayres, through whom we received such civilities, had been murdered by the rebels, the Cabanos, whom he attempted to dislodge from an Island at the mouth of the Rio Madeira, where they had barricaded themselves, and from whence they annoyed and plundered the vessels which passed up and down the Amazon. It was he who promised every assistance to our expedition, and deputed his brother Senhor Pedro Ayres from Manaos to Fort São Joaquim to compliment us on our arrival on the Brazilian boundary.

Septbr 26th On our reaching the mouth of the Mahu I had despatched two messengers overland to Pirara to inform the Indians of our arrival and to desire them to proceed to the landing place at the mouth of the River Pirara, in order to assist us in conveying our luggage to the village. I was up this morning before any one else stirred in the camp; the melancholy news which we had received the preceeding night had not allowed me to enjoy much rest, and I walked up and down the path before our tents which led to the village. I thought I saw an Indian peeping over the stunted bushes which are scattered over the Savannahs, but a second glance showed that I must have been under a mistake, as no human being was visible as far as the eye could recognize objects. But now there were three, nay four, five faces, one appearing after the other in different directions from behind the trees and vanishing as suddenly as their appearance had been. I was yet wondering whether these strange faces had evil designs on us, when my old acquaintance and guide to the Cannucku Mountains, Aiyukante stepped from behind the nearest bush and welcomed me according to their fashion and five or six others who meanwhile had approached from behind their concealment followed his example. I learned soon the reason of their strange manoeuvre. As Remiso the Soldier from Fort São Joaquim was well acquainted with the footpath which led from the Mahu to the village Pirara, I had despatched him accompanied by Gerard, one of the coloured men from the lower Essequibo, in quest of the Indians to assist us. The sight of the Brazilian was sufficient to awake mistrust, and the Indians supposed that their message to come and assist us, was merely a ruse to put them in the hand of the Brazilians, and to be carried as slaves to the Amazon. Therefore their precaution to reconnoitre before

---

[1] There is some ambiguity here as changes have been made to the original text so that it reads 'which the Portuguese call the Pizaza', thus making the name refer to the Pirara rather than to the rapids.

[2] Vieth and Le Breton had been left at the fort with instructions to descend the Rio Branco and then ascend the Rio Negro in order to meet Schomburgk and his party descending the latter river on their return from Esmeralda.

they approached our camp. A larger number of Indians had remained in a copse, where they had spent the night, not wishing to come nearer during dark, when they could not have used such precaution. The distance from here to the village is fifteen Geogr[l] miles over Savannahs much interspersed with swampy ground, chiefly during the rainy season, indeed when the rivers commence to overflow, they are impassable. When about half the distance from the landing place to the village, the Savannahs form elevated ground and which afford from its height a lovely Savannah view, bordered to the north and South by the mountain chains of Pacaraima and Cannucku and unbounded but by the horizon to the West. At the eastern foot of this elevation flows the Pirara, and is North of it joined by the Nappi which has its sources in the mountain Nappi, one of the Cannucku chain.

We reached Pirara at two in the afternoon and found our kind friend the missionary in good health and glad to see us. He had just returned from an excursion to the Rupununi where at Uruwa, in the vicinity of Curowatoka he intended to found a new mission.[1] The late cruel Descimento of the Brazilians and the planned surprisal of Pirara, which was only averted by my interference, had entirely unsettled the mind of the poor Indians, and Mr Youde judged wisely to prepare for the worst.*

*For the information of those who are unacquainted with the nature of a Descimento I observed that detachments of soldiers or the local militia are sent from the Amazon and Negro to surprise the Indian Settlements by night, and to lead those of the inhabitants who are not fortunate enough to escape into slavery. I was at Fort Sao Joaquim when such a Descimento arrived; they surprised some Wapisiana Settlements of the Takutu by night, set on fire their habitations and carried upwards of forty individuals, men women and children of all ages, into slavery. Whether these atrocities were not committed upon British subjects is at the present uncertain state of the boundary of British Guiana, difficult to determine. I am happy to say that many of them were afterwards liberated, I having appealed through Don Pedro Ayres to the authorities, others died at the Rio Negro, and some of the above could not be found.[2]

He was highly delighted with the promising fertility of the spot, which in case of necessity he had selected as the site of his mission. The soil of which he had carried a small sample left nothing to wish for and as an another proof he observed that a single plant of Yam (Dioscorea alata, Cur-ru-sa Macusi) had produced 80lbs in roots.[3] His mind was heavy and I myself could not deny that I thought a blighting storm was threatening the institution which a few months ago gave every promise to prosper.

An accident which befell my coxswain, a man on whom I could rely when necessity should demand it, obliged me to make a longer stay in Pirara than I should have wished it. This delay was irksome, as the weather was unfavorable for astronomical observations; and although there had been no rain of any consequence since July, the sky was more or less obscured.

[1] Uruwa is usually spelt Urwa and the Curowatoka is the River Kuratoka, a right-bank tributary of the Rupununi. For the events surrounding Youd's move to Urwa, see Rivière, *Absent-minded Imperialism*, Chapter 4.

[2] The reference to what later happened to the victims of the 'descimento', is a clear indication that part of the account was composed after the expedition was over, as Schomburgk did not meet them again until his return journey up the Rio Branco the following year.

[3] The yam, *Dioscorea alata*, may reach sixty kilograms (132 lb) and reach over two metres in length (*DCEU*).

It is a remarkable meteorological phenomenon that while almost constant rains, and violent thunderstorms, made our stay at Fort São Joaquim during the months of July, August, and part of September very unpleasant, there should have been comparatively fair weather at Pirara although the distance is not more than sixty miles in an easterly direction. During a stay of three months in Pirara, thunderstorms and those torrents of rain which mark the change of the season had been very frequent, and had given me opportunity to make a series of interesting meteorological observations. A number of 372 observations of Troughton's best mountain Barometer, which at that period was in excellent order, gave me for the height of Lake Amuku 519 feet; the missionary's House stands 80 feet above the small lake.*

*The means of all Barometrical observations was 29.411, the attached Therm. 26.8 Centigr. the detached 27.4 Centigr. Adopting the mean stand of the Barometer at Georgetown at 30.035 and the respective Thermometers at 27.7 and 27.8 the above result will be procured.

The mean stand of the Barometer & Thermometer was during the months of

	Barometer	Thermometer
April	29.500	82°.3
May	29.410	81
June	29.429	81.1

An accident befell my Coxswain Petersen,[1] who during our first Expedition up the Essequibo in 1835–6, and during the later which in 1837–8 extended to the Sources of that river, had made himself so useful, obliged me to make a longer stay at Pirara than I desired. A prickle of the Sawarai Palm (Astrocaryon Jauari Mart.) had entered his foot to a considerable depth, and rendered him for several days unfit for walking. I was meanwhile occupied to beat up for recruits for our intended journey over land to Roraima in which I was kindly assisted by Mr. Youde. Aiyukante was enlisted as chief guide, and his brother Uyamoni promised to be an able assistant, the more as he appeared to have some influence over the Macusis who formed our crew.

After their number had been completed, I was rather astonished to see a young Macusi, who to judge from appearance and size, could scarcely have completed his thirteenth year, press himself forward to be numbered among those who were to accompany me. I learned soon that he had been lately married, and much against his will. Indeed the young man, who had followed the wish of his relations, appeared to loath the object of his late union, and joined our expedition in order to avoid his bride.

October 8th. Somewhat before eight o clock this morning, our arrangements were complete, and we put ourselves in marching order. We had to march for three days across the Savannahs before we were to meet an other habitation, and had therefore to take provisions for that period with us. As we would be likely absent from any trace of civilisation for many months, we had to provide ourselves rather largely with such articles, as were not to be provided from the Indians, as articles for barter and payment of carriers and guides, medicines, wearing apparel, Instruments, &c. With regard to the latter, I had much to regret that the only Chronometer which I had with me during this expedition had stopped after our return from the Sources of the Essequibo, and my

[1] Presumably this is the same accident as that referred to briefly two paragraphs above.

pocket-watch was the only timekeeper. Our effects were packed in small tin-canisters, each of the weight of about from 20 to 30lbs, which the Indians lashed in that peculiar manner that the chief weight was sustained by the head. A broad band, either plaited of the young leaves of the Ita-palm (Mauritia flexuosa), or consisting of a piece of the bark of Lecythis was fixed to the burden and went round the forehead. In order to render the package of whatever description it might have been quite steady, other lashings went round the shoulders, in the way as our soldiers wear their knapsacks. This is the general method which the Indians, whether male or female, follow when carrying burdens.

All depends from the first step! This maxim becomes likewise applicable as far as it regards the Indians, who prone to sink under lethargy requires the more to be roused to action by any thing which strikes him as uncommon. On the recollection of such scenes, which though simple, are uncommon to him, his soul will feed for a much longer time than we have any idea. It becomes the topic during his journey; he is proud to have figured in the scene, be it even in so inferior a capacity.

Something of that description was wanting now. I had had some difficulty in procuring a sufficient number of men. The Macusis had been for years in war with the Arecunas, who inhabit the regions about Roraima, and although there had been no open hostilities for some time past, still a visit to their former ennemies, they thought, might be connected with personal danger. Many of those, who a few days ago, were willing to accompany me, looked back and it wanted a great deal of persuasion to make them adhere to their former promise.

Mr. Youde was to depart the same day on his visit to the Tarumas. I had given him a description of this tribe, and he was now anxious to follow my steps, and to learn whether there were any hopes to convert them to Christianity. The whole village had been therefore in an uproar from an early hour. Those of the Indians who were masters of Guns and powder had fired away since daylight. As already stated a little before eight o clock our column was put in marching order; everyone had been taught his place. Peterson marched at the head, carrying the British Union flag, which now had accompanied us for more than three years during which British Guiana had been explored under my command. It was to lead us beyond the British boundaries, into regions only known to the copper-coloured Indian, but we followed it unhesitatingly anxious to reach that aim, which was to form a connecting link between the researches of the greatest traveller of his or any time, and my humble endeavours. Esmeralda, at the right bank of the Orinoco in 3°11′N. Lat and 66°3′W. Long according to Baron Humboldt's determination, had been the last point which he visited on his remarkable journey up the Orinoco in 1800. Thirty eight years had since elapsed without that Geography had reaped any further information east of Esmeralda. It was now my wish to reach that point from the east; an undertaking which by the entire ignorance of the Indians, who were in our company or whom we hitherto had met with, was not without difficulties.

A number of other colours had been distributed among the Indians, and as we mustered, the camp followers included, thirty six persons, our banners and muskets, shouldered by the Indians in their gay feather caps, failed not to have the desired effect upon their untutored mind.

An hour's march brought us to the chief arm of the Pirara, after it has issued from the lake-like expansion, the Amucu; a name scarcely more known to the present tribe of Indians. We had to wade through it, and as it reached us to the neck, and the luggage had to be carried on the head, half an hour elapsed before we were on the opposite bank. Our path lay now through Savannahs in a northerly direction. The undulating ground which distinguishes the terrain South of the lake Amucu, ceases, and the clay which forms the sub-stratum does not possess the red colour, which is so striking about the village Pirara, and which it receives from an admixture of ferruginous ochre. Those rounded pebbles which are of shiny black which cover for miles the Savannahs on the partially elevated ground, are entirely vanished, and even those wonderful buildings of a minute insect, the Tumuli of the Termes of Guiana, are not more to be seen. These Savannahs are about 100 feet lower than the mission house at Pirara and are covered during the rainy season with water.

The march over a Savannah is at all times monotonous; similar stunted trees and bushes occur to repletion. The first consist chiefly of Curatella americana, and the latter of Malpighiae. We halted at 11 o clock on a sandy spot, which stretched for about half a mile in a north and south direction. These spots occur frequently in the Savannahs; they are generally from four to five feet higher than the surrounding plain, and trees and bushes are more numerous upon them. They are a favourite retreat for the herds of wild cattle during the mid-day's sun. Although sparely provided with foliage, they nevertheless afford some shade, and are preferable to the open Savannahs, where the sun darts his rays direct on his victim.

High above the trees and bushes too rose numerous Cacti their spiny limbs, their purple and pear-shaped fruit inviting us to quench our thirst. As handsome as the fruit appears, it is almost tasteless and by no means to be compared to the prickly pear (the fruit of an Opuntia) of the West India Islands.

We reached in the afternoon the River Mahu or Ireng of the Macusis, and continued our march along its left bank, following it upwards. Our Camp was selected on an open Savannah, and hunters were immediately despatched in quest of deer; they returned however unsuccessful.

At the setting in of night, we were surrounded by an ocean of fire; the hunters had set the Savannahs in fire: black columns of smoke were rolling onwards, and the noise of the hollow stalks of several large Gramineae, when in consequence of the heat, they burst, was almost deafening; and Cooper's beautiful and descriptive scene of the burning prairie, struck forcibly the mind.[1]

October 9th. We recommenced our march at six o'clock, and arrived at a distance of three miles from our nightquarter, at the part of the Mahu, where we had to cross it. The small river Unamara[2] joined it from the west. The Mahu was to[o] deep to be forded, and we had to use a small Corial which afforded only room for two people at a time, to convey ourselves and baggage to the rivers right bank. It was too tedious for a number of our Indians who plunged in the river and swam across; but as the current was very strong, many were carried far above[3] the harbour which they intended to make. More than two hours and a half had elapsed before we could resume our march. We followed the Unamara towards some naked mountains called Wuyeh-epping, which detached from the chain occupied the foreground. Their height surpassed

---

[1] James Fenimore Cooper (1789–1851). Schomburgk is probably referring to the description of a prairie fire in Chapter 23 of *The Prairie* (1827).

[2] Igarapé do Uanamará.

[3] Presumably Schomburgk meant 'below'.

scarcely 600 feet but they are remarkable for a huge block of granite which the Indians resemble to a deer, that Makunaima has changed it in stone.[1] It has been frequently observed that the inhabitants of Mountain districts are much more inclined to superstition than those of the plains. The fairies continue to exert mystic influence over the glens and mountains of Scotland, Rübezahl thrones on the Riesengebirge[2] and the fear for the Spell of the Witches of the Brocken who on Walpurgis night are on their way to join the revels on the Blocksberg[3] induces the peasant of the District to draw at the approach of midnight his bedclothes tighter. Thus superstition increased in equal ration with our approach to the Mountain chain, and while previously we had to wander for days without being told a single wonderful story, the relation of the remarkable occurrences during the sojourn of Makunaima and his two brothers on earth and the repeated metamorphose of living objects into stone appeared to have no end. At rock Toupanaghae awaits the son of Wakarampo the return of his father. Many a time stood at eventide of night the constellation of the Spirit of the Powis erect, and caused the glossy bird to break out in its measured but melancholic strain, but Eusékirang watched in vain the return of his father. As the door of his stony palace opened with the rising of the constellation thus it commenced to shut when the upper star inclined to the west, and when with the rise of the sun, even the most brilliant constellation of the southern hemisphere vanishes, Eusékirang returns despairingly to the interior fasts of his dwelling to await an other return of the favorable moment. Thus Generation after generation has passed away since the dispute of the three brothers and Wakarampo has not returned as yet. This was the drift of the tale which Aiyukante told me, when the valley of the [blank] opened and the rock Toupanaghae became visible to us.[4]

We observed some Indian huts at the foot of Wuyae but they were abandoned. The late descimento of the Brazilians had induced their former inmates to fly deeper in the mountains. The small river Unamara crossed our path again, we had to wade it where a large ledge of rocks formed a rapid. I observed here two species of Lacis rather an uncommon sight in so small a river. However the delicious fish the Pacu so fond of browsing on this its favorit herb were wanting.

In the afternoon we arrived at a bent of the mountain chain which continued from here. We had hitherto kept the outer ridge or most southern ridge of the mountain chain; on our left hand we had therefore detached groups of mountains remarkable for their desolate appearance while on our right loftier mountains but sparsely wooded

---

[1] Makunaima is a mythical culture hero of the Pemon and Kapon peoples who features in many of their origin myths.

[2] Rübezahl is a giant from German folklore who lives in the Riesengebirge Mountains, the source of the Elbe on the border between Poland and the Czech Republic.

[3] Brocken and Blocksberg are peaks in the Harz Mountains of Central Germany. Walpurgis Night is May Day Eve, 30 April.

[4] See p. 74 above where Schomburgk refers to Toupanaghae and describes it as resembling a hand. It has not been possible to relate the rather scanty details of this myth to any more recent and fuller version. Wakarampo is almost certain the same character that Theodor Koch-Grünberg calls Wakalambe (the whirlwind), and Ensékirang, Anzikilan (the Tinamou) who both appear as brothers of Makunaima in a Taulepang myth. The Southern Cross is often seen as a Powis in Amerindian mythology, as recorded in an Arekuna myth (see *Del Roraima al Orinoco*, 3 vols, Caracas, Ernesto Armitano Editor, 1981–82 [1917–24], pp. 41, 61). Native South Americans have a large body of celestial mythology. For a study of the subject with reference to Guiana, see Edmundo Magaña, *Contribuciones al estudio de la mitología y astrononomía de los indios de las Guayanas*, Amsterdam, CEDLA, 1987.

continued without interruption. We dipped now more in the chain itself. A large valley was before us, bounded on each side by precipitous and rugged mountains, crowned with wall-like masses of Trappean rocks or boulders which by their phantastic shape raised our attention and the whispering of the Indians, frightened at the supposed influence of the evil spirits whom they considered to inhabit these stony [monuments].

Our course was N.W. bW. through the Valley, which only sparely clothed with grasses had been until lately under water. Our path was therefore very uncomfortable. It turned somewhat more to the north, and we entered a basin like expansion, surrounded by high mountains and distinguished by three remarkable shaped masses of rocks. The summit of the high mountain Mara-etshiba has entirely the appearance of columnar basalt, and where the columns abruptly terminate rises a solitary mass to the estimated height of about 50 feet. This mass of rock [balks] somewhat out in the middle and has by the ever-fruitful imagination of the Indian been resembled to the Maraca,*

*An instrument formed of the fruit of the calabash tree, which is scooped out, and filled with pebbles, making a rattling noise when shaken.

the indispensable instrument of the Pi-ai-man, or Indian conjuror. Near the entrance to the valley and about sixty to eighty feet above the Savannah, are a group of Trappean rocks column-like, largest and most distinguished of them is called Canou-yeh-piapa, or the Guava tree stump. Half a mile further westward, and somewhat less elevated above the Savannah than the former stands an object which the traveller unacquainted with its nature, will consider some old large trunk of a tree, deprived of its leafy crown. It is however a rock like the former, and the wonder of the Indians near and far who name it Pourae-piapa, 'the cut-off tree.'

I looked with astonishment at this freak of nature, and doubted my guides, when they told me it was of stone. Straight rises the rock to a height of at least fifty feet. Its sides partly tinged by a red lichen, and on some places more weathered than on others, the illusion is increased by this play of colours, and one can scarcely divest itself from believing it to be some gigantic trunk, the head of which stricken by years or struck by lightning or the merciless tornado lies mouldering at its foot. A Jabiru (Myctetes Americanus) had selected its top to build its nest upon. We observed above the borders of the nest the head of the young one. At our approach its mother hastened from the neighbouring Savannah to its protection. The bird surrounded in girations the columnar mass, the circles became lesser, and at last it pitched on the rock, and stood sentinel balancing itself on one leg like our storks. I heard at that moment the report of a gun, the poor bird tottered and fell down the precipice. An Indian had stolen itself near it and shot it from its eyry.

It would have been a wonder if three such remarkable objects as the Maraetshiba, the Canou-ye- and Pourae-piapa had not given rise to some tradition. These mountains, it appears, have been the favourite spot of Makunaima, the good and high spirit – he lived in these mountains before he went travelling like Wakaranipo. He left his son Eusé-kirang for some time after him, however the latter followed his father, and it was on this journey that he arrived fatigued at the valley and observing the large tree, he cut it under the idea of its being loaded with fruits, but found himself mistaken. He was more successful with the Canou-yé or Guava the fruits of which refreshed him and he continued his journey to the eastward.

This mythological tradition is of great interest; indeed we may trace the distant allusion of Christianity in it. We have the father and son, the latter remains among the selected, as every tribe conceives himself superior to the other, for some time after the departure of the former but follows him ultimately eastward. The mother of whom we shall soon hear accomplishes the mysterious number three.[1]

We selected our nightquarters at a small streamlet which flows near Pourae-piapa and as soon as the necessary arrangements for our quarters had been made, I set off to visit this remarkable rock. The access to it is rather difficult in consequence of numerous rocks which lie scattered in fragments on the side of the hill and rendered the ascent uncomfortable. Arrived at the summit a scene of confusion presented itself. Sharp pointed rocks, many thirty feet long and scarcely six to eight inches thick, rose erect or were overlieing each other. They belonged to the Trap rocks, and were of the same nature as those in the valley of the Mahu, and at St. Bernard's in Tortola., Agave americana,[2] Bursera gummifera, Lecythideae, & the wild Iatropha manihot[3] occupied this interesting spot, while the limbs of a Cactus repandus clothed the base of the Pourae, and by its snow-white flowers and purple fruits contrasted strikingly with the stony column.

Our return to the camp was not so easily effected; the Indians had set the Savannahs on fire; and while our hungry stomachs appeared to brook no delay, to await the cooling of the embers, one of the most courageous pushed valiantly through the heavy columns of smoke and announced his success by a loud shout which was quite sufficient to encourage the others to follow him, and half suffocated by smoke and with every appearance of a chimney sweep we reached the banks of the little stream, which if we had waited somewhat longer we might have effected with much more comfort.

October 10th. After having continued our route over similar ground as the preceeding day, we ascended the hill Ina-mute for about four hundred feet in order to gain the saddle (mute in Macusi) which the mountain formed, and descended the opposite side into the same valley which we had followed before and through which the Unamara flows. As the mountains form an offset which extends considerable southwards, the path is shortened for several miles by this ascent, and the Macusi Indians express such passes by adding the word mute to the name of the mountain.

We approached in the afternoon a single hut, inhabited by two Macusis and their families consisting of fifteen persons. One of them was a handsome young man. His face was highly painted, and the cartilaginous part of the ear perforated by a piece of Bamboo, which was cut vertically on one end, and on the other slanting of[f], and of about the size represented (see Figure 10, p. 305).

He wore his hair long, and had it tied together in the manner of a queue by means of a long cotton string, the ends of which were strung round his neck and hung in large tassels over his back, and to which a number of Toucan Skins were fastened. At his command his wife brought several Calabashes filled with Paiwari, but our number was so great that the supply was exhausted before everyone had tasted of it. As the next

---

[1] It was a common assumption of the time that pagan mythology contained echoes of a past awareness of God and Christ. This was based on the biblical authority that all humankind was descended from Adam and Eve and the populating of the world following Noah's flood and the Tower of Babel meant that people everywhere retained at least a hazy remembrance of the Scriptures

[2] The Century plant, but this species is not listed for Guiana.

[3] According to the NMNH Checklist, *Jatropha manihot = Manihot esculenta*.

Settlement was only a few miles of[f] our host accompanied us thither, and having crossed the streams Kinote and Carrara, we arrived at five o'clock at Copoma, a Macusi Settlement, where I determined to rest for a day in order to procure a new supply of Cassada. The men were absent on a hunting excursion, and we found only females and children. However they promised to provide us with Cassada roots, if the women in our suite would prepare it into bread, as they themselves did not feel inclined for this extra labour.

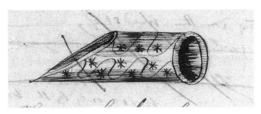

Figure 10: Robert Schomburgk's sketch of a Macushi decorated ear-plug made from bamboo. Included by permission of the Royal Geographical Society, London.

The Settlement, which according to my observations is in Lat. 4°3′38″N., is with the exception of the valley which affords an outflow to the Unamara surrounded by mountains, in many instances crowned by blocks, which the imagination and superstition of the natives have converted into objects of dread or into the habitation of evil Spirits. The mountain Ewa-ero was famed for a huge barbacot which Macunaima prepared with his own hands. A pile of stone has been resembled to that grating made of wood on which the Indians smoke or barbacue their meat. The mountain Maru-tuaca*

*Maru is the Macusi name for the Species of Tinamou which is peculiar to Guiana, and which the Colonists call Maam. Its loud but plaintive whistle resounds at [illegible] interval from the depth of the forest, and is as well an inhabitant of the coast regions, as of the mountainous tracts or woody knolls of the Savannahs.[1]

is famed for a large Maam which Macunaima made himself and transformed afterwards into Stone. These mountaineers are as vivid and fanciful in their imaginings as ours – no corner without its spirits and hobgoblins, and I regretted only that the little knowledge which I possessed of their language did not permit me to understand all these wonderful stories which they had to tell me about every stone which we met on our road that was of somewhat more than ordinary size, or fantastically shaped by nature.

October 12th. We started at ten o'clock. The Cassada, which we had procured was divided among the crew in equal shares with strict injunction that it had to last for a given period. Thus divided every individuals portion did not increase his burden considerably, while it would have taken three individuals to carry [provisions] required for the course of three days. We crossed now the Unamara, which we were told had its sources in an Ita*

*The Ita palm or Mauritia flexuosa, is only found in moist situations, and is generally an indication of morasses.

swamp. The previous two days we had kept the eastern side of the valley; we crossed it

[1] The Maam is the Great Tinamou (*Tinamous major*).

305

now in order to reach the opposite side; the valley was here [about three miles wide] and an offset of the mountain on the eastern side [runs] here in a S.W. direction across the valley leaving only near the western ridge an opening for the brook Tapirinduae which flows towards the Unamara. It has to pass over a ledge of rocks, which forms a small cataract. One of the Indians shot here a large Luganani or Sun fish. The Valley which we now entered, surrounded on all sides by mountains with the exception of the passage which the Tapirinduae had forced itself, had all the appearance of having been once a lake. This refers likewise to the valley through which at present the Unamara flows; or to express myself more properly the valley of the Unamara formed one of the northern bays of that extensive lake of the former existence of which the Savannahs between the Cannucu and Pacaraima mountains give such evident demonstrations; and it is more than probable that at some remote epoch these mountainous barriers upheld such an extensive sheet of water that the tradition of its existence has been transplanted to us in the fable of the lake Parima. The waters thus pent up burst their barriers and scooped out passages for the rivers which now flow into the Atlantic. This is not the place for those geological disquisitions explaining my reasons for these assertions and which may yet appear under some other form.[1]

We marched towards noon over rising ground, the hills closed the valley amphitheatre like and on descending we stepped from the tributaries of the Mahu to which river the Unamara flows, into the basin of its recipient the Takutu. After we had descended the hill, we continued our march along the Streamlet Murama-munda, following its course in a western direction. The mountains appeared better wooded than those we had passed the previous day, but the soil of the valley had every appearance of sterility, numerous Cacti and the viviparous Agave (Agave vivipara)[2] although affording an admirable appearance were nevertheless a sure proof of the great dryness of the soil. We entered again Savannah Valleys, a large mountain the height of which I estimated 2000 feet bore N.76W. and was about eight miles distant. This was likewise our course through the valley which was about two miles wide and is drained by the river Virua. We reached the latter at four o clock which we crossed; where we crossed it, I estimated its breadth thirty three yards. Its bed was full of rocks and contained at that time but little water.

The Virua empties itself a few miles above[3] the junction of the Mahu with the Takutu, in the latter river. It is the Manacaropa of the Portuguese maps, by which name it is however not known to the Indians. Its course is likewise longer than represented. We crossed it in 4°5′N. Lat. from whence its source is at least 30 miles further northward.

We observed three Indian huts before us; we found them however abandoned except by fleas and Tshigoes. A column of fine curled smoke, which we saw rising above the bushes on our left, spoke in the plainest terms of the presence of man. It were not the thick columns of black smoke, the effects of burning Savannahs set on fire by the Indian on his march; nay it was that light bluish smoke, which every experienced traveller will at once declare to be the consequence of a gentle wood fire encircling the much beloved

---

[1] Schomburgk did write on this subject, but not until 1845. See 'On the Lake Parima (The "El Dorado" of Walter Raleigh) and the Geography of Guiana'.

[2] Unidentified.

[3] Schomburgk meant 'below'.

pepperpot which our imaginings and a march since ten o'clock showed us filled with the greatest delicacies. Maipuri, Laba, Aguri, Paca,[1] the numerous family of gallinaceous birds with all their Orders and Suborders passed in review. In one point we were not quite mistaken; on turning the corner of the wood we saw a hut, which we found occupied by an Indian family consisting of twelve Indians, namely husband, his three wives and their progeny, eight children; of which the eldest, a boy, was scarcely more than five or at the utmost six years old. This is a single instance of a numerous family among the Indians where the husband lives in polygamy & there was every prospect that their number would be doubled in the future. Although rich in children they appeared to be poor enough in the necessities of life – neither bread nor corn was to be procured and I presume this was the reason that our Indians who generally selected their nightquarters in the huts, if we camped near a Settlement, slung their hammocks this night among the trees in the vicinity of our tent.

October 13th. We started at six o clock, the general hour for commencing our march, and followed for some time the banks of the Coya-oute, which flows in the Virua. Every brook which we passed afforded our Indians an apology for halting a few minutes in order to quench their thirst. The calabash which is tied by a string to the Akatauri[2] is quickly detached; after a piece of burnt cassada bread has been softened in the water it is kneaded with the hands, and an additional quantity of water having been put to it, they stir it about with a stick and drink it with delight as a substitute for Paiwori.

We entered an other basin like expansion by a narrow defile; the valley extended about a mile and a half; a pointed mountain bore S.84°W.; I estimated its distance six miles. The mountain ridge opened towards the W.S.W. and permitted a view of the Savannahs. At the distance of five miles an other mountain was pointed to us, which they call Saeraere, a name which the Indians appear to be fond of bestowing on heights. This is the third I know by that name; namely the Saeraere between the rivers Rupununi and Takutu, the Saeraere on the left bank of the Rio Branco, and the one just now alluded to. The Macusis told me that the name is of Wapisiana origin and signifies a bird. In the Macusi language *Saeraere* is the demonstrative or indicative *this* or *that*,[3] and would convey no sense. We kept the eastern side of the Valley and were at half past two at the foot of Marawa-epping. Here I halted to admire the picturesque ruins of a former castle, at least as such I should have taken these fantastic piles of stone which crowned the summit had I travelled in chivalrous Europe, but as even not the Ingas[4] have been known of having sojourned in Guiana, I was reluctantly obliged to consider that western towers and [their] ballestrades and walls in decay as a freak of nature. We stopt at the foot of Mavisi-epping sadly tired with our march over a bare Savannah and under a scorging[5] Sun which caused the Thermometer at 1 oclock exposed to its rays to rise to 127° F. The stream Mavisi has its sources among numerous boulders and ledges of gigantic size, and in its descent it forms a series of natural cascades, some of which are upwards of twelve feet high.

[1] Tapir, Labba, Agouti and Paca.
[2] A large carrying basket made from palm leaves.
[3] Compare this with the Carib-speaking Trio, *serë*, 'this' and *serërë*, 'this' with an emphasizer. Saeraere seems closer to the latter.
[4] Inca.
[5] Changed to 'scorching' by an unidentified hand.

October 14th. It being Sunday, I did not intend to travel, but besides that our camp had been selected where we could not expect protection against the sun when near the zenith, our guide had informed the Indians that a Macusi Settlement was at no great distance from our uncomfortable quarters which they appeared all desirous to reach; how far the prospect for a calabash with paiwori influenced them to come to their decision I know not, but we were soon after the deputation had received audience, in full march over Wairamura-muta and entered on our descent the system of the river Cotinga. We enjoyed from the small elevation one of the loveliest prospects over the Savannahs to the distant Mairari mountains,[1] along the foot of which our road was to lead us. We marched over a granitic ledge of rocks; when the hue and cry so peculiar to the Indians; a welcome in times of peace, defiance and the rush to battle in war, resounded from the valley. It was responded by our party, and Aiyoucante and his brother requested me much to take out our colours and to astonish their countrymen whom we saw walking through the valley. For the maintenance of order our Indians were drilled to the sound of the horn which served them as signal when to prepare for the march or the halt or execute any other common occupation of frequent occurrence. I found them apt scholars, and it saved me hereafter a great deal of trouble, chiefly as they got aware that I was determined to make them attend to it. I consented to their wish and while Great Britain's Union no doubt was for the first time unfurled in these mountains and headed our column a number of others of different colours, which I used as signals in my trigonometrical operations were distributed. The Indians whom we considered the inhabitants of the single hut before us, awaited us sitting on some rocks, and as much as they might have been astonished at our appearance, and at the probable object which led us among them, they did not express it in their features.[2] The Macusis of the Rio Branco recognised in the elder Indian a relative of their captain Cosmo, and there was now much talking. We were told that the hut before us was not more [.] [3]

[We] halted on the 15th on the banks of the Cotinga the river Cristaes of the Portuguese in the maps of former date. This river is generally considered a tributary to the Zuruma; the Indians, however, name the Cotinga, Cotinga to its junction with the Takutu, and consider the Zuruma or Zurum as they call it, a tributary to the Cotinga. Our camp was this night in 4°10′48″N. lat. and 68 miles W. of Pirara. Referring to Arrowsmith's late map of Colombia, we ought then to have been at the sources of that river, while I estimated its width where we crossed it 280 feet, and its depth from 5 to 10 feet. The Zuruma joins the Cotinga about 15 miles distant from here – the direction being S.S.E.

Hitherto we continued our march along the first ridges of the mountain chain; but after we passed the mountain Mairari (the highest of these regions) we turned more

---

[1] Serra do Merari.

[2] The conventional greeting among the Amerindians of the region requires the hosts to ignore visitors on their arrival, often for some length of time.

[3] The manuscript breaks off abruptly at this point (p. 44) and six pages have been inserted; they are composed of part of a letter written by Schomburgk, almost certainly to Washington at the Royal Geographical Society, from an Arecuna Settlement near Mount Roraima, and dated 17 November 1838. The first page is marked 'to follow 44'. The first and second pages are numbered 44a and 44b respectively. The second page is also numbered 2 and the remaining pages 3–6. The manuscript of the report takes up again on p. 45, on 19 October, thus there is a gap of four days. The only part of the letter reproduced here (parts of pp. 44a & b) covers those days.

to the N. An accident which befell one of the Indians obliged me to stop for a day, and I measured the Mairari trigonometrically, & found it 2817 feet above the Savannah and about 3400 feet above the sea. In lieu of following the longitudinal valleys of the Pacaraima chain, we now turned westward following the river Muiang,[1] one of the most considerable tributaries of the Zuruma. It had a turbulent course – numerous pointed rocks, resembling basaltic columns, obstructed its way forming cataract upon cataract. The direction of these rocks was S.76°E., the dip N.7°E., with an angle of about 75°. Our path now became fatiguing in the extreme – our feet blistered & injured by the sharp-pointed rocks; but if I, who wore shoes complained, how much more reason had the poor Indians accoutred only with light sandals. The first day of our mountainous path was marked by a serious loss; in descending a mountain torrent to try its temperature and in handing the thermometer to one of the Indians standing above, he slipped & fell with such force that the thermometer was broken; and I am now reduced to one. During the following days we crossed the Muiang several times.[2]

[The mountain Zabang] bore at half past Nine[3] N.9°W. along its northern foot flows the river Cotinga. We had to cross the Muiang another time and halted on its left bank in a shady wood for breakfast. Heliconias and Palms reigned here paramount; of the former I had one cut down and found it on measurement 58½ feet long, an immense height for that family of plants. When we issued out of the wood the hillocks which were undulating consisted of a white clayey substance mixed with minute fragments of Quartz. We were now quite near to the ridge which runs East and West and followed the Valley which it formed in conjunction with that ridge of which Aruwaiyang is the highest mountain. We entered a copsewood and observed at the entrance a tree belonging to the Labiatiae (Hyptis)[4] of much beauty and its leaves of a highly aromatic smell. The flowers were of a bright blue, the calix lake colored and the upper leaves of the spike changed from green through white into a pink color according as the rays of light fell on them. The tree was about fifty feet high – the trunk rugged and the wood hard. As we issued from the wood an Arécuna settlement of two houses was before us. When we were observed we were mistaken for Brazilians; the Women and children fled, each packing up their hammocks in the flight. The men made some show of defence, they rushed out with Guns and cutlasses; our guide was however recognised, and the most vociferous welcome was now poured upon us. From the noise with which their greetings were uttered, one who only heard without seeing them, would have judged them at least at daggers [illegible]. The Arécunas are fairer than the Macusis, and of the same make or shape.[5] Indeed they call themselves a brother tribe, although they have lately been at War with each other. As far as I can judge their language has much resemblance. There were eight men, the women I had no opportunity to number, as during our stay they never approached us except two ventured near our tents. Among the men there

[1] Rio Miang. Something seems to have gone wrong with Schomburgk's directions once again. The Miang flows into the Surumu from the north, and the flow of the latter is closer to east-west. Accordingly if Schomburgk was following the Miang his route would have been northerly rather than westerly.

[2] At this point the manuscript of the report starts again at p. 45 and continues in an orderly fashion until p. 56. A note states that it was received by the Royal Geographical Society on 22 January 1840.

[3] On 19 October.

[4] *Hyptis membranacea* (*Hyptidendron arboreum*), see van Dam, *Guyanan Plant Collections*, p. 27.

[5] Page 46 of the manuscript is blank save for two editorial versions of text deleted from p. 47.

was an old man whom I estimated upwards of sixty, the whole body was a succession of wrinkles, and as if to increase his ugly appearance he wore in each of his ears, the tusks of the large Peccary (Dicoteles labiatus) he was a famed Pi-ai-man or Conjuror and much known among the Arecunas and Macusis, who called him Zambara. Our latitude was this evening 4°29′N. and we were 103 miles West of Pirara.

October 20th. In continuing our route towards the mountains we crossed several brooks, tributaries to the Muiang which apparently drains the country between the Cotinga and Xurumu. The valley through which it flows from its sources was closed by woody mountains in the direction of W.N.W.; the sandstone ridge was about 5 miles distant, when we halted at the foot of mount Kinotaima, in order to rest for the pending ascent. For the first hour our road passed through wood, & the most fatiguing part commenced however when we came out of the wood and had to ascend a steep mountain covered sparely with grass. Our Indians with their burden although in no instance it was above 30lbs, were almost exhausted before we were half way, and it took us fully two hours before we had reached the summit, which I estimated 2000 feet above its foot, and about 3000 feet above the sea. I ascertained a number of bearings from its top and as we found a spring we halted at 11 oclock for Breakfast. While thus refreshing ourselves, we heard the hue of Indians and recognised three men from the last settlement we passed, with old Zambara at their head, in spite of his age the old Man must yet possess a strong stream of vigour in his veins. I did not find that he appeared exhausted, from ascending the steep mountain which formed an Angle of 33°.

We continued our march upon Tableland, only interrupted by soft undulating hills. The vegetation was here very interesting to a Botanist numerous Orchideae chiefly species of an Epidendrum, which I found for the first time at Ataraipu, with large umbells of a pink colour, and a variety of the same with white blossoms edged with rose, as well an other the stem of which was upwards of eight feet high, ornamented the mountain Savannah. I was much interested to find here the first arborescent fern in the Interior of Guiana, it was a Cyathea and their stem about 15 feet high before it formed itself in fronds.

In the afternoon at two o clock we crossed the Yawaira a tributary to the Carony, we had entered therefore the hydraulic System of the Orinoco which is divided from that of the Amazon by the ridge of Sandstone mountains which we had just ascended.[1] The Yawaira or Tiger river may be considered its most southern affluent.

It was about 40 feet wide and according to the Indians it falls through the Wairing[2] and Cuckenam[3] in the Yuruany[4] which is a tributary, or rather according to the Arecunas and Macusis is the eastern branch of the Carony. Before us was a hillock consisting of sandstone in horizontal beds. The particles of Quartz were very apparent in it and they were sometimes of a rose colour. The soil consisted of a red clay. We passed two huts once the residence of Zambara but even his far spread fame of being able to expel the evil spirit out of sick persons appears to have had no power over those who hovered over the region where then his residence was; several of his children, grand and great grandchildren died, and it bid fair chance that grim death would also touch him when

[1] This also means that Schomburgk had crossed into Venezuela.
[2] Probably the Río Uairen.
[3] Río Cukenan.
[4] Río Yuruani.

he timely removed with those who had been spared. Thus ascribes the superstitious Indian any causal circumstance to the evil influence of spirits, and removes his residence under the idea that his longer sojourn there will bring destruction to him and those who are related to him.

These regions of sandstone have their own Floras – every shrub was almost new to me, except some Melastoma[1] very few were in flower. If it were possible to transplant a Botanist among these bushes, without he were aware in which part of the world he had been conducted, the rigid leaves and tortuous branches would cause him to fancy himself in New Holland among the Melaleuca and Proteacea.[2] The most attractive was a shrub with rigid alternate leaves, and a flower like a simple Camellia, until a nearer inspection shows us that we have before us a flower belonging to the XIII Class of Linnes artificial system, nevertheless resembling Ternstramiacea in its concave and coriaceous sepals which are however persistent; its hypoginous stamens, its capsular fruit with central column, its alternate coriaceous leaves without stipulae, and its terminal peduncles, articulated at the base.*

* Note. It has since been ascertained to be a Kielmeyria.[3]

Interesting as the appearance of this shrub with its roselike flowers proved to me, it could not vie with an Orchidea, without doubt the highest yet described, and which for the gracefulness of its stem, the splendid configuration of its flowers, and its aromatic smell is perhaps not equalled among this most singular and most fragrant kind of plants. Long before we came to its vicinity, the Eastern breeze wafted the delightful odour towards us, and I looked curiously from side to side to discover the source of this fragrance. White like a lily, I espied at last flowers which raised on graceful stems above the surrounding shrubs. I hesitated to pronounce an Orchidea as strange and eccentric as this tribe pleases itself in its forms, but on coming nearer no uncertainty was further left, and Oncidium altissimum which rears its scape an unconsiderable height if compared with some Epidendrum was far surpassed in beauties and splendour. It has since been named Sobralia Elizabethea, in honor of H R H the Crown Princess of Prussia.[4]

We entered thick woods, crossing the Yawaira which has pathed itself a course between two mountains, not without turmoil the sound of its falling from ledge to ledge accompanied us for a considerable distance afterwards we had left its banks. On emerging from the wood, we had an other view of Roraima and some other mountains of the same formation. At the foot of the hill on which we stood we observed some huts towards which our march was directed. It was an Arecuna Settlement where we resolved to sojourn for some days.

October 21st The night proved very cold and the Thermometer stood at 6 oclock 61° and all of us shivered as if the cold had been under the freezing point. numerous Arecunas arrived in the course of the day from the neighbouring settlements; they had heard

[1] The Genus *Melastoma* is restricted to India and the Pacific, so presumably Schomburgk is referring to the Family Melastomataceae.

[2] *Melaleuca* is a genus of the Family Myrtaceae, but only occurs in Guiana as a cultivated or naturalized plant. *Proteacea* is a genus of the Family Proteaceae, but does not occur in Guiana.

[3] *Kielmeyera* is a genus of the Family Guttiferae (Bonnetioideae). It does not appear to have been reported from Guiana, but occurs in Brazil.

[4] The Epidendroid orchid, *Sobralia liliastrum*.

of our arrival and in the evening there were between sixty and seventy strangers round our tents, looking with wonder at us and the different objects of our baggage. They behaved very orderly, and were by no means forward. A severe thunder storm which raged about sunset dispersed them, but at our evening prayers they were silent spectators.

October 22nd. The Thermometer stood half a degree lower than yesterday and we felt ourselves very uncomfortable. The strangest object in the landscape is Roraima which at the distance where we viewed it from, appears like a dark wall. A mountain of less extent is somewhat further west. The intermediate space between them appeared to me like a large portal, through which clouds from the white fleecy, to those opaque black masses which obscure the sky and render day into night, issued without interruption, spreading over the country in all directions – towards sunset the clouds gilded on their edges and that ocean of fire where the luminary of the day sinks, to recall to life another portion of the world throwing its reflection on their dark matter formed a magnificent scene. Roraima offered then constant changes in its appearance, but perfectly cloudless, we had not seen it as yet.

October 23rd. We started this morning on our projected tour to the crystal mountains, and ascended for that purpose a densely wooded hill in a Southern direction,

Figure 11: Mount Roraima. From the original watercolour by Robert Schomburgk. Included by permission the Royal Geographical Society, London.

312

following a small limpid brook, with water to our taste as cold as ice. The Thermometer showed a temperature of the outer air at 8 o'clock of 65, the water of the brook was 63°. We entered a mountain Savannah and before us rose Pa-epping the name signifying a species of frog which has selected it as its favourite shade. The stratification of the sandstone was N.86E. and belonged to the elder formation. It showed itself in horizontal beds, and formed on the declivity of the hill terraces which we now descended for about two hundred feet where our guides stopt at a small hillock hundred and fifty to sixty feet in circumference which they pointed out as the crystal mountain and indeed the upper surface was covered by numerous rock crystals, much weathered from their exposure and comparatively of small size. The Indians told us we should find them larger by digging in the ground, but we were not more successful, as the largest perfect Crystal which we found after a few hours search was not more than an inch in length. They observed however that no doubt we were not sufficiently hungry, as when only in that state, the fine and large crystals were observable. My assertion that individually I ought to have found the largest, as having satisfied myself only with a cup of coffee at starting, I possessed now about the meridian height of the sun a keen appetite, went for nothing and considering further search as hopeless I set with good heart to a couple of Bananas and a piece of fresh Cassada bread which I found in our travelling bag. We returned in the afternoon with a number of small but clear crystals. An Indian brought me some more from an other place, which were larger and in some instances were variously combined. The Arecunas say that formerly there had been some of four or five inches in length and clear as water, but the Portuguese had carried them all away.

Nicolas Hortsman, I think was the first who made the existence of these Crystal mountains in Guiana known to Europeans.

We had in the afternoon another visit from the Arecunas from the neighbouring settlements, they had painted themselves for the occasion and as their features are by no means neglected by nature, they made in their way, a very good show. Many wore pieces of Bamboo fixed through their nose and chin, and in lieu of ear rings they had birds heads chiefly those of the Humming bird and a small creeper of a brilliant blue colour. Round their loins, they wore a girdle in some instances made of the hair of the Quatta or Coatta monkey (Ateles paniscus)[1] in others of the hair of their head, for which purpose they allow it to grow and cut it when of sufficient length they collect it carefully until they possess sufficiently, for which there is no great length of time necessary, as their growth of hair is uncommonly strong.

October 25th after a sojourn of some days at one and the same place, I find it always difficult to move at such an early hour as usually, and if the Indian be ever so many times ordered to prepare the previous evening for departure he is so reluctant to comply with the order, that he will always have something forgotten when at the moment of starting and he finds it necessary to unpack his load. It was therefore half past seven oclock before we left on our journey to Roraima. Half an hour after we crossed to the right bank of the Yawaira and ascended a hillock. The junction of the Yawairi with the Wairing bore from here S.67°W. distant about a mile. The Wairing is a small river, and drains a valley which divided from the Yawairi by a ridge of sand hills extends. The peak of Zabang bore S.76°E; it towered high above the other mountains in its vicinity. We

---

[1] The red-faced spider monkey.

passed a low swampy valley. overflowed during the rainy season by the Wairing and Cuckenam.

We halted at half past ten at an Arecuna hut at the left bank of the river Cuckenam, which about a mile and a half from here and in a WbS direction, is joined by the Wairing. I estimated the breadth of the Cuckenam 100 feet, its banks are upwards of 20 feet high, nevertheless there were sufficient proofs that it overflows them during the wet season.

The hut was inhabited by twenty five individuals, built round and so small, that I could not conceive how such a number could find place, much less comfort in it. One of the young men told me through our interpreter, that his father had been lately killed by a Kanaima. By this name is designated a person who, if such an expression could be used, has sworn the death of an other and does not rest until his object is accomplished. In this case poison had been administered which they extract from a plant, that according to their description, resembles an Arum. The substance which they extract is of a whitish colour, and is said to cause death at an earlier or later period, according to the quantity which the individual receives in his stomach. At the conclusion of his tale and having made many protestations of avenging his fathers death, he went into the hut and brought out a small Pakara or basket; he searched for some while, and took at last a package wrapt up carefully in some old rags – it contained two tracts of the London tract society,[1] and two French playing cards Coeur dame and Careau valet.[2] A strange association for so godly company. His father, he told us, had got them many years ago, when he was on a visit to Demerara. I understood from him that they prefer to descend the Siparuny to its junction with the Essequibo and that they want ten days to reach that river where it becomes navigable for Canoes. It appears they prefer that way to that of the Mazaruny, of which I could not hear anything of certainty from them.

We followed the Cuckenam upwards in a ENE direction and crossed it half an hour after in a small Canoe[;] our Indians showed themselves here expert swimmers and as merely the luggage had to be carried to the other side in the Canoe only half an hour elapsed before we continued our march on the rivers right bank. A Arecuna settlement was but a short distance from the river, where we halted for some time. The day after our arrival at the first Arecuna settlement they had despatched a messenger to the settlements on our road to Roraima to inform them of our intended visit, and to remove the fear, which our appearance might cause them. We found therefore every where Cassada and Paiwori ready for us. I counted 30 inhabitants, among them were three very handsome girls, this refers to their features as their embonpoint prevents their being acknowledged Indian Graces. The young men were likewise of very good appearance, round faces were prominent, and as their lips are not thrown up, but rather small it becomes them well.

We crossed at half past three the brook Amataima and stood soon after before an Indian hut. The people told us here that their Captain or Inapotoritong was at the next place, but a short distance from theirs where a Paiwori-feast had been prepared for our entertainment. We could observe the huts where we had been already discovered, and a

[1] Probably the Religious Tract Society, founded in London in 1799. In 1935 it merged with similar organizations to form the United Society for Christian Literature. The latter's publishing wing exists today as the Lutterworth Press.
[2] La Dame de Coeur, the Queen of Hearts, and Le Valet de Carreau, the Knave of Diamonds.

large crowd appeared to be on the tip-toe; some had ascended the roof of the hut, others had climbed upon trees, and a running hither and thither of the women and children showed the anxiety of all concerned. We came up with the place, and their Inapotoritong came forward to give us his hand, by this I immediately observed that he had been in the Colony, and a few words of Creol with which he paraded parrot like, left no further doubt. The assembly consisted of eighty and add to which our own company amounting with some hangers on from the last settlement, to forty four constituted a large assemblage. There was a grand display of gorgeous plumes and caps, and it appeared that the whole winged tribe had been set in requisition to furnish the most brilliant of their feathers.

Some wore in their lips those little bells made of the conch shell and on the cartilaginous part of the nose, many wore an oval piece of tin, copper or brass, and a few of silver, which being of the size of a crown piece, covered the lips,*

*This ornament reminds of the nose jewel against which and other ornaments the Prophet Isaiah denounces Gods judgement v Isaiah III v.21.

others who could not afford such an ostentatious display had satisfied themselves with putting a piece of bamboo of the thickness of a goose quill through it. Through their ears were put similar pieces of bamboo or the head of birds attached to a string were fixed to it. Their faces were highly painted, and round their neck they wore strings of Monkey teeth, chiefly of the Pisa, as well as those of the Peccary and a few very neatly executed necklaces of the Brazilian Porcupine (Hystrix Cuandu)[1] which they call Aru. To these necklaces were attached long cotton strings and fringes hanging over their back, and having at their ends a number of Toucan, Squirrel and other skins. A few had made incisions along their legs exhibiting the figure of the Grecian fret. The arms were tattooed in a similar manner. As it is the general custom of Indians, when they go on a journey, or to a feast, to dye their feet red to above the ankle, which gives them an appearance as if they wore red socks. Round their feet were tied piece of tin which made a tinkling noise when they walked.+

+v Isaiah III 16 & 18.

The women were less ornamented many had tattooed themselves by making an incision over their eyes, and from the corner of the mouth over their cheek which were stained blue. Their hair was either cut or some wore it hanging over their shoulders without any arrangement.

Towards evening the Arecunas commenced to dance there was no difference in their motion from the generality of Indians in Guiana. The dancers formed a half circle the hands were laid respectively upon the neighbours shoulders and then they moved gravely on; by the first step the right foot being brought forward, it was pushed hard on the ground by which those who wore tins or other ornaments on their feet caused a tinkling noise, the left foot was then brought after and put before the right; the right step'd sideways, and the left followed it, being put behind; thus they moved round accompanied by a monotonous song, being more a recitation than a song – the words were

> Roraima piaraboko tauria
> Cartejuta naewaribamui.

[1] All South American porcupines belong to the Family Erethizontidae of which there is a genus *Coendou*.

315

the only translation which I can give of it is

> Of Roraima the red rocked I sing
> Where with day break night still prevails.[x]

[x]Verbally   Roraima piarakobo tauria
Roraima red rocks I sing of
Cartejuta naewaribaumui
Day come where still dark

This was perhaps thousand times repeated, but chiefly the word Cartejuta in all its syllables separately and together. The words were seldom changed; but it appeared as if it were the duty of some of the dancers to form their improviso. I heard next[1]

> Roraima waikæ særunga
> Tunabi yau-ura, tauria.

which alluded to the waters which flows from that famed mountain Roraima, but which I have not been able to translate as I could not ascertain the meaning of the word waikæ. It appears that in their improvisos they use every poetical liberty, and change the word to cause according to their conception, euphony.

Nothing could disturb the dancers in their monotonous song and grave movements, around them the noisy merriment, occasioned by the exhilarating effects of the fermented liquor, was raging to the extreme; still they continued their dirgelike song and grave step.

I was sadly tired of their noise, song, and dance, and congratulated myself at about midnight, I saw them moving in the house. I thought now it will be over, and rest may yet be thy share; poor blind sighted mortal, their movement had only been made in order to adjourn to the house, where the song was changed in Amayæ, Waramayæ, Ecunoyo[,] a complaint as I afterward ascertained that some of their neighbours, who had promised to come, had not kept word. I fell at last in a feverish sleep Amayae, Waramayae, accompanied me to the god of dreams and I slept until daylight. Did I dream or was it reallty? The first sound which greeted me on awaking was Amayae, Waramayae, Ecunoyo, and by Jove this indefatigable votaries of Terpsichore were still moving to their monotonous song. When the sun rose they moved from the hut to the open space before the house, and after one or two rounds, they dispersed at last.[2]

At one of the settlements they had prepared a feast and we found a large assembly of people.[3] Among them was a stranger a Sarrakong from the Mazuruny.[4] He told me he travelled 7 days from Roraima to his settlement on the banks of the Mazuruny. I inquired naturally for the Coomarow in order to have a point with which to compare my

---

[1] The manuscript is in some disorder at this point. This is the end of p. 56 of the 'Report'; the next two pages numbered 57 and 58, appear to be a continuation of the 'Letter' of 17 November of which the first six pages were inserted following p. 44 of the 'Report'. After these comes pp. 57 and 60 of the 'Report', of which pp. 58–9 are missing. This p. 57, also numbered p. 13, is a direct continuation of p. 56, and has accordingly been relocated to here.

[2] Page 57 of the 'Report' ends here and is followed by two pages from the 'Letter', numbered pp. 57–8.

[3] This is the feast already described in the 'Report'.

[4] Serekong or Seregong, the Akawaio of the Upper Mazaruni. The name literally means 'the people here'. See Audrey Butt Colson, 'The Spatial Component in the Political Structure of the Carib Speakers of the Guiana Highlands: Kapon and Pemon', *Antropologica*, 59–62, 1983–4, pp. 73–124 (92).

observations with those of Mr. Hilhouse.[1] He told me he wanted 3 days to come from his place to the Coomarow – the path from this part to the Mazuruny passed Roraima. The Captain of the settlement where we sojourned gave me the same information, and it was afterwards corroborated by the Arécunas, near Roraima who pay frequent visits to the Sarrakong. He gave me the following itinerary – Leaving their settlement Awarrawayamostie, they travel the first day to the Maurisi, an affluent of the Yuruani – on the third day they reach the Cuyrara,[2] where it is navigable for small craft; on the 4th they reach the river Cucko[3] on the 6th, the Mazuruny, and the settlement of the Sarrakong on the 7th. From here it is 3 days further to the Coomarow. They enter the first day the Yaraina, an affluent of the Mazuruny from the east, the next day the Zinauwaru, and find, by passing over land, the Coomarow on the third day. Well acquainted with the mode of travelling, and making every allowance for the winding of its affluents, the nearest part of the Mazuruny is not less than 50 miles in a N.E. by E. direction from Roraima which gives a difference of 27.8 miles in lat., and 41.[9] for departure.[4]

The latitude of the east end of Roraima is according to my observations, and on which I have reason to depend as it agrees with all my trigonometrical operations at Uraparu and the astronomical observations which I made on my return there, 5°9′[40″]N. The point where the road from Roraima strikes therefore the parallel would be about 5·37N. Then it is still 3 days to the Coomarow in a N.N.E. direction. If I am not mistaken Mr. Hilhouse places the Coomarow cataract in 5·12N. I agree therefore much better with him in the longitude than the latitude.[5]

[*26th*. – Followed the southern foot of a range of sandstone hills, remarkable for their resemblance to fortifications on a gigantic scale. We crossed the river Wene & then turned north and ascended about 300 feet whence we saw Mount Zabang to the SE and the remarkable range of flat topped sandstone mountains of Roraima, more resembling basalt in their outline, rising like a wall in the NNE; passed over the saddle in Amauparu, so cleft & rugged in its structure, and so steep in ascent that we were obliged to tread in the exact steps that had been worn or perhaps cut out by the Indians. After descending we halted at the foot of Mount Waramatipu, a wooded hill 700 feet high, which from its dark foliage, appears almost black as seen in contrast with the light-coloured mural precipice of Roraima.]

We hurried round a small hillock and had a very pleasing aspect before us. The foreground occupied an Indian settlement, enclosed or barricaded as I might say, a practice which I had never observed before. The background occupied the wall like mountain wrapped in dark-clouds, wooded hills formed the frame to this picture. We arrived at the settlement called Arawayam at 11 oclock, it consisted of three square houses with gable ends and a round cabin. Only a few inhabitants were present the rest were in their

---

[1] The reference here is to Hilhouse's 'Journal of a Voyage up the Massaroony in 1831'.

[2] Probably the Kwiara River.

[3] Kako River.

[4] In a straight line, the distance is about forty miles which would make it fifty or more overland.

[5] An entry for 26 and 27 October is appended to p. 58 of the 'Letter', which appears to be in Captain Washington's handwriting. The original version for the former date, either in 'Report' or 'Letter' form, has not been found so the edited version is included here in [ ]. For the 27 October the 'Letter' (p. 58) and 'Report' (p. 60) versions exist and as they complement each other, the former is included in a footnote. As has already been noted, in the current ordering of the manuscript, p. 60 of the 'Report' follows p. 57, which is located after p. 58 of the 'Letter'.

fields. We learnt that this was the only inhabited place for many miles in circumference. I selected it therefore for head quarters, from whence I intended to make our excursions to Roraima. A short time after the Inapatoritong arrived with the remainder of his people and gave us welcome, and promised to furnish during our stay what Cassada bread we might stand in need of for the general articles of barter – knives, beads, razors &c &c. The afternoon elapsed with erecting small cabins constructed of Palm leaves, our tent cloths being so small that we could not enjoy any comfort in it, and served only where want of time or Palm leaves left no other alternative.[1]

On the 2 Nov[r] we started on our ascent of Roraima. We ascended several high mountains and descended on the other side, crossing frequently brooks which run towards the Yuruani. The mountains were thinly clothed with short grass, and a vivid vegetation only on the banks of the numerous rivulets which we had to [cross]. At mountain Kaimari I admired the regularity with which a number of boulders of different sizes were placed. If human hands[2] had put them according to line & compass they could not have been straighter. Their direction was S84°W.; and the breadth of the track about a mile. We passed in the afternoon the brook Doh, about 40 feet wide, and shortly after the Cuckenam from 30 to 40 feet wide, though within three miles of its source. At 6 oClock in the evening we were within a mile of the perpendicular walls of Roraima, and took up our night quarters in a hollow. It was with the greatest difficulty in procuring fire – the constant moisture which here prevails, renders the dry brushwood difficult to burn. The thermometer stood at 6 P.M. at 67.5, at 12 P.M. at 59 Fahr. Before sun rise and ½ an hour after, Roraima was beautifully clear and we saw it in all its beauty. At a height of 3700 feet above the Arécuna village of Awarrayam botte, the perpendicular walls begin to rise to a height of from 14 hundred to 15 hundred feet; their summit therefore is from 5100 to 5200 feet above Awarrayam botte; these walls as perpendicular as if erected with the plumb-line, & not by nature. Yet in some parts they are covered with low shrubs, which from the foot of the wall appeared as if suspended; and at the distance where it is impossible to discern distinctly giving to the reddish rock a dark appearance, as if affected by the action of the weather. These stupendous walls consist of boulders of a similar description long before we reached Roraima.[3] Those which belonged regularly placed on Mount

---

[1] The following is the account of 27 October from the 'Letter' (p. 58):
   'We reached on the 27 October, a settlement of Arécunas, called Awarayam botte. Contrary to what I had observed before as to Indian settlements, it was enclosed or barricaded. It consisted of 3 square houses with gable ends & a round cabin. They informed me that further towards Roraima there were no inhabitants, as their neighbours had gone on a journey. We were detained here 8 days by bad weather, during which time I only got two observations for latitude, by which we were on 5°4'N. Lat. The mountain of Roraima was almost constantly clouded and no day passed without thunder & lightening. I measured a base line in order to ascertain the height and distance of Roraima and the other mountains in sight. But for the data of my observations, I had to watch every favourable moment, and to repeat the observations according to the weather, in order to procure a mean result. All the heights hereafter mentioned are therefore extended from the settlement Awarayam botte, where according to a number of experiments, water boiled at 199.95° Fahr, though the thermometer was not of the nicest construction.'
[2] This the point at which pp. 57 and 60 of the 'Report', already included in this transcription, are placed in the manuscript. After p. 60 of the 'Report' there are a further eight pages of the 'Letter' of 17 November. They are numbered 59–60 and then 60a–f.
[3] There are some words missing from this sentence which should presumably read something like this: 'That these stupendous walls consist of boulders of a similar description we recognised long before we reached Roraima.'

Kaimari belonged to the same section, though the phenomenon of a perpendicular wall 1500 feet high is in Guayana, perhaps only peculiar to Roraima & the neighbouring mountains. Another remarkable feature is the waters which precipitate themselves thundering from this enormous height and flow finally into the three mightiest rivers of the northern half of South America – viz[t] the Amazon, Orinoco & Essequibo. Though the embouchure of the two former is 700 miles apart, the mountains Roraima, Iackenam, Ayang Catsibang, and Marima form almost a quadrilateral figure, of which Roraima the highest is the most north eastern.[1] This quadrangle occupies from S.E. to N.W. 10 geographical miles – the eastern end of Roraima is, according to my observations and computation, in 5°9′37″N. lat., and the north-western end of Ayang catsibang in 5°18′N. lat. Their greatest difference in longitude is between Roraima and the west end of Iackenam and amounts to 53 miles. N.W. from Ayang catsibang, at the distance of 2 miles, rises the rocky wall Irwakarina[2] to a height of 3600 feet. It is remarkable for an urn shaped rock on its eastern end, which on a pedestal of 3135 feet above the Arecuna village, is 466 feet high, and at its widest part 381 feet. Next follows Wayaca piapa[3] the felled tree, which Macunaima, like the Pourae biassa, cut during his journey through these parts.[x]

> [x]These heights have all been determined with the sextant and the plane speculum, provided with adjusting screw – tho' the sextant is not an instrument to expect such nice results as from a theodolite, I have in every case taken from 9 to 10 Obser[ns] & calculated the mean. These angles were determined from a base line at Awarrayam botte. The angle of elevation of Wayaca was one of those I could not procure, in consequence of the clouds always surrounding it.

Wayaca is less in height than any among the group, and resembles an obelisk with a truncated head. The three mountains, Cararingtebuh, Yuruaruina and Irutibuh[4] conclude the group. Cararingtebuh, the highest among them, is 4943 feet above the Arécuna village. I should have observed that north east of Roraima, the Waktibuh, or Sun mountain[5] belongs to this group, though it does not possess such perpendicular walls. The most remarkable amongst them remains however the quadrangle, and like as it points its five sides to the four quarters of the world.[6]

The Brocken in the Hartz mountains is an instance on a small scale of what we observe in Roriema, there is no doubt that the water arises in consequence of the vesicular vapours[7] being attracted and suddenly cooled by the rock, and the precipitation takes place almost constantly during the day, while the thunderstorms replace it

---

[1] This was changed to 'south-easterly' in the published version (p. 206). However, this is wrong as is Schomburgk's claim that the four mountains form a quadrangle. On the reference map Iackenam is Kukenaam; Ayang Catsibang is the eastern part of Mount Iwalkarima; and Marima is Maringma. They form a rough line from south-east to north-west in the following order Maringma, Roraima, Kukenaam and Iwalkarima.

[2] Mt Iwalkarima. It is not a separate mountain from Ayang Catsibang.

[3] Mt Waika-Piapu.

[4] Cararingtebuh is possibly part of Mt Ilutipu, Schomburgk's Irutibuh. Yuruaruina is possibly Mt Eluwarima.

[5] Probably Wei Assipu as *wei* is the word for 'sun' in several Carib languages. The 'tibuh' suffix on many of the names is probably derived from a common Carib word for rock or mountain; for example, *tĕpu* in Trio.

[6] These are definitely the words in the manuscript, but it is not clear what Schomburgk was trying to say.

[7] Schomburgk is probably using this term to mean clouds. There was a theory that minute drops of rain or fog were vesicular, i.e., hollow spheres.

during the night. When the latter did not resound through the valley, I have seen the mountain free from clouds. This is a rare circumstance during the day. While writing this I have been 4 weeks in its vicinity and during that time I have seen Roriema only twice free from clouds. Its rounded summit is overgrown with shrubs – this I ascertained on the top of a neighbouring mountain, for without wings the intrepid climbers of Peten Both[1] would not be able to reach its summit, The highest however is not a 100 feet, as at a distance of 3 miles, the extended angle between the top of the highest and where the wall becomes perpendicular, was only 8′ which would indicate a height of about 56 feet. Though so small the vegetation of the rounded summit aids the attraction of those colours which are charged with aqueous vapours. The circumstance that thick forests extend from the north of Roraima to the coast of the Atlantic, while to the south spread large savannahs, may be one of the local causes of the constant Humidity, as well as of the frequent thunderstorms of these Regions. It needs no words to describe the picturesque appearance of these mountains from which streams precipitate themselves from a height of 14 to 15 hundred feet in spray as fine as mist before they reach the basin excavated at the foot of the wall, but far over leaping it with thundering noise when swollen by the rain that accompanies the thunderstorms. On one of these occasions I had the good fortune to be near Kamieba which forms the largest cataract of the Roriema. Far famed is the Staub-bach[2] of the Swiss Alps but it stands alone. Roraima numbers 5, besides a number of smaller ones, which only flow after showers of rain. The neighbouring Icuckenam has a similar number, and Marima perhaps still more, the latter of which unite with the Aruparu.[3] Roraima is 3½ miles long but of inconsiderable breadth. From its eastern side flows the Coting or Cotinga, the Rio Cristaes of the Portuguese, uniting its waters with those of the Portuguese Amazon through the rivers Takutu, Branco & Negro. A little north of it the Cuya, a tributary to the Cuko which latter through the Mazuruny flows into the Essequibo. South of the Coting is the Aracabo,[4] an affluent of the Cuckenan. From the south western side of Roraima several streams precipitate themselves, which flow into the Cuckenam which latter has its source in the neighbouring mountain Icukenam, and flows through the Yuruani and Caroni into the Orinoko. The Yuruani itself which the Indians consider the head of the Caroni (Caroni-Yima) flows in numerous streams from the north-eastern side of Icuckenam, and is joined by others from its western side and from the mountains Ayang catsibang (literally louse-comb), Zarangtibuh, and Irisarkarima. The river Aruparu flows likewise in numerous streams from the rocky wall Marima and joins at 4 days journey from its source, the Cucko. The river Carauring, a tributary of the Yruani, flows from mount Carauringtibuh. The Cucko, one of the chief branches of the upper Mazuruny, has its source on the eastern side of Irutibuh, while the Cama[5] which flows from the western side, joins the Apauwanga[6] a tributary of the Caroni, north of the Yuruani.

To give an instance of the quantity of water which flows from the mountain, I have only to observe that the river Cuckenam near the Arecuna settlement, which is situated

---

[1] Who and what Schomburgk was alluding to at this point has not been identified.
[2] The Staubbach Falls of 1,000 metres, near Lauterbrunnen in Switzerland.
[3] Possibly the River Arabaru.
[4] Possibly the Río Arabopo.
[5] Río Camá.
[6] Río Aponguau.

at the foot of Roraima, about 3 miles from its source already from 50 to 60 feet wide near the savannah, [which] extends from that village to within a mile of its perpendicular walls, where the soil becomes first marshy and then changes into rocky glens and precipices. The marshy savannah abounds in the most curious & interesting plants, among them is an Utricularia, the most beautiful of its tribe. The root is fibrous, and from it arises generally one, but seldom two leaves on pellicles about 6 inches long, which bore a fleshy reniform leaf, inverted, the acute side being next to the pellicle. The stem of a dark purple colour rose to a height of 3 or 4 feet, and bore several flowers about 2 inches and a half in diameter, and of a beautiful purple. Its lower lip falls like a collar and is from 2 to 2½ in[s] wide. The palate is prominent, the throat open, dilated, bearded and furrowed with yellow. The upper lip or hood is large, bold at its margin and larger than the palate which it overshadows. The spur is longer than the plume, reserved and subulates the capsule in globose.[x]

> [x] I had nothing on my pedestrian tour to decide whether this interesting plant be new – in this case & should I receive permission it is to be dedicated to Baron Humboldt.[1]

The next plant of great interest resembles in its leaves the Sarracenia – they are radical, ventricose, about 5 or 6 inches long, the margin and veins of the upper leaves of a pink colour, ending in a short, vaulted and incurved appendix, precisely similar to those of Saracenia variolaris. But there was a great deviation in the flower; the stigma being neither dilated nor the stamen indefinite, consisting of from 27 to 32. In Saracenia each bears only one flower. In the present genus there are several and the seeds are winged. The flower resembles our snow drop, consisting however of from 4 to 6 Sepals which when of even number are placed in a [blank] manner, they are at the beginning white tinged with red, and become in course of time herbaceous.[2]

Of no less interest is a Cypripedium growing by the side of the Utricularia and Sarracenia in a marshy soil. I think it is the first South American species. The radical leaves were [blank] somewhat compressed and [blank] From the middle row the hairy and leafy stem to a height of from 4 to 5 feet bore on each peduncle several flowers. The lobe of the [blank] was triangular [blank] and of the size of the Sepals. The petals are narrow and longer than the Sepals. The flowers as well as stem and leaflets were hairy.

> If it prove new of which I have little doubt, and I receive permission it is to be dedicated to D[r] Lindley.[3]

I found numerous other plants in this remarkable mountain and which I have no space to mention. However I cannot pass over a Cleistia with a deep scarlet flower and stem & purple leaves.[4]

We returned next day to Awarayambotte and on the [illegible] road to Uruparu where we arrived on the 9 Nov[r] & where fever which broke out among several of our

---

[1] It was dedicated to Humboldt. Its scientific name is *Utricularia humboldtii*.

[2] *Heliamphora nutans*. For Bentham's description of this plant, see 'On the *Heliamphora nutans*, a New Pitcher-plant from British Guiana', *The Transactions of the Linnean Society of London*, 18, 1841, pp. 429–33.

[3] This is a marginal note without indication of where it should be located in the text. Here seems the most suitable place. The plant was originally called *Cypripedium lindleyanum*, now renamed *Phragmipedium lindleyanum*.

[4] *Cleistes*, a genus of Epidendroid orchid.

crew detained me. This was not to be wondered at as they were accustomed to the regular range of the temperature of the air which prevails on the Savannahs, and where the range is seldom more than 10° or 11° – the lowest daily state of the thermometer being from 75 to 78° & the highest from 85 to 90° in the shade. While we were on the elevated table land, it stood during the night, and in the morning from 60 to 63°, and rose at 2 oClock in the heat of the sun to which we were naturally exposed while travelling, from 105 to 110. This, connected with the moisture and rain to which we were exposed for 4 weeks, made the fever less surprising, and I only wondered that we ourselves have not yet felt its effects. It was impossible to leave the sick to their fate amongst strangers. They trusted me and left their homes, wifes and children to accompany me, but as I have been hitherto successful in treating them, I hope to recover the remainder in a few days so far that we can start on [blank].

I have called every information I could for our future tour, and the conclusion I have come to is, to start from here in a S.W. direction – this is the only region inhabited. According to the itinerary, received from the Indians, we reach the Parime on the 9th day (Rerariquare of the maps). We ford the Maijary on the 7th day – and according to my reckoning we reach the Urariquira in the vicinity of the former village [blank] 2 days from the mouth of the Urariquira.[1] The situation is certainly far different from what I supposed, nevertheless [blank] and delays which its visit has caused, it is a trifle if compared with the importance of its geographical situation. Here [blank] natural divisions of British Guayana, Columbia and the Brazils.[2]

I have added a coloured view of Roriema[3] and a detailed sketch of it. The latter requires every indulgence, being sketched on an empty biscuit canister – the most level space I had at command – for a ruler, I had the scale of a broken thermometer; it cannot possess the correctness which it requires. As a temporary map to let the Society understand what these hasty lines relate, it may prove welcome. Nor is the paper what I would desire – that useful article for communicating our thoughts to those distant from us – ink too is wanting and many other articles to render my work worthy of its destination, but I beg you to apologise in my name, and I am sure to receive the Council's indulgence if they consider that I am now 14 months from civilised society and the colony, and at present entirely in want of the necessary articles for writing and drawing.

I doubt if I shall have another opportunity of writing to you before March or April next year if it should, I shall avail myself of it.[4]

---

[1] The Rio Branco above its junction with the Takutu is called the Uraricoera, except for its headwaters where it is known as the Parima. The Parimé and Majari are both left-bank tributaries of the Uraricoera. The geographical information available to Schomburgk when he wrote this is clearly confused.

[2] Although there are numerous blanks in the manuscript at this point, Schomburgk seems to be excusing the time taken up by his detour from the route to Esmeralda by stressing the geographical importance of the Roraima region.

[3] The latter is a watercolour of Mount Roraima which is held by the Royal Geographical Society (LMS/RHS/1). It is obviously the model for John Bentley's almost identical illustration in Schomburgk's *Twelve Views in the Interior of Guiana* (1841). It is reproduced here, in black and white, as Figure 11, p. 312.

[4] The 'Letter' ends here and an editorial hand has written 'Note. So much of M[r] Schomburgks Diary was received in England on the [blank]. On the [blank] the Secretary received the following communication in continuation.' The manuscript continues at this point with the 'Report' at a page numbered both 17 and 61. This double numbering continues, although not every number from both sequences occurs on every page, until p. 108 or 152.

Nov 21st This morning was one of the coldest we had experienced in Guiana. The Thermometer at 6 oclock 59°. We started twenty minutes after seven, under many views[1] from the old Captain and his Wife who made us understand by Gesture and words, that we should be welcome, and that they wished to see us again. We were joined by some of the people from the place and retraced our steps towards Sampara's[2] abandoned hut. The path divided only a few miles south from it. I admired the strange yet rugged appearance of some sandstone hillocks which resembled in that respect those of trappean formation and no vestiges of the rounded forms, otherwise peculiar to that system of rocks, were to be traced. Some of the Indians had espied a bee nest and as they expected to find it rich of sweets, it was resolved to be secured. I was curious to see how this would be accomplished and our passing by had already disturbed the little colony and made the most of us scamper over stock and block. One of the Indians however after having put down his burden, crawled cautiously near it, having moistened his fingers with perspiration of his arm; he conveyed it to the entrance and commenced now to knock with his other hand which was moistened in a similar manner, at the lower part of the nest; all the bees, queen drones and labourers hastened to abandon it, without ever attempting to injure the destroyer of their colony. Having effected it with comparative ease, he plucked the nest from the branch to which it was fastened, and brought it to us. It was of a round form, somewhat larger than a childs head. The cells consisted of three tiers, the two upper filled with honey, the lower partly with larvae. The honey was very sweet and I might call it, almost in crystalized form, and possessed besides its sweetness, an aromatic taste. We commenced to descend Tariparu at 10 oclock; it forms one of the southern mountain of the sandstone ridge and is only a short distance from Mount Kinotaima which we had ascended a month ago (October 20). Tariparu is much steeper than Kinotaima, and not only fatiguing but frequently even dangerous, the numerous boulders of quartz, the companions of the sandstone, were heaped up, and an incautious step made them roll downwards to the danger of those who walked before, while at another time precipices of sixty or eighty feet, showed themselves to the right and left, leaving only a small path with a declivity of 42° and in some instances even more. Excepted some falls who exposed only the suffer[er] to the ridicule of those who witnessed it, we reached the brook Maese that flows at the foot of Tariparu, quite safe and selected it for our Breakfasting place. Where we issued from the wood we saw the peaked Mountain Arawayang before us; it bore then S.61°E., and towards it our course was directed. We had however previously to cross the wood that borders the Muiang.

Novbr. 22nd We ascended Aruwayang at least to the saddle which it forms with the neighbouring mountain as it were[;] it was a work fatiguing enough and we congratulated ourselves that the summit remained a stranger to our steps. The view was not uninteresting, we saw Mairari which we had passed a month ago, Saramaicka and Tarenni mountains[,] groups which we were to pass in a few days. We crossed several brooks which were flowing into the Inkarama[3] which is itself an affluent of the Muiang and descended for about 2000 feet into a mountain glen where the rush of water told us of a Cataract which the Warampa forms, which is likewise an affluent of the Inkarama.

[1] Changed on the manuscript by an unidentified hand to 'adieus'.
[2] Zambara, the old shaman. See p. 310 above.
[3] Probably Igarapé Ingamla.

In the fork which these two large brooks form near their confluence, we found an abandoned settlement, some of the cotton trees were loaded with cotton, our Indians fell eagerly over it, and collected what they could get hold of, in order to spin it at times of leisure, to cotton thread a most valuable article to the Indians for finishing off his arrows. The Inkarama was about 60 feet wide. We had to wade it for a good distance up the stream to discover the path on the opposite side, of which this side there was no vestage among the low bushes, which now over grew, what were once provision fields. After having continued our watery path for some time, we commenced to ascend the mountain Saraurayeng, and admired the prospect which opened itself to our eyes. On its summit we saw again these detached groups of mountains which girt the savannahs and among which we soon discovered Muritibuh by its towershaped summit. I saw here the white quartz regularly stratified, its direction being N8°W. At the Macusi huts at Canaupang built on a hillock surrounded by higher mountains, Mairari bore N59°E. we halted here for breakfast, and procured an additional quantity of yams, a welcome increase of our stock of provisions. We crossed in the afternoon the Zama,[1] a tributary of the Muiang and entered again mountain savannahs only moderately raised above the valley of the Xuruma. I saw those who went foremost departing from the regular course, and run towards a spot, where they looked with wonder and astonishment at some object. I hastened my steps, to come up with them, and found near the site of a cabin, burnt down by accident or malice, the skeleton of a man, which from all appearances had not been laying there more than three months. The bones were already bleached, those Harpies the carrion crows had done their work. Little was disarranged if we except the smaller bones. It was naturally that we concluded, that the person whose remains were thus exposed had come to his death by the fire which consumed the hut. But who can picture our horror, when that evening another tale was told us of his fate. We found namely the place which towards nightfall we selected for our quarters part of the Macusi families, who inhabit Canaupang and who were then on their way to the savannahs to make salt,[2] they consisted of twenty two individuals from the baby on the breast to the aged persons with snow white hair, and faltering step, nevertheless both extremes of the human life were not excluded from the journey to the savannah. They appeared very friendly, and told us through our Interpreter, that they were sorry they had not been at home, and though like ourselves on a journey, the Calabash with Paiwori was handed, and the smoking pepperpot seasoned by some small fish was put at our feet. We naturally asked about the skeleton, and why the bones were not buried. We were told it belonged to a middle aged man, once one of their inmates at Canaupang and whose children grown up, boy and girl were pointed out to us among their number; he had been stricken with blindness, he nevertheless accompanied them sometimes on their journey, or with the peculiar feat in blind people he directed his steps by the touch and knew to find his way to the provisions field. During one of these excursions he lacked however behind, and lost his way, and by the most unexcusable but not uncommon neglectfulness among Indians no person went in search of him until two days had elapsed, when they returned without having succeeded in finding him and no doubt he was no further thought off until they discovered him some time after in a

---

[1] Igarapé Zama.

[2] On some parts of the savannahs a salty substance can be obtained on the surface. The other sources of salt-like substances were the ashes of certain palms and water plants.

state of putrefaction, perished by slow famine. Who can picture the dying moments of this poor mortal. Surrounded by constant night, perishing inch by inch of hunger and thirst, his last cries mingling with those of the exulting Vultures at the approaching repast or which may have commenced already their feast before the last breath had escaped his lips. The thought is shuddering nevertheless founded on reality. And even after his body was discovered and his bones bleached by the sun, exposed to the sight of every one who passed that road, filial affection was not awakened in his children's breast to cover them with earth, even the aversion not only peculiar to the Indian, but likewise to many of the uneducated of our own race, which they show towards dead bodies, after life has escaped for some time past, is no excuse for his Children. The opportunity was too inviting to me to procure the skull of a Macusi, in such an easy manner, and I manouvered it happily enough to convey it to one of our trunks, without that an Indian got aware of it.

Nov 23 Our latitude was the preceeding evening 4°18N. We entered shortly after our starting the system of the Xuruma or Zurung; the brook Yanau flows in an E.bS. direction towards the low savannahs, which under the shouting of our Indians we entered at one oclock. We crossed the Yanau again, and directed our way towards the Xuruma which about 150 feet wide was much opposed in its course by rocky dykes and it forms numerous cataracts. These dykes are the connecting link between the mountain chain which we had just left, and the isolated and more southerly situated groups of Mampang and Muritibuh. We had to follow the Xuruma for some distance in a SSE. direction before we could find a place where we could ford it. Opposed by one of the dykes, it divided in three arms and formed an island to which part our trodden path led. We found it here only three to four feet deep and therefore not connected with danger to those who were not able to swim. Its rocky bed where now we were only ankle deep in the water, and by the next step fell to our loins, much to the detriment of our species, opposed some difficulties in traversing the three arms, and we were glad, as we had reached the most western bank. We marched from here more westward, and we were within two miles of the foot of the mountain group Mampang w[h]ere we admired the cascade formed by the brook Marai Kawanna, that precipitates itself perpendicular from a height of about three or four hundred feet. We had crossed the valley of the Zuruma in a SSE direction, its breadth was about five miles. We found now the country inhabited by of Wapisianas and halted at one of their settlements with nightfall.

Nov[r] 24th. Our path crossed numerous tracts of boulders and was fatiguing; soon after eight oclock we crossed the brook Warauwayang a tributary to the Marua (the river Parima[1] of the maps) at the banks of which we halted for breakfast. It was about 100 feet wide, and has its sources, as we were informed by the Indians, near the mountain group in Uracaima.[2] The Indians call this river the Marua and not Parima, by which name, or rather Paruima, they designate the Rio Branco of the maps from its sources (Urariquira) to its confluence with the Rio Negro. Large boulders which rose from 10 to 15 feet above its surface, rendered it easy to gain the opposite bank by jumping from boulder to boulder, those who waded it, went to their breast in water. The grass on the Savannah was very high, and my coxswain was nearly bitten by a rattle snake, upon which he came unawares. It escaped the blows which were aimed at it, however only for

[1] Rio Parimé.
[2] Serra Uraucaima.

a short time as the Indians set the Savannah in a large circle in fire. We selected our Camp at the foot of the mountain Marua where among huge boulders, higher than their cabins, there were two huts, inhabited by Wapisianas: we found only a few of the inmates at home, the greater part were gone to the savannah to make salt.

Nov 25th This being Sunday, we stayed. S.E.bE.½E. about 12 miles distant from the settlement Marua, there are on the banks of the river of the same name some very remarkable boulders of Granite which the Indians call Tamurumu.*

*This is no doubt a corruption of Tepu Mereme 'painted rock' in the Maypure language. M. de Humboldt discovered a similar rock a few leagues from Encaramada which rose likewise from the middle of the savannahs.[1]

The highest of which was designated to us as Macunaima's house, can not be less than from 3 to 400 feet, and to be covered with hieroglyphic figures, like the rocks at the cataracts at Warapouta and at Temehri and elsewhere at the river Corentyn. An accident prevented us from visiting them; in the afternoon one of our crew was brought in who had been bitten by a rattle snake. He was senseless and even after we had brought him too, a general stupor appeared to be spread over him. I had on the first instance, the wound, which was over the artery of the lower leg, sucked alternately by two powerful men, and as the consequence of its situation I felt reluctant to have it scarified. I rubbed it well with salt and sweet oil, Volatile Alkali being not in our possession. At the same time a ligature was placed tightly somewhat above the wound; sweet oil and salt were likewise given internally. As soon as he had recovered his speech, he complained of acute pain, not only in the wounded part, but likewise in his side under the arms, faintness of sight, and that his head seemed to turn with him, his pulse was small and rather irregular, and I feared much for his life. When he fell in a new stupor and ejected from time to time blood from his stomach, I administered him a dose of Castor oil, and had him covered with Blankets to produce perspiration, which after an hour was copiously effected, and his pains became less acute. [H]e told us he had been fishing at the brook, where the snake had jumped at him, and bitten him in two places; he meant however that the upper and lower fangs had inflicted separate wounds, he had met with the same misfortune some time ago, and told us that a small cup of milk from a Womans breast had saved him, this was procured for him and we tried to promote otherwise the perspiration and continued to rub the wounded part with sweet oil. It took us wonder that the leg was not more swollen, and if I except the spitting of blood that there was not more vomiting; it appeared even he felt no nausea before the castor oil was given him but his eyes were much bloodshot and it was evident that he did not possess their power. His limbs remained rigid, and he complained until late at night of the turning of the head, as our interpreter translated it.

Novr 26th Our invalid improved rapidly today – thought he continued to complain of vertigo, his pulse was less concentrated and more regular, and in the afternoon he asked for some nourishment. I gave him some rice, and as he was in the hands of his countrymen and relations, I thought I could give the necessary orders for leaving Marua next morning. The Wapisiana were not able to furnish us with provisions, and those which we had brought with us from Curupara were nigh at an end. [T]he

[1] Encaramada was the site of a mission on the Orinoco, a little upstream from the junction with the Apure. See Humboldt, *Personal Narrative*, II, 1907, pp. 177–83.

latitude of the settlement was 3.57.37N. the long^de 61°3W. We passed therefore the river Marua or Parima in 4°N. latitude, and already ten miles above its sources according to Mr Arrowsmiths latest maps of Colombia, while its real sources are 20 miles further North in the Uracaima mountains.

Novr 27th After having left to our invalid a supply of rice, the only aliment which I allowed him for the next three days, we continued our march over the Savannah, keeping the mountain chain at the right at a distance from 15 to 20 miles. Its general direction remained East and West. To the South we observed several isolated groups; among them appeared Cawaipassi to be the highest. Mount Muritibuh[1] bore in the morning S22W.: along its western foot flows the river Maiyari (the Majari or Majariera of maps). In the afternoon the group Toupae engtibuh and Waikamantibuh bore WbN. [T]he river Maiyari is turned somewhat eastward by this group, and flows as soon as it has overcome the impediment, along the foot of Waikamantibuh in a more or less south-easterly direction. In continuing our march over the Savannah we crossed the river Maiyari in 3°30′N Lat. 61°21′W Long^de, where it had a breadth of about 400 feet, and reached the next day a Macusi settlement called Carutza. The settlement consists of three round Cabins, and about fifty inmates, all Macusis; the river Parima or Rio Branco is within three miles of their settlement, and the mouth of the Maracca represented as a tributary of the former river about 12 miles in a S68½E. direction. [T]he Indians here say however that the Maracca is merely a branch of the Parima, from which it flows off West of the confluence of the Uraricapara and unites with it, as already stated, forming a large and extensive Island.[2] I hope to have opportunity to investigate this, which certainly would be of importance in the Geography of that river. It is not known here as the Urariquira, though they are well aware that the Caraiwa or Portuguese bestow the name of Rio Branco on it. Of the Villages Conceicão, Cajucaica, & San João Baptista,[3] nothing by tradition or vestiges is more to be discovered, though they flourish still in the latest maps.

The number of Women in Curutza surpassed far those of men, plurality of wives appears to be here more common than among the Arecunas. One aged man was pointed out to me, who had lately taken two sisters for his Wives – they were young and strong women, and each carried a boy of about a years age in their arms, which living testimonies certainly did not speak of declining age in their Father. The captain, a jolly looking personage of about 4 feet 10, and a rotundity which would make honor to a Dutch Burgomaster, had shown his followers a good example, and completed the trefoil; the oldest of his wives shows certainly an age of a greater number of years than her dread Lord & husband, while the years of the two others added

---

[1] In the published version (p. 214) this has been changed (correctly) to 'Wawatibuh'; from Schomburgk's position that day Mount Muritibuh would have borne approximately NNE. Although neither mountain appears on the reference maps, they are shown on Schomburgk's map (see Map 3).

[2] This is the large Ilha de Maracá. The distributary of the Uraricoera which flows round the north of the island is known today as Furo Santa Rosa. The Uraricapara is the Rio Uraricaá which flows into the Furo from the northwest. It was on the Uraricaá in 1773 that the Spanish sergeant Juan Marcos Zapata, with a small force of men, coming from Venezuela, founded the settlement of Santa Rosa. Later that year he also founded San Juan Bautista on the Uraricoera a little to the east of Ilha de Maracá. This Spanish venture into what is now Brazil was short-lived. The Portuguese soon heard of it, and mounted an expedition which brought an end to the Spanish presence in 1776 (see Hemming, 'How Brazil Acquired Roraima', pp. 310–13).

[3] Founded during the Spanish excursion south of the Pacaraima Mountains in 1773.

together, would only number his own. The hair of the old Woman are as white as snow, their growth lacks however not in strength and it gives her a strange appearance when she is occupied in her domestic affairs and she ties them together in a large queue. It appears upon her rest all domestic matters and though not now blessed with charms and not so smooth faced as her rivals she leads nevertheless the jolly Captain by the apron string.

December 3rd Our course turned towards the W.N.W.; we passed alternately copses of wood and Savannahs.

We were about 8 miles from the mountain group of which Toupaeeng is the highest. I estimated it above the Savannah 3000 feet the summit forming a wall like ridge, mostly consisting of rock and only sparely overgrown with wood; its southern end bore N39W, and the more North[r] N34°E. Waikamantibuh belongs to the same group, but is more peaked and shows no such rugged outline as the former. We passed in the afternoon the brooks Avariapuru[1] and Warapapura which flows scarcely half a mile asunder and joins the Parima[. S]hortly after four we reached a Zapara[2] settlement called Sawaekawari where we found a large concours of Indians, and we were informed that it were Purrigotos[3] and Individuals of some other nations from the Uraricapara, Merewari,[4] and from the vicinity of the Orinoco, and the Paraba (Paragua) the latter a tributary of the Carony: their number amounted to sixty and one all together. I soon recognised in the Purrigoto Captain, whose figure once seen could never be forgotten, the same person who three years ago told such a bundle of untruths about Lieu[t] Hainings and my fate to M[r] Brotherson whose indisposition kept at San Joaquim while we were occupied with the investigation of the upper Rupununy, I was therefore on my guard; it appeared that he intended to visit Pirara and the Corentyn. I am much afraid the latter for no good purpose, and it appeared to me that he practiced deception towards the poor savages, who had accompanied him and was leading them to slavery. These Indians consisted of Purrigotos, Guinaus,[5] Maiongkongs[6] and Oewakous.[7] The latter live in a perfectly wild state, at the sources of the Uraricapara, neither women nor men had any covering on them and their houses are still of lighter structure than that of the generality of the Indians[;] it appears they are still less attached to locality than other Indians in general, and fly at the appearance of any stranger. By what means the Purrigoto had succeeded in inducing them to accompany him I know not; those which I saw appeared very timid and about 4 feet 10 to 5 feet in height, they were slender, their eyes small, the face in general long, and their colour less dark than that of the other Indians.

---

[1] Igarapé Auaruparu.

[2] Also spelt Saparas. A Carib-speaking group similar to the Macushi. During the 18th century they were reported living to the west of the Rio Branco. The American explorer William Farabee found just three surviving Zaparas when he visited Maracá in the second decade of the 20th century. See *Central Caribs*, Philadelphia, University Museum, 1967 [1924], p. 242.

[3] Purigoto or Porokoto. Another Carib-speaking group, similar to the Macushi, living to the west of them either side of the Pacaraima range. Farabee reported them as almost extinct (*Central Caribs*, p. 246).

[4] Río Merevari.

[5] Guinau. An Arawak-speaking group which formerly inhabited the upper regions of the Caura and Merevari rivers. They no longer exist and have probably been absorbed by the Maionkong.

[6] Also known as Makiritare and Ye'kuana. A group of over 3,000 Carib-speaking Indians who live today in much the same area as Schomburgk found them; in the headwaters of the Merevari, Paragua and Ventuari rivers.

[7] Probably the Waika, a name used for the Yanomami.

The counterpart to them formed the Maiongkongs and Mauitzi[1] which I believe are sister tribes, and inhabit the Merewari and Paraba. They are from 5 feet 8 to 5.10 inches high, and even taller, their faces were round, the eyes set close together, and somewhat oblique, the forehead small and retiring, their figures broad and muscular, the eyelids furnished with long lashes; but the eyebrows as well as the beard had been plucked out – in one instance however it had been permitted to grow and though thin of respectable dimensions under the chin. It is a general practice among the females of the Caribis and other tribes of Guiana to raise the flesh of the calf and near the ankle, by tying, when yet young of age, bands round those places which are not removed or widened with growth. However I had not seen this Dandyism with men until I met the Maiongkongs, they have not only such bands round the leg, but likewise round the upper part of the arm where a kind of bracelet made of their own hair was tied; a similar band went round the leg under the knee. In lieu of a necklace they had a bundle of slender stems of a cryptogamous plant, a fern which they called Zinapipo, and to which no doubt talismanic powers are ascribed. Their waistcloths consisted of self manufactured laps, provided with fringes and dyed red. The Mauitzi resembled the Maiongkongs in dress and appearance. The Guinaus (Guinares) had oval faces, small heads, sharp features, and high cheekbones, the expression of their countenance was sedate and rather gloomy. We observed only few Women with them, but as we understood that a number had not yet come up to the settlement and were encamped at the Parima, I concluded that they might have stayed back with the others. A young Oewakou woman was much fairer than the rest and her eyes had a very soft expression, but her figure did not correspond with her features; she was short and muscular, and the head too small in comparison with the body. As I understood that they intended to proceed now by land and as the Zapara possessed only a small canoe, I applied to the old Purrigoto for his canoes; he did every thing in his power to deter us from proceeding further, and told us that starvation and sickness was prevailing higher up the Parima and Uraricapara and that we would find no people, and many other such tales; to which I knew to attach the necessary credence. He promised by presents &c. to comply with my request, and as I had found out that two of the Maiongkongs were only a short distance from the Orinoco I engaged them to accompany us, and as I had procured the old captain's permission for that purpose, they readily consented. Observations of α Cassiopeiae and α Eridani gave me as latitude 3°34′52″ for the Zapara settlement. [D]uring our observations the strange Indians were all ear and eye; they likely construed it that we were pi-ai-ing, and remained silent spectators – the old Purrigoto made however an exception, he wanted to shine before his people and show them that he was likewise acquainted with our doings. [T]he sky was very clouded however we pointed out several stars which he named; among others Achernar, which he called Irika, the three stars in the belt of Orion Kaikara, Aldebaran Wauyari-Yutta, the Pleiades Yumang, Capella Yawaiva.

Dec[r] 4th. This morning opened with the greatest disaster which for the sake of astronomical observations could befall me; in winding up my watch the chain burst and we were now without any time keeper, the misfortune admitted of no remedy, if I had sent back to the colony, two months would have elapsed, before under the most favourable circumstances, a messenger could possibly have returned, and the season[2] would have

---

[1] Virtually nothing is known about the Mauitzi. This is one of the very few references to them.
[2] The reference is to the season for travelling; which is basically the dry season.

been then nearly over. I resolved therefore to advance and act in the best manner I could, we had henceforth to judge the time and though latitudes by unenvied[1] attention were still attainable it was precarious with lunar distances. The traveller in the moist climate of Guiana ought to be advised to be provided with triplicate instruments on a journey of lesser duration than mine, and these instruments ought to be of the best construction. I had been peculiarly situated, and personal sacrifices to procure the most necessary instruments did not allow me to have them provided in a triplicate manner. A second watch which I had written for did not arrive and I was thus obliged to leave Pirara only with the one, the fate of which has just been related, as annoying as it proved I had to submit and to devise means how to counter check any errors which might arise from its want in my future observations. troubles come never alone is a trite saying.

Dec[b] 5th. We started at half past nine, and reached the confluence of the small river Paparu with the Parima an hour after; the old Purrigoto had accompanied us half way and returned apparently after a second thought. We found at the mouth of the Paparu four small corials but as it had been my intention to dismiss part of our crew, I considered them sufficient for our purpose. We were just preparing to load one when the old Purrigoto and his crew came with sack and bag and told me he could let me have only one as he wanted to go by water to Pirara. It was out of question that one was sufficient as with only a part of our baggage it sunk to the Gunwhales and I was determined not to be baffled by him again. a second Corial was taken possession of, and there is no doubt, that if I had wished to discharge only one of my pistols over their head, they would have soon desisted to carry the two smaller away, but as such an act though no harm had been intended would have been magnified, and construed in the worst manner by the Brazilians whose late conduct towards the Indians I had strictured, and though the old rogue deserved for his broken faith severe chastisement and the forcible capture of his Corials, I allowed him to slip through with two corials.[2]

After a storm follows a calm, the clamour and noise had now subsided, and means were to be devised how our corials might be enlarged. Our camp represented therefore in a short time the picture of a Dockyard in miniature. The Pirara Indians had been told that they were not to be dismissed until I were sea- or rather river- ready. Here were some employed to cut down Podai trees, the soft wood of which is particularly fit for light boards; others were seen dressing the boards with Cutlasses which served them as addices,[3] near some rocks others were occupied to make of clumsy pieces of Yarura wood, neat and light paddles, while the younger community were knocking Burra-burraro[4] sticks to be stripped off their coats, the bark forming a substitute for Oakum.

Dec[r] 6th. All was hustle this morning, and the corials were ready by 12 oclock. From the information which I had culled from the Maiongkong Indians, it appeared advisable to ascend the Parima. [O]ne of them was especially acquainted with the regions of the Orinoco, he told me of the Cassiquiare, the mountain Maravacca (Maraquaca)[5] and the

---

[1] Although underlined and crossed out, so not completely legible, this would seem to be the correct reading. Schomburgk presumably meant it in the sense of 'ungrudging'.

[2] This is one of the very few occasions on his travels that Schomburgk even contemplated force in order to get his way.

[3] Adzes.

[4] Possibly Buruburulli: *Licania divaricata*; *L. heteromorpha*.

[5] Cerro Marahuaca.

river Entuari (Ventuari). I thought myself therefore justified in trusting his information and changed my plan so far as that in lieu of the Uraricapara we were now to continue on the Parima, which river we entered at half-past one it was here about 300 yards wide, and much impeded by rocks which formed a series of rapids. Our course upwards was S.39°W. As soon as we entered the Rapids I found that the Corial was overloaded, and I had at this late hour to dismiss two men more; nevertheless she took in water at her sides when coming in the surge at the foot of the Rapids and Falls and felt uncomfortable. When we arrived therefore at the mouth of the river Yurumé[1] we landed, and having felled a Wanussuri tree (Cecropia peltata) of which two boards were dressed, we had them added (clinkered) to our washboards, and though it did not assist to accelerate her speed, she was rendered more safe and the siters were less exposed to get wet.

The river Yurume joins the Pari-ma from the N36W, its second reach turns however more Northwards. It is shallow at its mouth, much impeded by sandbanks and rocks and about 300 feet wide. In the Portuguese survey it is noted as the Idome. The Indians of the present day call it however Yurume; and of the village of San João Baptista, which is noted even in the latest maps, no vestige is more to be found. My astronomical observations gave me 3°30′40″N for the Latitude, differing but little from the latest maps, which the Portuguese surveys have served as foundation.

Decbr 7th A series of Cataracts which we had to surmount made our progress very slow. The Cataracts Mararitipang, Arukaima and Matiripang could not be passed without unloading the Corials and carrying the luggage overland.

The distance which we had made during the last three days amounted only to seventeen miles, and as I estimated our height at 111 feet above the Yurumé and our direct distance being scarcely fourteen miles, the fall amounted to eight feet per mile in a direct line.

We reached the mouth of the Uraricapara about nine oclock in the morning.[2] I found this river less in size than the Cuyuwini where it joins the Essequibo, and I estimated its width at about 250 feet. Its water was of the same colour as that of its recipient, and the current of equal strength, namely about 3 knots. Towards the end of the last Century, the Spaniards had at its right bank, but a considerable distance up the river, a small Fort called Santa Rosa, it was however already abandoned, and its site overgrown with bushes when the Portuguese surveyors visited it at the commencement of this Century.[3] The Latitude of its site was 3°50′N. and Mr. De Humboldt has drawn the attention of future travellers whose intentions it were to penetrate to the sources of the Orinoco particularly to this spot. If I had not met the Maiongkongs, who were now in my service, I should have no doubt attempted the ascent of the Uraricapara in lieu of continuing the Parime, but as not only the Purrigotos but likewise the Guinaus agreed in their accounts, that I should find not only the upper parts of the river uninhabited, but would have to turn far westward over land, I trusted this information, and chose the Parima as highway. The last reach of the Uraricapara is N.46°W.[4] and its course upwards appears

---

[1] Probably Rio Traida.

[2] Probably 10 December.

[3] Schomburgk is probably referring to the Portuguese expeditions into the region towards the end of the previous century. Two of these, that of Ricardo Franco de Almeida Serra and Antonio Pires da Silva Pontes in 1781 and that of Manoel da Gama Lobo d'Almada in 1787, reached the Uraricaá.

[4] This has been changed on the manuscript to 'S.46°E.' It is yet another example of Schomburgk's habit of recording the course of a river in the direction in which he was facing, rather than the direction of its flow.

to be NW., however near its mouth, a chain of small hillocks turn it to the SW. According to the observations I had taken the previous nights, the Lat^de of its junction with the Parima is 3°19′53, the Longitude deduced from observation at Marua and by dead reckoning 62°3′W. The Latitude according to Arrowsmiths map is 3.28N the Long^de [blank], this differs from my observation in Lat^de 8 miles, but I think I can depend upon my Latitude which was deduced from observations made the preceeding night of α Cassiopeiae and α Eridani, and any distance made this morning until 9 Oclock is too small to admit of an error there.

The river Parima before it is joined by the Uraricapara is about 200 yds wide, the same chain of hillocks which cross the Uraricapara traverses likewise the Parima, and not far from their junction the rivers form two large falls. The Purumamé Imérou[1] is without doubt one of the largest falls in Guiana and vies in size and picturesque beauties with William the Fourths Cataract in the Essequibo, and the large cataract at the Corentyn. this formidable obstacle to the navigation of the river, even in the small craft of the Indians, is about half an hour paddle from the junction of the two rivers. The river coming from the south, finds its course obstructed by the hillocks here already alluded to, and there is no doubt that it forced its way through them, and formed a break. The stratification of the rocks which were exposed to sight was S74°W. their dip S6°W. under an angle of 45°. The river narrowed to about 150 feet, divides into two streams, and precipitates itself a perpendicular height of 40 to 45 feet: the outflow being at the time when we reached it about 30 feet across through which narrow channel the whole mass of the Parima is forced. I have no doubt that during the time the river is full, it overflows this barrier, this was however not the case when we saw it. After it issued from this channel it turns Northerly and precipitates itself a second time about 25 feet, the whole fall amounting therefore to not less than 75 feet. In order to overcome this formidable impediment, no other alternative was left to us, but to haul the corials over the hillocks, which rose to a height of 350 feet. We observed that the same had been done before us by other Indians and thought the ascent was for about a third of its height almost under an Angle of 60°, and the Indians had to maintain themselves by steps, which had been made by predecessors, we had nevertheless the two corials and our luggage by four oclock in the afternoon on the other side of the Falls, and proceeded almost half a mile farther to a convenient resting place.

I repeated my observations for Latitude, and Camp was 3°18′16″N., the Southings which we had made since we left the Uraricapara amounted to 1′36″ which added to the former give for the Latitude of the junction 3°19′52″ differing only one second from last nights observations.

Decr 11th. I have noted already that I received from the Indians at the Zapara settlement the information that the Maracca is not a separate river but merely a branch of the Parime which flows off above the cataract of Purumamé, and joins the main stream again in about 3°22′N. Lat and 61°21′W. Longt. In maps it sources have been placed between the 2nd & 3rd parallel of N. Lat^de and 63° meridian W of G.[2] as the Indians of the Parima pretend however to have navigated this branch, we have no reason to doubt their assertion, and the Maracca is one of those instances of which the Amazons, and

---

[1] Cachoeira Parumaré.
[2] After the G (for Greenwich) there is a blank space before the period.

the Orinoco near its mouth offer many. Where the Maracca (which in the language of the Macusis, and their related tribes, signifies rattle) flows off, it is about 300 feet wide; its mouth is partly occupied by an island which leaves only a narrow channel on its right bank. The western hillocks, as I might call them in consequence of their tract preserving that direction throw numerous impediments in the course of the Parime and approach that river quite close, within a mile of the division or branching off. The largest hill is about 500 feet high, and bears from that point N61°W. and its distance is not quite a mile. Beyond that the river comes from S19°W and being opposed in its course by the mountains and narrowed in from both sides, it makes a large turn and divides into two branches, the mainstream of the Parima continuing again N24E. the Maracca flowing first S.70°E. & then NE. We passed shortly after the cataract Emenari where we had again to unload and to carry our baggage and our corial for a distance of 6 to 700 yards over land. Half a mile in a Southern direction from this fall the river is rejoined by a branch which like the Maracca has been flowing separately for nearly 20 miles. Our Indians told us that if we had selected that branch, it would lead us far to the North, and quite out of reach of the Zapara settlement which we hoped to find in the course of the day. We arrived there at one oclock, isolated from all other human habitations. Its access is barricaded by a number of falls and such a labyrinth of Islands that without the clue of thread of Ariadne one runs danger not to find the way back again. But the human beings who live here deserve such a sequestered spot; if the ugly club ever visited, it could not have boasted such an assembly of carricatures of the human face and frame. Whoever has seen those contorted and bizarre masks, the offspring of the Carnival in the most burlesque imagination, would have seen here their living prototype. A young man, apparently healthy, possessed a large tumour which occupying the right side of his face extended to the nose, and gave to that organ an immense protuberance, which hindered him to look straight forward and gave his eye an oblique direction. His face received in consequence such a frightful appearance, that even the knowledge of his presence gave one uneasiness, and one avoided to look in the direction where he was supposed to be. Blessed with the same share of curiosity as the others, he did not leave us until nightfall and many an unguarded look fell upon his face. The rest of the inhabitants suffered from inflammation of the eyes, squinted, presented the frightful picture of dropsy with its long drawn face and half open mouth, or were clad in sickly hue. Quite in concordance with their figures and faces were their voices, their welcome was squeaking and jarring to the ear, and their doings and actings so much 'en ton' with their general appearance, that a Hogarth would have found a study, a Lavater, an enrichment of his collections.[1] Nature pleases herself frequently in contrasts, she formed likewise here three exceptions. The Captain of this hospital like crew is an handsome and athletic man of pleasing manners (if such expression may be used if we speak of a Savage). The next which I shall mention is a pretty girl of tender age, who mirthful run from one to the other of the ugly faces and throwing her little arms about them. The third with the face of Girlhood, showed by her advanced figure, that she approached young Womanhood, without that her face possessed the regular features of

---

[1] Johann Kaspar Lavater (1741–1801). Native of Zurich and Christian minister. He had a theory that a person's character is revealed in his physiognomy, especially the countenance. He made collections of faces and people in order to prove his thesis. Many of his works were translated into English, including an autobiography, *Life of John Kaspar Lavater*, London, Religious Tract Society, 1849.

the antique statues, there was so much loveliness expressed in it, that I considered her the handsomest Indian girl I had yet seen – as if aware of the strong contrast, her handsome face and figure must cause among so much ugliness, she was only to be seen in the background and never forward like the others. Their settlement consisted merely of three huts and their inhabitants might amount to Forty. The houses were round, neatly thatched of Palm leaves, but did not end pointed as the Macusi houses, in general a hut ended with a passage for the smoke. The inside of their huts was clean, the only thing commendable among them. The Zaparas, it appears, have arisen from the intermarriage of Macusis and Arécunas.

They inhabit the mountains Toupae-eng and Waikamang, and there are likewise a few settlements along the banks of the Parima, and the solitary one just mentioned. Their whole number probably amounts to not more than three hundred. They do not differ in appearance from the Macusis, if in any thing they are more slender, and not so robust in figure. I had no opportunity of collecting any of their words. Their language differs however only little from the Arécuna and may be considered a provincial dialect of the stock of this region the Macusi. We found the settlement short of provisions, and they could not assist us with any except a bunch of Bananas, we continued therefore our journey next morning.

Decr 12th–14th One day has resembled the other in toil and monotony, as soon as we have surmounted one Cataract, the prospect of another opens before us, and tired out by such difficulty we are glad when the hour approaches, when we look out for a resting place. Although we labour uninterruptedly from half past six in the morning until 3 or 4 in the Afternoon our progress does not amount to more than three or four miles a day, and our height was now according to my calculation 400 feet above the Yurume. The river continued to be bounded by hillocks, stretching sometimes to its very edge and narrowing it, while otherwise its whole width is broken up by islands, and may amount from two to three miles excepting the far northern branches to which I have already alluded.

It is richly stocked with fish, Haimara, different species of Siluridae, chiefly Pimelodus,[1] and various others; among them abounds the Electric Eel (Gymnotus electricus) several of which were shot with arrows and measured from five to six feet.[2] During our progress through the falls, several of our Indians were frequently stunned by their shocks; they are eatable but so fat that I did not find them after my taste; one which measured five feet nine inches and was fourteen inches in girth, weighed twenty two pounds. The Macusis call it yaringra; the Guinaus Yarimina; the Maiongkongs, Arina.

Decr 17th. We passed this morning the mouth of the river Uruwé[3] which joins the Parima from the N.W. and drains no doubt the intermediate valley of the Uraricapara and Parima. It appears to be of the size of the Yurume: at a distance of a five day journey from its mouth it is inhabited by Kirishannas.[4] We landed at noon at a settlement of

---

[1] As already noted (see p. 283, fn. 1), the Siluridae is an Eurasian Family of catfish; most South American catfish belong to the Family Pimelodidae.

[2] Three species of *Gymnotus* are found in South America, but rarely exceed sixty centimetres. These examples are much more likely to be *Electrophorus electricus* which grows up to three metres in length.

[3] Probably Rio Puruè.

[4] Probably a Yanomami subgroup.

Waiyamara Indians.[1] As our guides informed us that from here eighteen days would elapse before we were to find an other human habitation, it became of paramount import that we should provide ourselves with provisions for so lengthened a period, the more so since ours were at the lowest ebb.

The settlement was some distance from the rivers banks, and after our tents were erected we proceeded thither. It consisted of two huts and the ruins of a third which had been lately burnt down. The Captain received us sitting on a low stool, surrounded by his Men, all armed with war clubs; after he had heard what our guides had to say about us and our intentions, he put a few leaves of Tobacco, in the dried [bark] of the Cookar-ally tree (Lecythis ollaria)[2] and having wrapped it up in the form of a cigar, and lighted it smoked it for a little while, and then handed it to me. I am no smoker, but to satisfy his courtesy I gave a few empty puffs and gave it to our guide. I was otherwise astonished at this custom, which I am well aware, is very common among the North American Indians but which I have not observed before among the Indians of Guiana. I accounted 45 Individuals but I was told that many were absent to clear a new space for Provision grounds; those which I saw looked sickly and haggard, and I observed two blind persons, and others suffered from sore Eyes, and one who was deformed. It appears therefore that the shocking practice that where any physical deformity occurs in a child when born, the Father puts it to Death, is not so general among the Savage Indians of Guiana as has been supposed, and it is to be hoped for humanity sake, that the shocking custom of which we are told by Humboldt that when twins are produced, one is always destroyed, has equally ceased. At least I have not been able to receive any authentic information of its continuance.[3] But what difference in their general appearance if we compared them with the healthful and stout Arecunas of the mountainous regions and the Savannahs! here we observed sickly and lean faces, others who apparently suffered of decline, but the most struck me the figure of the Women, young and old. It appeared as if the legs had not been made to support the body which was much produced above the line of gravity and appeared to be too heavy for those spider legs, and gave them not only a most ungainly appearance, but likewise an awkward walk. If I had only observed one instance, it would not have been remarkable but the whole womanhood of the settlement had not to show an exception which may be attributed to the circumstance that their isolated station forces them to marry in their own tribe and family. Their sickly hue must be ascribed to the insalubrity of the air along the rivers, which are subjected to periodical inundations and the bad, and often very scanty nourishment.

The principal settlements of the Wieyamara are along the river Mocajahi, the Kaiawanna of the Indians; we were informed that its distance from this settlement to the nearest of the Mocajahi was three days journey, or about fifty miles off; but I have no reason to think that this tribe is numerous, as they could only number three other

---

[1] Also Guimara or Uaiumara. Only a few references to this group exist and by the end of the 19th century the French explorer, Henri Coudreau *La France Equinoxiale*, II, p. 393, considered them extinct. It is just possible that they are the modern-day Carib-speaking Waimiri who now live to the east of the lower Rio Branco.

[2] This species of *Lecythis* is not reported from Guiana, but the vernacular term Kakaralli, as already mentioned, covers two species of *Lecythis* and ten of *Eschweilera*.

[3] Humboldt recorded the practice on the Orinoco *(Personal Narrative*, II, 1907, pp. 248–9). In the 1960s both the Trio and Waiyana of Surinam subscribed to the practice, although I never observed an incident of it.

settlements besides their own. They did not differ in physical appearance from the Zaparas, and their height was scarcely above 5 feet 6 inches. their language is in many respects different from that of the Macusis, and appears to abound in the ph, as Iphaeri, Kaephanari ears; they appeared to be little acquainted in numbers and they could not count further than five; for ten they say Tuphara[,] their intermediate numbers six to nine, I could not procure. Their Captain or Kaibisaika is known by the name of Marawai and had an intelligent face. Our question for provisions in the first instance had a denial but at the view of knives and beads, they considered and we succeeded in procuring twelve baskets with Cassada roots and several bunches of half ripe plantains. But it took almost a day and a half before that quantity was delivered, and of the stipulated number they brought first half, and after remonstration three baskets more were brought, and only the second day the remainder three were delivered. This quantity would have been with full allowance sufficient for five or six days. We had therefore to take in all commencement economical measures to make it last until we reached the Guinau according to the account of our guides 18 days journey from here.

The altitude of four stars when culminating gave me the Latitude for the Wieyamara settlement 3°14'48" since which I infer the Latitude of the river Uruwe in 3°14'30"N. and four miles East of the settlement.

Dec[r] 20th. We started this morning[;] the river continued to be broken up by rapids and islands. We passed at noon the brook Paruanna[1] which joins the Parima from the South by two [mouths.] We halted towards Evening near the spot where the Wieyamaras intended to settle; we found here 25 Individuals children included, inhabiting a temporary hut.

Dec[r] 21st. We discovered at eight oclock the bluish outline of the Marittani mountains in which the Uraricapara and the Paraba or Paragua have its sources; they bore N24W. The small river Akamea falls into the Parima from the South, the latter of which continued upwards with a breadth of about 400 yards, its banks low and its bed studded with rocks.

Decr 22nd The Marittaní mountains showed themselves this morning more distinct. They bore N b E distant about fifteen miles, the chain runs ESE & WNW, and as far as I can judge at this distance they belong to a similar sandstone formation as those of Roraima. I have already observed that they divide the hydrographical system of the Carony from the Uraricapara and Parima, and are no doubt the continuing limits between the mountains of the Orinoco and the Mountains Pacaraima or rather the continuation of the latter chain. I enquired after the Portage of Anocaparu,[2] however my Indians were not acquainted with it by that name. Paru signifies in the language of the Guinau a brook; and has no reference to a mountainous portage. The Marittana mountains are inhabited by a few Wieyamara, and the wandering tribe, the Oewaku.

Decr 23rd. We approached in the course of the day a chain of mountains which were the continuing of the Marittaní mountains, and which belonged also to the sandstone formation. Their height is from 2 to 3000 feet above the river, and the walls raise themselves frequently perpendicularly nevertheless they are clothed with bushes. The river

[1] Igarapé Paruaina.
[2] The River Anucapara, an upper tributary of the Paragua, appears on A. Arrowsmith's 1811 map, whereas the Portage of Anocapru is marked between the headwaters of the Paragua and those of the Uraricaá on J. Arrowsmith's map of 1834.

Parima flows along the Southwestern foot;[1] one of the mountains forms on its top a cone, like the Wayacca of the Roraima mountains; it is clothed with bush which gives it a dark appearance, almost black. This may have induced the Indians, besides its upright position to call it Coutta or Quatta (Ateles paniscus). The hill which is crowned by the cone is about 300 feet high and stands separate from the chain; viewed from a distance where the cone rises above the trees, that margin the river, it has a singular effect. Numerous blocks of granite obstruct the river they are mostly spherical and frequently one heaped upon the other.

At noon Mount Pakaraima bore N4°W, distant about four miles. It is a singular strayed mountain, and has been resembled by the Indians to a Pakara or Pakal, a basket but weather the whole chain has received the name from this one or from another of similar shape and resemblance, I cannot say.

I considered its height about 2000 feet and it consisted likewise of sandstone. The Ariwanna which rise more northwards follow the Pakaraima and are higher and steeper.

The brooks Kawanna and Irinikiari[2] flow from the Ariwanna mountains and joins the Parima[;] a path led formerly from the Kawanna to the Wai-ini,[3] a tributary of the Merewari; it is not more frequented and likely overgrown. The brook Irinikiari has water of a light yellow color, it was 3° cooler than that of the Parima. One of our guides a Guinau pointed at noon at a hill distant about 15 miles, where, he said the Paraba or Paragua had its sources. We halted at a Provision field which we were told belonged to the Kirishanna a wandering tribe like the Oewaku, though much more warlike and courageous. As nature has made thus, thus they go, without any artificial coverings. Now they live among the mountains until the game reduced by their depredation render their maintanance difficult and they resort to the river banks for fish, turtles, and Alligators; if indolence furnishs them, they clear near one of their habitual haunts, a small spot of wood, and plant it with Capsicum and Cassada roots, but long before it has come to maturity, they have frequent[ed] several other haunts and return only to reap their Cassada.[4] If the emigration is to be made by water, light canoes of the bark of trees are soon made, the wood offers numerous trees for that purpose and where axes are wanting recourse is had to fire.[5] As the Oewaku is despised by the other Indians, thus the Kirishanna is dreaded; he is aware of it, and if they fall in with other Indians not far superior in numbers, they demand at once such things in the possession of the strangers as pleased them most. No denial is accepted, as in that case the Poisoned Arrow is ready to fly from the strung bow. A part of Maiongkong who proceeded lately down the Parima, sent three of their number to hunt; they fell in with some Kirishannas

---

[1] There is a question mark in the margin at this point and the direction has been changed by an unidentified hand to 'south-eastern'. Given that the Uraricoera flows at this point south of east, the original appears correct.

[2] Possibly Igarapé Iniquiare.

[3] Río Guaña.

[4] This is an interesting and important observation since there has been considerable disagreement about when the Yanomami started practising agriculture; many authorities claiming that it is a relatively recent introduction. Furthermore it has been argued that the cultivation of cassava was an even more recently adopted practice; their earlier staple having been plantains. Schomburgk's evidence indicates that the Yanomami have been at least sporadic agriculturalists for a long time.

[5] Due to changes to the manuscript, more than one reading of this sentence is possible. The chosen one is as correct as any.

and out of the three two were killed, the third managed to escape, and brought the news to their party, who did not lose a moment to seek their safety in a rapid flight. There were no traces that they had been lately near their provision fields, and a number of woodskins or bark canoes which we found half buried in the sands along shore, proved that their wanderings had been directed towards the mountains. Though we did not actually watch the following night to guard against surprises, we slept with more care and vigilance, the more so since our Indians fancied they heard the sound of their trumpets, with which they signalize the presence of strangers.

Our camp was this Evening according to Account in 3°36′N. Lat and 63°17′W. Long. In Arrowsmiths map of Colombia to which I always refer as the latest production we ought to have stood there at the sources of the Parima; while its breadth according to trigonometrical admeasurement amounts yet to 288 yards, where it was free of rapids, and islands. The night proved like its predecessors for the past week cloudy, and unfit for observations.

Decr 26th. The water which hitherto was generally from 6 to 8° warmer at 6 Oclock in the morning than the atmosphere; it is now only from 1½ to 2°. This fact is likely to be ascribed to the frequent rains, which cool the water. The thermometer ranged from 72 to 74° at the same time.

I succeeded to procure this evening at least two observations, the mean of which gave me 3°40′N for Latitude, and agreed within 7″ with my accounts though six days had elapsed since I had been able to procure observations. The mountains Quebé and Quatata bore from here N.50°W. and N.45°W. The river flows between the two. They are from a 1000 to 1500 feet high, rugged, and formed like the preceeding. The sandstone shows itself in Horizontal Strata along the river, and forms dykes and rapids where it crosses it. The Massuaka Mountains towards which our course directed us bore at noon N.77°W., they appeared wall like, but clothed with wood, and had a NNE and SSW direction. We halted at two o'clock at the junction of Areekatsa[1] with the Parima. We were now to leave the Parima, and to ascend the Areekatsa. This river was of less size than the Uraricapara, and perhaps not more than 100 feet wide. It joined the Parima from the North West, and its waters were of a similar color as that of the former and its Latitude 3°44′N. The Parima continued with a breadth of 250 yards to the WSW., encompassed by mountains as hitherto, the blue outlines of which we could trace to a great distance.

The Arekatsa being comparatively so small its course was greatly meandring and in the commencement divided from the Parima only by a short neck of land. Its banks are low, sandy, and margined with numerous Palmtrees, among which I note a species of mountain Cabbage, the Coucourite, a few Manicolas and an other which resembles it and is called Ariha,[2] two species of Touro,[3] and a species which is very scarce within 100 miles of the Coast, the Popa,[4] I observed here in large numbers. The Sawarai so frequent along the Rupununy & the lower Rio Branco, is wanting, which would argue well for the soil, as the Colonists consider the soil by no means productive where it grows. A species of Triplaris, different from that of the coast and the lower rivers, was

[1] Rio Aracacá.
[2] Possibly Reho: *Euterpe stenophylla*.
[3] Possibly Turu: *Jessenia bataua* (= *Oenocarpus bataua*).
[4] Boba: *Iriartea exorrhiza*.

very common. We camped near a small Cataract which the river formed, however large enough to force us nevertheless to unload, and to carry the luggage over land. Our latitude was according to the mean of four observations two north and two south, 3°45′40″N., Longt by Acct 63°35′W.

We had again to unload our Corials at the Cataract Marisol, and to carry the luggage for nearly half a mile over land.

We found next day (Decbr 29th) that we could make no more progress by water; the Corials were therefore abandoned after we had entered the brook Kaimukuni, and some fleet messengers were despatched to the first Guinau Settlement, with directions to meet us with some small corials and some provisions of the want of which we suffered to the Aiakini a tributary of the Merewari, where we intended to embark again. We followed them over land next day.

Jan 1st 1839. The path led for the first five or six miles over mountains five to six hundred feet high, where we fell in again with the brook Kaimukuni the bed of which we followed upwards, the water now reached us to the ankles, now to the loins and under the arms, how glad were we therefore when we reached the half way hut, where our baggage had been deposited – the road had not only been fatiguing but likewise harassing in consequence of the wading, which much more fatigues than walking. This day was well apt to call forth recollections of bygone times, and while lying in my hammock, the Christmas and New years days for the last three years, since I commenced my wanderings passed by in retrospective views. Lieut Haining and myself ascended on Christmas day 1835 the [blank][1] in search of the Wourari plant and was then suffering under severe intermitting fever which attacked me, as soon as we reached the settlement where we purposed to halt for the night. The Christmas dinner consisted of Plantain soup and Cassada bread. The 1st Jan 1836 we were on the Rupununy, its water our beverage Cassada our meal. During Christmas day 1836 we camped at those series of Cataracts which we called after that holiday, and where on our return Mr. Reiss lost his life. At new years day 1837, I had the happiness to discover that wonderful flower the Victoria Regia. We were on Christmas 1837 at the river Essequibo where a pure brook meanders through the Acaray Mountains, our fare an antiquated Duckler (Plotus) and a piece of hard Cassada. At the following new years day, we were on our return, elated by the success which had crowned our endeavours to discover the sources of the Essequibo. Of our present Christmas, and new years day, the reader has received an account. I had scarcely arrived in the camp when a Bilious fever confined me for the following days. Three Indians of our small party were likewise attacked, and thus the 5th of January approached before we could think of starting. This delay was the more unwelcome since our last bread had been shared out the preceeding day and we had now to live upon mountain Cabbage and what fruits we could procure. Game was very scarce and with the exception of a few small fish our huntsmen returned unsuccessful. Although those who enjoyed good health were now experiencing the gnawing of hunger, we knew that in the course of a few days, our wants would be supplied but an other evil which had threatened us for some time, was now felt in all its force, it was the want of salt and we had not the slightest hope of procuring this condiment, which to us Europeans was of so paramount necessity.

---

[1] Kanuku Mountains on the first expedition.

We continued our journey on the 5th of January and left from the Kaimukuni, which had dwindled to a mere rill. We ascended a high hill and followed a path which connects the Kaimukuni with the Aiakini, the latter a tributary of the Merewari. These mountains which rise to a height of about 3000 feet above the level of the sea, divide the river Merewari and its tributaries from the Areekatsa and Parima. They are thickly wooded and range E. & W., we crossed them in a direction of N.bE. The height of these mountains forms no obstacle to the Indians of the Merewari from carrying their Corials and Canoes across them from the Aiakini to the Kaimakuni although the distance is about three miles.

We arrived at the Aiakini next day and found there the messengers we had sent forward with three small Corials, but no provisions; we were told however that the Guinaus had promised to meet us with some bread half way to their settlement. Mountain cabbage continued to be our food.

We entered the afternoon of Jan[y] 7th the river Merewari extended by rapids its breadth was not less than six hundred feet and though where unimpeded, the breadth amounted to only four hundred feet. I was nevertheless astonished to find so large a stream, the more so as according to the maps, its source is placed on 5°25′N Latitude and 64.47W. Long. Now we met it in 4°5′N. Lat[de] and 63°46′W. Long[de] by account, as for the last ten days not a single opportunity had offered itself to take an observation but our progress had been so slow during this period that the account could not differ much from the truth. To judge from the volume of its waters, and its course, its source must be at least 40 miles further northwest.[1]

This river is named Mareguare on the maps according to the Spanish pronunciation. The Indians call it Merewari; and it is a tributary to the Erivato[2] or rather where both unite they form the river Caurá.[3]

Though it was only two oclock in the afternoon, our progress was of short duration the small corial with Mr. Moriston[4] had preceeded us. The river continuing to form Rapids takes a turn, we passed it safely but at some rocks at its foot presented itself a picture of shipwreck[,] the small corial had run upon a rock and upset with the exception that all the luggage had got wet no other loss was suffered. The water was fortunately not deep, and those articles which had sunk were recovered.

The clouds dispersed towards Evening and I succeeded at last to procure an early observation of α Eridani, which gave for the Latitude of our situation 4°5′N. The Cataract where our camp was situated is called Cannicoan.

Jany 8th in consequence of the river being swollen we found it very difficult to pass the falls and rapids, and had several times to unload. The cataracts of Apai-shibí and Kributu were at least twenty feet perpendicular. Thanks to God they were safely passed. several brooks of small or large size joined the river from the mountains at the right and left banks. I shall mention only the river Wai-ina which coming from the ENE.[5] joined

---

[1] This has been changed to 'southwest' on the manuscript and 'S.W.' in the published version (p. 223). In fact the source of the Merevari is to the north-west from where Schomburgk was located and nearer to sixty than forty miles away. Although it is not possible to judge exactly where Schomburgk was, he cannot have been far from the position he gives.

[2] Río Erebato.

[3] On the official Venezuelan map (Dirección de Cartografía Nacional, Sheet NB-20–III) this is not so. The Río Merevari becomes the Río Caura well above its junction with the Erebato.

[4] Morrison.

[5] The general direction of the Guaña is from the ESE.

the Merewari at its right bank. I estimated its breadth at the mouth about 150 feet, and its last reach ENE, was about a mile long. Our guide told us it was inhabited by savage Indians, who did not permit any stranger to pass their camp. A path led formerly from the brook Kawanna (see Dec[r] 25) a tributary to the Parima to the Waiina[,] it is however not more frequented. We observed a ridge of high mountains at a distance of about 15 miles through which we were told the Waiina takes its course.

Hills from 5 to 600 feet high approached occasionally the Merewari they were clothed with wood and of rounded outline. The vegetation of its banks was luxuriant, numerous Palm trees, and the Heliconia gigantica[1] gave a diversity to the Vegetation. A corial hove in the afternoon in sight, it was hailed with delight, as we supposed that the people knowing in what straight we were, would come to meet us with provisions. We had rightly concluded, they brought us fresh Cassada and the favourite drink Paiwari. Our hungry stomachs [enj]oyed the simple fare as if it had been the greatest delicacies; we knew then what hunger was.

We left shortly after the Merewari and entered the brook Arvenima[2] joining the former river from the S.W. and pushed up its stream for a few miles, where we halted at the landing place of the Guinau settlement, which was situated on a small but steep hillock a short distance from the river. We found here two huts, with fifty people, mostly young and the females much predominated. They consisted of Guinau and a few Maiongkong. Young and old came forward to wave their hands, and if I should judge from the expression of their features, they appeared glad of our arrival. The place and its surrounding scenery reminded me much of the first Woyawai settlement which we visited. The surrounding mountains of the latter were however much higher. The place round the huts was as filthy as at the Woyawais and though an old man was occupied to clean it since we arrived, it had not failed to make its impression in its former unclean state.

I succeeded last night for the first time to procure observations, the previous four nights the sky was completely covered. The Guinau settlement is in 4°16′N. lat and 63°50′W. Long based upon those observations and the following geographical data. In the direction of N46W is the mountain Araba, its estimated distance being 30 miles, on its Eastern foot of which flows the Mérewari. The mountain appears to be formed of perpendicular walls of sandstone, it is rugged in its outline, but the distance is too great to decide without armed eyes whether it be wooded or naked; somewhat further West is the mountain Paramu, and about 25 miles from the former the mountain Pabaha, where they told us the rivers Cacara and Merewari had its sources. The Erevato, informed us the Guinau Indians, has its sources in the Marai etshiba Mountain near those of the Entuari (Ventuari) which river the Maiongkongs call Paraba.

The Erevato pursues a more north-eastern course. The information that the Mérewari is to be found ninety miles further South, than laid down on the latest maps will be of importance in the Geography of this region, and constraints the possibility where the Orinoco may have its sources to comparatively a small spot, reducing it to about 30 or 40 square miles West of the Guinau Settlement. The course of the Mere-wari is eccentric, this is caused by the parallel ridges of mountains through which it has

---

[1] Probably *Heliconia gigantea* is intended, but this species is not reported from the region.
[2] Río Abuenama.

forced itself by breaks, and it is consequently so much impeded that north and west from the mouth of the Aiakuni it is even not navigable for the small Canoes of the Indians who prefer to traverse by land the peninsula which its course forms.

N.59°W.[1] from the Guinau settlement stretches the sandstone Mountain Maratti Kuntsaban from WNW. to ESE., they separate the waters of the Paraba (Paragua, Paraua,) from those of the Mérewari. The Indians of the region bent on a journey to the Paraba haul their Corials to the N.N.E. in a direction of N.19°E. from here, over the mountains Pamuyamu and meet the brook Catsikare[2] a tributary of the Curuta[3] which flows in the Paraba. The portage of the Paraba Musi is well known to the Guinau and Maiongkong Indians.

The language of the Guinau is widely different from any of the other tribes which I have met with in Guiana, though it follows the general train in its construction. The words themselves appear to be derived from a different root. This refers likewise to the names of the heavenly bodies. There is no sound in their [dis]conversation[4] which bears resemblance to those of the Macusi, Caribi, Arawaak and other languages. We generally find that a star is called *Seriko, Serika, Serigu*; the Guinau express it by Yuwinti; the moon which is called *Nuna* by the Caribis, and *Capu-ih* by the Macusi, is named by the Guinau Ke-wa-ri. I inquired whether they knew whence they descended, and whether they had always inhabited these regions, but I could not receive any satisfactory answer. On my inquiry whether they had ever been visited before by Europeans or their descendant, I received a negative answer; they observed that the great and numerous Cataracts had likely prevented the Spaniards to ascend the Mérewari. They do not differ in manners from the generality of the Indians and appear to be blest with the same indolence. Their chief meal is in the Morning and Evening. A pot with fish or meat or for want of them greens boiled of the leaves of the Capsicum mixed plenteously with the fruit of the same shrub is placed before every head of the family of which the other male members and guests who may happen to be there partake with the master of the house; after the Lords of the Creation have finished, the Women and Girls take their places and satisfy themselves with the remainder. These meals were eaten before the hut, if the weather permitted it. I noticed a very neat kind of basket on which the Cassada bread was placed, they were round and of a concave form and embellished by the favourite figure of the Indian namely Grecques. The whole body of the Women was painted with a black dye (likely the Lana or Genipa americana), ankles knees wrists, arms and necks embellished with light blue beads, which appeared to be the favourite colour. They cut their hair short, and some wear trinkets of tin in their Ears. The faces of the Men were painted with the preparation of the Chica, they wore round their ankles, knee-joints and arms, strings twisted of their own hair others wore beads like the Women. Through the cartiligious part of the Ear was put a piece of Bamboo, one end of which was embellished with the feathers of the Parrot, Macaw, the black Powis, or they wore in lieu thereof the tusks of the wild boar hog; necklaces of the Monkey or

---

[1] As the Río Paragua lies to the east of the Merevari, Schomburgk probably has this direction wrong and meant N.59E.

[2] Río Casichara.

[3] Río Curutu.

[4] This is not a secure reading, but it looks as though Schomburgk has coined a word out of 'conversation' and 'discourse'.

of Peccary teeth were likewise common. I have already observed that their language is not well sounding; their speech is boisterous, and in their mirth they laugh still more so, ending in a loud scream.

It is most unfortunate for my purpose that the Maiong Kong, of the upper Orinoco, are at War with the Guinau and Maiong Kong of this region and the lower Orinoco. I could not procure guides those who have accompanied me refused to go any further, though I have offered them enormous pay; they are afraid of their lives, and say they will surely be poisoned if they went on.

A place by the name of Esmeralda, and a mountain by the name of Duida is entirely unknown to them, however through other localities which I mentioned to them, it appears they call Esmeralda Mirara, and the Duida Yéwunna mari. They know well the Maravaca which they described as a mountain like Roraima; it happens likewise that they know the Frenchman a M. Arnott, who I was told by Signore Ayres trades between Bararoa[1] & Esmeralda. As soon as the state of my invalids permits it are my intentions to cross the Peninsula which the Méréwari forms, and to penetrate towards the West in search of the sources of the Orinoco.

The weather has remained variable the range of the Thermometer has been at 6 oclock a.m. from 64 to 70 at 9 oclock from 78 to 80, at noon 80 to 84, at 3 oclock 85 to 88, at 6 P.M. 76 to 80.

Jany 14th We started from the Guinau settlement; this morning, after our baggage had been conveyed to the rivers bank I went once more to the Cabins of the Indians to wish such good bye, as had not come to our Tents. I became thus witness of a melancholy scene. The hut was almost forsaken, the only inmates were a young Indian woman, in her dying moments, her husband, and little boy. Death was settled already in her eyes; next to her hammock sat her husband calling her repeatedly, but she heard him not: the little boy assiduously employed to put heated rocks into a vessel with water that was standing under her hammock, and served in lieu of a vapour bath. When we arrived we found her suffering under a far advanced consumption. During the night when we were taking observations we heard her constant cough and her moans in consequence of her sufferings, and she became frequently our topic of regret. The night previous to our departure, her husband had acted as Piaiman, his conjuration appeared to have been of no avail. I left the hut with a heavy heart, they were all strangers to me, nevertheless the scene which words cannot describe would have led the stoutest heart to gloomy thoughts. We heard in the Evening by an Indian who left after us, that she lingered until noon.

After we had reached again the Merewari we followed its course upwards[2] in a northerly direction and passed several Cataracts. Small hillocks rose on both sides and hemmed it sometimes in, so that its breadth amounted in some places to scarcely hundred feet. We reached towards evening the mouth of the river Cannaracuna[3] which joins the Merewari from the W.N.W. Its water was quite black, and formed a strong contrast with the water of the Merewari which is of a reddish colour. We encamped near its mouth and I found the Latitude of the confluence 4°30′N.

January 15. We ascended now the Cannaracuna; the Merewari continued its course N.W. towards Mount Araba.

[1] Tomar on the Rio Negro.
[2] Schomburgk means 'downwards'.
[3] Río Canaracuni.

Jany 15[th1] The ascending of a small river is under all circumstances most monotonous but it is rendered much more so if that river be shallow or impeded by rapids – this was the case with the Cannaracuna, only when the high ridge of sandstone mountains came in view with its steep and cliffed sides, now ending in a small and to the eye even outline, now broken up and adopting manifold shapes, sometimes to be resembled to the gigantic Profile of the human head, to a turret, a steeple, the fir tree and many more for which an imaginative mind might find its prototype, only then were this monotony broken.

We arrived after noon where further progress for Corials became impossible. The river was for several miles broken up by large Cataracts and boulders between which the river lost itself and did not allow a passage for the smallest craft. We had therefore to leave our Corials and to continue our way over land. The unfortunate Warfare which there was raging between the tribes was the cause, as I already observed that I had not been able to induce any of our former guides to accompany us, and those which I brought with me were not sufficient to carry our baggage, we had therefore to leave a part behind, with the intention to send for the rest the following day. After a march of seven miles over steep mountains, and along their declivities, we reached a settlement of Indians consisting of two huts inhabited by Maiong Kongs and Guinaus, amounting in number to thirty two. Several among them, men and Women, had their body carefully painted with Lana. Along the spine went a broad line of this dye, the sides were embellished by labyrinth over the shoulders, and along the loins to the foot extended grecques, the intermediate spaces being filled out by dots, across the breast and stomach were a number of waving lines in reverse position, which were crossed by others. The arms were similarly ornamented. We were at the change of the moon. The weather was cloudy and in the Evening we had a severe thunderstorm. My hopes of having an extensive view from the elevated spot in which the settlement stood were not only frustrated, but I found it likewise impossible to procure astronomical observations. We had the following day to send for the remainder of our baggage. I was seriously indisposed and I fear me much that the horrid monster Dyspepsia was lurking behind these frequent indispositions, to which protracted fastings, insufficient or insubritious[2] and indigestible food had laid the foundation, but I ascribe it chiefly to the necessity of living for some time on Mountain Cabbage, a delicate dish where the necessary means are at hand to prepare it tastely, but highly indigestible when prepared in an insufficient manner. As we had to continue our road by the Cannaracuna, in Corials,[3] we departed next day without having been able to procure observations.

Jan[y] 17th The Inhabitants of this settlement had their landing place at the brook Yapecuna which about the distance of half a mile in a north eastern direct falls in the Cannaracuna. [W]e embarked therefore at the Yapecuna and descended it to the latter river. We approached the high ridge of sandstone mountains and I estimated Sarisharinima[4] as part of it was called about 4000 feet high. Their wall like appearance

---

[1] This is correct; the date has been repeated.

[2] This word has been crossed out and replaced in an editorial hand by 'bad', but it can be transcribed with confidence. Presumably 'insalubrious' was intended.

[3] Although it is not clear, what seems to have happened is that the Canaracuni is for a stretch impassable to corials and Schomburgk and his party having left their corials below the obstruction are now taking to others above it.

[4] Cerro Sarisariñama. They are over 6,000 feet high.

was not so smooth as Roraima, and they were likewise more covered with wood. If I can judge from the boulders which were lying near their foot, the sandstone was more crystalline. We left the Corials, which had to force their way through some rapids, and walked about half a mile over a Savannah a strange spectacle among thick forest which extends for several hundred miles in all directions. What are then the originating causes of a Savannah? If we adopt the peculiarity of the soil which nourishes merely grasses and a few stunted trees of the Genera Curatella Mabea & Malpighia, it is certainly peculiar that this soil should have been concentrated to this spot, an Oasis in a Desert. The reverse circumstance where tufts of wood are found on Savannahs is easier to be explained. During inundations the detritus has settled in consequence of local circumstances and the number of seeds contained among the drift matter germinate during the dry season, and are already of sufficient growth to survive the next inundation. I found the soil mixed with sand and void of vegetable earth. It was ochreous clay of almost a red colour. The Indians pointed out a few wild calabash trees (Crescentia cujetá)[1] which they said grew well here. We found at a short distance from this savannah, an Indian hut, constructed in the lightest manner, and open at the sides it appeared they were making a new provision field. The inmates amounted to nineteen, and among them we observed for the first time some Men and Women naked, without any covering, paint was the only foreign substance which they wore on their body. It proved a disgusting sight to us, and we left the place with every despatch[. T]he river meandered along the foot of the sandstone mountains, and rapids were almost continuous.

Jan[y] 18th We found one of the smaller Corials which had got the start before us, at halt. The people were assiduously employed to dig out of the clay soil the larva of an insect, which they were eating with their cassada bread. It appeared to belong to the order Hymenoptera Tribe Fassores[2] and was surrounded by a lump of clay, perfectly hardened like a shell. I did not feel inclined to follow their example, although I doubt little they are equal in taste to the larva of the Calandra palmarum or Grugru worm, which the French colonists consider a great delicacy.

We had to abandon the Corials again and to continue our path over land, it was of the same description as the other day, to me, an Invalid it was the more fatiguing; we made only about 5 miles that day. Arrived at the junction of the Kuihakuni we left the Cannaracuna, and followed the latter brook to a Maiong Kong Settlement, where in the evening a party of Arecunas arrived from the Carony.

Jan[y] 20th I discovered this morning that the eldest of the party who returned last night understood the Macusi language, and as the want of an Interpreter had already twice given occasion to mistakes and loss of time, I was most anxious to engage him, to go with us. He assented, if we would stay till next day, as he had been so long absent from his home, that he was anxious to spend at least one day there, to which we gladly consented. Though their language is so different, we have found hitherto in all settlements, Maiong Kong and Guinau mixed. The men distinguish themselves by their sort of dandyism. The Macusi, Caribi, Arawaak satisfied himself to secure a string of coral or red beads round his neck, and perhaps some white ones round the leg in the region of the Ankles, the Guinau and Maiong Kong wear however a profusion of them, and their

---

[1] *Crescentia cujete.*

[2] Although Fassores is the secure reading, Fossores was probably intended. These are wasps that live in holes in the ground.

favourite colour appears to be a light blue colour. When travelling or when they are not able to afford this [illegible][1] expense for this display, they satisfy themselves with wrapping strings of their own hair round ankles, knees, arms, and round the neck, sometimes they wear the rhizoma of a fern. I saw in several instances pieces of Wedgewood ware, which had been rounded and were worn fastened to the upper parts of the arm. But the general admiration [that] attracted the Indian was an old English uniform of the 86th Reg[t], once garrisoned in Demerara; how it had found its way to the confines of Colombia of this the old uniform itself could only give the best account. Their ears are generally ornamented by pieces of Bamboo from 4 to 6 inchs long, the end of which is embellished by feathers of the Parrot. I observed one who displayed crests of the Rock Manakin, several of which he wore likewise around the arms; this display would have been rather costly in England, where each skin of that magnificent bird is paid with from £2 to 3. He told us that they were very plentiful in the Sarisharinima Mountains. Their conversation is peculiar, now it continues with all volubility, and every striking circumstance is answered by the auditor with a grave and long "h – m" but often the relater himself stops with "h – m" answered by him to whom the speech is addressed, and re-answered by the former, thus six or seven "h – m"s may pass alternately before their conversation resumes again the form of words, and the wanted thread.[2]

According to several observations I found that we were in Lat. 4°27N. The weather had been fair for some days past, but the mornings were exceedingly cold, the Thermometer stood at 6 oclock a.m. from 59.5 to 62°.

Jan[y] 21/22[d]. Our march continued over mountains, the average height of which I estimated from 3 to 4000 feet.

We reached the Merewari at about noon, studded with rocks, and impeded by numerous falls, its breadth amounted to about 150 feet, its course was more or less SSE. We followed its left bank for several miles to the place where we were told we should find Corials; at our arrival we found only an old half rotten one, which we dispatched to the next settlement, a days journey down the river, in quest of more. Thus a new delay has arisen in consequence of false information.

If we think a line from the Guinau settlement, or rather the mouth of the brook Avenima to that spot where we met first the Merewari, we will find that it is 53 miles. From this we may judge of the considerable arc which the river describes from its sources, occasioned by the many obstacles which it meets to divert its [blank]. A large chain of mountains which stretch in the 4th Parallel of Latitude from NW to SE, turn it to the Eastward, and thus deprive the system of the upper Orinoco of its waters to which according to the nature of the division of the waters between the lower Orinoco on one side and the upper Orinoco and the Parima on the other, it strictly belonged. These mountains no doubt belong to the Sierra Mai, of the old maps; their average height is from 2 to 3000 feet, and they are thickly wooded; a counterpart from the sandstone mountains, the direction of which is East and West, and which form the connecting link between the Serras Parima and Pacaraima. The old man whom we had taken as our interpreter ran away with an other Indian during the night. We descended the

---

[1] The context would suggest some word such as 'considerable'.

[2] Schomburgk appears to be describing a particular form of language to which the term 'ceremonial dialogue' has been given. It has been widely reported in the Guiana region. It is used in special and formal circumstances such as for a welcome, the passing of news or for bargaining.

Merewari for about 3 miles and entered its tributary the Emekuni[1] which joins it from its right bank. Having ascended the Emekuni for 16 miles, we arrived at a Maiong Kong Settlement. Our journey now over land was to commence, the baggage was therefore disembarked and carried a short distance to an Indian Cabin inhabited by Maiong Kongs. The ground being elevated we had a prospect of a large chain of mountains at the distance of about 20 miles extending NNE to SSW. A high mountain was pointed out to me which bore NW, where we were told the Blowpipe reed grew in abundance. They called the mountain Mashiatte[2] and informed us furthermore that the river Paraba flowed in its vicinity. The Maiong Kongs Indians which almost exclusively inhabit these regions call the Ventuari Paraba. The sources of that great tributary of the Orinoco would be therefore further South than laid down in our present maps. Before however this information of the Maiong Kong Indians is confirmed by others, I do not lay much weight upon it.[3]

We saw in the Indian cabins several reeds of the blow pipe plant upwards of 16 feet long perfectly straight and free of knots. The arrows[4] which the Maiongkong Indians use are more than twice the length of the Macusi Indians, which are only twelve inches long. The arrow of the Maiong Kong Indians is twenty six inches and a half. At the distance of three inches from its point is tied some silk cotton fitted for the orifice of the blow pipe. The point is from 3 inches to 3½ inches covered with poison, from appearance like the Urari but which they call Cumarawa the Guinau Indians Maikuri. The arrow itself which is made of the midrib of the Coucourit Palm, is frequently orna-mented with Arnatto and Lana. The quiver in which they are carried, consists at the Macusis of basket work covered with Caruman,[5] and its orifice closed by a piece of deer skin. The Maiong Kong uses the spathe of a palm tree, closed at both its ends, and provided at one side, for the distance of 10 inches, with a slot by means of which he takes the arrow out. as our luggage had been proportioned for every carrier we had to replace the deserters; a task of great difficulty and I succeeded only after fair promises to induce two Indians to accompany us to the next settlement, a journey of two days. My observations gave me for the Lat[de] of the place, 4°11′21″N. As I found that we could not procure an increase of provisions, we left next morning, Jan[y] 26th. How should I describe the difficulties of the mountain road; the top of a mountain was no sooner reached when the descent commenced in order to ascend anew, as soon as the foot of the hill was reached. Our progress was slow, and the first attempt to hurry the carriers to a quicker step, was followed by a threat to strike off all together and to leave us in the midst of the wood. I found that I had not more to do with my well organized Macusis, but a savage tribe who were well aware of their superiority in number. We had therefore to preach patience to our wish of making rapid progress. The length ridges of the mountains, which during the first day of our march had a southwestern direction, changed more to WNW. and we had therefore to cross their axis; many of the moun-tains were conical and the average height of those which we crossed from 1000 to 1500

[1] Río Yemecuni.

[2] Cerro Masivari.

[3] The Amerindians were perfectly correct.

[4] Blowpipe darts.

[5] This is probably *karamanni* (*Symphonia globulifera*), a tree from whose resin a wax of the same name is made.

feet: much higher mountains from 2 to 3000 feet by estimation were however observed at our right and left side. How astonishing will it prove to Geographers in general, if they are informed we entered anew the system of the River Parima (Urariquera of maps) in 4°8′N Lat[de] and 64.50W. Long[de.] We erected our temporary huts on the banks of the Brook Birima, a small tributary of the Awarihuta[1] which flows into the Parima. I had hitherto doubted the information which I had received from the Indians of these regions that the Parima had its sources in the vicinity of those of the Orinoco; much of it has vanished since I newly entered the basin of the Parima, at a situation w[h]ere from the extant maps it could be so little supposed that this river should extend its ramifications so far North and Westward. I wondered to see our Indians as soon as our huts were erected, resort to the brook where they were most assiduously employed to dig up the ground along the waters edge with long sticks flattened at the end. On advancing nearer, I found that they were searching for worms which were concealed in the mud. Their body was contractile but when drawn out amounted from 12 to 15 inches; they were of cylindrical form, and annullated, the mouth was near the extremity naked and moved forward and backward as well with that extremity where the mouth was situated as well with that in the contrary direction. They resemble much our Lumbricus, or rather Gordius, only that they were much thicker, than those species which I have seen of the latter Genus. After the Indians had cleaned them of the mud which was attached to them, they eat them raw and apparently with much delight.[2]

We entered in the afternoon an Indian Cabin inhabited by ten Maiong Kong Indians, and as our provisions threatened an end we had to submit reluctantly to a days delay in order to lay in a new stock. The next settlement on our road was a journey of four days distant. From this place which according to my observations was in 4°5½′ Lat N. and by account in Long[de] 64°31′W. Mount Pawa,[3] where the Méréwarí has its source, bore N19E. its estimated distance being 55 miles; this coupled with former information I have thought myself warranted to place those sources in 4°58′N Lat. and 64°37′W. Long[de].; also about 30 m. south of the situation assigned to it in the extant maps: its farthest southern point is also however 85 miles farther southward than laid down hitherto. Next of interest was the course of the Parima, which at a distance of 40 miles runs East by Northward along a ridge of mountains, the highest peak of which the Kaiwinnima rises to the estimated height of 3500 feet and bore S40°E. from our position. This ridge extends for about 4 miles from SWbS to NEbN. and belongs as far as I could judge from a distance to the Sandstone Formation. Mount Pawa perhaps not less than

---

[1] Rio Auaris.

[2] The eating of earth worms is not widely reported in the ethnographic literature, but two of the major groups from this region, the Yecuana and Piaroa, do so today. As well as being eaten raw, the worms are boiled or smoked wrapped in leaves (see below p. 353). The worms are not eaten as a 'famine food' but as a delicacy. The Yecuana 'cultivate' them in so far as they spread them to places where they are not found. Two species of Glossoscolecidae earth worm are eaten. The smaller or 'motto' (*Andiorrhinus motto*), of which it is the case here, is found in a riverine environment; the larger or 'kuru' (scientifically unnamed), growing to four feet in length, is found in the forest. See Maurizio Paoletti et al., 'The Importance of Leaf-and Litter-feeding Invertebrates as Sources of Animal Protein for the Amazonian Indians', *Proceedings of the Royal Society, Biological Sciences*, 267, 2000, pp. 2247–52. For a rare earlier mention of the consumption of earth worms, see Wallace, *Narrative of Travels on the Amazon*, p. 201.

[3] This mountain is earlier (see p. 341) called Pabaha. Paba is the spelling which occurs in the published version (p. 230).

5000 feet high and which as already observed bore N19E. belongs decidedly to this group. The ridge from which it takes such an exalted rank continues E & W. S76E, distant about 5 miles is a remarkable peaked mountain, which the Maiong Kong call Arawatta, the Guinau, Biribu. All information I had collected hitherto pointed to a much further southern situation for the sources of the Orinoco as hypothetical Geography had hitherto allowed. The testimony of the Indians agreed all in that point that the Parima and Orinoco had their sources close together in the same chain of mountains. We hoped to be in seven days at their sources.

Jan 29 We crossed the river Awarihuta at a distance of a mile and a half from the Indian cabin. The Awarihuta is one of the most considerable tributaries which the Parima receives from these far north western regions. It was about 100 feet wide, its waters light coloured, and the current strong running over a gravelly and sandy bottom. Further Eastward it is inhabited by Macu Indians.[1] Its course as far as we could trace it from the mountain was S.E.bE. and the Indians pointed in the same direction when we asked them where it joined the Parima. The length ridges of the mountains which we had to ascend ran EbN and WbS. from which they scarcely varied a point; our road became more fatiguing in consequence of their great height. Rivulets pathed themselves turbulently a road towards the Awarihuta and formed in many places large cascades, exhibiting a coarse grained Granite in which large flakes of hornblende were predominant. In other places we observed a similar granite partly denudated of the Earth from which the water oozed in rills. In other places the granit was heaped up in boulders and formed crags and subteraneous caverns in which we heard the sound of running waters, these chasms were sometimes from 40 to 50 feet deep. All species of Palm have vanished nor is a Heliconia to be seen. Sirabally, Hya-hya,[2] Ackayari,[3] Tataba,[4] Ducaly,[5] Cumara,[6] Wallaba, and different species of Cackerally are the forest trees, which I have noticed very much[;] a mass of others, surpassing them in loftiness and size, were strangers to us. The Heliconia and palms, it appeared were replaced by arborescent Ferns. A high towering mountain which the Indians called Putuibirri, and which I estimated 5000 feet high remained to the right in westward of our path.

January 31st We entered today the system of the Orinoco, the brooks and streams which we crossed flow SWestward towards the river Ocamo,[7] a tributary of the Orinoco. A chain of mountains the blue outlines of which stretched NE. & SW. were shown us as our journey end; there, they said, had the Orinoco its sources. The locality surrounded by lofty and ombrageous trees where even the Zenith can not be properly observed, had not permitted me to take any observations, but as we are to reach next morning a settlement of Indians I hope to be enabled to procure observations. The weather has been fair, and we have every reason to be thankful as by the want of Palm or Heliconia leaves to secure us against the influence of rain, we should no doubt fare very

[1] Macu is a generic term in Amazonia for hunting and gathering bands. It is probable that a group of Yanomami is being referred to here.

[2] Haiahaia: *Sapium aucuparium*; *S. cladogyne*; *S. hippomane*; *S. jenmanii*; *S. paucinervium*.

[3] Acourie: *Licania densiflora*.

[4] Tatabu: *Diplotropis purpurea*.

[5] Dukali: *Parahancornia fasciculata*.

[6] Kumaru: *Dipteryx odorata*.

[7] The Río Ocamo flows southwest from the Sierra Parima to join the Orinoco at Santa Maria de los Guiacas.

badly during a torrent of rain. The mornings and evenings are cold and the Thermometer has at six oclock in the morning, seldom showed above 62° Fahr.

Feby 1st All our hopes and fond wishes are destroyed. We arrived this Evening at two Indian Cabins, inhabited by Maiong Kong Indians and found the inhabitants in the greatest consternation, and ready to leave the place; a party of Maiong Kong 20 strong had induced by signs of good will, which the Kirishannas who inhabit the mountains between the Orinoco and Ocamo, had shown to some of their tribe, undertaken to visit them partly for the sake of barter, partly out of curiosity. But scarcely had they made their appearance at one of their camps when the Kirishanna, who must have had knowledge of their coming fell from an ambush upon them and killed the whole party with the exception of four who found means to escape. These wild and savage Indians who do not allow any stranger be he either Indian, European or their descendants come near their camps, had immediately after surprised a Maiong Kong settlement only a days journey from the one where we then were, and killed every soul. The body of a Maiong Kong who had gone out to hunt was found killed with stones at a short distance from the Settlement, and these outrages of the hoard had set the whole community in alarm, and was enough to strike my crew with the greatest panic. I had to come to a quick resolution, with their hammocks slung round their necks they stood ready to depart, and to leave us and our baggage to our fate. I offered the chief man who acted as guide the best of what I had. I offered him my rifle, to which he had taken a particular liking and which was the present of a kind friend but nothing could induce them to give up their wish of returning if I should insist of proceeding further. Thwarted in my designs by the most untoward events I had to acquiesce though I stood at the threshold of the sources of the Orinoco. However they are no more a geographical problem, a single glance on a map on which my present tour is delineated will prove that the uncertainty of the situation is reduced to a square of less than thirty miles and even in that extent of ground much of the uncertainty is removed, as all strangers and inhabitants of the place remained firm and corroborated in their information that the sources of the Orinoco where at one of the mountains in the chain before us which they pointed particularly out to me. The Indians have promised to stay until next morning to allow me to procure observations, and if I should be successful I hope yet to be able to give the sources of the Orinoco their [correct] and geographical situation which that distinguished traveller, B[n] Humboldt, was himself prevented from fixing by a similar misfortune, frustrated, as he himself tells us, by the tribe of hostile Indians above Esmeralda who it appears are identical with the savage Kirishanas who had thus so unexpectedly thwarted my own views.[1]

February 2[d]. The weather did not permit me to take observations, although I was up the whole night, watching with anxiety. Every precaution had been taken to prevent our being surprised, and we were glad when the morning approached and we commenced our march to the northward, disappointed and chagrined of our bad success.

We had been fortunate enough to procure several baskets with dry Casada bread – prepared no doubt for their own journey – it was highly acceptable as without it we should have been short of provisions in a day. Our path led far northward. We were told, as it were now my intentions to proceed direct to Esmeralda that there were two

---

[1] See Humboldt, *Personal Narrative*, II, 1907, p. 467. He does not appear to have made much effort to ascend to the sources of Orinoco, feeling in poor condition and put off by stories of fierce Indians.

roads, the one leading westward being the more preferable, not only for shortness but likewise for the nature of being less mountainous but our Indians no doubt thought "Procul a Jove procul a fulmine"[1] and the northern was selected. Nor rested there their precautions; without that orders issued from me for that purpose, two and two were watching alternately the whole night. How shall I describe the monotony of our march, for it was rendered the more fatiguing by it. The eye did not sweep over boundless regions; arrested by lofty trees it did not extend above many yards. How delighted were we therefore when after having ascended a higher mountain than usual, we found ourselves on a granite platform of vast extent overgrown with alpine shrubs; Bromeliaceae, Orchideae, Commelincae,[2] and various other vegetable productions of high interest to a botanist. They distinguished themselves by their gigantic size a Bromeliaceae, the stem of which was propendent was from 12 to 14 feet in length before it spread out into leaves. As it was not its flowering season, I could not therefore determine to which genus it belonged. I considered it a Tillandsia. Several others of that genus find sustenance from the naked rocks which they clothed with verdure. Each formed a natural cistern containing upwards of a pint of water, that which was on the top, clear and pure, the remainder filled with residue and a slimy matter peculiar to the plant. The water is however well tasted and our Indians drank copiously of it. A Commelinaceae with leaves and a stem 4 feet long bore an umbel of yellow flowers, the delicate structure of their petals contrasted widely with the rigid Calyx. In Vernation, the umbel is surrounded by a spatha which like the buds perforate before they come to blossom. I recognised however several species which I had observed on Roraima. In many respects the flora of Mount Warima resembled that of Roraima, even the splendid Utricularia was not wanting, but as the rocky ground did not afford it the necessary moisture it grew from below the leaves of the Tillandsia where it found sufficient supply. It had a strange effect to see its stem adorned with magnificent blue flowers rising above the summit or crown of the Tillandsia. From these magnificent plants by which we were surrounded, I turned the eye to the landscape, spread like a picture before us. It swept to the North and eastward untill it was arrested by the Sarisharima mountains, along the foot of which we had toiled so lately, they stretched wall like from West to East; high towered Mount Paba among them, its summit was enveloped in thick clouds. In the East we discovered the mountains of the Merewari which by their North and South direction force the Merewari to take a retrograde course, and thus deprive the Parima of its waters. The prospect to the South and West was prevented by the mountains rising higher in that direction. We crossed a thicket and ascended about 200 feet higher, here opened the prospect to the South and West, and far on the horizon rise the Mountains Maravacca (Maraguaca) and Yaconnamari (Duida): at the foot of the first flows the Paramu (Padamo)[3] on the southern foot of the latter the Orinoco. At this distance their structure resembled much Roraima but I presume they are higher than that Mountain. Large columns of smoke rose in a S.E. direction, we were told that Macu Indians were settled there at the banks of the river Awari: further southward we observed the mountains of the Ocamo which we had just now left in full retreat. The

---

[1] 'Further from Jove, further from the thunderbolt.' It seems to have been quite a common saying and it has not been possible to attribute it to any particular source.

[2] Commelinaceae.

[3] Río Padamo, a right-bank tributary of the Orinoco down which Schomburgk is to travel.

Latitude of Warima is 4°0'14", Longitude deduced by account 65°5' West. These mountains with bare and naked summits stretched further northward. The rock is fine grained Syenite traversed in a W.bN. direction by numerous veins of quartz from one to three inches broad. We met here again thickets of Palm trees, the Manicole of the Coast regions. This Palm grows only in marshy soil, the ground received a sufficient supply of water from the granitic platforms. The granite mountains Warima form the division between the tributaries of the Parima and the mighty Orinoco.[1] After we had descended for about 1300 feet, we followed a rill which ran W.S.W. where it was about 30 feet wide, and crossed soon afterwards the brook Yawarui which flows in the river Matakuni a tributary of the Paramu (Padamo). [W]e crossed the Matakuni three miles further W.S.W. where it was about 30 feet wide. I find in Arrowsmiths map of Columbia a river Matakuni is designated a tributary of the Ocamo, though a river of a similar name and a tributary to the Ocamo might be in existence, the Indians whom I have hitherto met with know nothing of its existence, though we enquired for it when near the sources of the Ocamo. The Matakuni along which we wandered has its sources two days journey further north and falls in the Paramu. I am inclined to think an error has been committed in the above stated map.[2] We passed next day Feb[y] 5 over Mountains where Savannahs formed their summits. An Eupatorium[3] of moderate growth overspread large pieces of ground; its leaves were characterized by intense bitterness, combined with a slight aromatic taste. At some distance before us but higher than the savannahs, the ground had entirely the appearance as if covered with snow, and as the low bushes could not pride themselves of much foliage, the illusion of an early fall of snow, when the severe hand of winter has not stripped as yet entirely nature of her verdure, was perfect. On approaching we found that a species of Lichen, which densely covered the ground. It was of a pure white and I do not recollect now that we possess a single species in Europe nor have I seen another in South America which could vie with it in whiteness. Dieranum glaucuni and Hypnum undulatum among mosses come perhaps nearest, but they are whitish green. After the morning dews this Lichen is soft and pliable, but when the sun crowns his meridian height it becomes rigid.[4] We had great difficulty to find water, and it was already late before we found a small spring, near which we took up our nights quarters. It was very cold and the blankets gave us not sufficient protection. I rose at 2 A.M. and looked at the thermometer, it stood 57° F. In the morning at ½ past 5, it stood at 56°. We started early (Feb[y] 7) the motion of ascending we hoped, would restore our animal heat, really with the freshness of the morning, our hands and face, but chiefly the olfactory organ, had got quite benumbed, and a glance at our feet where the thick tufts of snow-white Lichen hid the smallest blade of grass made the illusion of a winter landscape perfect. We enjoyed a beautiful prospect

---

[1] If Schomburgk is where he claimed to be he was on a different watershed, the divide between the rivers that run south to join the Orinoco and those that run north to join the same river via the Ventauri. In fact, he was probably not as far west as he thought.

[2] The Río Matacuni rises between the sources of the Ocamo and Padamo and flows into the latter about twelve miles in a straight line above its junction with the Orinoco.

[3] A genus of the Family Asteraceae, but all the species of *Eupatorium* from Guiana have been reclassified under other genera.

[4] The following footnote appears in the published version (p. 233): 'The specimens which I brought with me have proved it to be the reindeer-moss (*Lichen rangiferinus*, L.), which at a certain elevation appears to be dispersed all over the globe.'

from the height of the next mountain. The morning was fair and cloudless and we saw the high mountains of Maravacca and Yaconnamari quite distinct, they bore from S45°W to S75°W an extent of 30° at a distance of no less than 40 miles. At a nearer distance the mountains stretched W.b.N and E.b.S and were met by transverse ridges going N.N.W. & S.S.E, along the latter flows the river Kuntanama.[1] It appears on these mountains as if savannah and wood contended for mastery, large patches of wood alternate with savannahs of similar extent; the grass of the latter was burning in different directions and the horizon was quite obscured by large columns of smoke. We observed at one of the summits an Indian cabin in S.W.b.W. direction, it was to be our journeys end for this day, but with our tired limbs we looked with dismay at the various chasms which yet intervened and which we had to descend and ascend before we could lay aside our staff. we found the path of a river which meandered southward through the narrow valley. It was the Kuntanama a tributary of the Paramu. We had to cross it before we reached the Indian settlement; it was about 90 feet wide and formed near the place where the Indians had made a bridge of two trunks of trees ballustraded by lianas a large cataract.

The Settlement consisted of two huts of Maiongkong and Guinau Indians, amounting to 23 souls, but a large party of Maiongkongs, who had returned from a visit to the upper Ventuari (called Parawa by the Maiongkongs) gave the place a populous appearance, there amounted to seventy men all in the prime of life. It appeared the people here had taken likewise the alarm with regard to the Kirishannas, large baskets of Cassada bread were hung up in various directions, while on a small barbacot we observed them smoking a great quantity of that species of Worm, which I already described and which I consider to belong to the Genus Gordius, fifty to sixty are wrapped up in Plantain leaves and preserved for times of need. The barbacot contained at least from one to three thousand of these worms, and from this we may conclude upon the vast numbers which are secreted in the mud along the rivers and brooks of these regions. We were successful to obtain another supply of Cassada bread, ready made, our journey on did not suffer any delay from want of provisions. We were obliged to leave without one of our Indians who was in such a weak state, produced by low fever, that we had to convey him in his hammock to the settlement. Sorry as I felt to leave him among strangers, his malady was of that kind, which even if he should recover, it would only occur after a lengthened period. The idea was prevalent that slow poison had been given to him.[2]

Feb[y] 8th Our march commenced with the ascent of Mount Kikiritza by no means an easy task, as it was very steep and about 3000 feet above the Kuntanama. Near its summit we entered again the regions of low bushes and tufts of white Lichen. Mosses are generally found only in humid places, but here bore everything the stamp of dryness, the soil rocky and marly, trees and shrubs of moderate height, and not planted by the hand of nature with the luxuriance of a tropical climate in thick tufts but far asunder, this profusion of mosses and Lichens was astounding. They consisted not only of the species just mentioned but others clothed the branches and trunks of trees, and covered the ground to such a thickness, that on taking a seat on this ground one might

---

[1] Río Cutinamo.

[2] As already mentioned (p. 39, fn. 1) the cause of sickness and death among Amerindians is more often than not attributed to human intervention, and is often thought to be the result of poisoning.

have fancied oneself to recline on the softest downy cushion. Mosses it appears therefore do not want a continued humidity as in this instance the rain and the mountain dew afforded them the only moisture. We reached at noon a Cabin with Maiongkong Indians; this settlement had only lately been erected. It contained however thirty two persons, the greater part of whom were young people. They had previous knowledge of our passing by, and gathered therefore some of the fruits of their new fields with which they presented us. Among others there were some pine apples, small of size, but decidedly they bore for sweetness and aroma the prize over any other I ever tasted previously. They far surpassed even those at Watu Ticaba which I considered then so superior.

In the direction of N½E at the distance of a mile and a half, rose a high peaked mountain, the Indians called it Aripani, and it was remarkable for a colossal mass of rock, which rose perpendicularly on its southern side. The brook Aripani flows along its foot and joins the Cuntanama.[1] We changed here some of our crew who were not capable to carry burdens over mountains; they caused a delay of several hours, and our distance made when the sun approached the horizon, consisted only of six miles in a geographical direction. I am aware that the Indians in cases of fever and other indisposition resort generally to bleeding, for which purpose they use the razor and make several incisions down the leg but I was not aware that bleeding was likewise considered a remedy against fatigue. I found our Macusis and Wapisianas to cut each others legs with a splinter of rock crystal, I thought that they used the latter as a substitute for a razor and offered them the lancet, but it was declined and I was informed, that a great deal of virtue lay in the crystal.[2]

The mountain which we crossed the following day continued in a N.N.W & S.S.E direction. Their summits must be sometimes exposed to terrible tornados, trees lay prostrate over large extents of ground. If so it should be willed, that man should happen to travel over places where such a scene of destruction occurs, whither to fly for protection? the crashing of the falling trees, the noise of the infuriated wind, all must combine to show how little hope there is for escaping death; He alone who governs the wind could afford protection. The number of trees which had fallen one on the other, were frequently so great that they formed barriers which we found it difficult to surmount. We observed there a number of that most beautiful bird the Cock of the Rock or Rock Manakin (Rupicola elegans) and I found opportunity to ascertain what the Indians had told me many times, but in consequence of its singularity I still doubted. The delays connected with our ascertaining the direction of our road rendering me generally one of the last of the marching column – on this occasion two Maiongkong Indians were with me when we heard at a short distance from the path, the twittering noise peculiar to the Rupicola, the Indians cautioned me and we stole nearer; before us was a spot about from four to five feet in diameter, cleared of every blade of grass, and smoothed as by human hands; on it capering a cock of the Rock in multifarious attitudes, now spreading its wings, throwing up its head, or opening its tail fan like, now strutting about, scratching the ground, all accompanied by a hopping gait, until fatigued, it

---

[1] Río Cutinamo.

[2] Scarification is widespread among the native peoples of Guiana, not simply for the reasons given here but also to provide prowess in hunting. A variety of instruments are used to make the incisions including the teeth of the agouti and bamboo slithers. The use of rock crystals makes good sense because of the association of rock with hardness and permanence, and these qualities with the endurance of a fit, well person.

gobbled some kind of note, on which one of those who acted as spectators took the field and relieved the dancer, which with self approbation retired to one of the low branches near the scene of action. We accounted ten cocks and two hens present and witnessed the exploits of them when the crackling noise of a piece of wood, on which I unfortunately placed my foot, told them of our presence and dispersed this company. The Indian who wishes to procure their beautiful skins, seeks for one of these places of their diversion, which in consequence of their bareness cannot be mistaken. When he has been successful, he arms himself with his blow pipe and poisoned arrows, and having previously constructed an ambush from branches of trees, he awaits with dawn of day the arrival of the dancing party. He does not commit destruction at the very commencement, but allows them to reach a certain height in their amusement, when off dash the poisoned arrow and the dancers capers are layed. Their ardour is so great, that they do not ascertain the cause of this sudden stop, but its place is immediately taken up by another, likewise doomed to fall a prey and thus four or five are sometimes killed, before they take alarm and fly away.

Senhor Ayres whom I have already introduced to the reader, told me it would be easy to procure in a district of short extent, near the river Uaupes from 200 to 300 skins during the season of fecundation, as it is then when the desire of a help mate urges them to enter the lists and to exhibit their beauty in these strange capers in order to win the affections of some favourite. We had gradually descended and found near brook Mahamé[1] which flows southward to the Kuntanama, Palmtrees and Heliconias; I do not think that our actual height excluded these so valuable plants to a traveller who with their leaves thatches his temporary hut, as we know that some species border on the limits of Perpetual;[2] it is therefore more likely that the soil is not favorable for their production.

Feb 10 Although the mountains continued in parallel ridges slightly deviating from N.N.W to S.S.E they are of less height and our descent has been considerable. The Atmosphere was warmer and the Thermometer had improved from 6° to 8° being formerly from 56 to 60 at 6 o'clock in the morning it ranged now from 64 to 66 which made a sensible difference. The white Lichen had disappeared, and the other species did not form compact turf. It was replaced at the height of 4000 feet by a species of Lycopodium,[3] which covered whole tracts and gave them the appearance of green Meadows. I saw this species for the first time which like most of its congeners is a prostrate plant. Among these patches there was likewise another species, the reproductive organs of which ended in apparent spikes, while on the former they terminated in branches. The latter reached a height of from 4 to 5 feet. We crossed the brooks Mantzaba and Marawai, and entered with it the system of the Paramu, at the banks of which river we arrived at three o'clock in the afternoon. I was disappointed in the Paramu I would have supposed it a much larger river. We met it first in lat. 3°49′40″N. and Long 65°37′W. where it was about 120 feet in width; its water of a muddy appearance, the current swift amounting to about 3 knots, impeded by numerous boulders of a coarse grained granite, which in these regions prevails at the foot and summit of the mountains, it rushed impetuously along and formed

[1] Probably Caño Machame.
[2] An unidentified hand has crossed out 'limits of Perpetual', and substituted 'alpine regions'. Perhaps Schomburgk intended 'perpetual snow'.
[3] Club mosses.

numerous falls. We found it in the maps under the name of Maquiritari or Padamo but the Maiongkong & Guinau Indians, who inhabit its banks call it Paramu. We camped on its left bank, while our Indians proceeded to the opposite shore to take their quarters in an abandoned cabin. The rain fell towards Evening in torrents, indeed it was sometimes as if the clouds had opened all their floodgates.

Feby 11 After our luggage and persons were conveyed to the rivers right bank we continued along it in a S.S.W. direction for several miles, and turned then in a more westerly direction to visit the settlement of one of our chief guides, a Maiongkong Indian. We crossed the small river Kurickanama, where it formed a very fine cataract, it flows in a S.S.E. direction into the Paramu. The Cuyaka along which banks we continued our course falls into the former; and on a small hillock which rises about 80 feet above its banks was the Indian settlement situated, which we reached at noon. It consisted of two large round cabins and a mud-house. The mountains surrounded the settlement and rose one above the other untill that part which the Maiongkong call Maravacca Huha, which bounded the scene. It appeared to me, as far as I have been able to judge of the group at a great distance, to be the highest among these regular ridges. They resemble in their configuration Roraima, they are however less steep and do not present an uninterrupted wall. The open place which surrounds the houses was peopled with Indians, anxious to show us their welcome. I accounted 64 individuals and was told that many were absent. They were well formed, and the greatest part of them perhaps not above twenty four years; they were painted and dressed like those of their tribe which I have already described, namely loins, ankles and knees, as well as arms surrounded by plaits of their own hair, while large bands of blue beads were tightly wrapped round the neck, the latter ornament gave them a stiff appearance and was worn by the youngest children and the oldest men. The women had the hair of their head cut short, but none represented the disgusting spectacle of perfect nakedness, as we had so frequently observed it among their tribe. After the welcome was over, the women appeared with divers fermented drinks which was followed by a whole array of little pots, filled with sauces and a like number of neatly plaited flat baskets on each of which there was a fresh cake of Cassada bread. The baskets are embellished with grecques and labyrinths, and the reed which is to form these figures is dyed black for that purpose. We did not observe any of the men possessing a gun, as he would have displayed it, but few were without cutlasses which they take great pride in keeping as clean as a soldiers sword. I need scarcely say that the cutlasses were all of British Manufacture. The Maiongkongs are inveterate smokers, while travelling with them across the mountains, and when we halted only for a short period, fire was immediately kindled, around which they squatted and prepared their cigars, the wrapper of which consisted of the leaves which surround the ears of the Indian corn, they commence to indulge "con amore" in their favourite amusement. As soon as a stranger arrives at a settlement, 5 or 6 cigars are offered to him by as many individuals, everyone of which has partly smoked a little while of it. It was therefore a severe trial for me to make seemingly a few empty puffs, and armed with a number of these cinders, I looked for the first opportunity to deposit them in some secret place, where they could not observe what ill use I made of these precious gifts.

The Maiongkong possesses a proud and upright bearing, the one end of his waistlap thrown over the shoulder, he stalks about as if the World was his own. He is not less inclined to Dandyism and takes particular pains to divide his hair over the front, with the greatest nicety. A War Club different from those of the Caribbees and Macusis is his constant companion, be [it] that he possesses a cutlass. The War club ends in a point and if he sit down or squat he thrusts it in the ground before him. Like all the Indian tribes they wake early and commence to converse with each other while lying in their hammocks. At 5 they take their bath in the neighbouring brook or river, as a settlement is never without one in its neighbourhood, the morning meal is meanwhile prepared by the women, after which they go to the field[,] to hunt, or indulge in their hammocks. the next meals are at 9 o'clock, at 12, & about 3, and make a grand meal at sunset; this we observed they took before the hut, when the little sauce pots formed one of the principal features. To these meals our crew were always called and as the settlement consisted of two divisions each of which had their dinners seperate, I need not say the guests who were invited to both were continually feasting.[1]

This Settlement is famed for the manufacture of baskets and blowpipes[.] I had at last the satisfaction of seeing the plant which produces those admirable reeds, which the Indians of Guiana hold in such high esteem as forming an indispensable article for the construction of their blowpipes. The reader of Humboldt's personal narrative will recollect that the Indians who returned to Esmeralda from the gathering of the Brazil nuts brought with them reeds which were from fifteen to seventeen feet long yet no trace of a knot for the insertion of leaves and branches were perceived but they were quite straight and smooth and perfectly cylindrical, and although they were of such high interest to M. de Humboldt, he could not determine to what genus they belonged.[2] I heard that these reeds were growing at the foot of Maravacca, and ascertained that it was a new Species of Arundinaria[3] which grows in large clusters like the Bamboo, the first joint rising without internodes in old Specimens from 15 to 16 feet at which height appear the first branches in a verticillated manner and continue [illegible] to a further height of thirty to forty feet at intervals of 16 to 18 inches. The stem is seldom more than 5 to 7 lines in diameter, and its own weight bends it in a graceful arch which much enhances its graceful appearance. It is peculiar to the Sandstone ridges of the upper Orinoco between the rivers Ventuari, Paramu and Mavacca. The Indians call it Curata, and the Maiong Kong and Guinau Indians who inhabit those regions are called the Curata people.[4]

The mean of 7 observations gave me as Latitude of the Maiongkong Settlement 3°47′ N. From this I estimated that of Mount Maravacca the highest of the group to be in 3°40′ N. L 65°48′W. L, and Kurianiheri, which is of pyramidical form and isolated in 3°18′ N & 65°W. The mountainous nature of the place and the thick woods which covered the hills did not admit of any baseline to be measured to ascertain the height of Maravacca. I estimate it however from 10000 to 11000 above the sea. Water boiled at the Maiongkong village at 205°.5 (about 3500 feet); the temperature of the air was

---

[1] This sentence also occurs in an alternative version. It reads: 'To these meals our crew were always invited, sometimes by several parties at a time, so that it seemed a continual feast.'

[2] See Humboldt, *Personal Narrative*, II, 1907, pp. 453–4.

[3] It was a new species and was named after Schomburgk, *Arundinaria schomburgkii (Arthrostylidium schomburgkii)*. See Schomburgk, 'Description of the Curata, a Grass of the Tribe of Bambuseae, of the Culm of which the Indians of Guiana Prepare their Sarbacans or Blowpipes', *The Transactions of the Linnean Society of London*, 18, 1841, pp. 557–62.

[4] The restricted area in which the reed grows made it a very important item in Amerindian commerce and it was traded across wide areas.

generally in the morning at sunrise from 59° to 61°; the highest stand of the thermometer shaded by the tent 88°; and at sunset from 78° to 80°. At 9 o'clock in the morning rose a slight breeze from the east which continued untill meridien height of the sun when it died away. Before we left the settlement we succeded to procure a great prize, a small calabash full of salt although I had to pay a thousand fold its value. Deprived as we had been of that article I would not have hesitated to pay double or treble that price. We procured it from some Guinau Indians who had arrived from the river Cunucuma,[1] their journey having been performed in four days, its distance was therefore about fifty miles in a westerly direction from the Maiongkong settlement. They told us that the breadth of the river was near their place about one hundred yards and that none but of their own tribe lived there. The Guinau like the Maiong Kong are famed for the manufacture of Cassada graters and they carry on a lively trade of barter with the neighbouring tribes of this indispensable article to an Indian household. The party consisted of four men tall and well made. Besides graters, they had a number of new hammocks and our Macusi Indians trafficked with them. My stock of merchandise was so reduced, that I could not give our Indians the articles to pay for their purchases; and though the Guinaus saw the Macusis for the first time, they nevertheless trusted to their word that they would send the payment by one of the men who were to accompany us to Pirara and whither I had ordered a new supply of goods. Their purchases consisted in Hammocks Cassada bread,[2] Waistlaps, girdles made of human hair, & ornaments of maccaw and parrot feathers; I procured a few bivalve shells from them which were from the Cunucuma and which they wore as ornaments. They belonged to a species new to me, and though they were perforated in order to fix them to a necklace of Monkeys teeth, they were not so injured by it as to render them useless for description.

We started[3] from the Maiong Kong settlement on Feby 15 and somewhat below the river Puruniama commences a series of Cataracts, here we met already with a disaster. One of the small Corials, in descending them, filled with water and sunk, and tho' the corial was recovered, her load was almost entirely lost, among other things of kitchen use we had much to regret our newly purchased stock of salt, & our set of Plates, which although not of noble metal and gorgeous workmanship, had rendered all the service of the costliest. A similar accident befell shortly afterwards another corial, they succeeded however to get her ashore before she sunk, and we got off with having her load thoroughly wet; the sun shone bright and this disaster was remedied. The river was not for the space of 300 yards free from Rapids and falls and some so large and dangerous that we had to unload the Corial five times and to carry the luggage overland.

Feby 16th The River continued the same; the falls amounted frequently to from 15 to 20 feet perpendicular height, and we had to unload repeatedly. We arrived about noon at the Cataract Marivacaru[4] the largest we had yet passed; the river precipitated itself here upwards of thirty feet over a ledge of rocks[;] we had naturally to unload and carry

---

[1] Río Cunucunuma.

[2] This has been changed to 'graters' on the manuscript, which, as described in the paragraph, were an important trade item.

[3] Although not explicitly said, it would appear that the expedition at this point took to travelling by river again.

[4] Probably Salto Caballete.

Corials and luggage overland. We had reloaded and followed the river in a E.S.E. direction when we saw at some distance before us I considered first to be a mass of white smoke, rising in circles above the ground, and I concluded that some of our Corials which had gone on before us had come to and kindled fires. These were my conjectures when I had the first glance of it, but I was soon undeceived, it was a sheet of foam, the river Cuntanama joining by a 'salto mortale' the Paramu. The prospect is highly picturesque, the Cuntanama comes from the South East[1] and on approaching its junction with the Parumu its bed is about thirty five feet higher than the latter river; it falls gradually fifteen feet, when at its mouth, the river being divided in two streams by a small island, it forms two formidable Cataracts of which the more southern is twenty feet high. The white foam to the eye apparently massive and dense, contrasts strongly with the dark colour of the Paramu, while clouds of mist, formed by the contest of the waters, rise high into the air, and hang like a veil over the verdure of clusters of Palms and thick umbrageous trees. No other instance is known to me where a river joins its recipient in such a turbulent manner. I estimated the breadth of the two falls three hundred yards; at their foot they had formed a large basin, on the southern side of which thick masses of sand were deposited which formed part of the detritus which the Cuntanama brought down from the mountains. It will he recollected that we crossed this stream Cuntanama on the 1st Feby in Lat. 3°57′20″N. and Long 65°19′21″W., its junction with the Paramu, according to my observations, in lat. 3°29′50″N. Long 65°3[4]′[15]″W its course is from thence therefore S.W bS. The Latitude of our camp this night was 3°25′56″N. the mouth of the Cuntanama being distant about 4 miles.

Feby 17th After we had passed the cataract Cacoanna[2] we entered comparatively smooth water, from the Puruniama to the Cuntanama the Paramu surpasses in the number and height of Cataracts any river which I have visited before and I was truly thankful to the Almighty that it had pleased him to conduct us safely in person to their end. Many were the moments which were passed under anxiety during the preceeding two days. The River widened now to about 150 yards its banks became low and dotted with sylvan vegetation and Clusters of Palms. We recognised the Coucourite, Curua,[3] Lou,[4] Popo,[5] Araho,[6] and several others which were unknown to us. From the mouth of the river Watamu[7] the Paramu turns far to the north and those perpendicular and wall like mountains, the continuation of Maravacca came now in view, only partially covered with verdure. The Sun reflected his rays on their bare walls and made them appear of snowy whiteness; Wataba Siru bore N.W.bN., its summit was wrapt in clouds, and it appeared an isolated mass of conical form. The Northern part of Yéonnamari (Duida) bore W.N.W. it extended however further South than our prospect would admit us to observe. Wataba Siru is considerably higher than that part of Yéonnamari which we had then in view, and I do not overrate it, if I say by 2000 feet. We halted at noon at a

---

[1] This has been corrected on the manuscript to 'north-east'.

[2] In the published version (p. 240) this is spelt 'Cavana' and on the accompanying map 'Cavanna'. It is probably the Raudal Cúa of the reference map.

[3] Kurua: *Attalea sagotii*.

[4] Lu: *Oenocarpus bacaba*.

[5] Probably Boba: *Iriartea exorrhiza*.

[6] Possibly Reho: *Euterpe stenophylla*.

[7] Río Botamo.

Maiongkong settlement. The owners of our Corials had conditioned that we should not take them further than to this settlement, and hopes were held out to me that I might purchase here a large corial, which had been just finished.

Feby 19th The Canoe arrived only today, it had been made near the pyramidical mountain Wataba Siru, and it had taken the Indians more than eight days to transport it to the Paramu; she was just large enough of size to suit our purpose her length amounted to 33 feet her breadth to five. The Owner was dressed up in high style; but his pride consisted apparently of a pair of suspenders, manufactured of silk and worked with representations of flowers. He told us that he had brought them from Angostura where he had been lately. He spoke a few Spanish words and appeared in every respect a very intelligent Indian. As much care as he had bestowed upon his own person to deck himself out in clothes, this extravagance had not extended to his fairer half who went à l'indécence. We agreed about the price of the Canoe, a part of which was paid in cutlasses, axes, calico, knives &c and all hands went to work to furnish her with temporary benches, as the fitting her out we delayed to our arrival at Esmeralda, where we hoped to find more conveniences for that purpose.

Feb[y] 20 We left this morning in our new Canoe; during the last three days we had had daily thunderstorms and rain and the river was risen upwards of a foot[.] Some Cataracts which are south of the settlement were passed without accident, the Canoe stood the heavy surge admirably and tho' of large size, was easily governed by the helmsman. We had every occasion to be satisfied with our new purchase, she was strongly built of Cedarwood[1] and more over very light, a quality which as I had not yet given up all hopes of proceeding by the Mavaca, adapted her well for being hauled overland. The Maiongkongs are famed boat builders and they have the knack to finish off with fire and axe in a shorter period than any other Indian tribe. The other Indians cede this point to them. At the foot of the last cataract of the Paramu, we were welcomed by a pair of fresh water Dolphins which accompanied us sporting and gambolling round the Canoe, now before, alongside, or behind us. I estimated the breadth of the Paramu 800 feet; its banks are low and the current much less than the preceeding day. Among the falls we had observed numerous Pacu, tho' of the same genus they differ in shape and color from the Pacu of the Essequibo & Mazaruni, they are of a dark color, blue approaching to black. Since we had entered smooth water & whenever we came to spots where the river was shallow we saw numerous species of the tribe Siluridae and others. On the banks of the river the gigantic Oubudi tree covered with bright scarlet fruit raised the desire to partake of them, and we repeatedly halted our Craft to collect what the wind or maturity had thrown on the ground; it would have been no easy task to climb the tree and pluck them fresh. The variety with yellow fruits was equally frequent. The heat was highly oppressive the thermometer exposed to the sun rose to 123°. The Sun was above 10° West of the Meredian when I noted around her disk a large halo 43°30′ in diameter, the circle was outside white and the inside tinged with yellow. Though I had frequently seen halos round the moon I had not previously observed one round the Sun. It accompanied the sun until that luminary was within 25° of the horizon. The day was hazy and towards North-east were heavy thunder clouds.

---

[1] Mennega et al. (*Check-list*), gives Red Cedar (*Cedrela odorata*) and White Cedar (*Tabebuia insignis*; *T. steno-calyx*), but a number of different hardwood trees are popularly called 'cedar'.

We reached towards sunset the river Matakuni. We had crossed it on 31 January[1] while travelling over the mountains. It was there only a small brook scarcely 30 feet wide, at its junction with the Paramu its breadth amounted to no less than 150 yards. The night passed with fruitless watching to procure the Meredian altitude of a star, during the earlier part of the evening thunder made every observation impossible, and it remained cloudy and hazy for the rest of the night. After 3 o'clock in the morning I procured a rather cloudy observation of α Centauri, which gave for the Latitude of the junction of the Matakuni with the Paramu 3°1′56″N. Longt. being by account 65°[39′illegible″]W. The rivers course therefore from where we met it first S.W.b.S.

I have already observed that in former maps the Matakuni is noted as a tributary of the Ocamo, but on inquiry I could not ascertain that there is a second Matakuni flowing into that river; the Indians were only acquainted with the tributary of the Paramu.

Feb[y] 21st We were before sunrise in our Canoo and expecting to enter in a few hours the Orinoco. The colour of the river Matakuni is white and it renders the Paramu much lighter in colour than it is above the Matakuni. There was no difference in the temperature of the two rivers the waters of both were 82° while the air was 73°. We were again attended by the Dolphin at least we fancied that they were the same which accompanied us the preceeding day, and under their escort we entered at nine oclock the Orinoco. The course of the Paramu had been lastly S.E., where it joins the Orinoco it is S.21°E. and it has a breadth of about 300 yards. The Orinoco above the junction is not much broader. The Latitude of the confluence, deduced from my last nights observations is 2°54′N. differing 18 miles from Arrowsmiths map where it is placed in 3°12N. Its course trends latterly to the east of south and not west of south as delineated in former maps. It becomes evident that consequently the course of the Orinoco is equally erroneous East of Esmeralda and the first decided proof is tendered by which entering the Orinoco from the Paramu where the majestic Duida or Yeonnamari of the Indians bears N.40°W.[;] according to extant maps it bears at the mouth of the Paramu N.33°W. When the Indians pointed out the mountains to me where they said the Orinoco had its sources and according to their information and my supposition, they ought to be in 2°45′N. Lat. I thought when referring to the Orinoco's course as laid down from Esmeralda to the Raudal de Guaharibos that it might make from its sources to that great cataract a sweep to the East but it is now my firm opinion that it keeps to its bifurcation more or less a W.N.W. course.

A few miles West of the Paramu the Orinoco widens to 400 yards and encreases its breadth from 5 to 600 yards. Numerous sandbanks filled its bed, and as it was predicted to us, we found difficulties to proceed, the river along its whole breadth only 12 to 15 inches deep, and we had to dig channels for our canoe in order to make progress. The river had so little current that in many places it appeared stagnant, and covered with scum and bubbles. Where the water was so shallow that it scraped the bottom, it turned up a species of fresh water Algae of a green colour and covered with mucous matter. The Dolphins had left us – the shallow state of the water did not allow them to pass the sandbanks. The Banks of the river were low and the adjacent country flat, and only now and then intersected by hillocks of moderate height isolated and densely wooded; but when the eye turned to the northward the Duida and its adjacent mountains raised their

[1] It was on 4 February, see p. 352 above.

361

head to the clouds. A pyramidical formed mountain of that chain was remarkable among the rest for its shape, but as our Indians were for the first time on the Orinoco they could not tell me its name. We heard a Dog barking on the right shore and for the purpose of receiving information we pulled towards the place. Our object was however frustrated by a fierce dog and apparently only tenanted by some females. We enquired in all the tongues at command to our Indians and self what the distance to Esmeralda might be but received only answers in some unknown tongue to us. Nor did we get a view of the tawny beauties. The Dog watched the door just kept ajar, like another Cerberus, and as loud as ever its barking was, the voice of the females surpassed its noise. We retreated followed now closely by friend Cerberus, which ever and anon showed the greatest disposition to inflict its teeth in the heels of the hindmost, who as cover to our retreat, had from time to time to stand, and to fight. After we had embarked and pushed off from the shore, the lately Invisibles made now their appearance and peeped from behind some trees at the Canoo and her Crew. Our camp was pitched on a sandbank opposite the river Wapo (Guapo)[.][1] Myriads of Sandflies swarmed round us like bees, and inflicted most merciless bites, they had been our torment since we had entered the Orinoco: and their torture combined after noontide with a heat of 130° in the sun to which we were fully exposed on the broad river and with no protection against it, we where glad when with the setting in of darkness their torment ceased and a gentle breeze fanned our burning faces. I procured that night four observations of northern & southern stars according to which we were in 3°7'2"N. Lat.

Feby 22nd We started at six o'clock full of expectation to see Esmeralda. Light fleecy clouds enveloped Mount Duida, but they vanished after the Sun had risen above the horizon, and we had for the first time a full view of these stupendous rock masses, partly illuminated by the oblique rays of the Sun, then only a few degrees above the horizon; the cliffs exhibited here the strongest light, while the adjacent part was thrown in deep shade. Our progress was not without difficulty; we got several times fast aground on sandbanks, and had to cruise from shore to shore to avoid shallows and to follow the eccentric course which the remaining current had [sco]oped out for itself. A fine Savannah extending to the foot of the mountains hove now in view which I knew from Humboldt's account to be Esmeralda, and some canoos tied to the river's bank, pointed out the landing place to us. With what feelings I hastened ashore I need not describe, my object was realized; and my observations commenced on the coast regions of Guiana, were connected with those of Humboldt at Esmeralda. I confess it with pride, that when my own physical powers threatened to succomb, when surrounded by dangers and difficulties of no slight nature, the name of that great Traveller, his approbation of what I had done hitherto, served me as encouragement and I went forward with renewed vigour. The emaciated form of my companions, and our faithful guides, the Indians, told me more than volumes, what difficulties we had surmounted; our number of those who had started with me at our embarcation at the river Parima was three less. The inclemency of the weather, the deprivations and fatigues to which we were exposed, while traversing the mountain chain, proved too much even for those natives. They fell sick and I was obliged to leave them under the care of friendly Indians. The sufferings of those around me, made me forget my own.

[1] Río Iguapo.

The village was a few hundred yards from the river's banks. We met half way to it the arcayde[1] or overseer who accosted us in Spanish[2] and bade us welcome. His attire certainly did not bespeak his dignity – merely a shirt formed of the bark of a tree called Marima,[3] which covered his loins. He led us to his Hut where his Wife, Children, and Grand-children were assembled and where we soon discovered, that for the present he was the only adult male inhabitant of the place. His Senhora had meanwhile put some smoked Fish and Cassada before us; her Husband was incessant in Enquiries after European affairs, and to shew us his Geographical knowledge, he spoke of France and Paris, England and London, Prussia and Berlin; he enquired which states were engaged in war, and what Ferdinand VII was doing in Catalonia. The change of affairs in Spain were great news to him and he could not conceive how a Queen could govern there; of equal won-der was the news of Donna Maria's ascent of the Portuguese throne.[4] He spoke of Napoleon, indeed he showed that he had a pretty good knowledge of Europe, and it did not last long, when he told me that he had been during the late revolution in Columbia a sailor in a privateer under a Catalonian commander, and had chiefly sailed in the Caribbean Seas, where though an Indian, he had picked up his knowledge but apparently no riches. After I had answered his urgent enquiries, I was naturally anxious to procure some information about my road. I felt loath to descend by the Cassiquiare as by that route Bararoa was at least 200 miles further, besides that the wretched state of our wardrobe made it less desirable to be seen by civilized people. I had sent a stock of Clothes from São Joaquim to Bararoa and the way by the Mavaca and Padauiri[5] was in every respect the more preferred. Another point of great import was that by selecting the Mavaca our sustenance might be defrayed from the remnant of our articles for barter, via Rio Negro we would have to launch out with Species, an article with which I had not pro-vided myself for such a case. The time of consideration which elapsed before old Antonio Yarumari pronounced sentence, were moments of suspense. As preface he told me that he was born at the Banks of the river Siapa, and was of the Ipavaquena nation,[6] I might therefore be well assured that he was well acquainted with the rivers and portages but that at the low state of the rivers we could not proceed by the Mavaca. He might have observed the disappointment which the information caused us, and as if to disperse all further doubt in the truth of his statement, he called some Indian name, on which a miserable half-starved looking being of an Indian made his appearance. His lean face, the upper lip cov-ered by a few straggling hairs, might have served as the beau ideal of an Indian Don Quixote. The figure responded to the face. It was no wonder that we had hitherto over-looked him and considered Antonio the only male inhabitant of Esmeralda, covered behind an Indian sugar mill, which occupied part of the room, he passed easily unnoticed.

---

[1] On the manuscript this has been corrected by an unidentified hand to 'alcalde'.

[2] At this point p. 108 or p. 152 ends, and the higher sequence of page numbers continues alone until the end of the manuscript. In other words the next page is just numbered 153.

[3] Bark cloth was often made from the same trees that provided outer wrappings for cigars, usually *Couratari* or *Lecythis* species. The Warao word for *C. guianensis* is Marimari.

[4] In Spain, María Cristina was at the time regent for her nine-year-old daughter by the late Ferdinand VII, Isabella II who ascended the throne in 1843. In Portugal, Maria II, daughter of Pedro IV of Portugal (Pedro I of Brazil) was on the throne.

[5] Rio Padauari.

[6] No information has been found on this group, but it is probably a phratry of the Arawakan people who lived, and still live in the region.

Antonio told us that this Indian was from Portugal, as he named the Brazils, and that he had journeyed several times with a frenchman[1] between Bararoa and Esmeralda. According their joint information the mouth of the Maravaca[2] is reached four days after leaving Esmeralda and that river is ascended for five days, when passing one day and a half over land, and passing a large mountain the river Siapa or Durowaca of the Indians is reached; it is followed only for a short distance, and one of its tributaries the Mandavaca is entered; by a short portage from here they reach the Brook Manehissen, which flows into the Marari a tributary of the Padauiri; the Marari once entered Bararoa is reached in seven days. But it was their decided opinion that meeting already difficulties enough in the Mavacca we would find it utterly impossible to pass the brooks, and there existed no path to perform the whole journey over land. This route, they said were only passable during the winter season (May to September) when the rivers were swollen. I saw no worldly reason which could have induced the old man to give me false information, even agreed that some of our party should have been averse to the Mavacca route, none could speak the Spanish or Portuguese, nor did he speak any of the Indian languages of my crew to suppose that he had entered in a conspiracy with them. I thought therefore it would be really heedless to take not his advice which appeared to be so honestly tendered and much against my will the Cassiquiare route was determined upon.

Thirty nine years had now elapsed since M. de Humboldt visited Esmeralda and found in the most solitary and remote Christian settlement on the upper Orinoco a population of eighty souls. The cross before the village showed still that its inhabitants professed to be Christians, but their number had dwindled to a single family, a patriarch with his children, grandchildren, sons and daughters in law. Of the six Houses which we found standing several were far advanced in decay and only three inhabited; but their plastered walls and massive well-finished doors, showed that not Indians had erected them. Before the building which we took to have been once the Church or convent, we noted a small bell hung up in the Gallery, it bore the inscription San Francisco Deasis Capp. 1769. Whatever the changes might have been which time and circumstances produced in Human works Nature had remained the same. Still raises Duida its lofty summit to the Clouds and savannahs interspersed with tufts of trees and the majestic Mauritia Palm stretched from the banks of the Orinoco to its foot and gives to the landscape that lofty and animated appearance, which so much delighted Humboldt when he viewed Esmeralda. A ridge of hillocks formed of heaped up boulders of granite, which represent the most grotesque forms or take the appearance of vast edifices in ruins, occupies the foreground and at the foot of this ridge, which is called Caquire, Esmeralda is situated. some pious hand has planted on the largest of the granitic blocks a cross – its airy form stands boldly in relief with the Blue Sky as background and heightens the picturesque appearance of the surrounding Scenery. It calls to mind that though nature and Man appear in savage state, there are still some in this wilderness, who adore the Deity and confess the Saviour crucified.

The highest point of the Duida is according to M. de Humboldt's measurement 7147 feet above the savannah*

*M. de Humboldt measured a baseline directed towards the Summit of the mountain in order to ascertain the height of Duida. I measured a baseline 2174 feet in length which run

[1] This is presumably the M. Arnott, referred to earlier (see p. 343).
[2] That is, Mavaca.

parallel with the mountain. The horizontal distance proved 44787 feet the double vertical angles at the extremities 18°8′37″ and 17°55′13″. The result of my admeasurements was at point A 7145 feet, at point B 7155 feet. This agrees so closely with M. de Humboldt's admeasurement that it appears almost accidental; it is the more remarkable, since the operations were carried on with the sextant.

or 8278 feet above the sea. The Indians of the rivers Paramu, Cunucumu, the Maiongkong or Maquiritares, in general call the Duida Yeonnamari, while they name Esmeralda Mirara which is very likely only a corruption of the former name. Towards the W.N.W. the mountains rise gently to the estimated height of 2000 feet, clothed with dense forests, from thence succeeded rocky cliffs, only here and there covered sparely with vegetation. The ridge extends in sinuous outlines towards the loftiest summit which bears N.30°W. from the village. Its lesser declivity likewise covered with wood, an unshapen rocky mass rises boldly to 4660 feet higher than the dense wood from which it elevates itself under such a high angle that it is impossible for a human being to climb the summit. From this point the range bends over to the NEb.E throwing out buttresses and escarpments which produce the semblance of a vast fortress. This similitude is increased by the low ridge of heaped boulders in the foreground, which imagination may form in the advanced circumvallations line of the gigantic works behind, works worthy of a race to attempt a second storm of Mount Olympus.[1] The most northern point of the Duida bears N.8°E. distant about 10 miles from Esmeralda, but another rocky mass of more wall like form rises Northward of Duida and stretches E & W leaning with its eastern arm on the river Paramu[;] further Northward follow the Mountains Wataba Siru, Ekui, Mariacca, Satawacca, and Marawacca, belonging all to the same system, the latter without doubt being the highest among them, and not less than 10,000 feet above the sea. Having ascertained that Roraima and the adjacent mountains consist of quartzose sandstone and that the Marittani and Sarisharima mountains as well as Paba belong to the same group, analogy deduced from the similarity of their appearance, told me to suppose that Marawacca were also formed of sandstone, and the specimens that Mr. Morrison brought from that mountain verified my supposition. Duida which evidently belonged to the same group could not be different although M. de Humboldt states it to be granitic, it wanted however proofs. An excursion to that part of the mountain where the dense wood ceases and the rocky mass rises almost perpendicularly was therefore undertaken & as in the former case it was found that as at Marawacca the sandstone rested on granite below and formed from thence the rest of the mountain. The specimens which were brought from here, were taken about 150 feet above that point where the mass commences to rise under a high angle, and the height was climbed not without danger by means of the scanty vegetation which covered the cliff. Numerous veins of quartz traverse this sandstone in divers directions and are analogous to those of the Crystal Mountains near Roraima. Thus a second error was committed with regard to the Duida when it was stated to be a granitic mass. The first gave celebrity and its name to Esmeralda[;] the rock crystals and chloritic quartzes which we find likewise among the sandstone group of Roraima, having been mistaken for Diamonds and Emeralds; although resting upon granite the upper part of the Cerro for a height of from 4000 to 5000 feet consists of quartzose sandstone. The small ridge

---

[1] A reference to the war between the Olympians and the Giants in Greek mythology in which the latter tried to storm heaven by piling Pelion upon Ossa.

Caquire the highest elevation of which does not amount above 200 feet, is formed as I already observed of heaped up boulders. These boulders are granite interspersed with large pieces of quartz of highly crystalline nature and veins of the same rock traverse frequently the boulders. Spots of dazzling whiteness are observable along the precipitous declivities of Duida when the atmosphere is clear and the sun reflects his rays on its walls, they consist no doubt of quartz, and the numerous fragments which are found at its foot on the savannahs and in the beds of streams which flow from it side, prove how frequent this mineral is. A very lovely prospect presents itself from the cross which has been raised on the large block of granite, to the north the high mountains their outline strong and bold near the spectator, and softening to the blueish tint of the atmosphere the further they receded. The course of the Orinoco upwards, could be traced for a considerable distance. A few isolated rounded hillocks of inconsiderable height rise on both sides of its banks, and others of similar form and height were observable to the West, otherwise dense forests covered the plains. Nearer to the observer was the village with its deserted appearance, the noon tide heat and prodigious swarms of sand flies,*

> *English Colonists misname generally the gnat of the Tropics Musquito. The Musquito a small fly as its name bespeaks, is a Species of Simulia, and is called in the Colonies Sandfly; the gnat or Zancudo of the Spaniards is a Culex.

kept the few inhabitants ensconsed in their houses; from the village stretch savannahs to the Orinoco, a few stunted trees, and where moisture had collected some Mauritia palms rise above the grass which formed a thick carpet. Numerous tumuli of a species of Termes, black like the soil of which they are erected and from three to four feet high, form too remarkable an object to be overlooked. Alluding to the converts which M de Humboldt found at Esmeralda during his visit he says "that they lived in great poverty and that their miseries were augmented by large swarms of musquitoes.".[1] The same observation holds still good, there was every evidence that the inhabitants were poor, and the number of sand flies, which proved from first dawn to the setting in of night, an unceasing torment, surpassed whatever I had seen in that respect. "Thus it is with us the whole year, and during the winter season, we are equally plagued at night by Gnats," said old Antonio. How can man endure these unceasing torments? and what interest can attach him to a place, where his stay is connected with such tortures? They are not accustomed to their bites by usage as we saw them as much occupied as ourselves to drive these bloodsuckers from their hands face and feet. In order to protect themselves in some regard while in their houses, they have a kind of latticed door before the entrance to each house, constructed of fine pieces of Palm wood, which admits light whilst it keeps in some respect the insects out. The house which we occupied not possessing such a commodity, I substituted my musquito netting, which answered the purpose still better. Old Antonio and his family did not cultivate the grounds near the vicinity of Esmeralda, he does not consider the soil fit for ground provisions, as worn out by long usage, their provision grounds are several miles distant. As he heard that our stay was to be from two to three days, he embarked in his canoe and promising to return the following evening, he started off for plantains. Good as his word we saw him make his appearance the next day, with some fine bunches of plantains, and a small basket

---

[1] Humboldt's description of Esmeralda is to be found in *Personal Narrative*, II, 1907, Chapter XXIV, and although there are frequent references to the swarms of mosquitoes and the poverty of the inhabitants, Schomburgk's words seem to be a paraphrase rather than a direct citation.

with the golden fruit of the Hesperides,[1] oranges and limes the first an unexpected delicacy to us, the second highly welcome to season our meals. He brought likewise some Brazil nuts and a fruit which he called Pentari – it was yellow, round, the size of a small apple and of a highly delicious flavor. I consider it a Sapotaceae, nevertheless I could not discover the bony seeds of that tribe indeed the whole inside was soft.

A line is drawn under the manuscript at this point and it is marked 'End'. In fact it continues to the foot of that page and the next page (pp. 161–2) with a summary of the journey from Esmeralda back to Georgetown. This is not included here as the full report is the subject of the JMS 6/29(f) that now follows. There are also to be found at this point some pages which belong with the papers relating to the first expedition and consist of notes concerning observations and collections and four pages which belong at the end of JMS 6/29(f) and have been returned there for this edition.

Manuscript JMS 6/29(f) had no original heading, but was given the editorial title 'Journey from Esmeralda on the Orinoco by the Cassiquiare to San Carlos, descent of the Rio Negro to Moura, ascent of the Rio Branco to Fort San Joaquim & return by the Essequibo to George Town, Demerara in March, April & May 1839'. It was received by the Royal Geographical Society on 16 March 1840, by which time Schomburgk had been back in Europe, and mainly in London, for six months. It is probably safe to assume therefore that it was written in London, and this may well explain why it is so much neater than any of the earlier manuscripts. It is in a copyist's handwriting with corrections and additions in Schomburgk's own hand, and these have all been included in the transcription provided here. The manuscript consists of ninety pages, but once again the actual numbering of the pages and their order are not straightforward; and as before these features will be noted where they occur. The report appeared in the *Journal of the Royal Geographical Society*, 10, 1841, pp. 248–67, under the title 'Journey from Esmeralda, on the Orinoco, to San Carlos and Moura on the Rio Negro, and thence by Fort San Joaquim to Demerara, in the Spring of 1839'. The published version is different from the manuscript mainly owing to numerous deletions from the latter and other editorial changes.

JOURNEY FROM ESMERALDA ON THE ORINOCO BY THE CASSIQUIARE TO SAN CARLOS, DESCENT OF THE RIO NEGRO TO MOURA, ASCENT OF THE RIO BRANCO TO FORT SAN JOAQUIM & RETURN BY THE ESSEQUIBO TO GEORGE TOWN, DEMERARA IN MARCH, APRIL & MAY 1839

Feby 25.[2] Our new canoe was finished this morning and rendered comparatively comfortable for the long journey we had before us. It was partly covered by a tent made of palm leaves and its size allowed us to look for a better protection of our luggage in

---

[1] In Greek mythology, the Hesperides were the daughters of Hesperus, who, with the aid of a dragon, guarded the garden on the Isle of the Blest in which golden apples grew. It is also the name for a class of plants which includes the orange family.

[2] The first four pages of the manuscript are numbered 87–90, and are actually the last four of it. They have been returned to that position in this transcription.

cases of rain. We left at one o'clock under many salutations from old Antonio who according to his circumstances had acted very hospitably towards us and our Indians. I had bought a sufficient stock of provisions to last us for ten days and hoped therefore to reach San Carlos in nine days. The Orinoco bears the same features westward of Esmeralda is it does Eastward of that village[;] numerous sandbanks frequently impeded our progress.

We passed successively the rivers and brooks Mantari, Cura, Sodomoni, and Tamatama;[1] the latter is almost currentless and resembles more an inlet than a river; before the Orinoco receives its waters, it forms a basin like expansion being on its S.W. side narrowed in by two ledges of rock of which the one on the right bank is called Solomoni the other Aracavacari. After having issued through this narrow the Orinoco expands again, takes a Western course (S.7°W.) and forms at the distance of 7 miles the remarkable bifurcation. The river divides namely in two arms the principal branch continues W.N.W. (the first reach N.74°W) and turns round the Sierra Parima while the lesser called the Cassiquiare or Cassisiare flows off southward to the Rio Negro. Baron Humboldt has given too explicit an explanation of this bifurcation which connects the Orinoco directly with the Rio Negro, as to elucid anything new from my observations; however it must be observed that the river Orinoco does not issue directly from a mountain chain where it forms this remarkable communication with the Rio Negro, but has been flowing for more than fifty miles through a comparative low country. The chain of which the mountains Maravacca and Duida are the highest elevations border its right or northern bank after it has been joined by the Paramu and as the stream could not affect a break through the formidable barriers it adopted a far western course to its bifurcation, the general direction from its sources having been previously W.N.W. Duida was enveloped in clouds and distant thunder spoke of an approaching storm: it prevented me from ascertaining its bearing from the mouth of the Cassiquiare it is about N.E. The width of the Cassiquiare when it flows off is only 100 yards, its current was sluggish, and did not amount to .7′ or 1.2 feet in a second. It winds in short turns southward, its banks are high covered with dense vegetation, but the trees by no means striking in height. Numerous high bushes of a species of Laurus called Siruabally in Demerara, the prickly Sawarai palm (Astrocaryum Jauari) girded the banks. The river was quite shallow frequently obstructed by sandbanks and studded with granite rocks and we found that our progress was not so quick as I could have wished. It will be recollected that M[r]. Vieth and M[r]. Le Breton proceeded direct from São Joaquim to the Rio Negro, they were to await me at Bararoa but as I could not foresee, whether circumstances might force me to change my route entirely, I ordered them in case I should not have arrived by the first of April to return to São Joaquim and, naturally anxious to arrive before their departure we had to use every despatch which geographical survey permitted.

Feb. 26th We passed the small streams Caripo and Pamoni[2] which joined the river from the East. South of Pamoni, I observed on some granite rocks, several figures consisting of circles and right lines – they were the first which I had seen during this Expedition; none were observed during our journey from Pirara to the Orinoco.[3]

---

[1] The Río Sodomoni and Caño Tamatama, both right-bank tributaries of the Orinoco are marked on the reference map (Sheet NA-20–IV), but the Mantari and Cura are not.

[2] Caño Caripo and Río Pamoni.

[3] While strictly correct, see p. 326 above.

Feby 27 & 28th The river without having much increased in width preserved its monotony. We measured the Current opposite the Curamini[1] but found it not different from the Mouth. South of the Curamini the Cassiquiare is stated to form an other Natural Canal with the Rio Negro, called the Itinivini, but this communication exists only during the rainy season when the waters of the Orinoco rush with impetuosity towards the Rio Negro and fill the bed of the Cassiquiare to overflowing. It was at this period that Baron de Humboldt ascended the Cassiquiare and found its current from 6 to 8 feet and even 11 feet 8 inches in a second and observed that there existed another communication through the Itinivini with the Rio Negro. In Feby 1839 when we passed it the water of the Cassiquiare appeared above the junction of the River Siapa frequently currentless and the banks where the Itinivini is said to flow off where from 10 to 12 feet above the level of the water.[2] Our camp was this evening in Lat 2°28'3"N. & Longt 66°43'6". The river flows now more eastward, its course being often eccentric and turns toward all quarters of the Compass. We passed in the morning of the 1st of March the outflows of the Lake Vasiva; they had black waters and the last reach of the principal outflow before it joins the Casiquiare is N69°E.

The Casiquiare like the Rupununi and Berbice possess numerous inlets several of them have been marked as rivers, of that description are Cuinuzaura, Dorotamaze merely currentless inlets of only a few miles extent. The brooks Catarico, Carie, Mumuni join from the rivers right bank or its western side, they have all black water and were generally from 2 to 3° colder than the Cassiquiare; this is no doubt to be ascribed to their being narrow and shaded by trees which scarcely admit the sun to have direct influence on the water. A large granite boulder, a little inside on the eastern bank, was remarkable for its size, it just overtopped the surrounding trees; the heights of which I estimated from 50 to 60 feet.

March 2nd A bar of granite rocks and several Islands obstruct the river and shut up one of the passages completely. This passage we had unfortunately selected and had to return to choose an other one.

At the distance 2 miles from these Islands, the direction being S7°W the river Siapa joins the Cassiquiare, its last reach being N85°E. The Siapa, Suapa, or Idapa which has its scources in the mountains Unturan is called by the Indians Durawacca. According to the information which I procured at Quirabuena it is much obstructed by falls and rapids which make its ascent uncommon laborious, even in small crafts, while larger ones can only frequent the river during the rainy season.

It scources are in the very heart of the Sarsaparilla country and though it is stated that the black waters of some of the inland rivers owe their colour to the roots of the Sarsaparilla the Siapa has nevertheless light coloured waters, scarcely a tint darker than those of the Cassiquiare. The Indians of Demerara where there is no Sarsaparilla attribute the black colour of some their rivers to the roots of Greenheart a valuable timber tree and a species of Laurus. The Siapa is abouth 150 yards wide at its mouth, and its Latitude is according to my observations 2°7'49"N. The Cassiquiare before it receives the

---

[1] There is an area called Curamoni marked on the reference map (Sheet NA-19–I), and to the west of it the Río Guaramoni.

[2] The Itinivini or the Caño Conorichite, as Humboldt also refers to it. It is marked on the reference map as a tributary of the Rio Guiania which rises near the Cassiquiare canal. It would appear that it does not connect directly with the Cassiquiare and that a short portage is required.

Siapa takes for the last 8 miles a far eastern course. A little southward of its mouth is an island with a solitary house on its northern point; it appeared uninhabited, but we met soon after some canoes with Indians who told us that we were only a short distance from Quirabuena the first village in the Cassiquiare.

We soon afterward landed there; it is situated on the rivers left bank and consists of about twenty houses. Quirabuena is likewise called Mandavacca. The principal houses form a square, the northern side of which is occupied by the church, a small but neat building, with plastered walls the roof thatched with palm leaves and a Portico in front. The houses of the Indians and Spanish Creoles who live here, consist likewise of plastered walls and thatched roofs; they have generally only one room and the interior bespeaks poverty. The Indians are from the Pauula and Marianna nation,[1] and though I believe that many were absent, I do not think there number amounts to more than eighty. We were met on shore by some of the Spanish or rather Colombian Creoles, the offspring of an Indian mother and the descendants of the former Spaniards. They lost no time to inform us that they were Patriots,[2] and after this preamble, numerous questions were put to us with the aim to satisfy their curiosity from whence we came and what led us here, and though we did everything to give them a description of our route, it nevertheless remained a riddle to them how we could have come from Demerara across the mountains to the Paramu or Padamo. They were well dressed in the attire of men of their class, but as something extraordinary though perhaps Spanish custom, their shirt sleeves were provided with ornamental trimming. I accompanied them to the huts of the Indians which though they exhibited no opulence but bespoke poverty, were kept clean & neat. The inmates were variously employed, some were spinning cotton, others fabricating hammocks, or a coarse kind of pottery of a whitish clay, which apparently is frequent along the Cassiquiare and alternates often with a red ochreous clay. The chief occupation of the inhabitants is however the fabrication of Hawsers and ropes which are made of the fibres of the Chique-chique palm (Attalea funifera),*[3]

*For this purpose large sheds are created for the manufacture of these ropes which they call Cabuja.

and during the high waters when the trade with the interior is most flourishing they are transported to Angostura. Their sale procures the fabricator the necessities of life for the ensuing year; his whole pride consists in exhibiting on Sundays and at the arrival of Strangers a fine suit of clothes. We were told that the Captain of the place was absent and that they had despatched a canoe to inform him of our arrival. His house was separate from the Square, larger than the others but the interior did not offer any differance

---

[1] No other reference has been found to the Pauula. T. J. O'Leary, *Ethnographic Bibliography of South America*, New Haven, Human Relations Area Files, 1963, lists two groups called Mariana; one part of the Witoto or Uitoto people of the eastern lowlands of Colombia and the north-eastern region of the Peruvian Amazon; the other part of the Yurimagua on the mainstream of the Amazon. On the other hand, they may be phratries of the Arawakan people who inhabit the area.

[2] Patriots were those opposed to Spain in the struggle for independence.

[3] The popular name for the *Attalea funifera* is Piaçaba. Chiquechique or Xiquexique is the vernacular name for Piaçabeira (*Leopoldina piassaba*) which is also used to make cordage. The name is also applied to a cactus found in the north-east of Brazil and for various species of the Genus *Crotalaria*, a member of the Family Fabaceae. See M. P. Corrêa, *Dicionário das plantas úteis do Brasil e das exóticas cultivadas*, 6 vols, Rio de Janeiro, Imprensa Nacional, 1926–78.

from the generality of the houses. He heads the Company of Militia which the fencible men of the four villages of the Cassiquiare form. While we were conversing three strokes of the bell announced noon; every one of the bystanders drew their hats and crossing themselves pronounced their Ave Maria's. Since the Revolution, the public cultus is left to the municipalities and they being so poor that they cannot maintain a priest, the whole service consists in recitals there being few who can read. There is at present from Angostura to San Carlos, no missionary in any of the villages even not in San Fernando de Atabapo, where formerly the president of the twenty six ecclesiastical establishments resided which at Humboldt's visit were at the banks of the Orinoco, Rio Negro, Cassiquiare, and Caura; the "good fathers" as they are still called by those whose recollection bears them back to the period of the mission, fled by the Cassiquiare and Rio Negro when the insurrection broke lose and returned to Europe. A travelling priest from Angostura which is at a distance of 900 Miles from these Villages pays them a visit at intervals of two or three years, and performs the necessary ceremonies of marrying and christening, and this is the only period when they hear mass performed by consecrated priest in their own church.

Opposite the village the Cassiquiare forms a rapid, it is however not formidable. The inhabitants informed me that the Cassiquiare rises 15 feet during inundations and an embankment as well as the higher situation of the village which is not less than 25 feet above low water, protects it completely. It was three o'clock, and as at that period the Captain had not arrived as yet, we had to depart without satisfying our curiosity what kind of personage he was.

I was anxious that day to reach S^t. Crux a village on the rivers right side. We landed there at Sunset[.] S^t. Crux is a late establishment having been removed from the banks of the Pacimoni.[1] It consists only of twelve huts and a few sheds for the manufacture of the Cabuja but few of the huts were built of clay the majority being merely constructed of Palm leaves. Fire had laid lately four houses in ashes. We were led to the Case del rey or King's house; by this pompous name a hut was designated which is destined for the accommodation of strangers and though events have converted the Colony into a republic the title has remained with the populace, and only the stanch republican, to whom even the allusion to any thing royal is irksome calls it the public house. We found our palace to consist of four naked walls and a few posts to fix our hammocks to. Every Settlement possesses a house of that kind and it is even previous to the erection of a place of worship thought of. This was the case in S^t. Cruz which did not possess a church – it appeared they wanted to make it up by crosses, and I accounted six large wooden crosses in different directions of the village. The people appeared to be so poor that they could not procure any provisions and we were comforted to our arrival at Solano[2] a whole days journey from S^t. Cruz. The Alcade estimated the population to 80 souls the Indians are from the nation of the Pacimonales.[3] We found the Latitude of S^t. Cruz 1°57′49″N.

March 3rd We started as usually before daylight; a fine moon affording sufficient light to steer clear of rocks and sandbanks. When day commenced to dawn we were

[1] Río Pasimoni.

[2] A place of that name still exists.

[3] Presumably a name deriving from the River Pacimoni or Pasimoni. Loukotka, *Classification of South American Indian Languages*, p. 229, places Pacimonari among the unclassified and unknown languages and notes it was 'once spoken on the lower course of the Siapa River, Amazonas territory, Venezuela'.

astonished by prodigious swarms of Ephemera or day flies. They directed their flight against the stream along the whole breadth of the river and the finny tribe anxious to secure such a delicate morsel, were seen in all directions to skip out of the water and to shorten the scanty time of existence allotted to the day fly. At the distance of 35 miles[1] from the village of S[t]. Cruz, joins the river Pacimoni the Cassiquiare from the east; its last reach being N79E its water is black and I estimated its width at its mouth from 280 to 300 yards. The flowing stream was narrowed in by numerous sandbanks from both sides impeding its course as far as we could see up the river. This sand is of a snowy whiteness and, contrasts strongly with the dark water. A solitary rock of gigantic size was observable from the mouth of the Pacimoni this rock was as we afterwards ascertained Humboldt's Piedra de Culimacari[2] which the present inhabitants of the Cassiquiare call Cerra Vanari. We halted two hours after at the village Buena Vista on the left bank of the Cassiquiare, it consisted of a square of twelve houses, the church occupying one side. A large crowd of people, all in their best attire, collected round us and stared with wonder at us and our Canoe. The population appeared to me larger here than in the two villages, which we had passed the preceeding day, and they distinguished themselves by greater forwardness and impertinence. While in Quirabuena and S[t]. Cruz they remained in respectful distance, they stormed I might say in Buena Vista our Canoe, taking completely possession of it and rumaging the baggage of the Indians, and only our presence prevented them from entering the tent and doing alike with our chattels.

At the distance of five miles from Buena Vista or thirteen miles in a western direction from the Pacimoni is on the left bank of the Casiquiare a highly remarkable granite rock which as already observed, Humboldt names Piedra de Culimacari, but which at present bears the name Vanari. Its chief Mass constitutes a gigantic boulder the height of which I estimated 150 feet, it is almost entirely naked and only here and there has a bush fixed its roots in the crevices, but at its foot reigns a thicket of Bamboos, Palms, Lianas &c. impenetrable without axe and cutlasses. While the chief mass astonishes by its size and circumference, some boulders to the right of it cause amazement by their peculiar figure. The one much less in circumference at the base than at the top, rises for upwards of forty feet, and bears on its summit another boulder. I might resemble this rock in appearance to Cleopatra's needle.[3] Partly on it reclines another boulder, larger than the former which bears likewise a second of smaller size on its summit, a third one which is isolated is somewhat to the right of the two former, less in size and less remarkable in figure. It was in the neighbourhood of this granitic mass that M. de Humboldt found opportunity to determine the Longitude & Latitude of the Cassiquiare, and its situation was according to his observations in 2°42″N. Lat & 67°13′26″W Long[t], and from these astronomical data he deduced the geographical situation of the confluence of the Cassiquiare with the Guainia and Fort San Carlos. I had been very attentive to the different courses of the Cassiquiare while descending it

---

[1] This figure has been underlined and in the margin has been written ' – ?3/'and the figure '3' occurs in the published version (p. 249). This is almost certainly correct and it is possible that the figure on the manuscript should have read 3.5.

[2] See Humboldt, *Personal Narrative*, II, 1907, pp. 409–10. On the reference map it is marked as Piedra Guanare o Culimacare.

[3] In the margin at this point an unidentified hand has reasonably queried 'why so'.

and with the exception of the first night after leaving Esmeralda, I have found opportunity to take every night observations for Latitude – while therefore my Latitude differed only 25 seconds from that determined by M. de Humboldt I was sorry to find a difference of 9 minutes 38 seconds (in degrees) in our Longitude. I should have adopted unhesitatingly M. de Humboldts determination of the Longitude of the rock Culimacari, if he himself had possessed better confidence in the observations which he procured for time and Longitude at that situation, and the error appears more plainly as Solano is laid down 21 miles West of Culimacari, nevertheless this distinguished traveller informs us, that he left the mission of San Francisco Solano at a late hour to make a short days journey* and rested at five in the evening+

*Humboldts personal narrative Vol V p 408[1]
+Ibid p 412.

near the Piedra de Culimacari. If the relative situation of San Francisco Solano and the above rock had been therefore correct, he would have made in that short period, twenty one miles, while at page 419 he tells us, that with all the activity of the rowers they could make in 14 hours only three leagues or nine miles.[2]

We landed towards sunset at the Village San Francisco Solano situated on the left side of the Cassiquiare. It is larger than Quirabuena but not so neatly built. The Indians are from the Cheruvichahenas.[3] The Square which likewise here, as in the other villages is kept clean and neat, has more an oblong form the church which occupies the Northern side is larger and we observed two bells, they hung too high to read their inscription. Our residence the royal house was likewise more extensive and had a kitchen attached to it, a table and bench were its furniture. The night was clear and I procured observations for Latitude according to which San Francisco Solano is 1°57′49″N.[4]

March 4th When day dawned we were already 3 to 4 miles from Solano. The preceding morning we were diverted about the same period by large swarms of Ephemera and we were today astonished by large numbers of goatsuckers (Caprimulgus) of white plumage spotted near the tail with black. Like the Ephemera they ascended the river. The Cassiquiare widens considerably on approaching its junction with the Guainia, and several Islands run along its right bank, and large bars of granite impede its course and allow only here and there an issue to the stream. At its mouth is a small Island on the left bank with a hut on its north eastern point. Though the waters of the Cassiquiare are much darker since they received those of the Pacimoni, they are far surpassed in darkness by those of the Guainia, and the sandy banks being in the latter of dazzling

[1] This is the first occasion on which Schomburgk gives a page reference when referring to Humboldt's *Personal Narrative*. Schomburgk used Helen Maria Williams's seven-volume 1814–29 translation of this work and all future page references in the text are taken from these volumes. This English translation, which is rather rare, is much fuller than the 1851 translation of Thomasina Ross, used in the editorial commentary and annotations.

[2] Humboldt, *Personal Narrative*, II, 1907, p. 410, gives the coordinates of Culimacare as 2°0′42″N and 69°33′50″W, whereas the rock, as shown on the reference map, is at approximately 66°48′W and just south of 2°N latitude. The distance between Solano and Culimacare is, in a straight line, about nine miles as measured on the reference map.

[3] No other reference has been found to the Cheruvichachenas, but they are likely to be a phratry of the Arawakan peoples of the region.

[4] This is very close to its position as marked on the reference map.

whiteness, they contrast very strongly with the dark surface of the water. From the confluence of the Casiquiare with the Guainia the river is called Rio Negro. The course of the Cassiquiare its windings included is from the bifurcation at the Orinoco to its mouth 176 Geog. Miles its Latitude 1°59′1″N. According to information received in San Carlos the four Villages Quirabuena or Mandavaca, St Cruz, Buena Vista & San Francisco de Solano, contain a population of 500 souls

The river Guainia comes from the N.W; though its last reach before it receives the Cassiquiare comes from N10E while the Cassiquiare comes from S61°W;[1] they form therefore at their confluence an angle of 129°. There is not much difference in the width of both rivers before they have united. The Guainia being not more than 50 to 60 yards wider; while I estimated the Cassiquiare at its mouth about 550 yards. I found the current of the Rio Negro sluggish, carrying the log only 32.5 feet in 15 seconds, the time in absence of a watch being measured by a simple pendulum 39⅓ inches in length; it must be however considered that the river was near its lowest level.

Two hours after we had entered the Rio Negro we landed at San Carlos; having passed between the right bank of the river and the Island of Mibita we had avoided the rapids of Uinumane. We were received on landing by Don Diego de Pina, Justice of Peace to the District. We put up at the Casa real or Casa Publica as the Justice pointedly observed when I named it by the former apellation. Though arriving at an early hour, I had resolved to stay that day not only for the purpose of providing our-selves with some necessaries, which I intended to procure in San Carlos, but chiefly under the hope of being able of procuring observations for Latitude. The village San Carlos del Rio Negro consists of 40 houses and a population of 400 souls, consist-ing chiefly of Indians from the Paniba Pure and Guarichina tribes,[2] the number of Zambos is inconsiderable and there are neither Negroes nor Mulattos. The square is not so regular as that at Quirabuena, but the church is much larger and has a well finished Portico; it occupies the eastern side of the square two streets on each side of the square running E. and W. The community under an Inspector appeared to be occupied in throwing up embankments and cleaning the village in every direction. This act of public labour was an uncommon sight to us – it is strange to the Indian who when necessary works for himself but not for the public good. On the right bank of the Rio Negro and opposite San Carlos is Fort Agostinho, it forms a square with bastions but in such a neglected state that the bushes which have grown up around it, almost cover it. The Cannons which are of Iron, are dismounted and the carriages in perfect decay. Without Commandant or garrison, its defence in case of necessity is left to the Militia of the district under their proper Commander. The low intrigues of the republic do not extend to these distant frontiers, they live in amity with the neighbouring territories, and there is every likelihood that the bushes will become trees and no axe be required for felling them to put the fort which they at present shade, into a state of defence.

---

[1] These directions are queried in the margin. In fact the Guainia does flow from a few degrees east of north just before the confluence, whereas the Cassiquiare flows towards, rather than comes from, the direction given. Accordingly the angle of their confluence is much less than given.

[2] The Paniba are almost certainly the Baniwa and the Pure the Baré; these are the two large Arawakan groups of the region. The Guarichina are probably the Guariquena, listed by O'Leary (*Ethnographic Bibliog-raphy*) as living in this region and closely related to the two former groups.

According to a trigonometrical admeasurement the breadth of the Rio Negro opposite to San Carlos is 1846 feet; I was shewn the mark on the embankment to which the river rises when it is highest; it amounted to about 15 feet, the period of its highest stand is the month of August. I did not succeed to procure any additional information to what M. de Humboldt observes about the upper part of the Guainia though Don Diego de Piná had travelled a great deal in the interior and had made it the object of his inquiry – he had not succeeded to procure any information which could be depended upon. Among other journeys which he performed he visited likewise the Raudal de Guaharibos,[1] the pillars of Hercules as M de Humboldt names them. The Guaharibos have retired further eastward and bear still the character of a hostile nation opposed to any stranger entering their territory, be it of their own colour, or be it European. The river, says Don Diego, is in the vicinity of the Raudale scarcely more than hundred yards wide and lessens considerably above the Raudal; the Rio Gehette being the last river of any consequence which enters the Orinoco. He argues perfectly with me that the Orinoco adopts a northern course from the Raudal. His ideas however with regard to its origin were still those of D'Anville.[2] He thought it issued from the Lake Parima. My journey has removed all doubts with regards to that point and it thanks its origin neither to a Lake Parima or Ipaca, but solely to a thickly wooded mountain chain. We know likewise that the river Parima or Rio Branco has its sources in the same chain or rather mountain from whence the Orinoco issues.

March 6th We had no native Pilot in our boat, we passed therefore the Island of San José[3] which forms the provisional boundary between the Brazils and the Republic Venezuela, without knowing it. Large Columns of Smoke which we saw issuing from a rocky Island, made us curious to ascertain the cause, it was a fishing Expedition from San Carlos, consisting of upwards of sixty individuals, men women and children and eleven corials and canoes. We landed sometime after at the solitary hut of Senhor Cordeiro, formerly a Lieutenant in the Militia, but who at the commencement of the Cabanno-war fled from S[t]. Isabel by the rivers Marawiha,[4] Pacimoni and Siapa to San Carlos.[5] He has since visited the mountain chain of these rivers a second time in search of sarsaparilla, and the information which I received from him about these regions is of the greatest importance.

Some time before we reached Senhor Cordeiro's habitation, we had observed a singular mountain which bore then S.28E., it appeared isolated and ended in three peaks, this was mount Cocui,[6] we did not reach it that day, night approached when we were only a few miles from it; our Latitude was 1°18′26″N.

March 7th We passed Cocui early in the morning; it is situated about a mile from the left bank of the river and consists of granite, its height was estimated from 8 to 900 feet. Steep and shelfy towards the south, no vegetation covers that side, on its eastern and western sides low bushes and a few trees are to be observed – it is a huge granite mass

---

[1] Raudal de Guajaribos. Guaharibo is yet another name, although rarely used today, for the Yanomami. These falls are on the upper Orinoco at approximately 2°17′N, 64°37′W.

[2] A reference to Jean-Baptiste d'Anville's map of 1760.

[3] Still so called on the Venezuelan reference map.

[4] Rio Marauiá. St Isabel is on the Rio Negro near the mouth of the Marauiá

[5] It is not clear whether this is the same Cordeiro who was commandant of Fort São Joaquim when Schomburgk first visited in the Rupununi in 1835 (see p. 62 above).

[6] Piedra del Cocuy.

the summit divided in three peaks when viewed from the NW., but when seen from the West, one of the peaks is hid and only two are observable. Its shelfy masses and almost perpendicular walls give it however from that side a more picturesque appearance. This mountain was the seat of the celebrated Cocui, who about the middle of the last century was chieftain of the Manitivitanos Indians,[1] a man famed in the traditions of the country for his cruelty and debaucheries. He was the implacable enemy of the Jesuits, and devastated their missions. A cavern is still shown at the mountain which has received its name, where he is said to have had its large harem, and where, as you are greatly assured by the inhabitants of these regions, he occasionally satisfied a peculiar predilection and devoured the finest and fattest of his concubines.[2]

Dr. Natterer[3] of Vienna who ascended the Rio Negro to the junction of the Cassiquiare, climbed to the summit of the mountain. M. de Humboldt when in 1800 at San Carlos met the son of Cocui, who was then Captain of the Indians of that village. The illustrious traveller assigning for the geographical position of Cocui, 1°40′N. which is 22 miles too far north of its real position.[4] An other mountain of less height is situated about a mile north-east of Cocui – it is remarkable for a huge boulder on its southern side. We observed in the afternoon a Chain of Mountains, the southwestern angle of which bore then S34°E. they were the mountains of the river Cababuri.[5] Threatened with a thunderstorm we used every despatch to reach Marabitana, and landed there at two oclock in the afternoon just in time to escape the weather.

San José de Marabitana, the frontier fort of the Brazilian territory, has a very neat appearance, when approaching from the north; the little fort and church occupy the middle and a row of houses extend along the banks of the river. The fort consists of mud embankments, palisaded around, and is defended by eight cannons of iron, two of which were English, they bearing the royal crown and the initials GR. The quartel or barracks occupied the southern side; it was a comfortable building and might have accommodated from fifty to sixty men. The Sergeant who acts as Commandant is from the line; the soldiers six in number are from the militia and settled with wife and children at Marabitana.

I succeeded to procure four observations of stars of northern and southern Declinations, the means of which gave me for the Latitude of San José de Marabitana 0°56′7″N. this differs from the extant maps 16 miles in Latitude. Marabitana being namely too far north from its situation. The somewhat elevated situation of the Fort offered a more extensive view than from the village. The Pirabuku mountains near the River Cababuri bore from here from East to S.30E., their distance being about 30 miles; isolated mountains like Cocui appeared to form the link of communication between the Cordillera where the northern tributaries of the Rio Negro have their sources and the mountains of the Sierra Tunuhy, near the sources of the Xié, Isanna,[6]

---

[1] No other reference has been found to the Manitivitanos but they were probably part of the Arawakan population of the region.

[2] This passage is very similar to that to be found in Humboldt, *Personal Narrative*, II, 1907, p. 392.

[3] Johann Natterer (1787–1843), an Austrian zoologist, spent eighteen years (1817–35) undertaking scientific explorations in Brazil. He was on the Rio Negro in 1830–31.

[4] According to the reference map Cocuy is on about 1°12′N.

[5] Probably Rio Cauaburi.

[6] Also spelt Içana.

and the left bank of the Uaupes. The Rio Negro takes from Marabitana for about 27 miles a western course, and turns only towards the South from the mouth of the River Xié. It receives six miles from Marabitana the small river Mahuala and two miles further the river Dimiti;[1] the latter has its sources near those of the Maturacca and by means of two streams, one a tributary of the Maturacca, the other of the Dimiti and a small portage, the Indians of the Rio Negro, Xie, and Isanna carry on a lively intercourse with those of the Maturacca, Cababuri, and of the whole Mountain Chain in that direction. I enquired likewise here about the direct communication between the Cababuri and Pacimoni, but the Indians of Marabitana were entirely ignorant of it, though some of them said they had ascended the Dimiti and visited the Indians of the Cababuri and Marawiha.

We halted a little while North west of the river Xie to exchange our pilot. We had been told by the Commandant that the one whom he gave us at Márabitana was not sufficiently acquainted with the river but that old Bernardo would answer every purpose. We passed the mouth of the river Xie which we estimated 150 yards wide. It comes from the N.N.E. where it joins the Rio Negro. On the right point of junction is the village San Marcelino consisting of six houses we did not halt to examine it, apparently it offered very little of interest. How different is the aspect of the Rio Negro from the rivers which we had so lately visited and where sometimes weeks elapsed before one met a human habitation, and though the villages have not the lively appearance of thickly inhabited places, and the river itself is not furrowed by numberless barks, they add diversity to the otherwise monotonous and frequently repeated scenery of inland rivers. We met towards evening canoes ascending the river. A young man of handsome appearance and figure looked for sometime with astonishment at us, and wishing us good day first in Portuguese, I was agreeably surprized when he addressed us afterwards in french. We halted the Canoes, and his first enquiry was naturally from whence we came – when I told him from San Joaquim do Rio Branco – he could not conceive how we could have performed the journey without embarking in Angostura, no person it appears, and I do not except those whom we met in San Carlos, have ever conceived the possibility of being able to cross from the Parima to the Orinoco, we are therefore for the present the wonder of the day. The young man was of birth a Portuguese, by the name of Castron, and his address, conversation, and knowledge of the French spoke of his education. I was therefore astonished when he told me that he lived at Marcelino where I think a man of his deportment is not in his place.*

*We heard afterwards that Senhor Castron was for political motives a fugitive from Portugal.

March 9th We had been camping in the wood, an approaching storm towards the preceeding evening made us prefer the wood to the open sand-banks where we would have been exposed to his fury. We had however to suffer for the partial protection the wood afforded us, all our luggage was covered with wood ants or Termites and had entered our canisters in large numbers. It took us several hours to get rid of them. Shortly after our departure we passed Sⁿ Joan Bapᵃ de Mabbe, a village of three houses. We observed in its neighbourhood a large Cuberta or decked Canoe,[2] she lays however

[1] Rio Demiti.
[2] *Coberta* is the Portuguese for the deck of a boat; thus the meaning 'a decked canoe'.

in ordinary as a vessel of her size can only pass when the river is high. It is during that period only, that the products of the forests Zarzas, Pucheri, Jalap, Balsam, Capaivi, &c[1] are carried to Para a journey of two months with the Current of the river and of six months against it. The River is south of San Joan from 900 to 1000 yards wide & islands divide the stream in several channels and numerous ledges of rocks cross it from north to south. About three miles North of N. Senhora da Guia it is so much narrowed in by ledges of rocks that its whole width does not amount to more than 400 yards. The village N.S. da Guia is situated on the right bank of the Rio Negro & consists of a church, a residence for strangers, and thirteen houses. About a mile south-west of Guia joins the river Isanna the Rio Negro from N49°W. Its last reach is from 3 to 4 miles long, its waters black, and its width near the mouth from 250 to 300 yards. Its course from its sources which are said to be in the Sierra Tunuhy is from West towards East and its upper part is thickly inhabited by Indian tribes. These poor beings were threatned with a *Descimento* of the nature and horror of which I have given elsewhere a description. An expedition had just then started up the Isanna in order to capture Indians under the false purpose of pressing them for the Navy's. It was the talk of the Country, and the expedition appeared to be of such an extent that we found some of the villages entirely tenantless or "pro tem" only inhabited by women. The village São Felipe[2] is only three miles from Guia – it consists of six houses and a church, and occupies a projecting point of the rivers right bank; and five miles further south is Sa Anna a miserable looking hamlet where the approaching night obliged us take our quarters, and we were well contented with an open shed as thunder rolled all around us.

The Brazilian villages along the banks of the Rio Negro are much inferior to those at the Cassiquiare and San Carlos on the Rio Negro. The houses are not so neat and front the river generally in a single row or are built in a straggling manner. If we are allowed to judge from outward signs, their religion is less zealous the numerous crosses of the Spanish Villages by which general name they are still designed although now a republic is wanting and one or two of those villages did not posses a cross at all. The churches are neglected and the places near them are overgrown with grass and unclean. But a period of more than seven years had elapsed since a priest had visited them and Padre Filipes present spiritual journey was the wonder of the day. S[t] Anna was only tenanted by women, the men had been drafted in the crusade against the infidels of the Isanna, to capture poor Indians at the contested Spanish boundary and to lead them in the interior of the mines as slaves. The Latitude of the place was according to our observation 0°17'11"N. and we flattered ourselves to cross the following day the Equator.

In the latest and best maps the mouth of the river Uaupes is about a mile south of the Equator; how astonished was I therefore as after two hours and a half paddling from S Anna, we were already at the mouth of the [Uaupés][3] – our distance made was then 9 miles our southings 8.6 miles[;] the confluence of that river with the Rio Negro is

---

[1] Zarzas is sarsaparilla; Pucheri is probably puxiri, pixurim, or pixuru, plants of the Family Laureceae; Jalap, or at least 'Jalapa verdadeira' is *Ipomoea jalapa*, but the name is applied to a number of plants. Capaivi has not been identified.

[2] There is a place called São Felipe marked on the reference map a little downstream from the mouth of the Içana, but such communities tended to be short-lived and there is no way of knowing if this is the same place referred to by Schomburgk. The names of many of the places he passed are not marked on the map.

[3] There is a blank in the manuscript at this point, but it is clear that Uaupés is intended.

therefore in 0°8′35″N. and has been laid down therefore 9 miles too far south in former maps.[1] The situation of Sª Anna at least as far as it regards the Latitude assigned to it, corresponded nearly with my observations – the great difference is therefore an error of the former surveyor which is scarcely excusable as the evidence of the eye might have directed him without watch or instrument that the distance south could not be seventeen miles. We ascended the Uaupes which is called Ucayari or Ucayali by the Indians for about a mile to San Joaquim de Coanne which we found a deserted village – the inhabitants had removed to Kai-wanna a settlement six days journey up the Uaupes where they carry on a lively trade in Sarsparilla, Cacao, Pucheri, &c with the natives. A short distance NE from the village San Joaquim, the Uaupes divides in two branches, the principal stream flowing N.E. and a smaller branch only navigable during high water flowing off SE.bE – in consequence of which an island of 5 miles in length is formed; but of the bifurcation which according to maps exists between the Uaupes and the river Curicuriari the inhabitants of these parts know nothing.[2] As already observed the Uaupes is called Ucayari and situation of its confluence according to my computation 0°.8′.35″N. Its waters are black like those of the Rio Negro and its width at its mouth may amount to three hundred yards. We found its current stronger than the Rio Negro being then 1.5 knots; the current of the Rio Negro where it was not increased by rapids being only .7 to 1 knot. We observed a group of peaked mountains called Wanarimapan; they were on the right side of the Rio Negro bearing S22E distant eight miles. The river is here narrowed in to about 400 yards by two bars of rock and high banks, however scarcely has it passed this partial impediment, when basin like it expands again to upwards of a mile with Islands on both its banks and studded with numerous rocks. The prospect with the group of mountains, and several isolated hillocks in the background is very lovely, and receives animation by several little cottages which are erected on the Islands and on the banks of the river surrounded by Plantain and Banana trees over which the graceful Paripe or Pijao Palm (Guilielma speciosa)[3] raises its pinnated leaves. The river Cocobiri joins from the south and further eastward a lonely chapel, called Santa Barbara, occupies a projecting point on the Rivers left bank. Where the River approaches nearest to the mountain Wanarimapan, bearing S. by W. two rounded islets occupy the middle of the river succeeded by several others of larger extent; a small hill the Cerro Aruyabai in the vicinity of Fort San Gabriel, bears S.E. and the river is disturbed by numerous rapids. This is a slight description of the scenery where the Rio Negro is crossed by the Equator. I had kept the traverse table with every precision which stood in my means, and I could therefore depend at least within half a mile on the spot where the Equator crossed it. We passed it not with indifference it was the second time during our present Expedition that we had crossed this imaginary line and more than fourteen months had elapsed since our feet trod over that spot, nearly nine degrees further eastward.[4]

---

[1] Schomburgk is perfectly correct in locating the confluence of the Uaupés with the Rio Negro north of the Equator.

[2] The Curicuriari flows parallel to the Uaupés, south of the Equator, and joins the Rio Negro to the southeast of São Gabriel da Cachoeira.

[3] *Bactris gasipaes*. The vernacular Brazilian name for this palm is Pupunha, but it is called Paripon in French Guyana (see Corrêa, *Dicionário*).

[4] See p. 249, fn. 3.

The river is now impeded by Rapids and falls; they follow in quick succession and a steady hand at the helm and quick eye is of the first importance. We possessed these excellent qualities in our old Pilot Bernardo, and landed safely towards sunset at São Gabrial.[1] When coming downwards the river, and about a mile from São Gabrial this little fortress affords a very picturesque view – it occupies a projecting hillock on the rivers left bank. Its walls are about 16 feet high and of stone, and it possessed then six cannons of iron, two of which were English. The half of these cannons were spiked. When the rebels the Cabanos were in possession of Manaos and the other towns on the lower Rio Negro the Commandant did not consider himself strong enough to defend the fort and fled to San Carlos; before leaving however the fort to its fate he spiked three of the best Guns.[2]

The political disturbances which rendered the magnificent Province of Rio Negro, a desert have likewise exercised their devastating influence upon S[t] Gabriel. Before the Brazilian empire became constitutional, and even antecedent to that period when still a dependency of Portugal, the commerce of Rio Negro was of importance, and several Towns and Villages of which at present in many instances only the name exists, extended along the rivers banks. Numerous boats were there plying between Grand Para, the Capital of the Estado and the upper Rio Negro, an inland navigation which for a distance of 1400 Geographical Miles did not offer any impediment. The largest Cataracts which the Rio Negro possesses is only a few hundred yards distant from S[t] Gabriel, and is so large that a loaded boat can not descend it without unloading. This is effected at the foot of a small hillock on which the Fort is built, from whence the Cargo is carried for about a mile overland to the lower port or embarcadero. At the time the commerce of the Upper Rio Negro was more flourishing houses extended along this road[;] only a few have remained, and are in a dilapidated state.

The Commandant, an officer of the Militia received us very friendly. We found the inhabitants in great alarm. I have already alluded to the Descimento or Slaving Expedition which the authorities of the District had ordered against the unhappy natives who inhabit the British boundary, a similar one had been undertaken against the Indians of the Rivers Isanna and Uaupes along the Venezuelan boundary and many had been carried away. Their tribes had sworn vengeance, and had sent a messenger, that they intended to burn the settlements along the banks of the Rio Negro, and that their attack was chiefly to be directed against Fort São Gabriel. The Commandant was in great consternation, he neither possessed a sufficient store of arms, nor did he consider the Garrison which consisted of only fourteen men, strong enough to defend the Fort. All the trees and bushwood had been cleared away from the hill to afford an open view, and to prevent the Indians of approaching the Fort without being seen. His situation was thus more precarious since all men in the neighbourhood, who were able to carry arms, had been ordered to the Isanna, on an other Descimento.

The great difference which I found in the geographical situation assigned to the river Uaupes when compared with my own observations made it highly desirable that I should procure observations at San Gabriel. For the last week the weather had been

---

[1] São Gabriel da Cachoeira.

[2] Page 21 ends here. The next page is numbered both 1 and 21a, and from here on the lower numbering system prevails although on some pages the numbering reverts to the old system. Thus on p. 4, a different hand has put a '2' in front of the '4' to make '24'.

very changeable, clouds obscured the sky daily and the rolling of the Thunder set in regularly towards afternoon and continued until midnight or later; observations became therefore precarious, and this was likewise the case on the present occasion. I watched from the setting in of night until 3 o'clock in the morning, but to no effect and if I had not resolved to stay another day, I would have had to depart without that desiderata, our observations at the night from the 11th to the 12th March give for Latitude 0.7.35S°.

The chief occupation of the Women of São Gabriel is in the manufacture of hammocks from the Miriti or Mauritia Palm. The cords after they are prepared from the fibres of the leaves are coloured blue with Indigo, Pink with the roots of the Mirapiranka tree, yellow with the fruit of Mankaratice,[1] and they receive an ochreous colour from the Urucku or Anatto. Green cords are produced by colouring them firstly blue, and steeping them afterwards in a decoction of the Mankaritice fruits. By means of their different tints, figures are made in the hammocks. I was told that a Woman with a sufficient quantity of cord prepared, finished a Miriti Hammock in three days. Their value is at Para and Manaos from 10 to 12 milreis or about 10 Piastres.[2] The Men manufacture Cordage or Piazaba[3] of the fibres of the Attalea funifera which constitutes one of the Articles of Exportation. The population is however scanty and does not amount to 200 souls.

March 12th our Canoes had passed safely the Cataract and stood reloaded on the place of embarkation. On our way thither I observed on a granitic ledge Indian figure writing, the more interesting since it was the first which I had seen at the Rio Negro. It consisted of labyrinths, and was remarkable for the depth with which it was cut in the rock, and although the footpath leads over these rocks, and thousands and thousands may have walked over it, the figure is by no means obliterated. Some attempt to imitate the figure at a later period and very likely executed with chisel and hammer, is nearly effaced, and puts the depth of the original the stronger in the eye.

We departed at eight oclock, and were carried rapidly forward by the strong current caused by continued rapids and falls, we were two hours after opposite the small settlement of Camanaos, where the falls cease. The sky looked gloomy, and the sun made only occasionally his appearance. The Thermometer when highest did not surpass 86°, and I had every apprehension for a complete change of the weather. We passed the river Curicuriari. A group of peaked mountains called Warigu, the highest of which rises to the estimated height of 2000 feet bears from here S by W. They resemble in their outlines the group of Cocui and Wanarimapan. The estimated width of the Curicuriari is at its mouth 100 yards. towards sunset we passed the Village São Pedro on the rivers right bank; it appeared deserted, neither man or beast were observable and the places before the houses overgrown with grass.[4]

March 13th The Thermometer stood this morning at 6 oclock only 75°.9 and the waters of the river Negro was 86°.3. Thunder was rolling towards the South, and the clouds

---

[1] It has not been possible to identify either of these vegetable dyes.

[2] In the published version (p. 255) this appears as 'about £3'.

[3] As mentioned earlier, Piaçaba and Piaçabeira refer to two species of palm, *Attalea funifera* and *Leopoldina piassaba* respectively. The name is also used for the brooms and brushes made from their fibres.

[4] Settlements along Amazonian rivers were often deserted and then recolonized. The reference map shows a settlement called São Pedro on the right bank of the Rio Negro, a little below the mouth of the Curicuriari.

crossed the river; an hour afterwards the rain fell in torrents. We met a family of half Indians, they had been up the Marié,[1] to procure clay for pottery. We bartered for some fruit called Yuccu by the Spaniards & which the Portuguese call Caqui,[2] chiefly for the purpose of procuring seeds to introduce the tree in Demerara. The seed is upwards of two inches long, in shape oblong, the stone or endocarp is Dark brown and possesses on one side a broad skar of a white colour. It is surrounded by a pulp of sweetish taste, by no means disagreeable. The outer coat which contains the seed possesses an acrid milk, and care must be taken while eating the pulp, that none of the milk comes on the lips or tongue, as it will smart for some time. The fruit is otherwise pear shaped but as I have not seen either tree or flower I cannot judge what plant produces it.

The river Marié which we passed under severe rain, joins from the SSW. I judged its width 200 yards, and the colour of its waters is black like that of the generality of the rivers which flow in the Rio Negro in these regions. I was informed that by means of a tributary of the Japura, the Indians travel from the Marié to the Amazon; it is perhaps the river Amoniu, which apparently has its sources in the vicinity of those of the Marié.[3] The Rio Negro adopts from the confluence of the Marié for [blank][4] miles a North Eastern course, its width is near the Village Wanawacca, where it is comparatively free of Islands, upwards of two miles, but its depth varies considerably the deepest parts surpass scarcely 10 feet, while frequently it shallows to 6 to 8 inches or forms large sandbanks. The shores are thickly wooded, Palms are numerous; but the height of the Forest trees is seldom more than from 60 to 80 feet. The majestic Mora of the rivers of Demerara is wanting to give the wood skirted banks a high appearance.

March 14th We broke up our Camp at three oclock in the morning anxious to arrive at an early hour at Castanheiro; we thought that a clear sky gave us sufficient light to find our way. Scarcely three miles from our Camp we found however the river so much studded with rocks and islets which formed occasionally rapids, that I commenced to repent our not having awaited daylight. We passed between this intricate passage without further inconvenience as that once or twice we run in a "cul de sac" and had to retrace our way to seek for another passage. These small rapids are the last obstructions which the river offers. When daylight broke we were opposite the Village of Massarubi generally called Porto de Maçarubi apparently almost deserted, only one house of the seven of which the Village consisted appeared inhabited. These empty houses, most of them already half in ruins and the housefloor overgrown with lank grass presents a true picture of the decline of the once populous river. The unfortunate rebellion and shattered state of the Province depresses the commerce which once occupied numerous individuals and the only cause of the depopulation which strikes the eye of the traveller every where. Four miles North East from Massarubi is the confluence of the river Cababuri with the Rio Negro; it has lighter water than the Rio Negro and its breadth amounts to about 150 yards, its last reach forming an Angle of 110° with the Rio Negro. By means of it a communication with the Interior is carried on, and as it has its sources in that chain of mountains where the Sarsaparilla abounds, it is sometimes visited by

---

[1] The Rio Marié is a right-bank tributary of the Rio Negro.

[2] The fruit of the *Diospyros kaki*.

[3] This looks quite feasible as some of the right-bank tributaries of the Marié rise within approximately fifteen miles of the Japura.

[4] The published version (p. 256) reads: 'for a distance of 45 miles'.

those enterprising individuals, who collect this medicinal roots in order to dispose of it at Angostura or Para. Though I found opportunity to converse on the subject of the stated bifurcation between the rivers Cababuri and Pacimoni, with Capitain de Melho, he was as ignorant of it as those I had previously consulted, and I fear much that it is imaginary, or consists only during the rainy seasons. The communication is carried on by means of a stream an affluent of the Cababuri and a short portage as already Lieut. Cordeiro observed who passed by the stream to the Pacimoni. We passed Carmo, once a thriving village, at present a desert; the less luxuriant growth of vegetation on its site and the want of trees prove that this was once a cultivated spot. No vestige of the former huts are more to be seen but as the village was built on rocks the frequent communication between the houses and the rivers banks had left the mark of the feet of the passers bye on the hard granite, and even time will find it difficult to remove these signs that the spot had once been selected for human abodes. The river adopted a Northern course from the Village Masarubi, it turns for a few miles SEbS and bends Eastward. During the latter course it spreads to upwards of three miles, and opens a long prospect towards four isolated mountains, which stretching North and South form now the perspective background to the peculiar scenery of the river which is by no means void of interest. We deviated from our course to visit St Antonio de Castanheiro, where we were friendly received by Senhor Joze Ferreira de Melho Captain of the Policiaes or Militia of the District. Castanheiro is on the left side of the Rio Negro and has a Church, a Residencia or stranger's house, and six dwellings there are only a few Indians of the Paré and Paui natives;[1] the population consists chiefly of the descendants of intermarriages of whites and Indian Women. Captain de Melho presides over them as Patriarch, and his house offers a picture of industry, a number of young Girls were diligent at the Cotton wheel, others manufactured hammocks while a number of boys prepared clay for pottery, which women and men formed with their hands in water jars, and cooking utensils. When their days work was finished, every one came forward to make her courtesy, and to kiss the hand of the Captain – we were there sitting on the bench before the house, conversing about multifarious subjects, and I as a stranger received likewise their greeting. Captain de Melho confirmed entirely the information of old Antonio Yarumari at Esmeralda, and congratulated us that we had selected the high road of the Rio Negro. The rivers Marawiha & Padauiri being at the present time impassable. We would find he observed, that even at its mouth the river Marawiha was almost choaked up with sand. When forced to relinquish my plan to proceed by the Mavacca and Padauri, I almost despaired to be able to add new information to the Geography of the river Negro; how far I had been mistaken in my conjecture shows already the situation wrongly assigned by extant maps to Fort Marabitana; the confluence of the river Uaupes, but a still more glowing error exists in the situation of the river Marawiha and the Village San Antonio de Castanheiro novo, that village being placed 26 miles too far Eastward and the river Marawiha to the West of Castanheiro; while it is in reality about 16 miles Eastward of Castanheiro. We passed the mouth of the river Cababuri at 7 oclock in the morning and landed four hours after at Castanheiro; in Arrowsmith's Maps the distance between the mouth of the Cababuri and Castanheiro is 55 miles, a sufficient evidence of the incorrectness of the situation assigned to it in that Map. The

[1] The Paré are almost certainly the Arawak-speaking Baré. The Paui have not been identified.

latitude of St Antonio de Castanheiro is according to my observation 0°·17'.32"S. Our Pilot whom we had taken at the Xié, was only to accompany us to San Gabriel, but as the commandant assured us, that there were no Indians in the vicinity of his Fort among whom he could select one as Pilot, he persuaded him easily to go with us to Castan-heiro. Captain de Melho who commands at that place, and whom I requested to procure another Pilot, commenced with the same excuse that there were no people, and ordered poor Bernardo to go with us as far as S^a Isabella.

March 15th passing the rivers Abuara and Inambu[1] we found the river, extended by Islands, from 3 to 4 miles wide. Current had likewise improved in rapidness and amounted to 1.7 knots. The river Marawiha joins the Rio Negro on its left bank. An Island almost 4 miles long divides the stream at its embouchure, and causes it to form two mouths. The larger part of its water flowing on to the Western Mouth. The Marawiha offers a high road to the Sarsaparilla mountains, but cannot be frequented for that purpose during the dry months of the year. It offers at its upper part a com-munication by one of its tributaries with the Pacimoni. The Rio Negro had been for some time free of islands, but East of the Eastern mouth of the Marawiha, rocks and islets commence again to impede its course, two miles further east flows a branch of the Rio Negro for a few miles southward and turns afterwards East, forming a large Island. We reached S^a Isabella[2] after dusk. It is situated on the left or northern bank of the Rio Negro, and not on the right as noted in Arrowsmiths map. Of the fifteen or sixteen houses of which the village consisted only two and the Residencia were inhabited. The church is large, and better built than those which we have hitherto seen along the Rio Negro. In the vicinity of S^a Isabel, but on the right shore the three rivers Uénévizi, Aiaana, and Urubaxi[3] join the Rio Negro at a short distance from each other. By means of the Urubaxi a lively communication exists between the Rio Negro and Japura. A trib-utary of the Urubaxi has its sources near the lake Maraki, from whence a river of the same name issues, which flows in the Japura.[4] I was told by Captain de Melho, that the Sarsaparilla abounds much more near the Japura, than either at the Uaupes or the Sierra where the Cababuri, Marawiha, and Padauiri have its sources.

March 16th The first information which I received at dawn was that the Pilot had made his Escape during the violent storm which raged during the night. When leaving Castanheiro Captain do Melho had lent him a small corial to find his way back again. We had taken it in tow, and when the storm set in, and he thought himself secure he had loosened it and escaped. I could not be angry with the man though he might have told me at once that he could not comply with my request to pilot us to the Padauiri, it would have been better than to steal clandestinely away. I resolved to proceed to the Padauiri without Pilot as with the exception of the Daraha[5] there was no river of conse-quence between S^a Isabella and the mouth of the Padauiri which I should have felt loath to pass without knowledge. We started therefore with my Coxswain as Pilot. We passed the river Daraha about 10 miles below S^a Isabel. It joins the Rio Negro from the North,

[1] Igarapé Abuerá and Igarapé Inambu.

[2] Santa Isabel do Rio Negro.

[3] Rio Ineiuxi, Rio Aiuanã, and Rio Urubaxi.

[4] The sources of the Urubaxi lie very close to the Japurá, but no river or lake called Maraki is marked on the reference map.

[5] Rio Daraá.

and is nearly of the same breadth as the Marawiha. It is much impeded by rocks and Cataracts, and uninhabited by Indians. Its sources are considered to be not so far North as those of the Marawiha and Marari. The Rio Negro is studded with rocks about the confluence of the Daraha and as they belong to the same group as those at Santa Anna and São Gabriel we may form [some idea][1] of the immense extent of this tract. It is very remarkable that though the waters of the river are of the darkest colour, none of the rocks which I have hitherto observed possess the black crust of Oxyde of Manganese so frequent in the rivers of Guiana. The black crust on rocks which are periodically immersed in the water, and the black color of water peculiar to several rivers, thank therefore their origin to different causes. The regions annexed to the river are by no means rich in smaller streams. The affluents which it receives are generally of large size and come immediately from the large mountains chain, and brooks or streamlets which naturally would have their sources at comparatively a short extent from its banks are only a few in number. The further we proceeded Eastward the more extended the river in breadth, the average of which may safely be stated to amount from 5 to 6 miles. when a long reach presents itself the river is blended with the horizon; and as if approaching land from seaward we see through trees, representing the optical illusion as if they were planted in the midst of the river.[2] In consequence of the low state of the river, sandbanks are very numerous, they represent however not more the dazzling whiteness which gave the banks of the Guainia, before that river was mixed with the Cassiquiare such a peculiar appearance.

March[3] 17th The Islands in the Rio Negro are now so numerous and of such extent that for some time past we had not seen both mainshores at once. this spectacle presented itself to day, and I estimated the breadth of the river as far as the somewhat hazy state of the atmosphere would permit 10 miles from shore to shore. The other day we saw the horizon blending itself with the water before and behind us, from which circumstance an idea may be formed of the extent and width of the reaches of the Rio Negro. Maps do not represent that river of sufficient breadth and though it does not continually keep that of 10 miles its average breadth from the embouchure of the Rio Marawiha is not less than five miles.

In consequence of the desertion of our Pilot we found great difficulty in discovering the mouth of the Padauiri, where we expected to meet Mr Vieth and Mr Le Breton who it will be recollected were to proceed by the Rio Branco to the Rio Negro, and had orders to await my return at Bararoa. We had since understood that they were at the Government rope manufactory which is about 9 miles from the mouth of that river on its right bank. We entered rivers which we took for the Padauiri at two different times but finding them entirely choked up with sand after we had ascended them for some miles, we were obliged to return. Two canoes which we had seen the previous days fled from us, and we were disappointed in receiving information. We were therefore glad

---

[1] Words are clearly missing from the manuscript. These have been taken from p. 257 of the published version.

[2] Although this passage is grammatically obscure, the phenomenon Schomburgk is trying to describe is clear. Because of the low, flat banks of the river, where water and land meet is difficult to discern at a distance and the impression is given of trees growing out of the water.

[3] At the top of p. 16 the following instruction occurs 'Include here the paragraph in { on page 17 March 17th'. This instruction has been followed here.

when we discovered on the morning of the 19th March an Igaritea[1] or large Canoe with sails which with a high wind in her favour, and attended by a smaller craft, came sailing up the river. As soon as they discovered our canoe, they intended to put about, and to escape, we succeeded however in cutting off the smaller craft, and having reassured them, we found that they had mistaken us for Cabanos, by which name the rebels are called, who are now in arms against the Brazilian Government. We found that we were about 6 miles below the mouth of the Paduiri.

The waves of the Rio Negro raised by the strong wind, were much higher than I would have expected to find them in a river. our return to the embouchure of the Padauiri against the current would have been therefore tedious and uncomfortable, if we had not decided to erect sail. A mast was soon constructed and fixed, and my tent cloth served as sail, a hammock as jib. We exposed therefore to the breeze a sail of fifteen feet height and ten feet width, and with the British Ensign on the stern, and a chequered signal on the peak[2] we commenced to plough the Rio Negro lustly and were in less than an hour at the mouth of the Padauiri.

Hid by Islands of various sizes, only those who are well acquainted with the locality may find the Padauiri without difficulty. An island of larger size conceals the mouth completely, and turns the stream directly to the East. The colour of the water would have guided us the previous day to that river, but occupied with the desire to intercept the Indians, we had in the heat of the chase paid no attention to the circumstance. When the waters of the Rio Negro come first in contact with those of the Padauiri, their directly opposite colours form a remarkable contrast, stronger than any other waters I have hitherto seen, otherwise the river is only of the third class, shallow and narrows within two miles from its mouth to 150 yards and North of the river Preto (Chié or Xiemerim of maps)[3] to 30 and 40 yards, we found it difficult to ascend with our light Canoe to the rope Manufactory. We flattered ourselves that in a few moments we should after a long and protracted absence meet once more those who formed part of our Expedition. We were however disappointed. Mr Vieth expecting from our long delay that we had returned to Demerara by descending the Orinoco to Angostura and to its embouchure, had left a few days ago, but as he was travelling slow we expected soon to overtake him.

The rope Manufactory belongs to Government and is placed under an administrator who receives twenty pr Cent of all that is manufactured. The labour is carried on by Indians who are taken from their homes for that purpose, and obliged to work for months without receiving any thing but their Victuals[;] under these circumstances it is no wonder that the Indians tries to escape his taskmaster, and during our visit all work was for want of Indians at a stand, and had been so for some time past. The administrator told me that he expected a number of Indians from the Descimento which had been undertaken to the River Isanna his application to the Captains of the district who are

---

[1] Igarité.

[2] Under the code of signals for the merchant service introduced in 1817 by Captain Frederick Marryat RN (1792–1848), the chequered flag had the meaning 'rendez-vous'. Given that Schomburgk was trying to meet up with the other members of the expedition, the signal was entirely appropriate. Marryat is better known as the author of novels for adults, e.g. *Mr Midshipman Easy* (1836), and for children, e.g. *The Children of the New Forest* (1847).

[3] On the reference map it is marked as the Rio Preto.

bound to procure Indians as labourers had been in vain. The tenth or Decimo of all Piazaba which is collected by the subjects of the Crown, is delivered by the Collectors who are appointed to receive the Decimo, to this Manufactory where it is fabricated in ropes and cables, besides if the number of labourers permit it fibres of the Piazaba Palm are collected in the adjacent woods. The Farinha a preparation of the Manihot or Cassada necessary for the sustenance of the labourers, is cultivated and manufactured by Women who belong to the Establishment, so that there is little or no expense connected with it. Before the Cabano war when Indians were more at the disposal of Government, there was an other manufactory further below, as however one could not sufficiently be supplied with labourers, the former was entirely abandoned. A soldier with orders from Government at Santarem,[1] was there at the Manufactory in order to convey what was ready to Santarem for the use of the numerous armed Schooners, which they were obliged to keep up for the protection of the Convoys which at stated periods proceed to Para.

March 20th It was so hazy this morning when we started from the Ropery that we could not see twenty yards before us. The inhabitants call this haze which it appears is periodical fumaça (smoke) and ascribe it to the burning of the Savannahs, although these are about four hundred miles distant, and in sooth thousands of square miles would have to be at the same time in fire to produce a smoke equal to the haze which had then hovered for some days in the lower atmosphere, but it is of no use to argue with the people as their fathers and grandfathers considered it to be smoke. The Thermometer stood during this period generally high in the morning, and varied from between 80.5° to 82°. The water of the Rio Negro which previously showed about that time a difference of 8° to 10° with the atmosphere was during the haze only 2° to 3° warmer than the atmosphere. A strong breeze from the East set in frequently already at night and increased the more the sun approached the Zenith until having passed it when it gradually died away, and about 2 or 3 in the afternoon the River was again as smooth as if it never had been agitated with waves, which in the morning made it resemble more a Sea coast, than the confines of a river.

In order to reach Bararoa where we thought to meet M[r] Vieth, we had to cross the Rio Negro; this could not be done in a direct manner as numerous islands and sandbanks intervene and we reached only Lamalonga next day about 3 o'clock in the morning. According to my traverse table the width of the Rio Negro is here 10 miles. Lamalonga on the right bank of the Rio Negro is about somewhat more than a mile to the Eastward of the mouth of the Padauiri on the opposite bank, while Bararoa is not less than 9 miles East of its embouchure, although it is generally considered to be opposite the River Padauiri.

Bararoa formerly Sao Thomar is in perfect decay.[2] It is situated on a high bank of the river; steps or rather ladders lead from the river to the houses. it possesses a church and the ruins of twenty houses, the church itself being in a ruinous state and the Belfery fallen in. It was declared a villa or Township at the declaration of the Constitution and the sign of having its own jurisdiction namely a gibbet is in front of the Church. The inhabitants which we met while there consisted of an old Negro woman and an Indian

---

[1] Santarém is a city at the mouth of the Rio Tapajós, on the Lower Amazon.

[2] This place does not feature under either name on the reference map, although it does appear on some maps; e.g., *The Times Atlas of the World* (2003), where it is called Tomar.

Girl and only one house bore the marks of being inhabited. What a difference between the Venezuelan Villages on the Cassiquiare and these places and Towns along the Rio Negro. The others inhabited by a happy race of Indians mixed with the descendants of the former Spaniards, please by their lively and neat appearance. On coming in sight of one of these villages, all appears life – Men and Women on seeing the strange canoe approaching run to change their coarse clothes with the best Sunday attires, and scarcely touches the corial the land when it is already surrounded by young and old, wishing the stranger a welcome and leading him to the Casa real trying on the way to procure as much information as will satisfy their curiosity from whence he might come, and where he purposes to go. Here it was different there were buildings who had been erected by human beings, but where were those who inhabited them? The lianas which covers the roof of the house, the high bushes, and grass before the door, which defy an entrance; the dilapidated state of the house itself, speak in plain language that many a day has elapsed since mirth and the bustle of domestic life resounded from its halls. May be the owner ruined in worldly affairs like his habitation roams somewhere else about to seek his livelihood, sickness may have committed its ravages amongst the former inhabitants or the Cruel Cabano war deprived the family of their prop, and distributed among strangers and relations the former members of the family and abandoned to the tooth of time their once happy dwelling. This was the train of thoughts as I made with difficulty my way through the high bushes and the sharp edged grass, which cover now what once might have been a street. After I had almost abandoned the idea of meeting a human soul I discovered the old Negro Woman in a small outhouse, and heard from her that Mr Vieth had left the same day he arrived on his way to Barcellos. She complained of her solitude, some people she said had gone to the field, the Justice of the Peace, the chief person in these Townships, to the other side of the Rio Negro, to build a Canoe with his own justicial hands, all law cases standing over for the present, until a sufficient number of people to form a quorum could be collected. So scarce was the human species about Bararoa, that lately a man accused of Murder was liberated by his Worship, as there were no people to guard him in Jail or to transport him to Barra or Manaos.[1] When leaving Mr Martins the administrator at the Ropery he had given me a soldier of the militia to Pilot me from Padauiri to Bararoa and from thence if we should not meet Mr Vieth to Mariewa or Barcellos[2] but scarcely had our Canoe touched the shore, when he profited by my absence to seek Men in the abandoned City, to make his escape. Our search for him was fruitless, and as I feared for the safety of our Canoe, which was exposed to the high waves beating against the weather shore, I did not hesitate to depart without a Pilot.

I observed near Bararoa a species of Palm along the shores of the Rio Negro, which I had not previously noticed. They grew in clusters of from 40 to 50, the stem slender, and set with prickles, rises to a height of 40 feet and bears a crown of fan shaped leaves. The tessellated and one seeded fruit removed all doubts of its being a Mauritia (Mauritia aculeata?). It is called in the Lingua Geral Maranna, and distinguished for its gracefulness and the large clusters in which it grows. As it appears to delight in the soil along the rivers banks, the current which frequently encroaches, tears whole clusters of[f], and they are frequently found lying with their heads immersed in water the roots high above

[1] Barra was the alternative name for Manaus in use at the time.
[2] Maiewa or Mariua was the alternative name for Barcelos in use at the time.

the ground on which they rest with part of their stems. The roots of such clusters are thickly matted together, and of a dark appearance. The second species which is frequently found in the neighbourhood of the former possesses pinnated fronds or leaves, and its stem is surrounded by numerous fibres, the fruit smooth one seeded and compressed. If I except these two species of Palm which preserve their livid Green, the vegetation looked dismal, the great drought which had been now prevailing for many months had deprived the trees of their green colour, or even stripped them of their foliage, thus representing the picture of Winter. In which direction we ever turned, we saw fire and smoke, and at night represented itself the splendid spectacle of seeing whole islands in a blaze; and numerous other fires larger or smaller in extent, according to the distance they were from the observer, conveyed the idea of an illumination on a grand scale. There is no doubt that many of these fires arose from the neglect of those who travel the river up and down, prepare their meals on one of these islands and on departing forget to extinguish the fire it spreads rapidly by means of the dry leaves which cover the ground, and the island is soon in a blaze, representing after the conflagration a dismal appearance of withered trees and bushes. It is however remarkable, how the fire reaches frequently small islands, which like an oazis is surrounded for miles with sand, the distance affording too great an obstacle to surmount as to believe that out of frolic they have been set on fire. The inhabitants say, that they arise from self combustion, and there is some probability in it, as the ground is often covered for feet with leaves and vegetable matter, which moistened by dew which is not wanting, be it ever so dry, commences to foment, and lastly, like this frequently happens with haystacks at home, ignite themselves. It appears not likely that the wind should have driven embers from other burning islands to such a distance. Equally detrimental as to the vegetation proved the great heat to the finny tribe, which penned up in pools being the only water which remained of the former inlet or flowing brook, died in large numbers and rendered the atmosphere in their vicinity pestilential. That strange species of Turtle the Mata-mata or Chelys fimbriata of naturalists abounded in those pools and might have been collected in hundreds. The disagreeable smell which it emits was however sufficient to deter us from taking any, although it is eaten by many and praised as tasteful as the large River Turtle.

March 22nd at sunrise the Thermometer stood 81°5 with a strong breeze from the East, the water of the Rio Negro was only two degrees warmer, and a similar haziness, as the preceeding days obscured the horizon. The river takes from the mouth of the Padauiri for about twenty five miles an ENE direction presented however otherwise a similar feature as the previous days, namely long islands, large sandbanks, low shores and the vegetation of withered appearance, the effect of long continued dryness. Since the white waters of the Padauiri have joined those of the Rio Negro, the latter have become a shade lighter. The granitic blocks and ledges so frequent about the upper Rio Negro have entirely vanished, and indurated clay in horizontal strata and strongly mixed with ochre, are only visible along the main shore. We passed the large Lagoon Warira or Arirão in which a river of the same name empties itself,[1] and arrived soon afterwards at numerous small cottages and houses, which fronted the river, and were inhabited by coloured, and a few white people. They extend for upwards of a mile, and

---

[1] Probably Rio Ararirá.

their number may amount to about Thirty. They are generally called Sitios,[1] and around them the owner plants his coffee, while for the provision ground (Roça) the most fertile spot in the vicinity is selected. May be the owner possesses a Town house in one of the Villas or Povoacãos, where he passes the high feast days or when the Priest pays his visit though short and far between otherwise the time is passed at the Sitio and this circumstance contributes much to the desolated appearance of the villages and Townships. These houses are built light and afford every comfort to the family which they stand in need off; the walls are merely of clay sometimes plastered, and the roof covered with palm leaves. Some outbuildings for kitchen, and the habitation of the Negroes or Indians if they possess any finish the Sitio. There are but few who possess Negro Slaves and I do not underate their number, if I observe that there are not more than from five to six hundred in the Rio Negro. A similar number of Indians are kept in Slavery, and used as domestics, field labourers and hunters.

I succeeded to procure here an Arroba (32lbs) of dried fish of the Pirarucu of the Brazilians or Warapaima of the Macusis (Sudis gigas).[2] Its flesh dried and salted forms one of the chief articles of trade of the rivers Negro and Solimoes or upper Amazon. This large fish which reaches a length of twelve feet is scarcely known to naturalists; its scales are of a considerable size, and of a beautiful crimson in consequence of which it is called Pirarucu or red-fish, in the Lingua Geral. In its dried state and slightly salted it is as tasteful as fresh. A great deal is exported to Para, and if the river is very dry, as it was at present, those who engage in the fishery make a handsome profit although the price at the Rio Negro is only from two to three milreis pr Arroba.[3] This fish is likewise plentiful in the Rupununy, it wonders one that our Colonists turn not this circumstance to account and carry the dried fish to Demerara where most likely it would command a higher price than Saltfish. The Pirarucu which by its size is easily observed while swimming in the water, is generally surrounded by a number of smaller boats and harpooned or they try to drive him on shallow ground, where it becomes an easy prey. The large scales strip off like a coat of mail, and it is afterwards cut in halves, and dried on stages in the sun.

March 23rd The Amplitude of the Sun when rising was 84°.15′ or E5°45N. The Thermometer 76° the water 85° with a clear state of the Atmosphere. The temperature of the Air had fallen 5° if compared with the previous days, while that of the water had risen 2°. The above amplitude gives for the variation of the Compass 4°54′E. which differs but little from all results obtained in those parts of Guiana which I have visited namely from the 56th to 68th Meridian and from the 7th Parallel of North latitude to the 2nd of south Latitude[;] indeed the differences may frequently have arisen from circumstances. Passing the river Quihuini[4] and the Lagoon Gunimaru, we halted at sunset at an isolated island. The river Quihuini offers during the seasonable months an other communication with the river Japura by means of the river Itavarana which joins the former below Marapi, it is however little frequented, the communication by the Urubaxi being preferred for all the others as it leads at once to the Sarsaparilla District.

March 24th We reached Barcellos at present called Mariua at an early hour, its aspect

---

[1] Sitio is the Brazilian term for a small, rural property.
[2] The Arapaima (*Arapaima gigas*).
[3] In the published version (p. 259) this sum has been converted into 12 shillings.
[4] Rio Cuini.

is not uninteresting. The church more extensive than any we had seen hitherto, is built on elevated ground and surrounded by several good looking houses, some Schooners and Sloops, which were anchored before the Villa added life to the picture. Barcellos had at the commencement of the present century from 10 to 12,000 inhabitants and was then the Capital of the Rio Negro and seat of Government. From the time that the latter was removed to Manaos or Barra and the latter declared the seat of Government for the Upper Amazon and Rio Negro, it dates its decay, and has at present scarcely more than twenty houses, the most of which are only inhabited during feasts and holidays. Several inhabitants engage in the trade of the river and are perhaps the only persons who could be called inhabitants of Barcellos as the greater part live on their Sitios and follow husbandry and the manufactory of ropes and cables (Amarra). Though Barcellos possesses like Bararoa, the sign of its own jurisdiction, and the right of judging and executing criminals, it has not now the sufficient number of inhabitants of exercising this right. We joined here after a separation of six months Mess[rs]. Vieth & Le Breton, and were glad to find them in good health. They had only arrived the evening previous, and M[r] Vieth was occupied to look over the collections which had been made in Geology and Botany. I was disappointed in the nature and number, although I do not attach any blame to him, the want of people and canoes to convey him to those places which might have proved interesting to a naturalist must bear the only fault of the scanty results of the Rio Negro. Delayed at Pedrero[1] and Barcellos by the promise of letters of recommendation or personal introduction, three months had elapsed at the lower Rio Negro when tired of the empty promises, he exerted himself individually, procured a canoe and Indians and repaired as far as Sao Gabriel[;] scarcely arrived there his crew deserted him and as the Commandant of the Fort could not make him hope to procure another Crew to proceed further, the contemplated journey to the river Uaupes which had been painted to us the Paradise for Naturalists was given up and M[r] Vieth returned to the Padauiri. He was loud in the praise of the kindness which he had received from private individuals but nothing had been done from the side of the Authorities although I was told that positive orders had arrived from Para to give every assistance to our Expedition. How little they were attended to proves in my own case, as I could not procure a Pilot through them from São Gabriel downwards, and unacquainted with the river and among a labyrinth of Islands, sandbanks and shallows, we had to err for nearly two days in order to find the Mouth of the Padauiri. It is an example on a small scale how much the orders of Government are disregarded, at the present unsettled state of the Province. Those in power be it ever so small or insignificant turn their little authority to their own Account. Self-interest is the spring of their Actions and in many instances (though I do not deny that there are exceptions) to the oppression and harassing treatment which the Indians received from these petty tyrants and their satellites must be ascribed the retirement of the aboriginal tribes from the banks of the river, to the wildest and remotest spots of the forests and mountains. It will prove therefore not amazing if I observe that from São Carlos to Barcellos I did not meet any natives, with the exception of the two Indians who fled from us, and who no doubt took us for Brazilians come to employ them under the name of public service for the benefit of our own purses. Thus the wish of the imperial Government to render every

[1] Moura.

assistance to us was entirely frustrated, not only with regard to Mr Vieth's Mission, but likewise in my own journey, and if I had not brought with me some of our Warrows and several Spanish Indians from the Guinau and Maiong Kong nation, all together to the number of twelve, months might have elapsed before we could have reached Barcellos and who knows how long we would have been detained there before the authorities would have procured us a crew qualified to convey us back to São Joaquim. Deducting our delays and the time we were looking for the Padauiri we had been twenty one days from Esmeralda, a distance of 575 miles according to the courses which we had run, about 27.3 miles in the average pr day. We could not have made such progress even under the most favourable circumstances if we had selected the Mavacca and Padauiri for our route. Our prolonged absence had not failed to produce anxiety for our security in the minds of Mr Vieth and M^r Le Breton, and this anxiety had been much increased by reports from Fort São Joaquim, that information had been received that our party, the Indians included, had been murdered by Savage Indians near the Orinoco. Shortly after my arrival we waited upon the principal inhabitants of the place. It was an agreeable duty to me to render them thanks for so much kindness and attention which many had shown to Mr Vieth & M^r Le Breton during their long stay in Barcellos, and I mention chiefly Senhor Rodolfo Pini and Senhor Coito who during the few days which we remained at Barcellos continued that kindness.

We had now to make arrangements for our departure to Sao Joaquim, and as I apprehended that provisions would be scarce at the sparely inhabited Rio Branco I resolved to provide myself at Barcellos, and bought besides salt fish Turtle, Oil, Coffee, about twenty baskets of Farinha. Each of these baskets contained a bushel, and weighed from 45 to 50 lbs, and the price pr basket was at the time of our purchase 1280 reis or about 4/7d. It is much higher in Manaos where a basket sells from 3 to 4 milreis and in Santarem, in consequence of the presence of the Troops, and that the generality of the Indians have joined the unfortunate conflict to the detriment of their little farms, it is often from 6 to 7 milreis and frequently not to be procured. As Farinha forms the only faecula for the nutriment of Man, and of other nutritive roots as Yams and Batatas, little or nothing is cultivated, its importance will become evident, and the failure of one crop, would produce Death and famine.

I can not leave Barcellos without mentioning that there lie on the bank since the time that Barcellos was the Capital of the Rio Negro, the materials for two land marks which were intended to be placed on the Frontiers between the Brazils, and the then Dutch Colony Demerara and the Spanish possessions. They consits of a coarse Marble, and have the Portuguese arms with the Inscription of João [blank] King of Portugal,[1] they are at present deeply burried in the sand, much injured by the weather and human hands, and there is now no likelihoods that they ever will leave their present situation.

The River adopts from Barcellos an ESE Course and its banks preserve their alluvial appearance with the exception of a large block of coarse-grained granite, which who knows by what accident came in the vicinity of Barcellos, no other kind of rock but indurated clay is to be observed. The river forms numerous Inlets interspersed with small islands. While we were at Barcellos it was on its lowest stand, lower than it had been in the recollection of Senhor Coito who was upwards of thirty years a resident at

---

[1] Probably João VI (1816–26), as the reign of João V (1706–50) seems too early for the erection of such boundary markers.

the river. The Rio Negro has the peculiarity, that if it once commences to grow, it does not sink again, and there are at no time of the year temporary swellings. The rising commences generally towards the commencement of March and it reaches the highest stand in June when it rises in ordinary cases from 15 to 20 feet but sometimes as Senhor Coito related to me 25 feet above its lowest stand. It falls gradually in the following months and is on an average level in September. The weather was unfavourable during our stay at Barcellos and I was not able to procure observations for Latitude. By the time of our departure in the afternoon of the 27th March the river had risen about ten inches, and as there was no rain as yet at the lower Rio Negro we ascribed its rising to the setting in of rain, at its upper parts, and perhaps equally at the Orinoco.

March 29th the inlets along the rivers right bank were almost continuous, the river had already risen so much that many of the Islets with which they were interspersed were inundated. A few sand banks were yet visible and those which reached above the water were crowded with Cormorants, the Razorbeaked Gull[1] and roseate spoonbills. We passed towards noon Aricari, Carvoeiro, or San Miguel do Rio Branco[2] pleasantly situated on the Rivers right bank. It consists of a church and about twenty houses partly fronting the river, partly situated along the banks of an inlet. Opposite to Aricari, it being generally known by this its Indian name empties itself a branch of the river Rio Branco after having received the river Xeremeveni or Seriveni[3] in the Rio Negro. It would be perhaps proper to say that a communication exists between the Xeremeveni and Rio Branco as to call it a branch of the latter, the connecting branch being only small, while the Xeremeveni is already a considerable river before it receives the waters of the Branco. It is generally used as the nearest passage to the Upper Rio Branco for those who live West of its embouchure and known under the name of the Boca Amajau.[4]

The wish of seeing Pedrero and to make the acquaintance of some friends who had been kind towards Messrs Vieth and Le Breton during their stay there, caused me to continue the Rio Negro and to cross from thence to the Lower Mouth of the Rio Branco. I was besides anxious to visit a small island about 10 miles West of Pedrero the Ilha de Pedra, famed for a number of Indian Hieroglyphs or picture writing. A very severe storm overtook us the other side of Aricari and we were obliged to wait in shore until it had abated its fury the waves running so high, that we feared our Canoes would have been swamped if we had ventured on the river. Nine miles East of Aricari we met again rocks in the river, the first since we had left Isabella. A few miles further the water of the Rio Negro assumed a Whitish tint, a sign that we were opposite the lower mouth of the Rio Branco. We halted that night on an isolated Island covered with a species of Eugenia with fruits of the size of a large Cherry. Their taste was by no means unpleasant. like its predecessors for the last week the night proved cloudy, and not fit for observations although we watched until three oclock in the morning for any favourable

---

[1] The Razorbeaked Gull does not feature in modern check-lists of birds. Because of the name it could be the Black Skimmer (*Rhynchops nigra*) which has a beak whose two parts fit together like a claspknife or cutthroat razor.

[2] Known today as Carvoeiro, it is situated on the right bank of the Rio Negro, opposite the mouth of the Rio Branco.

[3] Rio Xeriuini.

[4] Passagem Amajaú.

Figure 12: 'Indian "picture-writing" at the Ilha de Pedra'. From the *Journal of the Royal Geographical Society*, 10, 1841, p. 261. Included by permission of the Leeds Library.

opportunity and relinquished only our hope after the Centauri had passed the meridian. We soon afterwards started and reached the Ilha de Pedra with sunrise (March 30th).

The pictures which made this small island remarkable to us, are on its southern side, and are carved in hard granite boulders, and although the Atmospheric influence has not been without its effects, they are nevertheless several lines deep. They are numerous and consist of the representation of Men, birds, and Animals. On a large boulder thirteen figures representing Men are arranged in a line as if dancing[;] the most remarkable figures are however the representation of two Vessels under sail, the smaller resembling a two Masted vessel, the larger not unlike a large Galleon.[1] I have subjoined a drawing of both. It remains therefore no doubt that these picture writings have been made at a later period, and after the discovery of the Amazon when the vessels of the Conquistadores floated already on the mightiest stream of the world. It is not unlikely that the group of figures relate to an event of great rejoicings of perhaps the first arrival of Europeans on the Amazon.[2]

The Indians of the present day in the vicinity of Pedrero admit the antiquity of these figures and it appears the mode and manner how they have been produced has been preserved. They say namely that after a number of quartz pebbles had been collected a sufficient quantity were taken in the hand and the outlines of the figure which was to be executed having been traced in the rock with water, they rubbed with the pebbles up

[1] Others who have visited this site have failed to identify the ships which Schomburgk claimed to have found. See C. N. Dubelaar, *South American and Caribbean Petroglyphs*, Koninklijk Instituut voor Taal-, Land- en Volkenkunde, Caribbean Series 3, Dordrecht and Riverton, Foris Publications, 1986, pp. 44–5 and fn. 7; pp. 201–2.

[2] The manuscript does not contain the drawings that Schomburgk made of these figures, nor have they been located elsewhere in the Royal Geographical Society. However, the Society received them since they are to be found on pp. 261–2 of the published version and are reproduced here as Figures 12 and 13. It is difficult to interpret Schomburgk's comments about the rejoicing of the Native Amazonians at the first arrival of the Europeans, especially given how often he refers to the terrible treatment the Amerindians received at the newcomers' hands. Irony is not part of Schomburgk's repertoire.

Figure 13: 'Indian "picture-writing" at the Ilha de Pedra'. From the *Journal of the Royal Geographical Society*, 10, 1841, p. 262. Included by permission of the Leeds Library.

and down until the line had received the sufficient depth. Our trial to procure any impressions in that manner on the hard granitic rock proved fruitless[,] however there may be some dexterity connected with it, which we have no knowledge off. Our attempt would prove as abortive to extract fire from two sticks though it is a matter of comparative easiness to the Indians. I must however observe that the figures at this small island are by no means so deeply engraved as those at the Corentyn or at Waraputa on the Essequibo &c. They appeared if viewed at some Distance, as if they were merely traced with some chalky substance on the rock[;] only on approaching, it becomes evident that they are cut in the rock.

Pedrero, the former Moura during the Portuguese reign and Itarendaua or Place of rocks of the Aborigines by which latter name it is now called in official Documents, is about ten miles East from the Ilha de Pedra and is situated on the right bank of the Rio Negro. It was declared a Villa by the Constitution, but like Barcellos it does not possess the sufficient number of inhabitants to have its own jurisdiction in criminal cases. It shows the desolated appearance of the towns and villages in the Rio Negro in common, but on the present occasion all appeared life – it was the Eve of Easter Sunday and on the following Monday the muster of the Militia of the district was to take place. Numerous rowing crafts of all size from the smallest or Montaria to the large[1] Igaritea and Cuberta were fastened to the rivers banks over which a Schooner and Sloop which were moored at some distance from the shore, seemed to preside. The landing place was lined with people, whom curiosity had driven out their houses, though it was then raining. We were received by Captain Bemfico and Senhor Brandoã, and conducted to the former's house, where refreshments were served to us. Our satisfaction to see us so friendly and hospitably received was greatly damped by the various reports which were

---

[1] The page that starts here is numbered '44 or 65'. The following pages have one or the other pagination (and occasionally neither). For example, the next page is numbered 66, the one after that 46, whereas the one after that has no number. As will be noted below, although there are consecutive sheets numbered 65 and 66, there is actually a page between them that is missing.

afloat with regard to the new Mission at Pirara. M[r] Youd the Missionary it was said, finding that no success crowned his endeavours had been under the necessity to abandon his station, and even to fly to save himself from insults. It had been likewise reported that two Corials which had my collections from San Joaquim and Roriama on board were totally lost in the falls.

I had resolved to remain a few days in Pedrero. I was there much suffering from the bites which the insects during our journey over the mountains and at Esmeralda ... [.][1]

The river having grown we had to stem a strong current. We passed again the island of Rocks, and our sleeping place of March 29/30th and stood now for the mouth of the Rio Branco. Night had set in before we reached it, and as there are several islands, and the water of a pale color, long before we reached it, we were not aware when we entered the Rio Branco until it had adopted a northern course; with regard to that portion of the Rio Negro which extends from Barcellos to Pedrero or Itarendaua it is perhaps the least correct of my surveys as it is not based on astronomical observations though we had watched night for night we had not been able to procure an observation since the night of the 22/23rd March. It was one o'clock in the morning before we found a place suitable for our Camp, and having taken no nourishment since breakfast, it may be conceived that our appetite was considerable sharpened. The night proved cloudy like its predecessors, nor did fatigue permit us to continue our Vigil long after our repast.

April 3[d] & 5th the banks of the Rio Branco were high, and its bed at that time when the river was so low, much impeded by sandbanks, we were much assisted by the current of the Rio Negro, which apparently continued to grow, while the Rio Branco was getting still lower. The current of the former rushed therefore in the latter, and we felt this influence for upwards of thirty miles. The course of the Rio Branco in ascending was South, deviating sometimes a point or two on each side of it; otherwise its banks were highly monotonous. At the distance of twenty two miles from its mouth, we passed on its right bank the communication which exists with the river Xeremeneni and which constitutes the Boca Amajau. In the morning of the fifth, we landed at Santa Maria, a settlement on the right bank;[2] the night previous we had ascertained the Lat[de] 0°40′44″S and as we had made that morning about 4 miles N14°E the Latitude of Santa Maria would be about 0°36′54″S.

Duardo whom the reader will recollect as the Commander of the Descimento, has its residence in the vicinity of Santa Maria where we paid him a visit, anxious to see whether he had any late news from Fort San Joaquim in which we were however disappointed. He received us very hospitably and pressed us to stay for breakfast. His Sitio is surrounded by Orange, Coffee, and Cocoa trees, the latter bore the marks of the drought, the former were however loaded with the golden fruit, and we received permission to pluck as many as we desired. The Government at Manaos had lately

---

[1] The page marked 65 finishes here, but, as just noted, a page is missing and p. 66 is not a direct continuation. This page would seem to have contained information about Schomburgk's medical condition, a topic to which frequent reference is made in letters, but on which we have very little detailed information.

[2] An unidentified hand has written in the margin 'left?'. In the published version (p. 263) this has been changed to east (i.e., left) bank. It is also shown on the east bank on the map. Santa Maria Nova was founded in 1798 following the suppression of the uprising of the Amerindians settled in the village of Santa Maria, which was upstream near the present town of Caracaraí. When I was ascending the Rio Branco in 1967, I noted a place in this vicinity called Santa Maria de Boiaçu.

given orders, that the old Men Women and Children, who so unjustly had been carried away from their homes during the descimento, and who had been distributed among those who took part in that nefarious Expedition, should be released and sent to their homes. My arrival being then expected daily those at Santa Maria had declared when this news was communicated to them that they would wait until our party returned. Two men, five women, and two children were then in Sᵃ Maria left to themselves and almost starving. Our Canoes were almost overloaded. I procured however place for three in my own Canoe, and bought a small craft or Montaria for the remainder. Another party of seven were to follow the next day.

Santa Maria was founded at the commencement of the present Century by Duardo's father, and like San Felipe and Santa Barbara, peopled with Paravilhana Indians, shortly after the foundation they murdered their Commandants and the Portuguese who had settled with them, and the Government saw themselves under the necessity to send an Expedition against them, who conquered and sent them to the Amazon. The village was afterwards repeopled by Mura Indians[1] from the Amazon who however remained a short time and escaped to the woods. With the exception of Santa Maria and Carmo, no vestiges are more to be discovered of the former, only their sites are known, to the old people.[2]

April 8th The river did not offer any interesting feature; Sandbanks and Shallows continued, and as its bed was low, the banks were high, and we had to pitch our tents on the Sandbanks, not always pleasant when exposed to severe weather. The thunderstorms which almost regularly set in towards Midnight, gave us the benefit of a wetting. We landed towards sunset at N. Sᵃ· do Carmo, a small village on the right bank of the Rio Branco, famed for the number of Orange trees which are planted in front of it. The population appeared numerous, the Women constituted however the larger number. We met a great many Wapisianas, and Atorias here, who on a[3] former occasion carried away from their abodes by Descimentos, had been afterwards liberated and were now settled in Carmo. This certainly had tended to their civilization and this is the only reclaiming point in this cruel custom.

The night proved clear, and I procured four observations for Latitude, the means of which gave 0°16′35″N for Carmo, differing eight miles from Arrowsmiths Map.

The addition of seven Adults and two Children to our party, made me apprehensive that our provisions might not be sufficient for our journey. I was therefore glad to procure an additional supply of 200lbs Farinha and several turtles at Carmo.

---

[1] The Mura were first contacted living on the middle reaches of the Madeira River in the early 18th century. From the beginning they proved very resistant to pacification and sided with the rebels in the Cabanagem civil war of the 1830s. Several settlements of Mura exist today on the lower reaches of the Madeira.

[2] This a slightly garbled version of events. The Portuguese made various efforts to settle the Amerindians on the banks of the Rio Branco between 1776 and 1798, but as a result of revolts and desertions on the part of the Amerindians, they failed. Santa Maria Nova, the village Schomburgk refers to, was created in 1798 by Indians transported from villages higher up the Rio Branco. Carmo, or to give it its full name, Nosssa Senhora do Carmo, was one of the original villages and the only one to survive the various upheavals. Of the others, the first São Felipe was on the Tacutu and the second near the falls of Caricaraí; the first Santa Barbara was on the Rio Branco, about 20 kilometres north of the present Boa Vista, and the second also by the falls of Caricaraí. There were also various other settlements. For further details, see Farage, *As Muralhas dos Sertões*, Chap. IV, and Hemming, 'How Brazil Acquired Roraima', pp. 313–22.

[3] The pagination changes again at this point. This is the end of p. 48. The next page is numbered 70, the following three pages are unnumbered and the page after that is 74.

April 10th We were last night exposed to one of the severest thunderstorms I have experienced for some time, it blew almost a gale, and we had to use every precaution, that it did not blow tents and inmates in the river. By the high wind the tents did not afford any protection and we got what is vulgarly expressed a good sousing. Lightning and thunder were continuous, and the former so vivid, that we could see the smallest objects on the ground. We were camped at the mouth of the river Wariacura,[1] the Latitude of which I had opportunity to determine, before the storm set in; it was 0°34′17″N we had made therefore that day 17.7 Miles southing,[2] which if it be considered that it was against the current, and the river frequently impeded by Sandbanks and Shallows, to permit a direct course is a considerable distance. We had started from Carmo at 2 oclock in the morning, and with the exception of breakfast continued to paddle until ½ past 6 in the Evening. The observations at Carmo on the previous night and these at the succeeding at the mouth of the Wariacura were of importance to me as the determination of embouchure of the Catrimani or Caritarimani rests on them. We had passed its mouth about 11 miles NbE from Carmo, it was then almost choked up with Sand, and only a small rill scarcely 12 feet wide constituted the running water, a circumstance unheard of.

Several years ago people from Carmo ascended the Catrimani, and reached the Sarsaparilla country. At a journey of five to six days or about 60 miles from its mouth, it is inhabited by Pauishana Indians,[3] who carry on a lively trade of barter, on one side with the Indians near the Sources of that river, and on the other side with those of the Mocajahi and the Wapisianas at the Rio Branco. A path leads from the settlement at Catrimani to those of the Pauishanas at the river Mocajahi, and it takes them five days to walk from one river to the other. The bed of the Catrimani is much impeded by rocks and cataracts, during its passage through the mountains, and only navigable for small Canoes during the rainy season. Its last reach before it joins the Rio Branco is N67°W, and its breadth at the mouth during the time its bed is full, about 150 yards. A little above the Catrimani and on the same side joins the small stream Inivini[4] the Rio Branco.

April 12th We passed the mouth of the river Uanavau, Anava or Wanawau which has its sources in the vicinity of those of the Yuawauri a tributary of the Essequibo.[5] At its upper part it is inhabited by Taruma Indians. It joins the Rio Branco from the North East, but turns afterwards more eastward, following its course against the current. It appeared larger at its mouth than the Catrimani.

The rocks which we have hitherto observed in the river consists of indurated clays mixed with pebbles of quartz and some ochre. They appear sometimes stratyfied their direction being S11°W. We met the first granitic boulders on April 15th at a distance of [blank] miles from the mouth of the Rio Branco; the Yawattan mountains in the vicinity of the great fall bore then N51°E, the direction of the boulders is E. and W. as the generality of these tracts; the granite is coarse grained, quartz being prevailing.

---

[1] Probably Rio Aricurá.
[2] 'Northing' has been written in the margin which is obviously correct.
[3] See above (p. 287, fn. 1) concerning the problem of identifying this group.
[4] Rio Agua Boa do Univini.
[5] Rio Anauá. It has its sources near those of the Takutu River.

April 17th at Noon we had surmounted the difficulty which the fall had thrown in the navigation of the Rio Branco. The ledges of boulders which constitute it are Syenite, sometimes intermixed with granite which overlies them. The Yawuttan Mountains, or Serra da Cachoeira as they are generally called by the Portuguese, is at a distance of several miles from the left bank of the Rio Branco. The whole extent of the falls and rapids amount to about 7 miles, and it becomes necessary to unload the crafts at the largest which the Indians call Caruwanni. I estimated the perpendicular fall of the series in the course of the seven miles, about sixty feet[,] the largest, taking them separately, being scarcely 10 feet perpendicular and is much less formidable than the Itabally and Taminet falls in the Essequibo. In the afternoon of April 18th we had the first view of the Serra Grande, it bore then N25½E. its estimated distance being [blank] miles. We landed at sunset at the Sitio of a coloured Woman, where after an interval of five days (since April 13th) the night proved clear enough for observations. The Sitio, which its owner called Angelini, was in Latitude 2°18′16″N. The information of our having been killed near the Orinoco having been brought by Indians from the upper Parima, it was generally believed, and although strangers, our arrival appeared to cause general joy.

We travelled the night of the 19th April until half past one oclock and halted for rest at the foot of the Serra Grande or Caruma. The moon set as red as the sun used to do during the hazy weather at the Rio Negro and the wind was blowing in violent gusts, and as we were encamped on an open Sanbdbank, we found it very uncomfortable. We had passed in the afternoon the mouth of the river Mocajahi the Kaiawanna of the Indians[;] its Latitude deduced from observations at the previous nights was 2°24′58″N and 0°58′24″E from the mouth of the Rio Branco. Its last reach presents the remarkable feature of joining the recipient against the stream, though it is generally believed that a river which tends to enter another, either perpendicularly or in an opposite direction will by degrees change this direction and ultimately make itself entrance more downwards, or more in concordance with the stream of the recipient. The course of the Rio Branco is S.17°W. and it is joined by the Mocajahi from S.49°W. or with an angle of 32° against the stream of the former. I know no other instance of this description in Guiana, nor does it appear that it has changed its course and drawn more towards the perpendicular; the trees on both sides of its banks appear of equal age. The banks of the Mocajahi are inhabited by Pauishana and Waiyamara Indians, the first settlement of the former nation, Murumuru, is said to be fourteen days distance from the mouth of the Mocajahi, but as the river is winding and obstructed, a much shorter path leads from the Wapisiana settlement at the Wauwau to the Pauishanas. These two tribes keep up a constant intercourse, and the former bring generally spun cotton in exchange for dogs, Cutlasses and knives. Between the 63° and 64°th meridian and in about 3°N Latitude are a few settlements of Waiyamara. It is my opinion that the Mocajahi has its sources at the grand division of waters between the Orinoco, the Parima proper, the Catiramani and the Padauiri or in the southern angle of that group of Sandstone Mountains which branches off at the Marittani Mountains. I have already observed that a path of 3 days' journey, leads from the Waiyamara settlement at the Parima (Lat^{de} 3°15′N.) to those at the Mocajahi, where that river is said to be about 40 yards wide. it points therefore to a further western origin than delineated in recent maps. Indeed, from all what I have heard while at the headwaters of the Orinoco, the river Paraba, which has its source in the vicinity of Mount Tematiban and by which the

Indians in those regions descend to the Rio Branco is the Mocajahi in Portuguese Maps or the Kaiawanna of the Wapisianas.[1]

April 20th The wind blew in such heavy gusts that we made but little progress. It is remarkable that the wind at the Rio Branco, contrary to the Rio Negro, Amazon and Orinoco, blows generally downwards or with the current. The latter rivers, are margined by extensive woodlands; the Rio Branco for a considerable part of its course flows through Savannahs, which to the South and East are bounded by Mountains. We reached Senhora Liberadas who received us so hospitably at our excursion to Mount Caruma, at a late hour. The small Corial with the Wapisianas had not made its appearance for the last two nights, we were however not alarmed as we might easily conclude, that during the high wind which prevailed generally until two or three oclock in the afternoon, they could make no or little progress.

April 22nd We reached in the afternoon Fort San Joaquim. Seven months and two days having elapsed since we departed from it during which period we had made a circuit of about 2200 miles, a tract comprising the sources of the northern tributaries of the Tacatu, the western of the Mazaruni, the sources of the river Caroni, the northern tributaries of the river Parima, the sources of the river Paragua, the Parima proper, the sources of the Merewari, the Orinoco, Casiquiare, and the northern tributaries of the Rio Negro to the confluence of the Rio Branco, and reached ultimately our starting point by the latter river.

I have somewhere else observed that the Parima of the Aborigines or the Rio Branco of the Brazilians and former Portuguese has its sources not in the same mountain chain, but in the same mountain, from the western declivity of which the Orinoco issues – this is confirmed by the statement of all Indian Tribes along the upper Parima and the Orinoco, as I have now fixed the sources of the Orinoco, or Rinucu in Lat. [blank], those of the Parima are probably not more than one or two miles further East. that river adopts therefore in the commencement a north eastern course and receives its first tributary of consequence, the Awarihute[2] from the North. At the junction of the Arekassa,[3] which likewise flows in the Parima from the North, it turns more or less ESE. and skirts the group of sandstone mountains which continue towards the sources of the Paragua and Caroni or Yuruani; the junction of the Arekassa with the Parima occurs in Latitude 3°43′57″ and twenty miles from that point, the Parima possesses already a breadth of 288 yards; from Lat[de] [blank] Long [blank] to Lat [blank] Long [blank] it forms in its course the figure of an S and receives the tributaries Uricapara and Yuruma, sending from its Right or Southern bank a branch the Maraca which joins the Parima again in [blank] and has been considered in former Maps a separate river. Flowing towards the junction of the river Marua, (the Parima of Maps) in an Eastern direction, it receives previously the river Majary, named Mai-yary by the Indian tribes, and turns now southward to its junction with the Takatu. From this point to its mouth are according to my traverse table and following its winding 294 Geographical miles, offering during this course the

---

[1] This sentence is an addition in Schomburgk's handwriting. The Paraba he is referring to is obviously not the Paragua which is a tributary of the Caroni River. Presumably Paraba is another name for the Mucajaí or Kaiawanna.

[2] Probably the Rio Auaris.

[3] Rio Aracacá.

only impediment at the great falls, or Caruwannu of the Indians; it adopts from thence a southern course, deviating only slightly, and joins ultimately the Rio Negro in 1°26′S. Lat^de its whole course following its windings, amounting probably to no less than [blank] miles – traversing firstly 4° of Longitude and afterwards nearly 5° of Latitude. It is a remarkable feature of this river, which is by far the largest tributary of the Rio Negro, that already within [blank] miles of its sources it offers an average breadth of 275 Yards, receives afterwards the tributaries Uraricapara, Yarumé, Mai-yary, Marua, Takatu, Mocajahi; and has nevertheless in the vicinity of the Mocajahi a breadth only equal to that in Lat^de [blank] Long^de [blank] namely 250 to 300 yards. These tributaries, it appears, augment neither its width nor its depth, and these accessions to the recipient increase only its swiftness. During the time of the rains, the Rio Branco south of its junction with the Takutu, offers therefore a most rapid current, which in some instances amount from 4 to 4½ knots, and while during that period its mouth is reached from Fort São Joaquim it six days, it takes 18 to 20 days strong paddling to reach vice versa Fort São Joaquim. The upper Parima, namely west of its junction with the Mai-yary, will never be navigable to any craft, except the small corials of the Natives; the series of Rapids and falls are almost continuous, and the great Cataract Purumame places almost insurmountable obstacles in the way.

On entering the Takutu and standing for the Fort, we were surprised to observe to what insignificance it had dwindled during the drought. The flowing stream was restricted at its mouth to less than ten yards, and to a depth of 10 to 12 inches. This was then the river which in July and August the previous year, offered at its junction with the Parima a width of 690 yards, and an average depth of 11 feet. In order to keep up the communication between the respective shores of the Takutu, and Rio Branco, the inhabitants prefered the shorter process of wading to paddling in a Canoe.

We were welcomed by the Commandant and our old quarters surrendered to us. At the present state of the rivers it was impossible to proceed by water to Pirara, and the distance overland was too great to find it practicable to convey our luggage and collections by that way. Nevertheless I felt most anxious to be in Pirara. The information of one of my Corials having been lost in conveying letters, maps and collections was repeated by the Commandant. I received otherwise the information that letters and goods had arrived for me from Demerara, and that the people who conveyed them, had been awaiting me, for the last six weeks, in Pirara[. N]o person could therefore be more anxious to receive certainty with regard to my losses which might have caused the mishap with the Corial,[1] than myself; and only he who has lived distant from the civilized world, and wandered for months and months through the wilderness, may comprehend the eagerness to receive those communications from friends, and correspondents, which were said to await me at Pirara. Nevertheless the unfortunate state in which the bites of [illegible][2] insects had placed me, did not permit me either to ride on horseback, or to walk over land, and one small Corial which we had left in the charge of the Commandant had been lent out by him, and no other suitable one was to be procured, to venture the journey by water.

[1] This is an awkward sentence. What Schomburgk means is 'which the mishap to the corial might have caused'.

[2] The context suggests a word such as 'rapacious'.

The Montaría with the Wapisianas arrived only two days after us at Fort São Joaquim. As we supposed the strong contrary wind had not permitted them to travel for more than a few hours in the Afternoon. These poor liberated beings, left us the following day under the liveliest demonstration of gratitude in order to pursue their course to the Cannucu Mountains, where, as they told us they had relations.[1]

April 27th Our hunting craft returned this morning, but it was so ill-used that it took us more than half a day to put it in tolerable order. I embarked therefore in the afternoon at three o'clock, and provided with four good paddlers we forced our way over sandbanks and shallows, dragging the Corial by mainforce where the paddle was of no use. My unfortunate situation where sitting or standing proved alike painful did not permit me any other position than the horizontal, and the narrow corial did afford anything but comfort; we travelled therefore generally until after midnight, and reached the mouth of the Pirara already in the evening of the 1st May.[2]

We found Senhor Pedro Ayres at the head of the detachment of Militia who had taken possession of Pirara in the name of the Brazilian Government. How far they possessed right to such a step, it is not here the place to discuss; but as the orders of the Brazilian Government went so far as to order the Rev[d] M[r] Youde, the zealous Missionary to the Macusis, to leave these regions and to discontinue his religious instruction, in one word to *disperse* the mission, which promised such success, this forcible step is much to be regretted. Mr. Youde was absent, he had proceeded some months ago to Georgetown, and the Indians with the exception of a few had left Pirara. The former Chapel was converted into the barracks; and the building where the first germs of Christianity had been sown among the benighted Indians, was now the theatre of obscene language and nightly revels.[3]

Although it was but too true that my handsome Corial the Maconochie which had carried me so faithfully during former Expeditions had run against a rock, in descending Curibiru Cataract and carried away her bow, it appeared that the maps, papers, letters, were saved and thus my anxiety was relieved of a great burden.[4] The budget of letters, and newspapers, despatched by kind friends, brought in their train good and bad information, it is so seldom that our joys prove unadulterated by some alloy; grateful for the pleasure, and satisfaction which these afforded me which contained good news, the cloud which some others might have caused, was soon dispersed.

Nearly a year had elapsed since we had received information from the colony. The political changes which had occured during the interval were news to us of great

---

[1] At this point an additional, unnumbered page in Schomburgk's handwriting has been inserted.

[2] Schomburgk had referred to his ill health while at Moura, but it is just that page of the manuscript which is missing where he is apparently about to comment on it. There are also references to it in various letters to Washington, but he did not add much additional information other than that his complaint was the result of sandfly bites and he found it painful to move even from the canoe to his hammock. By the beginning of August he was recovering from the sandfly bites but was now suffering from a stomach disorder which had left him with a loss of appetite and energy. He later wrote that when he embarked for London he was feeling so ill that he expected to die on the voyage (RGS Corres 1834–40, Letters of Schomburgk to Washington, 3 May, 1 July, 2 August and 16 September 1839).

[3] For an account of the events surrounding Youd's removal from Pirara, see Rivière, *Absent-minded Imperialism*, Chap. 4.

[4] This was later found out not to be true and his reports, letters, etc., never reached Georgetown (RGS Corres 1834–40, Letter of Schomburgk to Washington, 1 July 1839).

interest, though perhaps they had long ago ceased to be of interest to Europe; scarcely were therefore the coloured people despatched who had transported a new supply of necessaries and had been the bearer of our letters, when I took advantage of the state of my feet, which had by no means been bettered by the walk over the Savannah, and sojourned to the Hammock, and to newspapers reading. The frequent arrivals in the Colony do not allow the events in Europe to accumulate; one political occurrence brought by this packet prepared for the subsequent brought by the next, but here the events of a year were lieing before one and I could follow leisurely cause and effect.

The first rain after three months drought fell at Pirara on the 3rd of May; and with it commenced the great change, the wind drew for a day from East to West, and calms and deluges of rain followed. My Meteorological Instruments were all out of order, the last Thermometer had been lost in Barcellos, so that with the best wish, I could not register the changes in temperature and weight of air.

The rivers commenced to swell, and in the middle of May the Savannahs represented a lake, out of which Pirara, which is about eighty feet above Lake Amucu, rose like an Island. Our Canoes with the Collections arrived only towards the end of May. They found the current of the rivers Tacutu & Mahu so strong that it had taken them twelve days to reach the mouth of the Pirara, which journey during low water I had executed in four days.

Having crossed the lake Amucu, the canoes were conveyed by a short land portage of a quarter of a mile into the Quatatta which flows in the Awaricuru (Wa'aecuru), a tributary of the Rupununi.

While thus occupied Mr. Youde the Missionary returned from Demerara, and the orders of the Brazilian Government having been communicated to him, he saw himself obliged to cede to force and to remove from Pirara. I need not describe the commotion which it caused among the Indians of that blighted mission and its neighbourhood! Our preparation being finished Mr. Youde, myself and party left on the same day.[1] The few Indians who had remained in Pirara to await the result, whether in reality their beloved missionary could be driven away by those Brazilians who had proved themselves so frequently Tyrants to their race, stood ready to depart, and when we left Pirara, I need not say under what feelings, they dispersed and left their peaceful dwellings where Christianity and civilisation had commenced to dawn upon them in possession of the Brazilian detachment.[2]

Our Canoes were floating on a tributary of the Rupununi; we had passed the small elevation which divided the waters of the great Amazon from those of the Essequibo, and carried with rapidity forwards we reached the junction of the River Rupununi with the Essequibo on the 11th of June at noon. During our ascent it had taken us twenty three days to reach this point from the Post Ampa at the lower Essequibo. In descending, assisted by a powerful current, we reached Ampa in five days, having made from forty five to fifty miles a day. We landed on the 13th of June at the Comuti, anxious to ascertain the height of those remarkable boulders which have received the name

[1] Youd left for Urwa, on the right bank of the Rupununi above Yupukarri, and thus it was assumed in British territory. Here he founded a new mission station, but following further threats from the Brazilians he abandoned it in March 1840 and moved down river to Waraputa on the Essequibo (see Rivière, *Absented-minded Imperialism*, Chaps 4 & 5).

[2] The page numbered 86 ends here. As mentioned earlier, pp. 87–90 are to be found located at the very end of JMS 6/29(e), and have been restored to their correct position here.

Comuti or Taquiari from the Indians. Their height as estimated by me at my first ascent had been doubted*

*v Journal of the Royal Geographical Society Vol VI p. 231 Editor's note.[1]

and as I could not divest myself of the idea, that they were really so high, if not higher, I was anxious to ascertain it, as far as it was practicable. The pile of rocks opposite to the Taquiari was therefore climbed and by means of a fishing line, we found its total height 146 feet. The Taquiari or Comuti is at least twenty feet higher. On our way up the hill one of the Caribis of our crew pointed out to us a boulder with Indian Hieroglyphics, which appeared to have escaped Doctor Hancock's attention. This was the highest situation where I had observed these picture writings. The boulders consisted of granite and the figures engraved on it are more regular than the generality of Indian Hieroglyphics. The accompanying figure[2] represents a compartment of this rock, and strikingly exhibits a similarity in its carving to that at Dighton near the banks of Taunton river twelve leagues south of Boston, to which American Antiquaries have ascribed Phoenician Origin.[3] A most interesting investigation remains to be accomplished on the Origin and symbolic nature of these picture writings, which personally I have traced over an extent of 388,800 square miles[4] or from the 56th meridian to the 68th West and from the 6th parallel north to the second parallel south. A mysterious veil covers their history, but before it is raised, no opportunity should be lost to take faithful drawings and measurements where ever they offer themselves.[5]

The river Essequibo was full to overflowing; the large Cataracts offered therefore no great impediment to our descent, and if I except some mismanagement in one of the Corials, by which it was put in jeopardy, we descended safely and without serious accident, all the Cataracts without unloading. We approached the Protestant mission at Bartika Point in the morning of the 17th. The hoisting of Flaggs and firing of guns from the shore gave us a proof of the kind interest the inhabitants took in our safe return.

At my return from my first expedition in the interior, I had the honour of being welcomed by the Lord Bishop of Barbados, at Post Ampa, who was then on a visit to the Protestant mission at Bartika Point. It was a strange coincidence that likewise on my present return, His Lordship tendered me his welcome when stepping ashore at the mission. In spite of a severe rain then descending His Lordship and retinue received me at the landing place, and I was only sorry in meeting this worthy prelate again that I had to communicate to him the first news of the dispersion of the mission at Pirara, in which

---

[1] This refers to the report on the first expedition where Schomburgk stated these rocks to rise perpendicularly 100 feet. An editorial footnote had noted that Hancock had described the perpendicular rise as fifty feet. Schomburgk clearly felt that his competence (and honour) were at stake. See p. 238 above.

[2] This diagram has not been located, nor was it published.

[3] The Dighton Rock is a ten foot by four foot slab of sandstone covered in petroglyphs. In the late-17th century, these were attributed to the Phoenicians.

[4] An unidentified hand has written 400,800 over the figure and in the margin there are various mathematical computations in the same hand.

[5] There is a large but inconclusive literature on South American petroglyphs. For an overview of the subject, see Dubelaar, *South American and Caribbean Petroglyphs*. Dubelaar concludes that, while there are no adequate means of dating the petroglyphs, the evidence all points to their being pre-Columbian. He also makes the point that 'Countless authors have published their ideas on the meaning and function of the petroglyphs they described; even of petroglyphs in general. We tried to make it clear that these interpretations are for the great part precarious' (p. 159).

he not only had taken the liveliest interest, but the foundation of which was partially to be ascribed to his instrumentality.

Twenty two months had elapsed since we passed the mission on our ascent of the Essequibo and bid adieu to civilised life and its comforts. During this period I had examined the River Essequibo to its sources, crossed the hitherto unexamined range of mountains which separate the basin of the Amazon on the south from the Orinoco on the north, and the Essequibo on the east, and travelling from there westward in the parallel of about 3° North Latitude reached the upper Orinoco and descended that stream as far as the former Spanish mission Esmeralda where I connected my investigations with those of Baron Humboldt, who reached that place in 1800 from the westward. Returning by the natural canal of Cassiquiare which connects the Orinoco with the Rio Negro, I descended the latter river to the mouth of the Rio Branco, ascended it to Fort São Joaquim, and entering its tributaries, the Tacutu, Mahu and Pirara, conveyed the Canoes by a short land passage or portage to the rivers which flow in the Essequibo and reached Georgetown in Demerara on the 20th of June 1839.

Thus is the internal navigation of one of the most magnificent Colonies under Her Majesty's possession, that I can not otherwise but direct the attention to the branchings and communications of the rivers which intersect that district of South America. By traversing the portage between the stream Quatatta and the lake Amucu, (which during the rainy season amounts to about seven or eight hundred yards) and [illegible][1] a canal of three miles length between the Guapore, a branch of the Marmore and the Madeira, and the Rio Aguapehi,[2] a branch of the Jaura and the Paraguay, an inland navigation would be opened between Demerara and Buenos Ayres, over an extent of 42° of latitude. The Napo, a tributary of the Solimoes, offers communications with Quito; the Ucayali with Cuzco; the Huallaga with Lima. Ascending the Rio Negro and entering the Orinoco by the Cassiquiare, its tributary the Meta offers an uninterrupted navigation to New Grenada and within eight miles of Santa Fé de Bogota.

If British Guiana did not possess the fertility which is such a distinguishing feature, this inland navigation alone would render[3] [it of vast importance, but blessed as it is with abundant fruitfulness this extensive inland navigation heightens its value as a British Colony & if emigration sufficient to make its resources available were properly directed thither, the port of Demerara would rival any in the vast continent of South America.]

****

In August 1839 Schomburgk sailed for England. He was in a poor state of health and confided to Washington, Secretary of the Royal Geographical Society, that he had expected to die on the voyage.[4] In fact, his health appears never to have fully recovered

---

[1] The context would suggest some word such as 'constructing'.

[2] Rio Aguapai.

[3] The remaining lines of the manuscript give the appearance of having been added by an editorial hand. Accordingly they have been placed in square brackets.

[4] RGS Corres 1834–40, Letter of Schomburgk to Washington, 16 September 1839.

and his correspondence during the rest of his life contains frequent reference to various ailments, including blindness, possibly the result of glaucoma.[1]

He arrived in England in mid-September, and except for a visit of few weeks to his family in Germany in the autumn of 1840, Schomburgk spent almost the whole time in Britain, where he took up residence at 19 Golden Square in London. He was quickly absorbed into the British scientific community and within a week of arriving in London he mentioned to Washington that he had been invited that evening (24 September) to attend a meeting of the Zoological Society.[2] He became acquainted with many of the scientists and other influential figures, and became a particular friend of Joseph Hooker and George Bentham. He also discovered that any presumed past failures had been forgotten as a result of his most recent success, and the Royal Geographical Society awarded him the Patron's Medal for 1839. Recognition also arrived from elsewhere; the King of Prussia honoured him with the Order of the Red Eagle 3rd Class, and he started to accumulate his numerous doctorates, honours and other awards.[3] He attended scientific meetings and sorted out his collections. He also organized an exhibition of ethnographic and other objects from Guiana which included three Amerindians whom he had brought with him: Sororeng, a Paravilhana, who was to accompany Schomburgk on his further travels; Saramang, a Macushi; and Corrienau, a Warao.[4] In addition, he was busy with his literary productions, and as well as the magnificently illustrated subscription volume, *Twelve Views in the Interior of Guiana* (1841), he also published *A Description of British Guiana* (1840), and the two-volume work on *Fishes of Guiana* for The Naturalist's Library (1841, 1843). It would not, however, be long before he found himself back in British Guiana.

[1] Ian Schomburgk (personal communication) informed me that this complaint runs in the family. Ian Schomburgk is Robert's great-grandnephew, the great-grandson of Richard.

[2] RGS Corres 1834–40, Letter of Schomburgk to Washington, 24 September 1839.

[3] A degree of commercialism was not always absent from the granting of these. In 1846, Schomburgk was appointed a chevalier of the Légion d'Honneur in return for the donation of a collection of plants to the Muséum national d'histoire naturelle, Paris. This was an exchange quite openly negotiated. See P. Daszkiewicz, & M. Jegu, 'Correspondence Between Adolphe Brongniart and Robert Schomburgk: Trading Natural History Collections for Honours', *Archives of Natural History*, 29, 2002, pp. 333–6.

[4] This exhibition was held at 209 Regent Street and after it was over many of the exhibits were acquired by Richard Cuming for his museum. The Cuming Museum, now located at 155–7 Walworth Road, London SE17 1RS, still holds some of this collection. It also has a copy of the catalogue of the original Exhibition, *Catalogue of Objects in Illustration of Ethnography & Natural History, Composing the Guiana Exhibition*, London, E. & J. Thomas, 1840.